GALLIA
BELGICA

GALLIA BELGICA

EDITH MARY WIGHTMAN

B.T. BATSFORD LTD

LONDON

© Edith Mary Wightman 1985
First published 1985

All rights reserved. No part of this publication
may be reproduced, in any form or by any means,
without permission from the Publisher

ISBN 0 7134 4609 9 (cased)

Typeset by Servis Filmsetting Ltd, Manchester
and printed in Great Britain by
Anchor Brendon Ltd
Tiptree, Essex
for the publishers
B.T. Batsford Ltd
4 Fitzhardinge Street
London W1H 0AH

British Library Cataloguing in Publication Data
Wightman, Edith
  Gallia Belgica.
  1. France – History – To 987
  I. Title
  936.4'02   DC61
  ISBN 0-7134-4609-9

Contents

Acknowledgements

This section had not been prepared at the time of the author's tragic death on 17 December 1983. Text, text figures, notes and bibliography were all complete and extensively revised for publication, and these have been left as they were written. The final selection of the Plates had not been made; here an arbitrary choice from the pre-selected material has been necessary. In the list of acknowledgements that follows many more names should have been cited, but, circumstances preventing this, those who do not receive individual thanks are asked to be indulgent. (*Editors*)

The late C.E. Stevens provided inspiration, and his personal library has been a mine of older references. In Belgica, this volume owes an immense debt, scholarly and personal, to M.R. Alföldi, C. Bémont, W. Binsfeld, J. Bloemers, S.J. De Laet, E. Frézouls, A. Hubrecht, M. Lutz, A. Mócsy, J. Moreau-Maréchal, R. Neiss, J. and B. Oldenstein, C. Rüger, S. von Schnurbein, and H. Thoen. Various British colleagues and, in Canada, C.M. Wells have aided greatly. The help and encouragement of innumerable other friends and colleagues, past and present, in Belgium, France, Germany, Luxembourg, the Netherlands, and Switzerland, as well as beyond the bounds of Belgica, is thankfully acknowledged. Many have supplied copies of their works. Earlier help is duly recorded in *Roman Trier and the Treveri*.

At McMaster University, M. Bottley, G. Harrod, R. Short-Michael and L.L. Neuru have acted as assistants at various stages in the compilation of text and illustrations; the Geography Department prepared the histograms. The final versions of the maps are again a tribute to the skilful hand of M.E. Cox. The photographs were taken by the author, except where specific mention is made. The Royal Ontario Museum, through the courtesy of A.H. Easson, has made available the photographs of coins in its collections. Indexes are by R. Short-Michael. L.L. Neuru and J.W. Hayes have seen the volume through the press, and express their thanks to the publishers for their patience.

Financial support and fellowships were received by the author from a number of institutions: specific mention should be made of grants from

McMaster University, Dumbarton Oaks (Washington), the Deutscher akademischer Austauschdienst (for work at the Römisch-Germanische Kommission, Frankfurt), and the Social Sciences and Humanities Research Council of Canada (and its forebears). The Royal Society of Canada provided a grant for indexing. The final stages of production of this volume were aided by contributions made by many friends and colleagues to the E.M. Wightman Memorial Fund; they are here warmly thanked.

History Department, McMaster University, Hamilton, Ontario, Canada

Figures

Plates

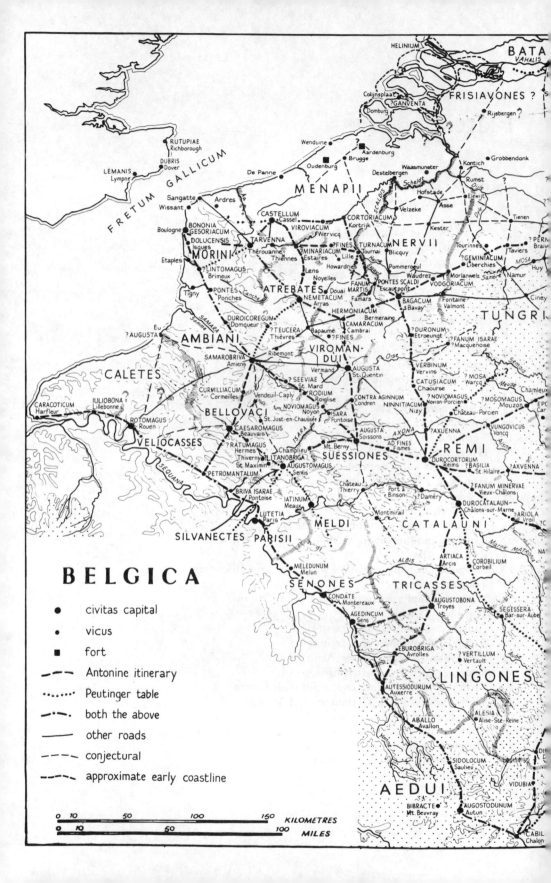

HELINIUM

BATA
VAHALIS

FRISIAVONES ?

Colijnsplaat
Domburg
?GANVENTA

Rijsbergen ?

RUTUPIAE
Richborough
DUBRIS
Dover

LEMANIS
Lympne

FRETUM GALLICUM

Wenduine ?

De Panne

Aardenburg
Oudenburg Brugge

Destelbergen Waasmunster
Scheldt Hofstade
Velzeke Asse

Kontich Grobbendonk

Rumst ?
Eliewijt
Tienen

MENAPII

Sangatte Ardres
Wissant
Boulogne
BONONIA
GESORIACUM
DOLUCENSIS
Isques
Étaples
MORINI
Théouanne
Thiennes
CASTELLUM
Cassel
VIROVIACUM
?Wervicq
TARVENNA
?FINES
MINARIACUM
Estaires Lille
Howardries
Lens
Noyelles

Tigny
LINTOMAGUS
Brimeux
PONTES
Ponches
ATREBATES
NEMETACUM
Arras
Douai
FANUM
MARTIS
Famars

CORTORIACUM
Kortrijk
TURNACUM
Tournai
Blicquy
Pommeroeul

NERVII

Kester

Tourinnes
Liberchies
GEMINIACUM

Taviers
?PERN
Brai

MOSA

Namur

Huy

Waudrez
Morlanwelz Sambre
PONTES SCALDI
Escautpont
VODGORIACUM

BAGACUM
s Bavay

Fontaine-
Valmont

Ciney

HERMONIACUM
Bermeraing
CAMARACUM
Cambrai

TUNGRI

Eu
?AUGUSTA

DUROICOREGUM
Domqueur

AMBIANI

?TEUCERA
Thièvres

Bapaume

?DURONUM
Etroeungt
?FANUM ISARAE
?Macquenoise

CALETES

SAMAROBRIVA
Amiens

Ribemont

VIROMAN-
DUI

Oise

VERBINUM
Vervins

?MOSA
Warcq

Chamieu

CARACOTICUM
Harfleur
IULIOBONA
Lillebonne ?

CURMILLIACUM
Cormeilles
Vendeuil-Caply
NOVIOMAGUS
Noyon
St. Just-en-Chaussée
Vermand
AUGUSTA
St.Quentin
?SEEVIAE
St. Mard
RODIUM
Roiglise
CONTRA AGINNUM
Condren
ISARA
Pontoise
NINNITIACUM
Nizy
CATUSIACUM
Chaourse
?NOVIOMAGUS
Novion-Porcien
Château-Porcien
?MOSOMAGUS
Mouzon
EPO
Car

VELIOCASSES
ROTOMAGUS
Rouen
CAESAROMAGUS
Beauvais
?RATUMAGUS
Hermes
Thiverny
St. Maximin
BELLOVACI
Champlieu
LITANOBRIGA
Mt. Berny
AUGUSTA
Soissons
AD FINES
Fismes
?AXUENNA
VUNGOVICUS
Voncq
REMI
AXVENNA

SEQUANA
PETROMANTALUM
AUGUSTOMAGUS
Senlis
DUROCORTORUM
Reims
?BASILIA
St Hilaire
?FANUM MINERVAE
Vieux-Châlons

BRIVA ISARAE
Pontoise
IATINUM
Meaux
Château
Thierry
Port à
Binson
?Daméry
DUROCATALAUN
Châlons-sur-Marne
?ARIOLA
Vroil
NA

LUTETIA
Paris

MELDI

Montmirail

SILVANECTES PARISII

CATALAUNI

Marne MATRONA

MELEDUNUM
Melun

ALBIS

ARTIACA
Arcis
COROBILIUM
Corbeil

SENONES
CONDATE
Montereaux
AGEDINCUM
Sens
TRICASSES
AUGUSTOBONA
Troyes
SEGESSERA
Bar-sur-Aube

EBUROBRIGA
Avrolles
?VERTILLUM
Vertault

LINGONES

AUTESSIODURUM
Auxerre

ABALLO
Avallon
ALESIA
Alise-Ste-Reine

SIDOLOCUM
Saulieu
DI

VIDUBIA

AEDUI
BIBRACTE
Mt. Beuvray
AUGUSTODUNUM
Autun
CABIL
Chalon

BELGICA

- civitas capital
• vicus
■ fort
– – – Antonine itinerary
········· Peutinger table
–··–··– both the above
———— other roads
– – – – conjectural
∿∿∿∿ approximate early coastline

0   10   50   100   150
KILOMETRES
0   10   50   100
MILES

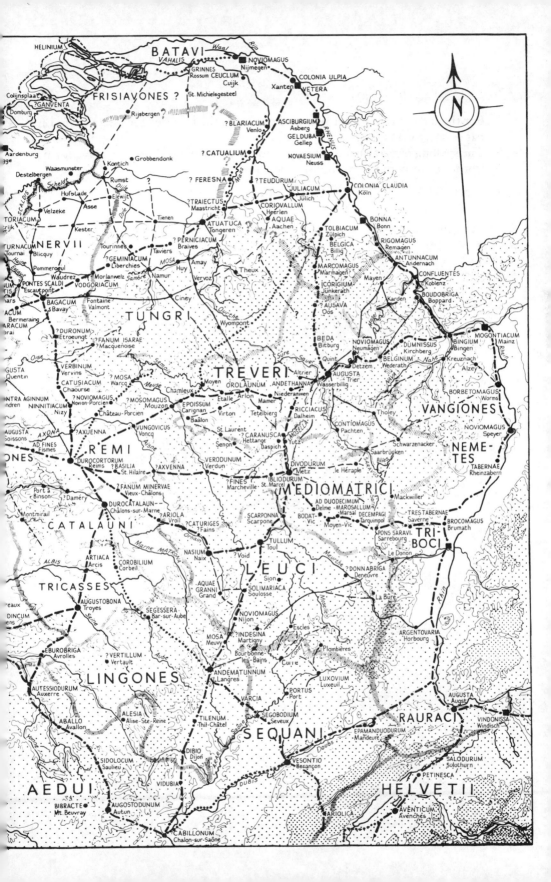

For the locations of minor sites mentioned in the text, see the index maps on pages 33, 70, 133, 184, 201, and 254–5.
The spelling of place-names follows modern local usage. For alternative forms (some more familiar in English) see Index.

I

BEFORE THE ROMANS

I The geographical background

The Roman province of Gallia Belgica comprised a number of distinct areas, and never possessed either at geographical or political levels a natural unity of its own. The administrative machinery of Roman rule lent at best an artificial unity, wholly imposed from above, its ostensible basis in pre-Roman ethnic or political facts open to question. A variety of landscape, peoples and traditions was the area's keynote in ancient times, as it still is today.

This variety is already present in the underlying geological formations which largely determine the superficial appearance of the country.[1] The broadest single feature is the saucer-shaped Paris basin, the outer eastern curve of which forms our area's central and western parts. Layers of varying hardness – limestone, chalk, clay and sand – were originally laid down by the action of a shallow sea, and subsequent erosion has left a series of ridges marking the edges of the harder (limestone) strata. It was the general inward slope of this basin towards its mid-point near Paris which determined the direction of flow for the Yonne, Seine, Aube, Marne, and Oise rivers and their tributaries, thus shaping the familiar river-pattern of the Seine basin. These valleys, especially in their lower reaches, allow easy communications except where (as happens to the Marne) they have to break through bluffs of harder rock. They have thus influenced from time immemorial the movements of man and the patterns of exchange which eventually led to the establishment of trading routes. It might appear logical that from an early time all roads should have led to Paris as centre of the dip, but in fact early medieval political forces were required to reinforce the mild pressure of the underlying geography. While the river valleys indeed provide convenient routes, communications between them are nowhere difficult, unless in the upper reaches of the Seine and Aube. The landscape is essentially gentle, occasionally monotonous, with many open plateaux of which the Champagne chalk-lands are representative. A traveller moving eastwards, into the wide crescent where the external strata of the Paris basin lap up against the much older, harder primary rocks of Ardennes and Vosges, will meet a more strongly articulated landscape. The upper valleys of Meuse and Moselle fall just within the outer edge of the Paris basin, but their flow escaped its attraction and retained a northerly course. The Meuse once had the Moselle as a tributary, until the latter's waters were captured by the Meurthe, an event which left the curious loop near Toul. Between Meuse and Aisne, the hills of the Argonne are one of the escarpments of the Paris basin; the Côtes de Meuse and Côtes de Moselle are also outer edges of the concentric formations, each of them forming natural lines of resistance against east-west movement. Further south, at the very edge of the Paris basin, the land rises to the Plateau de Langres, strategic crossroads and watershed, birthplace of Seine, Aube, Marne, Moselle and tributaries of the Saône.

In the east, south of the mineral springs in the Monts Faucilles (which divide Moselle from Saône), lie the high plateaux and jagged folded limestone of the Jura. Between Jura and Vosges the Belfort gap has played the same role in ancient and modern times, allowing communication between the elbow of the Rhine near Basel and the plains of the Saône valley. The presence in the Jura of iron-ore and, higher up, salt, once lent inherent importance to an otherwise inhospitable region. The parallel corridor which lies between the formidable south-eastern side of the Jura and the Swiss plateau, harbouring the Lac de Neuchâtel, was also of strategic importance in both prehistoric and Roman times, but lies beyond the area given detailed consideration here.

The eastern and north-eastern confines of our area are altogether more rugged than the centre, not only in appearance but also climate. This is here more continental in character because of greater distance from the tempering influences (already recognized by the emperor Julian) of the Atlantic – without enjoying any decrease in annual rainfall. North of the Belfort gap rise the southern (granite) and the northern (sandstone) Vosges. The latter are lower, but still form a barrier to communication between the Plateau Lorrain and Rhine valley. Passes, such as the Saverne gap near Strasbourg, are correspondingly important. In turn the Vosges give way to the hills of the Palatinate Haardt, (or Pfälzer Bergland), the largely slatey ridges of the Hunsrück and, north of the Mosel, the Eifel, part volcanic, part slate, part limestone and sandstone. Despite differences in underlying rocks, soils and appearance, the Eifel cannot in practice be separated from the Ardennes with their hard primary rocks (including granite), their variably wooded or bare ridges and upland marshy tracts – Caesar cannot be blamed for including both (and perhaps also the Hunsrück) under the umbrella of his Silva Arduenna. The hilly zones also have in common the intermittent occurrence of minerals, especially iron. Throughout this eastern section, ease of communication can never be taken for granted: passes must be sought, or ridges between steep winding valleys followed, while forests and marshy plateaux form additional obstacles.

North of the Ardennes a totally different geological zone with correspondingly different superficial appearance is entered. The plains of Hainaut and Flanders, with their fertile loess and less fertile sandy soils, along with the chalk cliffs and plateaux further west in the Boulonnais, Artois and Picardie, belong to the London basin and have their counterparts across the Channel.

The area which for a period of its history formed the Roman province of Belgica was thus a patchwork of disparate regions, the continuation or counterpart of each being external to the area as a whole. Natural boundaries to human activities can exist in the middle of a geologically homogeneous region, a good example being the Channel. Contrariwise, features prominent on any map of geology or physical geography may not be of such human significance as at first sight appears. The Rhine ostensibly provides a firm natural frontier to the east whereas, as will be seen, it linked as much as it separated (in addition to its function as a north-south highway) and became a frontier only with the special circumstances of Roman administration. Even the Channel and North Sea were less of a hindrance to the indigenous inhabitants of the West than to the military efforts of the Romans. The truest natural frontier lay within the area – the Eifel and Ardennes, which have throughout the ages proved a stumbling-block to would-be conquerors, and which created cultural distinctions in antiquity. It is not surprising if uneven movements of people, objects and ideas and consequent cultural variety are hallmarks of the area in prehistoric times. Centres of population and of power shifted from one part of the region to another over the centuries, and even Roman Belgica changed its boundaries for reasons of administrative convenience. This last fact, in its turn, causes ambivalence over the precise area of study, which in practice will fluctuate as its history unfolds.

It is of course surface geography rather than geological structures that influences the formation and behaviour of human groups. And even more than rivers and mountains, it is the presence of soils easily worked by primitive techniques, or alternatively more suitable for pasturage or the retention of forest cover, that affects patterns of settlement. Particularities of relief, soils and climate can further give rise to specific mentalities. There exist within the broader regions such as Artois and Picardie, Champagne, Ardennes, Lorraine or Vosges, a number of distinct separate '*pays*', some (Valois or Brie) with familiar names, others (Santerre, Thiérache, Barrois or Tardenois) less well known. These result from a feeling of common identity produced partly by common natural conditions and problems. '*Pays*' derives from Latin '*pagus*', and to these divisions a high antiquity is often ascribed, since they are at first sight territorial entities based on natural, not political conditions. Caution is however needed, for what appears to be natural may have a long history of development, with pre-Roman, Roman and medieval politics all involved. Within the context of the late Iron Age, it is occasionally possible to indicate the way in which boundaries were formed and maintained (or changed) by the interplay of geographical features and the mutual testing of strength between human political groupings.

Any attempt to reconstruct the ancient landscape must steer a course between generalizations and the detailed but localized information available from pollen analyses. In the first category falls the safe supposition that forest cover was, even in late Iron Age and Roman times, more extensive than now. To this day, the area of Belgica is noteworthy for the extent and richness of its woodlands, whether the deciduous forests of the Paris basin or the evergreens of Hunsrück, Vosges or Jura. But while many modern forests coincide geographically with ancient ones – for instance those of Thiérache and Arrouaise – caution is necessary. The forest of Compiègne is in some sense a descendant of an ancient one: yet the current size and dense, glossy verdure belong to the later royal hunting preserve. Ancient forest would be more open, mixed and scrubby in appearance, even if pollen counts show that oak and beech were dominant species in the Paris basin. The monotonous conifers of the hilly regions are also modern, though frequently in the same areas as ancient forests. The original upland forest was mixed, with both deciduous and coniferous trees; in the higher Vosges it included the larch. The extensive forests in ancient times largely coincided with the more rugged terrain – the higher parts of Burgundy, the Jura, Vosges, Palatinate, Hunsrück, Eifel and Ardennes girding the southern and eastern edges of the area, with the Ardennes extending towards the centre. Forest cover also extended to the north where, inland from the creeks and marshes of the immediate coastal region, it covered some of the sandy clays of Flanders as well as the loess of Hainaut, giving way to open, scrubby heathland in the Kempen (Campine). Caesar was to complain more than once of the way these northern woods could swallow up armies; in Hainaut, pollen analysis shows that beech increased in the immediately pre-Roman period, at the expense of lime and alder.[2]

Agriculture had already seen a long development before Greek and Roman writers began to regard Gaul as a land of exceptional richness and fertility. The late Bronze and early Iron Ages appear as periods of extensive forest clearance. Much of the country is indeed fortunate in its soils. Perhaps easiest for early agriculturalists was the light chalky soil of the Champagne Sèche, though it is by no means the most fertile. Pollen analysis shows that Champagne already in pre-Roman times had very much the same open character as today; the water-table was higher then because of greater precipitation, so that dryness was not such a problem. North and west of Champagne, virtually all of the Paris basin is (or was, before erosion) covered with fertile 'limon', similar to loess, heavier but more rewarding than the light soil of Champagne. In Belgica's southern and eastern fringes, pastoralism is likely to have played a greater role. Apart from the obvious upland areas, the plateau of Lorraine has comparatively heavy soil. Sheep, pigs and cattle would in fact be omnipresent, though the proportion of animal husbandry to agriculture and of one type of animal to another might vary with region and period.

Climatic variations, even if minor, affected the ancient farmer, especially

1   Map of Belgica showing modern regional geography

where the soils gave problems or where the growing season was short because of altitude. The climate in the eighth to second centuries BC was cooler and wetter than today. Thereafter a marked improvement set in, so that the first century BC was relatively warm and dry. This last period saw the gradual drying up of the extensive coastal lagoons left by the marine transgression known as Dunkirk I, a process which Caesar in a sense witnessed (without understanding it) when he encountered coastal marshes in the north.[3]

Any conquest involves three protagonists – conqueror, conquered and the land. The last is the essential backdrop against which all action takes place. After this brief survey, attention can now focus on the pre-Roman population of north-eastern Gaul.

2   The earlier phases of the Iron Age

In the seventh and sixth centuries BC there developed in central and western continental Europe a series of material cultures classified as the Early Iron Age. The name Hallstatt is generally given to these cultures from the Austrian site of that name, where the typical characteristics were first recognized. Apart from an ever increasing use of iron, one obvious characteristic of the Hallstatt period is the reflection of social differentiation in rich burials marked by a tumulus or barrow.

The burial customs as much as the new repertoires of objects form a clear contrast with the preceding latest Bronze Age cultures, called Urnfield from the characteristic large flat-grave cemeteries containing cremated remains interred in large pottery urns. Social differentiation was not entirely unknown, for some graves were marked out by a large quantity of grave-goods or by ditched enclosures, while a few hillforts suggest the command of subservient labour by an aristocracy. Nonetheless, the dominant impression (in comparison with later periods) is of social and geographical uniformity. One important exception is formed by the lower Rhineland, particularly east of the river, where Urnfield influences from the south remained minimal.[4]

Besides providing a fairly uniform base for later cultures, the Urnfield period raises some of the same problems of interpretation as the Iron Age. Was this culture spread by movements of people or did it evolve because contacts between largely stationary groups led to the spread of techniques and ideas? And was the evolution of Urnfield cultures triggered off around 1000 BC by conditions in the eastern Mediterranean, the first of several occasions when cultural change in central Europe is arguably connected with that other, southern world?

The arguments for seeing the creators of the northerly Hallstatt cultures as incomers were long supposed indisputable. To the indications of increased social hierarchy can be added the marked war-like characteristics of the richer graves, the greater use of horses by this upper class, and the fact that they normally inhumed where Urnfielders cremated. Modern archaeologists often stress the manner in which an aristocracy can emerge by internal evolution through the exploitation of fresh resources. Certainly, these were to hand, in north-eastern Gaul as around Hallstatt. Superficial outcrops of iron-ore exist in the Saarland, Eifel and Ardennes, Burgundy and the Jura, while salt springs are a feature both of the Jura and Lorraine (Seille valley). The control of new techniques of exploitation, especially of iron, could give to any group a marked (if not necessarily permanent) superiority over its neighbours. But if internal evolution happened at Hallstatt itself, the same pattern need not be expected everywhere. A good case for an incoming aristocracy can be built on the tumulus of Court St. Etienne (Dyle valley), one of a number of rich 'Hallstatt' burials in what can be considered a fringe area of the culture.[5] Horse-trappings, wagon-fittings and weapons are so similar to Bavarian examples as to suggest a central European origin for the objects and perhaps for their owner. Moreover the tumulus stands in a flat-grave cemetery where poorer, contemporary burials were still in Urnfield tradition. The tumulus burial might be of a local man who had acquired wealth and with it the exotic trappings that formed the visible signs of his membership in an élite, but then the accumulation of wealth in this remote northern area must be explained. On any view the distinction between rich and poor, presumably ruler and ruled, is very clear, as is the need for viewing rich burials within their surrounding context. The ideal of studying rich and poor burials together with the settlements to which they belong is unfortunately not yet attained.

Within modern Belgium, geographically distinct groups, each character-ized by aristocratic burials, can be distinguished, from the Ardennes in the south to Kempen and Limburg in the north. Other areas developed their own versions of Hallstatt culture. In Champagne the degree of wealth is rather less spectacular, as is the manner of burial, usually flat-graves with inhumation. The Hunsrück-Eifel started with a period of overlap between Hallstatt influence and its own version of the Urnfield culture (Laufeld), a pattern comparable with that of Brabant. Later, rich wagon burials with north Italian bronze vessels are found, and the area maintained a strong regional identity (hence the term Hunsrück-Eifel culture). Lorraine saw local developments in the Argonne and Seille valley, the former area maintaining cremation. The general impression is of a plurality of centres, with gaps between them.[6]

In any case, the more northerly areas cannot compete with the enormous wealth that is found in Burgundy and Württemberg (and to a lesser extent the Jura) in late Hallstatt times. This is best illustrated by the wagon-burial of Vix, where such luxury items as Attic pottery and Etruscan bronze beaked flagons were accompanied by a heavy gold diadem, perhaps of Greek manufacture, and a huge ornate bronze mixing-bowl, the product of the best archaic Greek workshops. Connected with the rich burial is the hillfort of Mont Lassois, a combination even better illustrated at the Heuneburg. Here too the tumuli contained Greek imports; more strikingly, the rampart was constructed in mud-brick, a wholly Mediterranean technique.[7]

The role of the Mediterranean world in stimulating developments north of the Alps is here at its most obvious. Trade with the Greek colony Massalia (Marseille) was, it is generally agreed, an important factor, with the hinterland supplying raw materials (timber, leather, wool, grain). The more precious imports were, however, not themselves objects of trade, but gifts to establish or cement a relationship. There are indications that not all exchanges took place via Massalia, the Etruscan flagon at Vix being one of a number of objects for which a route over the Alps is to be preferred. All such contacts benefitted the élite, provided wealth with which to secure control, and supplied visible symbols of it.[8]

Greek imports at Vix and the Heuneburg are dated to the second half of the sixth century BC. Around 500, this brilliant expression of cultural contacts came to a sudden end; destruction at both hillforts, as well as others in the Rhône valley, Jura and Lorraine, show it to have been a violent one. There follows a geographical displacement in the centres of wealth and power, along with a recognizably different material culture – new styles in art, new forms of weapons, brooches, pottery and ornaments. To these, and in consequence to the Later Iron Age in general, the name of the Swiss site la Tène has been given (again because the new style was first clearly recognized there). The two areas where the new culture can best be seen are, in order of both wealth and chronology, the Hunsrück-Eifel (with Saarland) and Champagne (more precisely the Département Marne, hence the label 'Marnian').[9]

Both the collapse of the older centres of power and the increased prominence of the northerly areas require explanation. Closer attention to the transition from one culture to the other in the north proves valuable. The Hunsrück-Eifel has produced no signs of any break in continuity, in marked contrast to the sites further south. Moreover, the new artistic styles were in part inspired by objects imported from the south – Attic vases, Etruscan bronze flagons decorated with palmettes, and other originally Greek motifs. Such imports now (the mid-fifth century) reached this area in much greater quantities than previously, and gave an impetus to indigenous crafts. Clearly new local workshops arose to satisfy masters who had acquired new tastes. Inventiveness spread to minor objects, such as the fibula with built-in spring, shaped basically like the modern safety pin, and fine pottery was now wheel-turned. The Hunsrück-Eifel aristocracy was apparently well-placed both to encourage such inventions at home and to receive them from abroad. In Champagne, the position is more complicated, for la Tène styles entered the area quite early but did not immediately replace older ones. In a number of cemeteries some burials have typical late Hallstatt goods, others have early la Tène. The phenomenon, much discussed, shows clearly that the products of new workshops overlapped for at least a generation with objects from the old. While there is no conclusive evidence from the excavation of whole settlements, disturbance seems slight. Further north, the picture varies, with the Haine valley showing signs of disruption, in that all the early la Tène tombs are on the opposite side of the valley from their predecessors.[10]

In any explanation it must be decided whether greater weight is to be given to internal or external factors. Among the former is the precarious nature of the ascendancy exercised by chieftains at Mont Lassois and elsewhere – the need to maintain a princely level of conspicuous consumption and gift-giving could eventually have overstrained the system. External causes may include collapse of the arrangement with the Massaliotes. A combination of internal and external causes seems likely, with attacks from rival groups not to be ruled out. Another side to the question remains – were movements of peoples involved in the formation of new centres of power and the spread of the new art styles? How did the new aristocracy emerge? On the evidence cited above for the Hunsrück-Eifel, Champagne and Belgium, this question will eventually be answered on a local rather than a universal level. Yet it is of wide import, since it bears, as will be seen, on the Celticization of Gaul. An aristocracy certainly developed with contacts so widespread that objects of identical style can be found in the Rhineland, Bohemia, and close to the Alpine passes.[11] And since this aristocracy's glitter belongs to northern areas, it deserves further consideration.

The Hunsrück-Eifel chieftains' graves (Fürstengräber) are remarkable for the quantity of gold, for the artistic quality of the craftsmanship shown (for instance in the gold torcs) and for the quantity of imports. The latter include jet, amber and coral, and also elaborate bronze wine-flagons of Etruscan origin. Copies of the latter, such as the coral ornamented flagons from Basse-Yutz, where the handle has been transformed into grotesque creatures and a tiny duck swims up the spout, are also common. Even more exotic is the silk (if correctly identified) from the Altrier burial, not otherwise one of the richest.[12] A hierarchy can be observed in the grave-goods of male burials. At the top come those (e.g. Weiskirchen) with gold-leaf ornaments inset with coral and amber, next those that include gold arm-rings. A two-wheeled chariot comes next, then those with sword but no chariot, sometimes still with tumulus. Below the tumulus level, and present only at attendant burials or in plain cemeteries, are those without sword, or without weapons at all. Sometimes the richer graves are connected with a hillfort, for instance that of Schwarzenbach with an early phase of the rampart at Otzenhausen.[13] Some hillforts show signs of habitation, while others served only as refuges. Nowhere, however, is a large group of wealthy graves associated with a habitation centre as at the Heuneburg, nor are the graves so outstandingly rich in imports. The mechanisms of acquiring imported status goods were probably different, with mercenary service in the Mediterranean world perhaps responsible rather than trade; flagons were preferred objects because the drinking of wine was symbolic of status. Little concerning the acquisition of wealth is really clear, beyond the fact that imports now came across the Alps rather than up the Rhône valley. A plausible explanation for the close contact with Etruria is the acquisition by the northerners of iron-working techniques which would then generate local wealth.[14]

However explained, wealth is also found in Champagne and north of the Ardennes. The Marne area, linked to the Rhineland by an old traditional route across the Argonne ('*chemin des Bretons*'), received imports, mostly bronze flagons, from that direction. Imports are fewer, gold less, but there are numerous chariot burials (still in flat-graves, with the wheels sunk into grooves) and some, such as la Gorge-Meillet or Somme-Bionne, rival those in the Hunsrück. The rich graves are found within large cemeteries suggesting communities of over a hundred people, considerably larger than the Hunsrück-Eifel norm of extended family hamlets. Social structure, while also hierarchical, cannot have been identical. The Ardennes ridges have produced a different pattern again, burial under stone cairns of warriors who normally have swords but rarely a chariot, a few grave-goods. It is north of the Ardennes that wealth is best seen, in the inhabited hillfort of the Kemmelberg (West Flanders) with its scrap of Attic pottery, or the rich burials of Eigenbilzen (Limburg) or Leval-Trahegnies (Hainaut).[15]

The burials of the Haine group show strong Marnian influences, but do not belong to the earliest phase of la Tène. Since the Champagne burials thin out considerably at this point, it may be that chieftains moved on to fresh fields. An alternative (accepting depopulation) is to see people from the Marne as among the Gauls who invaded Italy in the early fourth century. The graves of the late fourth or third centuries cluster more in the valleys, so that soil exhaustion or a sinking water-table are possible concomitant causes. In the Hunsrück-Eifel and Rhineland the wealthy burials went on longer, as witness those at Reinheim and Waldalgesheim, both containing noteworthy art pieces (and both of females).[16] Yet here too the richer graves kept shifting, and the Nahe valley, for instance, has numerous graves all of one short period. The aristocracy was in a sense international, and intermarriage between widely flung groups can readily be imagined. Yet the local groupings of which they must have been the centre were extremely fluctuating, continually dissolving and re-forming elsewhere. Only in the Haine and perhaps the Ardennes ridges can more permanent entities be envisaged. Otherwise, the élite superstructure erected over the basis of subsistence and upheld by far-flung contacts with the Mediterranean was a flimsy creation, and the day of settled political communities with fixed boundaries was still in the future.

3   Celts, Gauls, Belgae and Germans

Roughly contemporary with the development of the la Tène cultures are the first references to the Keltoi or Celts by Greek writers, who thereby raise questions on the application of ethnic names transmitted by literary sources to the cultural groupings recognized by archaeology. The earliest certain reference is by Herodotus (mid-fifth century), who knew that the Danube rose among the Celts and that they were also to be found in Spain.[17] Arguably of sixth-century date is a Periplus or description of a voyage round Spain in the direction of Britain, which survives in the later Roman version of Avienius. If comments on the Celts as a war-like race found along the Channel coasts were taken from his source then the name was already in use for the inhabitants of northern Gaul in the time of the Hallstatt cultures.[18] Herodotus' information probably implies the same, since Hallstatt but not la Tène cultures are found in Spain.

There is an indisputable general coincidence between the areas of Europe with Celtic (in the linguistic sense) place-names and the geographical spread of the Hallstatt and la Tène cultures. Both literary and philological evidence thus suggests that much of Europe was 'Celticized' by the sixth century, that is, inhabited by people who actually called themselves Celts (since this is presumably why the Greeks were given the name). Galatae, also used by Greek writers, is a different form of Keltoi, and is sometimes used (e.g. by Diodorus, a first-century BC historian using older sources) for the wilder and more northerly peoples, perhaps including those of later Belgica. The Romans used the word Galli for the Celtic peoples nearest to them (hence Gauls), and Galatae was often so used by later Greek writers while Keltoi (confusingly) was retained as a synonym for Germanoi (Latin Germani), meaning the peoples east of the Rhine outside the Empire.[19]

In what sense were the Iron Age inhabitants of north-eastern Gaul Celtic? Certainly descendants of the Urnfield folk formed an important substratum in the later population. To call these proto-Celts is to go beyond the evidence, but is not devoid of sense. But Celtic languages, and some sense of Celtic identity, may rather have spread during Hallstatt or la Tène times. And this brings back the question of incomers. While it is now recognized that the final stages in the development of languages take the form of lengthy interaction between a new and a pre-existing language, it remains hard to explain the spread of languages without the movement of some people. Most consistent with the archaeological record, especially in the north, is the movement of an aristocracy which brought with it a language as well as techniques and art styles. Nowhere is this more likely to be true than north of the Ardennes, where rich burials, as seen, stand out in an area where the poorer classes still lived in Urnfield traditions. Here, the aristocracy probably spoke one language (Celtic), the poorer folk another (the more so since Celtic place-names are rare here). The greater accessibility of Champagne, and its greater uniformity of culture, make it easier to imagine a common language developing. The Hunsrück-Eifel area retained elements of a pre-Celtic tongue, but it is also hard to believe that the aristocracy did not share a Celtic speech with the élites to the west and south-east. Personal names from inscriptions of Roman date show that a form of Celtic was the dominant tongue, and not confined to the aristocracy. All in all, the degree of 'Celticity' varied from one region to another, and, except perhaps in the north, strengthened with time.[20]

The comparative lack of Celtic place-names north of the Ardennes is one of several signs that this northern fringe never developed in the same way as the rest of Gaul. And this leads straight to the Belgae, their identity, geographical spread and to the probable reasons that led Caesar to consider them a separate people, different from the Gauls proper in both speech and customs.[21] Discussion of the problem will, however, gain in clarity if consideration of the passages in Caesar is postponed until after a brief review of other evidence.

While knowledge of la Tène cultures in France north of Champagne remains less detailed than in Germany or Belgium, there is no reason to suppose major differences in culture, apart from a comparative lack of hillforts north of the Somme. Hillforts are also virtually lacking in Flanders and Kempen. Gaulish coins (to be discussed later) thin out, and there are fewer pre-conquest types north of the Ardennes, though they increase to the west in

Hainaut and Artois. In the Rhineland, wheel-turned pottery, certain fibulae, and glass arm-rings become rarer towards the north, and there were perhaps differences in house-types. All of this suggests that there existed to either side of the lower Rhine, in Kempen and to a lesser extent in Flanders, a different type of social structure and culture. Along the lower Rhine even Urnfield influences were never strong, and north of the Ardennes the rich Iron Age burials are in a different tradition from the poorer.[22]

On the philological side, various types of Celtic place-names and early river-names fade out north of the Ardennes and Eifel. In their place are found others, believed to be neither Celtic nor Germanic, but older than either, and the spread of these continues east of the Rhine. Study of the names on inscriptions of the Roman period also shows an element that is neither Celtic nor Germanic, but as yet the third element of the personal names has not been related to the third element of the place-names.[23]

Both types of evidence show in different ways that north of the Ardennes and Eifel lay a zone of transition or fringe area. The westward boundary of this zone is ill-defined, by some criteria including, by others excluding, Hainaut, Artois and the Boulonnais – a fact that corresponds to geographical realities, since there is no clear barrier here.

The *Belgae* and *Belgium* of Caesar – the words are Celtic, and Belgae are 'the proud' or 'the boasters' – present different, not unrelated, problems. Of the people included by Caesar among the Belgae, some, such as Morini and Menapii, are clearly located in the transition zone. So too are the Eburones and perhaps others whom he classifies not as Belgae but rather as left-bank Germani. Other Belgae, the Ambiani, Caletes, Bellovaci, Suessiones and Remi certainly lie to the south of it, while there is doubt over Atrebates, Viromandui and Nervii. Some passages of Caesar, however, give a narrower meaning to Belgium, excluding Menapii, Morini, Nervii and Remi, so that Suessiones, Viromandui and Ambiani are left forming a heartland, with one or two immediate neighbours on either side.[24] Two conclusions follow. The first is that the heartland of Belgium is quite distinct from the 'zone of transition' with which it has sometimes been connected. The second is that Caesar's broader (and more usual) definition of the Belgae was probably grounded on the political conditions which he met in 57 BC, while the narrower Belgium he learned about later. Yet this does not explain why Caesar's Belgae should be different from the other Gauls, nor do place-names or broad archaeological differences at present promise a solution. It will however be seen that north-eastern Gaul was less developed socially and economically than the centre of the country, and this, along with the differences of dialect and custom likely in so large a country, might be reason enough for his statement.

The problem cannot be satisfactorily left here, for it seems that the Belgae were aware of themselves as different, and they had a reason which they were happy to present to Caesar – most of them were of German origin, they had crossed the Rhine in ancient times and settled after driving out the previous inhabitants. They alone had, in more recent memory, successfully resisted the raids of Cimbri and Teutones (with whom the Romans had had trouble enough). Closely linked with the Belgae in Caesar's account are other peoples dwelling in and north of Ardennes and Eifel who, he was told, called themselves Germani – the Eburones and other smaller groups. Caesar calls them left-bank (Cisrhenine) Germani to distinguish them from the others, and their presence was probably a surprise to him, since he had earlier believed that the Rhine was the boundary between Celts and Germans. To Posidonius of Apamea, the polymath traveller who discovered the Germans a generation earlier, they were simply a branch of the Celts who lived east of the Rhine. It is Caesar who first insists, for his own political purposes and almost certainly wrongly, that the Germans were a quite different people. Caesar presumably believed, however, and perhaps rightly, that the left-bank Germani had originally come from the other side.[25]

On the assumption that the stories told to Caesar had some validity, archaeologists long sought to discover special characteristics that might link Belgae and Germani. Early attempts were undertaken with the now discarded assumption that Caesar's Germani really were the ancestors of the later Teutonic-German speakers (who were then in fact hardly closer than the Elbe valley). Cremation as opposed to inhumation was an early candidate, until it turned out to be ubiquitous in the late la Tène period.[26] At present two suggestions hold the field. One sees the Germani as the first to cross the Rhine, perhaps as early as Urnfield times. The early la Tène princely burials north of the Ardennes are those of incoming Gauls, who formed an aristocracy and were related to the 'Marnians' in Champagne. The Belgae came in after the end of the early la Tène period in two groups, the more westerly forming Caesar's Belgium and the more northerly occupying the coastal zone.[27] All however had an origin elsewhere, somewhere in the middle Rhineland. This theory attempts to reconcile Caesar's statements (including the subservience of some Germani to the Belgae) with different archaeological groupings.

A second view has the Belgae crossing the Rhine in early la Tène times, bringing with them the potter's wheel and creating a new pottery style. The characteristic wheel-turned piriform vessel appears first in the Hunsrück-Eifel area and a little later in Champagne and the Ardennes. The Hunsrück-Eifel was the focal point of dispersion, and indeed its people did (according to Tacitus) boast of Germanic origin, though they were not counted as Belgae in Caesar's day. The left-bank Germans would then be people who went northward across the Ardennes rather than westwards to the Marne.[28]. This relies heavily on the connection between a particular style of object and the presence of incomers. In support it can be said that the area of the Belgae roughly corresponds with flat-grave cemeteries. Like the other, it presents a version of movements which could easily have formed the content of later tales, and the archaeological evidence allows for, even when it does not impose, the arrival of fresh aristocracies. At the same time, the final bonds between the people calling themselves Belgae must be political, and for this further evidence will be adduced.

There has of recent years been less interest in trying to reconcile Caesar and the archaeological picture. This is partly caused by a more sceptical approach to Caesar (who had his own reasons for painting Belgae and Germans as formidable foes) and, more generally, to tracing movements of people by archaeological evidence. If one must go further than the general conclusion that the Belgae were a fusion of relatively stationary people with more mobile aristocratic groups, should it not be in a different direction? One such possibility lies in the political developments in northern Gaul just prior to Caesar. Increasing interest is also being shown in the study of relations between aristocracies and their poorer countrymen.[29] From a study of the various societies in Gaul more light may eventually shine on the Belgae and the justification (or lack of it) for Caesar's statements.

4 The later Iron Age – cemeteries, settlements and hillforts

Throughout the Iron Age, cemeteries remain the most consistent single source of information. If the third and second centuries remain difficult periods to grasp, it is partly because the population itself was not geographically or numerically constant, and partly because a drop in Mediterranean imports makes precise dating much more difficult. The fading out of the Hunsrück-Eifel culture in the middle of the third century BC also seems connected with a drop in population, a generation or two later than the exodus observed in Champagne. This was still the period of Celtic expansion, with settlement in the Po valley as well as much wider raiding, in addition to attested mercenary service. Tenuous support for the involvement of northern Gauls is perhaps to hand in Bolgios, leader of a raid into Greece, and in Viridomarus, leader of the Insubres in Italy, who, according to Roman tradition, boasted of descent from the Rhine. Whatever wealth such activities generated does not show in the graves further north.[30]

The middle la Tène period (II in the French system, roughly equivalent to the German C), which covers the late third and most or all of the second century, poses problems in that the typical styles of fibulae and pottery are not ubiquitous. An important la Tène II cemetery at Pernant (Aisne) lacks parallels in adjacent areas and north of the Ardennes.[31] This differential distribution tells against a high degree of continuity in habitation sites. In this period incineration increases until it becomes the dominant rite, suggesting changing attitudes to death and burial. No longer equated with incoming 'Germanic' elements, it is thought to be a resurgence of older customs, never wholly submerged (least of all in the Ardennes and further north). This might mean a relaxation of aristocratic domination, and indeed the cemeteries give an impression of relative poverty (even when, as in the Ardennes, burial under tumulus was retained). Yet there are still a few chariot burials (e.g. les Pothées,

Ardennes) to suggest social stratification, and fine pieces of jewellery like the torcs from Frasnes-lez-Buissenal, near Tournai (though they were found in a later context).[32]

The final period of la Tène, chronologically equivalent in general terms to the first century BC, is also unevenly known. It is poorly attested in Champagne, but whether this simply denotes the preoccupation of many excavators with the more brilliant la Tène I material is unclear. One possible chariot burial (Armentières, Aisne) is known. In Picardie and Artois, as in Belgium, it is also too soon to make general statements.[33] The Saarland and Hunsrück provide a fuller picture. Here, the only problem is to distinguish pre-conquest from post-conquest material not showing Roman influence: the dates for some objects that had been pushed rather late are now creeping back into the earlier part of the century. Notably rich burials are again rare, though the chariot burial of about the mid-first century, close to a small hillfort at Hoppstädten-Weiersbach, testifies to minor aristocracy. Two aspects of the normal cemeteries are particularly striking. First comes the continually growing wealth observable in ordinary graves, which often contain a selection of good-quality wheel-turned pottery and sometimes spears, swords, bronze or iron fibulae and glass ornaments. Secondly, while small settlements of a few families are still normal, some communities (such as Horath and Wederath, on the lower, open Hunsrück ridges) reached the size of villages.[34]

The extension of our knowledge of settlements is an urgent task. Fortunately, Iron Age habitation sites are no longer synonymous with '*fonds de cabanes*', irregular depressions now considered to be annexes of dwellings or storage pits rather than dwellings themselves. Two types of late Iron Age settlement can now be recognized, the first very clearly, the second less so. Aerial photography in the Somme basin has rendered familiar the isolated

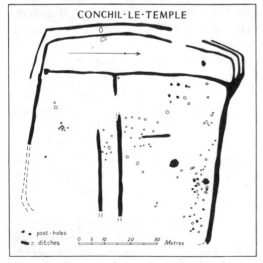

2   Plan of the enclosure excavated at Conchil-le-Temple (Leman-Delerive)

Gaulish farmstead, usually contained within a ditch system forming a double enclosure, with a ditch-lined entrance and sometimes fields and trackways.[35] The late la Tène date suggested at a variety of sites has been verified by the complete excavation of an enclosure at Conchil-le-Temple near the mouth of the Authie. Two rectangular houses, along with a variety of other post-holes and pits, suggest an unpretentious farmstead housing one or two families; the type of structure is also known from Bundenbach in the Hunsrück and from Rhineland examples.[36] These enclosures can be reasonably equated with the scattered *aedificia* observed in rural Gaul by Caesar.

A structure on a much grander scale, at first sight more fitting for Caesar's chieftains, has been excavated at la Verberie (Oise) – massive post-holes outlined a space 22 m × 12 m – but the function of this imposing building (the roofing of which was no mean feat) remains unknown. Unfortunately, the cemeteries belonging to the farmsteads remain undiscovered, whereas in the Hunsrück-Eifel the settlements going with the cemeteries are unexplored. Elsewhere, excavated habitation sites either belong to an earlier phase of the Iron Age or have not yielded complete plans.[37] It is clear that there were also nucleated agricultural settlements. Although the finest example, Kamps Veld at Haps, south of Nijmegen, is probably of early la Tène date, the waterside village of Mechelen-Nekkerspoel seems to be later.[38] There is thus no need to suppose that Caesar's *vici* were only clusters of farmsteads; the important question for the future is whether there were strong regional variations.

It is also clear that building traditions varied. The sub-rectangular four- or six-post hut is widely spread, as far north as Mechelen-Nekkerspoel and even beyond. The old classic site of Mayen offers something between these smaller houses and the more imposing structure at la Verberie. In Holland, a much longer, narrower, aisled structure which housed men and animals under one roof was the norm, and the houses of the Kamps Veld are a variation on this. Since the late Hallstatt house inside the small fortification at Beaufort, Luxembourg is related, it is clear that there is a broad zone where overlap might occur.[39]

The hillfort at Beaufort is one of the earlier ones of the region, spanning late Hallstatt and early la Tène. It also belongs to the smallest category, being 1.5 ha in area, and functioned as a fortified farmstead – two other buildings besides the one mentioned being visible. The early la Tène hillforts, whether or not permanently occupied, are normally not much bigger; Otzenhausen already falls in a larger category (10 ha).[40] The third century on present evidence saw a cessation of hillfort building and occupation, but unexcavated hillforts still far outnumber excavated. When the picture of depopulation presented by the cemeteries is put alongside, the two suggest an aristocracy which was either relatively weak or had less need to defend itself. By the second century defence was once more a consideration. The small hillforts of Erden (overlooking the Mosel) and Bundenbach (Hunsrück) were both constructed around the middle of the century, too early for the wanderings of Cimbri and Teutones, recorded in Roman sources, to have been the cause.[41] The reasons must lie in the internal development of society, with new growth in population and rivalry among chieftains. The refortification of Bundenbach in the late second century and the subsequent destruction around 100 BC can, however, be connected with the restless movements historically attested. Bundenbach still belongs to the smaller class of hillforts, the fortified chieftain's seat or *castellum* rather than the proto-urban *oppidum* of Caesar. The interior, the sole fully excavated example, provided for a chieftain and some retainers, lesser families and numerous storage-huts. The base appears predominantly agricultural; if the chieftain's wealth depended partly on the exploitation of nearby sources of iron-ore, this was not worked in the hillfort. By contrast there are signs of iron-working inside the small hillfort of Etival in the Vosges as well as in the larger one at Otzenhausen.[42]

While small hillforts are still found in the first century BC, the larger ones of 10 ha and upwards become more common, while a small number reach or exceed 50 ha. The date of their construction and the manner of their occupation is debatable. Two types of rampart construction are typical of the time of Caesar. For a long time the Gauls had experimented with timber-laced ramparts, and the type which Caesar describes as a typical *murus gallicus* differed from earlier types in having no vertical timbers showing at the front. Archaeology has added the fact that the timbers were often fastened together with nails, but has also shown that this type existed before the period of the conquest. The massive, simpler dump rampart, the material largely scraped out of a broad ditch in front, has been considered typical both for the period of the conquest and for the territory of the Belgae, and it is true that numerous examples occur precisely in this area. The dump rampart (called 'Fécamp' after a site in Normandy) is in fact more widely spread, but it is indeed a later development than the *murus gallicus*.[43] The hillfort Vieux-Laon (north of the Aisne near Reims) indicates this, since the first phase of the rampart was in *murus gallicus* technique, while secondary strengthening was of Fécamp type.[44] The faster construction technique may well belong to the period of the conquest, even if the *murus gallicus* was still in use.

What then can be said about the larger hillforts or *oppida* in north-eastern Gaul? While the construction of many may well have taken place before the conquest, the evidence for occupation in the first half of the first century BC remains limited. Yet there are indications from the Tetelbierg and the Donnersberg that the great fortifications which look as if they were intended to house and protect large communities did not stand empty.[45] It is not yet clear whether large hillforts were already serving as centres of artisan activity in the pre-conquest period, so that their proto-urban character remains to be demonstrated. The north-east lagged in this respect behind the centre of France (where Châteaumeillant and others show real urban characteristics). Also lacking as yet in the north-east are undefended centres of production such as Aulnat and Levroux. Yet the late la Tène wheel-turned pottery may well have been centrally produced, and the distribution of the collared fibula, for which there is pre-conquest evidence, suggests some centre in the Hunsrück or Pfalz. The time lag meanwhile remains, and while it need not be greater than one generation, the contrast with the brilliance of the early la Tène period is striking.

The uneven distribution of later hillforts on a map is largely due to the highly variable levels of archaeological research. There are many hillforts in Lorraine, especially between the valleys of Meurthe and Meuse, but they are undated. In the areas of most intensive work, the Hunsrück-Eifel and Ardennes, new examples are discovered almost yearly, and nowhere is the pattern complete. Only north of the Ardennes can it reasonably be suggested that the blank is real, and even here the Borgstad near Asse forms an exception to the general rule.[46] Belgium, north of the Ardennes, might be thought geographically ill-suited to fortifications, and it is certainly true that the Hunsrück-Eifel and Ardennes present optimum conditions. Yet Vieux-Châlons and Vieux-Reims show that plains were not an insuperable problem for fort-building, and in central France river-valley *oppida* are found.[47] Comparison and contrast between Champagne and northern Belgium can be taken further. Unlike the Hunsrück-Eifel, Champagne did not develop small hillforts in the early la Tène period, despite other cultural similarities between these two areas. The communities in Champagne may have been differently organized, with the landscape favouring the exploitation of agrarian resources and the pursuit of peace with immediate neighbours – excellent conditions for the development of political entities bound by mutual agreements. In northern Belgium, discrete, often widely separated aristocratic groups formed the earlier keynote, and a further time lag is wholly reasonable for the transition zone.

The sites of hillforts can to some extent be classified. Domination of the surrounding countryside is clearest at Vermand, Mt. César, Tetelbierg, Otzenhausen and (most of all) Donnersberg. Proximity to valuable natural resources is notable at the Tetelbierg, since the very hill itself contains exploitable iron-ore, and it also surveys land of a quite different character – a classic situation. Some may have formed on the boundaries of the developing political communities, an example being Gournay-sur-Aronde (Oise), between Bellovaci, Viromandui and Ambiani.[48] Of the low-lying *oppida*, Vieux-Châlons lies on an old route crossing the plateau of Langres, and Vieux-Reims on the river Aisne. Notable riverside groups are found on both Aisne and Somme, so close together as to raise a question-mark over simultaneous occupation, and the undated hillforts along the Meuse valley could form another such series. The centrality of certain *oppida* within a region will be discussed below.

5 Early coinage in Belgic Gaul

The adoption of coinage in the middle la Tène period was a further notable example of cultural borrowing from the Mediterranean world. The likeliest mechanism for Greek coins reaching Celtic lands is the frequent service of Celts as mercenaries to Mediterranean powers. Antigonus Gonatas of Macedon, for example, paid Gauls one gold piece per head for a campaign. In Gaul, the Macedonian gold stater originally issued in the mid-fourth century by Philip II and reissued by his successors provided the model for the main series of copies: the genius of Gaulish master-craftsmen then went beyond imitation to create bold, original designs.[49]

Belgic Gaul was the meeting place of two different currents. Copies of Philip-staters spread northwards from east-central Gaul and the area around Basel, while in the heartland of Caesar's Belgium, Tarentine gold coins of late fourth-century date were copied. The adoption of Tarentine types could have been due to some direct link between that city and the Somme valley, in the form of exploring Tarentine merchants. But the Somme valley itself had nothing to offer them, nor is there any indication that British tin (the most obvious attraction) ever passed that way. Related coins east of the middle Meuse also fit poorly into this idea. Only the fact that more than one Tarentine coin was copied suggests anything more than some curious fluke, and judgment may be reserved. These half-staters in due course died out, but not without issue, for a feature of Tarentine Hera's headdress appeared in Apollo's hair on the first northern copies of the Philip-staters.[50]

The adoption of coinage is hard to date, and opinions vary between the mid-third and the mid-second century. Only if an active role by Tarentum is demanded must the earlier date (before Tarentum's loss of independence to Rome) be preferred. There is no easy way of integrating coinage with other archaeological material, since the early coins are rarely found in any helpful context. Moreover there is no indication that minting was ever regular and continuous: the evidence is just as (perhaps more) consistent with short intense bursts of activity followed by lulls, and even relative dating can be difficult. As for the function of the coinages, there is agreement that they were not at first primarily commercial, but rather social. Coins were prestige objects that would be used in such transactions as the payment of dowries, the reward of signal services, or as offerings and gifts. The one literary reference shows an Arvernian chief from central Gaul scattering coins to his followers, thus giving a flamboyant display of his wealth while binding men to him by debts of honour. Moreover, the occasional discovery of iron currency bars shows that alternative ways of reckoning value were maintained. As for the source of the gold, there are indications that some were made from Greek originals melted down.[51]

Two important coinages of Belgic Gaul probably belong to the middle or the second half of the second century, and both show a mixing of the two traditions. Both are later than the earliest *philippus*-copies, some of which circulated just to the south, in north Switzerland and the Franche-Comté. The first group is found in the Hunsrück and Saarland, and has as reverse a man-headed horse (to be compared with the earlier man-headed horse on the lid of a flagon from Reinheim). The obverse, a fine head of Apollo, is close to the Swiss ones, but northern influence is betrayed by a trifoliate ear lobe derived from a Tarentine ear-ring. This series ('early Treveri') had no successors in the area, but almost identical coins occur in southern Armorica, whether because of emigration, a dynastic marriage or a wandering master-craftsman. The concentration of the first group in the Hunsrück corresponds well with that area's predominance in la Tène times. Roughly contemporary is a coinage with Pegasus reverse found on both sides of the Rhine between Koblenz and Mainz. Further south, in Lorraine, an idiosyncratic type with a Janus-head is found.[52]

The second important group are the first Somme valley staters, 'Gallo-Belgic A' or 'Ambiani *à flan large*'.[53] The broad thin flans allowed a marvellously luxuriant coiffure for Apollo, across which ran a spike derived from the Hera obverses. Numerous examples were found in a hoard at Tayac (Gironde) believed to date from before 100 BC. In its homeland it enjoyed a wide spread between Seine mouth, Soissons and the Pas-de-Calais (as well as in south-eastern England). While the distribution has its centre in the Somme valley, an attribution to the Ambiani of Caesar seems too narrow as well as anachronistic.

Gallo-Belgic A (to adopt the neutral terminology) influenced subsequent gold coinages on both sides of the Channel. Its immediate Belgic successors, Gallo-Belgic B, C, D and E, all have slightly different distributions. The first was struck from defaced obverse dies (of unclear significance) and appears at home near the Seine mouth. Gallo-Belgic D, a series of quarter-staters, has a more northerly spread, with one class quite far inland. The distributions of C (simplified from A, with thicker flan) and E (a uniface stater) are closer to that of A. Detailed examination of variants suggests that these might have their own areas of circulation within the whole.[54] With Gallo-Belgic F the concentration shifts to the south-east, and this coinage is attributed to the Suessiones because inscribed (Criciru) coins with an obvious concentration in the Soissonais are closely related. These last are ascribed to the period of the Belgic campaigns against Caesar.[55] There are further staters that belong to the same general family, most notably those with a star (Veliocasses), those where the obverse design resembles a Greek 'Epsilon' (Nervii), and those where the face has become an eye (Treveri).[56]

As a group, these coinages belong to the generation or generations immediately preceding the conquest, and the closer to the war, the more confidently they can be ascribed to one of the peoples mentioned by Caesar. The dating of the individual coinages is still disputed. A low dating, with many of the coinages actually ascribed to the resistance against Caesar, is giving way to a higher chronology which spreads them out between 100 BC and the conquest.[57] Whatever the chronology, the coincidence between the general distribution and the heartland of Caesar's Belgium – Ambiani, Suessiones and their immediate neighbours – remains striking. A spread north-eastwards to include Nervii as well as Morini can be observed, and at some point the Treveri also linked themselves to the group, while the Remi appear to have been excluded. Now at Caesar's arrival the Remi were linked with the Suessiones whose king Diviciacus within living memory had ruled on both sides of the Channel. It is clear that the coinages originated in the Somme valley, not the portions of Aisne and Marne valleys occupied by Caesar's Suessiones. But on the hypothesis of a southward shift of power in the generation immediately before Caesar the different types of information can be reconciled – the Suessiones rising to rule a hegemony in which they had perhaps previously been junior partners. It looks as if political manoeuvres reflected in the related coinages played a significant part in creating a Belgic brotherhood, and this must have been as important as any hazy recollections of a common origin. Meanwhile, to the south of the Hunsrück, the inhabitants of Lorraine (Caesar's Mediomatrici and Leuci), retained older styles of stater.[58]

By contrast with central and east-central Gaul, the north with its gold coinages was behind the times. Probably in the last decades of the second century, just after the Romans defeated Allobroges and Arverni, the peoples to the east of the lower Rhône adopted silver coins based on Roman prototypes. The idea spread, and soon coinages with a helmeted head on the obverse (originally Roma) were in use to east and west of the upper Saône. The date is again a matter for argument, but the coinage, which has numerous classes, could easily have had a long life. Bearing the name Kaletedu in Greek, and later in Roman letters, it circulated widely among Aedui, Lingones and beyond. A later and rougher coinage, with the name Togirix, originated in Sequanian territory, from where it also spread widely: this was still being struck at the time of the conquest.[59]

Along with the use of silver went the introduction of bronze coins, and this generally took the form of cast coins of high tin-content bronze, or potin. These coinages also spread up the Rhône valley; the earliest potin coins have Massaliote prototypes and may be of second-century date. One of the probable pre-conquest silver types, that of Q. Doci Sam. F., has potin counterparts, and another variety, sometimes known as the '*tête diabolique*', may have been circulating among the Sequani and Leuci before the arrival of Caesar. It is possible that other types, later common among Leuci and Remi, were also commencing.[60]

If the adoption of silver was already one step away from a prestige coinage towards a utilitarian one, potin provides small change and shows that transactions were increasingly reckoned in monetary terms. Central Gaul, where silver and potin were early in use, is not by accident the area which shows early forms of urbanization. In the coinage, the time lag between centre and north is again apparent. Not that it should be exaggerated, for the Suessiones and Treveri may also have had pre-conquest silver coinages, hard to date because they do not correspond with the others.[61] These are not, however, comparable with the massive emissions of central Gaul, and cannot have had the same effect on society and economy.

6 Society in Belgic Gaul

The essential basis of pre-Roman society in north-eastern Gaul, as in all pre-industrial societies, was the segment – probably a good 90 per cent – which itself lived little above subsistence level but provided the necessary nourishment for the rest. It is also the part about which even archaeology tends to inform us last and least, though progress is being made, as greater attention is paid to habitation sites, field systems and farming techniques, to the analysis of floral and faunal remains, to the demography as well as the dating of cemeteries. We know that emmer, spelt, rye, millet, barley and oats were all common, with bread-wheat rarer and buckwheat attested once (Bundenbach only), while vegetables and fruit were rather less varied than after the Roman conquest.[62] Analysis of animal bones has substantiated what might have been guessed, that the pig was the dominant domestic animal, rivalled by sheep and goats in the Paris basin and the cow in the north. The domestic hen was known, but not common, and wild animals and fish were a normal part of the diet.[63] Small squarish fields of so-called 'Celtic' type have been observed in Kempen, while larger fields are suggested by aerial photography in Picardie. There are indications in Rosmeer (Limburg) that a plough heavy enough to make cross-ploughing unnecessary was sometimes in use; the plough from the site of la Tène, however, is light, though iron-tipped.[64]

Eventually, more will also be known about spinning, weaving and other domestic activities which did not create great wealth. The maintenance of an aristocracy over a subsistence base can take forms which vary from one society to another. For the Celtic world it might mean control of basic substances and technology, and transactions with an external power that provided prestige goods. In northern Gaul control of iron ore was more important than that of salt, since the relevant parts of Lorraine do not display blatant wealth. In Champagne, the control must have been of agricultural surplus, and any such system is likely to have exhibited some of the features later found in Old Irish custom, such as the loan of livestock (or seed-grain) at an agreed rate of return. Aristocratic control over necessary imports – salt, or tin for the manufacture of bronze – is also likely. Skilled craftsmen presumably worked for the nobles – this is obvious for goldsmiths, and probably also at first for blacksmiths. Finer pottery, demanding the potter's wheel, was originally for limited consumption; habitation sites produce coarser local material, harder to date. Lower-grade craftsmen, such as the village potter, would also be peasants, exercising their craft only part of the time.[65]

The aristocracy benefitted also from religious sanctions of which we know nothing until we hear from Posidonius and Caesar of the Druids, men of noble birth. Yet the systems might easily get out of balance – a chieftain gave out more in gifts than he could amass, suffered defeat, had too many sons, or was unable to support his followers after a bad harvest. Hence arose warrior bands, or whole movements of people, for example mercenaries with wives and children.[66]

The third and second centuries were a period of transition to the societies which we meet in the pages of Caesar. For the Hunsrück-Eifel, Champagne and Hainaut, the decline of one aristocracy may have been followed, after a period of quiescence, by the emergence of another. Despite a comparative lack of imports – coinage apart – it was not a period of stagnation. Iron became more widespread, and the once prestigious metal was used to make fibulae for ordinary people. More types of pottery and other objects give the impression of being made in centres, and spread from there.[67] The control of skilled artisans may well have escaped from the nobility. A tension could thus be created between the interest of the nobles in maintaining their position and the potential for others to build new wealth and power. Any revolt against the nobility at most, however, amounted to the replacement of one élite by another. Some nobles doubtless adapted better than others. Among the means of adaptation was closer control of the agricultural base, and in an age where the population was arguably more stationary this would come increasingly close to control of the land itself, so that the chiefdom became more territorial. With time, the land would be regarded as belonging to an individual or family, rather than being held in common: hence Caesar's view that the Gauls recognized land ownership.

Both archaeology and literary sources suggest various steps in the hierarchical ladder of Gaulish society. Caesar, it is true, lumps all non-nobles together in an undifferentiated *plebs* which he dismisses as unimportant. But the observations of Gaulish customs recorded by Greek writers give more nuances, and there is the archaeological distinction between graves with and without weapons,[68] a distinction which should correspond to that between freemen and others, or free and base clients found in both Old Irish and Old Welsh laws. If the analogy is carried further then free clients might themselves establish control over land through customary use, and avoid a state of crippling debt and consequent dependence. They are candidates for ownership of the substantial yet unpretentious farmsteads of the Somme valley. In Old Irish law free clients paid a higher return on borrowed cattle than did base, because the borrowing was essentially a symbol of acceptance of another's suzerainty, not a matter of necessity. Base clients were often found in villages where they could be closely overseen by an agent of the chief. They owed labour services as well as food-renders, and might be called on to build or repair a fortification. It was very likely with such labour that hillforts were built, and the villages now appearing may be Gaulish equivalents to the Welsh ones.

That some villages consisted of freemen cannot of course be ruled out, and the small hamlets of three or four families are likely to represent free family groups. It will be of interest to see whether the area north of the Ardennes presents more villages and fewer dispersed farms than Picardie. The favourable climate of the last century BC would benefit all farmers, but the free families in dispersed homesteads could best profit from slightly increased surpluses.

Defence could also be a reason for the grouping of settlement, with peaceful times more likely to encourage a dispersed habitat and the claiming of new areas for cultivation. At the same time, peace did not necessarily serve the interests of chieftains. Much wealth and prestige must have stemmed from successful raiding, and it would be easier to dominate clients that needed protection. That minor warfare was an integral part of Gaulish society is indicated not only by ancient writers but by the quantity of middle and late la Tène swords that have been recovered, whether from graves, the dredging of rivers (including the Maas near Maastricht) or sacred deposits like that of the sanctuary of Gournay-sur-Aronde.[69]

The introduction of coinage to north-eastern Gaul brought another prestige item, created by the master-craftsman for his lord. Typically, we find another shift in the areas of special prominence: while early coins in the Hunsrück might be predictable, in the Somme valley they are not, and Champagne seems to have become, for a time, a backwater. Once again there is adaptation to a Mediterranean import, this time one of significance for society at large. Coinage was a two-edged weapon, for the techniques were not difficult to learn. While presumably gold coinage was closely controlled by the nobility, this is not necessarily true for silver, and even less for potin.

If a high dating is accepted for the coinages derived from Gallo-Belgic A, then the years around 100 formed a crucial period for the development of Belgic Gaul, when the foundations were laid for the country Caesar encountered in the 50s. If an external impetus is sought, it may be to hand in the attested wanderings of the Teutones, against whom the Belgae claimed to have offered organized resistance.[70] A period of external threat could offer ideal conditions for nobles to strengthen their position and for wider political alliances to be fashioned. It may yet be shown that a number of hillforts were built or, like Bundenbach, strengthened about this time.

The formation of the peoples or *civitates*, the political entities recognized by Caesar, must also be a product of this final period. Essential building-blocks for the *civitates* were smaller units, the *pagi*, which correspond to tribes, groups based on common religious customs, ideas of common descent, and later a defined territory.[71] Even the *pagus* was a far cry from the small groups of the early la Tène period, and itself represents a long development; petty local chieftains had to recognize the patronage of a greater one, and the latter's power had to be recognized as territorial. Accepted centres for religious observance and market exchange formed, the best example being Gournay-sur-Aronde, a boundary *oppidum* with sanctuary. Eventually, agreements between chiefs of *pagi* formed the *civitas* and the larger unit too came to have some sense of common identity *vis-à-vis* its neighbours. Once again a time lag in the north can be detected, for the *civitates* are notably smaller and often less cohesive than those of central Gaul.[72] Whereas many of the central *civitates* had initiated magistracies, in the north we still hear of kings (e.g. of the Suessiones), of paramount chieftains whose position might be challenged (the Treveri) or of war leaders (Nervii).

The hillforts are not unconnected with these political processes. It is clear from Caesar and from the coin record that some nobles found in the *oppidum* a means of increasing and maintaining their power in the face of challenge. In an ideal situation, we would see the political structure of a *civitas* reflected in the hillforts. Small hillforts like Weiersbach should be typical for the local petty chief, larger ones (Tetelbierg, Vieux-Châlons) for a *pagus*. It is not clear whether the inhabited *oppidum* representing the centre of a *civitas* really existed in the north before Caesar, though some possible examples will be seen. The classes of coins that are subdivisions of the main types may be *pagus*, not *civitas*, coinages.

Such, in general terms, was the road taken by the north-eastern Gauls, the Belgae and their neighbours, in the pre-Roman period. It was a society with its own social norms, but where the equilibrium of political groupings was uneasy. Petty warfare was endemic, and a graphic illustration of the carnage that might ensue is to hand in the Trou de l'Ambre near Eprave (Ardennes) where 75 men, women and children were savagely hacked to death and mutilated.[73] It had a long history of adaptation to Mediterranean influences, not the least of them coinage, even if greater advances had been made in south or central Gaul. It was a society in which Caesar could recognize many constituent elements and with which he could, to some extent, treat. Until now, contact with the Mediterranean world had been essentially on the Gauls' own terms, but this ended abruptly in the 50s BC.

2

THE CONQUEST

1 The political geography at the time of Caesar

The gradual transformation of early la Tène Celts into the Gauls of Caesar's day having been outlined, the political geography can be given in more detail, starting with Belgium narrowly defined. This wedge-shaped region stretching inland from the coast between Seine and Somme valleys to the middle reaches of Oise, Aisne and Marne comprised Ambiani, Bellovaci and Suessiones, with the probable additions of Meldi and Silvanectes in the south, Caletes and Veliocasses to the west, Viromandui and Atrebates to the north-east.

Boundaries are known approximately rather than precisely, on the one hand from Caesar, on the other from the medieval bishoprics which with minor variations were co-terminous with Roman *civitates*. Help can be forthcoming from place-names and Gallo-Roman inscriptions, and frequently later boundaries roughly correspond with natural features which at all times formed convenient frontier zones.[1]

Even if the ancient forests were sparser, lower and more varied than the later tended woods, Thiérache and Arrouaise (on the watershed between Escaut and Sambre to the north, Somme and Oise to the south) naturally separated the Nervii from Remi and, further west, Viromandui. Support is to hand in the occurrence of the Gallo-Roman place-name Fins (from *fines*) between Cambrai and Péronne, close to the boundary between the bishoprics that represent Nervii and Viromandui.[2]

These forests, by defining the northern frontier of the Viromandui (occupying the part of the upper Somme basin still known as Vermandois), also nicely delimited one sector of Belgium. Between Viromandui and the Ambiani of the lower Somme there was no such natural barrier. The Ambiani occupied Picardie, specifically the regions of Vimeux south of the Somme, Ponthieu to the north and the richer Santerre to the east, which the Viromandui may have coveted. Their name probably refers to settlement on both sides of the river. To the south-west, the Ambiani marched with the Caletes who gave their name to the Pays de Caux, the coastal part of present-day Seine Inférieure. The later boundary was here purely conventional, and an inscription from the Gallo-Roman sanctuary at Eu shows the presence of a minor people, the Catoslugi, between the two.[3]

To what extent Caletes and their southern neighbours the Veliocasses are to be considered Belgae is debatable. Caesar appears to attribute them to Belgium, their coins are of Belgic type and they joined the opposition to Caesar in 57 BC. Elsewhere, he lists the Caletes along with the Armorican peoples, and under the Roman Empire they were not, unless briefly, part of Belgica.[4]

Between Veliocasses, Ambiani and Viromandui, the triangular Beauvaisis belonged to the Bellovaci, the bravest fighters of Gaul according to Caesar; while this reflects their boastfulness, they were able to muster a large army. Wooded heights formed the frontier with Veliocasses, with the Bellovaci here dominating. Against the more powerful Suessiones to the east, however, they do not seem to have pushed across the Oise. This river through the centuries has formed a frontier: it is strengthened by marshes on the north-west side, by forests on the other, among them the extensive forêt de Compiègne, which sheltered both the hillfort of St. Pierre-en-Chastres and the sanctuary at Champlieu (already important in pre-Roman times). Across the Oise, the hillfort Gournay-sur-Aronde was most likely controlled by the Bellovaci against Ambiani and Viromandui: its sanctuary may have been the site of fairs open to all three people.[5] The Bellovaci, who straddle the route from Seine to Somme valleys, were clients of the central Gaulish Aedui in Caesar's time. Against their claim to dominance is also the lack of a specific gold coinage.

The Suessiones straddled two river routes, the Aisne and the Marne. The forests of the Oise valley to the west, and wooded heights along the Marne near Epernay to the south-east, seem to have marked their limits. Other boundaries are less certain. South-westwards lay the Meldi (not attributed to Roman Belgica) and the tiny Silvanectes or Sulbanectes (the form on an inscription) of whom there is no mention in Caesar. Both people were probably tributary, the Meldi to the Suessiones, the Silvanectes to the Bellovaci. Certainly, the latter's small territory, a depression surrounded by wooded heights, would have been easily dominated by a powerful neighbour.

A natural frontier was also lacking between Suessiones and Remi. The Remi admitted to Caesar that there had been a virtual state of union between them, and the easiest interpretation is that certain prominent Remi decided to gain independence from the Suessiones by joining Caesar. The Suessiones perhaps retained control of the Laonnois between Oise and Aisne (later given to the Remi), for this would fit Caesar's description of the Aisne as flowing through the far edge of Reman territory.[6]

The pre-conquest coinages of Belgium, and the reasons for attributing political meaning to their emission and spread (at least on the Gaulish side of the Channel) have been briefly reviewed. A fuller picture of the imports from Italy which were reaching parts of northern Gaul before the middle of the first century BC – wine amphorae, the occasional piece of Campanian pottery and bronze vessels – would be valuable. At present these are very thinly spread, yet sufficient to suggest that the Rhône-Saône corridor, and from there up to three possible routes, were bringing luxury objects as far north as Belgium, and from there perhaps by way of the Somme valley to Britain, in return for raw materials or slaves. If this is substantiated, then another thread in the development of the area will have been identified. At present, it is the sparsity of such items in the north as compared with the centre and south that is notable.[7]

Nonetheless, growing long-distance trade, and the desire of the aristocracy to control it, would accord with the clusters of hillforts along the valleys of Aisne and Somme. According to Caesar the Suessiones had 12 *oppida*, of which some five or six can be identified, four of them above the river valley. That one of these, Pommiers, had gained central significance is suggested on the one hand by its coin record and on the other by the fact that Caesar's taking it ended general opposition (accepting the usual identification of Caesar's Noviodunum). Vermand forms another central *oppidum*, as Incheville for the Catoslugi, and Mont César for the Bellovaci (unless some site like the Mont Capron close to future Beauvais was already in use). Among the Ambiani the situation is less clear. The nearest certain *oppidum* to Amiens is la Chaussée-Tirancourt, yet Caesar's references to Samarobrivae seem to imply occupation closer to the future Roman town of that name, on the elevated ground south of the river. No traces of this have come to light, and conceivably this lowest convenient crossing-place of the Somme had a name, which Caesar adopted, without having developed a fortified settlement. Even so, the people of Belgium show a greater tendency to centralization than either their northern or their eastern neighbours.[8]

To the east and south-east of Belgium dwelt in Caesar's time the Remi, a key people because of their early and consistent stand on Caesar's side. In Roman times, their territory extended from the Aisne valley northwards through the Laonnois to Thiérache as well as eastwards through the open chalky land of the Champagne sèche to the forested hills of Ardennes and Argonne. Their name is another boastful one, for it is equivalent to Latin Primi with loss of initial 'p' – i.e. 'the First'. Yet there are anomalies in this people, beyond the fact that they combined disparate regions of plain and hills, each with its own cultural tradition. Confirming the general impression of backwardness after the initial splendour of early la Tène is the absence of any gold coinage proper to the territory. Yet some of the earliest types of an extensive potin coinage were perhaps circulating before Caesar's time and Caesar certainly met a self-confident aristocracy.[9]

The impression is of a people poised for an upswing after a period of comparative backwardness – the future being guaranteed by their pro-Roman attitude. Illustrative of new contacts are Italian amphorae, bronze jugs and *patellae* found in cemeteries near Rethel (Ardennes). The connection with the Suessiones may have caused their inclusion by Caesar among the Belgae in the wider sense. In fact, the Italian imports and the potin coinage imply that they were now within the orbit of influences from further south, and the valley-bottom *oppidum* at Vieux-Reims may be another new development.[10]

If the Remi of Caesar's day did not control the Laonnois, they possibly controlled a larger area of the Marne valley than they did later. Caesar says that Remi were the first of the Belgic peoples he encountered, thus ignoring the people who by the fourth century were known as Catalauni, (derived from Catuvellauni). These must have been then a part either of Remi to the north or of Lingones to the south; archaeologically they belong more naturally with the Remi. One medium-sized central *oppidum* is attested at la Cheppe (Vieux-Châlons, *alias* the 'Camp d'Attila'.[11]

North of the hills and forests of Ardennes and Thiérache were peoples best called the northern Belgae, stretching from the Channel coast in the region of Boulogne eastwards across modern Belgium to the Meuse and Caesar's left-bank Germans. They are not a homogeneous group, although this is the region *par excellence* of the 'third language'. The Morini were called by Vergil, drawing on some earlier tradition, the remotest of mankind: their name means 'Sea Folk', and that of the more inland Atrebates perhaps 'Possessors of the Soil'. Both peoples were divided from the Ambiani only by a conventional frontier (the River Canche) – indeed, Hirtius considered the Atrebates to belong to Belgium. Both may have emitted some classes of the Gallo-Belgic coin series.[12] The Boulonnais and Pas de Calais are on geographical grounds alone obvious jumping-off points for Britain, and a settlement (perhaps pre-conquest) at Wissant has produced pottery showing a strong resemblance to types across the Channel. It is not, however, clear whether the Morini had developed *oppida*.[13] Their political unity in Caesar's time was enough to prevent certain *pagi* remaining in arms after others had surrendered, so perhaps the *civitas* of the Morini was a recent and insecure part of the Belgic confederacy. Yet they had an important source of potential wealth and power in coastal salt-pans.[14]

The Atrebates occupied Artois and a part of the Flandre français, and commanded two known hillforts, a large central one near Arras and a boundary site on the Escaut. The main inhabitants of Flanders were the Menapii, who in Caesar's time occupied marshy creeks and forest which proved almost impenetrable to his army. Caesar reckoned that they extended to beyond the Rhine mouth, but despite vast tracts of land their numbers, to judge from their military contingents, remained small. It may be doubted whether this sparsely inhabited region had developed any real stability or centralized control, though signs of a relatively homogeneous culture of middle and late la Tène date have been observed from De Panne eastwards. Pre-conquest coins are thinly scattered, mostly uniface and epsilon staters. The *oppidum* near Asse is therefore surprising, and since it lies south of the Scheldt is probably to be considered a northern outpost of the Nervii.[15]

Bounded on the west by the Escaut-Scheldt, Nervian land stretched across Hainaut, where the southern edges were demarcated by the forests of Arrouaise and Thiérache. To the east some ancient precursor of the medieval Forêt Charbonnière perhaps stretched north of the Sambre to form the first outcrop of the vast Ardennes forest which so impressed Caesar. But the Nervii probably stretched far enough into Brabant to contain the Dyle valley and also the area between Sambre and Meuse (suggested by their subsequent bronze coins). The area includes several distinct cultural groups, and Caesar's Nervii included smaller, presumably subjugated, tribes (Levaci, Pleumoxii, Geidumni, Ceutrones and Grudii) which probably formed *pagi*, since they were expected to contribute their own contingents to the army. While these may represent earlier la Tène peoples, no satisfactory equation of archaeological with tribal groups has been achieved.

One peculiarity of Caesar's Nervii stands out the more in view of the evidence for a previous horse-loving aristocracy. Alone of Gaulish peoples, the Nervii had no cavalry: indeed they built hedges (along the edge of forests or across open country) to act as a barrier to a mounted foe.

The formation of the Nervii into a *civitas* is perhaps reflected in the various groups of epsilon-staters. In Caesar's time they had a senate, implying an aristocracy, and their war-leader Boduognatus was thus a chief specially elected rather than a wielder of hereditary power. The *oppida* of which Caesar allowed them continued use are gradually becoming better known: with the exception of Asse, they lie on the Sambre or between it and the Meuse. Avesnelles, the most westerly, is also the largest (12 ha) of this group.[16]

Caesar stressed the unpopularity of foreign merchants among the Nervii, and indeed such objects as imported Italian amphorae have not been found so far north – again, the contrast with the early la Tène period is marked.

Eastwards beyond the Nervii were Caesar's Germani Cisrhenani – Eburones, Condrusi, Segni, Paemani and Caeroesi as well as the Atuatuci, the last supposedly descended from 6,000 wandering Teutones who had stayed behind in the north. These last are generally supposed to have occupied the middle Meuse valley, perhaps rightly, though the reasoning is suspect. No late incomers have been archaeologically identified (unless the use of caves as refuges, and the massacre in the Trou de l'Ambre, are connected). Many attempts have been made to identify their fortresses, especially the one in which Caesar besieged them in 57; most candidates are close to the Meuse, which Caesar does not mention. Also debatable is that Atuatuca, the later chef-lieu of the Tungri at Tongeren, must have belonged to them; since Atuatuca may simply mean 'the fortress' and Atuatuci 'the fortress people', the identification is not inevitable.[17] Changes which took place after Caesar, involving new folk from across the Rhine and reorganization of existing peoples, make localization difficult. This region had the least stable political geography of any within later Belgica, and since the pattern was repeated in the middle ages, bishopric boundaries are of no help.

The Atuatuci had subjected to themselves the Eburones, who owed them tribute in Caesar's time. Their localization is not straightforward either. Belgian archaeologists identify them with the cultural group in northern Limburg and Kempen (Campine) which showed such strong continuity from Urnfield times. This would certainly account for the propinquity of Eburones and Menapii mentioned by Caesar; the distribution of war-time staters attributed to the Eburones (a mixture of transrhenine and Treveran elements) also corresponds with this group.[18] But elsewhere Caesar says the Eburones mostly dwelled between Meuse and Rhine, and on this basis German scholars place them in the northern Eifel. The description of the Segni and Condrusi as lying between Treveri and Eburones then remains puzzling (the Condrusi gave their name to Condroz south of the middle Meuse). No cultural groupings can be isolated to suit the Eburones in the north Eifel. Possibly they were loosely grouped, for one explanation of their strangest institution, dual kingship, is that these commanded different areas. Both the people and their kings have names that are clearly Celtic, the Eburones being the 'yew-tree folk'.

Of the smaller peoples, apart from the Condrusi the only ones which can be certainly located are the Caeroesi ('Sheep-folk') who are the Roman Pagus Carucum, a subdivision of the Treveri, later the Frankish Pagus Caroascus. There is no etymological connection between the Famenne, a depression in the middle of the Ardennes east of Dinant, and the Paemani – which does not prove that they did not inhabit the region. One or other of these small upland peoples must have been descended from, or else succeeded to, the early la Tène group of the 'crêtes ardennaises'. After Caesar's time, all were attached to one or other of the major peoples.

The south-eastern fringes of the Ardennes, the Eifel and the Hunsrück were by Caesar's day occupied by a people calling themselves the Treveri, whose name may mean the 'river-crossers', and could apply equally well to Mosel or to Rhine.[19] For Caesar they were highly strategic, not only because they had considerable influence on their neighbours but because their land provided him with a means of reaching the Rhine. Possibly they regarded the Rhine as forming a boundary, and when they brought in 'Germani' to stiffen resistance to the Romans, Caesar of course presents the latter as a different people. More to the point, few of the Treveran 'eye' staters crossed the Rhine. But earlier types of coin, especially the pegasus stater, were at home on both banks, and pottery, fibulae and burial customs show a cultural continuum across the Rhine in the late la Tène period. Any restriction to the left bank was then a recent political development.

The Treveri do not show a stable political organization in Caesar, and had not advanced so far along the road to archaic statehood as the peoples of Belgium. We find squabbling over the paramount chieftaincy, and highly ambivalent attitudes both to Caesar and to the right-bank 'Germans'.[20] The hillforts likewise show an absence of centralization. Small or medium ones are numerous, while the larger ones that might merit the name *oppida* are notably eccentric – the Tetelberg to the west, and perhaps the enormous Donnersberg to the east. Pommern, on the lower Mosel, is almost certainly another, and new examples will doubtless fill in the gaps, but centralization at anything larger than the *pagus* level is unlikely. A silver coinage of uncertain date was struck first at Pommern, later on the Tetelberg, and the separate classes of 'eye' staters also suggest geographically distinct mints. Imported amphorae and bronze vessels here belong to the post-conquest period.

The remaining peoples have no claim to be considered Belgic. Nonetheless, the Mediomatrici and Leuci of Lorraine, upper Meuse and Moselle valleys were to become permanent members of Roman Belgica, and they also provided links between the Belgic area and east-central Gaul. The Mediomatrici are archaeologically the poorest known, with hillforts still requiring study – some of a group known south of Metz may be connected with boundaries between them and the Leuci. Hillforts of the Leuci consist of small ones in the Vosges, a potential *oppidum* quite centrally located at St. Geneviève (Essey) near Nancy, and the largest by far, Boviolles, far off to the west.[21] The Ornain valley which this last surveys was an important route between Champagne and the plateau of Langres, and the Roman successor of Boviolles was more imposing than the central city Toul.

Both peoples had gold coins derived from the *philippus* copies, but it is the use of silver and potin that links them more closely with the south. The Aedui of Burgundy controlled a passage to the Channel coast by means of clients like the Bellovaci; another route northwards led from Sequani or Lingones through Leuci and Remi.

The Lingones, Sequani and Helvetii were only grouped with the peoples of Belgica on temporary strategic grounds. All were of importance to Caesar for a variety of reasons. For Belgic Gaul they form the bridge to the south, be it Alpine passes or Rhône valley. It was the Helvetii who gave Caesar the excuse he needed to campaign north of the boundaries of the Roman province in the year 58 BC, and Caesar required no second invitation.

Before considering the conquest, however, can we gain some idea of the population represented by the Belgae and adjoining tribes? Archaeology as yet gives too flimsy a base, which only leaves the use of figures given by Caesar and extrapolation from Britain, where the evidence is fuller. Interestingly, the two approaches give results that are not too discrepant. The figure of 263,000 heads given by Caesar for the entire Helvetii – men, women and children – was supposedly taken from a recorded count, and implies a population of some 16 per km².[22] Conservative calculations based on other figures in Caesar suggest an average of 11–14 per km² throughout Gaul. Applied to Belgica, some 110,000 km², this gives a figure somewhat in excess of one million. The figure of 306,000 for the host assembled by Belgae and allies in 57 might imply a

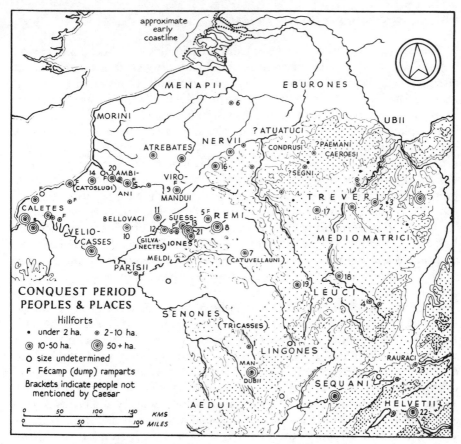

3 Map of the conquest period of Belgica showing peoples and places. Numbers refer to hillforts mentioned in text:—

1	Mont Lassois (Vix)	9	Vermand	17	Tetelbierg
2	Otzenhausen	10	Mont César	18	St. Geneviève
3	Hoppstädten-Weiersbach	11	Gournay-sur-Aronde		(Essey-les-Nancy)
4	Etival-Clairefontaine	12	St. Pierre-en-Chastres	19	Boviolles
5	Vieux-Laon	13	Pommiers	20	Liercourt-Hérondelle
6	Asse (Borgstad)	14	Incheville	21	Villeneuve-St. Germain
7	Vieux-Châlons	15	La Chaussée-Tirancourt	22	Bern-Enge
8	Vieux-Reims	16	Avesnelles	23	Basel

slightly higher population, depending on the ratio of fighting men to non-combatants (1:5, or 1:4). While this is high when compared with the archaeological record, estimates in Britain have recently suggested that a pre-conquest density of up to 11 per km² would be within reasonable bounds. If Caesar exaggerated, it certainly need not have been by a gross amount, and it is possible to take his figures as honest, if not necessarily accurate. The population of the north-east may then be put at somewhere between 1 and 1½ million with a reasonable degree of probability.

2   Caesar's encounter with the Belgae

C. Julius Caesar's political ambitions and the prodigious debts he incurred in their pursuit made it necessary that he should not only govern a province but also conduct a war. While the political background is of no concern here, it may be noted that but for events among the Helvetii, Caesar's war might have been in Illyricum, a province he held simultaneously with Cisalpine and Transalpine Gaul. As it was, Caesar could legally prevent the emigration of the Helvetii from being routed through the Roman province, but needed a pretext to attack them on land outside. Thanks to the Roman system of designating peoples outside their immediate control as 'friends and allies', a pretext was to hand. After Roman intervention in the 120s BC, (the origin of the Transalpine province) the Aedui were recognized as friends and even 'brothers' of the Roman people (perhaps mythology provided some strange link between them). These 'brothers' were now threatened by the Helvetii, and indeed the migration was connected with the attempt by the Aeduan noble Dumnorix to gain wide, unconstitutional powers over his own people and beyond.

The eventual defeat of the Helvetii in the Aeduan heartland brought Caesar tremendous prestige within Gaul, and strengthened the hand of the pre-Roman Aeduan chief, Diviciacus (brother and rival of Dumnorix). Caesar may have taken the opportunity to remind envoys who flocked to congratulate him that Rome, having previously defeated the Arverni, could claim some right of interference in Gaulish affairs even outside the Province, and in asking his permission to hold a pan-Gallic assembly the Gauls *de facto* acquiesced. The outcome presented to Caesar a technical dilemma, since he was asked to proceed against the incomer Ariovistus and his transrhenine Suebi who, invited across the Rhine by a faction of the Sequani, were a nuisance to others. But although Ariovistus too was a 'friend' of Rome, Caesar did not hesitate to take up the option, his definition of Ariovistus (despite his Celtic name) as a 'German' endowed with untrustworthy barbaric traits being merely the excuse. The stationing of six legions in winter quarters at Vesontio (Besançon) after the defeat of Ariovistus indicated that he was interested in further options, and was not going to retire peacably to the Province. The news that a coalition of Belgic tribes was mustering against him in the spring of 57 was not unwelcome, especially since he could claim that aggression came from the other side.[23]

Since the Lingones had already shown themselves to be friendly, a passage northwards and initial supplies for the army (now eight legions) were ensured. When the Remi greeted his approach by sending envoys announcing their people's decision to place themselves under his protection, he won a more northerly base and the justification that he was defending a further 'friend'.[24]

Large Belgic forces (whether or not the 266,000 claimed) mustered under the leadership of the king of the Suessiones, the strangely Roman-sounding

Galba, in Viromanduan territory, on one route from the Somme valley to Champagne. By sending a contingent of Aeduan auxiliaries into Bellovacan territory Caesar aimed at detaching a substantial body of Belgic troops. The Roman army crossed the Aisne somewhere north of Reims and encamped on the north bank. The Belgae marched south-eastwards, pausing to attempt the capture of the Roman *oppidum* Bibrax, probably Vieux-Laon, using a 'tortoise' of shields (an original invention, or borrowed from the Romans?). The abandonment of this effort in favour of opposing Caesar's lines, and the further abandonment of that when the outcome of skirmishes was unfavourable, illustrate the problems of leadership. The coalition was fragile, disbanding easily into individual components. This gave Caesar the ideal situation of facing the enemy piecemeal.

A rapid forced march westwards along the south bank of the Aisne brought Caesar to Noviodunum (almost certainly Pommiers, which he could reach by crossing the river at Condé-sur-Aisne) ahead of the retreating Suessiones, but even after the latter's arrival the sight of the Roman siege preparations was sufficient to bring about surrender.[25] The Suessiones were put under the patronage of the Remi and Caesar resumed his westward march. The Bellovaci surrendered without a battle in front of another hillfort, Bratuspantium, of uncertain location (the favourite candidate, Breteuil, has no certain hillfort). At the request of Diviciacus, the Bellovaci were treated leniently as clients of the Aedui: we are also told that ringleaders had departed to Britain, a documented example of an event that must have had many parallels.

Since the Ambiani offered no further resistance, Caesar was able to turn north-eastwards to face the threat in that area, the linked forces of Atrebates, Viromandui and Nervii. After three days' march in Nervian territory he learned that they were ten miles distant, behind the river Sabis. The identification of the river is disputed; the Selle, a tributary of the Escaut, is etymologically easier than the Sambre, but rather too small to fit Caesar's description of a broad stream, unless its ancient appearance was considerably different. If it was the Selle, then Caesar's route was not far from the frontier of Nervii and Atrebates. The Sambre would imply that the Belgae were falling back towards the hillfort at Avesnelles, in which case the crossing is likely to have been higher up the valley than the traditional location near Maubeuge.[26] Forests were a hazard to marching and fighting, and Caesar nearly lost the battle by underestimating the foe. A contingent of Treveran cavalry that was with the Romans (whether as envoys or auxiliaries) set off home with news of a Belgic victory, and it was only by extraordinary exertions that Caesar turned the tide. In a few days envoys came from non-combatant Nervians who had withdrawn further north into 'estuaries and marshes', offering surrender and begging for favourable terms. The Nervii were allowed to keep their land and strongholds: no mention is made of their allies but it may have been at this point that the pro-Roman noble Commios was appointed by Caesar to be king of the Atrebates.

There remained the Atuatuci, who had failed to join the Nervii in time for the battle, and who now concentrated their forces into one stronghold. From the description, it was a promontory fort or *éperon barré*, but the lack of any reference to a major river argues against the citadel at Namur and the Mont Falhize near Huy, both of them washed by the Meuse. Reoccupation of the earlier fort of Hastedon (St. Servais, just north of Namur) is a possibility. Other candidates are not lacking, but lie mostly in the Entre-Sambre-et-Meuse area, which probably belonged to the Nervii.[27] Once again investment with Roman siege equipment led to surrender, but since the Atuatuci launched a further treacherous attack, their treatment was correspondingly sterner, with Caesar claiming to have sold over 50,000 into slavery – a welcome source of revenue to himself and his officers as well as a terrible example to the Gauls. Throughout, Caesar sought to impress them – by speed, by superior techniques, by generosity or sternness as appropriate.

Only the Morini and Menapii still eluded his grasp as the campaigning season of 57 ended. But if Gaul was otherwise pacified, as he claimed, then he needed to turn either to Britain or to Germany. The disposition of his legions' winter quarters, spread out from the Belgae to the lower Loire, suggests an intention to campaign against Britain from the Loire mouth.[28] Preparations for this caused a revolt among the Armoricans, the suppression of which occupied the summer of 56. Caesar's trusted legate, Labienus, was left among the Belgae with a watching brief, especially against the ambivalent Treveri, but the only action there was a short, inconclusive campaign against the Morini and Menapii, led by Caesar in the late summer. Rather than surrender, they withdrew into forests and marshes. One legion may have been stationed among the Morini for the winter.[29]

Morini and Menapii were of no less concern in 55, since Caesar needed the use of their ports for a British expedition. Plans were once again postponed before unforeseen circumstances – Usipetes and Tencteri crossed the Rhine looking for fresh territory. Lands of Menapii, Eburones and Condrusi were invaded, and Caesar was quite prepared to pose as protector of all three – clearly, a pretext for an expedition into Germany was by no means unwelcome. The geography of the campaign sets problems. To trouble the Condrusi, the Usipetes and Tencteri must already have come southwards from their original crossing of the Rhine, but it is Dio not Caesar who tells us that they entered Treveran territory.[30] We do not know whether Caesar passed north or south of the Ardennes (or even through them) in his pursuit: any version creates difficulties. The final battle (for the sake of which Caesar technically broke a truce) is sited by him at the confluence of Rhine and Mosa, normally the Meuse. There is however no hint that Caesar had pursued the enemy back the way they had come (unless provided by the mention of women and children, unlikely to have travelled as far as the raiding parties). Mosa might here mean the Mosella or Mosel, a diminutive form. But there is no description of the Eifel ridges down which Caesar must in that case have chased the enemy, nor of the Treveri through whose land he must have passed. True, the bridge across the Rhine, the construction of which follows hard on the battle, is more likely to have been built between Koblenz and Köln than much further north. But Caesar may well have taken time to explore the Rhine mouth before coming south, and such omissions are not un-characteristic.[31]

The building of the Rhine bridge, a grand gesture and noteworthy technical achievement, occasioned the receiving into Roman friendship of the first transrhenine people, the Ubii. The short punitive campaign mounted against the Sugambri for helping Usipetes and Tencteri was however not a success, since the enemy disappeared into the forests. Caesar quickly cut his losses, destroyed the bridge and turned his attention back to the Morini and Britain despite the lateness of the season. A part of the Morini assured him of their peaceful intentions, while others still held aloof, gave trouble while he was away in Britain and only submitted after reprisals; they were made subject to Commios the Atrebate.

Caesar's simplicity of style leaves another problem of geography in connection with the expeditions to Britain – his points of departure. In 55 these were two or three in number: none is named, but his interest in the shortest possible crossing suggests that at least one, if not all, were north of Boulogne and even of Cap Gris Nez. Candidates for the ports of 55 are thus Wissant and Sangatte, because of their northerly position, because of evidence for a settlement at Wissant, and because old, arguably pre-Roman, roads, reach both places. It can also be argued that Boulogne with its estuary was then as now by far the most convenient harbour, and could hardly have been passed over; detailed arguments based on winds and tides have also been used to support Boulogne. Boulogne is the most generally accepted candidate too for Portus Itius, mentioned by Caesar as a point of departure in 54 BC. Yet arguments can again be made in favour of Wissant as Portus Itius, not least that Ptolemy gives Ition as a headland that is also the turning-point of the coast; if the name means 'port by the headland Ition', then Wissant fits. Changes to the coastline since ancient times can be used in favour of any of the locations, and it is to be hoped that archaeological discoveries will clarify the issue.[32]

While Caesar's narrative may be vague on geography (being written for those to whom it would present little interest), it invariably gives a clear, connected version of events, especially his own actions and the reasons for them. If these can sometimes be exposed as specious or misleading, it is usually from a study of his own words. His descriptions of the *civitates* of Gaul and their aristocracies are clearly valuable. What can archaeological evidence add? At first sight the answer might appear to be little, apart from supporting identifications already suggested by a combination of topography and Caesar's text. But this is partly because research is insufficiently advanced, partly because of misunderstanding over what archaeology can best do.

Archaeology from its nature gives a poor account of the kind of events that throng Caesar's narrative – diplomacy, marches and battles. Destruction levels can be clear enough, but their precise dating often depends on the written narrative. If numerous villages in Flanders were to show signs of destruction in the late la Tène horizons, then it would be reasonable to connect them with reprisals against Morini and Menapii. It can of course be risky to make such connections too early. It is tempting to suppose that the great ramparts of Pommiers and other hillforts were erected in 58/57 as the decision of the Belgae to resist Caesar was reached, and that the Remi built a new dump rampart at Vieux-Laon to protect themselves against either Romans or Suessiones. Even if this seems on balance likely, earlier dates cannot be ruled out, nor can we be sure that the smaller hillforts of the Treveri were a reaction to the Roman threat rather than to internal rivalries. It is the general picture that can be provided, not details or specific events. As the pattern within each region becomes clearer, it will be possible to bring the two different types of knowledge more meaningfully together.

The remains of Roman fortifications, known from aerial photography with or without excavation, pose their own problems. In form, they immediately stand out as the work of an incoming power – neat ditches turning careful corners testify to Roman discipline as do dump ramparts to native faith in the efficacy of size. The site north of the Aisne at Mauchamp fits nicely with the geography of Caesar's advance against the Belgae, and its 43 ha are arguably just enough for his six legions. Yet the *claviculae* at the entrances point to a later date, and Caesar's camp is arguably to be sought further downstream.[33] The problem is one that excavation could solve. So is the dating of the Roman bases near Breteuil, Folleville and Vendeuil-Caply, more likely Augustan than Caesarian. The Roman ditches which form an annexe against the *oppidum* at Liercourt-Hérondelle on the Somme are puzzling, for no siege is recorded there, and the function is not clear.[34]

Numismatics have already given much, with promise of more to come; the aid is mutual, for the appearance on coins of names mentioned in Caesar has provided pegs to help date the coins.[35] There is of course a need for caution. For a time it seemed that all coinages derived from Gallo-Belgic C were of the war years, effectively representing so many war-chests; now it appears that a pre-war origin must be allowed. Even some of the inscribed coins – the Nervian Viros, the Treveran Vocarant and Loucotios – may be pre-war, and it cannot be assumed that the inscribed coins are the latest of each series. It is clear from hoards that older coins were still actively circulating at the time of the war, but also that many series show an abrupt decline in weight and precious metal content. This last clearly fits wartime conditions – the need to strike as much gold as possible when stocks of good metal were disappearing as booty. Several hoards may date to the period of the war, the most striking being Frasnes-lez-Buissenal, where gold torcs were found along with Nervian staters (some with the name Viros). Even by themselves, the hoards would suggest a time of troubles.

Another phenomenon of the war years is the enormous spread of the central Gaulish silver coinages, most notably that of Togirix. There is a rough correspondence between areas of concentration and the legions' winter quarters: moreover, the earlier Rhône valley coinages are connected with a Roman demand that local communities raise military units and pay them. Almost certainly, the Togirix coinage was used to pay the Gaulish auxiliaries which Caesar attached to his legions.[36] The same phenomenon on a smaller scale may be seen in the silver coins of Commios found among the Atrebates. Bronze coins were also a product of the war years; the coinage of the Suessiones with legend Criciru appears in gold, silver and bronze. The coinages thus add a dimension missing from the written account.

3   Rebellions and pacification

Warfare and changes in the balance of power both within each *civitas* and between neighbouring *civitates* were nothing new in Gaul. Caesar's presence speeded up the process of change, so that the shifts that might otherwise have taken a generation were compressed into a few years. Since this was accomplished by an external power, there were pressures on the Gaulish nobles to accommodate themselves to the Roman way of life and thinking. Commios, Vercingetorix, (presumably) Togirix, and others spent time at Caesar's head-quarters. On the one hand this might lead to the Remi forming a free republic with a very Romanized bronze coinage.[37] On the other hand the resulting tensions could deepen factional differences, or even provoke wholesale revolt.

The Treveri were always a potential danger because of their excellent cavalry, their situation close to the Rhine and their ambivalent attitudes. That these attitudes sprang from internal factions must have been clear to Caesar since they sent envoys to complain about the Suebi, while later he heard persistent rumours that they were encouraging 'Germans' to cross the Rhine. Their flight from the battle against the Nervii was ominous, as was their more recent failure to send delegates to the assemblies which Caesar held annually.

It is understandable that in 54 he might judge it unwise to depart again for Britain without some tangible evidence of their submission. Haste, however, led to poor diplomacy and a clumsy interference in the Treveran power structure. The main claimant for supreme power, Indutiomarus, gathered his forces at Caesar's approach and withdrew into the fastnesses of the Ardennes or Eifel. His son-in-law and rival, Cingetorix, put himself at Caesar's disposition and swore loyalty to Rome; the presence of Caesar and his legions caused a majority of the minor chiefs to follow his example. Finding himself isolated, Indutiomarus eventually followed suit, giving specious excuses for his previous conduct. Caesar demanded Indutiomarus' son among his hostages, and further insulted him by having other chiefs pledge loyalty one by one to Cingetorix. The two men may well have derived their power from different *pagi* of the Treveri; indeed if a class of 'eye' staters without legend is rightly attributed to Indutiomarus, an eastern base is likely for him, whereas a westerly stronghold may have determined Cingetorix' stance.[38]

Caesar's taking of many Gaulish aristocrats to Britain (choosing, when forced, to kill Dumnorix rather than leave him behind) shows awareness that his hold on Gaul was insecure. The continual burden of provisioning the legions was another potential bone of contention. The summer of 54 brought a drought (visible in the tree-ring record) that caused a poor harvest and thus exacerbated the problem.[39] Caesar wanted to keep his legions in the north for the winter, but in order to lessen the burden he split them up rather than grouping them in accustomed manner. Three were in Belgium, that is among the Ambiani, Suessiones or neighbours, four others among Morini, Nervii, Remi and Eburones respectively – the last two or three forming a loose ring round the Treveri. Caesar himself stayed at Amiens, as if expecting trouble.

Much ink has been spilled over the location of the camps, especially the one among the Eburones, where the site, called Atuatuca, appears to have been an *oppidum*. This may have been a normal situation for Caesar's army (the first winter was at Besançon) and the site at Liercourt-Hérondelle might also belong to this year. The only topographical detail concerning Atuatuca, the existence nor far to the west of a narrow defile suitable for ambush, is too common a feature of the Ardennes landscape to be of assitance; thus the recent suggestion of Spa fits well enough but lacks archaeological confirmation.[40] The camp of Q. Cicero (the orator's brother), three days' march into Nervian territory, may have lain near the middle Sambre, that of Labienus on the borders of Remi and Treveri, perhaps just east of the Meuse.

The Eburones were in some sense clients of the Treveri, and neither of their kings, the older Catuvolcus or the younger and more active Ambiorix, was friendly to Caesar. Since they had never technically surrendered to him, they were within their rights in objecting to the Roman camp. It may be pushing the evidence too hard to suggest that the gold staters of the Eburones suddenly appeared in 54 in preparation for war, as they were clearly the current coin of this period.[41]

The Eburones opened hostilities against the Romans at Atuatuca, while the Treveri were still quiet. By a ruse (a supposedly imminent German attack) which deceived one of Caesar's less able legates, the Romans were lured out of their camp into an ambush from which only a few survivors struggled south through the hills to join Labienus. The easier westward route was taken by an exultant Ambiorix, who summoned the Atuatuci and Nervii to an attack on the camp of Q. Cicero. To this they laid siege – with a circumvallation and siege-towers (another technique imitated from the Romans) and used heated sling-balls to set fire to the thatched buildings. Only resolute and disciplined fighting kept the assailants at bay, while finally a message was taken to Caesar by a pro-Roman Nervian. Caesar's arrival with two legions diverted attention from Cicero, and the Gauls were tricked into a battle on unfavourable ground that ended in rout. News of Cicero's relief reached

Labienus, some 60 miles away, in less than 12 hours.

Unrest was now general, and Indutiomarus, encouraged rather than deterred, planned to strengthen his own forces with paid help from across the Rhine. A connection between these German mercenaries and the Treveran silver coinages with 'sitting man' is an attractive hypothesis. Cingetorix was declared a public enemy, but a precipitate attack on Labienus' camp was unsuccessful, leading to Indutiomarus' flight and ignominious death. Relatives continued the cause, with help promised by northern Belgae and Germani. Caesar, in the course of the winter, raised two new legions in Cisalpine Gaul and borrowed a third from Pompey. In March of 53 Cicero suggested to a friend on Caesar's staff that the Treveri were '*capitales*' or deadly (a pun on the *tresviri capitales* or public executioners of Rome – but also on the head-hunting habits of Gauls).[42]

Caesar's campaign was planned to neutralize the northern Belgae before an advance against Treveri and Eburones. The Menapii were finally brought to submission as Roman engineering skill was displayed in bridges and causeways, and were granted peace on condition that they did not aid Ambiorix. Reinforcements had meanwhile reached Labienus, and he moved forward into Treveran territory, camping just across a river from the Treveran forces. If (as Dio's narrative suggests) he had already moved forward before being reinforced, then the river could be the Mosel south of Trier: otherwise it must be identified with the Chiers or the Semois, with the whole action still confined to the western fringes of Treveran territory. A more central location would better fit the decisiveness of Labienus' ensuing victory and the immediate retreat eastwards across the Rhine of the anti-Roman Treveri together with their belated 'German' reinforcements. Cingetorix was reinstated with Roman backing, perhaps being given the status of king. No coins can be directly attributed to or connected with him, but a hoard of 150 Treveran staters found at Odenbach (southern Hunsrück) may reflect the events of this year.[43]

Caesar himself continued to detach the Eburones from potential sources of support. Crossing the western Ardennes (or skirting them to the south) he arrived among the Treveri after the final decisive battle and marched forward to the Rhine. The second Rhine bridge, a little upstream from the first, was again part show-piece, part threat. The Ubii protested their innocence and good faith, claiming that the Treveri had been helped by the Suebi. The last were as usual nowhere to be seen. Dio succinctly comments that Caesar accomplished nothing, while Caesar himself at this point in his narrative diverts the reader's attention with an extended ethnographical excursus on Gauls, Germans and the difference between them.[44]

Ambiorix proved almost as elusive as the Suebi, though Caesar's march into the Ardennes occasioned the suicide (or ritual self-immolation) of Catuvolcus, too old for guerilla warfare. Caesar divided his forces, sending Labienus and Trebonius respectively towards the lower Scheldt and the middle Meuse.

Caesar's own path is less clear, for he speaks in one breath of the Scheldt, its confluence with the Meuse and the extremity of the Ardennes where Ambiorix had taken refuge. (While the Scheldt was indeed linked by the Striene to the Meuse in ancient times, it flows well north of anything that could be called the Ardennes.) The search proved vain, and an attempt to use the Eburones' neighbours (Sugambri, from across the Rhine!) against them backfired when the latter started attacking the Romans instead. Caesar had to content himself with widespread devastation of the land and a claim of extirpation rather than a spectacular victory and a royal captive.

He must have been aware that trouble was brewing elsewhere, for the winter quarters of 53/52 were divided among Treveri, Lingones and Senones. Neither the Belgae nor the Treveri and neighbours played an active part in the great resistance of 52 led by the Arvernian Vercingetorix, until the latter was besieged in Alesia and a relief army was organized. Commios the Atrebate, now like many others renouncing loyalty to Caesar, was instrumental in gathering a Belgic contribution, in which the Mediomatrici joined for the first time.[45] The following year, undeterred by Vercingetorix' defeat, he helped form another Belgic coalition, sharing leadership with Correus the Bellovacan. Old jealousies complicated the plan of action, which initially involved attacking the Suessiones on the grounds that they were now clients of the Remi. Caesar's rapid approach caused the concentration of the Belgae and their allies, and one battle was enough to break the back of the resistance. This probably took place in the Oise valley near Compiègne, the archaeological evidence adduced for a location near Nointel (some 25 km to the south-west) being unconvincing.[46]

Various mopping-up operations remained – brief raids into the lands of the Eburones and Treveri, and vain attempts, going on into the winter, to capture Commios. Two versions of the latter's escape have been preserved: that M. Antonius agreed to his request never again to look a Roman in the face, and that he escaped to Britain by a ruse, making Caesar (who wintered at Arras) believe he had left by hoisting sails when his ships were still aground.[47] Since not all Roman agreements were honoured, both versions may be true. Commios is Belgic Gaul's equivalent to Vercingetorix, a Gaulish noble who turned against Rome after being close enough to Caesar and his legates to gain an acquaintance with Roman ways. Among the reasons for his later implacable hatred was the fact that Labienus, already suspecting him, had instigated an attempt on his life in 52, before the open outbreak of hostilities.

Caesar's later campaigns underscore the darker side of his relations with the Gauls. His diplomacy was often too obviously self-interested and hasty to do more than briefly postpone trouble. His desire to keep both Germany and Britain as potential areas for advance led to a merry-go-round of military activity to which Gaulish interests were perpetually subordinated. Resistance – which he treated as revolt, even from peoples who had not formally submitted – was neither unexpected nor necessarily unwelcome, since it could give him an apparently legitimate reason for increasing his army. Caesar tells us little of the booty, other than captives, which fell to him and his troops. But he came to Gaul with enormous debts and left able to distribute equally enormous bribes – indeed he brought so much gold back that the price of it fell in Italy. Such a quantity can only have come from the deliberate plundering of the sanctuaries where it might be stored along with other spoils of tribal warfare – the plundering of the treasure in the sacred lake of Tolosa (an earlier episode in Roman relations with Gaul) must have been often imitated.[48] The lightweight, impure staters of the war period, and their disappearance thereafter are a part of the same story, which may have been important in turning men like Commios against the person who was at once conquering hero and great overlord-patron. The rhetorical set-piece that later found its way into Orosius, portraying Gaul as a once beautiful woman, too ravaged by the raging fevers of war to raise her head again, had some basis.[49] Arguably only the sheer size of the population prevented its coming close to the truth.

The brighter side is to be seen in those Gauls who, even if from self-interest, did not desert Caesar, or who were won over to a pro-Roman stance. The year 50, when Caesar expected that he would soon leave Gaul, saw effort put into conciliatory gestures. Rewards included lands, rich gifts, status and perhaps Roman citizenship. Late coins with the legend Q. Julius Togirix suggest the last (however inexplicable the choice of Quintus), though for others the honour may have come only after military service in the civil wars which started in 49.[50] Had Caesar's diplomacy been of a higher order, there might have been a Julius Commios. One example of a contrary change in heart may be to hand in the Treveran Arda. His earliest coins are very lightweight gold staters (though his relationship to Treverans mentioned by Caesar is unclear). Later, he struck silver and bronze coins (one based on a Roman *denarius* of 49) and his centre was the Tetelbierg, where furnishings of a mint have been found. Bronze coins based on the elephant-*denarius* of Caesar, but bearing the name of Hirtius, were almost certainly also minted there, and the site was of great importance for the control of the Treveri in the post-war generation.[51]

Service in the Roman army, both during and after the war, was a powerful mechanism for increasing the adaptation of Gauls to Roman habits and society. To the Gauls, accustomed both to warfare and to mercenary service, the Roman army had an obvious appeal, the discipline and loss of independence palliated by regular remuneration. The magnificent ceremonial of Caesar's final solemn review of his army in Treveran territory – perhaps in view of the Tetelbierg – must have served as an advertisement as well as a threat. Not all of the thousands of men that he took with him on subsequent campaigns – partly as hostages – need have been unwilling to go.[52] Those who served as officers and those who meanwhile helped maintain peace in Gaul formed the bridge between past and future. Had Roman control been relaxed they would in any case have formed the next aristocracy, using the prestige gained through external contacts.

4 The aftermath: continuity and change

With the end of Caesar's campaigns consecutive narrative is also lost, and there follows a period for which written information is intermittent. The country was of interest to historians only if rebellions or invasions demanded military intervention, and of the accounts that were written not all survive. Otherwise, ethnographers and geographers (the best being Strabo) listed peoples and described the land, while the encyclopaedist Pliny the Elder collected assorted, often trivial information. The loss, though palpable, must be kept in perspective. True, Caesar allows insights into the politics of individual *civitates*. But his narrative is inevitably one-sided and gains value in proportion to the amount of archaeological evidence that can be mustered to provide a context or corrective. While the gain is mutual – literary precision lending a sharper focus – it is archaeology that provides the most consistent picture of a society in course of adaptation.

Although the general uprising that his enemies gleefully anticipated on Caesar's departure from Gaul did not take place, withdrawal of Roman forces from the north was indeed hazardous and usually gave rise within a few years to unrest.[53] Meanwhile, the archaeological record shows a remarkable degree of continuity, with major changes in settlement and a markedly new material culture occurring only after a generation. Indeed, only recently has a distinction between pre-conquest and post-conquest pottery (la Tène D1 and D2) become practicable. The relationship between Roman state and Gaulish peoples, and the various mechanisms of change deserve attention, even if the latter can often only be presented in hypothetical form.

The period can be conveniently divided, the first part coinciding roughly with the long series of civil wars at Rome, first between Caesar and Pompey, then between Caesar's heir (Octavian-Augustus) and Antony. So long as there were no major uprisings, Gaul was of little concern to the rulers of Rome unless as a recruiting ground. Attention was limited to appointing able men who could either forestall or deal with any problems. Before Caesar's triumph over Gaul had taken place in 46, the Bellovaci had already given further trouble (perhaps also the Menapii and Morini). 'Germans' too were a nuisance, occasioning the presence in the north of A. Hirtius (writer of the last book of Caesar's Commentaries) in 45–44. Evidence of his presence and success takes the form of bronze coins with his name and the title *imperator*, probably struck by the Remi.[54] Both Hirtius and his successor, Munatius Plancus, combined military with diplomatic actions, distributing favours where they were likely to have good effect. Plancus' activity, which included the foundation of Roman colonies planned by Caesar at Lyon and Augst to complement the one already founded at Nyon, was concentrated further south. This was also true of the men who governed Gaul on behalf of Antony between 43 and 40; they concentrated their attention on events in Italy. It is not surprising that Octavian, shortly after gaining control of Gaul, found it necessary to send his ablest general there. Besides fighting in Aquitania, Agrippa had to settle unrest in the north-east. His measures involved a further crossing of the Rhine, and this is generally connected with the settlement of the Ubii and perhaps other peoples on the west bank of the river. The first stages of the network of roads radiating from Lyon to Rhine, Channel coast and Atlantic should also be attributed to this governorship. The need for an improved system must have been clear, and the fact that Octavian even contemplated invading Britain in 34 suggests that communications were in good order.[55]

The success of Agrippa's campaigns is attested by the ensuing silence of the record for some half-dozen years. Later, trouble again broke loose and there is a growing body of archaeological evidence to suggest that it was on a serious scale. A new fortification at Kaster-Kanne near Maastricht is dated by dendrochronology to 31 BC, and suggests that resistance was wider than the written sources say. Occupied hillforts – including strongholds like Otzen-hausen – offered natural centres of resistance: there are hints that refortification occurred in sites varying from the tiny St. Dié to the massive Donnersberg. The warrior-graves of Trier-Olewig and Konz-Filzen could also belong here.[56] The Tetelbierg may have remained for a time in the hands of a loyal nobleman, since copies of Caesar's elephant-*denarius* again appear, but with the name of the new governor of the Gauls, C. Carrinas. Yet a destruction level dated by a coin-hoard belongs to 29 or just thereafter.[57] On the Roman side we know that timbers for a fort on the Petrisberg overlooking the Mosel valley at Trier were felled in spring or early summer of 30.[58] Carrinas celebrated a triumph 'ex Gallia', but not until 28, and the peoples mentioned by Dio are the Morini and the Suebi. M. Nonius Gallus was campaigning against Treveri and 'Germans' in 29, at the moment when Octavian closed the doors of the temple of Janus in token of ubiquitous peace. Perhaps the extent of the unrest was underestimated, and an attempt to keep the western Treveri loyal failed. Whether all of the northern Belgae were involved may eventually become clear.

That Augustus (when he visited Gaul in 27) found a need for organization is hardly surprising. The division of Caesar's Gaul into the three provinces which both ethnography and practical experience suggested (Aquitania, Lugdunensis and Belgica) probably belongs here, as does the institution of a census. Further consideration of Augustus' measures is however best undertaken after the archaeological pattern has been reviewed.

Down to 30 BC at least, the major *oppida* were continuously and more intensively occupied; indeed it is in this period that they attained urban characteristics, the Tetelbierg being the most obvious example. There are, it is true, some new developments. The site of Villeneuve-St.-Germain, in a fortified meander of the Aisne just east of Soissons, belongs to the post-conquest period; it must have largely replaced Pommiers as a centre of population, though the latter shows some continuation.[59] Other analogous shifts of site may yet be found. The name Caesaromagus (Beauvais) suggests the action, if not of Caesar himself, then of D. Brutus after the campaign of 46, and movement down from the Mont César would not be surprising. Remains of a very extensive but so far undated ditch system at Reims are perhaps to be fitted into this period.[60] Sites whose primary function was later religious seem to have been important centres of habitation and exchange, notably Champlieu (south-west of Soissons), Vendeuil-Caply (between Ambiani and Bellovaci) and Bois l'Abbé near Eu (mouth of the Bresle, just south of the Somme). All such sites are characterized by pottery of purely late la Tène tradition, and by increasing evidence that they housed mints.[61]

The coinage of this period consisted of silver, potin and struck bronze. The general picture is of continuity except for the absence of gold, which was no longer struck (formal proof is admittedly lacking) and barely circulated. In sheer quantity the larger cast bronze types are dominant. The commonest have diademed head and boar reverse (Leuci, probably minted at Boviolles); a man with spear and torc and elephant reverse (Remi); and, further north, a stylized branch ('au rameau', Nervii). Certain classes of another widespread type with two facing animals were manufactured at Villeneuve-St.-Germain, and there are numerous others with a more restricted circulation.[62]

The silver coins of Belgica were mostly rather small issues, of restricted distribution and imprecise date. Only one can be classed alongside the still widely circulating coins of Togirix and other contemporary silver from Lugdenensis. This bears the name(s) Ateula Vlatos and was already circulating in the 40s, since it was found in a mixed hoard (Vernon, near Poitiers) with Roman coins down to 45 BC. Widely spread north-east of the Loire, it is found on all sorts of sites and in several hoards down to the period around 30.[63]

Struck bronzes began to be produced with bewildering variety, gradually replacing potin. Widespread and more localized types can again be distinguished. Most numerous are two belonging to the Remi, with legends Remo/Remo and Atisios/Remos. Further east the Treveran coins of Arda held the field; less abundant types are ascribable to Mediomatrici and Leuci.[64] In the north, but still inland, are certain struck classes of the Nervian 'branch' coins, while the west was dominated by a type with running man.[65] A multitude of coins have a more localized distribution; some of these are only becoming known through excavations at such sites as Bois l'Abbé, Champlieu and Villeneuve-St.-Germain. A distinction can thus be made between coins which travelled widely and those which circulated at local, very probably *pagus* level. It may be surmised that the functions, if overlapping, were not identical. This conclusion is the more plausible since (except for potins) it is usually the more widely circulating coinages that have single or double names, indicating someone with official standing. Coins of Meldi and Mediomatrici have as part of the legend, Arcantodan, meaning 'magistrate of silver', and some of Remi, Mediomatrici and Veliocasses indicate the *civitas*.[66]

Taken together, the coins and sites indicate two processes at work. The first is the natural continuation of the tendencies, observable even in northern Gaul, towards urbanization, with the *pagi* and some *civitates* developing focal points where exchange and administration of justice could take place. Since the war had heightened political awareness and cohesiveness, despite casualties among the nobility, no surprise need be felt. Nonetheless, it seems that the tendency was accelerated by incorporation within the area of Roman rule, however loosely organized this may have been at first. The tribute that Caesar imposed on Gaul – the not unreasonable sum of 40 million sesterces – was in theory (on the analogy of all other provinces) to be paid annually.[67] Collection can only have been supervised either by local notables entrusted with the task, or by Roman army officers.

Parallels from other provinces suggest that such people, whether native or Roman, might rank as *praefecti*, and control one or more *civitates*: silence from Gaul is so far complete. Taxes, if not in kind, could only have been collected in Gaulish coinages, since Roman coins were reaching the north in insufficient numbers. The need to pay taxes would then stimulate the production of coin and the market exchange of goods for coin, thus favouring the growth of urbanized settlements which could also serve as collection points. Loyal chiefs from privileged peoples – the Remi are an obvious case – might be encouraged to produce coin as well as to collect it for Roman purposes. Such a system would readily give grounds for revolts, but can hardly have been rigid, since there was insufficient circulating coinage among Morini, Menapii and northern Nervii for it to have worked in the same way there as further south.[68]

Privileges in the Roman world were never far separated from duties, and from the start, loyal peoples such as Aedui, Lingones and Remi and even Treveri had supplied auxiliary troops for Caesar. Commios, before his defection, was once stationed with an auxiliary contingent among the Menapii. A reasonable hypothesis is that this system continued after Caesar's departure, with loyal chiefs policing their own and neighbouring peoples, or at least providing extra levies for the Roman army when intermittently required (for instance by Munatius Plancus).[69] While service in the Roman army might be paid in Roman coinage, native militia would certainly receive Gaulish, and the larger silver coinages would be minted for this purpose. Moreover Gaulish troops might be stationed in or near an *oppidum* – the clearest examples are Bern-Enge and Basel, but items of military equipment have recently been recognized on the Tetelberg, and the camp with double ditches at Vendeuil-Caply is on a native site, if not an *oppidum*. It is not unlikely that legionary contingents were also stationed in or near native *oppida*, for this is in keeping with the practice of Caesar and of the Romans elsewhere. The presence of military contingents, native or Roman, further encouraged the circulation of coin and the growth of *oppida*.[70]

Just how great a legionary presence northern Gaul saw in this period, even for specific campaigns, is uncertain. Also uncertain is whether Augustus made any changes in Gaul when he reorganized the army in the years following 31 BC (his final victory over Antony). Possible changes include new legions, changed bases, the payment of auxiliaries in Roman coin and a decrease in native forces. It is generally supposed that a marked increase in the military occupation of Gaul came a good decade later, after the end of fighting in Spain and just before the advances that led to the major German campaigns. Agrippa was again in northern Gaul in 20–19; further developments in the road network and general military dispositions are to be connected.[71]

It is not easy to date occupation levels with any precision between the years 30 and 15. Yet it may become feasible, since the number of northern sites suggesting an abrupt change not long after 30 is growing – destruction on the Tetelbierg, an end to occupation at Villeneuve-St.-Germain, a hiatus at Pommeroeul.[72] Between 30 and 15 the archaeological record changes considerably. Red-gloss pottery from N. Italy (*terra sigillata*, or Arretine, after Arezzo) started to arrive in the north, and almost simultaneously with it the products of branch plants in Lyon (the dating still debated).[73] Experiments led to the production, by a mixture of Italian and Gaulish techniques, of similar wares, some red, some brown, many black. The earliest examples in the north are from the Petrisberg at Trier, date to about 30 BC, and are hard to categorize: the better known varieties are a decade or so later.[74] To these 'imitations' the misleading name 'Belgic' or 'Gallo-Belgic' ware is often given, and such pottery was very likely being made south of Reims and in the Argonne before the end of the first century BC, though how much earlier is not clear. Lyon also exported thin-walled wares such as 'Aco' beakers from about 20 BC if not earlier, and as local potters throughout Gaul began to imitate Italian shapes the whole repertoire of pottery was diversified: the pottery from these experiments is sometimes called 'gallo-romain précoce'. Italian wine amphorae and the bronze paraphernalia of wine-drinking also arrived in increasing amounts, an illustration being the rich burials at Goeblingen-Nospelt (Lux.) where amphorae and bronze vessels were accompanied by both Roman and native styles of pottery, as well as fine swords in late la Tène tradition.[75]

In this period of 15 years, then, an upward spiral of southern imports and influences can be seen in northern Gaul, while at the same time the native coinages (especially silver and potin) thin out and Roman coins gradually increase (especially those of the new mint at Nîmes). The end of the civil wars and measures taken by Augustus in 27 or later, played their part, even if the causes cannot at present be disentangled.

It is clear that the presence of legionary troops in Gaul played a role both in attracting Italian pottery and in stimulating the manufacture in Gaul of types which resembled it. Greater clarity is reached with early imported lamps, which seem to have been almost entirely for military use. A taste for Italian-style pottery was then rapidly acquired by the Gaulish élite and from there was soon transmitted further down the social scale. Service in the auxiliary forces (possibly seen by the men buried with their swords at Goeblingen-Nospelt) was doubtless an important link in the chain which ended with various grades of Roman-style pottery, metalware and glass being relatively commonplace.

The very rapidity of this development makes it impracticable to use early *terra sigillata* as a simple criterion for identifying Augustan military sites in Gaul. Further research into the dispersion of the very earliest Italian imports and Gaulish equivalents may yet provide a new solution, and throw light on the organization of both army supplies and civilian markets.

If the presence of the army was a factor in the changing material culture, it was of even greater importance for the sites that were to become the Gallo-Roman *civitas* capitals, and for the roads that linked them. The building of roads was a normal and even necessary army activity and stretches of road flanked with V-shaped ditches known from aerial photography in the north present a military appearance. The laying out of roads may have been the chief activity for highly mobile legionary troops stationed in the hinterland of Gaul in the 20s, with Agrippa's second governorship in 20–19 BC concentrating efforts. Three hundred years later an Aeduan orator could complain that the roads served military rather than civilian purposes.[76] But along with this went the choice of sites for bases, even if not permanent. Now these bases ceased to be adjuncts to the *oppida* and took up rationally chosen sites controlling river-crossings or other strategic points. At Trier and Amiens there are indications of valley-bottom military sites near the obvious fords or bridging points, and the earliest bridge at Trier belongs to the year 18–17 BC.[77]

There was interplay between basic strategic geography and the need for political entities, and it was perhaps understood that each *civitas* would include one central site where military occupation would be temporary. Other bases lay between these central sites, the later *civitas* capitals, which were more than one day's march apart. Those at Breteuil, Vendeuil-Caply and Folleville (the latter two 12 ha and 16 ha respectively) are examples, along with Mirebeau east of Dijon; excavations have recently added a large (perhaps 30 ha) base at Velzeke, well north of the Bavay–Köln road.[78] When the army moved eastwards, during if not before Augustus' extended stay between 15 and 13, appropriate sites were ready for the civilian population, some of which had already assembled to provide services in the vicinity (coins were concentrated just outside the ramparts at Velzeke, as at Neuss on the Rhine). Augustan occupation at Arlaines, just west of Soissons, may indicate an intermediary stage between evacuation of the latter site for civilian purposes and withdrawal of the troops elsewhere. Many variations were possible; the hypothesis that most cities were preceded by a period of military occupation in fact goes beyond current evidence and will be confirmed only by future discoveries.

Precise dates are not yet available, but there are indications of a relative chronology. Logically, the roads attributed to Agrippa, leading from Lyon to the Channel and the Rhine, should have been the first to be laid out. An early date for the Langres–Trier road may explain why the site at Langres, usually presumed to be an *oppidum*, never descended from its inconvenient perch. The first road may have bypassed the site of Trier (where the advantage of a good ford across the Mosel was neutralized by difficult cliffs on the far side) by keeping to the left bank of the river from Metz northwards: later, the cliffs were cut, and the valley site could be used. The first road to the Channel may have been an improvement of the old Gaulish one by Autun, Sens and Beauvais. From the last, an early road went north-eastwards to Bavay via Vermand, whereas later roads aimed at St. Quentin, the new *civitas* capital.[79] The strategic importance of Bavay may have preceded that of Reims, through which later versions of the Channel coast road passed, via St. Quentin or Soissons. Around 20 BC the Bavay-Köln road was functioning as a major supply route to the Rhine, with a military stores base at Tongeren (which may have postponed the creation of a civilian capital) and outlying bases further north at Elewijt and Velzeke.[80] New Roman sites such as Bavay might, like

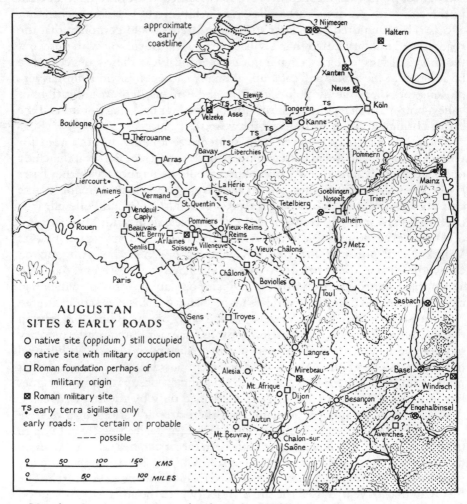

AUGUSTAN SITES & EARLY ROADS

O native site (oppidum) still occupied
⊗ native site with military occupation
□ Roman foundation perhaps of
    military origin
⊠ Roman military site
TS early terra sigillata only
early roads: —— certain or probable
            - - - possible

0   50   100   150   KMS
0   50   100 MILES

4 Map showing Augustan sites and early roads of Belgica the *oppida*, be centres of production for bronze coinages, and could have Celtic names (Bagacum).

Augustus' stay in Gaul occasioned further steps away from *ad hoc* arrangements with local chieftains towards a regular administrative pattern, where the local unit of self-government was the *civitas* and the local nobles responsible for it were organized in imitation of the senate and magistrates of Rome. But the cities which were indispensible, in Roman eyes, to the functioning of the new system were little more than building sites, and Augustus had to persuade the notables that it was their responsibility to remedy this, though he could help by putting army surveyors and manpower at their disposal, or by supplying architects. The time was not at all auspicious, since C. Julius Licinus, appointed to look after the finances of the Gaulish provinces, had created resentment by his unfair and extortionate demands, while the continuing effort to enrol the Gauls in a census was no more popular.[81] In the province of Narbonensis, the foundations for Romanized ways of life had been well laid by the foundation of colonies for Caesar's veterans (to which Augustus had added his own). The Three Gauls were very different. The personal element was here still of paramount importance, for the nobles viewed their inclusion within the Empire as a matter of clientship to Augustus, Caesar's heir, and had little understanding of the ideals of Mediterranean city life. There is no account of the many noble clients who must have approached their patron, to be disarmed by his diplomacy. Arrangements must have included the right to strike further coinages, for two very abundant types, in addition to some rarer ones, belong to the ensuing decade. The bronze of Avaucia, coined somewhere north of the Eifel, is widely found on military sites, while that of Germanus Indutilli circulated throughout the whole of Belgic Gaul.[82]

The offensive across the Rhine may have relieved discontents by allowing Gauls to serve on campaigns against a traditional foe – their neighbours. It is recorded that Nervian officers served with distinction. A more permanent answer to the need for bridges between Roman and Gaulish society was found in the great Altar solemnly inaugurated in 12 BC at Condate, the confluence of Rhône and Saône just north of Lyon. Lyon itself rapidly became a show-piece, with public buildings and amenities in Mediterranean style (and, from 10 BC, a mint). The annual ceremonies at the Altar, for which a day (1 August) significant in both Gaulish and Roman calendars was chosen, honoured with sacrifices both Rome and Augustus, thus linking known patron and more abstract power. The context was the old *concilium Galliarum* revived, with power to report directly to the emperor on relevant matters, including complaints against officials. The Gaulish love of glory was satisfied by the annual election of chosen delegates from each *civitas* and by them of a chief priest, the first an Aeduan, C. Iulius Vercondaridubnus.[83]

The northern Gaulish cities remained for a time shabby affairs. But the earliest monuments of which we have evidence are in honour of Augustus' beloved grandsons, and the *concilium Galliarum* presented to the emperor a massive gold torc.[84] Augustus should have been well pleased with this token of the Gauls' renewed clientship, symbol of their acceptance of inclusion in the Roman world and simultaneously a recognition of his own superhuman status.

3

THE FOUNDATIONS OF ROMAN BELGICA

Local communities and the province

The area conquered by Caesar, Gallia Comata or long-haired Gaul, was a loose appendage of the old Gallia Transalpina, requiring subsequent organization. Most arrangements at the local level, however, were probably made by him at the end of the war. The political geography of Roman Belgica was based squarely on the pre-Roman communities as perceived by Caesar, though with minor modifications that are not without interest.

The *pagi*, it is clear, still functioned as semi-independent units that could be easily regrouped. Some that had been tributary became independent *civitates* – hence the Meldi and Silvanectes, the former eventually included in Lugdunensis. The *civitas* of the Silvanectes has been thought a later development, due to Claudius. But while the area is tiny, Senlis functioned as an important road junction from an early period, and the easiest explanation of its name Augustomagus is promotion to *civitas* capital by Augustus' reign (the name Ratomagus given by Ptolemy being a confusion with Rouen, Rotomagus).[1] The Suessiones may have lost another *pagus*, the Laonnois, to the Remi. Since no early source mentions an independent Catuvellauni, they probably counted as a *pagus* of the Remi, whose loyalty was thus rewarded with an extremely large territory. Such arrangements suggest the hand of Caesar.

An area without any clear organization lay beyond the eastern Ardennes and Eifel, where devastation of Eburones and Atuatuci left a number of small groups. Eburones and Atuatuci disappear from the written record; their replacement, the Tungri, are first mentioned by Pliny. This name, perhaps 'the sworn ones' or confederates, may reflect their artificial origin, most likely the work of Agrippa and connected with his settlement of the Ubii.[2] The new *civitas* was enormous, taking in the Condrusi and the Entre-Sambre-et-Meuse area that earlier belonged to the Nervii. To the north, the Texuandri (mentioned by Pliny with the comment that they had several names) may have been another *pagus*: their name may be a Latinized version of Eburones (*taxus*, the yew-tree), though a theory connecting it with the right bank (of Maas or Rhine) is equally plausible.[3]

Rhine valley problems were often resolved by the settlement on the left bank of people from the other side. The Ubii were followed by the Sugambri, organized by Augustus' adopted son Tiberius in AD 8. South of the Mosel, Strabo and Pliny refer to Vangiones, Nemetes and Triboci (right bankers in Caesar). The Mediomatrici and Treveri, who in Caesar's time stretched to the Rhine, lost their eastern *pagi*; from the Treveri probably came the Aresaces and Caeracates near Mainz.[4]

Minor unlocatable peoples mentioned by Pliny are probably *pagi*, though their appearance in a list supposedly derived from official documents raises questions. The Chersiaci are specifically called a *pagus*, and the name is to be connected with the form Gesoriacum, one of the two names for Boulogne (referring to the harbour area). Inscriptions show that this *pagus*, like the *pagus* Condrustis, (Condrusi) and the Texuandri long kept independence as mustering groups.[5] The mention at Bois l'Abbé of a *pagus* Catuslo . . . allows identification of the Catoslugi, mistakenly said by Pliny to dwell inland.[6] Whether other *pagi* will thus emerge remains to be seen, for Pliny's list contains muddles both by author and by scribes.

Pliny treats the Rhineland as if it belonged to Belgic Gaul in spite of the military commands established there. Strabo, Ptolemy and inscriptions must be used if the boundary of the province to north and south is to be ascertained. Lingones, Sequani and Helvetii were within Belgica by the time of the German campaigns; the more northerly Alpine passes were by now opened up and it made sense to have all the major routes to the Rhine within the Belgic province. As Strabo remarks, emperors drew boundaries to suit administrative convenience. By the early second century, as Ptolemy shows, Lingones, Sequani and Helvetii were in Upper Germany, after a Flavian reorganization which established the two German provinces. The south-eastern boundary of Belgica then ran along a natural line, the Monts Faucilles and the Vosges watershed.[7]

In the north, Ptolemy ascribes the Tungri firmly to Belgica, but is unaware of the Frisiavones placed by Pliny in islands around the mouth of Maas and Waal, along with the Sturii and Marsaci. A second-century inscription (from Bulla Regia) makes it reasonably clear that the Tungri were in Belgica and the Batavi in Germania Inferior, but a faulty text leaves the situation of Frisiavones unclear. That the boundary with Germania Inferior lay west and south of the Maas rather than along it, thus including the Frisiavones in Lower Germany, seems geographically the reasonable solution, especially if a dedication by a magistrate of the Batavi at Ruimel-St. Michielsgesteel means that they lay partly south of the rivers. Marsaci and Sturii could be *pagi* either of Frisiavones or of Menapii, with the area west of the Striene then included in Belgica. There was no clear natural boundary in this area, unless the marshy Peel district

5   Map showing peoples, cities and main roads from Flavian times in Belgica

south and west of the Maas. In recruitment the boundary might be ignored, for the *pagus* Vellaus found in a cohort of Tungrians probably came from Veluwe, north of the great rivers.[8]

The decision to create a province Germania was taken by Augustus in the years following 12 BC, and was symbolized in the foundation of a new great Altar of Rome and Augustus at Ara Ubiorum (Köln). The various peoples along the Rhine now belonged to the new province. When territory across the Rhine was given up after the annihilation of Varus's army in AD 9, the strip west of the river was administered by the army commanders (from the reign of Tiberius, two in number).[9]

Differences in status among *civitates* probably go back to Caesar, for some follow rationally from his experience, and by early imperial times the various grades had very little meaning. The faithful Remi, like the Lingones, were rewarded with federate status. The neutral Leuci were declared 'free', though whether the theoretical immunity from tribute was long respected may be doubted; by the beginning of Tiberius' reign, if not before, tribute as well as troops was expected from privileged peoples.[10] The same status was given to Nervii and Treveri: conciliatory rather than harsh treatment was best for these large, strategically situated peoples. Silvanectes also enjoyed 'freedom', as did the diminished Suessiones. The other Belgae and the Germani Cisrhenani were left as *stipendiarii*, as (with less reason) were the Mediomatrici, but these unprivileged peoples were split up by the others.

These heterogeneous peoples now had to be forged into the reliable self-governing communities indispensable for the smooth administration of a Roman province. Throughout the Mediterranean world the normal form of local government was some form of the city-state, the aristocracy of which was responsible not only for law and order but for the construction of public works for no other reward than glory. The recognition that the *civitates* of Gaul could be treated as city-states seems a bold step perhaps initially encouraged by Caesar's need to concentrate on other matters. Yet backward parts of Italy had recently been in like shape, and Augustus may have gone to Gaul fresh from similar tasks in his homeland.

Both organization from above and changes in local attitudes were necessary. The centrality of the *civitas* symbolized by the capital city had to be firm, with nobles from the *pagi* providing a council and magistrates, while adopting the necessary Mediterranean values. Fortunately, emulation came naturally to the Gauls, and by the end of Augustus' reign schools had been established in Autun to transform the sons of tribal nobility into Roman gentlemen and old rivalries into appropriate civic behaviour.[11] One vast difference between Italy and the Three Gauls remained unbridgeable, a simple yet significant one of scale: Italian municipal territories averaged a few hundred km², those of Gaulish peoples might easily be 10,000 km². Only Narbonensian Gaul with its veteran colonies was comparable with Italy. To achieve a similar level of urbanization further north, every *pagus* would have had to become a *civitas* (an idea that is implied by passages in Plutarch and Josephus).[12]

Perhaps Augustus realized that colonies of Roman citizens would fit ill into the framework of archaic states, for he added none to the three planned by Caesar (though refounding the one among the Rauraci).[13] Pressure to conform to the Italian norms of a board with two or four chief magistrates (*duoviri* or *quattuorviri*) was not exerted: a *magister* at Trier, like an old-style *vergobret* among the Santones, may have been single chief magistrate.[14] Standard titles may later have become normal, for *duoviri*, *aediles* and *quaestores* are found. Of these, *duoviri* held supreme administrative and judicial power, judged cases among non-citizens (*peregrini*) and forwarded those involving Roman citizens to the governor. Normally the financial officials had the title *quaestor*, but a *duumvir ab aerario* is known from Trier. *Aediles* were responsible for public order. The council or *ordo* of decurions was nominally one hundred strong (though Tacitus talks, perhaps loosely, of over one hundred Treveran senators).[15] The manner of appointment of magistrates or decurions is unknown. In theory elections might be held, in practice offices would go round the eligible, and the council would be self-perpetuating, with the help of five-yearly magistrates akin to Roman censors. The system was, as before, aristocratic.

Civitates and the individuals composing them might differ in status. The initial norm was the peregrine or non-Roman community, with a sprinkling of Roman citizenship among those who had caught the attention of Caesar or Augustus, and who bore the name Julius as a result. Augustus then granted Latin status to some Aquitanian peoples. This ensured a small but steady increase in the number of Roman citizens (since the magistrates attained Roman citizenship subsequent to office), gradually enfranchising the élite while refraining from sweeping grants of Roman citizenship. How far Latin status was spread by Augustus or his successors cannot be easily determined, since there is no single criterion, either of nomenclature or of career pattern, which shows that a man belonged to a community with Latin rights.[16] It is not even easy to know if a Gaul had Roman citizenship, unless he has an imperial *nomen* or mentions a Roman voting-tribe.

Gallo-Roman nomenclature tends to imitate Roman style to the extent of having a *nomen* ending in -ius followed by a *cognomen*, even if the component parts are not Latin. But a person with a single name of Celtic derivation can still be a member of a Latin community and arguments about the status of particular persons or communities have to be indirect. A case has been made for regarding all communities with *duoviri* as possessing Latin status, since this was the general rule elsewhere in the Empire.[17] Contrariwise, places with non-Roman magistracies have been seen as peregrine. But the aristocrats of a Gaulish *civitas* might cling to ancestral habits, with or without the express consent of the emperor, while others might well have adopted a more Romanized style despite peregrine status. If they could imitate Roman names, why not the Roman style of magistracies? Much depends on the strength of native preferences and the extent to which emperors might conciliate Gallic nobles at the expense of irregularities. Flexibility would be well repaid if such a large country smoothly conducted its own local affairs.

Despite lack of proof, there are reasons for supposing that considerable areas of Gaul attained Latin status during the first century AD. One is the number of Roman citizens (e.g. priests at the Altar such as Q. Adginnius Martinus) who do not bear the names of emperors, another the toga seen on Gallic tombstones of first- or second-century date. In the mid-first century AD the emperor Claudius showed concern for the Gauls, by proposing that eligible men should follow senatorial careers.[18] It would be in keeping with his policies if he granted Latin status to many Gallic communities, and a scattering of Gauls with his tribe, Quirina, may be the result. This, however, remains hypothesis rather than proof, and since a number of the toga-clad Gauls are Treveri, the status of Trier becomes involved.

In Belgic Gaul, mention of a *colonia* is found among the Morini and the Mediomatrici as well as the Treveri.[19] Evidence from Lingones, Sequani and Helvetii, who belonged to the province at its widest extent, is also relevant. The last case is the clearest, for an inscription gives the title Colonia Pia Flavia Constans Emerita Helvetiorum Foederata. The name shows a Flavian foundation, but with contradictory indications, Emerita pointing to the settlement of veterans, Foederata to the status of the Helvetii. Aventicum seems to have been a compromise, perhaps with veterans in a Latin colony.[20]

All other colonies simply have the title of *colonia* followed by the people's name, with the exception of Trier which is sometimes colonia Augusta Treverorum, a fact that has led some to consider it an Augustan colony. The arguments in fact point rather to Claudius, for the first inscription to mention the colony refers to a career of Claudio-Neronian date.[21] The Sequani and Lingones came to imperial attention in the course of 69–70, and may have gained colonial status thereafter. With the Morini the only indication of date is very indirect: the father of a magistrate had the unusual name Sulpicius, which might point to the emperor Galba and the year 69.[22]

A confusing factor with *coloniae* in Gaul is that they do not cause the disappearance of the *civitates*; there are officials of the *civitas* who are later than others of the *colonia*. What then was the nature of the colonies? One explanation is to see colonial status as an honorific title, granted by emperor or assumed by the community, which in effect changed nothing. Avenches is an obvious exception, but at Trier too most people have seen a more than empty honour. Though no senior magistrates of the colony are certainly known, there are *augustales* or organizers of the imperial cult (as also at Metz), while augurs (normally confined to colonies) are attested for the Lingones, and there is a possible *duovir* among the Morini. The colonies did then have some form of separate administration, and this first solution loses credibility.

A second solution is to connect the colony closely to the central cities and to view them as colonies without *territorium* (though Avenches clearly had a territory). On this view the *civitas* continued to exist with its own separate administration. A practical objection is the complicated duplication of councils and magistrates. A more theoretical one is that to the Romans a colony was more than a physical town. Although special conditions for the Gauls can be pleaded, there is perhaps a solution which does not require it. If it is accepted that many *civitates* acquired Latin status, then there was little difference between them and the Latin municipalities elsewhere in the Empire. Yet the title *municipium* is never found in Gaul, perhaps a recognition that the Gaulish states were significantly different. If a *civitas* with Latin status was given the name and rank of *colonia* (increasingly considered desirable under the Empire), this need change little apart from the introduction of a few more officials, mostly religious, and perhaps a civic charter. It also represents a continuation of the Latin colonies of Gallia Cisalpina and Narbonensis – a practice generally outdated. The tribal area would, in official Roman parlance, be the territory of the colony, and there would be no need for two-tier local government.

The continued use of the term *civitas* may be due to Gallic attitudes. In course of time the novelty of colonial status wore off, the name was dropped and the underlying reality, that of the *civitas*, reasserted itself. The Gauls, in other words, were careless of Roman legal niceties, be it the status of communities or nomenclature.[23] Such an interpretation explains why, at Trier, the inscriptions mentioning the colony are either relatively early, or connected with religious organizations, or give an official domicile. Aventicum remains a special case.

It is then likely that all the major *civitates* in time possessed Latin status; it is certainly hard to imagine the Remi being left without it after the Treveri had gained it, and the same would hold good for Mediomatrici and Tungri. The number of relevant inscriptions is altogether very small, and more *civitates* may have claimed the title *colonia* than are at present attested. The uncertainties result not so much from poor preservation of the epigraphic record as from Gallic priorities. It is no accident that the fullest records – of Treveri, Lingones, Sequani, Helvetii – come from areas close to the Rhineland and thus more open to Roman influences disseminated through the army.

The *civitas* or *colonia* was then the organ of local administration, responsible for law, order and finances. Not least of the duties incumbent on council members were arrangements for the collection of taxes. These included the upkeep of roads and the maintenance of *mansiones* or inns for official travellers as well as the actual collection of money and of grain, hides etc. for the army.

The existence of administration at the lower level of *vici* and *pagi* is also clear from inscriptions. Among these subsidiary offices might be the administration of the central city itself, which, under its purely physical aspect, could be called a *vicus*; if it were large enough it might consist of several *vici* (Trier had a *vicus* Senia and a *vicus* Voclannionum, while Metz was similarly divided, and the Romanized *vicus* Pacis and *vicus* Honoris have been seen as a reflection of Mediomatrician colonial status).[24] Most *vici* of course were in the surrounding countryside, and some were centres for the rural *pagi* in which they lay. The *pagi* of Belgica also survived as political entities, and there was a proliferation of local organisms out of which the ambitious could proceed to the administration of the *civitas* itself, or even beyond.[25]

At the top of the political pyramid, linking together in one organization the *civitates* of all Three Gauls, was the *concilium Galliarum*, to which all sent delegates. On the one hand this was the refounding of an old Gaulish tradition, on the other, the Gallic branch of an institution which originated in the Hellenistic east and which was used to provide a focus of provincial loyalty. The central Altar at Condate, of imported marble with gilded inscription, was flanked by columns surmounted by figures of Victory and by statues representing each of the 64 *civitates*. Under Tiberius, an amphitheatre was added, and games became part of the ceremonies.[26]

The *concilium* was answerable only to the emperor himself. To be chosen a delegate was a coveted honour, to be elected high priest for the year the summit of a Gaul's ambition within his homeland. That we hear only of one or two high priests from Belgica is partly due to the bias of the record, but it is not impossible that the north produced fewer men whose status was guaranteed to impress delegates from the other provinces. Attached to the *concilium* was a treasury, the *arca Galliarum*, with its own financial offices, some of which were in due course filled by men from Belgic Gaul. Provision was also made for Roman citizens resident in Gaul to hold their own separate ceremonies. Overall, the institution must be judged highly successful, satisfying hunger for status, giving the necessary religious underpinning to new political allegiances and forging a pan-Gallic aristocracy with common interests.

2 The agents of central authority

The governors of Gallia Comata prior to 27 had been close personal associates of Caesar, Antony and Octavian, and the pattern was continued after 27, when Augustus was officially the proconsul of the Gauls, with legates to assist him. From Agrippa's second term of office in 20–19 to the beginning of Tiberius' reign, the known governors were virtually all members of the imperial house – Tiberius (16–15), his brother Drusus (13–11), Tiberius again (9–7 BC, AD 4–6 and 10–13) and later Germanicus (AD 13–17). Others must have filled the gaps, but not the commanders of the armies across the Rhine, who had responsibilities in Germany only. The emperor's relatives probably governed both Belgica and Germany simultaneously, with proconsular *imperium* and their own legates as required.[27]

Nothing is known of the legates of Belgica between Tiberius and Nero. Like Lugdunensis and Aquitania, Belgica remained an imperial province, and was governed by a legate of praetorian rank who resided at Reims. He had total responsibility for all civil administration (and for any small military detachments, for instance those policing the main roads) and attended to the more serious judicial matters. Non-Romans had no right of appeal from his judgements.

The first one known, the Spaniard M. Aelius Gracilis (*c.* 55–56), illustrates the potential jealousy between the legate of Belgica and the legates of the Rhine armies, who were more senior men of consular rank. Gracilis took exception to Antistius Vetus' proposal to use the Upper Rhine troops to dig a canal linking the Saône with the Moselle. Since the project was situated within Belgica, a tricky question of competence was raised. The scheme was represented as personal aggrandizement on the part of Vetus, and an appeal to the jealous nature of Nero prevented the inception of this interesting idea.

A few years later in 61, three legates of consular rank were engaged in a census of the Three Gauls: an inscription (from Boulogne) shows that Volusius Saturninus was in charge of Belgica. Almost certainly, each was simultaneously governor of the province with which he was concerned. A quarrel over status arose, perhaps the question of which should have the first seat of honour at celebrations in Lyon. (A later inscription shows that the order of protocol was Lugdunensis, Belgica, Aquitania, whereas in practice the legate of Belgica was usually the most experienced.) Another governor of Nero's reign, D. Valerius Asiaticus, belonged to a Narbonensian family from Vienne who had become powerful through wealth and the skilful exploitation of imperial patronage.

The Flavian period saw the recognition of the Lower and Upper Germany (now including Lingones, Sequani and Helvetii) as provinces, and brought increased military supervision within Belgica.[28] The legates of Belgica continued to be men especially favoured by the emperors; under Domitian, they included Q. Glitius Atilius Agricola and L. Licinius Sura, the latter a Spaniard and friend of Trajan. A pattern emerged whereby the governorship of Belgica, which ranked (*pace* protocol at Condate) among the highest of praetorian provincial offices, was speedily followed by the consulship. Previous experience of the area was valued; Licinius Sura is an example, since he had earlier commanded *legio* I Minerva at Bonn, and this sequence was repeated later by the Galatian Calpurnius Proculus.

Just as the overall administration of Belgica was only gradually standardized, so the early financial arrangements saw some *ad hoc* measures. Licinus, a Gallic or German freedman of Julius Caesar, was the first known procurator (assuming he had that title) in a period which saw considerable overlap between the posts of freedmen and equestrians. Chosen because of his experience with Caesar, he turned his native ability to fraudulent dealings (including a lengthening of the tax year to 14 months) sufficient to earn him a place in satire and history.[29] Under Tiberius the financial management of Aquitania seems linked with that of Narbonensis (although the latter was a senatorial province); Lugdunensis and Belgica (including the Rhine army districts) were perhaps likewise under the jurisdiction of a single procurator of equestrian rank. The first known, a prominent politician, P. Graecinius Laco, is simply said (by Dio) to have been 'of the Gauls'. So ambitious a person (he was given consular rank by Claudius) is more likely to have served in Belgica and Lugdunensis than in the less significant southern area; the procurator of Belgica was paymaster of the Rhine armies, and this lent importance to the office.

The first procurator specifically of Belgica is Cornelius Tacitus, probably the father of the historian, who is mentioned by the elder Pliny. It has often been conjectured that Pliny himself held the same office; this rests on the special knowledge which Pliny sometimes displays of northern Gaul and the Rhineland, and on literary testimony suggesting he held several high procuratorships.[30] From the time of Domitian, the title of the procurator was officially 'of Belgica and the two Germanies'. A further standardization is observable, in that this procuratorship ranked among the very highest of such provincial offices, being frequently the last post held before promotion to a higher level of responsibilities and remuneration. It is therefore understandable that the known procurators include ambitious and able men such as Sex. Attius Suburanus Aemilianus (in the 90s), who rose to senatorial rank and a consulship under Trajan. Inscriptions of minor officials from the procurator's staff show that his headquarters was Trier, a natural choice once the financial administration of Belgica and of the Germanies was linked. (The stone erected to M. Petronius Honoratus at Rome by two Treveri who regarded him as their patron is additional evidence.[31]) It has been conjectured that Trier also became the seat of the legate. By the time of the Gallic emperors, Trier was indeed the centre of administration. But the change from Reims, if indeed it did occur before the Gallic empire, took time, as is shown by an inscription set up to a legate by the Remi (complete with the title Foederati).[32]

The main task of the procurator was to ensure that taxes were duly assessed and collected, and to make money available to pay the Rhine armies. There was probably a separate procurator to oversee the *annona*, grain and other raw materials directly levied for the army, but none is known. The collecting of the $2\frac{1}{2}$ per cent on goods entering the Gauls (*quadragesima Galliarum*) was of greater concern to the procurators of Lugdunensis (Lyon was the main customs checkpoint) than of Belgica, though lead seals provide evidence of some customs activity at Trier.[33] The actual gathering of the taxes was done as far as possible without the interference of imperial agents; but the calculation by the procurator's staff of the amount due from each people rested on the provincial census. This was not itself within the competence of the procurators. During Augustus' reign, three censuses in Gaul were overseen respectively by Augustus himself in 27, by Drusus in 12 and by Germanicus in AD 14. Germanicus turned the completion of the process over to his legates, and from then on the normal practice was the appointment at intervals of special legates of consular rank.

The census was an enormous undertaking, involving the movement of many people to the central points of registration. Moreover, Gaulish customs concerning land, involving multi-ownership or a control which was strictly a holding in trust for clients rather than true ownership, did not correspond precisely with Roman legal practice. The stronger would naturally profit at the expense of the weaker: claims might have to be checked, disputes resolved, and there was ample opportunity for unrest to break out, as it indeed did in 12 BC. With time, the task became more routine. By no means all the censuses have left direct testimony, but by putting together available literary and epigraphical evidence, a picture of censuses at intervals of between 15 and 40 years emerges. Others may have taken place, but the intervals were not totally regular. The apparent absence of a census under Vespasian, a time of much general reorganization after civil war and revolts, may be due to a gap in the evidence. Domitian supervised one in person in 83, using it as a blind for the preparation of his German campaigns.[34]

The provinces were broken down into smaller areas, each with a procurator of equestrian rank in charge. Such procurators do not always specify their district, but within Belgica we know that the Ambiani, Morini and Atrebates formed one while the Remi formed another by themselves. The Treveri may have been numbered separately like the Remi, while the Suessiones, Bellovaci and Silvanectes, the Menapii and Nervii and finally the Mediomatrici and Leuci would all form natural groups. The inscription from Bulla Regia tells of another area which comprised Tungri, Frisiavones and Batavi and thus stretched over two provinces.[35] In the Germanies, the task may have been within the normal competence of the ordinary consular legates. The Bulla Regia inscription suggests close co-operation between them and the special consular legates of Belgica.

Wholesale delegation of the day-to-day administration of the Empire to the untrained leaders of local communities did not make for efficiency. The whole system was liable to all the abuses which occur when patronage is the determining factor in relationships and decisions. But in this way the Empire was run with a tiny number of officials, and the staffs of governor and procurator might be counted in the tens rather than the hundreds, some being soldiers detached for special duty (*beneficiarii*). Nonetheless, though they were numerically small, the status and permanent presence of agents of central authority made them important, especially in the early Empire, for introducing Roman ways of life to the provincials.

3 From Augustus to the Flavian emperors

The latter years of Augustus' reign were quiet in Gaul. The work of Drusus and Tiberius brought them to Belgica, and a garbled passage in Florus connects Drusus with construction work at Boulogne, which may have become a naval base for subsequent operations. Tiberius was there in AD 4, and the record of a congratulatory embassy shows that the name Bononia was already used for part of the town.[36] No Gallic unrest followed the crushing defeat of Varus in AD 9, and pacification must have seemed finally achieved. The return of Tiberius to the Rhine front in AD 11 doubtless helped. His journey through Gaul is presented by Velleius as a triumphal procession, and an inscription from Bavay records his passage.[37] Given the personal nature of the links binding aristocratic Gauls to their imperial patrons, the presence of Augustus' son and heir apparent was of importance. Tiberius was replaced by his heir Germanicus in AD 13, the year before Augustus' death: a hint in the poet Crinagoras that he had an early victory in Gaul, not Germany, could indicate unrest in the north.[38] New problems emerged within a decade, though not immediately after Tiberius' accession. Indeed, the numerous monuments set up to honour him suggest enthusiasm, unless due to the careful prompting of imperial officials. A marble head of Livia, Tiberius' mother, from some Tiberian monument at Trier, invites comparison with constructions at Saintes and Paris. Other monuments, like their locations – Naix and le Héraple – are more modest.[39] Dedicators at le Héraple were *negotiatores*, mere temporary residents in a village with little obvious appeal. This stone, dated AD 20, may have attested loyalty at a time when rumbles of discontent were already audible.

Tribute, debts and the arrogance of administrators are the reasons given by Tacitus for the rebellion which broke out among Treveri, Aedui and Turones in AD 21. All were privileged peoples, free or federated. They may have felt it the more keenly if Tiberius' tighter fiscal policies, necessitated by a low treasury, had indeed led to the suppression of immunities.[40] Special taxes, over and above the provision of troops, were probably collected to help finance the campaigns of Germanicus across the Rhine. The lack of any relaxation after the end of the campaigns, and the withdrawal (and subsequent death) of the popular young prince who personified the imperial house, would add fuel to the fire.

Debts and tribute are commonly given as causes for provincial revolts, but if they are stock items in the literary arsenal this does not make them the less true. Wealthy Italians were happy to lend out money at interest to provincials, as later Seneca did in Britain. Borrowing ready cash might be necessary for the payment of taxes. Unless a man combined adaptability, shrewd financial sense and good management of his resources in land and clients, the day of reckoning could be disastrous.

Closer attention to the Treveri reminds us that Gaul was still uneasily balanced between old and new traditions. Rivalry between the rebel Julius Florus and the loyal Julius Indus was not, Tacitus hints, suddenly born of the occasion.[41] Julius Indus was clearly ambitious, perhaps already an office-holder with access to high patronage, a likely target for jealousy that may also have had a traditional base in political geography. Indus married his daughter to another noble Gaul, Julius Alpinus Classicianus, whose name suggests a Treveran or Helvetian origin (as well as adoption from one noble family into another).[42] He himself had perhaps contracted a 'dynastic' marriage of the kind calculated to increase the wealth and influence of his family. Some such family ties may even have existed between Julius Florus, Julius Sacrovir and the other leaders of the revolt. Certainly, all instigators belonged to this same noble class, and internal rivalries may still have helped determine attitudes to Rome.

Had the leaders been able to win the entire support of their peoples, thus providing a focus of rebellion in each province, and had they acted in concert, the revolt might have been as serious as some at Rome evidently thought. In fact premature action among Andecavi and Turones was suppressed by the urban cohort from Lyon stiffened by detachments from the lower Rhine, which must have marched right across Belgica. The Aeduan Sacrovir showed the greatest shrewdness by taking hostage the noble youths at school in Autun, and with an improvised army of peasants and gladiators caused much anxiety.

Among the Treveri, Florus' fate was effectively sealed when he failed to win over the local cavalry unit to the massacre of Roman merchants at Trier. Caught between detachments of the Lower and Upper Rhine armies, he dispersed his forces and retreated to Eifel or Ardennes, where Indus and his troops pursued him until he committed suicide. The legions meanwhile defeated Sacrovir and his Sequanian allies.

A small hillfort (the Niederburg) with signs of occupation in the early imperial period has been identified on the Ferschweiler plateau north-west of Trier, an inaccessible area of cliffs and steep small valleys. Too close to the city to be the final retreat of Florus, it is possibly one of his bases and may underline the traditional nature of his support. Without Tacitus' account, this hillfort, along with possible destruction layers at Metz and Sarrebourg, would be the only indication of trouble.[43]

If measures were taken to ensure peace after the revolt, they are unrecorded. The assumption that the Treveri lost their 'free' status is based on an ambiguous passage in Pliny.[44]

Caligula (Gaius) probably understood the Gauls better than Tiberius. True, if Suetonius and Dio are right, he extorted money shamelessly. But he vouchsafed his presence at Lyon, his games and gladiatorial shows were well calculated to impress, and his other actions may have been less distasteful than the writers suggest. The Gauls may have preferred to believe that he himself (not one of his sisters) had been born among the Treveri in AD 15, a version of imperial family history given by Pliny.[45]

Caligula had other work in Gaul and Germany. Disaffection on the part of an Upper Rhine legate hastened his arrival, and campaigns were planned against both Germany and Britain. Neither a detailed account nor archaeological evidence for his troop movements exist. The one action for which he is given credit is the building of a lighthouse at Boulogne after the abandonment of the British plan. This is often identified with the 'Tour d'Ordre' which tumbled into the sea in 1644. Descriptions of the tower, however, suggest later building techniques, and Caligula's one may have been a lost predecessor.[46]

Claudius, while not a Julian, had been born in Gaul, at Lugdunum. Both Germany and Britain were to occupy his attention, but it was the invasion of the latter that brought him in person to the Gallic provinces. There is as yet no certain evidence for the troop movements that assembled an army at Boulogne for the crossing to Richborough, beyond possible military occupation at Kortrijk, Tournai and Arlaines near Soissons. By which branch of the road from Massilia to Boulogne Claudius later travelled is also unsure, and only a careful reading of Dio's account allows the inference that the emperor spent some months in Gaul on the return trip.[47]

Archaeological evidence shows that he and his agents busied themselves about practical but important affairs. Claudius and his army had probably found the roads in indifferent shape, the supposed cities, especially in the north, shabby affairs with wooden buildings, sometimes lacking a proper street grid. Improved roads were needed for troop movements; milestones show that work was done, though whether by the army or by the *civitates* cannot be told. Street grids were laid out at Bavay and Tongeren or existing ones extended, as at Trier.[48] The Sulbanectes expressed gratitude in a bronze statue with inscribed base, and the *vicani* of Marsal were among others who took similar measures.[49] Claudius accomplished a task which his father Drusus had begun – that of persuading the northern Gauls to adopt the outward forms of Graeco-Roman urbanization. To what extent he provided assistance in the form of architects, engineers or tax rebates must remain conjectural. Nor is it clear by what mechanisms stone suddenly became widely available to civilians as a normal building material, though army help may be suspected, and improved roads aided transport. Certainly, his attention bore fruit, for the physical appearance of northern Gaul altered considerably over the next decade. A change in attitudes is arguably symbolized by the Council's gift to Claudius – a gold crown, in contrast to Augustus' great torc.[50]

Claudius was later mocked for his desire to see even Gauls and Britons in the toga. Certainly, as has been seen, he concerned himself with the status of individuals and communities as well as with outward appearances. Not inconceivably some Gauls adopted the name Claudius simply to honour the emperor – illegal though it might be.[51]

During his censorship of 47–48, Claudius persuaded a reluctant senate that noble citizens from privileged Gallic *civitates* might become senators.[52] In practice few availed themselves of the opportunity, though one that did, Julius Vindex, was to play a fateful role. Arguably Claudius was trying to go too fast. Urbanism and urban attitudes were still of comparatively shallow growth in the north, and the Roman senators not altogether wrong in their distrust of semi-civilized tribal magnates barely divorced, despite the efforts of Augustus, Tiberius and Claudius himself, from such barbaric practices as human sacrifice and snake's egg talismans.[53]

Had Claudius been followed by a like-minded emperor, steady progress might have continued; the Saône-Moselle canal might at least have won a sympathetic hearing. Road improvements did continue for a time, for bridges over Mosel and Saar belong to AD 56 and 60. Nero's personal preferences being for the Greek-speaking provinces, he generally neglected the Gauls. Whether some unrecorded action provided a last straw is unknown; when the governor of Lugdunensis,the Aquitanian Julius Vindex, raised the flag of revolt against the tyrant in 68, many Gauls were ready to follow.

The complicated events of 68-70 saw three different, if connected, movements in Gaul and Germany. Vindex himself is a two-sided figure. He took counsel with leading Gauls (especially from Aedui, Sequani and Arverni) and was evidently assured of an uprising. But in his appeal to Galba to assume the purple he acted like a Roman senator. When, despite his hopes for Rhine army support, a pitched battle ensued near Besançon, the legions under

Verginius Rufus – always stationed, as Tacitus remarks, so that they could march into Gaul as well as Germany – defeated the ill-armed Gauls. But the feelings at grass-roots level did not die so easily. The Boii, a *pagus* of the Aedui, later produced a prophet, Mariccus, to lead a would-be Gallic independence movement, unable though he was to win over the aristocrats.[54]

The appeal of Vindex fell on deaf ears at Lyon as among Lingones and Treveri, who this time did not join the Aedui. Aristocratic loyalties as well as close ties with the army may have been responsible. Galba, once emperor, granted tax remissions and citizenship in the areas that had supported Vindex – the prominent Morinian Sulpicius may be an example. Treveri and Lingones were punished by harsh measures that included confiscation of territory (presumably given respectively to Tungri or Mediomatrici, Sequani or Aedui), and this aroused passions.[55] Appeal was made to the Rhine armies. Probably they knew of discontent caused by the empty victory at Besançon. Perhaps some even fancied themselves in the role of Vindex: the individuals mentioned by Tacitus mostly held posts that could have led to equestrian careers.

January of 69 saw the Rhineland armies and cities, the Lingones and Treveri, swearing allegiance to Vitellius while the rest of Gaul mostly supported Otho. The legates of both Belgica and Lugdunensis saw Vitellius as the safer bet, knowing that the armies would soon march. March they did, with contingents of Treveri, Tungri and others among them, and havoc ensued. Worst off were the Helvetii, who tried to oppose the passage of the Upper Rhine army detachments. But there was a massacre at Metz, without obvious pretext, and traces of destruction in the city may be attributable.[56] As the Lower Rhine army moved southwards through Toul and Langres to Lyon, it found itself caught up in the old rivalry between Lyon (which supported Vitellius) and Vienne (which had supported Vindex) as well as the revolt led by Mariccus. Following behind the main armies, Vitellius briefly held court at Lyon with ceremonies reminiscent in their splendour of Caligula.

Already the third disruptive element was waiting in the wings. Julius Civilis the Batavian was a Roman citizen with experience of the Roman army but with a grudge against Roman emperors caused by a brother's death and his own imprisonment. Cohorts of his fellow-countrymen formed an unruly part of Vitellius' army and were sent back from northern Italy to Mainz. Once Vespasian had been proclaimed and the Danube army had in his name defeated Vitellius, Civilis seized the opportunity of making trouble nominally on Vespasian's behalf. As he won over neighbouring peoples from inside and outside the Empire and with gathering momentum destroyed or immobilized the remaining parts of the Rhine armies he ordered the devastation of Treveran land. They, in anticipation, built a barrier, perhaps in the Nahe valley, against the advance of his troops from Mainz. News of Vitellius' death and of the fire on the Capitol at Rome changed the picture. This last episode was taken as an omen of the Empire's imminent doom and, we are told, brought Druids from their lairs to proclaim of Gallic freedom. In January of 70 the former champions of Vitellius among Lingones and Treveri made common cause with Civilis. While appealing for support to all the Gauls, they arranged the defection of Gallic auxiliaries marching with the first and sixteenth legions, the ranks of which had also been recently made up with recruits from Belgica. Julius Classicus, prefect of an *ala* of Treveri, donned a purple robe and the troops took the oath to the *imperium Galliarum*. Rhineland peoples (some, like the Ubii, with reluctance), joined the cause, as did Tungri and Nervii. But neither Civilis nor the Batavians took any oath, and Civilis with deliberately unkempt hair and native dress (if we may believe Tacitus) was pursuing his own ends.[57]

With only Tacitus as guide, argument over the motives of the leaders is obviously possible. The very Roman nature of the *imperium Galliarum* is illustrated by the rebel coinage, which has Roman images and slogans only slightly modified by obverse busts of Gallia. The ringleaders must be seen as men still caught between two worlds. They were more deeply imbued with Roman values than Julius Florus, thanks to the passage of time and their experience of Roman army careers. Julius Tutor was *praefectus ripae Rheni* under Vitellius and Julius Sabinus the Lingonian may, like Julius Classicus, have commanded an auxiliary unit (a connection between the latter and Julius Classicianus is not impossible). They were Romanized enough to want an empire, and ambitious enough to prefer to dispense patronage rather than to remain at the mercy of others. To this end they took risks which were far too great, given that the recent rifts between Gaulish *civitates* had not had time to heal, so that hopes of a united Gaul were more than ever unrealistic. Their experience, outside of their homeland, lay with Rhineland or at most with British armies. In this, they are to be contrasted rather than compared with the senators from the south such as Vindex or Antonius Primus (from Toulouse) who won Italy for Vespasian.

Success for the rebels depended on gaining support from the interior, holding the Rhineland and preventing the passage of armies through the Alps. The first goal was blocked by the Remi, who took the initiative in summoning an extraordinary council in their city and, in the course of stormy oratory, were able to sway the other Gauls against the Lingones and Treveri. They may even have surrounded their city with a vast bank and ditch (at present of uncertain date).[58] Tacitus shows the rebel leaders lacking in forethought and concerted action. Civilis busied himself in the north, Classicus, with the legions, simply held Trier and the Mosel valley, Sabinus pitched Lingones against Sequani in old-style tribal warfare, while Tutor made little effort to win the upper Rhine. The first to meet positive failure, Sabinus, defeated by the Sequani, took despairing refuge in an underground hide-out (where, concealed by a faithful wife, he became the subject of romantic legend). Tutor, unable to gain the upper Rhine, much less prevent the approach of Vespasian's armies, retreated before the twenty-first legion, lost much of his army and was defeated between Mainz and Trier. The legions at Trier withdrew to Metz, and with the arrival at Mainz of an army led by Petillius Cerialis, final defeat became simply a matter of time, though Valentinus made a valiant attempt to bar the approaches to Trier, and Cerialis came close to throwing away his victory by over-confidence. The rebel army put up a good fight in the battle at Trier, joined against the will of Civilis, but Cerialis' victory ended the *imperium Galliarum*, reducing Classicus and Tutor to refugee auxiliaries of Civilis. The latter, with the help of the transrhenine Germans, fought on for a while, and over a hundred Treveran nobles are said to have joined him rather than accept the Roman victory. Honourable terms for the Batavians were finally negotiated.[59]

The short term results lie in the military and administrative sphere. There was increased policing of the main roads in Gaul, attested by a scatter of military inscriptions. The fort at Arlaines, just west of Soissons (too large, and too far away from Reims to house a governor's bodyguard) was rebuilt in stone. The site may be only one of a number belonging to this period, a likely example being Mauchamps, where gateways with *claviculae* suggest a Flavian date.[60] Concern for the inner security of Gaul was thus combined with an expansionist policy aimed at bringing peace to the Rhine-Danube frontier.

Attention to communications included the stone-piered bridge across the Mosel at Trier as well as the one over the Rhine at Mainz. The battle at Trier must have involved an older bridge, and the new one may have been among the measures, both diplomatic and strategic, taken to ensure the quiescence of the area. Among the Lingones, there was a slightly later flurry of military building at Mirebeau, perhaps a new legionary fortress or a veteran colony. The colony among the Helvetii was founded and Lingones, Sequani and Helvetii were transferred to Germania Superior.

Short- and longer-term effects on the society of Belgica, and of the Treveri in particular, must however have been considerable. A great deal of confiscated land must have been made into imperial estates or sold: in the absence of any definite evidence for the former, preference may be given to the latter solution. Archaeological evidence for so major a change might be anticipated. In fact, the positive evidence for the revolt is confined to destruction levels in the Rhineland forts, with only the traces of fire observed at Tongeren, Metz and Sarrebourg to suggest that the unrest spread into Belgica.[61] Damage to the cities and villages was made good, and no obvious discernible break is to be seen in the countryside. Yet when attention is given to the body of inscribed and sculptured monuments, there does appear at Trier, Arlon and in the Treveran country a certain caesura between early Julio-Claudian monuments showing the clear influence of the Rhineland workshops and new styles developed in the second century; this could be the reflection of the events of 70, expressed through changes in ambition and patronage. The most clearly attested long-term effect was on the career patterns of Gauls within the Roman Empire, a question which merits separate consideration.

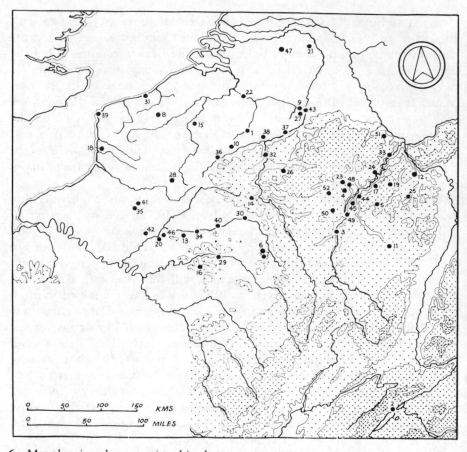

6 Map showing places mentioned in chapters 1–3

1	Court St. Etienne	18	Conchil-le-Temple	35	Breteuil
2	La Tène	19	Bundenbach	36	Maubeuge
3	Basse-Yutz	20	La Verberie	37	Huy
4	Altrier	21	Haps	38	Hastedon (St Servais)
5	Schwarzenbach	22	Mechelen-Nekkerspoel	39	Cap Gris Nez
6	Somme-Tourbe	23	Beaufort	40	Mauchamps
	(la Gorge-Meillet)	24	Erden	41	Folleville
7	Somme-Bionne	25	Odenbach	42	Nointel
8	Kemmelberg	26	Eprave	43	Kanne
9	Eigenbilzen		(Trou de l'Ambre)	44	Trier-Olewig
10	Leval-Trahegnies	27	Rosmeer	45	Konz-Filzen
11	Reinheim	28	Fins	46	Champlieu
12	Waldalgesheim	29	Epernay	47	St.-Michielsgesteel
13	Pernant	30	Rethel	48	Niederburg
14	Les Pothées, Rocroi	31	De Panne	49	Nennig
15	Frasnes-lez-Buissenal	32	Dinant	50	Hellange
16	Armentières	33	Pommern	51	Nickenich
17	Horath	34	Condé-sur-Aisne	52	Mersch

Contours indicated at 200 m, 400 m, 1000 m.

The Belgic aristocracy Romanized

According to Caesar, a Gaulish noble youth could choose to become a warrior or a Druid. The priesthood meant exemption from fighting and taxes and demanded a 20-year training which conferred enormous prestige along with both judicial and religious powers. Besides the obvious task of leading men in warfare (another avenue to prestige) the warriors or knights had, in the more advanced *civitates*, political options in the form of magistracies. As the aristocrat's private chest evolved into something like a public treasury, these included control of finances, but (if Caesar is right) the priests interpreted the law.[62]

The nobleman who could muster his clients for warfare easily adapted to service with Caesar, Pompey, Antony, Octavian and the Roman army. Some of the C. Iulii known from epigraphical and literary sources may have gained Roman citizenship in this manner, and not all need have been members of the very highest aristocracy, since merit and commander's patronage could bring rewards.[63] Not surprisingly it is in military service that continuity of career patterns from the period of the conquest into the Early Empire can best be attested. Not that continuity is complete, for definite links between service in the civil wars and the regiments later found in inscriptions are rare. Individual names are also few, and are not always given a precise rank: that of *tribuni*, given to the Nervians Chumstinctus and Avectius, who distinguished themselves under Drusus in 12–11 BC, is perhaps to be understood as meaning simply officers.[64] The reconstruction offered above for Gaul between Caesar and Augustus implies that irregular troops existed simultaneously with regular *cohortes* and cavalry *alae* recruited for service along with the legions.[65] In the course of Augustus' reorganizations the first were phased out. For the regular regiments, the recruiting base was sometimes widened so that the soldiers were no longer identical with the clients of their commanding officer.

The possibilities are well illustrated among the Treveri in the year AD 21. A cavalry *ala* described by Tacitus was recruited from among the Treveri but under Roman discipline: this is identified with the Ala Treverorum of inscriptions, and it continued to be recruited from and probably commanded by Treveri. From the body of men led by Julius Indus against the rebels there arose in due course a new regiment, the Ala Indiana Gallorum, which bore his name but was recruited more widely. Both regiments served in Germany, as did others from Tungri, Nervii and Lingones and more generally, Belgae. A pattern was thus established whereby Gauls gained experience of the Roman army without being posted far from home.

In the Julio-Claudian period, direct patronage from a governor or member of the imperial house must have been a normal requirement for advancement. Though only one is attested, other noble Gauls may have held the post of *praefectus fabrum* on the governor's staff, a position where they could be screened for promotion to command an auxiliary regiment. Those known to

71

have gone further remain few in number, but the Helvetian C. Julius Camillus held a legionary tribunate, as did a nameless Treveran from Mersch in the late first or early second century.[66] The career of Julius Alpinus Classicianus, procurator of Britain under Nero, remains exceptional, and it is a pity that we do not know by what earlier steps he ascended the ladder; his father-in-law doubtless helped. Less outstanding are the *praefecti ripae* (or *ad ripam*) *Rheni*, who had responsibilities for the various small peoples not yet raised to self-governing status. These included Julius Tutor and another Treveran (?Ti. Julius) Tiberinus, who may have gained citizenship under Tiberius.[67] Such men (or their sons) should logically have risen to emulate Classicianus; a career pattern which combined traditional emphasis on military prowess with integration into the Roman system was being worked out.

Roman practice also insisted that military and civic offices should be combined in a single career. Some inscriptions of Treveri show the pattern to be anticipated: a *praefectus* of a *cohors Aresacum* had held office as *quaestor* and as *magister* in the civitas Treverorum, and Tiberinus had some unpreserved office.[68] Both they and the later man from Mersch held priesthoods, whether local or at Condate. Military, administrative, judicial, financial and religious duties were all combined in a Romanized pattern.

High-ranking Roman careers normally included membership in priestly colleges, and Augustus had sought to increase the religious element in Roman political life. There was of course no place for druidic priests who, human sacrifices apart, gained status and judicial rights through long years of initiation and rote-learning. Augustus forbade druidic practices to Roman citizens, and this was enough to lessen their attraction further down the social ladder. The new Gallic priesthoods were closely linked to the body politic at either local or provincial level, and were connected more with ceremony than religious lore. Good examples of the local priesthoods are the flaminates of Lenus Mars and of Augustus held by the Treveran from Mersch. More problematical is the title *sacerdos Romae et Augusti* without mention of the Altar or the Three Provinces. Since this office was perhaps held by a peregrine at Metz (Taurus the son of Celer), it is arguably to be treated as local, but is also held by magistrates who may have been Roman citizens.[69] But even the municipal priesthoods were seen as the crowning achievement of a man's career, perhaps reached after, rather than before, the holding of a military office. Such men may have been delegates to the Altar, even if not elected as high priest.[70]

The number of prominent Gauls who bore the name C. Julius has been noted. The epigraphical record from Belgica is sparser than from Lugdunensis and Aquitania, but we have Treveran and Helvetian examples. Tacitus mentions no fewer than four other Treveri (all anti-Roman), a Reman (pro-Roman as ever) and a Lingonian. After the description by Tacitus of the troubled year 69–70, in which the Treveran Julii played a notorious part, literary sources come to an end. In later inscriptions, there are Julii in plenty, but no signs of aristocratic pretensions and some indications that the name was simply one of a common stock. The fate of the early Julii is of interest, since it touches on the continuity of the Gallic aristocracy apparently so well-established in the Early Empire.[71] The loss of literary sources of course produces a bias, but epigraphical evidence alone points to a change. Of course we do not know how many there ever were in any one people, nor whether there was a bias towards the peoples who supplied troops, nor how many perished or fled as a direct result of revolts. But since their name is such an obvious testimony to Julian patronage, it is hard not to connect their diminution with the end of the Julian line. It may be that access through patronage to military offices was an indispensable part of their status, and that without it they were unable to maintain their former standing. For this and other reasons – such as sheer failure to reproduce themselves – the aristocracy of early Roman Gaul may have made way before another, whose characteristics will be discussed later.

More important than the question of what happened to specific families is whether the Gallic aristocracy continued to function in the same way. If we look at the first century, part of the answer is clearly negative. Competition for civic honours or military commands in an imperial army might provide channels for competitive instincts, but it was hardly the same as the old system whereby the relative status of nobles was worked out in the course of internal feuding. While elements of this died hard – witness the enmity manifested between Julius Florus and Julius Indus, or between Treveri and Remi – it was no longer the dominant element. There is nothing to suggest that status had ceased to go hand in hand with wealth and with the control of land and clients; but the wealth now had to be gained and managed by acceptable Romanized methods.

While municipal offices and regimental commands were the prerogative of the wealthy, the Roman army also offered opportunities further down the ladder. Here too there was an obvious change, in that warfare was no longer undertaken on behalf of the local patron, but in an organized way and with predictable rewards. In the course of the Julio-Claudian period it became customary for auxiliaries to receive Roman citizenship at the end of 25 years' service. To this increase in status was added whatever the soldier had been able to save from pay or donatives, and the possibility of buying land. The arrangements which provided a bridge from Gaulish to Romanized society were also potential mechanisms of change.

Some of these Belgic Gauls Romanized through the army are attested by tombstones or votive inscriptions in the Rhineland. For the commanding officers, it is rather in the hinterland that we must look. Here, much depends on the dating of a group of large funerary monuments, of which fragments only remain. Decorated with friezes of shields and weapons, or with battle scenes, their style shows them to be products of the sculptors who worked for the army, especially at Mainz. Examples are known from Arlon, Chamleux, Nennig and near Maastricht, and they date from the second half of the first century, as does a grave with part of a cavalry parade helmet from Hellange (Lux).[72] While they are probably of army officers, there is no means of knowing whether the first ones are to be ascribed to indigenous Treveri rather than to incomers profiting from the flight of nobles in 70. A clear example of a largely Romanized family comes however from Nickenich in the Rhineland, where a relief (from a military workshop) showing four figures is connected with a walled tumulus and an inscription. The latter mentions a mother, Contuinda (shown in native dress) and her son, Silvanus Ategnissa who, despite his partly native name, wears the toga.[73]

If these examples show men of officer class, stone-masons from a legionary base might also put up a tombstone, in size like that of a serving soldier, for a shipper such as Blussus at Mainz. Another possible early shipper is Indus the Mediomatrican who dedicated a relief to Mercury at Trier, while a stone from Arlon (often called the 'schoolmaster') may show a waggoner with goad. The business of supplying the army, as well as serving in it, is already being expressed in the Romanized medium of sculptured stone. Further away from home, Remi and Lingones, probably traders, erected inscriptions in honour of Nero (just before the conspiracy of Vindex) beside the legionary fortress of Xanten.[74]

Service in the Roman army continued to be one option open to Belgic Gauls in the second century: it was, however, likely to be overseas, for the reorganization undertaken by Vespasian entailed sending Gallic regiments further from home, and placing them under normal Roman command. Of the officer class, much less is heard than might be expected. The Treveran from Mersch is a little later, and there is evidence from Tungrian territory of a continued military connection in the shape of ornamental daggers (*parazonia*) in rich graves.[75] The drying up of the first-century stream to a mere trickle, and the almost complete failure to rise to equestrian posts, is connected with the demise of the Julii. An aversion to serving away from home may be a partial explanation, and sheer prejudice against northern Gauls on the part of emperors and senators is likely. Later careers normally take purely civic form within the *vici*, *pagi* and *civitates* of the homeland or, if more ambitious, the *concilium Galliarum*. The idealized picture of an empire in which authority was shared by the provincials, inserted by Tacitus into Cerealis' harangue to the Treveri was, so far as the Belgic Gauls were concerned, that much less true than before. But if ambitious nobles had to redirect their aspirations, this had but little effect on the general development of the province.

4

URBANIZATION

1 Topography and early growth of *civitas* capitals

The sites of the *civitas* capitals were determined, it was argued above, by military exigencies in the period between Caesar and Augustus, and were already linked by an extensive road network when civilian functions became uppermost.

The town sites still varied in artificiality, for they might correspond closely, loosely or not at all to pre-Roman centres. Sometimes these might simply be perpetuated, the clearest example being Besançon; Langres and Metz may be similar. More often there was a shift in site, but sometimes only of a few kilometres, from a pre-Roman fortified settlement which had already gained central importance. Such a shift occurred at Soissons (from Villeneuve, rather than directly from Pommiers), Arras (from Etrun), Reims (from Vieux-Reims), while longer distances were involved at St. Quentin (from Vermand) and Avenches (from Mt. Vully). Caesar's use of Amiens as a headquarters may have given rise to an intermediary stage there (not however, on current evidence, in the valley bottom) and the same could be true of Arras. Elsewhere, the site was more obviously new and artificial. No nearby predecessors are known for Bavay and Tongeren, despite the names Bagacum and Atuatuca, and the site of Toul (Tullum) is rather far from Essey-les-Nancy. Cassel (Castellum) owes its name to a Roman description of this commanding site overlooking the plains of Flanders, and has no known predecessor. At Senlis there is a possible but unproven site nearby. The chosen site of Trier seems to have borne no relationship to previous political geography, but is again purely strategic.[1]

The city names do not necessarily reflect their early history. Caesar's Samarobriva (Amiens) and Nemetocenna (later Nemetacum, Arras) were not native centres – interestingly, both names refer to general topography (the Somme crossing, the forest). Caesaromagus, literally Caesar's market (Beauvais), may have been founded before Caesar's death: with Augustomagus

(Senlis), it represents the bilingual type of name found also in Augustodunum (Autun). Sites without predecessors were mostly given Celtic names, though Latin Castellum contrasts with Atuatuca. The three Augustae – St. Quentin, Soissons, Trier – were Augustan foundations to the same extent as Bagacum or Tullum; the initiative for the imperial name probably came from the local nobility.[2]

Further comparison between Trier and Toul is of interest. Immediately after the conquest, the most important site among the Treveri was, despite its eccentric position, the Tetelbierg: there is no indication that a more centrally situated *oppidum*, such as Castel, rivalled it. Among the Leuci, Boviolles in the Ornain valley was similarly predominant; it seems unlikely that the more central (but little known) Essey-les-Nancy could compare. Both major sites owed part of their prosperity to their geographical location – the Tetelbierg on the watershed between Meuse and Rhine, Boviolles on a route to Champagne from the plateau of Langres.[3] The traditional route was, however, replaced by a new road from Langres to Reims via Châlons, while the great strategic artery from Langres to Köln overshadowed all others. This last touched or crossed the Moselle at three points, the first and last giving rise to Toul and Trier. Once established, Trier's dominance was unquestioned, though a flourishing new minor town, Arlon, partially replaced the Tetelbierg. Among the Leuci the situation remained more complex.

The community from Boviolles descended into the valley to become Naix (Nasium, a nose or promontory, perpetuating the old name). Ptolemy, who normally gives one capital for each *civitas*, lists both Nasium and Tullum for the Leuci. Later, an official set up a dedication to the genius of the Leuci at Naix, and another inscription, if correctly interpreted, shows that the surrounding *pagus* had an *ordo* like that of the whole *civitas*.[4] It is clear that the primacy of Toul, the artificial Roman creation, was uncertain, in spite of its geographical centrality and its position on a major river.

All *civitas* capitals were road-centres. As has been seen, the overall pattern suggests that the main routes were laid out by about 15 BC. Certain adjustments, and the addition of the minor roads which formed a spider's web radiating out from each capital, may have come later. Thus Dalheim on the left-bank Metz-Trier road was already developing by 20 BC, while the absence of early Augustan material at Arlon suggests a later date for this part of the Reims-Trier highway. A link from Dalheim to Trier was developed in Nero's reign through bridges over the Mosel at Stadtbredimus and the Saar at Konz.[5]

A preference for sites on rivers, at points where these could readily be forded or bridged, can be observed. When the rivers are also navigable, as at Besançon, Châlons, Soissons, Amiens, Toul, Metz and Trier, they form a further integral part of the developed communications network. The Vesle at Reims, though petty compared with the Aisne, may also have been navigable for small craft. St. Quentin, Senlis, Beauvais, and Thérouanne, however, lie on streams too minor to be of use, while others have a totally different type of site.

Langres, the great road junction where routes arrived from Lyon and the Alps to leave for Rhine and Ocean, lies on a commanding promontory at the watersheds of Seine, Saône and Meuse. Similarly, Bavay is near the watershed of Sambre and Scheldt, and Tongeren beside the marshy zones of nascent streams. Cassel commands a whole area, Avenches a land corridor – all indications that land routes were initially paramount, and that the sites by river crossings owe their position to the need for the roads to cross rather than to the economic potential of the rivers. The predominance of land-locked capitals in the north, an area where water transport was later to be important, is noteworthy, as is the southerly position within their respective territories of Cassel and Bavay.

Throughout Augustus' reign, these sites may actually have borne fewer signs of incipient urbanization than the old *oppida*. Archaeological traces of so early a date are of course hard to identify on sites which have been occupied ever since. A large pit with material of the second decade BC, near the river-crossing at Amiens, could belong either to a military phase or to the earliest urbanization.[6]

How quickly a transformation took place is therefore hard to establish. Wooden buildings at Trier are late Augustan or Tiberian, and the same is true at Avenches. Since they have the orientation of the street grid, the latter must have been at least partially laid out, and sections across the central east-west street at Trier have produced only Augustan material in the bottom layers. The initial street grid here was enlarged under Claudius, while that of Avenches was extended at the time of the Vespasianic colony.[7] The original grids perhaps correspond to the common pattern in the central *insulae* (six in both directions with the central ones narrower). Elsewhere the extent of initial street grids and coherent planning remains very uncertain, though at Amiens central streets were also laid out by late in Augustus' reign. Further city-planning had perhaps to await the end of the German offensive, under Tiberius.

Early habitations were apparently not grand, and may have resembled the simple rectangular houses which are also found in the minor settlements. The dedication – probably one of many – to Augustus' grandsons at Trier shows that the occasional monumental building in stone – conceivably preceding the street-grid – was also erected.[8] These would clearly require the presence of architects from Italy or Narbonensis. While detachments of the army may have helped with the surveying and laying out of the street grid, the cost of buildings would have to be borne by the local notables, unless the emperor himself was prepared to make a contribution; as seen, the new towns were an exercise in public relations, the most obvious benefit (not to be lightly dismissed) being closer approximation to the conquerors' way of life.

At one or two cities, present evidence suggests that the street grid was not laid out before Claudius. One is Tongeren, where early material suggests a military supply base connected with Augustus' German campaigns. The *civitas*

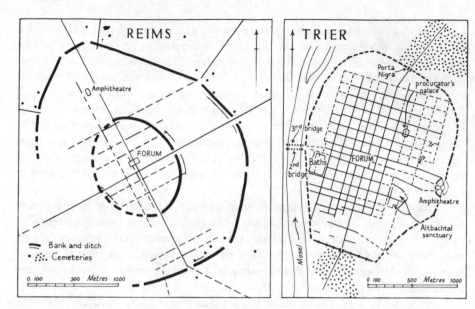

7 Plans showing the *fora* at Reims and Trier (Neiss, Schindler, Cüppers)

perhaps remained under direct military administration for much longer than the others, and the civilian site was not developed at first. A Claudian date is now also established for the street grid – a modest 15 ha – at Bavay. Considerable time thus elapsed before all the cities achieved an urbanized aspect.[9]

Frequently, the main roads were aligned with the street grid before entering the city, and sometimes, as at Reims, it seems that the orientation of the trunk road (here heading north-east for St. Quentin) preceded the town-plan. Perhaps at Thérouanne as well as at Reims, another trunk road ran at right angles to the first to form an intersection close to the town centre. The long, straight stretches of road must have been laid out from a *groma*-point at the junction. Here we have something close to a *decumanus* and *kardo*, though strictly these terms refer to the centuriation of land.[10] Elsewhere, main roads either aligned themselves on the streets only through modifications of line, or did not always intersect in the centre. At Amiens the primary road heading for the river crossing is oblique to the grid.[11] At Cassel, as at Langres, it is hard to see that any regular grid could have been adhered to in view of the steepness and narrowness of the eminences on which they sat: their plans must rather have resembled that of Lugdunum.

Whether the sites of public buildings, in particular the *fora*, were planned from the beginning is debatable. At Trier and Avenches the central *insulae* had dimensions different from the rest. The plan may have included the division of these into two rows of narrow *insulae* by the approach road, which would then abut on a wider area containing the forum. In practice, at least at Trier, further

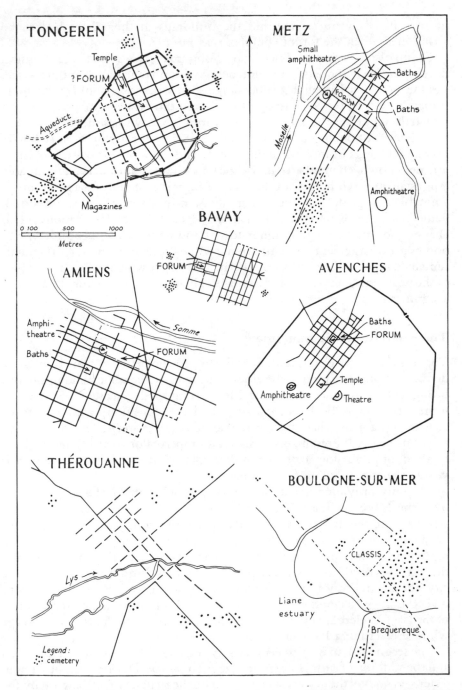

8 Plans of other cities in Belgica (Mariën, Bögli, Bernard, Seillier, Carmelez, Collot?)

narrow blocks were created and the buildings in them later had to be abandoned when the forum complex was built.[12]

Comparison between Trier and Tongeren shows that the physical development of the cities did not necessarily advance at a uniform rate, despite any official attempts to encourage this. Moreover, until Flavian times it may have been the converging of roads and the existence of a regular grid which distinguished the *civitas* capitals from minor towns, rather than any full complement of public buildings. The date of their furnishing with elaborate private buildings is also hard to determine, and again probably varied. There are no known counterparts in Belgica to the extraordinary, presumably Augustan, peristyle houses at Bibracte.[13] About the middle of the first century a notable change did however occur, apparently within a very short period, namely the use of stone rather than wood (at least for foundations). This change took place in cities, minor towns and countryside; henceforth, city houses grew larger and more luxurious, while those of the minor settlements remained much as they had always been. The rich town house was now a part of the northern Gallic scene, and the second half of the first century also brings a significant crop of mosaics.

2 The capitals: public monuments

The century between Claudius and the Antonine emperors brought a definitive transformation to the cities of Belgica. The public buildings which brought them resemblance to the Mediterranean city arose everywhere, if somewhat erratically. By their nature and their position in modern town centres they are often hard to date, so that no reign-by-reign development can as yet be charted. Presumably individual emperors or their legates used the methods of persuasion attributed to Agricola in Britain by Tacitus, and their words sometimes fell on fertile soil.

The only early monument that can be precisely dated is the second bridge over the Mosel at Trier. Tree-ring dating of the wooden piles that were rammed into the river bed as a foundation for the stone piers show that work began in the year AD 71. The new bridge was more than a functional replacement for its 90-year-old predecessor. For the traveller leaving the city, the vista was rounded off with a decorative hemicycle on the far bank. On the city side, an archway spanned the point at which the street turned slightly to meet the city grid (another archway performed a similar function to the north of the city).[14] Here are monuments which contributed to the urban landscape while also setting a Roman stamp on the recently rebellious city.

The second half of the first century saw considerable expansion of the cities, and the addition of extra, sometimes irregular *insulae*. During Claudius' reign, Trier was said by the geographer Mela to be the richest city of Belgica; by the end of the century it had expanded further, especially to the north. Amiens likewise grew rapidly, and if it indeed reached its full size of about 150 ha by AD

100, it must for a time have rivalled or even outstripped Trier. At Bavay, the new grid was a clumsy addition on a different orientation from the old, the result bearing no comparison to Trier and Amiens. The third big city of the province was Reims, where details of the street-plan unfortunately remain uncertain.[15]

With expansion went improvements. Wooden underground drains appear at Amiens, stone vaulted ones at Trier. These amenities were however sporadic, and open gutters probably remained more usual. Porticoed streets became the norm, fronting public and private buildings. By the later second century, public buildings normally included *fora*, baths, aqueducts and temples, frequently amphitheatres, theatres and monumental archways.

The *fora*, symbol of Romanity and distinguishing feature of administrative centres, consisted of a series of related buildings. Their organized space fulfilled religious, judicial, administrative, social and economic functions (even if a more northerly climate did not encourage the outdoor life of the Mediterranean world). The Gallo-Roman *fora* are not rigidly planned; while there are common elements, even the few examples known from Belgica show variations.

The position of *fora* within the street grid is normally central, and sometimes provides an architectural focus to one of the main streets. At Trier (as at Avenches) this was at the expense of blocking the path of the main roads through the city centre. Aesthetic considerations here predominated over any inconvenience, and the main roads had to shift a block to the east and south. At Bavay the forum lay south of the main entrance road, at Reims just to one side of the main intersection. At Tongeren and Amiens it is unclear whether a main street turned or ran through the forum.

In Gallic *fora* the incorporation of three elements was normal – a courtyard with single-roomed shops or offices, a second courtyard with a temple, and a basilica for the dispensation of justice. A *curia* or meeting place for the local *ordo* might be provided, but is not always identifiable. The best-known *fora* are those of Bavay and Trier, which also present both peculiarities and striking common elements.[16] In each place the basilica seems to have lain at the east end, that of Trier being notably long and narrow. This gives a sequence, from east to west, of basilica, commercial area and (probably) temple surrounded by porticoes. These last were built on two levels, with a *cryptoporticus* below a higher one. Both also have a rectangular projection at the westernmost end, interpreted as the *curia* or senate house even though it is separated from the basilica. The resemblance between the two buildings could be better tested if more were known of the Reims forum, which also had a *cryptoporticus*. The purpose of these has been much debated; remains of painted wall-plaster, some of it imitating marble, strongly suggest that they were not simply utilitarian storage rooms. Their practical function was probably not uppermost in the minds of the designing architects; they represent a grandiose solution to the problem of erecting an impressive monumental complex on sloping ground,

9 Plans showing the *fora* at Bavay and Trier (Biévelet, Cüppers)

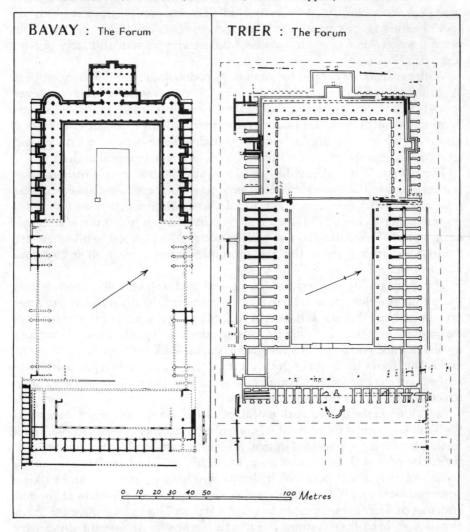

BAVAY : The Forum   TRIER : The Forum

0 10 20 30 40 50   100 *Metres*

without regard to the northern climate. An inscription from Nîmes suggests that they might sometimes house the headquarters of guilds. This could equally be the function of the spacious rooms in the central portion of the Trier forum, of dimensions rather grand for ordinary shops.[17]

The Trier forum, because of underlying remains, cannot be earlier than the last quarter of the first century; both it and its Bavay counterpart could belong to the early second. At Amiens the exceptionally long and narrow forum is thought to be Flavian (a late Flavian date is indicated at Paris). The late first century perhaps saw a wave of forum-building, each city anxious to comply.[18] Experienced and imaginative architects must have been employed.

The next building to be *de rigueur* was the public bath-house. The culmination of monumental bath-building is found at Trier, where the huge Barbarathermen occupy space equivalent to four *insulae*, lying on a strip of land which had been artificially made up in the mid-second century.[19] The plan was not complicated; the sequence of cold, warm and hot rooms, the first and last furnished with sunken baths, is traditional, and the flanking symmetrical wings are remarkable only for the number of rooms and the size of the twin heated swimming-pools. The decorative aspect of the architecture deserves more comment. Thanks to seventeenth-century accounts, it is clear that the exterior was as elaborate as the interior. Rows of niches with pediments enlivened the large wall-spaces, and further decoration included foliage and putti in stucco. This exuberant decorative detail has its counterpart in contemporary funerary monuments and monumental archways. Either incoming architects knew how to cater to the tastes of Gallic patrons, or northern Gaul had developed its own architects capable of designing large and complex structures. The interior of the baths was more in the Roman tradition, with much use of marble and good replicas of classical sculptures.

Trier probably had public bath-houses of more modest dimensions, like the early second-century baths at Amiens. Metz certainly had at least two sets of imposing baths, one boasting a circular swimming-pool. An inscription corroborates what would otherwise remain guesswork – that such buildings were indeed endowed by local notables; swimming-pool and courtyard were donated by a man who had served as *sacerdos* of Rome and Augustus.[20]

Given the extravagance of bathing establishments in Trier and Metz, the site at Soissons known as the 'château d'Albâtre', which has produced hypocausts, second-century mosaics and third-century marble statues might well be the principal baths of that city.[21] Bath-houses certainly became exhibition grounds for the acquired taste in monumental architecture.

As the custom of using baths, both private and public, took hold, the need for water supplies must have increased dramatically. Whether baths or aqueducts came first is not immediately apparent. Small aqueducts were present from an early stage of urbanization, for at Trier lead water-pipes have been observed in early street levels. At first, springs within easy reach of the city seem to have been utilized: how the Barbarathermen were supplied is not clear, for the largest of the Trier aqueducts appears to be late Roman in date. The most imposing remains and the fullest information come from Metz, where the aqueduct from Gorze, with a *nymphaeum* where it entered the city, was provided by a group of *seviri Augustales*.[22] A *castellum aquarum* or collecting reservoir, from which water would then be dispersed, would also be necessary. All cities may be presumed to have had aqueducts, and when desired, as near Bavay, the more sophisticated siphon, as opposed to arches, might be employed to bring the water across a valley.[23] Inside the cities, provision was made at regular intervals for the attachment of pipes to lead water into private houses. The provision of a public water supply may have allowed the Gallic cities to support a larger population in more tolerable conditions; an auxiliary supply in the form of wells was also widely available.

Baths were probably restricted in availability and appeal; a wider public was certainly reached by the amphitheatres. These are known in varying degrees of detail from Trier, Metz, Amiens and Senlis; at Tongeren the site of one is suspected and at Reims there is indirect testimony. In all probability, the other cities were similarly endowed.

Amphitheatres are sometimes placed on the very edge of the city grid, but this need not indicate their relative date in the scheme of urbanization. The amphitheatres of northern Gaul were frequently built into the side of a hill to avoid the need for elaborate vaulting. In Belgica this is most obvious at Trier, while at Senlis a natural valley was exploited. No logical reason is known for the position of the amphitheatre next to the forum at Amiens. The site at Trier may have been so used from an early date, for there are traces of a wooden predecessor below the later stone edifice, which itself dates from the end of the first or the early second century. At Reims, Metz and Amiens, topography and remains suggest a greater use of vaulting. The shape of the buildings also varies from an elongated ellipse at Trier to an almost circular form at Amiens, where an unusual façade was added at a tangent, on the orientation of the street grid.[24]

If amphitheatres were normal, the same does not hold good for theatres. At Trier, no trace of one has come to light apart from the small earth and timber theatre (with stone seats) located in the Altbachtal sacred precinct. There is a larger stone-built theatre across the valley by the side of the imposing temple dedicated to Lenus Mars. This well illustrates the general impression given by Gallic theatres, that they are a less integral part of urbanism than of religion. At Avenches, an apparently urban theatre is closely associated with a major temple, and that of Soissons was perhaps similarly linked.[25] Curiously rare in the cities of Belgica is the more obviously non-classical type of theatre-amphitheatre or theatre with arena which is found in big sanctuaries such as Grand, and is normal in Lugdunensis, though the Soissons theatre perhaps had a wall separating spectators from orchestra. Influence from the Germanies is the probable reason for the two types of monument remaining more distinct.

Amphitheatres and theatres were important partly because of the sheer numbers of people from town and countryside who could gather together when spectacles were given. Their mere existence would intensify the recognition of the city as the focal point for the surrounding region. Scenes on mosaic pavements testify to the popularity of the arena among the rich, and suggest that traditional combats between gladiators and exotic beasts formed part of the fare. In theatres, pantomimes or some form of enactment of the myths central to Gallo-Roman religion may have been the usual entertainment.

The production of spectacles, and the provision and upkeep of buildings called for the expenditure of large sums. Inscriptions from Belgica only

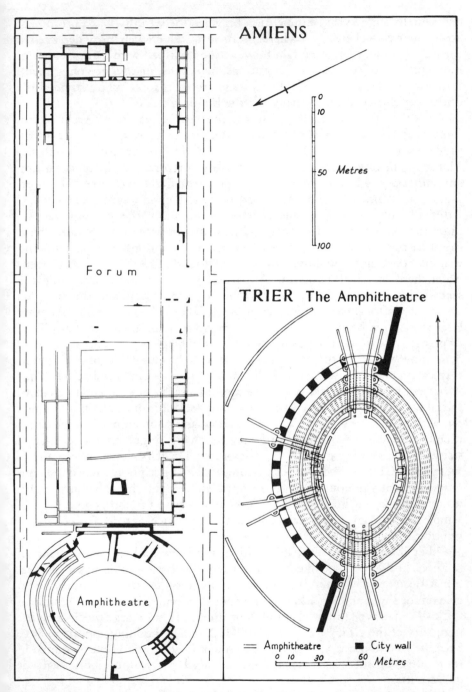

10 Plans showing the Forum at Amiens and the Amphitheatre at Amiens and Trier (Massy, Cüppers)

occasionally suggest that competition between the wealthy was a prominent aspect of city life, here as elsewhere. Stone seats, which were provided even in earth and timber theatres, might however be inscribed with names, either of individuals or of collective organizations such as the *iuventus* or young men's fraternity of Trier. In all likelihood these are the people who provided the outlay for shows, if not actually for the building itself.[26]

The other form of spectator sport, the circus, was rare. Architectural remains at Trier suggest a late Roman date, though there are arguments for a predecessor. At Soissons the circus, ascribed by Gregory of Tours to the Merovingian king Chilperic, was presumably of Roman origin. Since visiting administrative officials would no doubt particularly welcome the sports familiar to them, it would not be surprising if Reims was also equipped.[27]

Of all public buildings the religious ones show the greatest variety, illustrating at one end of the spectrum the strong impetus to Romanize and at the other the vigorous persistence of indigenous traditions. It is again at Trier that the best architectural remains are to be found. The temple 'Am Herren-brünnchen', perched across the Altbachtal valley from the amphitheatre, seems to have been of classical type; if an inscription dedicated by the *haruspices* is correctly associated with it, then it was of the god Mars Victor. Another large inscription bearing the names of some sixty men, members of a college, or perhaps decurions, may testify to others who helped erect it or embellished it in some way.[28] In the valley below lay a great cluster of shrines of non-classical type set up to numerous indigenous or semi-Romanized deities. They varied enormously in size, with the larger ones set in monumental precincts, but all were of Gallo-Roman type – a square, rectangle or polygon sometimes set within an ambulatory. The dedicators and worshippers varied from members of colleges to more ordinary folk who might offer a terra-cotta statuette of a mother goddess to their protecting deity. That other temples were scattered throughout the city is indicated by inscriptions. The god Lenus Mars, especially honoured by the Treveri, elicited from his adherents a mag-nificent shrine on the far side of the Mosel, where the indigenous type of temple was given a classical pediment to produce a true Gallo-Roman hybrid.[29]

Other Belgic cities probably had a similarly varied complement of religious buildings. One likely place for wholly classical buildings is the *fora*, but at Beauvais a lavishly decorated example stood to the north of the street grid on the slight eminence known as Mont Capron. At Tongeren a temple of Gallo-Roman type (but perhaps with pediment) lay in a large precinct on the periphery of the grid.[30] The period of lavish temple building appears to have been the second century, with the monumental aspect sometimes acquired in the course of successive rebuildings financed by various individuals or collectivities.

A variety of other public works enhanced Gallic cities and created an appearance familiar to visitors from other areas, in spite of such peculiarities as the Gallo-Roman temple. There is some evidence for fountains and honorific statues, the latter infrequent. A Severan building with a wide apse at Beauvais was some kind of public amenity, perhaps a library. Some cities had monumental archways gracing the entrance to the city centre. At Trier these performed the aesthetic function of masking the point at which the approach roads, coming in at an angle, joined the street grid. Those at Reims are of later date (second-century) than the ones at Trier and delimit only a small area. One, the highly decorated Porte de Mars, survives, partly restored. The cycle of the seasons is portrayed in a series of vignettes decorating the ceilings of the archways, while the exterior has further elaborate detail, partly architectural, partly figured, as in the analogous Porte Noire at Besançon.[31]

A few cities had yet more official buildings. Reims and Trier required a complex to house the legate and procurator respectively; remains of the procuratorial palace are probably to hand in the richly decorated remains of a substantial house at Trier, adjoining an apsed hall which could form an audience chamber. The governor's palace at Reims may have been in the area of the later Cathedral. Tongeren had a long drawn-out building which seems to have formed an official magazine, perhaps for storing grain and other produce for subsequent shipment to the Rhine armies. It lay to one side of the street grid, and was rebuilt on that site even when the city wall had come between it and the town.[32]

The great amount of space taken up by public buildings of unnecessarily monumental aspect distinguished *civitas* capitals from lesser agglomerations and shows how, after a rather slow start, the northern Gauls adopted the forms of the Mediterranean city. The grandiose nature that civic projects might reach is nowhere better illustrated than in the bridge, Barbarathermen and city wall of Trier. The building of a new bridge started in the years 144–152, and this time wooden caissons allowed the foundations of basalt to be laid directly on bed-rock. The road from the new bridge aimed directly for the south side of the forum, avoiding the previous need for a zig-zag course. The line of the street determined the outer wall of the Barbarathermen courtyard, showing that the baths were not yet completed. Hardly had the new bridge been completed than changes were made to it, shortening it on the city side and adding gateways on both sides of the river. This in turn is to be connected with the city wall, which ran up to the gateway on the city side. Given the enormous length of the wall (in practice indefensible) and the manner in which it is linked with other urban improvements, it appears to be another monument to civic pride as much as a defensive structure. This is also the effect made by the surviving Porta Nigra, imposing yet rather too open for effective defence. That a few of the many quarry marks found are common to Barbarathermen and Porta Nigra is another indication that they were not far apart in date, raising the possibility that the prominent citizens responsible for the buildings also owned or controlled the big sandstone quarries that lay just across the river. Yet the pottery from the building levels of the Porta Nigra shows that it was not finished much, if at all, before 200 – half a century later than the start of work on the bridge.[33]

The great 6.5 km wall at Trier was not the first in the province. That distinction is claimed by Tongeren, where the wall of 4.5 km cuts through no layers later than the early second century and is believed earlier than the second-century stone version of the long store-houses. Since the city wall was preceded by a ditch and palisade, it is possible that a need for defence was felt at the time of the Batavian revolt. The stone version is however just as likely to be a symbol of status, with permission to build granted by a sympathetic Trajan or Hadrian. As with amphitheatres, so the inspiration for the building of city walls is to be sought in the Germanies, not least in Köln. The third city wall of Belgica, that of Metz, already belongs to a different world where defence was a real consideration and funerary monuments might be torn down wholesale to provide building material.[34]

3 The capitals: private buildings, cemeteries and suburbs

The problems of archaeology in towns which have a continuous building history of close on two millennia are even greater for private houses than for public buildings. This lends especial value to Avenches, where medieval and early modern town did not cover the Roman city. Thérouanne may be analogous, since the post-Roman town was destroyed in the sixteenth century. Otherwise knowledge tends inevitably to be haphazard, dependent on modern building programmes which also destroy what they uncover.

Not surprisingly, little is known of buildings constructed before the use of stone became normal. From Avenches, however, it can be shown that early houses near the city centre might have porticoes and that artisans might work just behind. House plans and functions may have differed little between capitals and *vici*.[35] From an early date two types of house may however have developed along separate lines. The first, narrow, rectangular and simple, reflects the attraction of artisans towards any urban settlement, regardless of its status. Something grander is to be anticipated once local notables were persuaded to spend time in the urban centres, and to denote their status with elaborate town-houses. At present, however, the evidence does not determine whether large houses were first erected in city or countryside.

At Trier, finds of Julio-Claudian date are scattered beyond the original kernel of the street grid, and buildings sometimes appear to have preceded streets. Here, if anywhere, large town houses of an early date would be in place, and there are indications of them from about Claudian times. Spacious buildings of Italian design complete with peristyle were built in the later part of the century. At Avenches, the late first-century properties were already large, each taking up a significant portion of an *insula*; the area which had previously housed artisans was devoted to a single enormous town-house adjacent to the forum. Beauvais and Reims have produced a similar picture.[36]

While such houses saw subsequent internal remodelling, the basic elements persisted for a century or more, and were thus a fixed element in the town-scape. An indication of the embellishment and rebuilding of rich houses can be gleaned from mosaic pavements, which became a regular feature. While mosaics of first-century date are quite few, there was a general flowering in the second century, which at Trier continued without intermission into the third. There is great variation in numbers from one site to another. Trier has produced over a hundred, the runner-up, Reims, just under fifty. Metz and Bavay have almost twenty apiece, Amiens some ten. At Soissons, mosaics have mostly come from the so-called Château d'Albâtre. Virtually none are known from Beauvais, nor from Arras, St. Quentin, Cassel, Thérouanne or Toul, while Tongeren has produced only five. Naix, however, and a few other *vici* such as Nizy-le-Comte have them, a reminder that the centres of *pagi* might usurp some of the functions of the central cities. Boulogne, with its unique status as port and base for the British fleet, can also boast several.

Such variations in number should bear some relationship to fact, and their rarity in the more northern cities should indicate that less money was lavished on town-houses. Either fewer people had the necessary wealth, or those who did chose to use it otherwise. The great wealth of villas and rich tumulus-graves in the Tungrian countryside suggests that for them at least the latter is the explanation. There is also a chronological difference to be observed, for whereas the majority of mosaics from Trier belong to the late second or third century, the majority of those in the western part of the province are earlier. The contrast between Amiens (which seems to have reached its peak by the early second century) and Trier is striking. In the latter city, the rich third-century town-house with peristyle and fine mosaic floor (showing a charioteer and horses) below the courtyard of the later Kaiserthermen is typical.[37]

The existence of houses occupying a substantial portion of an *insula*, combined with the rather even spread of mosaics in Reims or Trier, suggests that population in the central parts of the cities was never dense. There are in fact hints of open spaces at Reims, Amiens and Soissons. Nowhere as yet is there any indication of apartment-block dwellings, though a relief from Dijon may show a town-house with modest shops and dwellings along its frontages. At Trier and Reims more modest houses, constructed wholly or partly of timber or mud-brick, have been found in less central areas.[38]

As the city centres were given over to more lavish buildings, artisans might be forced to withdraw to a sector on the outskirts of the grid. At Trier, where potteries had been established in the southern part of the town from a date early in the first century AD, a flourishing potters' quarter developed. Whether other activities such as metal- and stone-working were concentrated in the same area is not clear. Evidence from Tongeren suggests that such activity could be scattered, though always at a discreet distance from the centre. At Reims, the manufacture both of pottery and of bone objects was concentrated in the southern end of the city.[39]

There is sporadic evidence for the plying of such crafts from many of the cities, and some such activities presumably went on in all. The cities were perhaps the centre for certain forms of production – the finer provincial bronzes or bigger monumental tombstones.[40] Trier also had a distinctive mosaic workshop, the products of which are found throughout the region; of the other cities, only Reims might boast the same. There is evidence for ware-houses along one of the exit roads at Avenches, and these must also have existed at Metz and Trier, along the river from which the *nautae Mosallici* made their living. Yet archaeological evidence for industry in the cities is not often on a large scale.

While the prime residential area of the Gallo-Roman city was near its centre, there could be small distinct settlements outside but in close proximity. Burials or masonry remains, considered to be villas, exist to the north and south of Trier, and the same may explain the cemetery at La Horgne au Sablon south of Metz. Across the Mosel from Trier lay a rather larger settlement known from inscriptions as the Vicus Vocclanionum, with its own cemeteries and cult areas. Such a development may have been commoner than is realized: whether such physical separation brought with it feelings of suspicion and even hostility towards the city-people proper (as happened in early medieval Soissons) we shall never know. There were cemeteries across the river from Amiens, while at Arras a suspected suburban quarter (the medieval Méaulans, derived from Mediolanum) down near the river may have been separate from the main city. That Metz had a suburb across the river was natural, since one of the roads to Trier stayed on the left bank throughout. There may also have been a further community at Sablon, around an important sacred area, the Mediomatrican equivalent of the Lenus Mars precinct at Trier.[41]

It is from Metz and Trier that there is evidence for possible internal divisions, also called *vici*, within the cities. An inscription from Trier mentions a Vicus Senia, while the two *vici* of Metz have the more formal, Romanized names of Pacis and Honoris.[42]

Effectively, it was the cemeteries which, in the absence of walls, demarcated the cities under the Pax Romana. According to Roman religious practices, the burial of the dead within settlement boundaries was forbidden, and this accorded with Gaulish custom. Allowance was very clearly made for the subsequent growth of the cities. Whether or not a formal boundary sanctioned by religious ceremonies was drawn around the provincial towns, it is clear from Trier and Reims that the cemeteries were planned at a healthy distance – about 1 km – from the city centres. At Trier, where expansion was greater to north than to south, the later city wall cut through a cemetery in the north and enclosed another small one in the east. Evidence for the comparative decline of Amiens in the late second and third centuries comes from the discovery of burials within the previously inhabited area.[43]

Although there are a few exceptions, the cemeteries normally stretched on either side of the main exit roads. A variety of monuments – altars, pillars, flatter *stelae*, walled areas and simple ditched enclosures – presented itself to the passer-by, a variety which would itself differ according to the particular city and its custom. Further research may show that there were distinctions in death as in life, with certain areas of cemeteries reserved for the wealthy.

4 Small towns and villages

Belgica also contained a wide range of population centres varying from small towns such as Naix and Arlon to remote rural hamlets. Those near the one end of the scale are best considered as aspects of urbanization, whereas at the other end lies a rural phenomenon. In practice, a reasonable dividing line can be established on criteria of function, topography and status. Functionally, villages where artisan activity and secondary services were as important as agriculture can be classed as urban. Topographically, the distinction between villages on or near roads and those away from them corresponds well with the first criterion. Finally, a *vicus* to the Romans was a community capable of having its own administration. In practice all inscriptions mentioning *vici*, *vicani* or magistrates of a *vicus* or *pagus* come from villages along the main roads.

Since villages on main roads served as staging-posts, a number of them are mentioned in the Antonine Itinerary (thought to have been prepared for the emperor Caracalla) or in the Peutinger Table (a copy of a later road-map). Some are mentioned on the road-indicator known as the *milliarium* of Tongeren, on a more dubious example (perhaps a copy of an authentic map) from Macquenoise or on inscriptions set up in the village itself.[44] Most of the places known from epigraphic or literary evidence can be located. Archaeology has added a large number of villages, most notably among Tungri, Nervii and Menapii, for which no ancient name is given. In French-speaking areas, the ancient name can often be reconstructed from modern toponymy, and some such examples are also preserved in the Mosel valley. The names are in general Latinized Celtic, occasionally incorporating such well known roots as -magus (Noviomagus, Noyon and Nouvion) or -dunum (Verodunum, Verdun), or simply taking the name of the river on which they lay (Mosa, the Meuse).

The most difficult villages to classify lie beside sanctuaries. When the sanctuary is very rural and the settlement small, the religious element was probably predominant; such places are not considered here, even if some minor artisan activity may have gone on. Vendeuil-Caply or the Tetelbierg, however, while undoubtedly of religious importance, were also considerable population centres, and can reasonably be included. The fact that marketing functions were often bound up with religious does however render distinctions rather artificial.

Like the capitals, villages might or might not have pre-Roman origins. Just less than one-fifth have produced evidence to create a presumption of Iron Age beginnings. The best documented in Belginum (Wederath, Kr. Bernkastel), where a substantial portion of the cemetery is of pre-Roman date, suggesting a community of some 40–50 families. Its site is a low but commanding ridge of the Hunsrück, and the topography attracted the Roman road that in turn assured the community's continued existence.[45]

Other settlements with pre-Roman roots are *oppida* which survived the conquest. Some (e.g. Pommiers) had a limited life, while at Vermand the roads leading to it show that the fortifications continued to shelter a permanent community. La Cheppe (Vieux-Châlons) continued to be occupied in spite of Châlons – indeed it may be the Fanum Minervae of the Antonine Itinerary, surviving partly as sanctuary, partly as road station. The best example of a Roman village within a Gaulish *oppidum* is however the Tetelbierg. The bulk of the archaeological material from this site is in fact of Roman date, but late la Tène fibulae and pre-conquest coins go with pre-Roman occupation. Excavations have unearthed houses of the period 50–30 BC – large rectangular timber buildings some 7 m × 15 m, with the narrow side facing a street. These were soon replaced by houses built partly in stone, and with cellars, though the long narrow plan remained typical. A smaller, untidier village in a hillfort lies near St. Dié, at la Bûre. Here a traditional community in a remote spot absorbed Roman influences only slowly.[46]

The decades following the conquest saw a rapid increase in the number of villages, particularly along roads. A number of them may replace military bases, though only at Velzeke is this certain. Along the road between Bavay and Köln, Waudrez, Liberchies and Braives have all produced either pottery or Gaulish coins of Augustan date; Liberchies was flourishing by the middle of Augustus' reign. Dalheim, south-west of Trier, had a number of wooden houses by about 15 BC and the same story comes from the Mont Berny and Carrière du Roi, two villages on the relatively non-strategic road between Senlis and Soissons.[47] The same general period saw the supplanting of Boviolles by the roadside valley site of Naix (Nasium), and by the end of Augustus' reign Arlon was rising on what was now the main route from Reims to Trier to challenge the Tetelbierg. The two generations following the conquest therefore represent a period of rapid change.

Not all the detectable changes occurred within this initial period. Sites producing nothing earlier than Claudian pottery suggest another major phase of development in the mid-first century AD. This coincides with further evidence for road-building (attested both by milestones and excavations) and some temporary military activity to which ditches at Kortrijk and Tournai bear witness. Cemeteries also show changes in the settlement pattern around this time. Those at Fouches and Chantemelle (B. Lux.) may be of villages which were somehow displaced at this time.[48]

By the middle of the first century AD the road network was in place, and the minor settlements were strung out along it at intervals which vary from 7 to over 40 miles. This neat picture does however require qualifications. Major, and some minor rivers attracted settlements in the absence of main roads. The Meuse valley saw villages at Stenay, Dinant and Huy, and there were several settlements between Trier and Neumagen, on a road which followed the loops of the river. Whether Destelbergen and Waasmünster (on Scheldt and Durme) or Tigny (on the Authie) were linked to the road system is unclear. The recent discovery of a small inland harbour at Pommeroeul has graphically demonstrated that the waterways in the Low Countries had a life of their own, giving rise to numerous small population centres. Many *vici* were on both transport systems, being situated at the point where roads crossed rivers: a good example is Dieulouard-Scarpone, on the Moselle, where a pier is known.[49]

Occasionally, there are settlements either a little way off the main roads, or else on roads so minor that the settlement may have been prior – for instance Ciney (Namur), Lens, Noyelles or Ardres (Pas-de-Calais). Most villages so situated are, however, those where the function of sanctuary was predominant. A number in the Monts Faucilles owed their presence to mineral springs, and in due course developed as spas, with great bath-houses not unlike the modern counterparts below which they often lie. The healing waters were of course sacred to divinities: hence the big sanctuary of Borvo at Bourbonne-les-Bains.[50]

One village, Boulogne, had a unique position. The lower town, Gesoriacum, was technically a *vicus* of the Morini which happened at the same time to be a major sea-port. Little is known of it apart from its cemeteries. There is no evidence that it was highly urbanized in form: urbanization connected with the end of the route to Britain took place further south, at Amiens. The high town, Bononia, was from Claudian or Neronian times a base for the *classis Britannica*, and under Trajan this gave rise to a regular stone fort. Yet Boulogne attracted to it people like Sulpicius Avitus, magistrate and priest of the Morini, and there can be little doubt that Gesoriacum grew at the expense of the land-locked Thérouanne.[51]

The roadside *vici* obviously acted as *mansiones* and *mutationes*, places where accommodation and horses were available to travellers. Places mentioned in the Antonine Itinerary were perhaps officially bound to offer these services for the *cursus publicus* at the expense of the local *civitas*, which also had to see to the general upkeep of the public roads. But no doubt nearly all villages had their inn, no matter how uncomfortable and insanitary. Little is known of such buildings at present, the only identified inn being a late Roman one at Chamleux, where rooms opened off a court into which carriages could be driven by means of a wide entrance. Despite the existence of a cellar with ample storage of amphorae, the level of comfort was obviously low.[52]

The larger *vici* had magistrates and an organized community life. *Quaestores* are found (Belgium), and there are other dedications made by *vicani* corporately, or on behalf of them by a magistrate. The *iuniores* (Young Men's Brigade) of Bitburg denote social stratification and pretensions to Romanity. This is one of several indications that the *vici* served as centres for surrounding *pagi*. That a *pagus* cult-centre might be situated in a major *vicus*, thus paralleling the relationship between *civitas* and capital, is also shown by a dedication from Belginum. There was thus an outlet for local pride, and a focus for the corporate bonds expressed in local cult practices. Naturally, every *vicus* would have its own shrine or shrines, even when it was not a *pagus* centre.[53]

That a need for local marketing facilities was important in the development of *vici* is clear. Some may have started by supplying temporary army bases and exploiting the opportunities for reciprocal exchange brought by the long-distance army suppliers. Post-conquest Gaulish coins are typically found in large numbers in *vici*. Aerial photographs of Vendeuil-Caply suggest the presence of a forum building comparable to that of Alesia, though whether this served as a market centre or merely reflected local pretensions cannot be known. Periodic marketing will have occurred in connection with religious celebrations; whether regular periodic marketing in the form of the Roman *nundinae* occurred in the Gaulish provinces is simply unknown. Much of the buying and selling which went on in *vici* was of individual artisans' items in the front of the very workshops where they were manufactured. Nevertheless, *negotiatores* or merchants set up an inscription to Tiberius at le Héraple, and shops stocking quantities of imported *terra sigillata* pottery have been found at Pachten and Braives. How much exchange of agricultural produce went on, and what proportion of all exchanges involved money, can only be a matter of guesswork. Careful analysis of the coin records may bring clarification.[54]

One function of all village-type settlements was undoubtedly the manufacturing of certain objects and the refining of raw materials. Evidence for the production of salt was for long based largely on place-names such as Marsal (*Marsallus vicus*) in Lorraine, coupled with the stray occurrence of clay containers connected with 'briquetage'. This, while increasing in clarity, has now been overtaken by the evidence from Flanders and the Pas-de-Calais. Salt refining from sea water was practised at Ardres (on a secondary road reaching the channel coast at Sangatte) and some small communities along the Belgian coast may have depended entirely on it.[55]

Salt remained of necessity localized, and could be compared with the forestry which probably supported the hamlets or villages in the Vosges. Pottery manufacture and metal-working are on the other hand so ubiquitous that there is hardly a single report on excavations in a *vicus* which does not mention evidence for one or the other; the economic implications will be discussed later. Some *vici*, notably Tournai and Thiverny (Oise) were connected with quarrying, and there may be other examples to discover; a situation on a river was almost a *sine qua non* for such activity.

Iron-working and smithying were not surprisingly the commonest activities concerned with metal. Evidence varies from a few lumps of slag or ore, to a complete forge at le Héraple (Moselle) or small bowl-furnaces (Courtrai, Thionville). A clear impression of the items produced is not available – presumably a range of goods for domestic use, items connected

with vehicles and transport, and agricultural implements like those of the so-
called 'peasant's hoard' from Tarquimpol. More rarely, there is evidence for
the working of bronze, and it is clear from discoveries at Pachten (Saar) and
Daméry (Marne) that such little workshops could also be used to provide cast
silver coinages in periods when officially coined money was in short supply.

Metal-working demanded an ample water supply, and the number of wells
found in *vici* has often received comment. Water was needed for other
purposes too, quite apart from a drinking supply. At a few *vici* (e.g. Ardres, St.-
Maximin, Schwarzenacker) activity connected with cloth has been recognized. The number is surprisingly low, sufficiently so to raise the question of
whether loom-weights have gone unrecognized or whether the double-beam
loom, which does not require them, was normal.[56]

Clearly there was much artisan activity in the villages, and on a reasonable
assumption the village potter and blacksmith supplied the needs not just of the
village itself but also the surrounding countryside within a convenient radius.
Were the needs of the local villa estates then largely supplied by the *vicus*, or
were the larger of them at least self-sufficient with regard to pottery, tiles and
metal-working? These and related questions will be further discussed below.
Most important, did a majority of the villagers earn their livelihood most of
the time from artisan activity, or did they normally combine this with
agricultural concerns?

It is tempting to see in the villagers numbers of small men making good,
practising crafts in return for monetary rewards and thus freeing themselves
from the constraints which an earlier form of traditional life and patronage
imposed on them. It has been pointed out that there are often villas within a
kilometre of the *vici*, which tells against the cultivation of large areas of land by
the villagers, as does the comparative rarity of agricultural implements and the

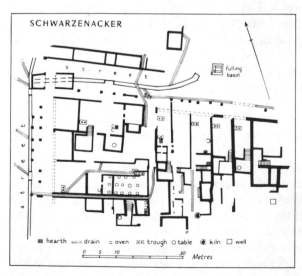

11 Plan showing the *vicus*
of Schwarzenacker
(Kolling)

95

unsuitability of the average *vicus* dwelling for the storing of vehicles or the stabling of larger animals. It has also been suggested that the *vicani* would largely sell their products to a free peasantry, and would thus form part of an economy which can be considered separately from that of the larger self-sufficient estates.[57]

The picture is likely to have been more complex. The closeness of the nearest villas need not be seen as denying agricultural activity to the villagers. They had room for vegetable patches behind their houses, and a relief from Arlon – admittedly one of the largest and most prosperous *vici* – suggests market gardening as a lucrative activity, while another shows the figure of a ploughman. One obvious function for villagers is as day-labourers at time of ploughing and harvest. But in addition to this some might have owned or rented plots among the villa farms. Nor were they necessarily free from all constraints of traditional patronage, though they may have received a higher percentage of payments in money than peasants on estates. While it is likely that much long distance trade passed them by, there was still money to be made from services, or from selling manufactured items to a trader or middleman who had a ready market for them elsewhere.

In any case, the *vici* were not simply or invariably a world of 'little folk'. The magistrates at least were men of standing in the surrounding countryside, and therefore landowners. Their nomenclature suggests that they were of the same class as the men who put up big funerary monuments or became decurions. Wealthy people must have endowed the shrines, and more especially the cult theatres or the public baths which some (Mamer, Lux.) possessed. At Naix and Nizy-le-Comte, wealthy men lived in the village, for both have produced the unusual luxury of early mosaics. Such men would be patrons of the village in a general way, even if the nature of the bond cannot be defined more closely.[58]

The *vici* certainly were a typical feature of Belgica. At present just over 150 are known, or roughly a dozen for each *civitas*, and the total was no doubt considerably higher, perhaps as much as double. In appearance, as in size and function, they varied, yet presented common features. Some were simply spread out along the main road, or along the arms of a fork or crossroads; the larger ones had a rudimentary grid pattern, though a certain amount depended on topography (a regular grid could not be imposed on Arlon's steep hills). At the outer edges were the cemeteries, again along the roads. To one side of the centre was a sanctuary or sanctuaries – Belginum seems to have had a major one at each end of the settlement. Towards the centre, the buildings were long and narrow, with the narrow end facing the road. They often combined a shop or workshop in the part nearest the street with dwelling quarters behind, or perhaps over, and a long enclosure behind that. Sometimes more spacious houses were found, some of them reminiscent of the smaller villas; examples are to hand in Saarbrücken and nearby Schwarzenacker, but whether this betokens a higher degree of wealth or a greater involvement with agrarian pursuits is unclear. Public buildings were much less in evidence than in the *civitas* capitals, but might include, beside the temples, a cult theatre and a bath-house; aqueducts are also known. One unusual building at Schwarzenacker has been interpreted as the meeting place of a guild because of its strange plan and the discovery of a metal object which could have been a guild symbol.[59] The general impression must have been a mixture of down-to-earth untidiness and pretentious attempts to emulate the *civitas* capitals.

5   The functions of towns in Belgica

Every focus of population deserving the name town or village had certain common functions, among them facilities for marketing and production of certain classes of goods. Leaving aside questions of status, to what extent were the *civitas* capitals radically distinct from the smaller centres?

Like villages, *civitas* capitals were marketing centres for the surrounding countryside, arguably servicing wider areas or providing more specialized facilities. The production of ceramic and metal goods was dispersed throughout both *vici* and capitals (not to mention rural centres). Bavay, Reims, Metz and Trier all produced Gallo-Belgic pottery in the first century after the conquest. Only Trier followed this up by becoming a major producer and exporter of *terra sigillata* and other fine wares, supplying a fair proportion of the fine pottery needs between Mainz and the Rhine mouth. The potteries in other capitals, on present evidence, continued to work mostly for the local market, though Bavay may have produced some more widely ranging coarse wares and was a manufacturing centre for bronze box and furniture fittings.

Given that, *prima facie*, the *citivas* capitals were not necessarily more productive than the villages, a fuller enquiry into size and probable population is warranted. If the public buildings are subtracted, were the *civitas* capitals much larger and more populous than villages?

Investigation shows two distinct categories, with only a small degree of overlap. For the villages, an area of between 10 and 20 ha is normal, to judge from the better known places. Among these is Belgium, where there seem to have been some 60 strip-houses (recognized from the depressions formed by their cellars) divided between the two sides of the road. If 50 were simultaneously occupied, this would give a total population of about 300. This is a little more than the figure suggested by the cemetery, which has some 2,000 graves for an estimated ten generations (the existence of another cemetery is not excluded). Successor to a pre-Roman village or villages, Belginum remained quite small, and buried its dead in traditional fashion, reserving inscriptions for the sanctuaries which were patronized by the wealthy. Schwarzenacker, with a more Romanized and prosperous appearance, perhaps reached 25 ha, as did Arlon (where very little is known of the actual village, as opposed to the cemeteries). Of the regular roadside *vici*, only Tournai and Naix were substantially larger, reaching some 40 ha and, given evidence for a regular street grid, resembling the smaller *civitas* capitals.

Vendeuil-Caply, which combined the functions of *vicus* and important boundary sanctuary, attained a quite exceptional 100 ha, helped by two theatres, temples and a forum-like building.[60]

The capitals turn out to be quite variable. Normally, it is the developed city of the second and third centuries that is best known, with a complement of public buildings that rarely occupies less than 5 ha and may reach 10–15 ha. Sometimes an estimate can be made of the area originally gridded, or of the development reached within the first century AD. At Avenches the original grid arguably covers some 25 ha, though later expansion doubled that figure. At Bavay, only some 15 ha was originally laid out, but considerable expansion then took place to give a city estimated at 40 ha; Arras and Thérouanne are reckoned to have reached about the same figure. Metz, hemmed in by its cemeteries, reached some 60–70 ha (not counting suburbs), while Tongeren after a late start expanded from some 50 ha to about 75 ha. The plan of Reims is still all too little known, but on the evidence of mosaics it was over 200 ha, and thus in sheer area the largest city of the province. The other two obviously large cities are Amiens, which grew to some 160 ha perhaps by the end of the first century, and Trier. By the mid-first century the street grid at Trier covered 60 ha and finds of that date cover an even wider area. At maximum extent it perhaps reached almost 200 ha.

There is still room for argument on the density of building and of population. Figures of up to 300 and even 500 persons per ha have been suggested, but are certainly to be rejected as fitting only the crowded urban conditions of a much later age. The few rich town-houses of which the plan is substantially known show that they could take up a whole *insula*, 0.5 ha or even more, and this does not suggest densities of over 50–100 persons per ha. Parts of the cities might well of course be more densely occupied, but it is to be noted that the strip-houses of Belgium, admittedly well spaced out, give some 25 persons to the ha; it may be questioned if anything over 100 was normal, and the average was probably less.[61]

This gives for the average city a population of between 2,000 and 5,000 inhabitants, with only Amiens, Reims and Trier possibly in the 10,000–20,000 category. Even so, this is well in excess of the few hundreds suggested as average for villages. Granted that there was more need for household servants and for service trades in the capitals, the figures raise the possibility that many city-dwellers were highly dependent on a small number of wealthy people. Whether donations were frequently made on occasions such as weddings, deaths or gladiatorial shows remains unknown, since no inscriptions record this facet of city life.

At the same time, the total number of people in villages within any one *civitas* would equal or surpass the inhabitants of the capital. The impression of a high village population in the north, among Nervii and Menapii, is to be connected with the absence of northern cities. Since *per capita* productivity among villagers was higher than among city dwellers, taken as a whole they represent the principal focus of industrial activity in the province. Yet adding villages and cities together still leaves a probable nine-tenths, a minimum four-fifths, of the population elsewhere in the countryside.

One obvious difference between capitals and villages lay in administrative function. Though some *vici* had local magistrates and were centres for surrounding *pagi*, this did not normally affect the paramount position of the capital, meeting-place of the *ordo* for the entire *civitas* and recipient of the patronage which produced the public buildings.

From this fact, combined with the Mediterranean attitude that made the city the natural focus of all civilized life, various consequences stemmed. The capitals became centres of education (though how early the Trier schools were established is uncertain) and dissemination of Roman ideas.[62] Members of the imperial administrative staff, retired veterans, money-lenders and traders helped; few would dispute that knowledge of Latin and literacy were more widespread in capitals than elsewhere. When the distribution of inscriptions and reliefs is studied, Trier and Reims, it will be seen, stand out for the way in which the city dominates the territory in sheer numbers of monuments, especially funerary. Arlon's urbanized character again shows up in an unusually high proportion of funerary monuments.[63]

Although in social status and as centres of Romanization the capitals were paramount, their economic function can, as has been seen, be questioned. Doubtless they were largely dependent on their rural base, the rich town-houses being normally built by magnates out of the profits from rural estates, the official buildings also thus financed. A good deal of the produce consumed in the capitals was probably brought directly from estates. The question still arises whether production of untraceable goods (e.g. woollen garments) was concentrated in capitals more than in *vici* or on estates. The stone monuments, which must be consulted in lieu of other archaeological remains, are ambiguous. Most of those that depict the production of cloth or garments come from the countryside or from *vici*, though it has been argued that the production of the Secundinii family shown on the Igel column may have been centred on Trier rather than the estate.[64] Certainly, the population base was there, but whether it was so used is more doubtful.

A static model of the city as a parasite on the countryside may however be too simple, especially for Metz, Trier, Reims and Amiens. The last three show the greatest growth in area, the first three have produced most evidence for the concentration of service trades. It may be surmised that the presence of a more mixed population, including foreigners, was one reason. At Reims, a rapid development in the first to early second century could have been sparked off by the presence of the governor and his staff. Excavations, and the smaller number of later mosaics, suggest that building activity slowed down after the middle of the second century. Although Pomponius Mela says that Trier was the richest city of Belgica, its physical development may at first have been slower than that of Reims: later it enjoyed a building boom that went on into the mid-third century. There was, it is true, spasmodic building elsewhere (e.g. Beauvais and Soissons), but the forum at Amiens (though rebuilt after fire damage in the late second century) lay in a sorry state, filling up with rubbish, while cemeteries encroached on the street grid. While inscriptions and a famous isolated find, the Amiens *patera* (showing, like the British Rudge cup, the names of forts on Hadrian's Wall), show that the connection between the city and army traffic continued into the second century, decline clearly then set in. None of the other cities shows continuous expansion like that of Trier.[65]

Much depends on the view taken of long-distance trading and traders in Gaul. It is clear that Metz and Trier were affected by the Lyon-Rhine artery, with its prolongation to Britain. What mattered was not the importation of luxury goods, which reached nearly all capitals to some degree while simply passing through the *vici*, but rather the manufacture, handling and selling of goods. It is hard not to see some of the wealth of Metz and Trier stemming from this source. The possibility that Trier began to usurp Lyon as the trading capital for northern Gaul is to be seriously considered even in the absence of cogent epigraphic testimony. Of the cities of Belgica, Trier certainly has the best claim to be regarded not as an empty status symbol, a pale reflection of imported Mediterranean ideas or a mere parasite on the countryside, but as an active generator of wealth through production and trade. Without the Rhine frontier, however, this development could never have taken place.

To sum up, the degree of urbanization in Belgica depended on three main identifiable factors. The first was a connection with officialdom. The presence of governor and procurator at Trier and Reims, and the importance of Amiens for the connection with Britain, helped bring about the extraordinary early development of these three. The second was adoption by local notables of the idea of urbanism, and acceptance of the particular site marked out as capital. Toul and Cassel were failures in this respect, the first because of rivalry from Naix, the second because urbanization simply did not take root. The third was marketing and producing for an area notably larger than that of the average *vicus*. Bavay makes a surprisingly good showing here, but Trier wins by a very large margin, while also being at the top on the other criteria. Yet the Treveri, however wealthy and however urbanized by the standards of Belgica, failed to produce the knights and senators that might have been expected of them. By this very Roman criterion of status, the urbanization of Belgica remained a qualified success. By another criterion Gaul was also, by Roman standards, under-urbanized. Those of the larger *vici* which were *pagus* centres would in Italy or Africa have become capitals of independent *civitates*; but even Naix and Tournai took no more than tentative steps in this direction. To Roman eyes a failure, to a modern viewpoint the unpretentious *vici* are a more healthy reflection of a country where the economic base, despite the arguments made above, remained overwhelmingly rural.

5

RURAL BELGICA IN THE EARLY ROMAN EMPIRE

The Julio–Claudian period: continuity and change

At one very basic level the conquest brought little change to the countryside of Gaul, for in order to live, the inhabitants had to continue its exploitation. Thereafter, the interplay between continuity and change becomes meaningful: were the same sites occupied, did settlement types remain the same, did the pattern of ownership and exploitation change significantly, and if so, how suddenly? Some questions are answerable by archaeological means, others only by hypothetical argument. Close attention to the century after the conquest is required, despite difficulties in the archaeological record.

Until recently this was virtually blank before the latter part of the first century, which saw an upsurge in the building of the solid stone-foundationed complexes (dwelling with surrounding yard) to which the term 'villa' is conventionally applied. The great exception was always the site at Mayen where the earlier hut was replaced by a larger and more solid rectangular structure (foundations in stone, but lined with weight-supporting posts) perhaps within the reign of Augustus. This semi-Romanized technique indicated a family remaining in occupation of their land and adapting to new conditions.[1]

There is still no other excavated and published example of continuity that ousts Mayen (actually in Germania Superior) from its position as *locus classicus*. But at a growing number of places continuity is relatively well attested or at least very probable. For the most part the conclusion rests on pottery, and at best – as at Haccourt (Liège) or Auve (Marne) – only a few post-holes have been recovered from any pre-Roman building. Test excavations in the Somme valley have given a Roman date for at least some of the ditched enclosures usually called 'native farms'. An exception is the large rectangular wooden building, of complex plan, set within ditches at Condé-Folie (Somme); this is of particular interest because late la Tène pottery is associated with a building which appears Roman in style.[2] In fact this highlights two problems. Residual pottery from an earlier building can easily appear to be associated with a later one, and at Condé-Folie the rectangular building lies at a strange oblique angle to the enclosure. In addition, many types of pottery span the conquest period and can only be dated more precisely by the absence or presence of associated Romanized types. Ambivalent pottery has been noted at Creil-le Houy (Oise), as also in the lowest levels of a number of known villa sites in Belgium, France and Germany.³ This ambiguity prevents any close evaluation of the extent of continuity for the time being.

One or two sites remind us that later occupation of the same spot may not mean straightforward continuity. At Meerberg te Val-Meer (Limburg) a gap has been suspected between earlier (pre- or post-conquest) occupation and the villa, and at St. Maurice-aux-Forges (Meurthe et Moselle) a similar gap lasted for at least a century. At Horath in the Hunsrück a villa grew up very close to a late Iron Age settlement, but continuity, while likely, remains unproven. Some native farms (e.g. Conchil-le-Temple) did not show continuity into post-conquest times.⁴

Yet continuity there sometimes was, however difficult to describe with precision. Cemeteries in Champagne (such as Bouy, Ecury-le-Repos and Vert-la-Gravelle) were in use from late Iron Age into Roman times, and the same phenomenon has been noted near Trier (Biewer, Detzem) and in the Saarland (Lebach, Freisen and others). Most of these are large enough to suggest a nucleated settlement rather than a single homestead. Such cemeteries tend to die out in the second half of the first century AD, a fact which must be connected with the upsurge in villas with farmyards at this time. The untidy Roman hamlet outside the tiny late la Tène fortification at Landscheid (Kr. Wittlich) is another indication of continuity in a nucleated settlement, and a similar pattern is indicated by the hillfort and cemetery of Hoppstädten-Weiersbach. The contrary phenomenon, a settlement which did not continue into Roman times, is probably to hand in the unfortified site of Staberg te Rosmeer (Limburg); yet continuity is possible between Iron Age hut and Roman villa in nearby Rosmeer itself.⁵

That continuity appears stronger for hamlets than for farmsteads and is more evident in cemeteries than in habitation sites need not surprise. Nucleated settlements were probably the most stable element in the countryside, and even they tended to have a limited life before dying out or shifting position. Isolated houses need only shift their site slightly and excavation of the later stone villa will miss them. Limited excavation with the Roman period as principal objective will thus inevitably underestimate continuity. The comparative rarity of continuing smaller cemeteries (though examples are known from the Saarland) does however indicate shifts of population.

If continuity is still a grey area, the last few decades have added considerably to knowledge of the early Roman predecessors of the well-known large stone villas – the type of establishment which should be connected with Julius

Sacrovir and his kind, whom Tacitus believed to have country residences to which the word villa could apply. There were indeed substantial Julio-Claudian wooden buildings in the countryside, and on a scale very different from Mayen. The best example is Velaines-Popuelles (Hainaut), where part of a building with two wings has been found under the later stone replacement. Pottery included much in the late la Tène tradition, but some which was clearly Roman. Likewise, pottery from the early wooden period at Kerkrade (Dutch Limburg) included *terra sigillata* of Augustan or Tiberian date, and a wooden phase at Seeb (Switzerland) was Tiberian.[6] In what manner, if at all, agricultural buildings were attached to these habitations is unknown. It may be that there were associated hamlets; the cemeteries mentioned above might belong to such dependent settlements, subsequently dispersed.

The ownership of land is a much more difficult question. Censuses would establish not customary rights but ownership in Roman legal terms (even if technically non-citizens had only the lesser right of *possessio*). Since ownership of land was the principal determinant of wealth, it must be supposed that the Julii, for instance, had established title to large areas. Newcomers to this landed aristocracy there must have been, in view of the upheavals of conquest, yet this made little immediate difference to the system whereby nobles expected their upkeep to come from the labour of clients. Non-noble free families, who under Celtic custom probably owned land in common, had either to establish joint title, split their holdings up or allow one member to become the full owner. The post-conquest period may have allowed them to move into fresh or unoccupied land, even if some (at Mayen) remained where they were. It is unlikely that the people of the hamlets would normally be able to establish title to land, unless in areas without established chiefs, but it is possible that villagers in Flanders and Kempen were the equivalent of homesteaders elsewhere.[7]

In addition to the census, other external agencies could cause limited disruption. Land might be bought by Italians, but the epigraphic record of the province does not suggest a major foreign element. Arguments from place-names derived from -acum or -iacum, a common Gallo-Roman type of estate name, cannot be used, since those which appear to incorporate Roman names (Antoniacum, Flaviacum, Albiniacum, Paternacum) could have been the property of Romanized Gauls.[8]

Later, there was certainly land in Gaul which ranked as property of the emperor, administered by his procurators, and in all probability some existed from the beginning. The one instance attested by an inscription lies in the Vosges, an area which could be exploited for forestry and hunting but which is unlikely ever to have supported a large population. Other marginal areas may have been similarly treated, especially if they contained mineral resources, since mining areas were often imperial preserves. Although direct evidence is lacking, it is likely that parts of the Eifel, Ardennes and perhaps also the Saarland formed imperial estates.[9] Alternatively, areas on the boundary between the various territories could also have been public land of the *civitates*, and the ownership of sacred areas may also have been public. Further areas of imperial land might come from confiscated property. This is less likely at the time of the actual conquest, when Caesar probably used it to reward his supporters, but the estates of later rebels may have passed into imperial possession, and some Gauls may also have bequeathed land to the emperor.

While it may not appear in the Romans' best interests to disturb the pattern of landholding, it was of course within their power to do so. The land of a people who surrendered technically became Roman public land until returned to a properly constituted, recognized body politic. Portions of it could be retained by Rome, or later confiscated if it was decided to plant a colony. Such land might be surveyed and centuriated (the Roman term was *limitatio*) into regular units, the classic type being squares with sides of 2,400 Roman feet (about 710 m): this enclosed 200 *iugera* (approximately 50 ha) but could be further sub-divided.[10] This system could with reason have been employed at Nyon and Augst, and later perhaps at Aventicum.

In fact, traces of regular alignments have been identified not only in the land of the three colonies mentioned but also in the territories of Tungri, Ambiani, Remi and Treveri (western fringe). The claim that these represent centuriation must be examined, and, if accepted, its import for the countryside of Belgica. Even at Avenches, problems are posed by the absence of regular squares and the presence of more than one orientation. These different systems, if accepted, must represent resurveying.[11] Possible occasions for centuriation among the Tungri are the creation of the *civitas* by Agrippa, the aftermath of the Batavian revolt (in which the Tungri were involved though not prime movers) or, conceivably, an assumption by the city of colonial status. Here again, more than one orientation has been observed, some but not all parallel to the roads. Any reason for centuriation of the land of the federate Remi is hard to find, and the presence yet again of several systems, only partly based on the roads to Trier and St. Quentin (which form a right angle) raises the question of whether strict centuriation is really involved. Certainly, if it was done officially, it seems that some form of measurement other than squares was employed, and that all the flatter areas of the country were treated alike, regardless of status. The Augustan census is then the likeliest occasion, in which case the recorded outcry is understandable, even if the land was thereafter returned to the original owners.

Closer investigation of the evidence, to ensure that the perceived orientations really are dominant and form coherent systems, is desirable before conclusions are finally drawn. Among present examples, many could have resulted from a gradual alignment of field boundaries in accordance with roads, rather than from strict *limitatio*. Better evidence that rural habitation sites are in close connection with the supposed system is also desirable. Even if the alignments are essentially Roman, explanations involving massive expropriation must be treated with reserve. Owners may have received back in the form of neat rectangular parcels land which previously had untidy or imprecise boundaries. Much of it could also have been done piecemeal by civilian surveyors acting on behalf of the *civitates*; their job might include the reallocation of surveyed land and even the settlement of disputes.[12]

Even in areas without such general alignments, the appearance of the countryside did gradually become more regular, with field-boundaries and farmyards more frequently – though not invariably – rectilinear. Nothing did more to effect this change than the appearance of the substantial stone-built country houses or villas which are often considered the most typical feature of the Gallo-Roman countryside.

2   The growth and development of villas

Review of the evidence to hand suggests that roughly one half of the villas in Belgica were built in the second half of the first century AD. The figures record, not new habitation sites, but the sudden mushrooming of stone buildings. Many establishments may have had earlier periods in wood, and some new buildings (Haccourt, Liège) were still of wood in the middle of the first century. It is not at present feasible to suggest what proportion of stone buildings were on old or new sites. None of this alters the fact that these decades saw great building activity in the countryside, and that stone was becoming increasingly the norm, just as in the towns and larger villages. Even Haccourt, of wood at the time of Claudius, was rebuilt to a larger scale in stone by the end of the century.[13]

To what extent this activity was encouraged by Claudius and his governors is uncertain. More was involved than persuading the Gallic landowners to see the advantages of comfortable country-houses. For the upsurge of building activity to take place, quarries had to be opened and roads (in addition to rivers) be capable of transporting heavy loads; no doubt the attention given to the road system by Claudius helped. Architects, stone-masons, carpenters, plasterers, painters and manufacturers of roofing-tiles must all have increased in number to meet demand. Along with this building activity may have gone clearing of woodland and cultivation of fresh areas, for villas are sometimes found on relatively infertile land that was previously (and subsequently) not used for agriculture.[14] Whether this brought clashes between the old Celtic custom of ownership through prolonged unopposed occupation and Roman ideas of possession can only be a matter of surmise.

A comment is necessary on the meaning of the word villa. Two concepts of essentially Italian origin underlie the word. The first is that people of means, who would in a Mediterranean city-state have a role in municipal organization and spend much of their time in the town, should nonetheless also have a comfortable dwelling on part of the land which was the basis of their wealth. The second is that this dwelling should be the centre of exploitation of the surrounding land, and be no mere pleasure house but the focus of an economic unit. Villa and land (*ager*) together formed the organized estate (*fundus*) and

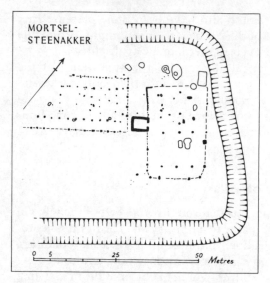

0   5   25   50   *Metres*

12   Plan of the site at Mortsel–
     Steenakker (de Boe)

were thus inseparable. Any substantial rural habitation may then be called a villa if there are signs that it was also the centre for surrounding agricultural activity. Yet the Romans would not have used *villa* but rather *casa* of the humble thatched cottage-farmhouse of a small peasant farmer, regardless of whether he owned the surrounding land. Conventionally, therefore, the use of the word is confined to buildings showing signs of wealth and Romanization, the latter expressed in the architecture. Thus a homestead with sub-rectangular huts and irregular enclosures, even if built in the first century AD, is not thereby a villa. A substantial wooden building, on the other hand, as has been argued, may deserve the name, and it is likely that many more await discovery in the northern areas of the province, where local sources of building stone were lacking.

Less clear-cut is the site Steenakker te Mortsel (Antwerp) where two roomy rectangular wooden buildings, from which only a series of postholes remained, were set within a small ditched enclosure. One building had a central hearth, a narrow corridor-like room at one end and another big partitioned area (perhaps for animals) at the other; from this a wooden stairway led to a stone cellar. Despite a few tiles in the cellar, the main roofs had not been of anything more solid than thatch, and there is little trace of Romanization in the buildings.[15] 'Farm' or 'homestead', in Latin the more neutral *aedificium*, thus seems more applicable than 'villa'. Yet in this area, where stone was less readily available, such farms might be similar in their economic role to the outwardly more Romanized establishments usually recognized as small villas.

Confusion may also arise from the use of the terms *villa urbana* and *villa rustica*. Ideally the word villa should be applied, as usually by the ancient writers, to the whole complex of buildings, and the *pars urbana*, the main dwelling, separated from the *pars rustica*, the attached farmyard, though it is hard in practice to avoid a looser usage.

That villas were indeed intimately connected with the exploitation of the land has long been recognized, if only occasionally debated. Older excavations tended to concentrate on the main house (which offered mosaics or other attractions) or to uncover whatever part first came to light, so that it can be hard to determine whether the 'villa' of an older excavation is the main dwelling or not. Nevertheless the nineteenth century already provided Anthée (Namur), where the farmyard buildings stretched for some 600 m behind the big house, and where the manufacture of enamelled *fibulae* was believed (wrongly, it has since been shown) to supplement agricultural concerns. At Fliessem (Kr. Bitburg) too the existence of a farmyard was shown, and surface traces strongly suggested a similar arrangement at Oberweis (Kr. Bitburg). The exemplary excavations at Köln-Müngersdorf showed a rather different type of layout, in which the main dwelling was not so clearly separated from the subsidiary buildings, and one enclosure wall surrounded both.[16] Further excavations, and more strikingly aerial photography, have finally established the ubiquity of the farmyard. Indeed, while a few farmyards had no main dwelling (Fresnoy and Liancourt, Somme) there are no certain large rural dwellings existing in isolation, even if sometimes the arrangement diverged from the norm – as at Nennig and Wittlich where topography militates against it.[17]

The greatest uniformity is displayed in the Somme valley, where the layout of some 600 villas is known to a greater or lesser extent.[18] The principal dwelling is usually situated at the head of a long yard lined with subsidiary buildings. This yard can be rectangular (Estrées-sur-Noye) or trapezoidal (le Mesge) in shape. Sometimes the whole is enclosed by a perimeter wall, but the main house is often set in a separate courtyard. Not surprisingly, the degree of demarcation increases in proportion to the size of the house. The grander it is, the more likely it is also to be set upwind from the farmyard and surrounded by its own garden. The axiality often visible in the planning of the house is sometimes increased by a prominent central feature – shrine, dovecote or well-house – in the wall dividing house from farmyard.

The lack of a constant ratio between the size of the dwelling and that of the farmyard points to differences in social arrangements. Common to most Somme villas is a secondary dwelling (to judge from its plan) within the farmyard but near to the main house (also a feature at Anthée). Apart from this, there is no reliable information on the use of the buildings, though at Grivesnes investigation of a dark patch of earth mixed with cinders corroborated the idea of metal-working. Depressions outside the enclosure walls were used for the extraction of clay (the main construction material above foundation level) and perhaps thereafter as ponds. That the enclosure walls were in no sense defensive but simply demarcated the yards and prevented the free passage of animals is clear, since they sometimes run between the buildings rather than outside

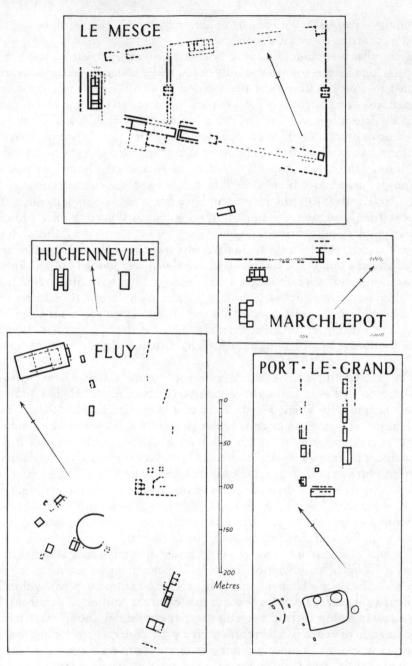

13 Plans of villas in the Somme valley (Agache)

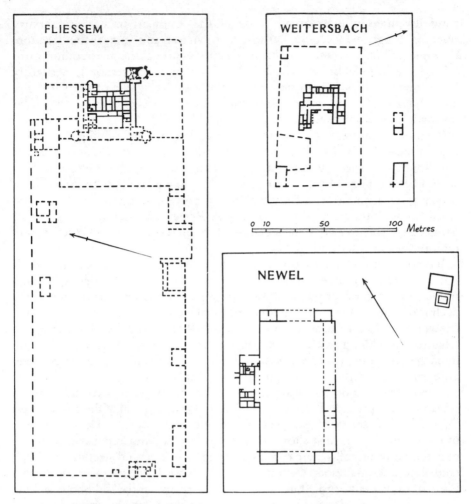

14   Plans of villas near Trier (Cüppers)

them; sometimes, as at Aubigny, walls are replaced by a ditch.

Given the general regularity, peculiarities of form immediately stand out –
the little dwelling at Blangy-Tronville with a series of untidy enclosures, the
house at Huchenneville which is not in the same axis as the yard or the scattered
buildings at Fluy. Since the same general plan is found as far afield as
Switzerland as well as in the Ardennes and Eifel it was certainly widespread and
clearly met requirements well. Its apparent uniformity should not however
obscure variations which may be of importance. Even in the Somme, the
difference between the small, simple main dwellings and the more luxurious
ones is striking, and clearly militates against any idea of uniform social
conditions. Villas in the territory of the Treveri and Tungri contain on the one

hand dwellings which surpass those of the Ambiani in size and luxury (Nennig, Rognée, Haccourt, Bauselenne te Mettet) and on the other far more examples of small dwellings set firmly near the centre of the surrounding yards (Weitersbach, Goeblingen-Miécher, Ittersdorf and many more). A slightly larger one like Newel may be situated along the long side of the yard, and Voerendaal, while it grew considerably in size, never had a very clear distinction between dwelling and farm-buildings.[19]

To these variations in plan must be added differences in building materials – chalk foundations with wood and clay walls in the Somme, limestone or sandstone in the Mosel valley, Eifel and Ardennes – though the effect of these would be minimized by exterior plaster. All alike contribute to a picture of steady growth in dispersed settlement – a pattern suggesting tidiness and efficiency within the conditions of the *pax Romana*. Sometimes, a village or hamlet gave way to a villa; the meaning of this in terms of social structure will require further discussion below.

It is not yet possible to follow in detail the growth of individual farmyards. It thus remains a hypothesis, albeit a likely one, that the larger ones represent a movement of rural population away from less organized settlements, the decline of which is seen in the gradual disuse of large cemeteries such as Lebach, Biewer and Detzem near Trier or Ecury-le-Repos and Vert-la-Gravelle in Champagne. Along with reorganization, in all probablility, went a more intensive (as opposed to extensive) exploitation of the land. Further hypotheses arise out of the typical development of the villa dwellings.

The small buildings which are often found either as the main dwelling or as a subsidiary one provide a convenient starting point. Typical of the commonest 'basic house' is the predominance of a single central space. The fact that it usually contains a hearth shows that it was roofed, and represents a multi-purpose room or hall where cooking, eating, working and sleeping could all take place, and small domestic animals might enter. It was, in short, the Gallo-Roman equivalent of the 'but' or all-purpose room, in the old Scottish 'but-and-ben'. Only at Mayen however do we find the older hut simply enlarged and straightened out. The rooms which were subsequent additions at Mayen are more often found as an integral part of the original plan. These are the corridor or verandah along the front with small square wing-rooms at either end, a plan which gives the classic simple 'Portikusvilla mit Eckrisaliten' or 'villa à galérie-façade' (Bollendorf, Goeblingen-Miécher, Sauvenière, Jette, Serville, and many others) which is particularly characteristic of the Treveran region. In the Somme, a significant variant is noticeable, although the long corridor-verandah, with or without wing-rooms, is extremely common. The large basic room often appears in duplicate or triplicate (e.g. Marchélepot, Blangy-Tronville), a feature which is also found in the earliest stage of Voerendaal. While the duplication of wing-rooms suggests a striving for Romanized architectural symmetry, the duplication of the main room suggests that the dwelling was intended for more than one family, indeed for family groups. The possibility that such rooms did serve identical functions remains however to be tested by excavations.[20]

Another frequent feature of the 'basic house' was a cellar under the front corridor, reached by stairs from the main room. The whole plan, with cellar, may be seen as the provision in Romanized style of housing adapted to Gaulish customs, including the use of pits or sunken huts for storage. Normal additions also include extra rooms and corridors, the expansion of the wings outwards and small bath-suites, more often than not with a furnace stoked from the central room. Such growth, often over a period of a century or more, clearly reflects modest wealth used to provide extra comforts.

This, in turn, suggests the owner-occupied villa of the moderately prosperous family. The growth may be quite substantial – witness the provision of extensive agricultural buildings along with separate bath-house and extra rooms at Voerendaal, or the wings which at Weitersbach almost enclose a courtyard (cf. Modave). Such changes however differ from more radical transformations such as the replacement (second century) of the first masonry habitation at Haccourt by another several times larger and on a different orientation. Here the only plausible interpretation is wealth coming from a source other than the exploitation of the immediately surrounding farmland alone.

Even the first masonry period at Haccourt could hardly be classified as a basic house, for the range of rooms flanked back and front by a verandah stretched for some 60 m, and the large room at the centre already looks as if it served as a grand reception or dining-room rather than an all-purpose living-room. From an early time there existed a grander form of the basic house plan, even if some of the elements are the same; the first stone period at Haccourt is very close to some of the medium-sized buildings in the Somme valley. At many large villas (Jemelle, Bauselenne te Mettet, Téting) the original form cannot be so easily isolated.[21]

The date at which the truly luxurious house made its appearance is a vital and debated question. Growing evidence suggests that it was within the first century, if barely before the middle. At St. Ulrich (Moselle) an extensive bath-house is dated to about Claudius' reign. There are possibly first-century mosaics at Bous (Lux.), and Anthée together with some Swiss villas which were probably already large and rich before AD 100.[22] Finest of all is Echternach, where the first main house was already huge, with bath-house, wings flanking an ornamental pool, and a central reception room with marble-clad walls and a finely carved marble basin. Dated to about the reign of Nero, it arguably might have been constructed after rather than before the Batavian revolt. Yet its position is remote enough from the main roads to suggest a native Treveran, and this is even truer of the villa at Mersch (source of the inscription with equestrian career).[23] Echternach is the earliest example of the plan which stretches to palatial dimensions the same elements of centrality, porticoed front and projecting wings that are found in the small villas. Above

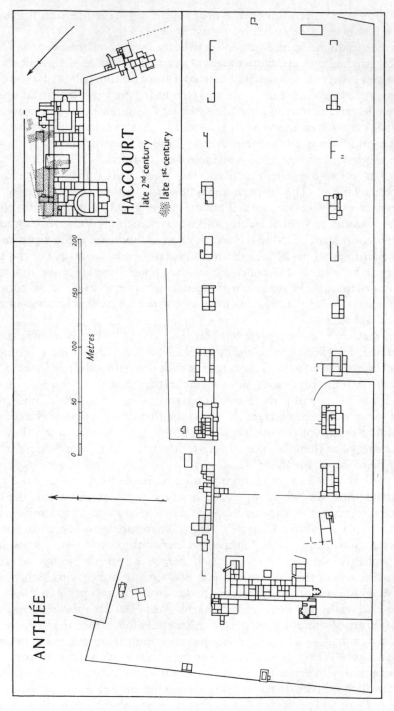

15 Plans of villas at Anthée and Haccourt (de Boe, Mariën)

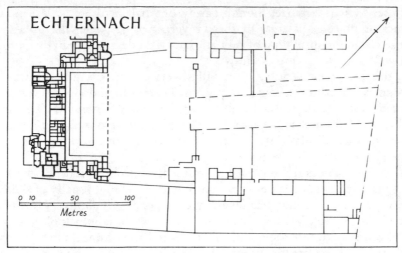

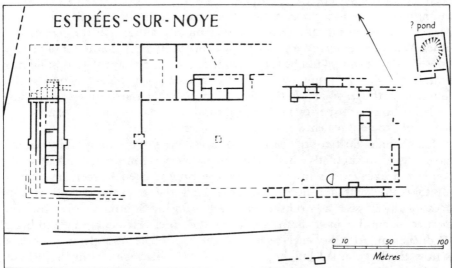

16 Plans of villas at Echternach and Estrées-sur-Noye (Metzler, Zimmer, Agache)

all, it proves the existence of villas that were luxurious from the start, as opposed to those which grew to luxury by stages.

Peristyles and courtyards were frequently incorporated into the large villas. The ranging of rooms round a central courtyard, however, was rarer in the north, despite examples at Rognée and the second periods of St. Ulrich and Vieux-Rouen (Somme). The predominant plan remained the stretched winged-corridor type, and the majority of truly imposing dwellings, with mosaic floors and marble decoration, belong to a phase of development in the second or even the third century. In the Somme valley, about one villa in 20 impresses by its sheer size, though barely one half of those have produced mosaics or marble. In areas of the Treveri, perhaps one villa in ten was extensive, and the sprinkling of rural mosaics is far denser than in the Somme, with well over 50 examples known.[24]

By the late second century, large villas were certainly standard features of the countryside, without being ubiquitous. There is an undoubted correlation between areas of fertile soil and their growth to luxury dimensions. The Entre-Sambre-et-Meuse area suggests that other exploitable resources might provide a basis for such displays of wealth, for traces of iron-working have been frequently observed in the proximity of villas.[25]

While less can be said about the development of the farmyards, it is clear that they generally contained at least one subsidiary dwelling, usually of the basic house type; indeed, Anthée had several such dependent buildings. Elsewhere – Voerendaal, Newel, Weitersbach – the subsidiary buildings look like barns and accommodation for animals, but only at Köln-Müngersdorf has there been any really systematic attempt to establish function. Even small villas might have some living accommodation apart from the main dwelling – at Mayen and Weitersbach a two-roomed building about half the size of the other. While these facts give no simple way of estimating the number of people housed – and it should not be forgotten that some may have shared buildings with livestock – it is quite clear that the housing of people was one of the functions of the farmyard. In the larger Somme villas, the subsidiary dwelling probably housed the person in charge of the day-to-day business of organizing the work, the equivalent of the Italian *vilicus* or bailiff.

The extreme rarity of the basilican or aisled type of building which might have offered an alternative basic house plan deserves comment. Lack of well-conducted excavations may have made it appear even scarcer, and aerial photography will not necessarily reveal all the relevant details. It can occasionally be seen as a subsidiary building in the Somme farmyards, and isolated examples have been found in the Eifel, Hainaut and Limburg (Wollersheim, Attenhoven, Neerharen-Rekem).[26] The most striking example is now the large aisled buildings at Seeb. Here, however, as in the second building at Steenakker te Mortsel, the impression given is of a large interior space where the main function of posts was to support the roof rather than to subdivide the space, as also in simpler buildings at Oelegem. The first building at Steenakker, where the rear portion only of the house was aisled, suggests more of a division by function. It is thus closer to the houses found in the frontier zone in the Netherlands and north Germany (e.g. at Rijswijk and Fochteloo). There is however no parallel in Roman Belgica to the extremely long, narrow aisled houses which normally house a peasant family at one end and their livestock at the other, despite the Iron Age predecessor at Beaufort (Lux.). Any attempt to link the aisled house to a common social structure must be tempered by the fact that the more northern settlements were, or grew into, hamlets, whereas Mortsel appears isolated.[27] The limits of the various house-plans, and their social connotations, still largely defy definition.

3   Other rural settlements

The isolated stone-built villa, solid and easily recognizable, has dominated research to an even higher degree than once it did the Gallo-Roman countryside. Alternative forms of settlement were long considered merely exceptions that proved the rule. One possible alternative has, after much controversy, been largely disbelieved or ignored. Old excavations in Lorraine's *maren* or *mardelles* – the rather regular, frequently water-filled hollows encountered where they have not been destroyed by ploughing – certainly left much to be desired. The vast majority are probably natural geological phenomena, born of the Keuper rock in which they are mostly found. *Mardelles* in Picardie are believed to have served as quarries for marl, or as ponds. Nevertheless, *mardelles* at Leyweiler and Altrip (south of St. Avold) produced worked wood, hearths, Roman pottery and tiles and an unexpectedly regular lining of clay at the bottom. While the depressions may have served as dumps this implies habitations close to hand, and in areas apparently without villas. There are also secondary burials of Roman date in earlier tumuli in one area where *mardelles* are thickly distributed, and old-fashioned foresters' huts of the region, a larger version of which could have covered sunken dwellings, bear considerable resemblance to the steep-roofed hut tombstones which are frequent among the Mediomatrici.[28]

Further evidence for rural settlements of a different type also comes from the Mediomatrici and Leuci, in the form of untidy villages strung out along ridges of the northern Vosges foothills, an area of red sandstone which has since reverted to forest cover. Over 30 of these hill villages have been recognized,

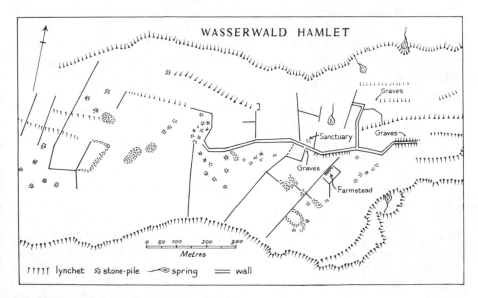

17   Plan of a rural settlement in the Wasserwald (Fuchs)

the best known being above Lutzelbourg and Wahlscheid. Sometimes a main and subsidiary streets are visible; in the Wasserwald they are lined with stone banks and wander with an un-Roman casualness. The clearest house-plan consists of four cell-like rooms side by side, each opening onto the little walled yard. (The plan has parallels in the artisan's quarter at Bibracte.) The villages had walled cemeteries which contained the small hut-shaped tombstones with steep gables which should logically reflect traditional building. Occasionally there are inscriptions or relief busts of the defunct. The Wasserwald settlement (as probably most of the others) also had its own sanctuary area, with a crudely sculpted Mercury and riding Jupiter on a column. All settlements are surrounded by field systems, demarcated by terraces or low walls.[29]

Although such villages show little Roman influence beyond the use of *terra sigillata* and the sculpting of the soft sandstone, neither they nor their cemeteries have direct pre-Roman roots. Rather, they grew in the course of the first century AD and continued through the second into the third, and are thus contemporary with the growth of villas. If this whole area was in fact an imperial *saltus*, the villagers would be lowly tenants of the emperor, perhaps under the general charge of a *conductor*. The absence of Iron Age occupation, implying that the land could not reasonably be claimed as the property of private individuals, would have facilitated such a development. Moreover, a Roman version of the Celtic ownership through undisturbed occupation may well, like the *lex Manciana* known from Africa, have made the exploitation of new areas attractive.

Until recently the Vosges villages were without clear parallels in Belgica, though hamlets were known in the Auvergne. The site near Landscheid (Wittlich) has since shown that the Mediomatrici had no monopoly. It too lies on marginal land covering red sandstone, since reverted to forest; pollen analysis suggests that grain crops were never a major part of the settlement's economy, which probably depended on stock-raising. The simple cottages are relatively spacious, the largest measuring 21 m × 13 m, and one comparatively rich burial testifies to social distinctions. Moreover, since the hamlet lay just outside a small hillfort of late la Tène date, there is a strong likelihood of continuity, until the hamlet died out in the second century. Other such settlements very likely await discovery; there are hints of their presence in the border zone between Belgica and Lugdunensis, and their equivalent in wood has been found at Oelegem near Antwerp.[30]

In addition, nucleated settlements lying close to a villa are known, the best example being the 13-hut iron-working hamlet of Morville through which ran an aqueduct leading towards the nearby villa at Anthée. At Vellereille-le-Brayeux the full plan of the villa is not known, and the tile kiln and wattle-and-daub huts could simply be a part of the regular farmyard.[31] Cemeteries, especially in Belgium, also suggest the existence of hamlets which were not roadside villages and may therefore have been the dependencies of villas. A cemetery at Hachy (Belgian Lux.) representing a community of some 60–70

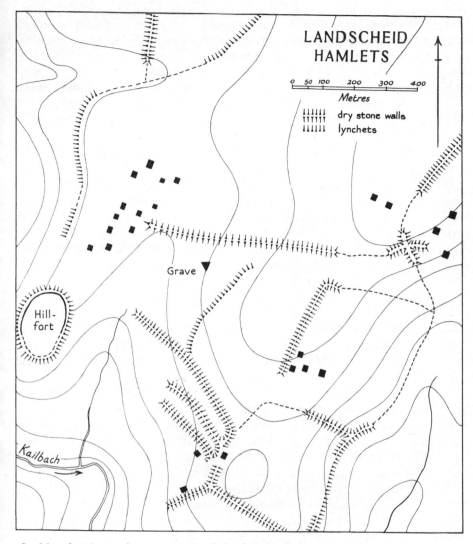

18 Map showing settlements near Landscheid (Schindler)

people, though close to a main road, seems connected with a nearby villa rather
than any *vicus*. Remoter and larger is that of Cutry, south-west of Arlon, with
some 600 burials, and rural cemeteries of similar dimensions are not lacking
among Nervii and Tungri.[32]

  In the Somme, traces of nucleated settlements are infrequent. At Fluy, the
untidily scattered buildings cluster around a sub-circular construction and may
denote a special centre connected either with crops or livestock. At
Moyenville, Fresnes-Mazancourt and Chilly, irregular constructions might be
hamlets. Whether the extraordinary flowering of villas in some parts of the

area left no room, or no need, for the coexistence of villages – the farmyards of the Somme villas are unusually large – remains a moot point. Soil conditions are such that ditches and other slighter remains appear most clearly on valley edges where the chalky underlying rock is less deeply covered. Here many traces of field systems and enclosures have been located, including some complex sites with the appearance of hamlets, such as Riencourt, 'le Croc'.[33] Dating evidence for individual sites is still awaited, but many of the irregular enclosures and field systems are certainly of Roman date.

There is also epigraphical evidence, if of debated import, pointing to rural communities other than villas. Saarland dedications include two by the *coloni Crutisiones* and *Aperienses*, though without informing us on their settlement. In the Ardennes near Bastogne a fragmentary inscription mentions a Curia Arduen [nae], and reinterpretation of another from a sanctuary near Foy-lez-Noville suggests a Curia Ollodagi nearby (though *centurio* is a possible reading). With other dedicatory inscriptions mentioning *curiae* from the area nearer Köln, these show the existence of recognized groups centred on native cults, and here may imply special organization in the context of imperial estates.[34] Such cult associations, whether or not with pre-Roman roots, bring us very close to the basic realities of rural life, where religious customs were the social cement of community life. The fact that rural hamlets in these areas have yet to be found does not imply their absence. On the other hand, many villas are known from the Ardennes, and clearly the area was not one of villages alone.

The majority of known villages occur either in the border zones between *civitates* or in less fertile areas. Yet large cemeteries with hundreds of graves in such diverse areas as Hainaut, northern Lorraine and the Soissonais suggest that grouped settlements remained a normal part of the landscape. Rarely are villas so closely grouped as to exclude other forms of settlement. The clusters that can be seen along the roads east of Amiens in fact have areas behind them sufficient for woodland, pasture and dependent settlements, and traces have been observed of many indeterminate remains.[35] Nonetheless, the trend to dispersed settlement militated against villages – witness the early cemeteries that died out. Even if many villagers were relocated within the villa system, perhaps actually living in the larger farmyards, a break with tradition, and very likely religious custom, is implied. Cemeteries closely connected with villas (the best example remains Köln-Müngersdorf) tend to be small, with 50–60 graves over several generations, which suggests a fragmentation of communities; the size of cemetery connected with the biggest villas is still unknown.

Agricultural hamlets were not of course the only relatively un-Romanized rural settlements. The Somme basin had many 'native farms', simple wood-and-clay homesteads within irregular enclosures and field systems. Typological development suggests that double enclosures where the inner one is regular in shape, and those that are virtually rectilinear, are most likely Roman in date.

This is borne out by indubitably Roman buildings within similar enclosures – a medium villa at Faubourg de Montières outside Amiens, a smaller one at Blangy-Tronville and at Prouzel two small stone buildings. A characteristic funnel-shaped entrance has been dated to the late la Tène period at Condé-Folie but may well have continued in use. Near Erondelle a double rectangular enclosure contains a hut site in each half, the un-Romanized equivalent perhaps of the small villa houses with duplicated main room, or of the main house and subsidiary dwelling. At Port-le-Grand, where a villa is positioned very close to a native farm enclosure, it would be of particular interest to know if both were contemporary. Another interestingly ambivalent site near Mayen has a large two-roomed house for principal dwelling, resembling the cottages of Landscheid. There were subsidiary buildings attached, and a small cemetery with eight ditched enclosures containing almost 20 burials. The field system surrounding the farm and the area naturally demarcated by streams and a road, amounted to some 100 ha, about the same area as that exploited by many villas.[36]

Further work is required to determine whether these less Romanized farms are an economic function of the poorer soils, or illustrate the poverty of social dependency and exploitation. Clearly they were inhabited by people who adopted minor aspects of Romanization but lacked either the ability or the incentive to go further. Clearly, too, this could be as true of people living in isolated farmsteads, the successors of Caesar's *aedificia*, as it was of the nucleated villagers. A fuller picture from Flanders and Kempen will be of the highest interest here. If the farmstead at Steenakker te Mortsel is typical, then here too a dispersed rural pattern prevailed between the various larger agglomerations. At some point this must meet with the tradition of small agricultural villages (Wijster, Rijswijk) known to be the norm only a little further north, and overlap would be natural. This northern area, so near the frontier of the empire, promises an increased understanding of the interaction between Roman administrative requirements and the settlement patterns of ordinary provincials.

The rural economy: human and ecological factors

Despite the record's limitations, archaeology presents the outward changes in the countryside and hints at regional variations which will become clearer with time. To gain an inkling of how rural Belgica functioned as a complex system of human and ecological factors, we must however direct attention to different questions. Population density and the level of technology are the human side of the equation, soils, crops and domestic animals the other.

For any population estimate of pre-Roman Belgica, either the figures given by Caesar have to be used as a base or the attempt abandoned; the older, higher estimates (15 million for the Three Gauls) that were for a time wholly rejected no longer seem absurd, though a more conservative view was taken above.

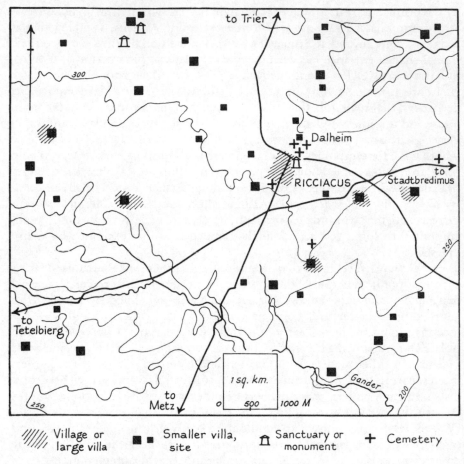

| ///// Village or large villa | ■ ▪ Smaller villa, site | ⛩ Sanctuary or monument | + Cemetery |

19 Map showing settlements near Dalheim (Metzler, Folmer)

Evidence from pollen for major clearances quite early in the Iron Age, with only minor fluctuations thereafter, is certainly consistent with high rural populations practising agriculture, stock-breeding or a mixture of the two.[37]

A drop in population may be normal after a conquest involving much loss of life and disruption, but no hard evidence either supports or disproves this. The remarkable growth of proto-urban settlements shortly after might mean a redistribution, but it could only have taken place if the rural hinterland were in sufficiently good shape to support the growth – a hint perhaps that losses were quickly made good.[38]

In the Roman period, the growth of villas is liable at first sight to suggest a growth in population. In fact the eye is in danger of deception, for the villas simply stand out because of their construction materials. Moreover, it is evident that only a fraction of the less Romanized settlements – whether farmsteads or hamlets – needed for a total picture are known. A better picture can be gained from cemeteries, assuming that what we have is reasonably representative of the whole; these, while insufficient to suggest a specific population density, do suggest an increase between the first and second centuries.[39] The regular distribution of villas would allow at least a minimum estimate to be formed (since they often appear to command areas of between 50 and 100 ha), if it were clear how many people they housed and how many were simultaneously occupied. While the figure need hardly rise above ten for the smallest, it could easily run to a hundred or more for an elaborate establishment where even the building would require many hands for its upkeep; such an establishment would however command a larger area. In fact, the villas do not necessarily imply much increase over the 11-14 persons per km^2 suggested for the late pre-Roman period. For an increase, a minimum of 15 per km^2 average over the whole countryside would be necessary, with cities and villages added on top.

Now it is certain that wider areas were brought under cultivation in Roman times, for expansion on to poorer soils not previously used can be clearly demonstrated.[40] It seems unlikely however that a figure double that of the late Iron Age could have been reached, much less surpassed: a figure of some 20 persons per km^2 is already higher than was reached in the Middle Ages, and was not surpassed until the eighteenth century. This would give for the approximately 110,000 km^2 of Belgica a total of some 2.2 million, which is in keeping with the more conservative recent estimates for Roman Britain.[41] While figures remain at best an educated guess, further work will establish more firmly the limits within which the truth should lie. Fluctuations from one area to the next are obviously to be expected, with sparsely inhabited boundary forest compensated by rich plains or an abundance of villages. It is already fairly clear that the population was higher than in the early Middle Ages, when chronic shortage of manpower is a common theme, and this fact demands that a drop occurred either during the Later Empire or immediately thereafter. Whether epidemics took a toll as early as the later second century, as is vaguely suggested by literary sources, may one day be established from analysis of bones.[42]

As for agrarian technology, no implement is more important than the plough, and much ink has been spilled over possible improvements between Iron Age and Roman times. The patchy evidence does suggest that improvement took place, though not because of Roman introductions. Fossil fields in Flanders show that already before Roman times a light plough that entailed cross-ploughing gave way to one that did not, and when Roman fields are identified they are usually long, even strip-like, rather than square.[43] While no archaeological evidence for a wheeled plough has ever been found, Pliny's statement that this was in use north of the Alps in an area he enigmatically calls 'Gallic Raetia' (perhaps the Rauraci and Helvetii?) deserves to be taken seriously. While it is unlikely that the wheeled plough was known

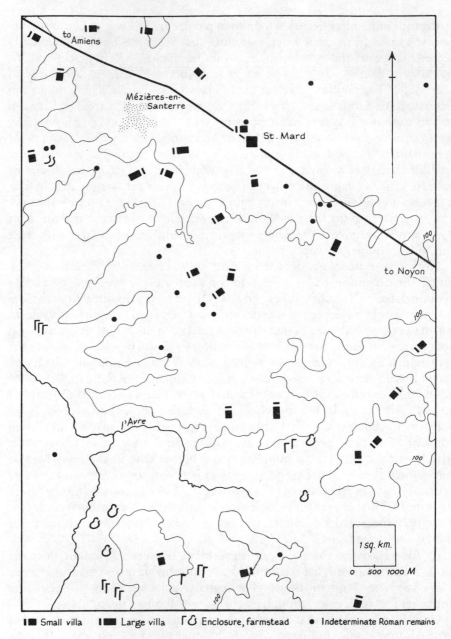

20 Map showing settlements near Amiens (Agache)

south of the Alps (as commentators have sometimes deduced from a passage of Vergil), its use in Gaul and Britain is confirmed by a medieval commentator quoting a fifth-century writer. This need not imply that it became the norm, nor does Pliny's passage allow any specific connection with the Belgae.[44]

Many variations in the plough are possible. Iron objects from a ritual hoard at Gournay-sur-Aronde (Oise), explained as pre-Roman coulters, in fact look more like iron tips for the share of the bow-ard (*araire chambige*). Whichever they are, they indicate an improvement over a plough without iron tip. Coulters do occur in Roman contexts, sometimes along with long-tanged shares, shaped like blunt spear-heads, that would also fit the bow-ard. A bronze model from Köln indicates that the bow-ard might have two flat extensions fanning out from the tip. Whether these could be used to turn the soil is uncertain (they perhaps flattened the earth after sowing). The other share commonly found, the broad flanged share, is also invariably symmetrical: in due course it should become clear whether this is of northern or Mediterranean origin.[45] Its breadth fits Pliny's description of the wheeled plough's share, which, he says, enabled it to turn over the soil. The two improvements, broad share and wheels, could nonetheless occur separately. The broad share possibly went with a different form of beam and stilt, but the difference is immaterial. Both were essentially ards, and even Pliny's statements need not imply the asymmetrical earth-turning medieval plough (*charrue*), since wheeled ards (*araire avec avant-train*) are quite feasible. By cushioning the effect of uneven ground, the wheels put less strain on ploughman and yoke.

One advantage of the wheeled plough, according to Pliny, was that if followed by harrowing, it avoided the need for labour-intensive manual raking after sowing. That such a plough does not (unlike the mechanical reaper) figure on monuments is surprising, since the need for two or three pairs of oxen should have been no drawback on large estates. Yet thus far only the simple bow-ard with two oxen is depicted, and we also see men breaking up the clods of sown fields manually.[46]

Since the long share and perhaps also the broad share may have been in use before Roman times, and the wheeled plough may or may not have been widespread, were improvements in the Roman period of real significance? The answer is probably affirmative, but is rather to be sought in the much greater availability of iron. Spades as well as ploughs were now iron-tipped, iron mattocks replaced digging sticks, and scythes (the Gallic scythe is mentioned by Pliny as larger and faster) became common.[47] The number of implements recovered in excavations is already enough to suggest this: it would be much higher still if more farmyards were investigated. (Iron implements when old would of course be returned to the blacksmith to be reforged; old stock not yet re-used may be represented by a depot of agricultural implements including plough-shares at the *vicus* of Tarquimpol.[48]) It certainly seems likely that every small villa would have its own plough, with iron share, and oxen to pull it, even if further down the scale ploughs might be shared.

The most spectacular Gallo-Roman invention was the reaping machine or *vallus*, mentioned by Palladius (a fifth-century Gaulish writer) as well as by Pliny and confirmed by representations at Reims, Virton and in the Mosel valley. These leave uncertain some details of the wheel-mounted box, the shape and size of the protruding comb of teeth which ripped off the ears, and whether they were of iron. More important are debates on the reasons for and the extent of its use. Like the wheeled plough combined with the harrow, it clearly saved labour, though not without a cost, since the straw was not harvested along with the grain: similarly the improved scythe mentioned by Pliny cut the grass some way up the stem. Both were used, as might be guessed, on large estates. Do they therefore imply labour shortages, either chronic or seasonal at harvest time, in addition to a canny desire to save labour costs? No firm answer can be given. It may be noted that until now the countryside around Reims has not shown the same density of occupation as around Trier: the *vallus* was however known in both places. While the use of the machine does not suggest a teeming pool of labour that could be drawn on at short notice and low cost, the paramount concern might have been to get the harvest in fast in the face of uncertain weather. It also suggests that the grain could fetch a profit that overcame the loss of the straw, which may imply both good yields and a ready market.[49]

Whether the *vallus* ever saw widespread use, rather than remaining a rare curiosity, can be debated. Even so, it is clear that improvements might occur to technology on rich men's property, while at a lower social level only the wider availability of iron was significant. Neither this increased availability nor the mechanical inventions were, however, enough to produce any dramatic breakthrough, and their full potential may have been inhibited by adherence to custom.

Any statements on crops and animal husbandry could until recently only be based on the *obiter dicta* of Pliny or else be educated guesswork at best helped by extrapolation from known medieval conditions. Now, results from analyses of pollen and seeds are increasingly offering confirmation, qualification or entirely new knowledge. For the area of Belgica itself, they are still regrettably few, but can be supplemented by results from the Rhine valley.

In the choice of grains, not only did the proportion of wheat to other grains rise, but modern bread-wheat began to rival spelt as the main type, while emmer and einkorn declined. The increase in bread-wheat may have been caused by army preferences, since it took much less threshing than other types and did not require prior scorching (the Romans did not know that it was less nourishing). Future analyses will show whether this trend occurred throughout Belgica and the other Gauls, or was less marked there than in the military zones. Production of rye increased slightly while that of barley generally declined. Yet finds from Neuss show that barley as well as wheat was delivered to the army. At least one grain, buckwheat, went out of use so thoroughly that it was held to be a medieval introduction until identified at Iron Age Bundenbach.[50]

From an anecdote of Pliny it is known that spring sowing of grain could be found among the Treveri, a phenomenon he attributed to the failure of a previous autumn sowing. Discounting the probable misunderstanding, many scholars have inferred the use of a three-field system of crop rotation, into which spring grains normally fit. This remains a hypothesis, and the system, even if known, may have remained exceptional rather than normal. Its adoption would certainly have improved agrarian productivity while saving manpower. Totally uncertain are the yields that might be expected: these are usually thought to have lain between 1:3 and 1:5, that is, higher than the often abysmal yields recorded for the early middle ages but considerably lower than what was normal in Italy; lower, too, than those recently recorded in simulated ancient conditions at Butser.[51]

A variety of pulses, root-crops and other vegetables is attested. Some types of peas and beans were imported rather than indigenous, though the distinction can be debated. Root-crops included carrot, parsnip, beets and turnips (the last mentioned by Columella, and probably largely used for fodder). Cabbage, a spinach-like plant, and lettuce are found along with celery, which may have been used for religious as well as dietary purposes. Garlic, coriander and dill were certainly imported, savory, mustard and thyme probably indigenous. A greater variety was achieved partly through the cultivation (for the first time, or more intensively) of native species.

The same phenomenon can be seen with fruit, where cultivation of native strawberries, raspberries, plums, cherries and apples (the last again singled out by Pliny) went along with the importing of peaches, southern types of plum and not least the vine, which cannot be shown to have reached this area before Roman times. Figs and olives may have been imported for special purposes, but a later literary source (the emperor Julian) shows the fig growing (with difficulty) near Paris. To native nuts such as the walnut was added the edible chestnut, which Pliny says had reached the channel coast by his time. A very different plant, flax, was also more extensively cultivated in Roman times, and over a very much wider area than might be guessed from Pliny's brief reference to Morini and Caletes.[52]

Some changes may have been initiated by army wants and by knowledge gained from army service. An example of local development is afforded by a well at Irrel, north of Trier, where levels with second-century pottery showed a greater number of fruits than first-century samples, and suggested intensive fruit-gardening.[53] Along with this more varied and healthy diet belong the changes in pottery styles which indicate adoption of Romanized methods of cooking and eating – jugs for oil, mortaria for rubbing and mixing, and flat plates. For drinking, native habits largely prevailed – the closed beaker which required two hands to use and fitted ill with the recumbent position preferred by the Romans.

Besides the preferences of any segment of society, another general factor may have aided the establishment of southern fruits such as the vine and even the olive in early Roman times. Examination of the weeds from Irrel suggests that the climate was on average drier in the second century than the first. This is the continuation of a trend that set in during the late la Tène period, and roughly corresponds with the drop in sea level relative to the Flanders coast. Descriptions by Caesar and Tacitus of poor harvests due to drought correlate well with low points on the tree-ring graph, though evidence for intermittent severe flooding of the Rhine in the first century AD shows variable conditions. Peat-bog pollens of southern Denmark concur with the evidence from Irrel in showing that this warmer, drier climatic phase lasted through most of the second century, then suggest the onset of a markedly cooler and damper phase around AD 200.[54] While generalized data of this kind give no information on the year-to-year variations which affect the farmer, they suggest that optimum conditions were followed by a more difficult period. Repercussions would be especially felt in marginal or hilly land.

Animal husbandry of course continued to be an important part of the rural economy, and it too sparked occasional references in the written sources, not least those that show the Gauls' reputation as great eaters of meat by Roman standards. Pliny says that Morinian geese were appreciated in the capital, though we may wonder how many of the latter actually got there on their own feet (and under military escort) as he would have us believe. The popularity of Gallic and specifically Belgic woollen garments elicited frequent testimony and raises the possibility of an increase in sheep-farming to meet demand for a staple export.[55]

Analyses of faunal material are unfortunately still few, and again tend to come from the Germanies. At present they give information only just beyond the obvious – that cattle, sheep, goats and horses were kept, all smaller than modern beasts but larger than those of the early Middle Ages. It is generally assumed that stock-breeding had considerable effect.[56] It is also inferred that the animal manure was better used, alongside the traditional practice of marling. The most probable new import is the domestic cat: dogs large and small had already a long history. The domestic fowl has also been found in a pre-Roman context, though its availability probably increased. Numerous questions remain to be investigated; one is whether the predominance of cattle in the Rhineland and Netherlands was due to the proximity of the army with its need for hides, another whether areas particularly suitable for sheep rearing (such as Artois, Picardie and the Hunsrück) were in fact so used, whether the Lorraine plateau, known today for cattle and cheese, was similarly viewed in ancient times, or whether mixed farming was in fact the rule throughout.

Unknowns may outnumber knowns, but some advance can still be made towards reconstructing typical farm-units. The small to medium villa surrounded by an area of between 50 and 100 ha is so common that it must represent a naturally convenient unit. Moreover, the less Romanized farmstead near Mayen seems to have about the same area available to it, so that Romanity of architectural structures need not correlate with area. On the basis of figures given by Columella for the ploughing of 200 *iugera* or 50 ha (two ox-teams with two ox-hands and six labourers), cautious calculations can be advanced. It must first be remembered that not all the area was necessarily cleared and cultivated – indeed for 50 ha to be under plough the farm would have to be considerably larger. While it may be theoretically dangerous to generalize from the single description we have of a Gallic estate – the fourth-century Aquitanian farm of Ausonius – it is no less so to ignore it. Two-thirds (700 *iugera*) of Ausonius' estate was woodland, with ploughland (200 *iugera*) vineyard and meadows (100 and 50 *iugera*) making up the remainder. For a farm of 50 ha, the amount under plough could be anything from 10 to 30 ha, but is unlikely to have been larger, and even a 100 ha farm could have as little as 20 ha under plough in any one year. Moreover, the Italian sources may offer the wrong social model, an owner who did not himself work but employed slaves or labourers.[57]

The small villas of Roman Gaul might better be compared with later French farms, such as an eighteenth-century one in Artois known in detail from documents. This was 37 ha in area, of which 22 ha was ploughed with the power of three horses (a team and a spare) and was under intensive cultivation. Pasture for horses and two mares, nine cows, three heifers, two calves, two bullocks and a bull took up much of the remainder along with a vegetable garden behind the house. Ten pigs and various fowl completed the livestock, while the farmyard consisted of stable, byre and barns grouped round the dung-heap. The house consisted of kitchen, back kitchen, rooms for boys and girls and a main bedroom which also served as work-space and for ceremonies. The owner and his wife, one boy, three girls and a servant ran the farm.[58]

Not all details are of course transferable, the biggest single difference being horse-power and an improved plough. Nonetheless, the small villas look like single (in the Somme sometimes double or triple) family dwellings, with space at most for a few helpers. The arrangement of the rooms was certainly different, with sleeping and dining for the owner/occupier and family being the functions most readily attributable to the wing rooms. Secondary dwellings make it clear that additional hands might be housed nearby: under what conditions, and whether free to marry or not is unknown. A subsidiary family, perhaps a junior branch of the main one, is possible. The total number on this model would be unlikely to pass 15, with likely *minima* and *maxima* of 10 and 20. An alternative approach is the detailed calculations based on possible crop yields and calorific requirement which have been undertaken in connection with a settlement at Rijswijk in Holland, where farming was considered mixed, but with emphasis on stock-raising; results are not inconsistent.[59]

On present evidence, then, a main family, a subsidiary family (at most two), one or two hands or slaves and perhaps additional seasonal labour seems a reasonable reconstruction of the human occupants of a small villa. Two (better three) draught oxen, a dozen or more cattle, sheep and pigs (using woodland for forage), a few goats and some domestic fowl would form the animal components (not to forget a dog or two, perhaps a cat). Two basic points must be borne in mind. It seems likely that farm unit sizes would base themselves on the amount of land that an ox-team could conveniently plough, which in Gaul may normally have lain between the 10 ha mentioned enigmatically by Pliny in the context of the wheeled plough and the more optimistic figure of 25 ha given by Columella. Secondly, the number of animals on a farm could not be too low if adequate manure was to be available.

Some further implications may be mentioned. When a villa bigger and obviously richer than the small basic one is surrounded by an area no greater than 50–100 ha, it is virtually certain that the owner either held additional land elsewhere, was in fact the owner of surrounding tenant-occupied farms, or else had some other source of income, for instance industrial activity. Contrariwise, when a farmstead failed to become a small villa, either the land was too small to produce a reasonable surplus after whatever taxes and renders were owing, or incentive to Romanize was lacking for some social reason. Finally, villages may be required among the villas to provide a pool of seasonal labour.

5   Rural society and the agents of change

One of the consequences of inclusion within the Roman Empire was a notable increase in the production and marketing of surpluses from agriculture and stock-breeding. The joint demands of the army and Italy transformed some of these goods into items for long-distance trade, as will be seen. An attempt can be made to follow the consequences for agrarian society, once land was subject to tribute but was also a source of potential monetary gain – moreover an asset that could be bought and sold in a manner previously inconceivable and bequeathed in ways not necessarily in accordance with traditional custom. What level of change is reflected by the archaeological record?

Wealthy Gauls who had established ownership of large tracts of land, and who had clients at their disposal, were faced with the question of how best to utilize land and manpower. Encouraged to take an active part in the growth of new cities at the same time as they began to feel the weight of taxation, many had a double-edged sword put into their hands in the form of cash loans from Italian money-lenders. The incentive towards efficient running of their estates was strong, even if erstwhile warriors turned to farm management with reluctance. If their clients included freemen, these might be treated as tenants, with parts of the estate turned over to them as separate farms. Unfree clients were more likely to remain clustered on the part farmed by the owner, with the help of a slave- or client-bailiff. Both types of client could be encouraged to extract more from the land – by clearing new areas, adopting the iron-tipped plough and improved manuring – in the interests of all. Some of the farms that gave rise to small villas may have been so created, the villa itself perhaps being built by or with the help of the estate owner (as an extension of the *instrumentum* normally provided) to render tenancy more attractive and increase his revenues.[60] Similar farms and small villas may equally have belonged to lesser free landowners who were able to derive sufficient profit by their own exertions (aided by a few clients, slaves or a junior branch of the family) to build in Romanized style.

As for the unfree tenants, the hypothesis that their settlements were rearranged has support from the cemeteries, and the natural place to seek them is in the larger farmyards and remaining dependent hamlets. While there was opportunity enough for the disruption of peasant communities or denial of a patron's responsibilities, the existence of new opportunities in villages and cities probably made humane treatment prudent. Such folk may have continued to work some land on their own behalf and were in practice *coloni* like some of the small villa-dwellers, only of lower status. Whether the inhabitants of 'native farms' formed an intermediate group of *coloni* must remain uncertain, but close dependence on a larger landowner would be one good explanation for their condition.

The working of estates by slave labour has often been attributed to the Gallo-Romans, and in Narbonensis a number of slaves are mentioned in rural inscriptions. Since slaves from slave-gangs are unlikely to be so commemorated, the likelihood is that these were slave-bailiffs, a figure found both in Italian and Celtic custom. In Belgica, not only are mentions of slaves and *liberti* fewer (and later in date) but they occur almost exclusively in cities. An apparent exception, the *familia* Vindonissae from near Joinville (Hte.-Marne) could arguably have been serfs or tenants rather than slaves proper.[61]

This is not to deny that chattel slavery existed, for it was normal in Celtic as well as Italian society, and to the obvious source, prisoners of war, could be added debtors. The real question is rather one of proportion and use. Plentiful labour, some of it tied and only just above slave status, renders it unlikely that slaves formed a major part of the work force. Though slaves could have been employed for certain agricultural tasks, including the herding of animals, the house and garden is where one would expect to find them. Fetters found in one smallish Somme villa show that constraints might be imposed. The building of villas thus need not mean the total abandonment of traditional customs, nor does the (sometimes exaggerated) regularity of the small villas mean that society had somehow become egalitarian. Rather, it is a phenomenon connected on the one hand with more intensive cultivation and on the other with the desire to be more Roman.

Scattered fragments of evidence, none in itself conclusive, can be taken to mean that land tenure continued to be regulated as much by customary as by Roman law. Not least of these is the absence in West Roman vulgar law (which stemmed from practice not theory) of the Roman concept of contractual lease and the presence of a double claim to ownership which could derive from Celtic custom. Yet it seems inevitable that the Celtic patron-client relationship should be watered down, whether simply through changing conditions (military service to a chief was no longer appropriate) or by acts of will. As land changed hands, by inheritance, sale or confiscation, the lower grade of client-*coloni* almost certainly went with it, so that hereditary ties would be broken.[62] The cost-conscious landowner might disown clients – perhaps trying to save labour with devices like the reaping machine. Another might fail to thrive, become indebted and be forced either to sell or to rebel. The rich Treveran landowners of the second century may be descended from those who profited from confiscation and redistribution after 70 AD. Nonetheless, there are hints of estates around Mersch and Echternach which may have remained geographically intact right through the Roman period.[63]

For smaller landowners, one aspect of Celtic custom would have to be discarded or counteracted if prosperity were the aim – partible inheritance among male heirs, which militates against the gathering of wealth and can lead to dire poverty. One of the differences between small to medium villas and un-Romanized farmsteads might be success or failure in evading this constraint. We do not know whether dowries might include land lower down the social scale as well as at the top, so that clever marriages might bring at least moderate wealth, if at the cost of dispersed holdings. Women perhaps brought movable goods rather than land under normal circumstances, but might inherit in default of male heirs. Average family size is also unknown, though inscriptions and reliefs suggest that large families were not the rule, or at least that surviving children were few.

With time, dispersed holdings would become more normal, cottars without traditional land rights might be commoner, and there could be more reliance on the labour pool in the villages. Some landowners undoubtedly increased their wealth by involvement in production and trade, and it is in this context that the enormous growth in size and richness of many villas must be set. Men of increasing wealth invested profits in their country dwellings, emulating those who had been able to build luxurious villas from the start. The eventual commercialization of rural relationships, depicted by the use of coinage on reliefs at Neumagen, is the culmination.[64]

As indicators of wealthy proprietors, probably of decurial (or equivalent) status, mosaics are of considerable interest. Is it possible to single out a group of greater wealth, the few outstanding families that might dominate magistracies and aspire to equestrian rank? The answer here may not lie so much with mosaics as with sheer size and luxury at an early date. Echternach, Mersch and St. Ulrich are the obvious examples, and of Mersch we know that it was occupied in the early second century by a Treveran who performed equestrian military service. People of the highest rank should naturally have been first to give serious attention to their country-houses, before the enlargement and beautification of villas became widespread.

Further down the scale, the small-to-medium villas remain a striking phenomenon. Whether tenants or owners, the occupants certainly were no depressed peasantry. Connected funerary monuments range from the relatively simple to the elaborate foundation at Newel, where the accompanying *tumuli* are probably several generations of the same family. More modest family cemeteries might take the form of small ditched 'Grabgärten'.[65] The monuments of villa-dwellers are generally of a higher quality than the gravestones from the Vosges villages. Along with the more prosperous *vicus*-dwellers, the first group form a rural middle class, somewhere between peasant and small gentry, and were probably the mainspring of the small-scale rural commerce that centred on villages and rural fairs. The attention devoted to them in the history of research is not wholly disproportionate, for they are one of the most characteristic features of the Early Empire, and their high degree of visibility a response to Romanized conditions.

How are such responses to be summed up? In the early days, and at highest social levels, imitation of Italian practice and the adoption of a new value system were clearly important. Thereafter, there is an increasing (though not absolute) correlation between the appearance of villas and exploitable resources. The most obvious is light-to-medium fertile soil suitable for the growing of grain – hence the clustering of villas in the limestone areas of the Eifel or of Luxembourg just north and west of Trier, in the Santerre east of Amiens and the loess areas of Hainaut. By contrast the heavy clays of the Argonne and Champagne humide remained free of villas, as did the dry plateaux south of Soissons and sandy Flanders. Their density in the Entre-Sambre-et-Meuse area indicates that mineral resources formed an alternative or auxiliary source of wealth. The areas without villas probably saw a less lively and profitable exchange of goods and services.

The growth of villas was thus an economic as well as a social phenomenon, yet stopping short of radical change and total disruption. It was the development under favourable conditions of the existing base, with a continuity modified yet real, but with the profits from exploitation counting for as much as original social status. Development was not invariably successful: the solidity of the stone buildings may give an illusion of greater stability than was attained. In areas with a high density of villas, not all need have been simultaneously occupied. Preliminary investigations in the Somme valley have suggested that some were quite short lived, occupied only for a generation or two. Time will tell whether it was the entire villa complex or only the main houses that knew such vicissitudes, and will also bring more information on the permanency or otherwise of the alternative types of rural settlement.

Already, comparison and contrast between Picardie and the area of Trier is instructive. In both areas the late first and early second centuries were crucial for the establishment of villas, but whereas in the former a number were apparently abandoned by the end of the second century, the Trier villas continued to grow in size and wealth if not in absolute numbers. The continued growth of villas corresponds with what might be termed the secondary sector of urban growth – not so much the public monuments as the building and decoration of wealthy town-houses. Rather than any pattern of opposition between town and country or transference of interest and resources from one to the other, the evidence suggests a parallel development, with the most favourable conditions in the eastern part of the province.

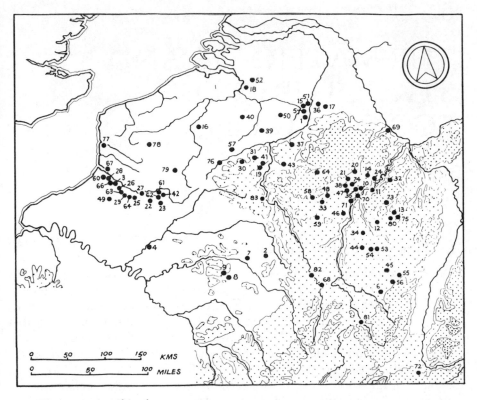

21 Places mentioned in chapters 5–6

1	Haccourt	29	Fluy	57	Vellereille-le-Brayeux
2	Auve	30	Rognée	58	Hachy
3	Condé-Folie	31	Mettet	59	Cutry
4	Creil-le Houy	32	Weitersbach	60	Moyenville
5	Val-Meer	33	Goeblingen-Miécher	61	Fresnes-Mazancourt
6	St. Maurice-aux-Forges	34	Ittersdorf	62	Chilly
7	Bouy	35	Newel	63	Riencourt
8	Ecury-le-Repos	36	Modave	64	Foy-les-Noville
9	Vert-la-Gravelle	37	Modave	65	Prouzel
10	Biewer	38	Bollendorf	66	Erondelle
11	Detzem	39	Sauvenière	67	Port-le-Grand
12	Lebach	40	Jette	68	Pagny-sur-Meuse
13	Freisen	41	Serville	69	Brohl
14	Landscheid	42	Marchelepot	70	Igel
15	Rosmeer	43	Jemelle	71	Grevenmacher
16	Velaines-Popuelles	44	Téting	72	Laufen-Müschhag
17	Kerkrade	45	St. Ulrich	73	Hambach
18	Mortsel	46	Bous	74	Welschbillig
19	Anthée	47	Echternach	75	Schwarzerden
20	Fliessem	48	Mersch	76	Pont-sur-Sambre
21	Oberweis	49	Vieux-Reims	77	La Calotterie
22	Fresnoy	50	Attenhoven	78	Labuissière
23	Liancourt	51	Neerharen-Rekem	79	Bourlon
24	Wittlich	52	Oelegem	80	St. Wendel
25	Estrées-sur-Noye	53	Leyweiler (Leyviller)	81	Epinal
26	Le Mesge	54	Altrip (Altrippe)	82	Commercy
27	Blangy-Tronville	55	Lutzelbourg	83	Charleville-Mézières
28	Huchenneville	56	Walscheid		

133

6

THE MATERIALS AND STRUCTURES OF ECONOMIC LIFE

1 Exploitation of mineral resources

Direct measurements of changes in production and marketing is not possible for the ancient world. Indications – if rough and subjective – can be gained from the contents of museums, which tend to support the assumption of all-round increases in the Early Roman Empire. Literary sources inform us that manufactured items from the Gallic provinces, especially woollen garments, supplemented and gradually supplanted the long-established export south-ward of slaves and raw materials.[1] The bulk of the evidence is, however, archaeological, very direct in its testimony yet requiring arrangement and interpretation. Inscriptions and reliefs, in addition to other classes of objects (above all pottery), give assorted pieces of a complex jigsaw puzzle, never quite enough to show without argument which of two or three possible pictures is the correct reconstruction.

More important than simple questions of quantity are the mechanisms of exchange and the socio–economic relations behind the visible phenomena. The role of state demands in stimulating agrarian production has already been touched on, though further discussion is warranted. The vital question is the extent to which increased production brought social change, and freed the economic processes from the constraints of a pre-industrial social framework. The relationship between land-ownership, production and trade is also at issue.[2]

Production and marketing obviously took place at many levels. At that of subsistence economy, with household production and exchanges in kind or services, people by-passed the market, or operated below it. At the top are the manufacture in bulk of goods destined for profitable sale, the members of recognized trading corporations known from inscriptions, the owners of huge funerary monuments showing capacious ships, piles of amphorae or barrels. Ideally, each level of operation should be treated separately. Since interpretation of the archaeological record is needed to determine the levels, an easier alternative is adopted here as a first step — that of discussing the various categories of materials, with attention to the probable type of organisation. Some categories — wood, salt, iron — represent a continuity of age-old exploitation. Others, such as the quarrying of stone, were new departures.

Little exploited before the conquest, stone forms an obvious hallmark of the Roman period. The main resources are concentrated in the eastern part of the province, where limestones and sandstones of varying quality are frequent. Coarse limestones are also found in Champagne, but less in chalky Picardie or the sands and clays of Flanders. The Iron Age peoples used stone only sporadically for such purposes as fortifications, and undressed lumps sufficed. Organized quarrying, the dressing of stone and the use of mortar came only with the Romans.

Quarries must have opened on a small scale during the reign of Augustus, with exploitation either by military detachments or by civilian entrepreneurs from Italy or Narbonensis. Some of the earliest were in the Moselle valley above Metz, at Jaumont and Norroy (near Pont-à-Mousson). Stone for the monument connected with the imperial house at Trier, as for Rhineland monuments of all kinds in the first century AD, came from here. An explosion in the use of stone occurred around the mid-first century, whether or not the result of any official encouragement by Claudius. Everywhere except in Flanders and Kempen stone became a normal building material, though timber and clay were still widespread above foundations. Although the Rhine armies also used Brohltal tuff, Norroy limestone remained in use, and during the Flavian period was directly quarried by legionary vexillations. Inscriptions are thereafter silent, leaving it in doubt whether exploitation then passed into civilian hands. While the stone went as far as Nijmegen, its distribution away from the river route diminished after the first century as other quarries were opened up for local use. A little of the limestone found along the Rhine is thought to come rather from the Meuse valley in the region of Verdun, demanding either lengthy transport down the Meuse and up the Rhine or a brief overland portage from about Pagny-sur-Meuse to the Moselle at Toul. A limestone that enjoyed wide distribution as a good-quality building stone is the dark, marble-like stone of Tournai, all the more valuable in a stone-poor area.[3]

The second and third centuries saw the development on a larger scale of many quarries that may have started earlier, satisfying local civilian needs. Quality was of less importance than ready availability and with it lower cost. Coarser shelly limestones were used at Trier even for good-quality statuary (plaster and paint could cover defects), while building materials saw a gradual changeover from the hard fine limestones (still used extensively in public buildings) to the softer sandstones which could be quarried just across the river from the city. In Lorraine, stone of the type found at Savonnières-en-Perthois (where traces of Roman working have been observed) was widely used, and further east, so was the soft red sandstone of the Vosges. To the north-west, rough limestone was quarried in the Oise valley, while, near Arras, underground galleries aimed at the better quality chalk. Many minor quarries in southern Belgium are thought to have been worked in Roman times. Studies that would more precisely match stone and quarries are still needed.[4]

Luxury stones, mostly marble, were imported for ornamental use in cities or the richest villas. Belgica and the Germanies also had their own specialized types. Basalt for the piers of the second bridge at Trier was brought from the Rhineland: its origin was probably not the quarries near Mayen (where preserved remains are more consistent with the production of smaller items) but a newly discovered Roman quarry between Namedy and Brohl. Curiously, some stone for the piers was also brought from the Meuse valley. The basalt suggests collaboration by the army of Upper Germany, always possible for major civilian undertakings but in Belgica not actually proven by inscriptions (unless perhaps those of the Trier Porta Nigra). Lying within Belgica but much less well known are the quarries at Theux (Liège) where bitumen imparts to limestone the appearance of black marble; it was used for mosaic cubes at Trier and doubtless elsewhere (various local stones and even pottery were also so used).[5]

Direct information on the organization of the industry is lacking. Some quarries, particularly those used by the army, were probably imperial property, but this is quite consistent with civilian contractors. Private ownership is more likely for those that started life later. At Mayen-Kottenheim, the division of the working areas into many small pockets suggests numerous small concerns. Indirect comparison can be made with the multiple quarry marks on the sandstone blocks in the Barbarathermen, bridge and Porta Nigra at Trier. While the mark MAR is common to all structures, it is only one of ten or so found in each, showing that for the completion of major public works a number of firms were called into service.[6]

Blocks for the Porta Nigra were probably delivered with architectural features already roughed out, implying collaboration between quarriers and architect. Neighbouring Lugdunensis offers a mason's workshop in the quarry at Tintry near Autun, where capitals, columns and millstones were roughed out. The widely exported products of the Mayen lava quarries, primarily millstones, were hauled in rough shape to Andernach for finishing. Near St. Dié in the southern Vosges, individual millstones were cut off column-like blocks and finished on the spot for distribution by river and road within a radius of some 50 km. Smaller workshops still are to be found in the northern Vosges, producing sandstone tombstones and votive reliefs for very local use.[7]

Various levels of organization can then be discerned, from military to local. Larger enterprises, state or private, may have employed slaves (or criminals), but free labourers working for hire are also quite conceivable. Smaller concerns could have been family businesses, examples of the small-scale private enterprise that is often seen as characteristic of Roman Gaul.[8] Unknown factors are whether the army concerned itself with the transport of stone coming to it, whether this was exacted by corvée, or whether stone was bought from enterprising civilians. The status of the sandstone quarriers at Trier is debatable. Some of the contracted names are easy to parallel in local nomenclature and could be those of prominent citizens. Who profited, and by how much, is not revealed, for no one boasts on a funerary monument of being the owner or contractor of a quarry. If private ownership is assumed, the operation was presumably profitable. Further down the social scale, the virtual absence of tombstones depicting stone-workers contrasts with the number depicting smiths and other artisans.

The most obvious secondary craft dependent on stone is that of stone-carving. Unfortunately, the organization of workshops remains elusive. Sculptures frequently show a particular treatment of eyes or other features which in theory should facilitate recognition of other works by the same person or workshop. In practice such connections are surprisingly rare, and are easier to make among non-figured monuments, e.g. a group of small gravestones at Metz. The battle-frieze tombstones of Arlon, Mosel valley and Rhineland, together with sculptures by the same hand at Metz and Alzey, show that in the first century AD sculptors might be itinerant. At a later period the same is suggested by a Mercury from Mt. Essey with a curious loin-cord also seen on those from the Donon.[9] The growth of workshops in major *vici* is shown by the sculptures at Arlon, some of which have a strong family resemblance and are closer in style to those from Reims than to the monuments of Igel, Neumagen and Koblenz. Soulosse, hardly as important as Arlon, also produced a group of tombstones related both in general shape and details of the figures, suggesting an active if perhaps short-lived workshop. Other stones from Soulosse, in a 'primitive', flat style have analogies at Thil-Châtel but are quite distinct from other flat figures at Langres, although it is nearer. The combination of size of monument and quality of workmanship found in Trier and its vicinity is hardly if at all paralleled elsewhere. Even if some of the great sculptured tombstones stood in the country beside roads or overlooking the Mosel (as at Grevenmacher), they obviously point to highly skilled workshops based on Trier. The possible use of blocks delivered from the quarry in standard sizes, attested in the Rhineland, remains to be investigated.[10]

Stick-like figures, the crude busts or simple house-shaped stones often carved in soft Vosges sandstone called for no great specialization, and could have been produced by masons or even enterprising peasants. A higher degree of training was obviously called for by the finer monuments, as also by the adornment of buildings, including rural sanctuaries. Further comparison both within the two groups and between them may yet show the extent of the skilled stone-carver's mobility and specialization.[11]

Neither simple building activity nor the production of sculptured monuments rose in a smooth curve. Between the reigns of Claudius and Hadrian, building was everywhere intense, with the countryside little behind the cities.

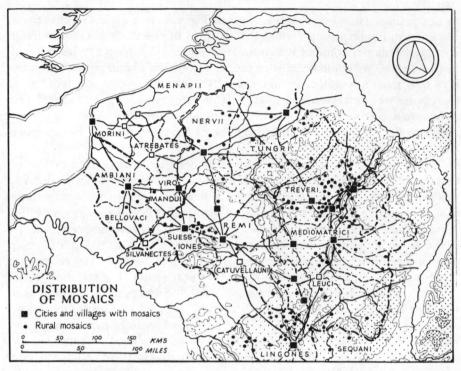

22 Map showing distribution of mosaics in Belgica

Thereafter there is less sign of continued activity in the western half of the province, beyond the occasional reconstruction of a damaged building. There may also have been fewer new buildings in Trier and the surrounding area, but additions to old ones certainly went on apace. Meanwhile, the production of sculptured monuments rose steeply in the second half of the second century, so that some redirection of effort from masonry to stone-carving is possible. The vast majority of monuments are however in the east, despite adornment of rebuilt rural sanctuaries at Ribemont-sur-Ancre, Champlieu and Fontaine-Valmont.[12]

Mosaics offer a valuable complement. The first century produces a scatter, mostly in cities (Bavay, Amiens, Reims, St. Quentin, Trier). The second century saw increased activity along with the adoption of more complicated figured patterns. Many floors were laid in villas, but this was not at the expense of the cities and villages. The densest spread is among the Treveri, though there is also a noticeable group between Reims and Soissons. A difference can again be observed between eastern and western parts of the province. In the latter, as many mosaics date before the mid-second century as after, while in the east, particularly in and around Trier, later floors are more numerous. Between the mid-second and mid-third centuries the Trier-based workshop was particularly prominent, laying floors as far away as Grand.

Present evidence thus shows no simple story of urban decline with transference of energies to the countryside but rather illustrates an increasing divergence between the eastern and western sections of the province.[13]

The exploitation of Belgica's commonest mineral, iron-ore, by contrast continued an old industry. Good quality ores were frequently near surface level in Entre-Sambre-et-Meuse, parts of the Ardennes, southern Belgium, Luxembourg and Lorraine; poorer ores were also available in Flanders. The extent of any mining by galleries is unclear.

Technically, iron-working was hardly more advanced than it had been previously, nor did it noticeably differ from iron-working outside the Empire. A variety of furnaces was employed, from more or less open types to the commoner shaft furnace. Shafts of varying height and width were sometimes built into stone packing and had various arrangements at the bottom for the production of sufficient draught (by bellows). The slag normally flowed into a pit, rather than being tapped.[14]

Two types and scales of production can be clearly determined. In the first, the ore attracted workers to it, while the second is small scale working usually within a village community. A good example of the first lies in the Swiss Jura, while large-scale working in southern Belgium is attested not by excavated furnaces but by huge slag heaps (the so-called 'crayats des Sarrasins' south of the Sambre valley), most of which disappeared in the nineteenth century. Condroz, Famenne and the Entre-Sambre-et-Meuse all saw considerable activity, and these are areas with many villas.[15]

Activity on a smaller scale is well attested in *vici*. Its regular occurrence in the north – Destelbergen, Waasmünster, Blicquy, Ardres and others – in spite of the poor quality ores, shows an effort towards local self-sufficiency. On the Tetelbierg or near Thionville it is more natural. While much of the activity in *vici* may have been smithing, the presence of slag points also to smelting. Iron-working connected with smaller villas is rare; no other example is as clear as the small furnace at Laufen-Müschhag in the Swiss Jura. The connection between large villas and iron-working is best seen in one Somme valley farmyard, and in the small hamlet with smelting furnaces at Morville, considered a dependency of Anthée.[16]

At the local level, smithing was sometimes profitable enough to be represented on monuments, found in such varied places as Trier, Scarpone and the hilltop settlement of la Bûre near St. Dié. Dedications to or representations of Vulcan in *vici* (Sarrebourg, Bitburg and Daspich) or near villas (at Hambach, Welschbillig and Schwarzerden) may also reflect smithing. Free workers rather than slaves are suggested by the dedication to their patron by the *fabri ferrarii* near Dijon.[17]

Mines were frequently imperial property, and the lack of any direct link between mining and the imperial *patrimonium* in Belgica may be due to gaps in the evidence. The *concilium Galliarum* also owned unlocated iron mines and had special officials to administer them. A connection between land-owners and mining can well be argued for the Entre-Sambre-et-Meuse and adjacent areas. The working here was on a large scale, while the settlement pattern is of villas, and moreover of villas that grew to luxury proportions in an area not blessed with fertile soils, proximity to a city or even good communications. If the villa-dwellers were *conductores* rather than owners, they were nonetheless wealthy, perhaps combining land-ownership with contracts. A connection between this large-scale iron-working and army supply is reasonable. At a lower level, small villas and farmsteads were probably often dependent for their needs on the nearest *vici*, where smelters and smiths might both be present. The need of further excavation in farmyards of all sizes is, however, clear.

By contrast with iron, lead (with or without silver) was scarce in Belgica, though mining near St. Avold might be the origin of the high number of lead coffins noted near Metz. Lead for coffins at Amiens most likely came from Britain, while that perhaps used for the Bavay aqueduct siphon could with equal ease (or difficulty) have come from Britain or Lower Germany.[18] Tin must also have been imported from Britain.

Copper and zinc ores, mined in the Saarland-Eifel and Eifel-Ardennes respectively, were commoner. Extensive underground mining near St. Barbara (Saarland) seems to have been divided into individual operations, one labelled as the *officina* of Aemilianus. Near Kordel, copper-mining took place immediately adjacent to quarrying; the name MARCI (Marcus, or Marcianus) applies to both and suggests private ownership or contracting of both enterprises together. Imperial ownership is perhaps more likely, though not proven, for the boundary zones with zinc ores in the higher Eifel and eastern Ardennes.[19]

The path of the ores, once extracted, can be followed only to a limited degree. Traces of bronze working have been found in the countryside (Narcy, Hte. Marne), but most activity seems again to have been in the *vici* (there is no foundation for the often-cited fibula production at Anthée). Furnaces in *vici* were multi-purpose: thus one at Pachten could be used for small objects or for fake coins. Bronze statuettes may have been made at or near Blicquy, but the best evidence is for smaller objects – bronze appliqué masks at Nimy, decorative box-handles at Bavay.[20] Where the bronze and enamel fibulae, which have standardized designs, were actually made remains to be seen. *Civitas* capitals are likely, by analogy with Bavay, to have seen their share of such work. Most dated bronze-working belongs to the second and third centuries, though plain fibulae, some of which simply continue late la Tène traditions, were manufactured without interruption. Similarly, though the zinc ores may have been exploited earlier, the best attested use is for the production of brass buckets somewhere in the lower Maas valley in the third century ('Hemmoor' type).[21]

That indispensable material, salt, was of course also exploited. The two principal areas of activity saw the employment of different methods. In Lorraine, as in the Jura, salt springs had been used since pre-Roman times. The Seille valley south-east of Metz saw extensive salt-works near Vic-sur-Seille and Marsal, with remains from 'briquetage' spread over areas of up to 100 ha. The use of shallow clay containers raised on clay supports was a technique going back to pre-Roman times, though whether a reference in Pliny is to this or to a more primitive technique of pouring salt water over burning wood is unclear. Air photography in Lorraine also suggests the more developed 'marais salant' technique, where artificial channels led the salt water to evaporation pans. Along the North Sea coast, saltern construction to trap water at high tide started in pre-Roman times at De Panne, and was then continued at Zeebrugge, Raversijde, Ardres and elsewhere. Less advanced methods were also in use, and Varro also mentions the burning of certain plants to obtain salt.[22]

That salt-production went well beyond local needs is shown by first-century inscriptions set up at Rimini by the *salinatores* of Morini and Menapii, to honour as patron an ex-centurion from the legion at Neuss. The three *negotiatores salarii* of Colijnsplaat, one of them a Treveran, may also have had army connections, for two of them had headquarters at Köln. The record is again silent on questions of ownership, and there is no obvious geographical correlation between salt-production and villas.[23]

Fossil fuels, while occasionally found in the coal-rich Saarland, were not mined for deliberate use, and the main fuel remained wood. Since wood was also used by builders, wainwrights, and for innumerable objects from statues to dishes, the industry centred on it must have been among the biggest, although by its nature leaving few archaeological traces. Eventually, pollen sequences will surely reveal substantial clearing of forest cover in many areas in the Roman period. Again, large landowners stood to gain from the natural resources of their estates, even if some of the Eifel and Ardennes forests were public land or imperial property. How the supply of wood to craftsmen was organized is also unknown. Wooden objects are frequently depicted on funerary monuments great and small, but only rarely was one erected by a craftsman himself (a carpenter at Metz, perhaps a wainwright who also made yokes at Senon, while at Sarrebourg a M. Tignarius derived his name from his craft).[24] Even skilled wood-working remained at artisan level and did not bring much more than a modest livelihood. Any profit must have been to the landowners who controlled the supply.

2 Clay products

The industries based on wood and on clay could hardly contrast more sharply. Both activities were widespread, but while the one is recoverable only with care and good luck, the other leaves a highly visible trail of virtually indestructible potsherds.

The general history of pottery importation, production and exportation in Belgica, as in the rest of Gaul, is well known. The importing from early Augustan times of *terra sigillata* from northern Italy to meet military and élite demand was quickly followed by its manufacture at Lyon and in southern Gaul. Amphorae were imported for the sake of their contents, normally wine from Italy, olive-oil and fish-sauce from Spain. Local pottery production went on, but Roman shapes might be adopted, and the better potters hybridized known techniques with Roman preferences to produce the so-called Gallo-Belgic ware which often closely imitated the prized *terra sigillata*. In the first and second centuries AD, *terra sigillata* manufacture moved by stages closer to the Rhine armies, Gallo-Belgic ware declined and the container picture is complicated not only by Narbonensian amphorae but by the widespread use of barrels. Coarse pottery, increasingly (from its shape) implying the adoption of Roman habits of cooking and eating, was produced for immediate and less local consumption.[25] Belgica was transformed from an importer to an exporter of fine wares, while as always self-sufficient in coarse.

Allied to pottery, but as new as the other was traditional, were clay tiles. Whether introduced by the army or percolating northwards from Narbonensis, they are the natural counterpart to stone, and their introduction and use should run parallel. The prohibitive weight of tiles meant a strong incentive for local production, and they were sometimes produced near villas, as at Vellereille-le-Brayeaux. The evidence for the Early Empire shows kilns, often in groups that may be termed brickyards, established in rural areas and exporting their products over a radius of some 25 km by road as well as water – a good example is the tilery at Hermalle-sous-Huy, stamped tiles from which are found at Braives, Amay and Vervoz-Clavier. Tiles might also be manufactured in cities; of those identifiable as products of Bavay, some travelled along the natural river route towards Namur (by analogy, a barge with a cargo of tiles on the Therain could have been coming from Beauvais).[26] Clearly by the second century they were a commercial product, whether specially commissioned or bought in bulk from stockpiles. Tile-stamps are not readily intelligible, though probably contractions of personal or place-names. Public tileries, e.g. of the civitas Leucorum (at Toul), also existed. Only in the Saarland are there contracted *tria nomina*, Q. Val. Sabe. and Q. El. Appi, suggesting imitation of the Italian practice whereby estate owners ran (either themselves, or through a contractor) tileries, and a tile kiln is known near a villa at Mürlenbach (one slave's name is found in the same general area). Distribution of these products was clearly by river. Other rural tileries were perhaps more independent concerns, for they can produce more than one stamp, suggesting small consortia of artisans. Yet these must have worked out arrangements with landowners for the use of the land, so that a financial interest and a measure of control on the latter's part is likely. At Speicher and Mittelbronn, tiles were produced alongside pottery, but there is no evidence for consistent links. The vast majority of tiles are of course unstamped.[27]

Pottery production also varied from household to commercial level. A first-century kiln beside the small villa at Laufen-Müschhag (Swiss Jura), which fired wares of miserable quality and was abandoned after a short life, illustrates the former. Many coarse wares, like tiles, had a modest area of distribution outward from the centre of production. The *mortaria* stamped Brariatus may have been made either at Bavay or at Pont-sur-Sambre; distribution along the river is sure in either case. Two other first-century manufacturers of *mortaria*, Q. Valerius Veranius and Summacus, subsequently moved their workshops from Bavay, the former perhaps migrating to Britain.[28] One coarse ware noted in the Blicquy cemetery, called 'savonneuse' from its soapy feel, was probably made in Nervian territory, though not at Blicquy itself. Another was made in the village, and can be distinguished from similar types made at Howardries or in the Entre-Sambre-et-Meuse area.[29] It is probable that *vici* were normally centres of production for such coarse wares serving the surrounding rural areas. Almost every *vicus* that has been partially excavated has produced kilns; the wares often require further study, but vases with appliqué masks, common in Nervian territory, were made at both Blicquy and Liberchies.

Cities also produced coarse wares and often developed potters' quarters (Bavay, Reims, Trier). Other centres lay in the countryside, where the clay rather than an established settlement was the attracting force. La Calotterie on the Canche and Labuissière can now be added to previously known examples such as Speicher north of Trier. Production at Labuissière started in the first century but reached its maximum only in the second, delivering a type of grey coarse ware previously assigned to Arras. A wide number of shapes were manufactured, whereas some workshops, e.g. Bourlon between Arras and Cambrai, specialized more in jugs and bowls. Overall, this period sees increasing standardization, so that not only are the products of different centres quite similar but there is evidence for 'services' of the same shape in different standard sizes. At Labuissière several types of kiln were in use, and a total of 250 kilns puts this in a different order of magnitude from *vicus*-workshops. Sudden expansion of another coarse ware is documented at Amiens, where types that formed only five per cent of deposits dated to about the reign of Marcus, rise to 60 per cent a little later: the clay indicates an origin among the neighbouring Bellovaci.[30] The hypothesis that landowners, not simply independent potters, were involved in control of production, and that local politics as well as supply and demand might affect distribution, is consistent with this phenomenon, if hard to prove. Interestingly, much of the distribution of these medium-range coarse wares must have been done by road rather than water.

Overall, it looks as if household production of coarse wares gave way to the local or semi-industrialized, although production in the out-buildings of large villas remains a further possibility. More organized production, where availability of clay, water and wood were the determining factors, was a new development for coarse pottery, though not for fine. The physical aspect of such centres is largely unknown. Labuissière, which must have had quite a huddle of dwellings, did not give birth to a *vicus* in the strict sense of an organized community. That some *vici* may have owed their origin or growth to industrial concerns is however not ruled out for such untidy agglomerations as Florange-Daspich-Ebange and some sites in the Maas and Scheldt valleys. Terra-cotta statuettes of deities, another typically Gallo-Roman product, may have been produced in *vici* which, like Altrier, had important sanctuaries.[31] Nonetheless, a hypothetical dichotomy between independent artisans in *vici* or cities and controlled workers on estates may be justified, whether or not the manufacture of pottery was a full-time occupation.

Between coarse wares and *terra sigillata*, the fine ware *par excellence*, lie classes of pottery which combine Roman and native traditions and belong to table rather than kitchen wares. These include relatively unknown types such as the imitations of so-called 'Pompeian red' ware made at Blicquy.

The combination of traditions is best seen in the important class of pottery awkwardly and inaccurately called Gallo-Belgic – awkwardly, since the label is not always used with precision, inaccurately because the pottery was also made outside Belgica. Most Gallo-Belgic pottery is either black (*terra nigra*, fired in the traditional reducing atmosphere) or red (*terra rubra*, fired in the oxidizing technique favoured by the Romans from about 30 BC), though various browns and mottled shades are found. *Terra nigra* is technically a continuation of the black-gloss late la Tène wares, except for the introduction of a range of open shapes, particularly plates. To complicate the definition of the ware, it was sometimes produced in the same workshops that made early types of Gaulish *terra sigillata*, most notably at Lyon but also, slightly later, at Vidy. Occasionally, poor *terra sigillata* can hardly be told apart from Gallo-Belgic, though normally the latter has a softer and less glossy finish.

That the production of Gallo-Belgic pottery originated in supplying the Roman army is a widely accepted hypothesis. One early centre was in Switzerland, perhaps directly stimulated by influences from north Italy. Both forms and potters' names in Switzerland tend to be more Roman, and in general the products resemble *terra sigillata* so closely that they have been called 'imitation'. The earliest known production of Gallo-Belgic ware further north is among the Remi. At Thuisy, south of Reims, six out of seven kilns are considered Augustan, while kilns in the Argonne area started almost as early. It is not clear whether such pottery might travel quite far (like the wares of Italy and Lyon) or whether the discovery of identical potters' stamps at Reims and Nijmegen rather indicates movement of potters (there was a need for this, since available native pottery in the lower Rhineland was inadequate). The names of the more northern potters tend, in contrast to the Swiss group, to be single and Celtic.[32]

Later, numerous centres arose. Workshops started at Trier and Metz by Tiberian times, and other places in Lorraine (Daspich, Boucheporn, Bliesbruck) followed suit. The group on the Vesle south-east of Reims continued production (Thuisy, Sept-Saulz, Prunay) and other kilns, some of them in *vici*

(Amay, Braives, Clavier-Vernoz) started up further north. With a more restricted number of forms, the ware continued to be produced into the second century; continuing popularity was after the initial period enjoyed by the black wares only. Production as a whole declined after the Flavian period, and a connection with the events of 69–70 has sometimes been surmised.[33]

Gallo-Belgic pottery absorbed and redirected the energies of skilled indigenous potters. A few, notably among the Helvetii, continued for a time to produce painted wares with designs on white background in the pure late la Tène tradition; the pottery in this area had specific regional characteristics and will not be further followed here.[34]

The second century brought other types of fine ware drawing on indigenous traditions. Most obvious are the dark colour-coated drinking beakers, which testify to the persistence of local customs in beverages and drinking habits. One of the largest centres was Trier, where top-quality black beakers, often indented and not infrequently carrying painted mottoes, were a hard glossy black. More ordinary beakers, often with a rough-cast finish, have been ascribed to the Compiègne area and to the Argonne. This type of pottery reached British sites in small quantities, exported by way of the Seine and (for Trier) the Rhine.[35]

The fine table ware *par excellence* in all the northern provinces was red-gloss *terra sigillata*, which became popular among the civilian population soon after its initial introduction. Manufacturing centres gradually moved from southern Gaul to the north-east, closer to that large steady consumer, the army. By Flavian (if not Neronian) times potters were established in Lorraine, having migrated, to judge by their decorative repertoire, from central and southern Gaul. The earliest production was grafted on to an existing Gallo-Belgic industry at Boucheporn (Moselle) on the Metz-Worms road (not far from a rich villa, though a connection cannot be proven). This then became one of the largest producers of eastern Gaul (with some 30 kilns and 60 potters' names known at present). Two of the most prominent potters, Satto and Saturninus, appear then to have set up a new workshop at Chémery and perhaps also Blickweiler before finally settling at Mittelbronn, which started in the middle of the second century just as Chémery faded out.[36] Movement and experimentation appear typical of the east Gaul workshops. Satto and Saturninus seem to have had extraordinarily long working lives, and perhaps their stamps continued to be used by firms which they founded. Minor second-century workshops of this east Gaulish group were at Eincheville, Eschweiler Hof, Laneuville-la Madeleine (south of Nancy) and Haute-Yutz, the last two being on the Meurthe and Mosel: all remained insignificant compared with the Rhineland establishments, especially Rheinzabern.[37]

Another group of workshops was founded in the Argonne, the hilly, forested area between Meuse and Aisne valleys that was traversed only by the Reims-Metz road, but where good clays were plentiful. The biggest producer here was Lavoye (up to 70 names known) where *terra sigillata* started production in Hadrianic times, but did not entirely supplant earlier Gallo-Belgic. (Indeed, the same kilns, as at Vidy, may have been used for both types.) Pont-des-Rèmes, Avocourt and les Allieux were less than half the size, and there is a trail of yet smaller concerns, not all identified. Individual potters either moved around within the group or there was much borrowing of stamps. Even if grouped together, the Argonne potteries, like the Lorraine ones, never reached the scale of la Graufesenque or Lezoux in South and Central Gaul.[38]

In the Argonne, the clays attracted artisans to an area without good communications. The opposite can be observed at Trier, where a workshop or workshops started in the first half of the second century, with the production of plain wares preceding that of decorated. Communications were of course excellent, but production never grew above medium size.[39]

The names of the east Gaulish potters are overwhelmingly native. Analysis of the potters' names from Boucheporn shows that over half are indigenous and only one quarter clearly Romanized. The evidence for working in groups coupled with high mobility suggests that the workshops were formed by associations of free potters. A degree of dependence on richer folk is not thereby ruled out, for some form of agreement with landowners was necessary, whether a money rent or share of products. The potters themselves, whatever their degree of freedom, did not make particularly high profits from their trade. No organized *vici* grew up around the kiln sites, which conspicuously lack the funerary or votive monuments which would denote modest prosperity. A *fictiliarius* at Metz almost certainly dealt in pottery even if he also produced it, and had a favourable location in a major city.[40] Pottery was both made and shipped in massive quantities, but it was shipping and selling that was profitable. Whether this was sometimes combined with control of the basic resources by landowners cannot be demonstrated.

The production and marketing of fine wares, especially *terra sigillata*, differ in important respects from that of coarse pottery. They could not simply be produced by peasants turning their hands to the pot-shed in spare moments, and from the start aimed at a wider market. Of the products of Satto and Saturninus, it has been estimated that a mere 8 per cent were sold locally, the bulk going to the Rhine and Danube.[41] Study of this more sophisticated branch of the industry inevitably leads to questions of trade-routes and traders.

No less important than the origins and growth of the pottery industries in Belgica is their duration and their decline. The second half of the second century, despite the tendency to standardization, was not a period of steady growth. This is least marked in coarse pottery, where old types simply continued in production although sometimes (as at Labuissière) with lowered volume. The replacement of one workshop by another can be seen at Boucheporn and Chémery, which wound down just as Mittelbronn, situated that much closer to the Rhineland, started up. A number of the smaller east Gaulish workshops were short-lived, including one at Luxeuil. Mittelbronn

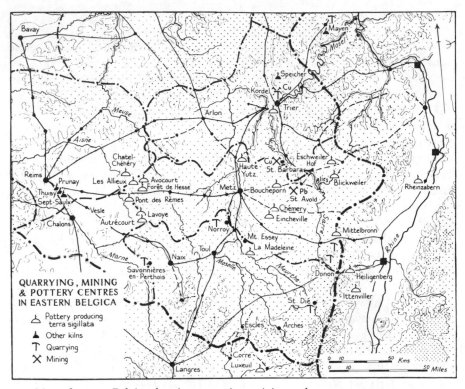

23 Map of eastern Belgica showing quarrying, mining and pottery centres

itself may not have survived the second century, although it recovered from a destruction dated to 160 AD. Production in the Argonne continued, but less figured ware was produced, and there was a return to traditional repetitive decoration, along with a diversification of effort into beakers and barbotine-decorated wares some of which are still little-known. The one place without any diminution of production is Trier, where both *terra sigillata* and beakers continued at strength until the mid-third century and beyond (the *terra sigillata* is complicated by the use of old moulds). In western Belgica, by contrast, a study of the imported fine wares shows the virtual cessation of central Gaulish *terra sigillata* around 200 AD, whether caused by decline of the potteries, changes in organization of the trade or the competition produced by glass and metallescent wares.[42]

Glass, which became increasingly popular as fine table ware in the second and third centuries, was not manufactured on any great scale in Belgica, though Amiens or its neighbourhood may have been home to the third-century barrel-shaped vessels associated with the name of Frontinus.[43] The one great centre of production and export lay outside the province, at Köln. Window-glass may have been produced locally, in villas or *vici*.

3   Agricultural products

There can be no doubt that incentive to improve agricultural output came from the twin sources of taxation and army supply.[44] Regular production of a surplus (previously used only for the social purpose of maintaining *clientelae*) now had to be undertaken if the producer himself was not to suffer.

During the limited period when an army was actually stationed in Gaul, produce may simply have been commandeered, but the developed military system involved payment. How long Belgica continued to supply the army with grain is debatable. For a time, until agriculture in the Rhineland was developed, supplies from the hinterland may have been necessary. At latest by the Flavian period, they will have been largely superfluous, at least for Upper Germany. The Somme valley, conveniently placed to ship goods to either Lower Germany or Britain, may have continued the supply, but it is difficult to imagine that transport of grain by land was profitable. Moreover, it is likely that there was a change in consumer, with the growing cities forming a higher two well-known barrel-laden ships. The distribution of actual amphorae also agriculture in their immediate vicinity.

The need of vines for rather more specialized conditions as well as more skilled labour naturally restricted their spread. Funerary monuments and vats for the treading of grapes show that vines reached the Mosel valley and Rhineland in the course of the second century AD, if not before. Domitian's attempt to curb provincial wine-production had no lasting effect. A spread into some parts of northern France is believed to have taken place, and climatic conditions for this were favourable in the first two centuries AD.[45]

Home-grown northern wine did not totally replace southern varieties: both were probably necessary to supply the thirsty armies, and imported wine may have been preferred by the Gauls themselves. The monument (or monuments) from Neumagen show both a pyramid of Narbonensian amphorae and the two well known barrel-laden ships. The distribution of actual amphorae also shows them passing through Trier, perhaps being loaded from smaller to larger craft, and then continuing to the Rhine frontier and even to Britain. Barrels pose a problem, for analysis of wood in Harelbeke near Kortrijk shows silver fir and larch, the latter a tree then only at home in the Alpine foothills or the higher Vosges; perhaps it will eventually be shown that larch barrels held Rhône valley wine, and that other types were available for northern produce.[46] Testimony to the scale of the wine trade comes from numerous *negotiatiores vinarii* as well as the distribution of amphorae; since barrels are rarely recovered, no comparison of the container bulk is possible. The scale of beer production and trade is likewise a matter of guesswork, but involved a retired sailor, who would draw on his connections with the Rhineland, as well as inhabitants of the rural hinterland. The overland transport of beverages in large 'tanker' barrels is suggested by reliefs from Langres and Neumagen.[47]

No evidence indisputably connects production of wine on estates and trading; yet it would be natural for landowners who marketed their own surplus to turn through the means of agents to wider trafficking. Trade within Gaul may have originated as Narbonensian estate owners imitated late Republican practice in Italy by controlling the manufacture of the wine and its containers, thereafter financing the shipping.[48] The involvement of Treveri in the wine trade at Lyon and the likelihood that the Neumagen merchant was a Treveran should indicate business interests ranging far beyond the limits of their own land or that of relatives.

While the Moselle was certainly the main artery of the wine trade, other routes must have been used. The Meuse was well suited to supply the centre of the province, and it would be interesting to know if the medieval tradition that supplied southern Belgium from Burgundy, northern from Bordeaux was already common in Roman times.

Except for woollen goods, trade in animal products has left no traces. Menapian hams and Morinian geese are known only from Martial and Pliny, and this allows no real estimate of their importance. The enormous need of the army for hides is an established fact, but the implications for Belgica are hard to trace, especially as army needs were increasingly met from the Germanies. To counteract this, the amount demanded by the civilian population for shoes will have increased. Also vanished without trace, apart from a possible oblique reference in Pliny, is the breeding of ponies for the army in the Eifel and Ardennes.[49]

Information on the woollen industry is, by comparison, copious. References to the heavy outdoor garments made in Gaul (especially the 'sagum') begin with Strabo, occur among satirists a century later, and reappear in Diocletian's Prices Edict. The figured monuments nearly all show Gallo-Roman dress, with sleeved tunics for both sexes, hooded outdoor cloaks of varying lengths and fullness for men and a variety of under-tunics, scarves and shawls. Heavy table-cloths and curtains or hangings are also often shown. Some scenes are connected with the actual production or sale of cloth or garments – cloth is examined on a relief from St. Wendel near Tholey, a finished tunic on one from Stenay and the cutting and sale of cloth is found at Reims and Arlon. This evidence is mostly from the Treveri and Mediomatrici, though Atrebates and Nervii are also explicitly mentioned in the written sources along with the Lingones, Bituriges and Santones. The scattered reliefs of Belgica come from both countryside and villages, those of other provinces more often from *civitas* capitals. The culmination of them all is the Igel monument with its scenes showing the testing, baling, shipping and selling of cloth.[50]

Debate surrounds the wool trade's organization. In addition to household production for immediate needs, there may have been an estate-based cottage industry, the work carried out by poor clients for the use and profit of their lords. Cloth production also took root in villages and some cities. To the reliefs can be added a fuller's shop at Schwarzenacker (complete with a piece of preserved cloth). While the extent to which village activity was controlled by estate owners can always be debated, the villagers themselves could not provide enough wool to support specialized fulling or dyeing (probably shown in reliefs from Arlon). Where the spinning and weaving was done remains a mystery which further excavations in villas and villages may partly solve. The small number of loom-weights from either type of site (an exception is Ardres) is at first sight strange. Part of the answer may lie in the technology, for the two-beam vertical loom would leave no archaeological trace.[51] In any case, estate production aided by the dispersal of some of the processes into the villages seems likely.

While cloth and clothing were obviously sold locally, the wide market for finished clothing arguably demanded some co-ordination of small-scale production. The trickle of clothing reaching Italy from Gaul became a steady stream by the late second and early third century, and is well symbolized by the name Caracalla given to the emperor who commonly wore the garment of that name. Haphazard activities of small traders, perhaps including the attested *vestiarius* from Germany, probably gave way to the more organized channelling of goods.[52] In this, either middlemen and perhaps specialized markets had a role, or the business was undertaken by the larger estate producers and their agents. Further development, giving to the whole industry a highly organized and specialized character, is conceivable.

Debate centres on the Igel column, where cloth is shown being handled on a scale too great to reflect the produce of any one estate. One interpretation has raw wool imported from as far afield as Aquitania or Spain in order to achieve quality as well as quantity; this is shown arriving on mule back. If wool did arrive in bulk, its processing would require large numbers of hands, both unskilled and specialized, and could best be effected by tapping the labour pool of the nearby city, Trier. The involvement of the Secundinii of Igel ceased when the cloth was finished and inspected, for it was then shipped elsewhere for cutting; since the boat shown on the base is being hauled upstream, logically this last process took place up-river, on the road to Italy. (A Mediomatrican *negotiator sagarius* at Milan shows the involvement of that people in the Italian trade.) The scale and specialization is akin to that of the medieval wool trade, the sophistication higher than generally thought appropriate to the Roman economy. The Secundinii are here seen as primarily businessmen, whose investment in land, conveniently located for their needs, was secondary.[53]

This view of the Secundinii is not without problems. The amassing of wealth from next to nothing, as opposed to the addition of wealth to wealth, was quite exceptional in the ancient world. Equally consistent with the monument and more in tune with ancient realities is a view of the family as primarily landowners and only secondarily dealers in cloth. Indeed, if their estates were multiple, the cloth could still be the product of family property, the business element little more than the marketing of surplus. A middle road is to see their activity as partly estate-based, but combined with the buying of wool from elsewhere, and centred on Igel because it was near Trier. The scale and complexity of the operation is not thereby denied, nor the commercialization (including the likelihood that the cash transactions seen on monuments involved piece-work). But the emphasis is reversed, with the wealth from marketing more firmly anchored in land – the same pattern that has been proposed for quarrying and mining. The greatest impetus to use manufacturing and marketing to add wealth to existing wealth would of course naturally be among those landowners who were not quite of the highest rank, or among younger sons (the name Secundinii might even denote descent from a second son). Their appearance near Trier is yet another reminder that this was a particularly favourable area for the generation of wealth.

Trade routes, marketing and traders

The Early Roman Empire incontestably increased the amount and variety of goods that travelled through Belgica on their way to market. To this end, natural waterways and the improved Roman roads were utilized, and both must be reviewed. A start may be made with the Belgic part of the great river system which impressed Strabo as divinely ordained because of the regular way in which it watered the land and facilitated the movement of goods.[54]

Strabo laid little emphasis on the routes to the Rhine because he was more interested in the old-established trade-route to the Seine and Channel coast than in the new exigencies being created by the Roman army. As the troops moved forward to the Rhine, the easiest and shortest supply route was by means of the Doubs, since this involved only a short and simple portage through the Belfort gap. The Saône route was more complicated. The Saône itself would be navigable for small craft to about Corre, and some probable traces of Roman attempts to canalize the stream have been observed. Even from Corre, the Coney might have been taken for a short distance. Sooner or later, however, one of several possible routes had to be taken through the hills, one debouching at Escles, where there was a small community. From Escles, another series of hills had to be traversed to reach the Moselle in the region of Châtel-sur-Moselle below Epinal.

The region between Corre and Escles is seamed with roads of evident antiquity, though for none is Roman origin clearly established.[55] The region has also produced a few mosaics and a noticeable sprinkling of inscriptions and reliefs. A group of these from the upper Coney valley suggests that an alternative was to follow that valley to the end and join the Moselle at Arches (which has produced very classical reliefs). It is presumably the Coney valley (taken by the southern branch of the Canal de l'Est) that Antistius Vetus had in mind for the ambitious scheme of linking Saône and Mosel. While the portages were tricky, once the Moselle was reached, all but minor troubles were over. Below Metz it was swelled by other navigable streams, the Saar

(Sarre) from eastern Lorraine and the Sauer (Sûre) from the Luxembourg Ardennes. Larger ships could thus be used downstream from Trier.

The other great river of Belgica, the Meuse, should have been navigable in ancient times at least as far up as Commercy or St. Mihiel. It was linked by a short and easy portage to the Moselle at Toul, and by a longer and less convenient one to the Ornain and thence to the Marne. Evidence for use of the higher reaches of the river in Roman times is, however, lacking. It is only from Verdun that *vici* are regularly found at intersections of Meuse and the roads that cross it, and only from Namur down that settlements are frequently found on its banks. Tributaries of the Meuse, most obviously the Sambre but arguably also the Ourthe on its way down from the Ardennes, were also navigable.

The Escaut/Scheldt and its tributaries were of course also open to traffic, and it is from one of them, the Haine, that hard evidence comes in the form of harbour installations and riverboats at Pommeroeul. Both dug-outs and flat-bottomed barges were in use, the latter reaching nearly 20 m in length.[56] In western Belgica, Marne, Aisne, Oise and Somme were all usable as well as some smaller rivers.

The greater river routes were in Roman times all roughly paralleled by land routes. The road network of Belgica was dominated by a great triangle consisting of Langres-Trier-Köln in the east, Langres-Reims-Amiens-Boulogne in the west, and Amiens-Bavay-Köln in the north. These roughly corresponded to the Saône-Mosel, the Marne-Seine and the Sambre-Meuse systems respectively. From Reims, a number of roads fan out providing optional ways of going north and a series of links to Trier, Metz and Toul. The latter all cross the Meuse, the only major river not doubled by a main road; it also passed through difficult country around Charleville-Mézières and, except in its lower reaches, did not head directly towards major cities or army bases.

Water transport, besides cheapness, had the added advantage of being considerably faster downstream, though slower in the other direction. While the pulling power of mules harnessed with yokes in Gallo-Roman manner may have been considerably greater than usually estimated, water transport was still obviously attractive for heavy or breakable cargoes.[57] Indeed, the whole long-distance network of Belgica, leading to the middle and lower Rhine, depended on the fact that it was obviously preferable to ship goods up the Rhône to Lyon rather than to haul them over the Gd. St. Bernard to the Swiss lakes and rivers.

The relative use made of land and water routes is thus a question of some interest. Evidence of two kinds is available, in addition to the discovery of boats and harbours as at Pommeroeul and Dieulouard-Scarpone.[58] Inscriptions and reliefs form one category, while the other is analysis of the dispersion of transported goods. From Neumagen comes the famous depiction of large vessels with over 40 oarsmen, almost, if not quite, of sea-going character, and corresponding well enough to Ausonius' later description of such craft. It may be doubted that ships of this size could be used above Trier, where much reloading from smaller craft would take place. Other types of ship are shown, including one with sails far from any river at Jünkerath. A smaller craft is shown at Bollendorf on the Sauer, while medium-sized loaded barges may be seen on the base of the Igel column, or again far from rivers at Virton. Traffic at different levels from the local to the long-distance is obvious. Yet the monuments equally give evidence for transport by land – straining mules at Neumagen, mules pulling a huge barrel at Langres, pack-mules with bales of cloth going across hills at Igel.[59]

A not dissimilar picture emerges from inscriptions. *Nautae* are found in such natural places as Metz, and may be presumed at Trier (though only specialized *proretarii* or pilots are attested). A Rhône-Saône shipper also appears between the various river systems at Dijon, and a dedication to the genius of the *utriclarii* (probably raftsmen) at Bard-le-Régulier on an overland portage from Autun to the Seine.[60] The guilds of shippers were thus also connected with the overland routes. Yet if the portage from Saône to Mosel was not easy, the overland route from Chalon-sur-Saône via Dijon and Langres to Toul was very awkward, involving several uncomfortable gradients, not least at Langres itself – a hill which must have had every wagon driver wishing that the capital of the Lingones had been moved down off the plateau. This road is hardly comparable to the flat Rhône valley one Strabo says was preferred to the strong river current on the upstream voyage. Nonetheless, it looks as if the route, however irrational, was in fact used even for bulky goods.

Pottery, it rapidly becomes clear, travelled in bulk overland as well as by river. Dispersion of goods from *vici* or from isolated rural potteries often had to be by road. Some of the east Gaulish production centres are quite surprisingly land-locked, Chémery being some 40 km from either Saar or Mosel, and Boucheporn not much closer. Chémery's replacement, Mittel-bronn, also lies well away from rivers and clearly aimed at sending its produce by road through the Saverne gap to Strasbourg. The Argonne kilns were also awkwardly situated, though both Meuse and Aisne were attainable. The rivers do not however seem to have been a primary factor in the distribution of their products, and proximity to the Aisne did not bring expansion or longer life to Pont-des-Rèmes. From Lavoye a great deal of pottery travelled overland, westwards to Reims, eastwards to Trier, and only thereafter by river to the middle Rhine. Some destinations, including cities (Bavay, Tongeren and Reims, to say nothing of rural sites) could of course only be reached by road, but the interesting point is the impression that neither kiln-sites nor transport were organized rationally around considerations of transport costs.[61]

Viewed as a whole, the distribution of *terra sigillata* within Belgica in the mid-second century is in fact (to a modern mind) neither wholly rational nor irrational. Preliminary analysis discerns two distinct areas of distribution. That the western area, especially near the coast (Amiens and Boulogne) was primarily supplied from central Gaul is no cause for surprise, but as far inland as

Bavay there is little change. Tongeren seems to lie on an invisible line, with Central Gaul and the Argonne equally strong, while south of the Meuse Argonne ware dominates. The centre of Belgica was thus poised between two routes carrying pottery from the Allier region to Britain and the Rhineland respectively. Terra-cotta statuettes of deities, especially mother-goddesses, travelled along with the pottery.[62]

Various irrationalities are to be seen in the long-distance pottery trade that supplied the army. Despite geographical proximity, products from Trier and the lower Rhineland reached Britain only in negligible quantities. Argonne and other east Gaulish wares could also easily have travelled to Britain once they reached Mosel or Rhine, but did so only when the organization of the central Gaulish distribution network was disrupted at the end of the second century. Rheinzabern's capture of the Danube market in the late second century (despite competitive efforts from the Satto/Saturninus workshop) may thus not be entirely due to location on the Rhine. Perhaps the strangest distribution anomaly is that of the globular wine amphorae from Narbonensis, the type seen at Neumagen. Distribution of the vessels suggests that they went via Doubs or Moselle to the Rhine, and only then on to Britain. The British route was, if this is true, merely the irrational lengthening of one originally designed for the Rhineland, and the failure of pottery from Belgica to take the same route is all the stranger.[63]

A few points can be made in summary. Transport by land and water involved people at the most disparate social levels – from the wagoner or bargee to the wealthy trader or shipper. More goods were transported by land than appears to the modern mind reasonable, and goods did not invariably travel in the directions that might be anticipated. For all that, the western part of the province, where a certain failure to develop can be detected after the initial wave of Romanization, may have suffered from not being on a major waterway to the armies; all indicators point to the importance of the traffic bound for the Rhine armies by way of Saône and Mosel.

Indications of the various levels at which marketing took place have by now emerged. The *vici* served passing traffic and local needs; artisans and farmers would also meet in the fairs that were held at sanctuaries. The long-distance trade in non-luxury goods brought such items as pottery and glass, while exotic items simply passed through *en route* for army bases, cities or rich villas (though the presence of cotton cloth at Pachten is to be noted). The larger villas were probably more independent of the local networks, while their owners were to varying degrees involved in the long-distance and luxury trades as consumers, producers or organizers. Such men also had one foot in the cities, where they could buy and sell. Most cities did not generate great wealth by manufacture, which tended to be dispersed rather than concentrated. Trier went further in this direction than any other, and was also an important reloading point, with some form of customs control.[64]

One contentious issue is the connection between wealth from trade or manufacture and wealth from land. It is often supposed that the large landowners of the first century AD gave way to a new aristocracy that has beeen described as 'entrepreneurial' or as a 'bourgeoisie', for whom land was an investment for acquired wealth. An opposite view sees the economy as wholly controlled by social relationships and the search for status, with land not only the only major source of wealth but the highest social determinant. Most of what appears to be trade is thus reduced to the selling of surplus.[65]

Support for the first view has been sought in the distribution of villas (which at first sight is too dense to suggest large estates) and in their growth from comparatively small to luxury dimensions (which implies an increasing wealth). A connection between their increasing luxury and the exploitation of resources remains likely, and the link (however tenuous in any single case) between growing villas and growing manufacture and trade tells against any too static view of economic conditions. A middle course suggests that wealth from manufacture and marketing was secondary but nonetheless real. Moreover the processes involved helped free some people from previous social restrictions by turning social relations into economic ones. A few people like the Secundinii were also taking the first steps towards freeing the economy from the constraints born of dispersed small enterprises. Effectively they replayed the role of the Roman *equites* or knights who formed an enterprising class in Italy during the Late Republic. If this caused a clash of values they may have been content to take a back seat in the competition for the highest civic and religious honours.

The inscriptions mentioning shippers and traders are not inconsistent with such a view. Theoretically the two were separate, the shippers (*nautae*) taking their name from the rivers which they plied (Rhône, Saône, Mosel) and the traders (*negotiatores*) from a specific class of goods – wine, beer, pottery, fish-sauce, salt, clothing or grain. In practice interests were often combined, especially wine and pottery with shipping. Both *nautae* and *negotiatores* formed guilds, the grandest being the *corpus splendidissimum Cisalpinorum et Trans-alpinorum*. Patrons of other guilds included knights or decurions, e.g. the Viromanduan L. Besius Superior or the Treveran Apronius Raptor. It has been argued that the simple guild members were of lower status and lesser wealth, neither large landowners nor of sufficient status to hold municipal office, yet the names found on inscriptions show them to have been a highly Romanized sector of Gallic society.[66]

The inscriptions recording *nautae* and *negotiatores* cluster both spatially and chronologically. Geographically, the Rhône-Saône-Mosel axis stands out, with the majority of inscriptions at Lyon, followed by Trier, Mainz, Köln and the islands south of the Rhine mouth, where the important sanctuaries of Domburg and Colijnsplaat mark points on the route between the Rhine and Britain. Shipping and trade from Lyon northwards was in the hands of Gauls; the majority of those who specify an origin was from Belgica, with the Treveri providing almost as many (some ten) as everyone else combined. A tight connection between the great trade-route leading to the Rhine armies and the appearance of boatmen and traders on inscriptions is evident.[67]

Chronologically, the inscriptions reached a peak in the late second and early third centuries. While the *nautae* of Paris, the *negotiatores* of le Héraple, or the Remi and Lingones found at Xanten in Neronian times are reminders that such organizations had an early start, nearly all other monuments, when datable, fall in the later period. At Domburg and Colijnsplaat, standardization suggests a single workshop for many altars, and epigraphical criteria are consistent with a date within some 50 years on either side of AD 200.[68]

The close link with army supplies may not simply reflect the laissez-faire growth of trade. Arguments have been advanced for seeing the *collegia* as directly responsible to the emperor and his agents. The shipping of goods to the army would in that case be part of their official *munera*, undertaken in lieu of other forms of tax payments. Lack of profit is not thereby implied, since soldiers had to buy most of their goods and had cash for non-essentials; trading with civilians, while secondary, was also lucrative. Traffic was however to some extent state-directed.[69]

Another contentious issue is the extent to which a market economy was created. That some steps were taken it would be hard to deny. The primary mechanism behind the circulation of coinage may well have been the transformation of provincial taxes into pay for soldiers and officials followed by redispersion of the money in return for goods. Nevertheless, the circulation was sufficiently lively that inequalities were for the most part ironed out, so that the cross-section of coins available between one part of the province and another, or even between neighbouring provinces, was much the same. Penury of small change led to phenomena such as halving or forging, showing the demand for coin. The sheer volume of circulating coin was considerably higher than in the early Middle Ages, and the extent of coin-loss in *vici* points to a considerable degree of monetization. It would not be surprising if further study shows a more intense circulation of coinage in eastern Belgica than in the centre and west, and the 60,000 coins documented for Trier almost certainly far outstrip those of any other city (even allowing for favourable modern conditions).[70] The frequency of reliefs showing payment in cash or the counting of money in Treveran territory might then be a reflection of realities and attitudes, not just an accident of survival.

The conclusion that eastern Belgica profited and changed as a result of production and trade aimed at the army is unavoidable. The trails of inscriptions and small monuments that mark the roads and passes leading from Lorraine into the Rhineland suggest activity relatively low down the social scale, and widely dispersed. Wood, wool, leather, iron and grain may all have made their way eastward through the hills to be exchanged for coin that was then spent partly on inscriptions and reliefs. The evident prosperity around the middle Meuse may be connected with the use of that river from Dinant northwards. The principal gainers were however clearly the Treveri, and more especially the city of Trier. The extraordinary growth of the city from the second half of the second century may well have been connected with the beginnings of decline at Lyon. Whether some shifting of the balance northwards was an almost inevitable course of events or was due to specific actions (for instance against Lyon) taken by Septimius Severus may be debated. The process in fact seems to have begun somewhat earlier, but may well have accelerated in Severan times. That Trier became the economic capital of Gaul in the third century is no new suggestion, but re-evaluations of the evidence seem consistently to point in the same direction.[71] An interesting difference between the two cities can be discerned. Lyon had functioned almost as an extension of Italy in the northern Gauls, one testimony being the high number of freedmen and Greek names. Trier shows much less Mediterranean influence in nomenclature and underlying social structure, even in civic values. A greater generator of wealth than any other city in Belgica or even (Lyon apart) in the Three Gauls, it remained an essentially northern city.

7

ROMANIZED BELGICA

1 From the Flavian to the Severan emperors

Even during the period on which Tacitus wrote, the Gallic provinces earned notice only when revolts affected the emperor and the armies. Lack of information subsequent to AD 70 is not then entirely due to the failure of other writers to take up the pen that Tacitus laid down. After the first abortive Gallic empire the Gallic provinces settled down to a century troubled by few newsworthy incidents, but rather characterized by slow modifications to society and economy effected by absorption into the Roman Empire. The evidence for these is inevitably archaeological, since the questions involved, while very proper to a modern historical enquiry, were not so regarded in ancient times. Moreover, provided the imperial framework did not fracture, the acts of emperors were largely irrelevant to these processes – as Tacitus, in the speech he puts into Cerialis' mouth, hinted they should be.[1] After 70, visits from emperor or members of his house were rare; the presence of the governor and of a small number of troops with policing duties sufficed to preserve calm.

Belgica, because of its proximity to the frontier, was more liable than the other Gallic provinces to occasional interruptions of the peace. A revolt against Domitian, involving the legions at Mainz and Strasbourg, was suppressed in 89 by the legate of Lower Germany, A. Bucius Lappius Maximus, who had previously supervised military activity at Mirebeau when commander of the eighth (Strasbourg) legion. Trouble in the towns of Germany under Nerva is hinted at by later writers. Repercussions in the hinterland of Belgica have been supposed on the basis of burnt layers observed (but on an insufficient scale) in Saverne and Metz. A dedication to the *concordia civitatis* at Metz suggests that the concord was at some time threatened, but the monument cannot be ascribed to any specific event.[2]

The administration of the province proceeded smoothly along established lines. One governor, Ti. Claudius Saturninus, is known because he corresponded with Hadrian on a point of law. A later one, C. Sabucius Maior

Caecilianus, had served as *legatus iuridicus* in Britain – doubtless an advantage, since Belgica was not considered to merit a separate *legatus iuridicus* of its own. The census was administered as before, at intervals of between 15 and 30 years. Procurators continued to include ambitious men; two later became prefects of Egypt and one, M. Bassaeus Rufus (in the 160s) rose from the centurionate to become praetorian prefect at Rome. The son of another, L. Alfenus Senecio, held the governorships of Syria and Britain under Septimius Severus. Belgica thus continued to be a significant province for those whose eyes were fixed on advancement.[3]

The reigns of Trajan, Hadrian and Antoninus were, in general, times of considerable (if not precisely dated) building activity in both town and countryside. That indefatigable traveller, Hadrian, should have seen each of the great roads of Belgica, since he went fom Rhône to Rhine, from Rhine to Boulogne and after his British tour from Boulogne back to Narbonensis. Few cities could therefore have escaped his attention, and he is said to have had an entourage of architects and engineers.[4] Excitement and ceremony there must have been, with a decking out of cities to greet the imperial presence, even if no stone archways or other buildings can with certainty be ascribed to his visit. The most ambitious urban projects, the bridge and great baths at Trier, belong to Antoninus' reign.

Although the present picture lacks sharpness, it shows that throughout Belgica further steps had been taken along the road to urbanization, with local notables persuaded to adorn their city and to spend time in well-appointed town houses; emulation, in Greek *philotimia*, now took urban form even in the north. Further south, it was even getting out of hand, for *curatores* appointed to oversee city finances are attested in Narbonensis from the time of Hadrian. For Belgica, the sole example is of third-century date, but concern for financial affairs is shown by minor procurators of the Antonine period.[5]

The reign of Marcus Aurelius saw a renewal of incidents that attracted the attention of writers. Between 172 and 174 both Chatti from across the middle Rhine and Chauci from further north were repulsed by Didius Julianus, then legate of Belgica (later, briefly, emperor). Almost the only certainty is that the Chauci did not come by way of the lower Rhine, since sites there show no signs of destruction, nor does any kind of interruption appear in *vici* along the Bavay-Köln road. Raids by sea-borne pirates are perfectly possible.[6] The coin evidence sometimes cited for both events has to be used with caution. While there are hoards of this period, some were buried later than the supposed events; other hoards ending (or apparently ending) with Marcus or Commodus may have been deposited after a devaluation in 194. Their non-recovery would then have to be linked with some later event, such as the troubles surrounding Clodius Albinus. Also debatable is the archaeological evidence for destruction at this point. Burnt layers have been reported at a number of sites, both urban and rural, in the north and north-west of the province (including Amiens, Tournai and Arras). The danger of attributing scattered chance occurrences to one single recorded event is apparent. Yet if the numbers continue to mount, and if general conflagrations are proven, they may eventually support the idea of piratical Chauci. The start of military occupation at Oudenburg and perhaps Aardenburg (both among the Menapii, and originally near the coast) around this time indicates measures against some sea-borne threat.[7]

Arguably more serious was the unrest recorded in enigmatic terms among the Sequani, since the fact that no external foe is recorded suggests internal unrest. No details are known, and it is unnecessary, if tempting, to relate the incident to the serious problems of Commodus' reign, when so-called 'deserters' wars' also cannot be defined with precision. The main literary source, Herodian, is given to rhetoric and this must be allowed for in his account of an army of deserters and discontents terrifying Gaul, Germany and Spain. Yet there is independent evidence for unrest of some kind. An inscription refers to a 'siege' of the eighth legion at Strasbourg (probably in AD 185), and a writing tablet found at Rottweil in Upper Germany shows the legate of that legion judging serious (though possibly still routine) charges against civilians.[8]

The second century thus shows, on the one hand, peaceful enrichment, and on the other, hints of incipient trouble from within as well as from without, perhaps indicative of social imbalance. Unrest may have been exacerbated by the epidemic spread by the army under Marcus Aurelius, assuming that it spread to Gaul as well as Germany. Again there are no details and as yet no archaeological evidence except a rather later multiple burial at Destelbergen.[9]

In the absence of documentary evidence, it is difficult to pierce the smooth surface presented by funerary monuments and apparently thriving villas. Was all this accomplished at the expense of turning a part of the population off the land and chaining the rest more relentlessly to it? Was the population in some areas increasing beyond its comfortable limit? Such questions can be raised rather than answered, as also the possibility that the weather was already beginning to worsen in coastal areas, causing bad harvests.

The north-west was also the area most directly troubled in 196/7 by the march of the British army under Clodius Albinus to Lyon and, after its defeat by Septimius Severus, back again. The episode, so reminiscent of 69/70, is known only in bare outlines. The extent of reprisals taken by Severus against Lugdunum and Lugdunensis, which he had formerly governed and where he might have expected the ties of patronage to hold up, are debated, but peace was not ubiquitous. The deliverance of Trier by the legion from Mainz in 197 raises the possibility that some areas of Belgica held out for Albinus. As late as 205, an inscription shows the legion at Bonn taking action against unspecified 'rebels'.[10]

Under the Severi, the administrative posts in Belgica were given to men closely connected with the new dynasty. L. Marius Maximus Perpetuus Aurelianus (later to turn imperial biographer) had helped Severus defeat

Albinus, and thereafter had an extraordinary command of Belgica combined with Germania Inferior. C. Iunius Faustinus Postumianus, an African supporter of Severus, took over shortly after. It was a period of activity, with a census being held shortly after Severus' victory and much rebuilding of roads and bridges in preparation for the emperor Caracalla's German campaigns. Around 220, an easterner probably connected with the female side of the dynasty, L. Iulius Apronius Maenius Pius Salamallianus, was vice-legate of Belgica before his praetorship.[11]

The early Severan period brought no dramatic changes; even the granting of citizenship to provincials leaves no clear traces in the epigraphic record. The general impression is however gained that the north-western part of the province was less flourishing than previously. In the country, villas not long built were deserted, while in the cities there are fewer new town-houses with mosaics; at Amiens, the inhabited area shrank markedly, and cemeteries encroached on the street-grid. In the east, the contrary is found. Reconstruction of roads and bridges attested under Caracalla (with distances now recorded in Gallic *leugae*, leagues of $1\frac{1}{2}$ Roman miles) surely helped, but the single most important factor was probably that the soldiers were richer than before; this wealth in turn stimulated monetary circulation and economic activity in the immediate hinterland.[12] Of the datable stone monuments, an unduly large proportion belongs to this period, and they give valuable information on careers, on nomenclature and on the Romanization of the province.

Careers inscribed step by step are in fact extremely rare, and mention of any kind of offices less frequent than might be expected in so sizeable a body of epigraphic material; it was perhaps of importance only in certain contexts (for instance, at Lyon much more than in any northern city).[13] Many men of decurial status must remain unknown simply because they did not care to mention it even on their funerary inscriptions – it was a fact of life, like the physical location of their estates.

A Viromanduan, C. Suiccius Latinus, who was *praefectus legionis* of the eighth legion (an office that dates him to the early third century), *curator* of the *civitas* Suessionum and an *inquisitor* connected with the finances of the *concilium Galliarum* thus becomes the more remarkable. He was also *sacerdos Romae et Augusti*, probably (although it is not stated) at Lyon; there is no mention of municipal offices which would normally have preceded the priesthood. Another Viromanduan knight, also connected with the finances of the *concilium*, at least summarizes his municipal career in the common short form *omnibus honoribus apud suos functo*. He was also patron of the *nautae Ararici et Rhodanici* and thus combines all three civilian elements that are normal for the period – the *concilium Galliarum*, the municipalities and the corporations of shippers and traders.[14]

Belgica produced, so far as is known, no senators, and these two Viromandui are at the very top of the social pyramid.[15] Municipal careers are also very poorly attested. One Treveran, Q. Secundius Quigo, actually held magistracies among the Aedui; he had previously been *sevir Augustalis*, perhaps at Trier, and thus shows that a man could rise from the lower rank of the sevirate to that of the higher magistracies. Arguably, his presence at Autun was connected with trade, for this was the norm for rich Treveri away from home. Another *sevir* from Trier, resident at Lyon, was a freedman, very likely also connected with the trading corporations (the inscription is broken). A freedman origin for the family of Quigo cannot thus be ruled out.[16]

The members and patrons of the corporations who do not mention any municipal offices raise questions of status. The infrequency of such mentions might indicate that the ordinary members were of lower rank than decurions and, *a fortiori*, than magistrates. If, however, decurial status was often passed over in silence, no conclusions can be drawn. The Treveran decurion C. Apronius Raptor, member and later patron of the *nautae Ararici*, patron also of the wine merchants of Lyon, can then be seen as the norm rather than the exception, an indication also that members and patrons were not from entirely different social levels.[17] Corporations themselves varied in status, and it is highly unlikely that the Treveran M. Sennius Metilius, member and prefect of the highly distinguished *corpus splendidissimum Cisalpinorum et Transalpinorum* did not rank with a magistrate of the Treveri (if indeed he had not been one). Sex. Vervicius Eutyches, a mere *vestiarius* (perhaps of freedman origin), was not comparable, yet to judge from other careers, there was no absolute bar against his family rising to higher levels. The corporations seem to provide exactly such opportunities, and their close connection with the municipal aristocracy can be as well argued as their separation, the more easily since they do not seem to be wholly separate in Italy.[18]

Status and wealth, while connected, were not the same thing. A freedman or decurion could be as wealthy as a magistrate, *sacerdos* or even knight. Outside patronage was clearly required for the latter honour, to which few attained. The extent to which the *sacerdotes* and magistrates differed in either wealth or status from the upper ranks of the traders and *corporati* is doubtful: at the very least, passage from one to the other was certainly possible, even if individual careers including both are not frequent.

2   Monuments and Romanization

Various criteria can be used to establish an index of Romanity, whether for regions, cities, rural sites or individuals. Among the materials that lend themselves to such study are the stone monuments – statues, reliefs and inscriptions. Though catalogues inevitably lag behind the actual state of discoveries, they allow for quantification and comparisons between different cities and regions. Carving and inscribing stone was unusual before the conquest, and almost unknown in the north: it is essentially a Roman introduction. The first stone–cutters and sculptors came north from the Po valley or Narbonensis during Augustus' reign. In the Julio-Claudian period workshops were well established in the Rhineland, supplying monuments for the army and occasionally for civilians. The Mainz workshops were particularly ready to take up commissions in the hinterland; early military grave monuments and togate statues among the Treveri, statues of deities from Sommerécourt and Naix among the Leuci betray their hands or at least influence. In the course of the second century we then find local or regional workshops with their own traditions, some derived from the Rhineland, some showing influences from the Hellenistic world, some tapping indigenous sources.[19]

The steady trickle of first-century monuments later became a regular stream, broadening out noticeably after about AD 150. Dating of individual monuments is, with rare exceptions, at best approximate, though a reasonable relative chronology can often be worked out. Few Belgic Gauls saw the need to add consular dates to inscriptions; those that did were clearly influenced by the neighbouring Germanies, where dates are much more frequent and can provide pegs for styles of lettering or carving. The vast majority of datable monuments from the Germanies falls into the period between 140 and 260, and it is safe to suppose the same for Belgica. This is certainly the period which emerges as predominant whenever regional studies are undertaken.[20] If the period from Augustus to 260 be divided roughly in two, three-quarters of the monuments belong to the second half. Moreover the end of the monuments is an abrupt one. A curve illustrating the adoption of the custom would show a long flattish period at the start, a steepening rise from the mid-second century and little if any flattening out before a steep drop in the third quarter of the third century.

The general geographical distribution of monuments is also uneven. Among the Gauls, Belgica is second only to Narbonensis in overall density of monuments, while remaining below Germania Superior and the southern part of Inferior. Within the province itself, about three-quarters of all monuments come from the three eastern *civitates* Leuci, Mediomatrici and Treveri (in ascending order). It is natural to connect this general phenomenon, like the narrower one of dated inscriptions being mostly among the Treveri, with the proximity of the army.

Various sources of bias may of course have affected both the number of monuments that were erected and the number that have been preserved. These include the availability of stone (especially sandstone, which does not fall victim to the lime-kiln), and the presence of an established antiquarian tradition – though areas without it, such as the Monts Faucilles, have nonetheless preserved monuments, despite attempts by local priests to destroy anything that might be construed as heathen (a custom not confined to rural areas). Naturally large-scale excavations in Trier and Metz have produced many stones at one fell swoop, as have late Roman fortifications where the foundations were of reused monuments. Bias due to such accidents of research

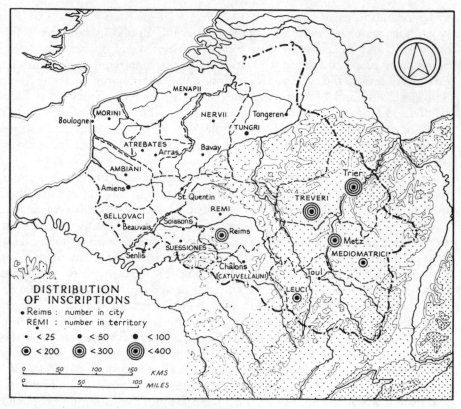

24 Map of Belgica showing distribution of inscriptions

is thus most likely to occur in urban centres, and it is there too that ancient monuments most risked re-use in medieval buildings. Yet the number of monuments often (though not invariably) corresponds with other criteria for the development of a city – no one would ever doubt that Trier was more urbanized and had more monuments than Toul. In short, it seems reasonable to conclude that the record of monuments as we have it is not so far from being a representative selection as to render it unusable, especially if analysis concentrates on the larger bodies of material. Significantly, inscriptions cluster in or near cities or major *vici*, along roads and, to a lesser extent, rivers.

Analysis of the distribution in cities, roadside *vici* and the rural hinterland shows that patterns of use might vary strikingly from one *civitas* to another. This is best illustrated by Remi and Leuci. The Remi have produced more inscriptions than reliefs, and they are strongly concentrated in the capital at the expense of *vici* and countryside. With the Leuci, the rural hinterland dominates in every category except that of funerary reliefs. Toul, though the capital, makes a poor showing; here, the monuments only confirm the other evidence for the failure of the Leuci to develop a strongly urbanized *civitas*-centre. Since

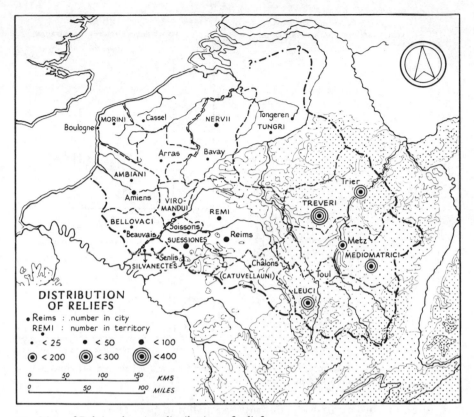

25 Map of Belgica showing distribution of reliefs

urbanization is one aspect of Romanization, the Leuci were, in this respect, less Romanized than the Remi. Among the latter, the status of the city as an early provincial capital must have emphasized the urban centre as the place for monuments (especially inscriptions). Among the Mediomatrici and Treveri inscriptions are also strongly clustered in the city; reliefs are less so, and here the Mediomatrican countryside predominates over the city. The Treveran picture is obscured by the difficulty of knowing how many Neumagen monuments came from Trier: the higher the proportion from Trier, the more the city predominates. The rural hinterland of Trier has also produced a goodly crop of inscriptions and reliefs, the former clustered to the south, west and north of the city. The rural inscriptions of the Mediomatrici are mostly well east of Metz, in the Sarre valley and the passes which lead from there through to the Rhine.

Elsewhere, the numbers of monuments are smaller, but the same patterns can be detected. The Suessiones had a scatter in the countryside, nearly all in the Aisne valley along the main roads. Ambiani and Morini show more of an urban concentration, but among the latter this is not at Thérouanne but at Boulogne, and the doing of the fleet. The Tungri have inscriptions dispersed

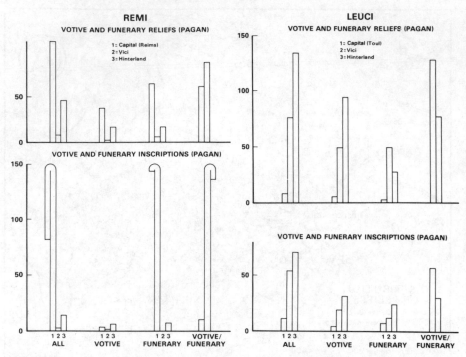

26 Analysis of the distribution of pagan votive and funerary reliefs and inscriptions amongst the Remi and Leuci

throughout the countryside, but only a small number. The comparative lack of monuments in this area is interesting in view of the other evidence both for wealth and for service in the army; very few of their tumuli have produced inscriptions. Perhaps some have disappeared and others were of wood, yet the lack of influence from the stone workshops of Köln or Bonn remains striking when contrasted with the situation south of Ardennes and Eifel. Weight should probably be given to the traditional origins of burial under tumulus, despite the architectural features (e.g. the ring-wall) which were undoubtedly introduced from outside.[21]

Varying levels of Romanity can be illustrated in another way. Along with strong urban centralization of monuments tends to go a higher proportion of inscriptions to reliefs and of funerary monuments to votive. This confirms what might be suspected, that the sculptured portrayal of a deity was the type of monument requiring least mental adaptation on the part of Gauls. Portrayal of deities in semi-anthropomorphic guise was not entirely strange to the traditions of Celtic art, and there was no need to commit the deity's name to writing. Not surprisingly, the rural areas also showed a penchant for the funerary relief without inscription, frequently in the form of the small house-shaped monuments that are so common in the Vosges foothills.[22] For long enough, writing and Latin alike may have been rare outside urban or military

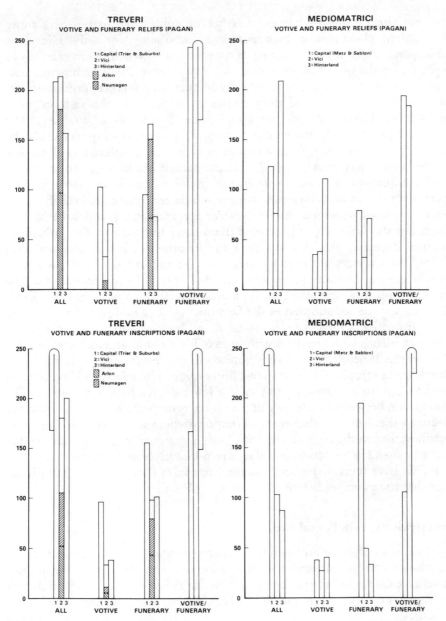

27 Analysis of the distribution of pagan votive and funerary reliefs and inscriptions amongst the Treveri and Mediomatrici centres. The writing of names, whether of deities or mortals, is a more Romanized phenomenon than portrayal, involving not only a level of education but also the overcoming of superstitions. Two different reasons can be given for the spread of inscriptions into rural areas. The attachment of the Gallic aristocrats to their rural base meant that they were as prone to erect monuments in the area of their estates as in the city: the fashion, once introduced, filtered down the social scale in the usual manner. The involvement of people further down the scale with army supplies can also be adduced; this seems the likeliest explanation for the proliferation of modest inscriptions as well as reliefs in the eastern part of Mediomatrican territory.

If comparison is made with Britain or the Danubian provinces, the overwhelming impression is the extent to which inscriptions and reliefs were a normal part of provincial life.[23] Neither the mentalities which demanded them nor the skills which produced them were limited to a few urbanized centres. If greater precision in dating can be attained, it will be possible to follow the chapters in the story more closely, and see just how quickly or slowly the use of Latin for inscriptions did spread in the hinterland. The uneven spread of monuments in Romanized style remains to be considered. That they were not adopted in the far north need cause little surprise, quite apart from the comparative rarity of stone. Interestingly, there is a rough correspondence between the distribution of inscriptions and mosaics. In some *civitates* the fit between the two is noteworthy, Treveri and Suessiones being the clearest examples. Ambiani have, however, produced a sprinkling of rural mosaics but no inscriptions, and so to a lesser degree have the Tungri. The connection between the density of monuments in the eastern *civitates* and the route to the army is reinforced. Perhaps nowhere is this connection more manifest than in the inscriptions and reliefs (some pretentious, most not) that are to be found in the Monts Faucilles, a remote and uninviting area that would certainly have remained apart from the currents of Romanization but for the fact that the portages between Saône and Moselle ran through it.

3 Inscriptions, reliefs and society

Studied as a corpus of archaeological material, inscriptions and reliefs allow conclusions on the pattern of Romanization. Taken separately, the inscriptions give names and the reliefs show how the Belgic Gauls thought it proper to represent their deities or themselves. From both, further conclusions emerge.

The inscriptions of Belgic Gaul do not provide any families like the one from Saintes which shows four generations from Epotsorovidus to C. Julius Rufus. But nomenclature does run the gamut from fully Romanized style (C. Julius Primus, C. Apronius Raptor) to peregrine names that would be barbarous tongue-twisters to any Roman (Cletussto, Bloturix or Carathounnus, the latter variously spelled).[24]

The simplest way of analyzing Romanity is to distinguish individuals with the full Roman *tria nomina* (*praenomen*, *nomen* and *cognomen*) from those possessing *nomen* and *cognomen* only and from the large group that have a single name. That there are variations from one *civitas* to another is not surprising. The Treveri, with 25 per cent *tria nomina*, have the most Romanized nomenclature in the province. The Mediomatrici actually have proportionally fewer (nine per cent) than Nervii, Morini and Ambiani, the probable explanation being that the habit of inscriptions was in the latter *civitates* confined to a smaller range of people. The Remi, with only 1.5 per cent, have a strikingly low proportion; this could be an accidental result of the particular cemeteries discovered there.

In all except Leuci and Suessiones, the most Romanized form of name is concentrated in the city. Examples from the rural hinterland record the land-owning classes on their estates. Any idea that the Romanized names belong largely to incomers is not borne out. A few strangers can be readily detected – a procurator at Trier, soldiers at Norroy – because they mention their profession. Others, with good Italian names, may not be Gauls (especially if they mention a tribe). But the majority are natives, or immigrants at most from other parts of Gaul. Names starting Ti. Attius or T. Ianuarius end up with Andecarus or Tasgillus for *cognomen*, and many *nomina* turn out to be only superficially Romanized – Solimarius, Dagissius, Teddiatius and their like are found in both urban and rural areas.[25] On a minimum estimate, over a third of the Treveran *tria nomina* must belong to natives and the majority of the others contain elements frequently found in Gaul.

The Treveri stand out even more clearly in the second category of names, double names without *praenomen*. Forming 35 per cent of the total body analyzed, they are the largest category in the *civitas*. Only the Tungri, with some 25 per cent, come close, the Mediomatrici having only 15 per cent. Dropping of the *praenomen* increasingly crept into inscriptions, so that by the second century even soldiers used the shortened form (as at Trier and Boulogne).[26] But while there are many neutral elements, examination shows that most double names must be of Gallo-Romans, since frequently at least one part of the name is non-Roman. Among the Treveri forms like Urissulius Campanus, Camulissius Aprilis, Cattonius Secundinus, Indutius Veriugus Excingonius Secundus, Blussinius Sennaugus, Secundius Ibliomarus leave no doubt. Four freedmen of unknown origin adopted names of this style from their patrons, and would be indistinguishable had they not mentioned their status.

The Mediomatrici have more neutral names, e.g. Genialis Saturninus, but also offer Capellinius Caprasus and Benignius Tasgillus, while the Tungri produce Velugnius Ingenuus. The Treveri were, however, the specialists in what is called the pseudo-*gentilicium*, or *nomen* made up from a native root but given the Roman -*ius* ending. That this form of name remained only semi-Romanized is shown by its failure to be handed on to subsequent generations

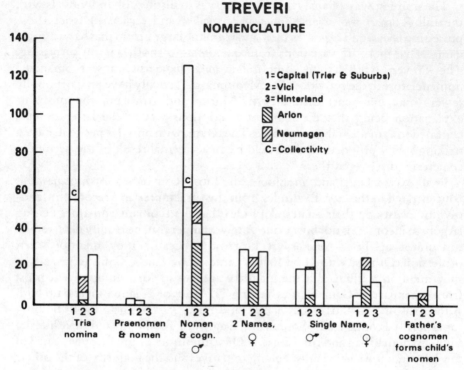

28 Analysis of nomenclature amongst the Treveri

in Roman manner. Rather, a son or daughter forms a new pseudo-*nomen* out of his father's *cognomen*; the double name is thus a superficially Romanized version of the single name with patronymic which was normal to the Gauls. The son of Camulissius Aprilis is Aprilius Iustinus, of Catulius Martialis, Martialius...., of Censorinius Andecarus, Andecarius Nocturnus. This habit is also found with some *tria nomina* – L. Senilius Sacratus' son was L. Sacratius Sacerianus; M. Restonius Restitutus' children were Restitutius Aurorianus and Restitutia Auroriana.

The custom of forming a new *nomen* with each generation was not confined to the Treveri, as isolated examples elsewhere make clear. A Veliocassian trader, Placidus son of Viducus, is probably the same man as M. Viducius Placidus, having meantime gained citizenship as a result of the Antonine Edict. The Tungran legionary Victorius Victorinus had a stay-at-home brother Acceptus, son of Victor.[27] Whether the double name invariably or even usually denotes Roman or Latin status is however a complex question. Numerous Treveri had only a single name of peregrine type, yet arguably there are too many examples of the double name for it to be the sole prerogative of magistrates or even decurions. Moreover, while the majority of such names are in the city, they have a wider spread, and are particularly frequent at Arlon. This suggests that it was primarily a fashion, indicative of aspirations to Romanize without total loss of tradition. The Mediomatrici meanwhile developed their own style, which included besides 'neutral' Roman names considerable use of the imperial *nomina*. That not all were descendants of men enfranchized by Caesar and Augustus is suggested by the variety of *praenomina* and by ladies named Julia married to a Matto or Miccio; some Belgic Gauls used the name Julius just like any other.[28] In the same freehanded way Marcus or Sextus might be used as names, not *praenomina*.

Although any single instance is ambiguous, there are many indications that the Gauls were careless over the forms of nomenclature. Often they abbreviate on inscriptions. The son of Julius Victor is given as Florentinus, but was presumably Julius Florentinus. That conclusions from names like Aquinius, which strictly ought to indicate origin in the Italian city Aquinum, cannot safely be drawn is made clear by Urissulius Campanus, whose son would be Campanius. Geographical names, along with others from months (Januarius, Aprilis), seasons (Aestivus) or numbers (derivatives of Secundus are the commonest) seem to have formed components of a general provincial

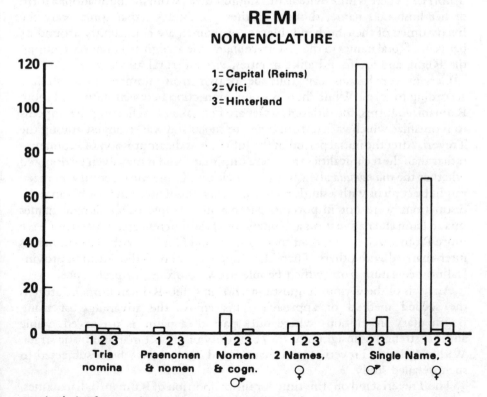

REMI
NOMENCLATURE

1 = Capital (Reims)
2 = Vici
3 = Hinterland

29 Analysis of nomenclature amongst the Remi

mixture. Individual names can always pose unanswerable questions: was Atilius Regulus at Arlon the result of school-room classics?[29]

The single name remained the norm for the vast majority of the recorded population: only among the Treveri are they less frequent than others, while their predominance among Mediomatrici (despite colonial status), Leuci and Remi is overwhelming. Strictly, these names are proper to peregrines, and provincials could legitimately adopt more Romanized forms after the early third-century Antonine Edict. The difficulty in dating individual inscriptions is a hindrance. But the evidence does not suggest that everyone imitated M. Viducius Placidus. There is no reason why the years following the Antonine Edict should be more poorly represented among Mediomatrici than among Treveri, though the possible bias introduced into the urban record by the huge but not rich southern cemetery of Metz-Sablon requires further research.

The majority of women mentioned on inscriptions also have single names, regardless of area. Evidence does not suffice to show whether the second name, when it exists, was given haphazardly or whether one derived from the mother's name might be added to one derived from the father's. Occasionally part or all of a woman's name is given a masculine form – Iulinia Popillus, Senorix.[30] There is little evidence to suggest that a woman might adopt a form of her husband's name, though another possibility is that some were the freedwomen of their husband. Names of women are consistently around 25 per cent of total names in the eastern *civitates*, rise as high as 35 per cent among the Remi, and are found alike in cities, *vici* and rural areas.

Certain conclusions can thus be drawn from nomenclature studied according to form. While there is some connection between status and more Romanized forms, the different styles are best taken as reflecting the impetus to Romanize which varied from *civitas* to *civitas* and was strongest among the Treveri. After the initial period of the Julii, it was the impression of Romanity rather than the technicalities that were important, and it may even be doubted whether the *tria nomina* always denote a citizen. In the third century a citizen might be content with a single name, whether out of ignorance or because the distinctions were not important. Meanwhile, people using double names mixed Latin and native roots as if unaware of the difference; sons need not have more Romanized names than their fathers, and families with Roman names inter-married with others. There developed a pool of Gallo-Roman provincial nomenclature from which people drew according to preference.

Analysis of the various linguistic strands in Gallo-Roman nomenclature is the second method of approach. This enjoys the advantage of using fragmentary inscriptions where only part of a name is preserved, while another strength is insight into the continuity of pre-Roman linguistic strata. Within Belgica, Treveri, Mediomatrici and Tungri have been subjected to such detailed study.[31]

The Treveri stand out this time for the proportion of Roman/Italian names, which averages 63 per cent throughout the *civitas*, rising to 72 per cent in the

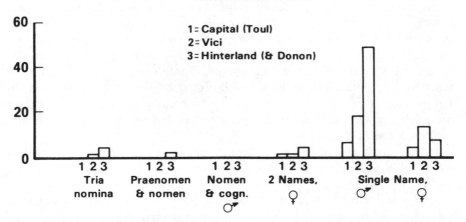

MEDIOMATRICI
NOMENCLATURE

1 = Capital (Metz & Sablon)
2 = Vici
3 = Hinterland

▨ Soldiers at Norroy Quarries

LEUCI
NOMENCLATURE

1 = Capital (Toul)
2 = Vici
3 = Hinterland (& Donon)

30 Analysis of nomenclature amongst the Leuci and Mediomatrici

city. Despite their penchant for imperial *nomina*, the Mediomatrici end up with only 50 per cent of their components Roman, as do the Tungri. With 33 per cent the Mediomatrici emerge as strongest on Celtic components, the Treveri having only 16.5 per cent (highest density in rural areas) and the Tungri 11.5 per cent. The last have about 17 per cent Germanic names, the Treveri barely two per cent. All have many (between 15 per cent and 20 per cent) names which appear to be neither Roman, Celtic nor Germanic, some of which can be reasonably attributed to a pre-Celtic stratum.

Any simple division into Roman and non-Roman elements, however, tends to overestimate Romanization. Analysis of components rather than of whole names copes poorly with double names which mix the linguistic elements. Moreover, many of the elements classified (on linguistic grounds) as Roman are, on closer examination, part of the Gallo-Roman general provincial stock. Some names, like Iullus, can be either Roman or Celtic, which may explain the frequent use of Julius as an ordinary name. Others are so close to Celtic words that their popularity is to be so explained – the root *marco*- (a horse) probably lies behind not only Marcus but also Marcellus and others, just as Marius and derivatives are to be seen in the light of *maro*- (great), found in less Romanized names such as Ibliomarus. The suffix *-inius* was close to a Celtic one and led to derivations like Auctinius, Saturninius (which linguistically are Roman) as well as Cattinius or Camulinius (classifiable as Celtic). Names in *Ursus*, particularly prevalent among the Treveri, are translations of native names in *Arto*-, a bear. Local fashions can be spotted, including the use of names from names of the months among the Mediomatrici. While using Latin forms, they are as much a genuinely provincial development as the Latinizing of Celtic names or Celtic patronymics. Attention thus directed, the impression gained can be very different.

No less interesting are the purely Celtic names. A whole range of 'speaking' names can be perceived, with references not only to battle (Cingetius), strength (Nerta) and power (Ollognatus) but also to animals (Biber, a beaver) and deities (Esunertus). Composite names with heroic implications did not altogether die out – Bloturix, Dagomarus, Donnomarcus, Magiorix. Persistence of the Celtic language is thus well illustrated.[32] Yet the names take on Latin inflections, the continued use of names does not necessarily imply regular use of the spoken tongue, and the degree of Romanization involved in any inscription must not be underestimated.

Ideally, analysis of provincial nomenclature requires to be more subtle than either of the simple approaches. It should also be borne in mind that knowledge is limited to a tiny proportion of the population – arguably some 0.1 per cent, even of the Treveri. If what has been preserved represents between one tenth and one hundredth of the original material, between one per cent and ten per cent of the overall population were ever mentioned on inscriptions.

Just as general relationships can be seen between nomenclature and status, so there are rough correspondences between types of sculptured monument, wealth and social status. Variations in wealth are most easily followed in the funerary monuments, though it is clear that marble statues adorning a rural shrine (as at le Châtelet, between Leuci and Catalauni) mark the commission of a rich landowner. A tombstone in the form of a large altar was judged suitable for Julius Classicianus when he died at London in the reign of Nero. The so-called *testamentum Lingonis*, describing in detail the memorial arrangements which a certain Julius wanted, shows that an altar might be only a part of a more elaborate scheme, set in an orchard with an artificial pool. Such ramifications were suited to the spacious country estate. In the more crowded cemeteries of Lyon, a simple altar, smaller than that of Classicianus, continued to be the norm even for the wealthy. From Neumagen come much more elaborate altars, giving way in the course of the second century to the sculptured 'pillar' monument incorporating architectural features – a version of the military officer's tombstone mixed with ideas coming from other parts of the Empire. The culmination is the multi-storeyed sculptured Igel column, still standing 30 m high from stepped base to the Jupiter-and-Ganymede group which crowns the steep roof.[33]

Because of the geographical bias discussed above, it is only in the eastern *civitates* that we frequently see the defunct portrayed. Generally there is a solemn group with the head of the family in toga if he possessed the citizenship, otherwise in the long-sleeved Gallic tunic-coat. The surrounding scenes may refer either to mythology or to daily life, and both can be found together, as at Igel. Reference is made to leisure (hunting, the circus) and often to activities which increased wealth – baled cloth, amphorae, barrels, the tilling of the soil and the sale of its produce. The mythological scenes sometimes (as at Igel) have a clear reference to hopes for an after-life, the portrayal of daily life is an equivalent for the burial of objects to ensure wealth in the hereafter. Some men specify themsleves as *negotiatores*, one or two from Neumagen were *seviri Augustales* of Trier, but no mention of decurions or magistrates is found on surviving monuments of this type.

The one certain grave of a decurion, the Tungrian Vitorius Caupius, took the form of a tumulus in the Ardennes. His was not even one of the bigger: the huge tumuli along the Bavay-Köln road contain an amazing assortment of precious items including carved amber and rock-crystal, gold jewellery, knife-handles of jet and gold – in addition to pottery, glass and bronze vessels. A few have produced the *parazonia* or ornamental daggers of military officers. Other alternatives open to the rich were funerary chapels such as those known from the slopes above the Mosel, or a revival of chariot-burial. Tumuli and chapels could better adapt to the new custom of inhumation that spread from the Mediterranean in the course of the second and third centuries and occasioned carved sarcophagi, some in marble.[34]

The element of display, after death as in life, was of course important. There is no indication that one type would be favoured by people from the status of decurion upwards, another by those who, while wealthy, were of lower social standing. Probably more depended on regional tastes and the availability of skills. Nonetheless, the showy type of sculptured monument might well have a special appeal to the *negotiator* who was not a decurion, while the tumulus might best typify tradition and the stability of rural roots. The foundations for a sculptured monument beside the modest villa of Newel show that such memorials were not always accompanied by other blatant forms of wealth. This was a curiosity in its own context, being surrounded by simple tumuli, less obviously wealthy than the tumulus of Berlingen (Limburg), which was also connected with a villa but contained compasses, pen and ruler to suggest an occupant who was also a surveyor or architect.[35]

Perhaps the most striking feature of the sculptured monuments is not that elaborate ones were commissioned by the wealthy but that the custom spread well below the summit of the social pyramid. There is no abrupt transition in type. The monuments of the western Treveri (many stemming from the later walls of Arlon and Buzenol) include some that differ from those of Neumagen only in a few details, in the absence of the toga, and in their smaller size, appropriate to a minor aristocracy. Below the scaled-down Igel 'column' we find simpler monuments where the emphasis is on the couple or family in the central niche. These, with variations, are typical for larger *vici* (e.g. Scarpone, Soulosse) but can be found also in the countryside and in *civitas* capitals (Metz and Reims). Often there is no hint of a specific occupation, and if the man holds a purse or a set of tablets this merely refers to his well-being: these people could be small landowners. Occasionally this is made specific, as by the side-scenes of hoeing and fruit-selling on a small pillar at Arlon.

Frequently, however, a trade or profession is shown, and we find that clothiers, carriage-makers, coopers, blacksmiths, pottery-sellers, veterinarians and perhaps bakers erected modest monuments.[36] This does not necessarily mean that the people were simply artisans, for they could be the owners of small businesses, employing others even if also plying their trade themselves. Nor does it mean that all successful artisans or small landowners were at all periods able to erect monuments. Not only does the evidence suggest that most are later than the mid-second century, but it is quite consistent with intermittent bursts of activity rather than permanently established workshops. Moreover, many villages seem barely to have been touched by the habit, but continued to bury their dead in traditional fashion, in ditched enclosures (the poor man's tumulus) or at most with temporary markers.[37]

Further down the social scale are monuments with roughly carved busts, those with a simple rough inscription or the house-shaped monuments. The last are particularly common in the Vosges, where they usually have steep gabled roofs and small doors indicated. A rather finer type found among the Treveri has a semi-cylindrical top and perhaps depicts a chest rather than a house.[38] Simple busts are found everywhere, inscriptions are more frequent in the cities and villages but still occur surprisingly often in the hinterland. Here it looks as if we are dealing with peasants and poorer artisans who were themselves also peasants. *Grosso modo* there is a correspondence between these simpler monuments and the single names, often of Celtic or at least non-Roman type. Yet while a Vosges peasant can be imagined carving a plain monument out of soft red sandstone during the winter months, it must be asked just how far down the social scale the stones finally reached. To substantial independent peasants, yes, to the poor dependent workers or clients on some villa estate, no. Access to stone and to skills, also exposure to the army and to passing foreigners all contributed. It must again be remembered that the stone funerary monuments reflect only a small percentage of the population (perhaps some five per cent for the best represented areas). Over a large area of the province the visible means of indicating the status of the dead remain unknown. Nonetheless, the passage of time changed the distinction between those whose tombs were clearly marked out and those who had no such distinction. In the first century, the dividing line lay between what might be termed the 'officer class' and those below. By the late second century, most people of independent status were at least potentially above it, and this socio-economic change is one part of what is usually called Romanization.

4 Religious aspects of Romanization

Inscriptions and reliefs also provide a corpus of material for the study of Gallo-Roman deities. Since they not infrequently offer names and attributes that are manifestly non-Roman, they lead straight into a very disputed territory – the identity and function of the native deities named or portrayed. The Romans themselves were not troubled by such questions. By a process described by Tacitus as 'interpretatio Romana' they assumed correspondence with the nearest Roman equivalent. Thus Caesar tells us that the Gauls worshipped above all Mercury, as inventor of the arts, traveller's guide and helper in commercial transactions. Next came Apollo, Mars, Jupiter and Minerva, deities connected with healing, war, the sky and the teaching of crafts. Dispater, god of the underworld, was a mythical ancestor. Later Romans might have concurred, for on the monuments Mercury does indeed emerge as the most popular Gallo-Roman deity, followed by Apollo. Though Mars and Minerva are rarer, representations of Jupiter do not always correspond with Roman ideas and there were gods or divinized heroes not mentioned by Caesar. This did not imply the wholesale adoption of foreign gods but rather a process of assimilation, never quite complete. Effectively, the equivalence of Roman deities was largely adopted by the Gallo-Romans themselves, certainly by those of them that erected monuments. Two Viromanduans serving in the Praetorian Guard at Rome could describe their homeland gods as Jupiter, Apollo, Mercury, Diana, Hercules and Mars.[39]

Reliefs showing deities not fully Romanized give hints of Gaulish myths or folk tales. These do not allow a single convincing interpretation, nor is it certain that standard versions ever existed. That the stories involved gods, heroes and animals, that humans or gods could be transmogrified into beasts (e.g. the three birds of certain reliefs) and that there was a connection with seasonal festivals is likely.[40] Dilution of mythology and customs was inevitable under Roman rule, even if the ubiquity of the aristocratic Druidic priesthood can be debated. Influence from Roman concepts was also natural, and the exact relationship between names, art-forms and underlying concepts must often remain mysterious. Lack of a precise fit between Roman and Gaulish deities is often clear: modern scholars studying the monuments have as much trouble as ancient scholiasts (glossing a line of the poet Lucan) in deciding whether Esus and Teutates were respectively Mercury and Mars or the other way round.[41] Gaulish gods often had more than one aspect: their functions were less clear-cut than those of the Graeco-Roman pantheon, and they were more localized. Yet no striking differences between the Belgae and other Gauls show up, though among the northern Tungri links with the lower Rhineland can be detected.

An effort to relate inscriptions and reliefs to the few written texts is natural, if fruitful only to a certain point. Archaeological evidence for religious beliefs and practices also includes a range of symbolic or votive objects, figurines in bronze and terracotta and of course the various shrines and temples in which the gods were honoured. Various levels of Romanity are easy to distinguish. The loss of so many wooden statues (preserved only in exceptional circumstances such as the springs at Luxueil) is unfortunate, since those that remain are on average less Romanized in art-form than stone representations. Bronzes, even when crudely made, predominantly show Roman deities, and exceptions are still Roman in art-form.[42] Even terracotta statuettes often depict deities in a Graeco-Roman guise – Mars, Minerva, Cybele with her crown and lions. Common to both wood and terracotta are portrayals of small men in hooded cloaks, clearly a Gaulish figure, yet in the terracotta versions often clutching the scroll of Greek Telesphorus.[43] Also common in terracotta are standing or seated mother goddesses with swaddled or suckling infants, without parallel in the official Roman pantheon. Religion at grass roots level is however best glimpsed through the much later Christian writers who denounce various superstitious practices. Attention to the whole gamut of evidence – including the bones from sacrifices and their disposal – within an excavated context will also prove valuable: all too often the more obvious classes of object are studied in isolation.

Bias in the inscriptions and reliefs has been discussed. Nonetheless, they remain the richest and most tractable body of material. Insight into the less Romanized strata of beliefs is more readily attained from reliefs than from inscriptions. A stone of first-century date at Trier shows on the side a wood-chopper attacking a tree in which are a bull's head and three large birds. Comparison with an inscribed stone from Paris shows that this figure is Esus, the bull Tarvos Trigaranus. The front face shows a nude Mercury, Roman in character apart from the torc around his neck and a female consort at his side; the simple inscription mentions Mercury only.[44] The style suggests a craftsman from one of the Rhineland military workshops producing a commissioned piece with a deliberate conflation of elements. Other products of this period of experimentation include the male and female deities, sculpted

1 View of the Argonne *(chapter 1.1)*

2 Aerial view of Bray-les-Mareuil (Somme).
The outline of a large, isolated farm *(aedificium)*
is revealed, dated to the end of Gaulish
independence (Photo courtesy Roger Agache)
(chapter 1.4)

3 An aerial view of Conchil-le-Temple (Pas-de-Calais). The circles are Bronze Age funerary and ritual enclosures; the rectangles represent an Iron Age habitation (Photo courtesy Roger Agache) *(chapter 1.4)*

Coins (Photos courtesy Royal Ontario Museum, Toronto) *(chapters 1.5 and 2.4)* Various scales; diameters indicated

4 Gold quarter-stater, Hunsrück/Saarland region ('early Treveri'). Mid to late second century BC (13.1 mm)
a Obverse: laureate head of Apollo
b Reverse: man-headed horse

5 Gold quarter-stater, middle Rhineland. Later second century BC (15.8 mm)
a Obverse: head of Apollo
b Reverse: Pegasus

6 Gold quarter-stater of the Ambiani ('Gallo-Belgic AB2'). Late second–early first century BC (13.6 mm)
a Obverse: laureate head of Apollo
b Reverse: horse

7 Gold stater of the Ambiani ('Gallo-Belgic C'). *c.* 90–60 BC (17.7 mm)
a Obverse: laureate head of Apollo to right
b Reverse: disjointed horse

8 Gold uniface stater of the Ambiani ('Gallo-Belgic E'). *c.* 90–55 BC (18.5 mm)
a Obverse: plain
b Reverse: disjointed horse

9 Gold stater of the Treveri. *c.* 75–55 BC (18.2 mm)
a Obverse: 'eye' pattern
b Reverse: horse

10 Cast potin coin of the Remi. *c.* 50–20 BC (?) (21.3 mm)
a Obverse: man with spear and torc
b Reverse: 'elephant'

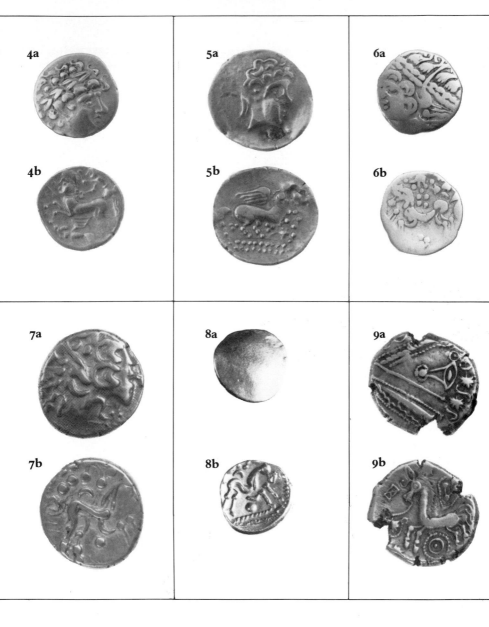

4a

4b

5a

5b

6a

6b

7a

7b

8a

8b

9a

9b

10a

10b

16 The amphitheatre, Grand *(chapter 4.2)*

17 Vermand, the site of a Celtic *oppidum* and later Roman town *(chapter 4.4)*

18 Hypocaust, Viel–Evreux *(chapter 4.4)*

19 The remains of a villa at Bollendorf *(chapter 5.2)*

20 Hunsrück grabgarten with barrow on the left *(chapter 5.5)*

21 *Mardelle* in the Vosges *(chapter 5.3)*

22 Gate post in the Vosges *(chapter 5.3)*

23 & 24 Two funerary monuments, both from Soulosse, show markedly different levels of adaptation of Roman styles (Musée d'Archéologie Gallo–Romain, Metz) *(chaper 6.1)*

25 Kiln, Marilles *(chapter 6.2)*

26 Sculpture showing a vegetable shop (top) and farm labourers (bottom) (Musée Luxembourgeois, Arlon) *(chapter 6.3)*

OPPOSITE ABOVE
27 Rural trackway in the Vosges *(chapter 6.4)*

OPPOSITE CENTRE
28 Marble sarcophagus of a young man depicting a lion hunt (Musée St Rémy, Reims) *(chapter 7.3)*

OPPOSITE
29 Tumulus under a grove of trees, Tienen *(chapter 7.3)*

30 Funerary monument to Caratulla, daughter of Satto from Scarponna, in the shape of a house (Musée d'Archéologie Gallo-Romain, Metz) *(chapter 7.3)*

31 Tools of the family trade are depicted on this funerary monument to Carianus, son of Bellianus and Felix, son of Carianus, from parents Bellianus son of Bondillus and Augusta, daughter of Crobus (Musée d'Archéologie Gallo-Romain, Metz) *(chapter 7.3)*

32 Dedication to the bear-goddess Artio carved on rock in the countryside near Bollendorf *(chapter 7.4)*

34 Limestone group of Jupiter riding over fish-tailed giant (Musée d'Epinal) *(chapter 7.4)*

33 Sculpture showing a bearded tricephalic god, probably Mercury, depicted with a cock and a ram (Musée St Léger, Soisson) *(chapter 7.4)*

35 Sculpture depicting Apollo, Cernunnos and
Mercury: a mixture of Gaulish and Roman
beliefs and art forms (Musée St Rémy, Reims)
(chapter 7.4)

36 Statuette of Intarabus in bronze (Photo
courtesy Musée Luxembourgeois, Arlon)
(chapter 7.4)

37 Altar to Sucellos and Nantosuelta
(Musée de Sarrebourg) *(chapter 7.4)*

38 Sculpture depicting Epona, goddess of
horses (Musée d'Archéologie Gallo-Romain,
Metz) *(chapter 7.4)*

39 Late Roman city wall, Beauvais *(chapter 10.1)*

40 Late Roman city wall with tower, Senlis *(chapter 10.1)*

in the round, from Sommerécourt north of Langres. The draped, cross-legged god with torc had sockets in his head for antlers that may have been removable according to the season. Both the god and goddess are accompanied by ram-headed serpents, yet the goddess betrays Mediterranean influence by the pomegranate in her right hand. Another striking group is a mother-goddess from Naix, a grim wrinkled old woman with two smaller, younger attendants. All of these, despite their subjects, are markedly more Roman than the undatable little pillar-like bust from Euffigneix (Haute Marne), executed in a flat but decorative style that is wholly Celtic and died out without succession.[45]

Reliefs of second-century date tend to be more polished in style and blander in content. There are however a few exceptions. A cross-legged and once antlered figure appears at Reims, flanked by smaller figures of Mercury and Apollo; a small bull and stag drink from a stream of coins pouring from a money-bag on his lap. On a Tetelbierg relief the same elements are seen with a more Romanized genius-figure. Mercury and Apollo are conflated on another stone from Reims where Mercury holds a lyre and one figure has two heads, one bearded, the other unbearded. Ram-headed serpents accompany a Mercury at Beauvais. An attribute of Mercury, the cock, appears with the bearded triplicate heads that are found near Reims and Soissons, and the triple-head is connected with three mother-goddesses, Romanized as the Fates. A link can thus be traced not only between Mercury and Esus but between Mercury and the antlered god which the Paris pillar identifies with Cernunnos. Chthonic associations appear in the serpent and the Fates, and in Vosges folklore that sees the stag as presager of death.[46]

The late second and third centuries brought the emergence of styles that were more primitive, though indubitably based on Graeco-Roman norms. The sanctuary on the Donon, watershed of the northern Vosges, has produced a naked Hercules-like figure, a wolf-skin over his arm, and accompanied by a stag. A god with a sword is found both on the Donon and at Escles on the Saône-Moselle portage. Sometimes seen as a renaissance of pre-Roman cults and priesthoods, these phenomena rather reflect the ability of people lower down the social scale to commission stone monuments.[47]

Inscriptions clarify some issues and complicate others. Simpler criteria of Romanization can be applied, for a Celtic name (Bugius, Ouniorix or Icovellauna) is less Roman than Apollo Grannus or Lenus Mars and these in turn than simple Mars or Mercury. Yet the relief of Mercury–Esus from Trier reminds one that formal criteria may mislead.

Wholly native names and features are characteristic of both gods and goddesses, but especially the latter. Males include Sucellus, sometimes assimilated to Silvanus, whose name may refer to his attribute the mallet, and who is seen as a deity of the underworld or as connected with the cooper's trade.[48] Intarabus and Sinquas are woodland deities found among the Treveri and southern Tungri. Goddesses are very varied, including Arduinna of the

Ardennes (but Vosegus is male). Vercana is associated with springs at Wahlscheid and Bad Bertrich, and Sirona, often linked with Apollo, is another of this company, some of whom are portrayed with the attributes of Hygeia. Many other goddesses have no topographical connections but are rather providers, as shown by their fruit-baskets and by personification as Abundantia or Fortuna. Birth and death doubtless also fell within their domain.

Depiction in triplicate is rarer in Belgica than in the Germanies, as are the names Matres or Matronae; the Matronae Cantrusteihiae of Hoeylaert (near Brussels) are reminiscent of their Rhineland sisters. Two goddesses meriting mention are Nehalennia with her dog, who presided over the seafarers' sanctuaries at Domburg and Colijnsplaat, and Epona. The latter's name means horse, as Artio means bear; in Belgica she is usually shown mounted. Related by her baskets of fruit to the less specific mother-goddesses, she is frequently found in *vici* and her worship was carried to Rome by travellers or Gallic members of the imperial cavalry guard.[49]

Other goddesses are found mostly as consorts of male divinities. Rosmerta and Sirona, the consorts of Mercury and Apollo, are widespread, others more localized; Ancamna and Inciona, found with Mars near Trier, fall into this latter class along with Nantosuelta, who accompanies Sucellus at Sarrebourg. Association of a god with a goddess is a typical feature of the Gallo-Roman pantheon, occurring frequently with Mercury, Apollo and Mars. Mercury and Rosmerta are found together from an early date, as is shown by the relief at Trier; her name, thought to mean 'the great provider' shows her to have the characteristics of a mother goddess. The link between Sirona and Apollo is found only in monuments of the second and third century.[50] This development, with its hint of a new hierogamy, throws doubt on the usual assumption that Gallo-Roman religion was unable to generate new mythologies.

Characteristic of the central members of the Gallo-Roman pantheon is the addition of a native name to the Roman one, to give Mercurius Visucius, Abgatiacus or Bigentius, Mars Cnabetius, Exsobinnus or Vegnius, Apollo Grannus. Many are again localized, so that Mercurius Clavariatis or Vassocaletis can be detected as strangers to Belgica. Lenus Mars was the chief god of the Treveri, honoured at his central shrine near Trier by the various *pagi*.[51] Mars Camulus was especially honoured by the Remi, Mars Segomo by the Sequani – part of the evidence that makes reasonable an identification of the Gallo-Roman Mars with the original Gaulish Teutates, whose name means god of the *tuath* (people). Mars is however very rare among the Mediomatrici, where the local Teutates was probably Romanized as Mercury.

Some Celtic surnames appear to be descriptive labels of a deity's function; the clearest is Jovantucarus, 'caring for (or dear to) the young', applied to Mars near Trier and Mercury near Tholey. While the functions of Gallo-Roman deities may have become more specific under Roman influence, they were never wholly precise, nor did they correspond exactly to their Roman counterparts. Healing was a primary function of Apollo (often associated with medicinal springs) but also of Lenus Mars, while a striking relief from Montiers-sur-Saulx attributes healing to a goddess.[52] Mercury, it has been seen, had many aspects. The art-forms do not allow a distinction between identification and mere association – perhaps reflecting a real lack of clarity.

Jupiter well illustrates the complex phenomena of assimilation. Inscriptions make it clear that he was the counterpart of Taranis, mentioned along with Esus and Teutates by the scholiasts on Lucan. In Belgica he has no native surnames, but is sometimes shown with the wheel rather than the thunder-bolt.[53] A clear connection also exists between Jupiter and the rider-god who crowns a column above a base depicting various divinities, usually rather Romanized. Inscriptions, when they occur, are to Jupiter, and since he does not figure on the bases he is most probably identified as the rider himself (who was sometimes replaced by a sitting Jupiter). The god is usually shown riding over (or supported by) a fish-tailed giant, and the dualism between sky and earth appears to be expressed. Both Roman and Celtic roots are attested for the idea of the column. Imperial iconography, perhaps also Mithraic, was incorporated into the riding figure, the finest examples of which are highly dramatic and forceful.[54]

When Jupiter appears with Juno and Minerva as one member of a small marble Capitoline Triad at Trier, it is reasonable to see a genuine importation of a Roman deity, an expression of Romanity and urbanism. Asclepius was introduced to Trier in spite of the healing functions already performed by Lenus Mars. Other exotic deities are Mithras, Isis and Cybele. The clustering of Mithraic finds along the Rhône-Saône-Mosel axis suggests that travellers, including traders, were as much responsible as the army. Three of the six Mithraea (Schwarzerden, Saarbrücken and Trier) lie near to the great trunk route, while those of Mackwiller and Angleur are close to Upper and Lower Germany respectively, that of Sarrebourg on another road to the Rhine army. The highly specialized ritual, appealing to those who combined a sense of social hierarchy with a need for salvation, did not keep Mithras apart from Gallo-Roman deities. He might share a precinct with them, or be associated with the Sun and through him with Apollo. How far Isis and Serapis (known only from Soissons) were integrated, is unknown. As for Cybele, in Belgica she mostly appears in the form of terracotta statuettes and was so assimilated to local mother goddesses that her independent recognition and worship might be questioned, but for a mention at Metz. The figure of Attis, her young consort, was widely adopted into funerary iconography, as were the zodiac and various forms of astral symbolism. Dionysiac imagery was also widespread; when it is found on objects such as box-handles the religious content is hard to estimate.[55]

The cult of the emperor and his house is generally considered a purely political phenomenon creating aristocratic alternatives to Druidism. Cults with political functions need not however be wholly devoid of religious content. There was a real need to 'mythologize' the emperor and to express

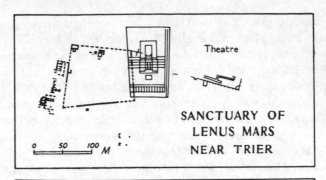

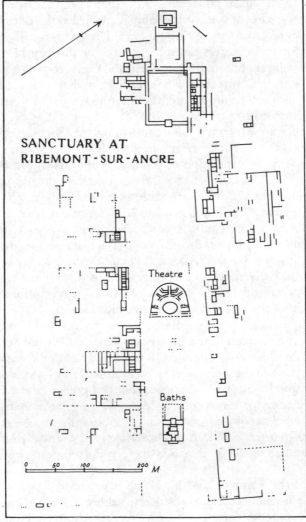

31 Plans showing the sanctuary of Lenus Mars near Trier and the sanctuary at Ribemont-sur-Ancre

loyalty in religious terms. This may have fitted with the ascription of heroic, semi-divine status to Caesar as conqueror. The frequency of dedications mentioning the spirit of the emperor or his divine house (if reduced to a formula) suggests their virtual incorporation into the elastic Gallo-Roman pantheon.[56]

As housing for the various divinities, wholly classical temples were as rare as purely Roman gods. The temple 'Am Herrenbrünnchen' at Trier (perhaps to Mars Victor) and that on the Mont Capron at Beauvais are both placed curiously far from the centre of the city. Knowledge of the temples of Asclepius and of Jupiter Optimus Maximus in Trier itself, or of the temple that probably accompanied the theatre at Soissons, would be helpful, as would indications of the places accorded to the imperial cult. The principal temple of Tongeren was of Gallo-Roman type, a square cella with ambulatory set in a precinct. That of Lenus Mars near Trier was in its developed form a curious hybrid combining ambulatory with classical pediment; the same may be true at Ribemont-sur-Ancre east of Amiens, a sanctuary which may also have had political functions within the *civitas*.[57]

The normal temple everywhere is the Gallo-Roman one, a Romanized form of the simple rectangular shrine which goes back to pre-Roman times. The ambulatory which was usually added presumably allowed adherence to traditional ritual, which may have rendered immaterial the precise outward form of the deities. Gallo-Roman temples of varying size are found in cities, villages and countryside. Excavations show them to have been among the earliest stone buildings, since an early first-century date is indicated at Ribemont-sur-Ancre. Alternatively, early wooden forms might be replaced in stone only later in the first century. Others (e.g. Fontaine-Valmont) were built on virgin sites in the mid-first century or later. The more elaborate sanctuaries often owed their developed form to rebuilding and ornamentation in the course of the second century, when this was clearly one expression of patronage. Additional buildings for priests and pilgrims might be provided.[58] Theatres remained optional, though found in the Altbachtal and the Lenus Mars sanctuary, and attested by inscriptions at several villages (Bitburg, Wederath, Pachten, Nizy-le-Comte) and rural sanctuaries, especially among Ambiani and Treveri.[59]

Major sanctuaries are frequent in *vici* which were also *pagus*-centres and on the boundaries between *civitates* – Eu, Vendeuil-Caply, Champlieu, Fontaine-Valmont, Tholey-Wareswald, le Donon. Other major (and many minor) shrines developed on the site of springs – Heckenmünster, Bourbonne-les-Bains (named after the god Borvo) with its enormous bathhouse. Grand remains a total mystery. Perhaps the richest shrine in Belgica, it had besides a large theatre an apsed building with an enormous third-century mosaic and a huge precinct-wall with towers. Yet the water which might have explained the worship of Apollo had to be brought in by aqueduct, and pre-Roman origins are not attested.[60]

SANCTUARIES ETC., EASTERN BELGICA

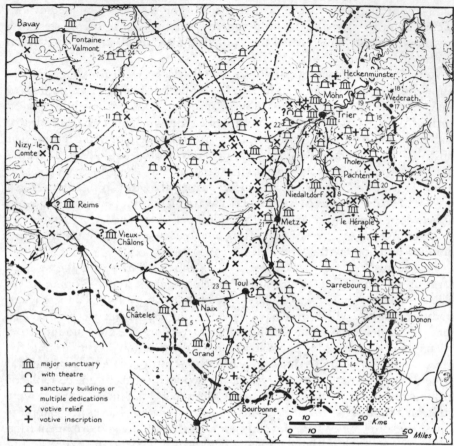

32 Map of eastern Belgica showing sanctuaries, reliefs and inscriptions

1 Sommerécourt	10 Belval Bois-des-Dames	19 Niederemmel
2 Euffigneix	11 Montcy-St. Pierre	20 Bierbach
3 Wahlscheid	12 Gérouville	21 Ste. Ruffine
4 Bad Bertrich	13 Sion	22 Altrier
5 Montiers-sur-Saulx	14 Mt. Avison	23 Sorcy-St. Martin
6 Mackwiller	15 Drohnecken	24 Matagne-la-Petite
7 Velosnes	16 Gusenburg	25 Matagne-la-Grande
8 Merten	17 Hottenbach	
9 Deneuvre	18 Hochscheid	

Hills were frequently sacred, and a number of these were old hillforts (Sion, Mt. Essey, Otzenhausen, Velosnes), testifying to the relationship between settlement and shrines. Often there is no clear connection between shrine, settlement or topographical features. Among the Ambiani and Treveri, where some 30 or 40 shrines are known, sites on slopes are almost as common as those on hills or ridges. Temples can be related to villas at Newel and Fliessem, to hamlets in the Vosges, and the Jupiter giant columns are often related to

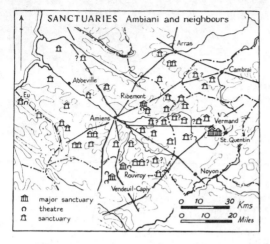

33 Map showing sanctuaries amongst the Ambiani and their neighbours

settlements. Probably every village or hamlet and the larger villas had some communal sacred spot. Roman roads certainly helped determine which sanctuaries grew large and elaborate.[61]

No simple correlations exist between deities and type of sanctuary, while Mithraea were recognizably distinct, yet stood cheek by jowl with other shrines. It might be anticipated that gradations in the Romanity of deities would appear between town and countryside, but this is not attested by inscriptions, which rather show regional variations; the authors of stone monuments were too evenly Romanized for such distinctions to show. Only dedications to *genii* (usually of a collectivity) turn out (with few exceptions) to be specific to *vici* and cities, along with dedications to the imperial house. Even eastern gods like Mithras are found in rural areas.

Finally, what of the choices of the worshippers, who vary from administrators at Trier to men and women with single Celtic names in the depths of the countryside? The preferences of administrators were variable, but a minor procurator at Trier is known through his dedication to the imported Asclepius. Soldiers sometimes mention the imperial house along with Roman, exotic (e.g. Jupiter Turmasgades), or Gallo-Roman (and at Tongeren possibly Germanic) deities. Mithras drew both Roman knights and more ordinary worshippers. High-ranking Gallo-Romans worshipped Mars Camulus at Reims, Lenus Mars at Trier, Vulcan at St. Quentin, which is not to say they did not patronize local rural gods on their estates. Colleges of craftsmen at Trier linked the Augustan *numina* with Epona, Aveta and Intarabus, while *vicani* acting collectively preferred more Roman gods.[62] People with single peregrine names do not on the whole mention the emperor, or concern themselves with *genii* and exotic gods. On the other hand their taste ran more to Roman divine names than to native, as if to make up for their own lack of Romanity. There are thus a very few glimpses of correspondences between the heavenly and the earthly pyramid, and a hint of social aspirations.

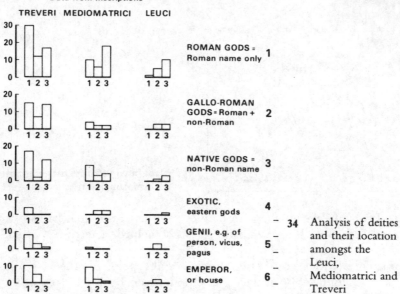

DEITIES/LOCATION

1=Capital 2=Vici 3=Hinterland
Data from Inscriptions

TREVERI MEDIOMATRICI LEUCI

ROMAN GODS = 1
Roman name only

GALLO-ROMAN
GODS= Roman + 2
non-Roman

NATIVE GODS = 3
non-Roman name

EXOTIC, 4
eastern gods

GENII, e.g. of
person, vicus, 5
pagus

EMPEROR, 6
or house

34 Analysis of deities
and their location
amongst the
Leuci,
Mediomatrici and
Treveri

At the level of reliefs and inscriptions, the outstanding feature is the inextricable mixture of Roman and Gaulish elements in Gallo-Roman religion. The phenomenon has a political, social and artistic as well as a religious aspect, and must be viewed against the non-proselytizing nature of Roman paganism. Emulation of the conquerors came naturally, initial impulses being strengthened by education and the training of the aristocracy in Roman ways. Stone-masons were more readily able to depict Graeco-Roman deities for which there were familiar models. Yet the reliefs from Paris and Trier show that they could deal with Gaulish mythology when requested, and that there was, for a time, a genuine attempt to portray non-Roman ideas. Whether this was officially discouraged, by Claudius as part of his effort to stamp out Druidism or by Vespasian after AD 69/70, is unknown. The trend which might have continued to depict and name Esus, Cernunnos and others did not develop, but gave way to more Romanized versions which probably affected, when they did not already reflect, concepts. The vaguely defined function of Gaulish deities and the expectation of ancient paganism that other people's gods roughly corresponded to one's own, certainly helped, perhaps also common elements in mythology (e.g. cattle-stealing) or similarities between the labours of Hercules and the exploits of Gaulish heroes. Later, the astral element in some cults may have fused with a similar element in traditional beliefs. Meanwhile priests had laboured to reconcile Gaulish and

Roman calendars, and festivals might be slightly adjusted (as probably from 1 May to 30 April, the Roman Floralia, at Bitburg).[63]

5 The socio-economic dimensions

Romanization stretched from careers, religion and education through a wide range of material goods to such basic matters as crops and diet. While the apparently all-embracing nature of the changes should not obscure the fact that they represent one more chapter in the long history of contacts between the Mediterranean world and the north, it is of importance to consider how deeply the structure of society was affected.

There is no question of incorporation within the Empire bringing with it radical changes of population. The landowning classes, as can be seen from inscriptions, were essentially indigenous, and *a fortiori* those below them. The majority of foreigners were birds of passage. Their number may even have diminished with time, as the Gauls themselves became the craftsmen, producers and traders – there is no need to see in the Greek-derived names of the second and third century large numbers of orientals, for some belonged to freedmen, others to the devotees of cults.[64] The temporary incomers were not evenly dispersed; the main road to the Rhine armies saw most of them.

Individual Belgic Gauls left their province in various ways. Treverans and later more especially Tungrians and Nervians saw service in the army, mostly in the northern provinces; Belgic Gauls may also have served among the *equites singulares*, the emperor's bodyguard, at Rome. Among civilian travellers, the Treveri were outstanding. Lyon, headquarters of the various shipping corporations, acted as a magnet to those who were involved in army supply, but they are also found throughout Gaul and along the Danube frontier.[65]

The prestige accorded to objects from the Graeco-Roman world, and their consequent imitation by local craftsmen, had a long history, but old patterns were not exactly repeated. The imitators had previously been master-craftsmen fashioning precious objects for aristocratic patrons. The exclusive nature of this relationship was already eroded in the late Iron Age, as craftsmen catered for a wider range of customers. The loss of political freedom dealt a death blow to traditional art not because it immediately altered the relationship between patron and craftsman but because it introduced a new system of values, based on emulation of the Roman way of life. This behaviour pattern was further encouraged by Roman education. Along with loss of self-determination also went incorporation into a vast free-trade zone. A range of desirable goods could be too easily acquired from eager traders, and status symbols started to take new forms such as Roman-style offices or funerary monuments. Opportunities for the ordinary craftsman were meanwhile enormously enlarged.

The value accorded to imitation by all ranks of society and the enormously increased markets are prime reasons for that standardization of culture, the large-scale production of derivative articles that elicit wonderment (or boredom) from the beholder. A few objects are generally admitted as exceptions, for instance, the multi-coloured enamel fibulae which so curiously revive an old technique in the second century. Some types of pottery also managed to combine traditional shapes and quality with production for a wider market. It should be remembered too that we lack the patterned Gallic textiles mentioned by writers. Even in so Romanized a medium as sculptured stone the derivative element can sometimes be counterbalanced by enough originality to produce provincial masterpieces such as the rider-god from Merten or some of the figures from Neumagen.

In some areas of life, traditional beliefs, practices and values not unnaturally died harder. Funerary customs remained essentially indigenous until the adoption of inhumation in the second and third centuries, the placing of Charon's obol in the mouth of the deceased, or the erection of Roman-style monuments being superficial changes only. The apparent re-emergence of native deities in the late second and third centuries indicates a retention of the traditional, made visible because stone monuments became available to a wider social spectrum.[66]

Education and the adoption of a supposedly superior culture do not necessarily alter the structure of society. Army service too can raise a limited number of individuals a notch or two higher while returning them to a society which continued to function as before. If other young men of standing were mustered into *collegia iuventutis* and allowed some paramilitary ceremonial, this did no more than provide a stabilizing factor.[67] The whole political organization, with councils, magistracies and Latin rights and semi-political priesthoods, encouraged a conservative search for status; it might keep the aristocracy turned towards Rome while deepening the gulf between them and the lower levels of society.

Changes in the rural base were probably of more long-term importance than alignment of the aristocracy to Roman models. As seen, traditional patterns were modified, if unevenly, as the villa system developed and relationships commercialized, with consequent erosion of old customary rights. We cannot readily tell to what extent this was balanced by the traditional forces of rural religious groupings. The proliferation of small villas shows the existence of a class of reasonably independent peasant-farmers who could erect monuments and who may have largely escaped, in good times, from any bonds of clientage. While this is the continuation of a tendency already visible before the conquest, the conditions of the *pax Romana* allowed it to go a good step further.

The comfortable peasant class and their urban or village equivalents, the successful artisans and small traders, form an interesting phenomenon. They show every sign of profiting from the more monetized economy. To judge by the solemn way they clutch their purses on tombstones, their wealth was to them both real and important, a compensation for the status they could not

claim. Archaeological evidence from the *vici*, and from the pottery manufacturing centres, suggests a higher differentiation of labour than in pre-Roman
times. It may be assumed that more people spent a higher proportion of their
time in occupations other than the basic production of food, even if the village
smith might still have his cabbage patch or work as harvester. It was not only
the line between those that could and could not afford monuments that slid
further down the social scale. More people could procure bronze statuettes of
deities, however miserable, for dedication at a sanctuary or to decorate a
household shrine; more people had fine pottery on their table and shoes on
their feet.

If there was any mechanism at work which can be called dynamic, it lay in
the need to pay taxes and the opportunities born of supplying the army (and
the cities). The extraordinary development of the eastern part of the province
is testimony. It also shows that a certain mentality had to be present: the
Menapii did not become so Romanized on the basis of their iron and salt.

It can be argued that the wealthier elements of society benefitted from
supplying the army, and that there was a close link between landowners and
the wealthier traders and shippers. Had the business not proved lucrative and
been important to them, they would have been less at pains to flaunt it on their
tombstones. If this is right, an aristocracy of landowners and military officers
in the first century gave way partly to one of landowners and military
suppliers.

Interesting figures for illustrating social mobility are the freedmen, who
might start as the agents of big landowners in their commercial enterprises
and end up in the municipal aristocracy themselves. Since freedmen very easily
became indistinguishable from other members of society through the styles of
Gallic nomenclature, their number may be greater than is realized.

Thanks to developments in middle and late la Tène times, Gaul already had
a reasonably developed system of production and dispersion of goods even
before the conquest. Production could readily be increased to meet new
demands without necessitating radical changes – hence the free potters of the
Gallic industries as opposed to the slave system temporarily introduced at
Lyon by the Italian firms. Given all this, and an aristocracy part of which was
quite prepared to increase its wealth through various enterprises, everything
needed for an early form of capitalism seems to be in place. Yet nowhere did
industries or businesses go on from strength to strength through successive
generations. Rather, they flourish for a limited time, and then fade out for
reasons not necessarily commercial.

The opportunities for capitalism were never taken up, unless in a piecemeal
and impermanent fashion. Out of a high level of pre-industrial market
economy the next apparently logical stage thus fails to emerge.[68] Capital
remained just too strongly anchored in land, and any adoption of Roman
ideals of status certainly encouraged this. The closest point to capitalism was
however reached among the Treveri, with the Secundinii and their like. Had

the legal opportunities for corporate ownership or banking been more fully exploited, had production of goods been further concentrated, much later developments might have been anticipated. As it was, the second and third centuries saw a complexity and a dynamism never previously achieved.

8

THE GALLIC EMPIRE

1   Background

The third century was, as has been seen, a time of unequal development in Belgica, with not all parts sharing in the prosperity which the eastern part of the province enjoyed along with the Germanies, a prosperity which reflected increased army pay and spending power.

There are, it is true, aspects of monetary history that are hard to understand. An absence of fresh bronze coinage circulating in Gaul from the time of Marcus Aurelius onwards is well established. The reasons for this, also noted in northern Italy, are obscure. From Caracalla onwards the continual debasement of the silver coinage, now increasingly taking the form of *antoninianus* or double *denarius*, also becomes marked. This is connected with the problems of paying the army, but its effects on provincial life are unclear. Circulation of coins with the real value of their silver content well below their face value may have led to price inflation, but caution is needed in the drawing of conclusions which, on modern analogies, seem reasonable enough. Price increases may have merely reflected the coins' lower intrinsic worth.[1]

In the course of the third century, Gaul experienced tendencies which were part imperial, part local. Three interlocking trends can be observed – changes in the central imperial system, social developments in Gaul itself and a new series of attempts on the part of German peoples to break through the frontier.

Sharply reflected in third-century imperial succession is a serious breakdown in consensus over how to reach imperial office. No longer was birth, adoption or senatorial background coupled with high military office a necessary requirement. Besides senators (e.g. the Gordians), knights (Macrinus) and even soldiers rising through ability (Maximinus Thrax) were successful contenders for the purple by the middle of the century. Armies proclaimed the particular favourite of the day, hoping that the immediate favour of donatives would be followed by other gains. Increasingly, legitimacy was purely a function of success, and little else distinguished would-be usurper from reigning emperor.

In ideology, a sharper distinction might be drawn, and failures vilified by protagonists of the successful. One traditional vilification was to see them as bandits (*latrones*), tantamount to ranking them as outsiders to civilized humanity, but implying little about their real activities. The successful were, not surprisingly, army men.[2]

Such developments were a logical continuation of trends in Roman society and imperial ideology. The endless search for status made the imperial office a goal at which anyone with sufficient power could aim. Parallel tendencies have been observed in municipal life, best documented in the east. There was a general cessation of the particular search for prestige which had until now fostered public buildings and inscriptions. Municipal magistrates were sometimes virtually appointed by governors. Satisfaction was no longer thereby achieved; the goals for men of ambition were set higher and the local élites sought to move into wider circles. There is irony in the fact that these developments were accelerating as Rome celebrated (AD 248) her millennium, symbol of unchanging permanency. Emperors were perhaps not unaware of change; the wider use of equestrians in positions of government (especially connected with Gallienus) was a recognition that the highest classes were virtually one as well as an attempt to avoid the usurpation of senators with armies. No equestrian *praesides* of Belgica are known by name, though the existence of one, with seat in Trier rather than Reims, is implied by the dedication of a staff member at Niederemmel.[3]

This same period saw outstandingly wealthy Gauls, and it would only be natural if they too were avid for the power that only high, preferably imperial, patronage could bring. Knights and senators from the three Gallic provinces had remained few in number; no senators and only a handful of knights are known for Belgica. It must have looked as if first-century prejudices (perhaps recently renewed under Severus) constituted a permanent bar. The career of T. Sennius Sollemnis of the Viducasses shows how Gallic aristocrats might attempt to rise to equestrian status by catching the eye of a governor. A few, like the Viromanduan L. Besius Superior, succeeded, but Sennius had to rest content with gifts of seal-skins rather than tribunates. He remains the most explicit example of a local magnate endeavouring to climb the next steps of the ladder. In status he was, with his municipal career, already much higher than men (such as the Secundinii) known from Treveran monuments: yet the Mosel valley may have seen the stirrings of like ambitions. Some Belgic Gauls recorded their gratitude to official patrons – for instance the Mediomatrican C. Sacconius Adnatus to Timesitheus, a praetorian prefect whose career included Gallic procuratorships under Alexander Severus – but without known results. A *bellum civile* is recorded in Gaul in about 250, and this episode may conceal some otherwise unknown usurpation of higher power, and so provide a forerunner of the Gallic emperors. A unique contemporary coin found in Lorraine, bearing the legend MARC SILBANNACVS, could be connected.[4]

The frustrating situation might barely have changed but for the movements of the Germanic peoples, which brought a military threat at times sufficient to necessitate a visit from an emperor (Alexander Severus, later Gallienus) or the speedy acceptance of the German army's imperial candidate (Maximinus). The reasons for the increased German menace are debated; population pressure, exacerbated by exhaustion of the soil, is preferable to any chain reaction set in motion by the distant Huns. Proximity to the frontier had affected the nearest Germans without bringing them a full share in the increasing prosperity of the Roman provinces. It is very possible that worsening climatic conditions were another factor. In any case, it is in the early third century that new Germanic confederacies make their appearance, the Alamanni ('All-men') troubling the frontier from the Taunus southwards, the Franks (probably the 'Free') further north. They had reached a phase where it was of great importance to their leading men to increase prestige by successful raids. As time went on the waxing confederacies provided still more dangerous foes. Already they had learned from experience of the Roman Empire: their organization and weaponry had improved, and they developed an acute sense of exploiting the Empire's weaker moments.[5]

The Alamanni started giving serious trouble in the 230s, the Franks some two decades later. For the Gauls, the most significant episodes were the campaigns of Gallienus against both Alamanni and Franks in 255–257; he was celebrated as *restitutor Galliarum* on coins of 256 after the winning back of the Agri Decumates. Belgica and Germanies were now well supplied with coinage produced by the new mint at Köln, closely connected with the campaigns (and probably melting down old issues to create larger new ones with a reduced silver content). Although information is confined to military events, Gallic aristocrats must have realized that the presence of an emperor was not only necessary to security but also allowed a range of patronage to which they had had all too little access. Gallienus' son, left in Köln when he himself departed, is an indication that the need for an imperial figure in Gaul was recognized. The young Saloninus was not, however, a sufficiently powerful figure, and in 259 or 260 Postumus, the commander of a part of the Rhine army, was hailed as emperor by his troops. The occasion is said to have been dispute over the apportioning of booty brought back from across the Rhine, but there were underlying conditions favouring such moves.[6]

2   Emperors and their reigns

M. Cassianus Latinius Postumus thus defected from the Central Empire to rule an area centred on Belgica and the Germanies. His origin is unknown, with Gallic birth possible but unproven. Yet although a military man elevated by an army in a manner long become traditional, he is clearly represented as ruling the Gauls with their full consent, as if Gallic endorsement of the army's choice was of great moment. Perhaps the approval came from Trier and adjacent areas, whose fate was closely linked to the frontier zone. Although his empire included Britain and, at least nominally, Spain, his main headquarters remained at Köln. The mint of Gallienus now struck for Postumus, its products including a remarkably fine *aureus* with a three-quarters-face bust of the emperor. It was probably also Köln that witnessed the ceremonies consequent upon his consulships, and other manifestations of imperial presence. The rank of Trier is unclear, though the mosaic inscription recording Victorinus as tribune of the praetorians suggests official functions. The value of a capital behind the frontier, in a province that was both civilian and Gallic may have become clearer under his successors. That a mint of Gallic Empire date functioned at Trier is made highly probable by the inscription of a procurator most readily dated to this period, but whether instituted by Postumus or Victorinus is still debated.[7]

If Postumus laid claim to the whole of the Empire, he wisely took no practical steps in such a direction. *Roma aeterna* on coins suggests that he considered himself the legitimate ruler of one part of the whole. His immediate task was the protection of the west, more narrowly the Germanies and Belgica. The deity often figuring on his coins is the appropriate hero Hercules, sometimes with the surnames Magusanus and Deusoniensis known from Batavian sanctuaries.[8]

Postumus was a military man, but of his successors (or would-be successors) Laelianus and Marius, little is known, though the latter is described as a brawny ex-blacksmith. Postumus was supposedly killed by his troops in the course of opposing Laelianus' usurpation. The chronology is confused, and it is tempting to link the other usurpers' actions with special favours shown by Postumus to Victorinus. M. Piavonius Victorinus, indicated by the coins as successor to Marius, was a man of a different type. Even without the dubious corroboration of the sources, his provincial *nomen* and common *cognomen* suggest that he came from a Gallic family, and his officership in the praetorian guard of Postumus was probably not the only basis for his ambition. His influential and wealthy mother Victoria is known almost entirely from the Augustan History. Her role in assuring (by largesse to the army) the accession of Tetricus after the violent death of Victorinus is, however, also mentioned by Aurelius Victor, so that she is perhaps not simply a literary figment, despite her absence from coins. Tetricus' name, C. Pius Esuvius Tetricus, shows him to be a Gallic notable, and reliable sources have him as a senatorial governor of Aquitania. His sharing of power with his son is vouched for in the coinage, and his coin legends place less stress on the army, and more on personifications such as Concordia and Hilaritas.[9]

Tetricus may be seen as the culmination of a Romanized Gallic aristocracy – a Gallo-Roman with a senatorial career claiming Roman imperial power in a way that Vindex could not do. But he had been preceded by others with diverse claims, and there was no way of preventing further attempts. Hints of those – the 'mutinies' said to have disturbed Tetricus' reign – are preserved: it may be that Tetricus' control of the army was at best precarious, his support geographically limited. There is no way of knowing the full number of attempted usurpations, given unsatisfactory sources. It is inherently likely that the plot which killed Victorinus came from a would-be ruler rather than a wronged husband, and a certain governor Faustinus (presumably of Belgica since his seat was Trier) was causing Tetricus trouble at the time of the latter's defeat by Aurelian (in 273 or 274). Given their dependence on the trade route to the army, it would be logical for the Treveri, and anyone acting as their patron, to oppose any emperor who did not sufficiently favour the Rhine armies.[10]

No precise reconstitution of events is possible, even the dates and lengths of reigns being subjects of debate.[11] In general terms, Postumus is everywhere represented as a successful military man who defended the Rhine frontier vigorously; Victorinus too was seen as energetic and competent. Archaeology shows the taking of defensive measures, since the earliest fortifications in the hinterland of Köln and along the Bavay-Köln road belong to about Postumus' reign, and an inscription testifies to the erection under Victorinus of a *burgus* near the lower Mosel. To the same period also belong the first irregular hilltop fortifications, discussed below. Germanic incursions are indeed mentioned for Postumus' reign and for the period just after his death.[12]

Postumus and Victorinus also had their problems with the Central Empire; the first had to meet an army of Gallienus, the latter to cope with the defection of Autun, a defection quite probably caused by jealousy at the sight of the favour lavished on Trier and the north-east. Tetricus eventually surrendered to Aurelian in the course of a battle forced on him near Châlons; the location suggests that he had abandoned most of Gaul. He was also prepared to abandon his position, and duly lived to govern Lucania after figuring in Aurelian's triumph. One probable example of a supporter – the Trier mint official – whose career also continued is known.[13]

Various attempts have been made to date and localize Germanic invasions more precisely from the Gallic Empire coinage and coin hoards. Coins of Postumus certainly celebrate victory over the Germans and the restoration of the Gauls, and those of Victorinus and Tetricus keep up the martial theme. The hoards, however, have been wrongly interpreted, and unfortunately cannot be used to pin-point invasions. The reasons for this deserve further consideration.[14]

Even if the hoards containing the coinage of Tetricus in massive quantities be temporarily left aside, those ending with coins of Gallienus, Postumus and Victorinus are extremely numerous in Gaul, especially in the north and east. The total runs into the hundreds, and it is hardly surprising that the assumption of a close connection between invasions and the hoards has been made. A general connection between times of trouble and failure to recover buried money is both reasonable and sometimes demonstrable. To suppose that invasions were always the immediate cause of deposition is, however, a further step; it has been shown for other historical periods that known hoards need not very precisely reflect trouble-spots.[15] Moreover, there were other likely reasons for the deposition of many third-century hoards.

There are problems intrinsic to the hoards themselves as well as to their interpretation. Only in a fraction of the whole is the date of the latest coin established: less than 5 per cent have been properly studied, while all too often only a handful of coins have been seen. A further trap is hoards consisting of several parts, with different metals buried separately; quirks of circulation can make the end dates of the parts different. The problems are most clearly illustrated by the numerous hoards ending with Tetrican *antoniniani* and copies thereof (often called barbarous radiates, because they are poor copies of types showing the emperor with radiate crown). These may occur in thousands, yet a very few coins of Aurelian, Tacitus, Probus or Diocletian show that deposition in fact took place well after the death of Tetricus. It is now recognized that imitations of Tetricus were produced in the intervening period, and that these hoards belong as a class to the 280s. Dating based on a small sample of coins from a huge hoard is thus liable to mislead. Until classification of the hoards into certain basic types has been taken further, lists and maps are poor guides.[16]

Conclusions based on the distribution of hoards also require re-examination. The bulk of hoards comes from northern and eastern Gaul, with relatively few being found south of the Loire. Hoards of this period are also frequent in Britain, and since no major invasions of Britain are known, these hoards cannot reflect actual incursions.

Throughout the third century, hoards mirror the vagaries of circulation. Bronzes stopping with the Severi may have been buried long after, since comparatively little new bronze reached Gaul. *Denarii* were hoarded for their silver content, the more so after they went out of production in the 240s. *Antoniniani* of any period prior to a devaluation were collected. Hoards ending just prior to the latest issues of Gallienus may thus be the result of devaluations rather than invasions. Postumus' own devaluations near the end of his reign resulted in more collecting and deposition, not necessarily connected with either Germans or the problems of succession. Finally, hoards ending with Tetricus and imitations were probably collected for different, but still monetary reasons.

The reformed coinage of Aurelian, by which he attempted to bring order out of chaos, did not circulate much in Gaul, despite the opening of a mint at Lyon to replace the one at Trier. Gallic Empire coinage, supplemented by local imitations, still comprised most of the circulating pool. It is surmised that eventually this was demonetized, and so turned into useless base metal.[17] Burial may have been consequent to this; concealment of possession may have been desirable. That a form of prejudice against the Gallic Empire coins was involved is suggested by the Central Empire coinage contemporary with it, which, also debased, circulated much longer.[18]

What then are the informative aspects of coins and coin hoards? First, the propaganda element of the coins, not excluding Postumus' initial attempt to keep up silver standard of the *antoniniani*. Sheer inability to keep up the necessary volume of silver coinage, even debased, is already evident in his later devaluations, and the *antoniniani* of Tetricus finally had fewer than ten parts per thousand of silver. The weight of the rare gold *aurei* likewise declined.[19]

As for the hoards, if they cannot give precise information on invasions, they can on coin production and circulation. The observation that the Gallic Empire hoards regularly have a higher percentage of 'good' coins (judged by silver content) than do coins from sites suggests that many hoards represent conscious savings and not merely a random chunk of circulating coinage. It can be shown that the Gallic Empire coins were dominant only in the central-east and north-east, with reasonable quantities reaching Britain. Imitations are also largely confined to northern Gaul, the Rhineland and Britain, the Rhineland having fewer than the other areas.[20]

The distribution of the coinage, and the production of imitations by a host of local mints, are arguably the most significant aspects. The concentration of official Gallic Empire coins in the proximity of the Rhineland points to the underlying cause for the mints' very existence – the need to pay the army. Circulation of coin was probably altogether more intense in the north-east, as soldiers' pay was exchanged for goods from the hinterland. Unfortunately, nothing is known of taxation under the Gallic Empire, and the extent to which it was collected in kind or in money. The series of devaluations suggests problems in supporting the army without any recourse to the wealth of the eastern provinces; interest in the silver mines of Poitou could be the reason for Gallic Empire *aurei* found in this region, for gold coins tend to denote the immediate circle of the emperor.[21]

The local production of imitation coins was not a new phenomenon. Cast copies of early third-century *denarii* had been manufactured at a variety of places (including the *vicus* of Pachten), partly to supply a need and partly because it was a coin on which forgery could bring a profit. Cast and struck imitations of Postumus' bronzes are known, and some of them were produced by a fair-sized mint that was nonetheless irregular, and which lay in the north-east.[22] After the death of Tetricus the fashion reached mammoth proportions. While many productions circulated only locally, others went further afield, their travels exemplified by coins from the same dies found at St. Mard (Virton) and in Britain. One unofficial mint was near Sarreinsming (northern Vosges) in a small settlement close to a villa and very likely dependent on it – a precious indication that behind the imitations were perhaps big landowners taking the law into their own hands.[23]

Finally, do the hoards cast any light at all on the troubled nature of the times? Here it is the extent of non-recovery that is the significant fact, and there are more hoards from this period than from the preceding two centuries. Moreover, some hoards are of silver plate, including one from Chaourse near Reims. Only with the hoards of the 280s was non-recovery possibly a result of their inherent worthlessness, and even so re-use as scrap metal might have been anticipated. The overall extent of non-recovery still suggests problems, but these were not exclusively military, and it will be through a better overall understanding of money supply and circulation that the meaning of the hoards will eventually be worked out.

3   The aftermath

After the battle of Châlons-sur-Marne, the Gauls were once more united with the Central Empire. Yet a tendency towards separation was again shown when, after the death of Aurelian and the brief reign of Tacitus, the Gallic provinces supported Florian against Probus. We can only guess at the jealousies and discontents which pitted supporters of Aurelian or Florian against others. Florian's diminution of the frontier troops, or simply the absence of an emperor, caused the Germanic peoples to judge the time ripe for further incursions.

The exact date and, more importantly, the extent of these invasions are hard to determine. Most authors only mention them in the context of Probus' subsequent campaigns, though making it clear that Gaul was in the hands of barbarians; the emperor Julian believed that 70 cities were rescued. The impression given by Eutropius and Zosimus is that these were more serious than any previous incursions, and involved Franks, Vandals and Alamanni. Yet not only Orosius (who had a special Christian axe to grind) but also Aurelius Victor stress the earlier invasions under Gallienus. Between calumny of Gallienus, praise of Probus and possibly spurious details, facts are difficult to extract.[24] The weight accorded to the invasions of 275–6 by modern authors rests on a shaky foundation, since it has consisted mostly of adding to the literary sources the inappropriate data of coin hoards and the many observed instances of destruction of sites by fire, dated almost by tradition to these years. There is indeed much cumulative evidence of destruction by fire in both towns and countryside, but it cannot be dated to a single year nor necessarily attributed to invaders. The literary sources do, however, suggest that larger numbers of Germans were involved, and that they stayed within Gaul rather than returning with their booty.

Again, it is difficult to prove that Probus fully deserved his reputation for rebuilding prosperity and confidence, though it is very likely that many city walls went up during his reign. The literary tradition paid particular attention to his encouragement of provincial vineyards, difficult to verify through archaeology. The settlement of barbarians on the land attested by the Augustan History may also be factual.[25]

In some ways more telling, despite obviously non-factual ingredients, is Zosimus' story that presence of the emperor sufficed to end a famine and brought a magic downpour in which grains of wheat fell along with rain.[26] However rationalized (were hidden stores suddenly opened up?) it demonstrates the belief that the emperor could work supernatural wonders. It also raises a possible correlation between bad harvests and invasions. Yet Probus did not supply Gaul adequately with his official coinage, nor was he even able to put an immediate stop to efforts at usurpation. The defeat of a usurper (or usurpers) in the neighbourhood of Köln shows the lower Rhine army still interested in promoting local rulers.[27]

The usurpers are generally regarded as a hangover from lengthy military and political crisis. But, as has been argued above, the whole phenomenon of usurpation can be viewed differently. The narrow band separating usurpers from the characters described in less complimentary terms as brigands can be nicely seen in one Augustan History discussion. The criteria were clear enough – if a local dynast wore the purple, struck coins in his own name and issued edicts he was a usurper and if not, he might be dismissed as a mere brigand.[28]

In this same context another contemporary Gallic phenomenon is to be approached, since it may be more closely connected than is normally supposed. After the death of Probus in 283 the sources talk of internal troubles in Gaul that had to be suppressed by Maximian, appointed in 286 as Caesar of Diocletian in the west (and shortly after raised to be fellow-Augustus). These troubles were a source of embarrassment to our only contemporary sources, the Panegyrists, because it was equally improper to mention and to omit them, and the people involved are vaguely described as rustics, a band of ploughmen and shepherds turned infantry and cavalry. It is from later epitomisers that we learn that they were called Bagaudae, a word probably derived from a Celtic root *baga* meaning war.[29]

These Bagaudae have usually been seen as homespun warriors, involved in a peasant revolt caused by various real hardships – invasions, famine, and (doubtless) taxation. The enemy, it is supposed, were the big landowners, also the state and its officials.[30] Landowners were indeed the people best qualified to survive both invaders and the march and countermarch of armies, simply because their control of land and labour guaranteed them basic produce and the means of building fortified retreats. But this very fact made them the obvious place of refuge for the poor and needy, and in ancient society times of want were prone to knot more tightly, rather than to loosen, the bonds of mutual support between rich and poor. The Bagaudic leaders known from the sources, Aelius and Amandus, are more likely to have been powerful land-owners than rebellious peasants. Thieves and highwaymen there might be, but (as Ausonius later reminds us), such people could also be in the protection of landowner-patrons. Aelius and Amandus should perhaps be classified as usurpers, for the existence of coins with their names has been claimed. There is also a unique coin with the name Domitianus, unattested in literary sources.[31]

A good case can be made for linking this phenomenon with the situation that had produced the Gallic Empire. The 'brigands' may have risen to power by none too lawful or peaceful means to be local tyrants, their power based on control of land and clients. Unlawful seizure of property and men can be imagined among their activities, withholding of taxes a likely offence against official powers. They mostly stopped short of minting coins with their own names, and may or may not have worn the purple. Lack of an army is one obvious reason. The many unofficial local mint-workshops may however have produced coinage at the behest of such local magnates, who could then distribute it by paying retainers.

Such an explanation of the Bagaudae provides a thread of continuity across the period of 'crisis'.[32] It does not, however, thereby deny that there was much disruption and unrest. The evidence for destruction, by whatever hand, is simply too strong, and a society that regularly pulls down its funerary monuments to build the foundations for city walls is breaking psychological links with its own past. Among the evidence for disruption is the cessation of monuments, including the votive sculptures and reliefs apparently necessary to rural well-being. The latest dated votive inscriptions belong to the 240s, but giant columns and smaller sculptures were erected until at least 260. Their end can with difficulty be attributed to a change in aristocratic values, and may testify to the collapse of the army supply system and of the service trades that it fostered.[33]

Before the Gallic provinces were finally placated and subordinated to a ruler in the new northern capital at Trier, there was to be one final usurpation of full-blown military style. Carausius the Menapian rose through sheer ability to become a military strong-man. When Maximian found that expeditions by both land and sea were necessary to suppress the Franks and other Germans, the latter sphere of operations was entrusted to Carausius. In 286 or 287 he claimed the purple, winning over Britain. In addition he kept more than a foothold on the continent, controlling Boulogne, and, it has been argued, winning over the legion at Xanten. Maximian's expedition against him in 289, with a hastily built fleet, was a failure, and may even have allowed him to increase his continental empire: Boulogne perhaps housed a mint.

Constantius Chlorus, created Caesar in 293, had to devote strenuous efforts to defeating both the usurper and the Franks, who by now were Carausius' supporters, ready to invade on his behalf. Constantius' winning of Boulogne (by building a mole across the harbour mouth) gave him a vital fleet base, eliminated or severely reduced the usurper's continental area but also occasioned the further usurpation of Allectus. Coins of Allectus are found on the continent, and may point to a continued if limited control (hoards at Noyelles-Godault and Amiens). Not until 296 was a successful campaign mounted, and the delay illustrates the trouble that could be caused by an able usurper controlling a large fleet and army in an area where his local knowledge and *clientela* could be useful. Celebrations for Constantius' eventual victory included the minting at Trier of gold medallions as donatives, the best known (showing London greeting Constantius) coming from the Beaurains hoard near Arras.[34]

With the defeat of Allectus, the problem of usurpers was settled for two generations. Mistakes like the appointment of Carausius to his homeland area were avoided. The establishment of an official, recognized capital at Trier afforded a new focus for the political life of the Gauls. The creation of a permanent mint there in 293–4 also meant that there was a steady supply of coinage, and the local coin-workshops were rendered obsolete. So too, with members of the imperial house always nearby, were pretenders whose main basis for power was fighting the Franks or Alamanni. The conditions of the reorganized Empire were now in place.

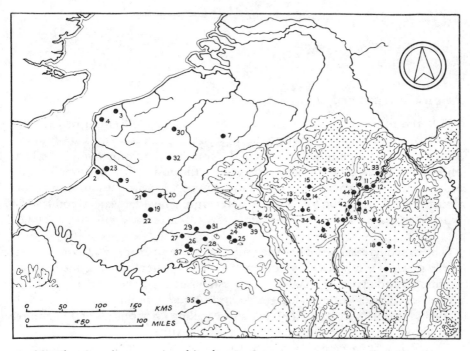

35   Map showing places mentioned in chapters 8–13

1	Sarreinsming	17	Berthelming	33	Bengel
2	St. Valéry-sur-Somme	18	Rouhling	34	Longwy
3	Marck	19	Laboissière	35	Villeneuve-au-Chatelôt
4	Marquise	20	Athies	36	Trois-Vierges
5	Sotzweiler	21	Warfusée	37	Armentières (Aisne)
6	Robelmont	22	Montdidier	38	Biermes
7	Soignies	23	Nouvion-en-Ponthieu	39	Seuil
8	Irsch	24	Crépy	40	Omont
9	L'Etoile	25	Beine	41	Wiltingen
10	Stahl	26	Oulchy-le-Château	42	Temmels
11	Schweich	27	Mercin-et-Vaux	43	Palzem
12	Leiwen	28	Blanzy-les-Fismes	44	Wintersdorf
13	Florenville	29	Vailly	45	Audun-le-Tiche
14	Thiaumont	30	Annappes	46	Audun-le-Roman
15	Warnach (Tintange)	31	Passy	47	Welschbillig
16	Remerschen	32	Witry-en-Artois		

9

NORTHERN GAUL AND THE LATER EMPIRE

1 Belgica reorganized

While the reforms of Diocletian were often the crystallization of existing trends, his reign can still be seen as a turning-point. Thereafter, the Late-Empire stage was set, though modifications by Constantine and others might still be important. No aspect of the changing scene – the position of the emperor, the reorganization of provinces, taxation and army – was without significance for Gaul. There is, however, a problem in determining how far general conditions (known in theoretical form from legal sources) actually apply to particular regions.

The ever-increasing gulf between subjects and emperor – now companion of the gods, as symbolized by prostration – can be viewed alongside the far-reaching administrative changes. Both established for the emperor and his chosen colleagues an unchallengeable and almost tangible authority. Diocletian's reforms were the outcome of a sure feeling for the needs of the Empire and, above all, for the imperial majesty of the ruler.

Diocletian was accused by the Christian writer Lactantius of chopping the provinces up into little pieces in order to have more officials than previously (the result of the multiplication is shown in the so-called Verona list). Two Belgic provinces were created, with Belgica Prima embracing the *civitates* along the Moselle (capital Trier) and Belgica Secunda (capital Reims) the more westerly peoples. The Tungri were now a part of Germania Secunda, the remodelled Germania Inferior, which would otherwise have been only a strip of land perpetually threatened by the Franks (conceivably the redrawing of this boundary took place earlier). Each of the two provinces was governed by an equestrian *praeses*, as had probably been normal since Gallienus.[1]

Reorganization involved more than multiplication of provincial governors. These men had until now been the emperor's direct representatives, appointed by him and (in imperial provinces) answerable only to him: appeals from their jurisdiction went straight to him. A whole new administrative stratum now effectively severed this direct connection. Moreover, in military provinces a single man had been responsible for civil and military affairs. These were now normally separated, yet the fact that reorganization of civilian provinces was no less thorough than that of military shows that separation of civil from military powers was not the only concern.

Just as Diocletian turned his own rule into that of a college of emperors, two senior and two junior (the problems he faced in Gaul must have helped to suggest this solution), so too he multiplied the office of *praefectus praetorio*. These *praefecti* were now the supreme civil and military officials, each attached to one member of the imperial college and responsible in this instance for the Gauls with Spain and Britain. Their deputies, *vicarii*, looked after the smaller dioceses, of which the Gauls formed two, the southern Viennensis and the northern *diocesis Galliarum* containing the two Germanies. The latter, the new Sequania and the various divisions of Lugdunensis and Belgica, was however directly administered by the *praefectus praetorio* from Trier. To him provincial governors were now responsible, and appeals from them went to his court; the governors were now at the bottom of an administrative pyramid.

Despite lower status, the governor's duties were not diminished, since he was now responsible for financial matters and thus combined the duties of legates and procurators. The pyramid of financial responsibility depended from the *comes sacrarum largitionum* through lesser *comites*, though taxation (discussed elsewhere) lay within the sphere of the *praefectus praetorio*.

The modifications made by Constantine are sometimes seen as more radical than the system itself. At the very pinnacle of authority, the tetrarchic system of four rulers fell victim to natural human ambitions. Winner in the struggle, Constantine reverted to the family dynasty, and had his sons Crispus and Constantine proclaimed as Caesars in 317, even before he was sole ruler. Although Crispus was resident in Trier until his death on charges of treason in 326, the correlation between an imperial college and prefectures broke down. The prefectures remained, but became purely territorial, the permanent features of an administration in which the imperial family was the movable part. At the same time, prefects lost military powers as these were more sharply divided from civil. Compensation took the form of increased status, for Constantine frequently appointed senators as prefects, or promoted men already in office. The more important provincial governorships were also given to senators, and the two Belgicae, like the Germanies, were governed by senatorial *consulares* (though a *praeses* is attested for Belgica II as late as 326). Equestrian rank was now only one grade in a hierarchy of office distinguished by titles.[2]

In the long run this was to allow a build-up of power among senatorial families that had deleterious effects for the Empire, since senators could avoid responsibilities at the local level, and frequently at the fiscal. For the Gallic provinces the changes may not have seemed important, except that a senatorial governor was a more satisfactory patron, and there were more governors to dispense patronage to ambitious men, be it the granting of a minor administrative post, the favourable adjudication of a law-suit or an introduction to some potentate.

At the local level, provincial capitals apart, little had apparently changed. The *civitas* was still the unit of local self-administration, run by the *curiales* and magistrates chosen from among them (though perhaps by appointment rather than election). Owing to the general lack of inscriptions and the omission of civil offices from Christian tombstones, there are no details for the cities of the Belgicae apart from one possibly late magistrate of Trier.[3] Curial status became, like the professions, a hereditary office which was less attractive not simply because it was more burdensome but because it no longer sufficiently answered the quest for status. In the fourth century it was less a matter for pride than a duty to be avoided, and it is unlikely that northern Gaul escaped the trends that can be documented elsewhere. One option was to climb to the top of the local ladder, becoming one of a select group called the *principales*, an inner ring that ran city affairs in their own interests. The humbler *curiales* were not so far above the great divide separating the lower *humiliores* from the *honestiores*, and the fact that they were forbidden to avoid duties by enlisting as soldiers shows that they might and did. Meanwhile, the increasingly complex administration opened up for the *principales* a new range of choices, including minor (and even theoretical) posts on the staff of governors.

The civil service hierarchy was analogous to the military; offices were called *militiae* and brought similar privileges such as freedom from curial duties. Timely words and donatives could ensure coveted advantages, and ambition for status took some apparently strange new turns.[4] Admittedly, the evidence for the Belgicae does not allow us to study such processes in detail. There is also only a presumption that the cities' financial affairs were regulated by a *curator*, originally an extraordinary official appointed by the emperor but increasingly a normal part of the municipal scene. Nor is it known whether it proved desirable in due course to appoint *defensores*, high-ranking (often senatorial) officers whose theoretical duty it was to protect the ordinary people of the city from abuses. If a provincial council existed, it was probably dominated not by the municipal aristocracy, but by the senatorial.[5]

The *civitates* of the Later Empire were the continuation of their predecessors, with minor modifications. In two, perhaps three, instances new territories were formed from earlier *pagi*. The western area of the Mediomatrici, centred on Verdun, became the *civitas* Verodunensium and the area around Boulogne (previously the pagus Gesoriacensis) the *civitas* Bononiensium. The independence of the Catalauni may have come earlier, but is only clearly attested for the Late Empire. The date of these changes cannot be precisely determined, since information in the *Notitia Galliarum* belongs to the very end of the fourth century. The elevation of Boulogne, the strategic importance of which has been seen, might have occurred after the partial destruction of Thérouanne in 275, but a better argument could also be made for a date after the defeat of

Carausius, or during subsequent reorganization of the Channel coast defences. Boulogne henceforward had the status of a defended city, though its harbour could still be used as a fleet base.[6]

Had the splitting up of *civitates* been done consistently, other candidates would have suggested themselves, especially the western Treveri around Arlon and the north-western Remi around Laon. Behind the decisions may lie lobbying by notables who identified their interests with the rise to independence of their *pagus*. More puzzling are Cambrai and Tournai, now respectively the *civitates* Camaracensium and Turnacensium. While the independent Bononienses left a reduced Morini centred on Tarvenna, the fate of the Menapii and Nervii is unclear. The exposed position of Cassel and the very radical reduction of Bavay should mean that Tournai and Cambrai were replacement capitals for the whole *civitates*, yet the naming of military units after Nervii and Menapii shows that the names did not immediately disappear, and possibly the old *civitates* continued for a time.[7] The final change may then have recognized the *de facto* situation that the northern part of the *civitates* concerned could no longer be regularly administered. One hint of further, otherwise unrecorded changes has come down. The compiler of the *Notitia Galliarum* felt the need to specify that the capital of the Leuci was Tullum. The ambivalence in the fourth century lay not between Toul and Naix but between Toul and Grand. Two Constantinian milestones at Soulosse give a distance which fits the latter place, and milestones usually measure from the capital. Grand, probable site of Constantine's vows and subsequent generosity to Apollo, may have enjoyed a temporary elevation.[8]

Two other trends are visible in the Later Empire. The first is for the word *civitas* to denote quite unambiguously the city rather than the people or territory. Three centuries of Roman rule had led to an increasing emphasis on the administrative centre as opposed to the people or territory. This is found even on milestones, the distance at Soulosse being given from the *civitas* Leucorum. As a corollary, the cities became known by the name of the people, and the old place names, whether Celtic or Roman, fell into disuse. Most died out altogether, so that the medieval and modern names are derived from those of the peoples – Amiens, Soissons, Reims, Trier, Metz. There are, however, exceptions. The new *civitates* stressed their centre (Bononia, Turnacum) in a different way. On the other hand, four original place-names survived, namely Cassel, Bavay, Thérouanne and Toul. All four are places where urban life does not seem to have developed very far, so that there could, however strangely, be a connection between a more evolved urbanism and the winning out of the territorial name.[9]

While the theory of local administration can be pieced together, the absence of local evidence renders it hard to assess the practice. It may be questioned whether all cities had a complement of *curiales* who resided in the towns. The smaller towns offered neither amenities nor space, and there is yet no evidence, except at Trier, for wealthy suburban houses.[10] The paradox inherent in the position of the curial class can be seen at its sharpest in Belgica. On the one hand, the need to regulate the collection of taxes made their existence necessary to the central administration which, for good reasons, shrank from putting the whole routine into the hands of officials. At the same time ambition was being funnelled elsewhere, and in the north the conditions for city life on the Mediterranean pattern no longer existed throughout. Yet Salvian in the early fifth century depicts (though probably drawing on Trier) thriving and rapacious curials extorting an unfair burden of taxes from the rural poor, rigging the distribution in various forbidden ways.[11] The curials well reflect wider problems. The administrative staff of the Empire had increased partly to enhance the authority of the emperor by surrounding him with a larger *comitatus* or court. There was no corresponding increase in efficiency, for the Empire still relied heavily on officials who had other means of livelihood. Abuses and inefficiency were therefore endemic. The stream of legislation forbidding irregular practices simply allows us to see what was commonly done, for the laws could not be enforced in a society where patronage remained the key form of relationship.[12]

2 The army, defence and the Germans

The army and the defensive system were also remodelled by both Diocletian and Constantine. Details are often disputable because of the lack of strictly contemporary evidence. Most of the information comes either from Ammianus' description of the army under Julian, or from the lists of commands provided by the *Notitia Dignitatum*. This refers primarily to a later period, though mentioning units which go back to Diocletian. Moreover, combining the information on military offices given in the *Notitia* with the archaeological remains of defensive systems is not simple.[13]

Overall, Diocletian's main change was the separation of military from civilian commands by the creation of *duces* to command the armies. Not all provinces required a *dux*, and the military command of a single man might stretch over more than one. It is uncertain whether a *dux* was created for each of the Belgic provinces. Only one of Belgica II is unambiguously attested and that for a late date (in the *Notitia*); the existence of the other depends on dubious argument from a tetrarchic inscription at Trier. *Duces*, like *praesides*, were under the overall control of the *praefectus praetorio*. This changed when Constantine created the military supreme posts of *magister peditum* and *magister equitum*, while leaving the *praefecti praetorio* responsible for recruitment and supplies. Constantine's other reform, the creation of a mobile field army, has attracted greater attention in both ancient and modern times. The historian Zosimus bitterly contrasts the strengthening of the frontiers by Diocletian with their weakening by Constantine in favour of the new mobile troops. The bias of the writer, a pagan, is however obvious. Just as Lactantius the Christian implied that Diocletian had quadrupled the army (modern estimates suggest that it was not even doubled), so Zosimus later sought to hold Constantine responsible for the loss of the Western Empire.[14]

As in so much else, Constantine was building on earlier foundations. Under the Tetrarchy, the number of troops attached to the person of the emperor had multiplied to include the *protectores*, an élite domestic corps, and various *scholae* (probably also the legions named *Joviani* and *Herculiani* after the tetrarchs' protecting deities). Out of this *comitatus* and the need for Constantine to march against imperial rivals arose the mobile field army, the *comitatenses*. The number of soldiers along the frontier, the *limitanei*, was diminished, the total size of the army somewhat increased (but, since legions were now only 1,000 strong, not by so much as might appear). Although units could be moved from one division to the other, the two parts of the army went separate ways. The *comitatenses*, regarded as the élite, were normally billeted on civilians – a form of taxation – while the *limitanei* became more settled soldier-farmers.[15]

The whole practice of frontier defence in northern Germany and Gaul had, however, changed considerably since the days when auxiliary forts strung out between legionary bases had sufficiently ensured peace. Developments are most obvious in two areas – the creation of coastal forts roughly corresponding to others on the British side of the Channel coast and the emergence of a system of defence in depth behind the Rhine.

The Channel coast forts did not spring suddenly into being in the early fourth or even the late third centuries, but had origins stretching back another full century. Oudenburg had turf rampart phases as early as the second century, and in ancient times was situated on a coastal headland. Probable companions were Aardenburg, also in Menapian territory and the Brittenburg (of uncertain date, now below the sea off Katwijk). Rebuilding after 275 (except at Aardenburg) made the sites part of a chain that stretched around Britanny to the Atlantic coast.[16]

Not all links are known, and there are serious problems in trying to integrate the sites with the locations and commands given in the *Notitia Dignitatum*. To start with, Boulogne is unexpectedly absent, though it must have remained an important fleet base. Even if it was a fortified city with billeted troops rather than a military base *per se*, a mention of the fleet would be expected, and this has led to a suspicion that the list is simply incomplete. The position of the listed fleet base, that of the *classis Sambrica* in locus Quartensis or Hornensis, poses other puzzles. While Sambrica might denote the Sambre, there are strong arguments for supposing that the Somme (Samara) is intended. The likeliest site is St. Valéry near Cap Hornu, where a late Roman fortification may lie below the medieval walls. Stamped tiles of the Cl(assis) Sam. . . have also been found at Etaples on the Canche. There remain the sites Marcis (described as being *in litore Saxonico*) and Portus Aepatiaci. The former is generally thought to be either Marck or Marquise in the Pas–de–Calais, while the latter may be Oudenburg. The Saxon shore forts, of which Marcis was one, were essentially fortified fleet bases with an additional garrison that could be, as here, of cavalry. Those of the Tractus Armoricanus, further west, were defended cities with an additional military function, akin to Boulogne or Amiens; the latter was the base of a heavy-armed cavalry unit for the first half of the century.[17]

While there is probably more than one phase in the arrangements as described, they cannot at present be disentangled. There is confusion, too, in the *Notitia*'s commands. The Count of the Saxon Shore has a title that suggests creation by Constantine or his sons, and the high rank would be consistent with a command originally including forts on both sides of the Channel. That the continental sites are under the control of the *Dux tractus Armoricani* and the *Dux Belgicae Secundae* is likely to reflect later modifications. But the former of these two commands is not internally consistent; the full title is *Dux tractus Armoricani et Nervicani*, yet despite mention of a *limes Nervicanus* immediately below, the provinces over which his command specifically extends do not include Belgica. There may then have been a period when a single *dux* had control over the internal fortifications of Armorica and Belgica II; the area was then split when the coastal commands were added to the others.

In the hinterland, the development of frontier defences in depth began under the Gallic Empire. The provision of fortified posts along the road from Bavay to Köln remains the best known feature, along with the *burgus* near Liesenich; other examples will emerge, since these early posts were built in earth and timber. While the measures show awareness of the weakness of a linear frontier, it is not clear how the posts were garrisoned. They functioned as a series of watch-towers combined with fortified stores-bases. The rebuilding (in masonry) and extension of the system probably started before the Tetrarchy, though additions to it were made by Constantine and later by Julian and Valentinian, until the major north-south and east-west roads behind the Rhine frontier were protected.[18]

Fortified stores-bases and watch-towers remained an important part of the system, and not every fortification need have been fully garrisoned. Liberchies II (Brunehaut), which has produced a copious coin sequence, clearly was. Built in the early fourth century at latest, it had a garrison throughout most of the fourth century with the exception of the period 350–380.[19] The site, identified as Geminiacum, gave its name to the occupying unit, the Geminiacenses, who appear in the *Notitia* after a subsequent move. The Geminiacenses are, it has been argued, a formation of the later fourth century, and therefore represent the later garrison. Belonging to the same period should be the Cortoriacenses (Courtrai) as well as the Musmagenses (Mouzon) and Turnacenses (Tournai). Larger garrisons, this time the legions Menapii and Nervii, were probably originally stationed at Cassel and Bavay before being upgraded to the *comitatenses*.[20] If the surviving names are representative, there were more garrisons in the north than behind the middle Rhine. They are also a reminder that the Bavay-Köln road was only part of a larger system, still imperfectly understood. The fact that the system stretched across two provinces, Belgica II and Germania II, was no bar to command by a single official; by the period of the *Notitia* this was the *Dux Belgicae II*.

The Bavay-Köln road was never intended to function as a linear frontier, but as a fortified road within a broad frontier zone. Recent discoveries suggest that the lower Rhine frontier was maintained until at least the period of Valentinian and Gratian. Moreover, the probable existence of fourth-century fortifications at Gent and Brugge underlines the fact that the territory north of the road was still protected. Toxandria, between the lower Scheldt and Maas, was from the time of Julian occupied and defended by federate Franks.[21] Other peoples of Germanic origin, whose status will be discussed below, were settled both south and north-east of the Bavay-Köln road, as well as in the hinterland. They played an important role in the overall scheme of defence, by peopling the countryside with soldier-farmers.

The system of defence in depth had a dual function. One was to ensure the arrival of vital supplies to the army stationed along the forward line, the other to help chase out any invaders who had penetrated that line, while depriving them of the food held in the forts. The forward line itself, as always, controlled the movement of Germanic peoples, keeping it as far as possible to a minimum. Although much of the campaigning in the fourth century involved the Germanies rather than the Belgicas, a summary of relations between Romans and Germans is not irrelevant.

Roman emperors clung to the idea that punitive expeditions across the Rhine were an essential part of regulating relationships with the German peoples. In fact, while this allowed for the semblance of victory and the psychological boost of celebrations, such campaigns were not particularly useful, and might even be counterproductive. If there was indeed chronic overpopulation in the frontier zone immediately beyond the Rhine, Roman reprisals which destroyed crops and prevented normal exchange would only drive the peoples to greater desperation. Famine at least once weakened the Germans subsequent to an invasion, but it may also have been a cause.[22]

In practice, the emperors had long come to terms with the fact that intermittent displays of strength could not exclude from the Empire determined peoples whose ambition it was to gain entry. From the time of Gallienus the sources mention arrangements, often specified as *foedera* or treaties, and the descriptions often make it clear that the Romans were not really negotiating from strength. Peace sometimes involved the ceding of land to certain groups in return for their help in keeping others out. Gallienus' treaty in the 260s seems to have been of this kind, and the discovery of gold coins of the Gallic Empire in Free Germany suggests another, with peace achieved through payment. Probus sometimes ceded land to barbarians, and whether or not he did so on the lower Rhine, by Constantine's day there were Franks on both sides of the frontier. The only settlement unambiguously described is that of the Franks in Toxandria (after a display of strength) by Julian in 357, but it is likely that we simply lack details on others.[23]

Rather more is heard of German prisoners, because the terms were more unambiguously Roman. In keeping with the policy which demanded victories with appropriate celebrations, a number were thrown by Constantine (and doubtless others) to the beasts in the amphitheatre in Trier. Others were doubtless sold as slaves. Others again were settled on the land inside the Empire, so as to increase the number of peasants. At first (according to a panegyrist) distributed among private landowners, they then appear in later legal sources as occupying land of special status, *terrae laeticae*. They remained eligible for military service, and thus formed a new pool for recruitment at a time when depopulation on the one hand and fiscal pressure to keep peasants firmly in their place created a dearth. Auxiliary units bearing the names of *civitates*, e.g. the *sagittarii Nervii*, may have been recruited out of *laeti*.[24]

The settlement of *laeti* went back until at least the time of Probus, but the great period of recruitment of these and other Germans was under the Tetrarchy and Constantine. Some, like the Bructeri and Salii, bore names that clearly displayed their origin, while others are found giving tongue to German war-songs in battle. A peace treaty made by Constantius II with the Alamanni in 354 is known to have included recruitment as one of the conditions. Although Gallo-Romans were still recruited, the auxiliary portion of the new army consisted overwhelmingly of Germans. It can be argued that this is the more successful part of Roman policy towards the Germans, and that the comparative peace of the latter part of Constantine's reign was due to it.[25]

Peace was not permanent, nor the arrangements without risks. The worst disruption came in the middle of the century, when both Franks and Alamanni invaded Gaul in 352–3. Destruction layers from a number of sites, along with coin hoards (this time more plausibly connected with invasions), give some substance to the claim that Julian found a wide strip west of the Rhine laid waste.[26] Imperial political problems were involved. The usurper Magnentius, of Frankish descent, was raised to the purple in 350 with the help of the largely German army. Constantius II was suspected of having intrigued with the Germans against the usurper.[27] It took hard campaigning by Julian before acceptable conditions were restored and the Rhine in its lower reaches was made safe for Roman supply ships. But neither lower nor middle Rhine could be maintained as a boundary, and the 360s brought campaigning by Valentinian, the early 390s by the Frankish *magister militum*, Arbogast.[28]

Meanwhile, *laeti* would return after service to their *terrae laeticae*, while other Germanic veterans probably swelled the Germanic element in the countryside. The problems of connecting the archaeological evidence for a Germanic element in the countryside with the groups of Germans known from the literary sources are discussed below.

Arbogast well illustrates another aspect of Roman policies. Well born or able Germans could rise to the very highest military offices, and within the fourth century there are over a dozen examples in the offices of *magister militum*, *peditum* or *equitum*. While aristocratic birth might be desirable, the strong-man Charietto, a Frank who conducted guerrilla warfare against other

Franks between Trier and the Rhine, became *comes* of both Germanies under Julian. Not infrequently these able and ambitious men saw service in the imperial bodyguard, and thus the court at Trier was for many of them the scene of a schooling in Roman ways. For some of them, including Arbogast, marriage was with members of respectable provincial families, while others (e.g. Stilicho) were connected to the imperial house. Edicts forbidding mixed marriages were enforced, if at all, only for those of lower rank.[29]

Integration of Germans into northern Roman provincial life thus took place at various levels in the countryside of Belgica and at the court in Trier. Imperial policy had some positive results, if also its limitations. Given Roman imperial ideology, more could hardly have been achieved in translating a perceived threat into a new source of strength for the Empire.

3 Emperors and Gauls

Few imperial achievements of the early fourth century are more remarkable than the way in which Constantius (even more than Constantine) captured the loyalties of the Gallic provincials. This is both illustrated and explained in the Panegyrics which have come down to us because they were collected and preserved in Gaul (probably by the schools of Autun) and which are one of the main sources.[30]

Maximian was celebrated as an energetic and successful soldier.[31] Constantius, with successes against both barbarians and Carausius, was just as much the victorious general, but is in addition awarded an enthusiasm and affection not evoked by Maximian. The fact that Constantius resided at Trier whenever campaigning permitted allowed the Gauls to feel that he was in a very special way their own Caesar. His own actions did much to underscore the advantage, for he is shown as clearly responsive to the needs of the provinces. No sooner had he regained control of Britain than he imported skilled craftsmen into Gaul to help with the restoration of the battered cities; attention was then given to peaceful tasks such as the restoration of the schools at Autun. Ruins inhabited only by wild beasts gave way, we are told, to peopled cities which seemed like so many islands of civilization arising like Delos from the sea – truer for some cities than others, but Constantius earned the reputation of general restorer and refounder.[32]

In Trier, assurance that the Gauls were viewed as an integral and important part of the Empire took tangible form as the massive walls of the great palace enclave, almost certainly started in Constantius's time, arose. It would be surprising if the new birthday of the city, piously celebrated by Constantine in the later summer of 310, was not an institution of his father. The schools of Trier itself were presumably also restored, and the city became in addition the focus of all court ceremonial. The jealousy felt by the notables of Autun is palpable, and the attention given also to that city a wise response.[33]

The gold medallion struck to commemorate the triumphal entry of

Constantius into London refers to him as *redditor lucis aeternae*, and the sentiment is echoed in the panegyrics. The sun, to whose rays he is sometimes compared, shone all the brighter because of Constantius' god-like gifts to lesser mortals.[34]

While the Gauls set great store by the presence of a ruler among them, and doubtless enjoyed the festivity and solemnity of ceremony, they were not merely influenced by outward appearances. The court of the *praefectus praetorio* at Trier had a staff of some hundreds, and the imperial court was larger. It was natural, and wise, to fill some posts with Gauls. Thus Eumenius (of a Greek family settled in Gaul) was *magister memoriae* (the most important post in the palatine secretariat) to Constantius before retiring to head the schools at Autun. The orator who performed before Constantine in 310 may have held the same office and had an eldest son employed as *advocatus fisci*. Mamertinus, panegyrist to Maximian in 291 and perhaps a native of Trier, may be the father or grandfather of the later Claudius Mamertinus whose discourse of thanks to Julian for a consulship in 362 is preserved in the same collection.[35]

It was to Constantius that the Gauls looked as their great patron, fit founder of a new dynasty. When Constantine was hailed *imperator* by the British army on his father's death, he was welcomed in Gaul because of his parentage, and indeed the panegyrist of 310 turns to the son only after a lengthy survey of the father's deeds, and stresses the facial resemblance that made it seem as if Constantius had not left them. Constantine had already established his military reputation with victories over the Franks. The respect that he was believed to pay to the Gallic Apollo – perhaps here too following in his father's footsteps – doubtless also won him sympathy. He was well repaid, for the story spread that Apollo had appeared to him in a vision accompanied by Victory, offering the laurel crown that presaged his sole rule. The fortunate temple is not named, but the geography of the incident fits Grand.[36]

The achievement of the success promised by Apollo increasingly distanced Constantine from Gaul, and after 315 his visits there were limited to brief stays at Arles. That city was not however a rival to Trier. Constantine's eldest son, Crispus, was installed in the latter city as Caesar (along with his half-brother the younger Constantine), and continued the imperial duty of warring against the Franks. After Crispus' execution in 326 Constantine II remained there, though replaced for a time by Constantius II. Not only did the northern Gauls still have their Caesar, but the Trier mint continued to strike gold, which was normally produced only where the emperor himself was residing. Moreover, the administrative staff of the court grew larger under Constantine: additions included the *magister officiorum*, who co-ordinated other palatine *officia*.[37] From the latter part of Constantine's reign the church also began to emerge as a new dispenser of power and patronage, though this phenomenon may have been confined to Trier and perhaps Reims, where the church grew under the aegis of imperial court and provincial governors' entourage.

After the abdication of Diocletian, Gaul was one of the most stable regions of the Empire and, after 320, one of the most peaceful. The sons of Constantine had only, like the Julio-Claudian emperors after Augustus, to maintain the bonds of patronge between themselves and the Gauls. This was not, in the long term, to be. At first the dynastic squabbles affected the Gauls little, and even the death of the familiar Constantine II and his replacement in 340 by the unknown younger Constans caused no visible disturbance. Yet it seems likely that Constans' unpopularity spread among Gallic notables as well as the army, and that some supported the plot which in 350 proclaimed as emperor Magnentius. It is probably significant that the plot came to fruition at Autun, Trier's rival city.[38]

Born shortly after 300 in or around Amiens, Magnentius was the son of a Frankish (i.e. Laetic) mother and a British father; Laetic status inherited from his mother would ensure military service, though not the good Roman education also credited to him. His usurpation, followed by Constans' flight and suicide, went smoothly. He gained control of the mint at Trier, and coined also at Lyon, Arles, and, on a smaller scale, at his native Amiens. His brother Decentius was left in charge of the north while Magnentius marched to his defeat by Constantius II. Rivalries between the cities of Gaul are further illustrated by the behaviour of Trier. Preferring a member of the Constantinian house to the emperor created at Autun, the city went over to Constantius. Under the leadership of one Poemenius, an official or local notable, the gates were shut against Decentius and the mint struck for Constantius before that emperor reached Gaul.[39]

There followed a period of confusion The Alamanni under a strong king, Chnodomar, had caused trouble as early as 352, if certain coin hoards can be so closely pressed. Constantius campaigned against them in 354–5, but came to terms. Matters were not helped by the usurpation at Köln of Silvanus, an able military Frank, now *magister peditum*; the aftermath left Gaul without a strong hand. When Julian, from a collateral branch of the Constantinian house, was suddenly created Caesar in 355 and sent to Gaul, he found a general scene of devastation, and had to start afresh to stabilize the military situation and to win the confidence of the Gauls.[40] Despite his eastern upbringing, this younger member of the Constantinian house was given a tumultuous reception, particularly in Vienne.

Although we have much detail from the pen of Ammianus Marcellinus (an eyewitness), little is known of Julian's actual dealings with the Gauls, except that these were hampered by the unfriendly *praefectus praetorio*, Florentius. One condition of the successful prince, victory, he fulfilled already in 356, with both energy and acumen. The Alamanni had penetrated so far into the interior as to threaten Autun, and he initially joined the troops waiting for him at Reims with difficulty. Bold use of a minor road was successful, and advance from Reims in the direction of Strasbourg, with a minor engagement near Tarquimpol, saw the Alamanni pushed beyond the Vosges. A march down the Rhine to beleaguered Köln, and thence through Trier to winter quarters at

Sens enabled him to display himself on the various fronts, to endear himself to the army, and to bring both comfort and practical aid to the provincials. The next two years brought a repeat in slower motion. In 357 the Alamanni were decisively beaten at Strasbourg, while spring of 358 brought land and sea operations to pacify the lower Rhine, troubled by the Frankish Salii, and the settlement of Toxandria. A further punitive campaign into the old *Agri Decumates* and the building or rebuilding of fortifications crowned the military part of his endeavors. Ammianus explicitly mentions sites on the Rhine and others (not certainly identified, but perhaps including Cuijk) on the lower Maas, but it would be natural if some *castella* guarding roads in Lorraine also belonged to this period.[41]

Julian's main recorded act of wise government concerned taxation. He refused to permit the supplementary levies that were the regular means of making up deficits, and equally refused to remit accumulated arrears, on the grounds that both customs damaged the poor. By administering the collection of taxes from Belgica II without interference from officials, he showed that fair collection could bring in the requisite amount.[42] Since officials were mainly employed for the taxes of senators, it must have been with the powerful that he dealt, and doubtless he offended some and pleased others. The straightforward, unsophisticated nature of the Gauls pleased Julian, and his own directness may have been welcome to some of them.

Julian may have been greatly helped by Saturninius Secundus Salutius, a senatorial Gaul of philosophical interests who, having been assigned to Julian as an adviser, became a friend. Of others who attended on Julian or whose careers were advanced by him we know Claudius Mamertinus and Jovinus, later appointed *magister equitum* and perhaps a native of Reims.[43] In this way Julian continued the work of his predecessors. In other ways, which are harder to estimate, he may have altered certain balances. His total avoidance of Trier was most probably due to the presence there of Florentius and his court, but his choice of Sens and Paris as winter quarters would lead to fresh, if undocumented, developments in patronage. As it was, Julian had to deal with a strange new kind of power in the person of bishop Hilary of Poitiers who, because of his resolute stance against Arianism, was sent into exile at the beginning of Julian's time in Gaul.[44]

Acceptance of Julian as a new restorer, akin to the ideal perfect prince, may then have varied from place to place. The first stage of his accession to the position of Augustus, challenger of Constantius for Empire-wide dominion, is shown as the traditional military affair, instigated by the German and Gallic troops that did not wish to be sent east as Constantius had bidden. The innocence and unwillingness of Julian was probably not so great as officially depicted. At a later assembly in Paris, to which he had invited civilians as well as soldiers, all joined in hailing him 'Julian Augustus', and Ammianus makes him out to be the provincials' as well as the army's choice. In 361, when he marched east, Gaul was again deprived of an emperor, though the efforts of

Charietto (now Count of both Germanies) and Jovinus (*magister Armorum*) kept order until Julian's death. Salutius, meanwhile, was *praefectus praetorio* in the east, and was even offered the purple on Julian's death.[45]

Because of a further movement of Alamanni into Lorraine, Valentinian came to Gaul in 365 to face a situation similar to that of a decade before. Victories near Scarpone, Metz and Châlons were to the credit of Jovinus, and again demonstrated the importance of Reims and east-west communications. Horror that the Gauls might find themselves without a present emperor led to scheming when Valentinian fell ill at Amiens, and that city now witnessed an imperial acclamation as the young Gratian was elevated to rule with his father. Soon Trier received both father and son (367).[46]

To Trier in particular the new dynasty brought renewed, even increased, splendour. Buildings were erected, improved or altered, while the mint once more functioned to capacity. Not even in Constantine's day had the city housed such a cosmopolitan throng of officials and notables and been so closely in touch with the different currents of intellectual and religious life. True, a sensitive Italian senator and man of letters such as Symmachus might shudder at the Gallic weather and maintain that Valentinian's preference for Gaul was simply a proof of his devotion to duty. But at no point did the city more deserve the title of Belgic Rome, given it on a lost inscription or epigram.[47]

With the sole rule of Gratian (from 375) and in the person of Ausonius the full potential of imperial patronage for Gallic provincials was realized. As the best known of the professors at the school of Bordeaux he was picked by Valentinian to be Gratian's tutor. His enormous influence over the young emperor was thereafter used to rid the court of many of Valentinian's particular supporters and to bring back into favour the senatorial class of whom Valentinian had been suspicious. Not only did he himself rise through the prefecture of the Gauls, then of Italy and Africa, to the consulship, but a half dozen members of his family, including his aged father, held high office. The Gallic landed magnates had never been so successful in their quest for the prestige brought by service to the imperial house. The short-lived nature of the phenomenon, the manner in which Ausonius' patronage ceased with his retirement just as abruptly as it started, is however a measure of the tenuous, personal and unpredictable nature of imperial favour.[48]

The same reign was remarkable for the presence at court of able, educated and powerful men of Frankish extraction – among them Mallobaudes and Richomer (both for a time *comes domesticorum*), Bauto (*magister militum*), Merobaudes (*magister equitum praesentialis*) and Arbogast, the nephew of Richomer. The whole balance of the Empire, to judge by its most important officials, was shifting further north. When 378 brought the death of the eastern emperor Valens at the hand of the Goths, Gratian's appointment of Theodosius as co-ruler shows a realization that the west needed its own visible emperor. At the same time, Belgica was the passive scene rather than a major active contributor, unless the Franks be counted as being by this time Belgic provincials.[49]

The great majority of the Gauls involved in running the Empire still came from the centre or (even more overwhelmingly) the south and south-west, with only a handful from the north-east. Even Jovinus, who retired to Reims after a long and honourable career, is not certainly a native, although Reims was a place where patronage might operate. Among the correspondents of Symmachus at Trier, the would-be historian Protadius with his brothers Florentinus and Minervius were probably natives, but the point depends on the interpretation of an ambiguous phrase. For one at least of the Syagrii prominent under Gratian, Lyon has a better claim than Soissons, base of a later member of the family.[50] As for the schools of Trier (doubtless closed from the 350s till the time of Valentinian and Gratian) only chance remarks of Ausonius on Belgic orators and the dedication of a poem give a hint of their activity; there is no evidence that the high salaries offered by Gratian attracted professors equal to those of Bordeaux.[51] Those northern Gauls who had risen to equestrian status in the third century had surprisingly few successors; ambitions for the most part must have been tempered to more mundane levels. There is a real sense in which the resplendence of the northern capital came from borrowed finery.

The reasons for the usurpation of Magnus Maximus, *dux* or *comes* in Britain, are not known in detail. If the Britons had dreamed of their own emperor, disappointment lay ahead, since Trier soon became his capital. More obscure are the reasons for the lack of organized resistance in Gaul, where he had almost immediate success and acceptance, after battle near Paris. No doubt Gratian's recent lengthy stay in Milan (between 381 and 383) was a contributory factor, and the arrival of Maximus with his army (at Boulogne?) was perhaps less of a surprise to some high-placed people than it was to the emperor; perfidy is mentioned by a later panegyrist to Theodosius. There may have been a general reaction in some quarters against the pacific Gratian.[52]

Accounts of relations between Maximus and the Gallic notables disagree. The panegyrist congratulating Theodosius on Maximus' defeat is an obviously biased source, portraying a greedy and bloodthirsty tyrant who killed or ruined the rich for the sake of their fortunes. A more charitable judgement is passed by Sulpicius Severus, perhaps because of the fervent Catholicism of both Maximus and his wife.[53] Ausonius and his circle were removed from power, but less is known about their replacements. More information is to hand on Maximus' dealings with churchmen. Already under Valentinian the prestige of Martin of Tours had risen to the point where he could demand an audience with the emperor on his own terms, and expect a polite reception. Martin was also prepared to disagree openly with Maximus on the treatment of the so-called Priscillianist group which, he held, should have been a purely ecclesiastical affair. The great efforts to win Martin round after the execution of the heretics testify to the holy man's power at court.[54] Meanwhile, the most powerful churchman of the age, Bishop Ambrose, was acting as emissary of the court of Valentinian II at Milan, where a number of Gratian's clients had taken refuge.

The eventual defeat of Maximus was due to the generalship of Arbogast, to whom Theodosius then entrusted the reconquest of Gaul. There he defeated the son of Maximus and also campaigned against the Franks – by his birth his fellow-countrymen but against whom he bore a grudge. Growing tensions between Arbogast and the young Valentinian II led to the emperor's premature death and to the proclamation of Eugenius, a cultured man without military pretensions. Along with the great pagan senatorial families of Italy, Eugenius and Arbogast were defeated by Theodosius, with a largely Gothic army and leaders that included the Vandal Stilicho.[55]

Arbogast had attempted to renew the west as it had been under Gratian, with a cultured emperor and a strong military man to keep order. Theodosius was less sensitive to the needs of the north. Neither the emperor himself nor Honorius, the son to whom he confided the west, went there. The decision that Trier should cease to rank as a capital may not have been made immediately: the discovery of bronze weights for standardizing gold *solidi* of Honorius shows an intent to have the mint striking in all three metals. In practice, no gold coins of Honorius were ever produced at Trier, and this points to a policy change taken very shortly after Theodosius' death and the beginning of Honorius' reign in 395.[56] The palatine offices left Trier for Arles, and this explains why, in 402, Symmachus in Italy had difficulty in finding anyone who could bear a letter north to Protadius. The court of the *praefectus praetorio* may have left at the same time, but it can also be argued that it stayed until *force majeure* prevailed in the form of the invasions of 406/7.[57]

The connections between emperors and Gauls were not thereby severed. The reign of Theodosius is remarkable for the number of prominent Gauls who, following the example of a few who had taken that route under Julian, moved to office in the east during Gratian's reign or accompanied Theodosius to Constantinople after the defeat of Maximus. Prominent among them was Flavius Rufinus, who rose to be principal adviser to Arcadius as Stilicho was to Honorius.[58]

Nonetheless, a chapter was ending. Gaul no longer was awarded the special position within the Empire that alone kept the northern provinces and Rhine frontier in stable condition. That great Frankish generals were no longer in favour is, after Arbogast, understandable enough. With the nearest imperial court in Milan and the praetorian prefect no closer than Arles, prevention of northern usurpers and upkeep of the Rhine frontier were alike impossible. Stilicho's visit to the Rhine in 396, though brief, may have been effective in the short term. Little can be said about the Rhine frontier in this period; in the absence of the psychological and strategic support of a nearby court and generals, its days as an effective system were numbered, and it is the more amazing that the definitive invasions did not come before the very end of 406.[59] The withdrawal of the courts spelled, not least, the end of the special status of Trier and its effectiveness as an outpost of Mediterranean culture in a northern land.

The sources on fourth-century Gaul, because of their literary nature, inevitably tell us most about the aristocracy. It is only from Salvian, writing in the early fifth century, that we have information on men of curial status, who were well below senators in status yet equally a long way above the bulk of the population (hence, from below, they could appear as so many petty tyrants).[60] The 'international' nature of the provincial aristocracy is unduly stressed at the expense of any regional characteristics that might show if a broader sample were available: even Salvian's *curiales* behave much as *curiales* might anywhere in the Empire. Unfortunately, in the Later Empire such people, at the lower end of the spectrum of *honestiores*, become much more difficult to define, as do the shopkeepers and artisans who formed the more respectable element among the *humiliores*. This is largely because the stream of inscriptions and reliefs dries up except for one narrow and peculiar channel – the Christian epitaphs of Trier. If an impression is to be gained of the population of the province as a whole, it is to the evidence for urban life, rural settlement patterns, religious and funerary customs, production and trade that recourse must be made.

10

THE LATE ROMAN CITIES

1 Survival and fortification

The study of urban centres in late Roman Belgica is inevitably an evaluation of change, and the task is rendered more complex by the need to link the material remains with the values of late Roman society. The symbolic value of cities and city life also underwent a transformation that rendered obsolete some typical earlier features. In all of this, Gaul was both a part of the wider Empire and an area with its own particular conditions. This is particularly true of Belgica, because of its proximity to the frontier and because along its northern coastline even the physical geography had proved inconstant.

Before wider questions can be discussed, the late Roman urban topography of Belgica must be presented. Continuity between the late Roman and medieval urban centres often obscures this, so that a clear picture of late third-century decline and destruction, or the extent of subsequent restoration cannot always as yet be obtained, and we must do without a detailed view of how the cities were divided into public and private space. The one invariable rule is that each city was now fortified, but the space enclosed within the walls ranged from 70 ha at Metz to less than one tenth of that at Senlis (to omit here as an aberration the 285 ha of the earlier walls at Trier). Are the smaller fortifications to be viewed as tiny walled towns or rather as citadels with the town proper spread out around? It can even be questioned whether the word city is always appropriate. Yet it is best to keep it as the equivalent of the Roman *civitas*, a word which was now strictly applied to the administrative centre. The *vici* – now also mostly fortified – should once more be included, for comparison and contrast, in any discussion of late urbanism. The dividing line was indeed sometimes crossed, as former *civitas* capitals slipped from the higher status to the lower, while Boulogne and Verdun became *civitates*.[1]

Typical problems of evidence arise already with the extent of destruction to communities in the second half of the third century. Literary sources in sweeping terms attribute general devastation of cities as well as countryside to various German invaders, especially after the death of Aurelian, and give Probus credit for restoration of 60 cities (effectively, all the capitals of Gaul). But, as seen, the date 275 may have been wrongly stressed at the expense of other, earlier events.[2]

Archaeological reports too quickly give the impression of widespread destruction. Cities and villages where a destruction layer (often clearly more than domestic fires, since found at various points) attributable to the second half of the third century has been found exceed those where excavation has brought no such testimony to light. A good example is the fill of a cellar on the Tetelbierg, where assorted débris including bronze and iron fragments, a shield-boss, a horse's skull and much nearly whole pottery had been flung pell-mell along with burnt material (coins to Tetricus). The number of centres lacking excavations is however still roughly one third of the total. Moreover, in places as far apart as Grobbendonk (Tungri) and Château-Porcien (Remi) the evidence specifically suggests abandonment without destruction.[3] At present, no consistent factor of location, size or type seems to distinguish sites with evidence of destruction from others.

Among the *civitas* capitals, destruction layers have been noted in virtually all that have seen excavation on a reasonable scale; they are clearest at Trier, Amiens, Reims, Beauvais, Arras and Tongeren – despite the presence of walls around the first and last places. The conclusion drawn from Tongeren, that there was some intra-mural as well as extra-mural destruction, not necessarily adding up to systematic devastation, holds good generally;[4] there is no need to imagine every building being involved in a great conflagration. Moreover, the strict contemporaneity of destruction levels has not really been demonstrated, nor the risk of attributing any mid-to-late third-century burnt layer to a supposed 275 holocaust avoided.

The archaeological evidence is thus not as free from bias as might be wished. Nonetheless, unless it can be shown that the layers have been quite wrongly dated, the combined testimony for a catastrophe to urban life towards the end of or after the fall of the Gallic Empire remains impressive; the fact that the events so mirrored escape precise formulation or dating does not make the results any less real. Destruction may in fact have occurred on a variety of occasions. Some was perhaps the result of earlier incursions, an example being Schwarzenacker, where the coin series (as perhaps also at Sarrebourg) stop in 260; at Amiens a date as early as the 250s has been suggested for an initial destruction followed by others.[5] Some may not have been caused by invaders at all: whatever view is taken of the Bagaudae, it is clear that the internal equilibrium of society was gravely shaken, and disturbances in cities as well as countryside may have resulted. Another possible culprit is the central imperial army, whether engaged in quelling resistance or indulging itself by looting. Finally, the demolition of buildings prior to the erection of fortifications may sometimes have been mistaken for hostile acts. Architectural pieces as well as dismantled funerary monuments certainly found their way into the new foundations, but the clearing of buildings around the projected line would be necessary.

Had destruction merely taken the form of accidental fires, the permanent damage would have been less, for rebuilding on the old lines could have taken place quite rapidly. Some such resilience is for a time visible; minor reconstruction took place within the Amiens forum in the middle of the century, and may have survived the 270s without further damage. The first walls to close in the Bavay forum probably date to a period when civic life was still in reasonable shape. At Famars, a disused bath-house seems to have been used for other purposes (a flour-mill?) prior to destruction. It is clear that the trouble eventually went deeper. Human skeletons in a well at Amiens indicate actual loss of life, to be put alongside the failure to recover buried coin-hoards.[6] An estimate of the numbers that were killed, slowly by famine or disease if not quickly at the hand of external or internal foe, is obviously impossible: the overall population may in any case have been in decline. Perhaps more important is the shock to the fabric of society, well illustrated by the readiness to throw funerary monuments as well as buildings into foundations. Local government was clearly in disarray. The withdrawal of surviving landowners from the cities to rural retreats is a likely part of the story, perhaps the rapid acceleration of an existing trend. It has been noted that most cities had stopped growing, that monuments were, even in the late second and early third centuries, not always well kept up. At Amiens, a drastic shrinkage had occurred by the middle of the third century; the connected encroachment of cemeteries on the street-grid shows a growing disregard for urban proprieties. By the end of Tetricus' reign, the inhabited city was about a quarter of its former size.[7] Even without the troubles, some other cities would also have declined. As it was, two or three decades accomplished the work of a century and, last but not least, the decision to fortify the cities made reconstruction on the old lines impossible.

With the exceptions of Tongeren, Trier, the fleet base at Boulogne and the sanctuary of Grand, the cities and villages of Belgica were still unwalled at the time of the Gallic Empire. It seems at first reasonable to see in the two first circuits the realization that permanently peaceful conditions could not be guaranteed; yet, as argued above, questions of status were probably as important as those of defence, with initiatives taken by local notables gaining permission to erect walls as an addition to the complement of public monuments. Boulogne was a special case, and at Grand the wall may be a spectacular *temenos* or sacred precinct.[8]

In the later third century, it is harder to deny that considerations of defence were important. Villagers rather than city-dwellers were the first to whom new necessities became apparent. Along the Bavay-Köln road, the centres of Liberchies, Braives and Taviers were levelled under the Gallic Empire to make way for wooden fortlets, while village life continued for a time on the periphery. If an inscription from Bitburg is correctly interpreted as referring to a tower (*farator*), the first steps were taken as early as the 240s. Other small fortifications in stone, at Senon and St. Laurent-sur-Othain, have been dated early, but the evidence is less compelling and their position on minor roads does not appear to demand priority. A more likely candidate exists in the small blocking walls around the forum at Bavay.[9]

The movement towards fortifications in all capitals and selected *vici* seems to come after the Gallic Empire. When a stratigraphic relation has been observed, it shows the walls set over, or into, burned or levelled earlier buildings (the Porte Bazée at Reims is the best example). Coins of Aurelian, Probus, Carinus and Diocletian found in the mortar of the walls (at Amiens, Beauvais, Toul and Famars) are generally consistent with the epigraphic evidence attributing the walls of Grenoble to Maximian and Diocletian and the tradition preserved in Gregory of Tours which saw the Dijon walls as the work of Aurelian.[10] Certain groups of walls can be identified on grounds of building technique and plan, but this does not give a date. A carbon 14 date from a wooden pile below the later wall at Tongeren (260 plus/minus 50 years) at least rules out a much later date in the mid-fourth century. A story of Constantius I being pulled up into the walls of Langres is given by Eutropius, and it seems probable that the main group of walls round capitals was completed by or in his time. Smaller links in the chains (Jünkerath, Bitburg, and Neumagen) may well have come later (as the connection between Neumagen and Constantine given by Ausonius, if taken literally, suggests) and some final additions (e.g. Saarbrücken) are known to be of mid-fourth-century date. The date of the northern outposts at Gent and Brugge is unknown.[11]

The chronological vagueness unfortunately bears on the interpretation. It is hard not to see the circuits as defensive, though there is a real discrepancy between the strength of the curtains and bastions and the actual capacity of any army other than the regular Roman one to lay serious sieges, while to usurpers the walls might offer strong-points as much as hindrances. Allowance must be made for the current tastes in military architecture, developed in the Eastern Empire, and for the sheer desire to impress. Walls could be conceived as 'gifts' of emperors to their subjects, and could not be undertaken without imperial approval. A decision from on high may be envisaged, and fits the circumstances of the late third century in Belgica better than competitive initiatives from the municipal worthies. Aurelian and Probus, whose reigns saw the building of the late defensive wall round Rome itself, are obvious candidates. If the majority of destruction layers turn out to be correctly dated to Aurelian's reign, any real start before Probus can be ruled out. An argument (in addition to Eutropius' story) for the walls' existence by Constantius Chlorus' time derives from his siege of Boulogne, where the older walls were in too poor a state to offer protection, and at latest Carausius should be seen as the builder. Support may be found in the absence of any precise reference to city walls in the panegyrics where Constantius is lauded for restoration of buildings, even if coin evidence makes it clear that actual building operations continued on some sites until this time.[12] On balance, then, the main initiative can be ascribed to Probus, and a time-lag allowed for completion.

The method of construction also bears on their significance. There is normally a striking contrast between the foundations and the visible parts of the masonry. Time and effort were spared on the former by copious use of *spolia* from public buildings and funerary monuments. The latter amounted to desecration of graves, a step of no little consequence. On one hand this clearly suggests hurried local effort, on the other the turning of an official blind eye, or imperial edicts actually allowing the destruction of monuments to this end (later laws stress that the reutilization of material from old buildings should be kept to a minimum, while the destruction of funerary monuments was expressly forbidden). We are left to imagine any protests that may have occurred – or were disruptions to local society so severe over the years that there were relatively few descendants to care for their ancestors' memorials? Some interesting inconsistencies are visible: the destruction of a rural monument overlooking the river Mosel at Grevenmacherberg contrasts with the preservation of that of the Secundinii at Igel, only a few miles downstream, and not all urban cemeteries were affected.[13]

By contrast, the upstanding portions of the walls were normally built with great care. Small stones and tile courses were used to give a tidy and durable facing on a rubble and concrete core, and at Amiens the exterior of the walls was plastered. There must have been much quarry-work, organized quite differently from the gathering of stones for the foundations. Some of the walls show such similarity that the same designers and even the same pool of labour are indicated. A striking group is formed by Beauvais, Senlis and Soissons, while the walls of Amiens differ from the others both in overall design and in detail.[14] It is reasonable to see here the work of army detachments brought in to supplement civilian effort.

The upshot was a series of formidable strong-points. Many variations are found, with rectangular or sub-rectangular plans (Beauvais, Soissons, Pachten, Bavay, Amiens) being rather less common than roughly oval layouts or plans that took advantage of high ground (Senlis, Arlon and many others). What all had in common was thickness of curtain-wall (a minimum of 2.5 m, usually 3 m or more) and frequent external towers or bastions, whether semi-circular, circular, square, hollow or solid (Amiens, where towers have not come to light, is an exception). The need to provide a glacis round the exterior must have still further changed the face of the cities. Whether ditches were provided is unclear, though probable. On the inside, building ramps (rather than regular banks) have been detected at Beauvais and Reims.[15]

Not least were changes in scale. The great exception here is Trier, whose 6 km circuit, enclosing 285 ha, remained as it was. At Metz, too, the greater part of the originally inhabited area was included in the 70 ha that was walled, though the south-eastern quarter was cut off. By contrast, the 45–50 ha late circuit at Tongeren enclosed about one third the space of the earlier one. A

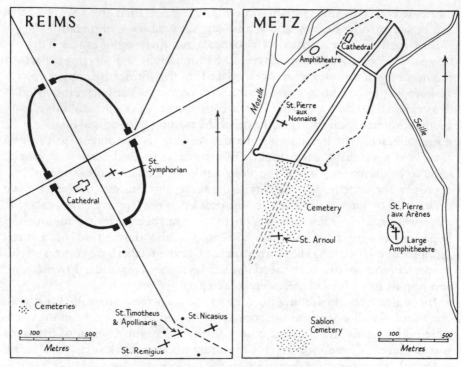

36 Late Roman Reims and Metz (Neiss, Collot, Gauthier)

greater real reduction was experienced (despite its status) at Reims, where the walls now joined the earlier monumental arches to enclose some 60 ha.[16]

There was a great gap between these larger circuits and the next group, bridged only by Amiens which, with some 20 ha, was easily the second in Belgica II. The main cluster in both provinces lies around 12 ha (Toul, Verdun, Soissons, Beauvais, Boulogne, probably Thérouanne and Arras, with the largest being the newly upgraded capital, Tournai). Senlis and Châlons are notably smaller (the first 6 ha, the second probably less) and information is not yet available on St. Quentin and Cambrai.

No explicit information on the population of any of these cities is of course extant. Sheltering, or boosting the morale of, the civilian population was only one consideration, the overall aim being to ensure a chain of fortified supply bases. That a local population strongly led might create a larger walled area can however be suggested, and administrative needs would be another factor.

The size of fortifications in *vici* is instructive. To judge by Bitburg, Neumagen, Jünkerath, Pachten and Taviers the norm lay just above 1 ha, smaller ones belonging either to the very early phase of fortifications or (Saarbrücken, Scarpone) to the mid-fourth century. The larger ones are of some interest. At Bavay, at first only the area of the forum, some 2 ha, was fortified by the addition of an encircling wall, at a period soon after the Gallic

· FORTIFIED CITIES

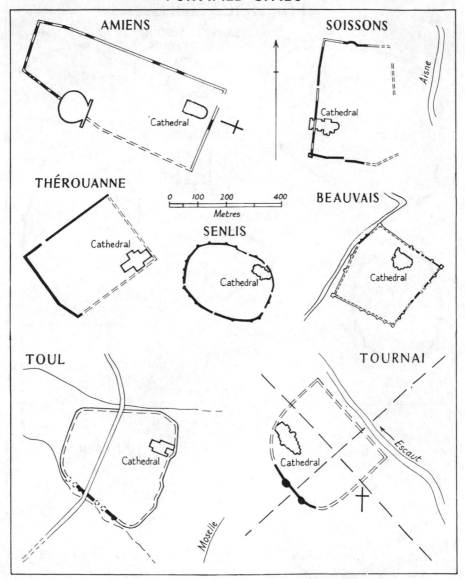

37 Plans of fortified cities in Belgica (Blanchet, Ancien, Liéger, Lemen, Vanvinckenroye, Massy, Bernard). Medieval cathedrals superimposed

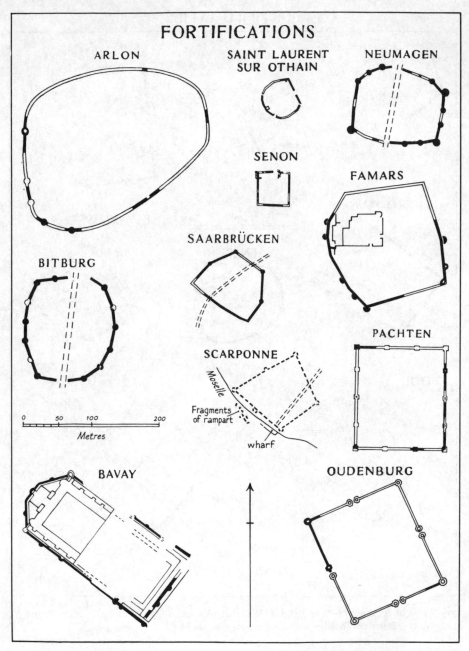

FORTIFICATIONS

ARLON

SAINT LAURENT SUR OTHAIN

NEUMAGEN

SENON

FAMARS

BITBURG

SAARBRÜCKEN

SCARPONNE

Moselle

Fragments of rampart

wharf

PACHTEN

BAVAY

OUDENBURG

0   50   100   200
Metres

38 Plans of fortifications in Belgica (Leman, Mertens, Biévelet, Grenier)

Empire. Later the size was doubled, the whole being enclosed within a more solid wall with bastions. Whether there was a division between military and civilian use remains to be demonstrated. The area compares with some 4.5 ha at Arlon, one of the larger *vici* of the Early Empire but now outstripped by Verdun and Tournai. The largest *vicus* fortifications are among the Medio-matrici, where Sarrebourg, le Héraple and Tarquimpol (credited with 14, 12 and 8 ha respectively) attain the normal size for capitals.[17] The importance of the route to the Rhine frontier accounts in part for the size of Metz, the roads leading eastward from that city to the Rhine, for the surprising size of Sarrebourg and the others.

To what extent was it a primary function of any of the fortified sites to house a permanent military unit? A clear answer can be given only for Oudenburg, where the military design and the high proportion of male burials show it to have been a true fort. Boulogne is ambivalent; although the Late Empire walls were essentially a rebuilding of the earlier fort of the *classis Britannica*, it was now also an administrative centre. The 12 ha enclosed leaves space for a military enclave alongside a supply base and civilian centre, and it is also possible that walls ran down to the shore of the estuary from the 'high' town, Bononia proper. One other city, Amiens, had a semi-permanent garrison in the form of *Ursarienses* and the *catafractarii Ambianenses*, but they were perhaps stationed at St. Acheul, some 2 km to the east, rather than in the city itself (though it was reputedly at a gate of Amiens that St. Martin gave half of his military cloak to a beggar). Normally, it was the occasional passage (probably attested at Châlons) rather than the permanent stationing of an army unit that took place. Nonetheless, this constant possibility of interference made the cities less attractive places to live, especially since the billeting of soldiers in civilian houses was normal in the Later Empire.[18]

The small size of most walled areas inevitably gives an impression of reduced population and a diminished civic life, which is only reinforced by the dismantling of monuments. The impression may be correct, yet deduction from reduced size alone is improper. If, in spite of military considerations, the walled centres were not forts, to what extent did they have the physical semblance of cities, with a considerable urban population?

The question can be approached from a different angle. Most late Roman fortified centres became medieval walled towns, and the evidence for direct continuity is usually strong. When the topography of the medieval city becomes easy to grasp, the fortified centre functions as a citadel, and although it may be densely inhabited, much of the population lived outside it in *suburbia* or suburbs. If this situation be read into the late Roman evidence, it makes the continuity between late Roman and medieval city that much stronger, and it means that no conclusions regarding population and civic life can legitimately be drawn from the mere size of the fortified areas.[19] The questions bear on the concept, function and topography of late Roman cities in northern Gaul. A start can best be made with topography.

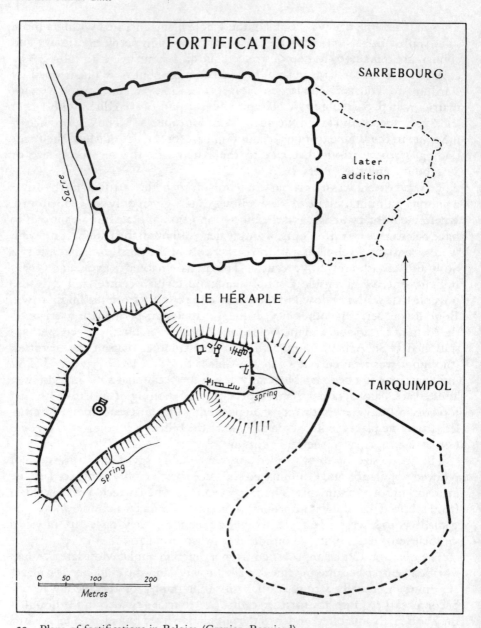

FORTIFICATIONS

SARREBOURG

later
addition

Sarre

LE HÉRAPLE

spring

spring

TARQUIMPOL

0   50   100   200
Metres

39   Plans of fortifications in Belgica (Grenier, Beaujard)

2   Urban topography

A reconstruction of late Roman urban topography must evaluate the extent of settlement outside the walls and the nature of buildings and habitation inside. Argument back from medieval conditions will not suffice, since it assumes what must be proven. Moreover, the case for each city must be argued as far as possible on its own merits before generalizations are made.

For northern Gaul, extrapolations are often made from Paris. Here, a good case can indeed be made for the continued existence on the left bank (the site of the early Roman city) of a community in the Later Empire, even though the main fortified area was the 13 ha Ile de la Cité. The earlier Paris forum was perhaps arranged to serve as a secondary fortification and burials continued to take place in the nearby south-eastern cemetery.[20]

In the cities of Belgica the evidence is less persuasive. The argument made for Senlis rests on the tiny size (6 ha) and a supposition that suburbs attested later, grouped around churches and cemeteries, had late Roman roots. While this is not impossible, archaeological proof is still lacking. The clearest example at present is Amiens. No general ring of suburbs surrounded the *castrum*, for burials of late Roman date encroach on the previously inhabited area, coming quite close to the centre. Only in the south-east of the original city is there space for limited occupation between the walls and the earlier cemeteries. There was certainly burial at St. Acheul (whence come Amiens' early Christian grave stones) and this, 2 km outside the city, is likely to reflect a separate community which can be seen as a rather distant *suburbium* (earlier burials and tombstones, including military ones, come from the same area). The cemetery on the north bank of the Somme also continued, but the dead could be from within the walls. The honorary mention given to Amiens by the historian Ammianus, *urbs inter alias eminens*, remains surprising.[21]

At Soissons, where the fortified area is smaller (12 ha) a suburb across the north bank of the Aisne has not been demonstrated, and at Beauvais a cemetery outside the *castrum* to the north-east may, but need not, be suburban. The cemeteries at Tournai would allow for some extramural habitation. At most other places the evidence has yet to be sought. Reims and Metz are in a different category, in that the size of the walled area was sufficient to enclose a fair-sized community and thus create a walled town rather than a citadel. At Metz, continued occupation on the left bank of the Moselle is indicated, but any extramural settlements to the south and east may have taken the form of villas rather than larger communities, a pattern found at Trier.[22]

The existence of suburbs as a general rule thus remains open to question, and they scarcely housed a significant enough population to make up for shrinkage of the centre. At Amiens, the Late-Empire cemeteries are small compared with the earlier ones, some of which were completely abandoned. True, the period involved is shorter, and simple inhumations without grave-goods, frequent in the fourth century, may have been less consistently reported; this does not outweigh the impression of a reduced urban population. Even at Metz and Reims only one out of the various cemeteries saw extensive use in the fourth century, in both places the one to the south of the city. At Trier alone do both big cemeteries remain in use and suggest a population no less than in earlier times.[23]

When evidence permits, the *vici* tell a similar tale. Of those reasonably well known, almost one third show no signs of occupation in the Later Empire, though the phenomenon is more marked in the north (Tungri, Nervii, Menapii) than elsewhere: Treveri and Mediomatrici show a high survival rate for *vici*, whether fortified or unfortified. Among Ambiani, Bellovaci, Remi and Suessiones the evidence does not allow for calculations; some *vici* of the Soissonais were still inhabited. Overall, just over one third of unfortified *vici* do show occupation in the fourth century. It is however often limited or special – a few buildings or a part rather than the whole site as at Mamer and the Tetelbierg. Only one or two fourth-century coins have been found at Schwarzenacker, and at Wederath, only a few inhumations (one of an official with a gold fibula) have been found to go with reported fourth-century coins. A not infrequent pattern, too, is for coins to fall off rapidly after the house of Constantine.[24]

Interestingly, fortification did not invariably prolong the occupation of a site, though again the negative evidence is largely from the north, along the Bavay-Köln road. Elsewhere, continuity of various types is found. The larger *castra* (to use the terminology of the *Notitia Galliarum*) sometimes saw intra-mural occupation, and functioned as small walled towns. This is best attested at le Héraple, where buildings were up against the fortification. It is likely at Arlon, Sarrebourg and Tarquimpol, probably also at the smaller Scarpone, where the inhabitants included men buried with weapons (a similar cemetery at Daméry on the Marne may indicate that it too was fortified). At Pachten, on the other hand, excavations revealed nothing inside the walls, but some settlement outside. In Picardie, as also elsewhere, *vici* may have survived only to be hidden by medieval successors, and no details are available.[25] A different pattern is revealed at Williers-Chamleux, where a small village in a valley (including a modest inn) was overshadowed by a fortification on the height above. Sometimes (Virton and Château Renaud) there may have been a shift of population to a higher, defensible site. The evidence, however patchy, is certainly most consistent with an overall drop in the population of *vici*, individually and collectively. Sacred sites (Rouvroy, Vendeuil-Caply, Fontaine-Valmont) did not fare any better, and at best had very impoverished structures, as at Ribemont-sur-Ancre.[26] To summarize, most *vici* south-east of the Meuse survived whether fortified or not, those of the Bavay-Köln road were reduced to strongpoints and elsewhere the record is uneven.

With the exception of Trier, and possibly Metz and Reims (where a little crowding could have made up for lost space), urban and village population was then reduced. To what, is another question. Eighteenth-century censuses show densities of between 100 and 200 persons per ha for the areas within the late Roman walls. By this time these had long been crowded city centres, and the figures can only be regarded as maxima: it is unlikely that densities in excess of 100 to the ha were found in late Roman times.[27]

Archaeological aid towards reconstructing the internal appearance of late Roman cities is (Trier apart) still meagre. Sometimes (Amiens) the forum area was included within the walls, but this is not always sure; at Beauvais, the fortification was built eccentrically, in an area of sporadic earlier building. In any case, public buildings did not necessarily retain their previous appearance and function. The monumental complex at Beauvais served as a quarry. That living quarters were constructed within the Bavay forum is not surprising, since the walls contained little besides that edifice, but something similar happened at Amiens. Moreover, part of the forum area there was levelled in the second half of the fourth century and the space devoted to metal-working on such a scale that an identification with the imperial armament factory (sited at Amiens in the *Notitia Dignitatum*) becomes almost unavoidable.[28] The space may then have remained public property, while being diverted to more urgent practical tasks.

Space becomes even more restricted if it is supposed that cities normally housed within their walls a cathedral church and bishop's residence. The discovery of a large apsed building beneath the cathedral at Tongeren raises the possiblity of ecclesiastical complexes. At Soissons, the local legend that the cathedral was built over a pagan temple has not yet been archaeologically proven; at Reims, there are indications of late Roman buildings under the cathedral, but of uncertain function, while at Metz local tradition (unsubstantiated) has an early cathedral below the present one. It will be seen that the intra-mural cathedral perhaps became the norm in Belgica only in the fifth or even sixth centuries, Trier being a certain exception, Reims and Metz possible ones.[29]

At Metz, another building which was later undoubtedly a church (St. Pierre-aux-Nonnains) lies in the southern part of the city, on high ground. It is an aisleless apsed hall, clearly modelled on the imperial auditorium at Trier, and incorporating tiles with the same stamp. If not a church, it must have been a large public building, perhaps connected with the administration of justice by the governor. If this explanation is preferred, then a secular purpose for the aisled basilica at Tongeren becomes more likely. Yet it is not clear that buildings of this type were normally erected for the occasional use of governors in cities that were not provincial capitals. When possible, Roman custom suggested the use of existing buildings, whether public or private (since any suitable residence could simply be commandeered). Occasional literary references to a *praetorium* could as well refer to the function as to any specific buildings. The whole question thus remains open.[30]

Knowledge of private residential buildings also remains sparse; there is (Trier apart) a total absence of late mosaics. At Beauvais, the houses found over the Severan monumental building were of poor quality, strengthening the impression that the late Roman cities were shabby. Even in central Reims, a fourth-century habitation over an earlier mosaic was of lower quality. Yet a paved street at Bavay shows that some care was still taken with public amenities. For Reims there is a clear reference to old paving in a Merovingian saint's life, at Trier numerous actual examples. In general, it can be presumed until otherwise proven that the street grids were adhered to, even if over a limited space, though adjustments might be made and roads were created behind the ramparts. The fortifications themselves, particularly when the number of gates was restricted to two or three, of course entailed alterations in the approach roads.[31]

The erection of new monumental buildings within the walls seems to have been confined to the larger circuits. The most obvious example, the palace complex at Trier, will be dealt with separately. At Reims, the donation of a bath-house by the emperor Constantine (location unknown) must have helped give that city an appearance befitting a provincial capital.[32] At Metz, the controversial apsed building was certainly monumental. Such buildings must have underlined further the gap between places that were effectively walled cities and those which were little more than strong-points.

Even at Metz and Reims the walled community was cut off from some earlier monuments, notably the amphitheatres. At Amiens, the amphitheatre was incorporated into the walls, because it lay unusually close to the centre. Openings to the outside were blocked and the monument thus served as a bastion; limited use as a place of assembly and even spectacles is not thereby totally ruled out. Elsewhere, amphitheatres and theatres were now outside the walls, as much as 0.5 km distant at Senlis.[33] Did such extramural monuments still function? The only city besides Trier to produce definite evidence is Metz. Here, too, the cellar of the large amphitheatre probably belongs to the very late third or early fourth century, since it produced stamped tiles of the type used in Trier at this period (and mural mosaic fragments are more likely to belong to this time than earlier). The second, smaller amphitheatre, close to the walls near the river, probably saw more use. Later, the large amphitheatre was the site of a church (St. Pierre-aux-Arènes), and Christian epitaphs suggest a cemetery from the fifth century. There is, however, a considerable gap between this and the tradition that has the church commemorating an earlier martyrdom in the amphitheatre.[34] Probably there was a period of disuse between an ambitious restoration, clearly presaging the continuance of traditional city life, and its use as a place of Christian cult. The other cities remain mute on the use of earlier monuments now outside the walls or, for that matter, inside. What arrangements existed for public ceremonies (especially those expressing loyalty to the emperor) are simply unknown.

Common to many of the late Roman cities, regardless of size, was a phenomenon which may not at first have been very noticeable but was to form an important bridge to the medieval towns. In the course of the fourth century, though more clearly in the fifth, the growth of cemetery churches was taking place. The exact beginnings are hard to date: ideally even the more reliable medieval traditions should be tested against archaeological evidence. In any case, the original small funerary chambers would not be a very noticeable feature of the urban landscape, since not significantly different from pagan counterparts; their architectural importance was in no proportion to their increasing effect on the life of the communities. Only archaeological evidence will be able to show whether there were occasionally, as tradition would have it, *vici Christianorum* clustered round some of the more important shrines in the fourth century, or whether the proper distance was kept between habitations of the living and the dead until a later period. The latter seems inherently more likely; the concept of the *vicus Christianorum* is indeed retrojected to Roman times by Gregory of Tours, but is probably anachronistic.[35]

In conclusion, change to the cities was major, but a clear distinction (leaving Trier aside) can be drawn between Metz and Reims and all the others. The latter were genuinely reduced in terms of inhabited area and population, and suburban settlements, even where they existed, were small. Much of the earlier cities was probably given over to market gardening or even agriculture. To complete the contrast, it should ideally be demonstrated that at Reims and Metz the greater part of the enclosed area was occupied, and that there were not vacant spaces within the walls. Strictly, this cannot be done, but where building projects were actively undertaken, more civic life and a greater urban population may be supposed; at Metz this can be supported by the extensive continued use of earlier cemeteries. At Metz, and also Reims, burials did not encroach too badly on previously inhabited areas – though burials outside the Porte de Mars at Reims show that this was not an absolute rule. In any case, cemeteries no longer presented the same appearance since the destruction of the old monuments. The chamber with sarcophagi was now normal for the rich, and wooden coffins (or none at all) for the poor.[36]

Even at Reims and Metz there is a high probability of disused buildings in various stages of dilapidation between cemeteries and walls. Without assuming that the cities of the Earlier Empire were always in an excellent shape, we may have to conclude that the later cities were, in comparison, melancholy places that did little to reflect the Mediterranean ideal. Hints of this are occasionally found in literature – Ammianus' comments on the ruins of Aventicum, Julian's on the much reduced Vesontio or Symmachus' praise of Valentinian's dutifulness, which led him to spurn pleasanter areas of the Empire for one blessed neither by populousness nor fine city monuments (and with a wretched climate to boot).[37]

3   Praesentiae tuae munera: late antique Trier

The exceptional position of Trier, while rooted in the past, owed most to the period of the Tetrarchy. If the city had been favoured by the Gallic emperors because of its strategic position behind, yet close to, the frontiers, there is no sign of any official programme of that period. The mosaic floor mentioning Victorinus belongs to a private house, and leaves in doubt what edifice the emperors used as a palace — perhaps that of the procurator.[38]

The city walls, too long to be effectively defended, failed to offer sufficient protection in the 270s. Testimony for destruction comes mostly from later levelling and dumping of burned débris in various parts of the city, and to this may be added (with caution) an orator's comment.[39] The fact that no smaller circuit of walls was built within the larger one, as at Tongeren, is of some interest. Perhaps such a reduced circuit would have come into being but for the decision that Trier should be capital of the northern Gallic diocese and an

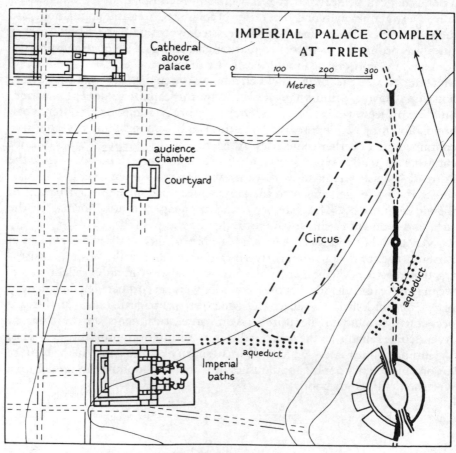

40   Plan of the imperial palace complex at Trier

imperial residence where rulers would stay whenever state business allowed. Trier had already known emperors, and to grace the city with a regular imperial presence was a wise idea. It was with Constantius' arrival in 293 that the mint also started, and was soon pouring forth a high volume of coinage, including, besides gold propaganda pieces, a quantity of the new reformed bronze. Probably it was Constantius who gave Trier the new birthday, symbol of a new era, that was celebrated in panegyric.[40] Architecturally, the new age was symbolized by the creation of a palatial enclave consonant with the city's acquired dignity.

As at the other new capitals, Milan and Aquileia, the buildings were grouped together, here in the eastern sector between Altbachtàl, amphitheatre and city wall. The space was ample, and the projects to scale. The new imperial baths (Kaiserthermen) were comparable in size to the lavish old Barbarathermen; imperial munificence had to equal or surpass private. Thus Trier contained two of the largest sets of baths in the Empire outside Rome, the new ones with their compact mass and emphasis on domes and apses well illustrating recent trends in architecture. For their construction, fine old private houses (with no signs of previous destruction) had to be levelled. Vast quantities of limestone were brought from quarries in the Eifel, and for use in bonding courses as well as roof a huge mass of tiles provided, some of them stamped with new names (of places or people). Started not earlier than 293, the baths seem (from coin evidence) to have been long in the building, and in fact, like many a grandiose enterprise in the Roman Empire, never reached completion, since there is evidence neither for the firing of furnaces nor the installation of water-pipes. They remained, nonetheless, one of the most prominent monuments of Trier, being adapted for some other purpose later in the century and again in medieval times.[41]

To the east, on conveniently level land, lay the circus, included by one panegyrist among the imperial gifts to the city. A reconstruction of an existing monument, it was now adorned with statues of the emperors and Caesars. Imperial patronage also brought improvements to the amphitheatre: wood from the beams and elaborate stage machinery of the cellar belong to the 290s, and a literary reference testifies to its continued use.[42] It was later believed that the amphitheatre had functioned as a triumphal entry to the city, but whether any remote memory of imperial ceremonies, rather than sheer invention, is to be seen remains uncertain. (Triumphal gateway it could scarcely be, without an access road.)

Among the palace buildings, pride of place went to the great aisleless apsed audience chamber now known as the Basilika, perhaps then the *basilica palatii* or, from its function, the auditorium. Originally rising amid a complex of buildings long invisible (though the vestibule lasted until the seventeenth century) it created, with its vast, richly decorated and well-lit interior, a fitting frame for the throne of emperors who were perceived as closer to deities than to their subjects. For one orator, concerned to link the building with

Constantine, it was the *sedes justitiae*, seat of justice personified.[43]

At a more prosaic level, the huge building (some 60 m without the apse, the half of that in breadth and height) beneath its plastered exterior, marble and mosaic-encrusted interior, was composed of countless tiles set in mortar, and must have occasioned a great upsurge of tile-production. The tile-stamps, again a mixture of personal and place-names (but with the latter prevailing) overlap with those from the baths but more closely with those from the fort Köln-Deutz, epigraphically dated to Constantine. While this date must be generally right, the exact time of start and completion cannot be closely determined. The orator who mentions the seat of justice also attributes the circus to Constantine, whereas an honorific inscription to his father as Caesar suggests an earlier date.[44]

Extensive buildings and courtyards surrounded the great basilica. In front of the entry-hall stretched porticoes and probably gardens. Part of the strip separating baths and basilica was covered by buildings, a fragment of which has been detected below the museum.[45] From below the cathedral, in the other direction, come indications of a more private part of the palace in the form of wall and ceiling paintings. Whether the heads that are framed between gift-carrying *putti* are personifications or portraits of Constantine's family has occasioned much debate. In any case, the extensive use of purple for cloth and jewels indicates a connection with the imperial family.

The room that had contained the ceiling-paintings was destroyed and levelled to make way for an extensive new building convincingly identified as the northern part of a great double church. Medieval tradition held that the first cathedral at Trier had been built when the devout Helena, mother of Constantine, gave her house for the purpose. For long this was dismissed as pious legend or, if taken seriously, gave rise to a search outside rather than inside the city walls. The double church raises the chance that the tradition enshrined a kernel of truth. Since Helena died about 328, much depends on dating. It is equally important for an alternative view, that the churches were founded by Constantine in remorse following his execution of Crispus (his son) and Fausta (his wife), thought to be involved together in some intrigue.

If the paintings show Constantine's family, and particularly if they are to celebrate the marriage of Crispus to Helena the younger, a destruction soon after the executions of 326 becomes plausible. Personifications, on the other hand, demand no such tight dating. In fact the arguments for an element of portraiture (perhaps mixed with personifications) are strong. Yet this by no means guarantees that the building of the cathedral followed within a year of 326. Coin evidence can hardly be pressed so closely, though a general connection with the aftermath of Constantine's family tragedy may be held as probable.[46]

The imperial enclave at Trier could be felt in more than one way as the gift of the emperor's quasi-divine presence. For people of all classes there were solemn processions and ceremonies, all the atmosphere created by the presence of the court. And since the near-divine status of the emperor was as much a reflection of widespread popular feeling as an imposition from above, this may indeed have lent an aura that it is hard for a secular age to grasp. The envy of other cities can be heard through the orators of Autun, who had to plead for an imperial visit for their city.[47] The result of envy and competition from within Belgica is expressed in the Constantinian baths of Reims, perhaps in the amphitheatre at Metz and more certainly in the basilica there, a smaller version of the one at Trier. Both are cities that either Constantius or Constantine must have visited. While the emperor's presence was itself important, so were the enduring buildings which he might endow. It is a sign of the age that public buildings were now financed not by local notables vying with one another to adorn their city but by successful appeals, often through oratory, to the highest authority.

There was of course another very different aspect to imperial buildings and the presence of the court. Buildings meant employment, and while some of the specially skilled craftsmen may have come from elsewhere, the majority would be local, coming at furthest from countryside or neighbouring city. It is of interest that the Trier school of mosaics was not totally interrupted, and that on grounds of style alone it can be hard to distinguish mosaics of the mid–third century from those of late third- or even early fourth-century date.[48]

In addition to the employment created by their corporate presence, the members of the courts as individuals also provided hands with cash, and mouths with food. The repercussions for both city and surrounding countryside are obvious, even if the population suggested for late Roman Trier has almost certainly been much exaggerated (it is not infrequently put at well over 50,000, implying an unlikely density of over 200 to the ha). Service trades must certainly have been more fully occupied than in other cities, the amount of cash in circulation much higher. The demands made on the surrounding countryside might be bad or good, depending on whether supplies were simply exacted by way of taxation – by extraordinary indictions – or whether they encouraged rural–urban exchange. The extent of rebuilding and occupation in the countryside, it will be seen, sounds a positive note. Yet large estates might belong to senators, court officials, or the imperial fisc and some of the production of goods for court and army was done by state factories. The traders, for whom there is limited evidence, may have dealt largely in luxury goods. The manufacturing of tiles seems to have been controlled by a wealthy few. At Trier itself, the making of pottery of the type known as 'Weinkeramik' continued, but export was not on the same scale. On balance, Trier may have been more of a 'parasite' on the country than previously.[49]

Nonetheless Trier was a vastly different place from surrounding cities in the province. Moreover, the effect on urban topography did not stop at the palace enclave. There is evidence for rebuilding of the municipal basilica in the forum. To the east of this, two large buildings, each occupying a small *insula*, could have been official.[50] There is a generous sprinkling of fourth-century mosaics throughout the city. Some old houses went on in use, with or without rebuilding. The Altbachtal sanctuary flourished, at least until the time of Gratian, and has produced a particularly high number of coins of Constantine and his house. Throughout the city, streets were paved with limestone for the first time. Some wealthy men preferred to live outside the city, and rich suburban villas were to be found on both sides of the river, comparable to the house of Ausonius near Bordeaux. Some were not far from the edges of the urban cemeteries, which still expanded. One feature that Trier shared with other cities was the gradual growth of Christian funerary chambers into places of meeting for the faithful. The burial places (real or supposed) of the early bishops gave birth, by stages not closely datable, to churches.[51]

Status, and a life closely dependant on the presence of the court, was not without hazard. Usurpers in the form of Magnentius and his brother were followed by the Alamanni and, worse, the pagan Caesar Julian who was at odds with the *praefectus praetorio* and also so hated Constantine that he perhaps made a point of neglecting Trier. Good times returned under Valentinian and Gratian. New building projects included extensive alterations to imperial baths, which perhaps became palatine barracks, and to the cathedral, which now gained its great square core. Down near the river, with access through an unknown gate, great warehouses were constructed on the edge of the built-up area of the street grid. Gratian's reign may be seen as a heyday, partly thanks to all the information provided by his mentor and client Ausonius. As many prominent men walked the streets as under Constantine, and the times seemed no less secure. Ausonius' own terse word-picture of a peaceful city feeding, clothing and arming the Empire must have seemed most appropriate.[52]

A sharp eye might have seen signs of the times that were not the result of imperial patronage. The great municipal baths may no longer have functioned as such; by the end of the fourth or the early fifth century, they served as habitations or barracks.[53] Barely enough is known of the porticoes lining the streets to tell if they were encroached on by shabby private buildings as happened elsewhere. Municipal properties may or may not have been well maintained. We know nothing of Trier's civic life and administration in this period; court and church alike overwhelm it, and we know more about bishops and churchmen than city magistrates. The reign of Gratian saw the construction of streets over a ravaged Altbachtal, for which change credit must be given to St. Martin as well as to the emperor.[54]

Symmachus might employ a sneering commonplace that by implication denigrated Trier along with the rest of Gaul. Yet epigraphical evidence combines with literary evidence and the occasional study of skeletal material to show that fourth-century Trier had a varied and cosmopolitan population, in which Gauls were only one element (though probably disguised by new fashions in nomenclature). After the murder of Gratian, Trier saw usurpers rather than legitimate emperors, and often in the absence of the imperial court the great buildings must have stood largely empty. Yet the mint continued in regular operation until the death of Theodosius in 395, and the city remained the seat of the *praefectus praetorio Galliarum*. So long as the Rhineland had to be protected, Trier's strategic importance did not drastically decline. The city continued to present an appearance that visitors from other provinces would have recognized as typical of the Mediterranean urban *koine*, with a northern flavour detectable under the imperial overlay. It also played an interesting new role, as Germans of princely family rose high in the Roman army and intermarried with local families to produce, albeit in small numbers, a new nobility of mixed ancestry. The date of the withdrawal of the prefecture to Arles is, as has been seen, debated. The Rhine frontier was drastically breached in 406/7, and the first of several armies of Germans advanced on the city, this time Vandals, Alans and Suebi, later Franks. The people of Trier must have regretted their enormous walls as they huddled for safety in the amphitheatre. Destruction layers observed in buildings and streets may belong to this or the subsequent sackings of the city by Franks. The mint continued to function spasmodically, but passing usurpers and loyal generals must have found a ghost of the previous city.[55]

4   The function of cities

So far the emphasis has been on change, and the gulf that appears fixed between Trier and the next grade of city, and again between Reims or Metz and Châlons-sur-Marne or Senlis. Yet all cities by definition still served as administrative centres, with the local *curiales* responsible for them. Tax rebates offered by Valentinian to ensure upkeep of fortifications are a reminder both of continuing local responsibilities and the problems that might require imperial intervention.[56]

Presumably then, parts of public buildings in the city centre were still used for administrative functions, even if other areas of public space were diverted to new uses – the storage for shorter or longer periods of the supplies that represented taxation in kind, the quartering when necessary of troops that were too numerous to disperse among private households. Thus functions appropriate to the new age of insecurity and imperial control were grafted on to old.

The extent to which the system of decurions and magistrates still functioned regularly can of course be doubted, although in theory the rank of *curialis* was a hereditary burden. In the later fourth century, the *defensor civitatis* makes his appearance, gradually becoming more powerful, and probably more ubiquitous. Increasing concentration of power at the local level in the hands of the few influential *curiales*, and of individuals acting as patrons of the *ordo*, could also be found. To an ever greater extent, the cities may have been *de facto* dominated by a few people, even a single high-ranking family. The Syagrii of fifth-century Soissons are the logical conclusion of such a process, even if a lengthy connection with the city cannot be documented.[57]

Yet it is clear that cities no longer played the same role in the life of the local aristocracy. Until at least Severan times they had been persuaded that to beautify them was the most appropriate way of expressing their rivalries. They had learned the Mediterranean way of channelling ambitions: local feuds had developed into *philotimia*, the competitive civic virtue on which ancient cities depended. Archaeological evidence for the cities of northern Gaul, however inconclusive, suffices to show a drastic dilution, if not a disappearance, of these corporate civic values. Eloquent voices are also to hand in the literary circles. Ausonius shows that the Gallic aristocracy, like their Italian cousins, set greatest store by their rural possessions, and that city life and business were regarded as a chore from which escape was made as quickly as possible.[58] The people of greatest means sought to avoid civic responsibilities, preferably by joining the senatorial class and so gaining immunity from anything except an honorary position.

Compared with the rest of Gaul, Belgica produced, as has been seen, comparatively few senatorial families, and those confined to the Treveri, Remi and Suessiones. Yet the same attitude may be supposed prevalent, and to have militated against the restoration of the cities to their former grandeur. A distinction may have to be drawn in Belgica, however, between an area where the change was largely one of values and an area in the north where the whole economic substructure of city and countryside had been attenuated. Interestingly, this had the effect of confining late Roman urbanism almost to the same areas that had started to develop it in pre-Roman times.

What of the economic function of the later cities? Clearly, sheltered behind their walls, they served as gathering points for the produce of the countryside. This was however a surplus which they did not themselves consume, but which was redistributed by imperial officials. If a general drop in urban population is accepted, then the function of the city itself as consumer was thereby diminished. Did they still serve as markets, and even produce goods?

It is difficult to avoid an impression of overall diminution of economic activity, and this is in no way lessened if the *vici* – or *castra* as the fortified ones were now termed – are taken into account. Most of the evidence in the smaller centres of pottery production and metal-working belongs to the Early Empire. Yutz was the probable source of the ADIVTEX stamped tiles, but this was clearly controlled by a big landowner or an imperial official. Trier's 'Weinkeramik' was reduced in both quality and quantity.[59] For wool, we have the state factories or *gynaecia* established at, or controlled from, Trier, Metz and Tournai, and the two capitals, Trier and Reims, had gold and silver thread workers (to supply officials) as well as armament factories (also found at Amiens).[60]

Evidence for the secondary sector of service trades is also virtually lacking for the Later Empire. Caution is required, since the lack of evidence is in part due to changing funerary fashions. The dying out of funerary monuments depicting or naming individuals and their professions is, it can be argued, as much due to a change in values as to different economic realities. Yet only at Trier are stone sarcophagi really frequent, and a drop in the service-trade of the funerary stone-masons can perhaps be taken as symptomatic of the whole. Certainly, there is no evidence that artisans any longer had the wherewithal to announce themselves to posterity by means of a stone monument.

It cannot of course be held that no production was centred on the cities. But what we know of is either at a lower level than previously or is essentially government-organized activity, such as the factories, which indeed provided a means of livelihood, but not marketable products. Except at Trier, the evidence for long-distance luxury trade is also less than for the Earlier Empire. The range of luxury items available in the imperial city may be aptly symbolized by an exquisite translucent shallow bowl carved out of agate.[61]

Yet such observations should be placed within a wider context. Was there not already a selective economic factor at work in the Late Empire *civitates*? If Cassel may have been abandoned or demoted out of considerations of insecurity, the same does not apply to Bavay. Thérouanne and Tongeren kept their status in the fourth century, but declined thereafter, as did Arras. In each case, the replacements, Tournai and Cambrai, like Verdun, were situated on navigable rivers whereas the demoted city was landlocked. [62]

Arguably, the first stage of the selective survival of cities was conditioned largely by administrative and military exigencies. Cities on rivers were that much better placed for the easy transport onwards of goods assembled there for redistribution. On the other hand, given that the army could simply requisition private transport as necessary, geographical location should not have been of great moment. Perhaps then the growth of the riverbank sites, the decline of the others, was already sufficiently evident by the third century to influence official choices. The period 260–285, when all evidence combines to suggest a general condition of *sauve qui peut*, may have seen a further differentiation, helped by a failure to keep roads in good repair.

Certainly, it is the riverbank sites that show the greatest continuity and are the first to show a revival of economic life in the early middle ages. Dinant, Namur, Amay, Huy (the last showing signs of continuous artisanal activity from late Roman into Merovingian times) and Maastricht testify to the importance of the Meuse as Cambrai and Tournai to that of the Escaut/Scheldt. There is certainly a sense in which later economic geography was pre-figured in the fourth century, and this lends support to the view that a certain, albeit low, level of economic activity persisted throughout and that the sites never quite sank to the passive, essentially pre-urban form that has sometimes been suggested.

For their future, however, no feature of the late Roman cities is so important as their becoming the seats of bishops. By employing the Roman administrative divisions as a basis for its own structure, the church contributed equally to both change and continuity. In Belgica, the rate of change must not be exaggerated, for this was, along with Armorica and Britain, the far north. As will be seen, not all cities were certainly the seat of bishops in the fourth century, and even at Trier there is no evidence for them taking an active part in civic as opposed to ecclesiastical affairs. The existence of intra-mural cathedral churches before the fifth century is debatable, with the exception of the imperial capital. If, however, a certain time-lag manifests itself in the north, the important point is that the gradual strengthening of the church was not halted by events of the fifth century. It is in this period that two distinct, and at first sight contradictory, trends can be most clearly seen in the north. On the one hand, the day of cities in the Mediterranean sense was already over, even if remnants of Roman civic administration did survive. At the same time, the last feature of the city to spread out from the Mediterranean was just completing its conquest, and the hybrid product of these processes was to give birth to the medieval town.

11

THE COUNTRYSIDE IN THE LATER EMPIRE

1 **Desertion, flight and hillforts reborn**

An inhabitant of second-century Belgica who had awakened from a magic sleep two centuries later would have found the rural scene much altered. The extent of his disorientation would have depended considerably on the region. In the Eifel north of Trier, landmarks would be identified relatively fast beneath superficial changes. In the north-west, even behind the coastal areas rendered unrecognizable by the marine transgressions, ruins were probably as frequent as inhabited farms. Parts of the Condroz and Hainaut were in like shape, while the higher Ardennes had likely reverted to forest. In Lorraine or the Soissonais, the traveller might have felt more at home. Everywhere he would often have found new hamlets and villages that were subtly different in character from the old ones. He would also have found that many hilltops had been fortified by an array of walls, banks and ditches, some but not all sheltering small permanent communities. The overall impression of a lower density of people would be unavoidable, though more obvious in some areas than others.

The stages by which these transformations took place are obviously important, and the third century emerges as a crucial period. It is often claimed that the majority of villas went up in flames in the course of the 275–76 invasions, and that from this destruction many of them failed to re-emerge. A critical examination of the evidence is in theory simple, in practice rather less so, for the number of well excavated sites is small. Conclusions have sometimes been drawn from unstratified material or even coin-hoards without a precise context. Re-examination of old material, and the collection of new, is gradually bringing clarification.[1]

Unquestionably, some villas did suffer violent destruction in the second half of the third century, and a hypothesis of frequent accidental fires strains credulity as far as acceptance of hostile acts. The best documented destruction levels come from the Eifel, Hunsrück, and Saarland – from small (Bollendorf, Sotzweiler), medium (Newel, Weitersbach) and large (Horath, Oberweis,

Echternach) sites – and the same story is found among the western Treveri (Robelmont). Since the number of coins found in villas is normally small, dating to any given year is not possible. At Haccourt, a destruction of around 275 demonstrates that damage was not confined to the Treveri. Other Belgian villas with no evidence of later occupation could have been either destroyed or deserted, and the same holds good for the villas of Lorraine (though the destruction of the Mithraeum at Mackwiller indicates violence, as do traces of fire at a villa and hamlet near Sarreinsming).[2] In the west and north of Belgica, evidence for destruction as opposed to desertion of rural sites is not yet so sure.

Even in areas where destruction is attested, it was less than wholesale. Sites in the high Eifel escaped, as did some in the Saarland (Ittersdorf) and Luxembourg (Goeblingen-Nospelt). The palatial villa of St. Ulrich near Sarrebourg was not destroyed, though it may not have maintained its old level of luxury.[3] Overall, the evidence indicates desertion, or a drop in living standards, as much as destruction. Desertion can also be exaggerated; apparent absence of coins between 275 and 295 need not mean a gap in occupation, if there are coins of Tetricus or imitations. To complicate the issue, the pottery of this period is relatively poorly known.

In spite of qualifications, the evidence still indicates desertion of many villas in the north and west (of over 600 sites found in Picardie by aerial photography, a tiny number have produced fourth-century pottery). It is less impressively attested in the east, particularly among the Treveri, and perhaps also in the south (Suessiones). Paradoxically (at first sight) the region with best attested destruction has also the lowest rate of desertion.

Closer attention strongly suggests that the desertion of rural sites did not simply begin at the time of the invasions (even if the time bracket be 259–76). A number of sites, small in total, but significant for the beginnings of a trend, were deserted already in the late second or early third century. The best known example is Estrées-sur-Noye (which may have been inhabited for little more than a generation), and to this can be added, besides others from the Somme valley, Noyelles-Godault (an example the more striking because the nearby *vicus* saw fourth-century reoccupation). Soignies (Hainaut) failed in the late second century, and Irsch near Trier was not occupied beyond the earlier part of the third (Newel may also have lain untended for a time).[4] It is highly probable that more such examples will come to light.

Although the desertion of sites in the second century is not yet as broadly or securely based as is desirable, the consequences of its acceptance are important, since desertion in the third century can then be seen as the continuation, doubtless accelerated, of an existing trend. The beginnings were perhaps more marked in the north-west than elsewhere, but the eventual number of abandoned sites is hardly less impressive among Nervii and Tungri. Recent studies here have increased the sites showing signs of habitation in the fourth century, but still show almost 80 per cent of them abandoned, and north of the Bavay-Köln road the figure is probably higher. Among the western Treveri, around Arlon, the survival rate remains low, and even in the centre of the *civitas*, just north of Trier, it may not have gone beyond 50 per cent of all sites. Among Mediomatrici and Leuci further research is required, while in the Soissonais an impression of greater continuity is, as will be seen, based rather on cemeteries than sites.[5]

A sliding scale between the west and east, north and south of the province, may be tentatively accepted. What kinds of explanations are then appropriate? There is no mystery over the coastal areas of Flanders or the low-lying areas by the mouths of Canche and Somme. The marine transgressions (known as Dunkirk 2) had drowned the immediate coastal area and rendered a further area marshy: fingers of the sea crept as far inland as Ardres, and left Oudenburg on a peninsula. Coins show a population still in place under Postumus, whereas the lack of later hoards suggests a date before 275 for the disaster, perhaps triggered by one or more spectacular storms. (This followed, however, on a period from the late second to early third century which had seen a marked increase in the occupation of the coastal zone, a reminder that not all areas behaved alike.[6])

No such simple solution applies to the plateaux around Amiens. The failure of the city itself has already been noted. Had this resulted from transference of interests and building patronage out into the countryside (a phenomenon traced in third and fourth-century Britain), then the villas should have increased in number, size and luxury, not decreased. The fate of this area could, however, in another way be linked with Britain, or the Rhineland. If production of grain for the armies or markets there had caused the boom of the late first and early second centuries, their self-sufficiency would have the reverse effect. The local urban markets were also at best in steady state. The profit to be made from agricultural surplus may have been insufficient for the continued support of the artificially large number of imposing structures built upon it. Whether erosion and inadequate manuring were contributory factors is hard to estimate: impoverishment of the soil is less likely here than in the poorer, sandy regions of Flanders and the lower Rhineland, but not impossible if the effort of growing cash-crops had led to an imbalance.

The same explanation may be considered for regions near the Meuse which could have been affected by the self-sufficiency of the Rhineland. Ultimately, the question will need to be reviewed in a wider context, since some areas of Lugdunensis were similarly affected by desertion of rural sites in the third century. It must also be borne in mind that desertion of certain sites could represent one stage in the process whereby land changed hands to produce larger multiple estates for a smaller number of richer landowners. Yet if increasing numbers of pollen samples show, as a few already do, that forest was encroaching on cultivated areas even in the middle of the Roman period, then the hypothesis of a real (and early) decline in population and agriculture will be substantiated.[7]

Alternatives to a single, general catastrophe theory with the barbarians as prime movers are then available. Yet they should perhaps not be overstressed, for the barbarians were both a constant threat and at times an actuality. Even if the coin evidence be left to one side, the building of clearly unofficial rural fortifications started already in the reign of Postumus, and can only reflect insecurity. Moreover, destruction in the countryside can be more devastating and permanent in its effects than in urban settlements, if stores are lost as well as current harvests, and famine can rapidly become a reality. Best able to survive would be landowners with multiple holdings, not all of which were affected, or those who had already stored supplies away in a strong-point. Nonetheless, had destruction or flight been confined to a single incident, recovery would have been more widespread and rapid. It is the lingering of the foe within the frontiers and the addition of other longer-term problems that render the picture more sinister.

The defeat of Tetricus and the ensuing imperial abandonment of Gaul left a country ripe for internal trouble, especially once the barbarians had created a temporary disaster area. It was suggested above that large landowners who survived the troubles might effectively become local 'tyrants'. Further trouble in the countryside could have come about as one band met another, or the imperial army. In the north, a part of Belgic territory came under the control of Carausius. This, and the campaigns of Maximian and Constantius against him, were further reasons for disruption in the north-west.

It may never be possible to unravel into a coherent account the intertwining problems and their effects. It should, however, become clearer which areas were more affected by early desertion of sites, which by actual destruction. Refined dating for the latter (based on pottery as well as coins) should also prove possible, and this in turn gives a clue to the cause. As Belgica is more fully set within a wider context, it will become apparent whether it is the lower survival rate among western sites or the high among eastern that more requires comment and explanation.

If the only visible rural change was a smaller number of occupied villas, it might still be possible to minimize it. As things are, it often cannot be demonstrated that the farmyards were deserted when occupation ceased in the main house, and continued occupation of farmyards would indicate scattered estates passing increasingly into the hands of fewer absentee landowners. Transformations of a more far-reaching kind, albeit unevenly spread across the landscape, are however suggested by further concatenations of evidence.

The serious interruption of the peaceful conditions that had been conducive to dispersal of settlement caused what might, given Gaul's long-term history, be anticipated – a return to the old expedient of fortified hilltops. This might entail the refortification of a site where ramparts of Iron Age date (Buzenol) were still visible or the choice of a new one. Among the earliest is Nismes-Viroinval, where an *éperon barré* was created by a double ditch and stone rampart in the reign of Postumus: the coins do not go beyond the Gallic Empire, but the pottery suggests a more than occasional occupation. It lies in an area of south-west Tungrian territory that seems to have seen little actual

LATE HILL·FORTS

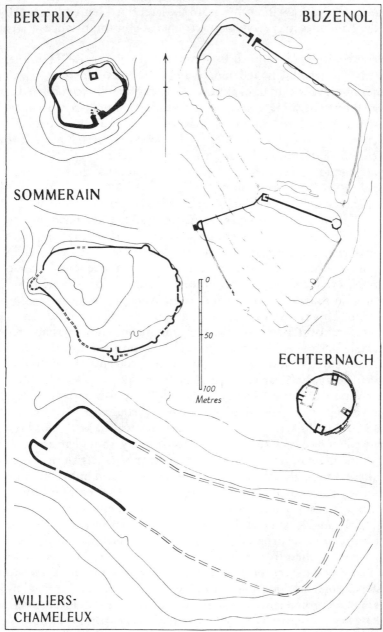

BERTRIX

BUZENOL

SOMMERAIN

0

50

100
Metres

ECHTERNACH

WILLIERS-
CHAMELEUX

41 Plans of late hillforts (Mertens)

destruction – a nearby villa at Treignes survived, a villa and sanctuary at Matagne-la Grande saw intensive use in the later third century. A nearby road across the Ardennes may have begun to increase in importance as a route to Köln.[8]

Other early irregular hillforts lie above the Mosel near Zell, Hontheim and Pünderich. The trend was well underway by the end of the third century, and further examples come to light almost yearly as sites hitherto undated turn out to be late Roman. Dating is variable. Sometimes a fourth-century, even a late fourth-century date is indicated (Château-Renaud above Virton, Vireux-Molhain overlooking the Meuse in the French Ardennes).[9] Many sites were occupied only intermittently, and finds are sometimes sparse. The custom clearly took hold, and any threat to security might cause the building of a new fort, or the reoccupation of an old.

Plan and technique were highly variable – *éperons barrés*, ring-walls, double enclosures, towers of all shapes (sometimes added as afterthoughts) were admissible. The area enclosed might be over 1 ha (Buzenol), but was much more often less, comparable with the smallest grade of pre-Roman hillforts. Earth ramparts might be raised, especially in a first phase, but the use of stone was regular. Frequent, but not ubiquitous, was the use of *spolia* which, like the milestone and funerary monuments from Buzenol, might be dragged over several km. This re-use of funerary monuments again shows an amazing disregard for normal family and religious proprieties, perhaps reflecting considerable lack of continuity in rural land-owning families. (The remains of a large monument so looted, apparently before the end of the third century, have been excavated near Grevenmacherberg.[10])

The position of some fortifications, well away from roads, is enough to suggest that private initiative, not official requirements, was at work. Occasionally the link is closer. A tiny circular walled area at Echternach is probably connected with the huge villa 500 m away, though it is barely the size of one of the main house's wings. The fortification 'Kaasselt' is some 1500 m from Altrier and made use of funerary monuments and burnt building stones from there; it presumably offered protection to the community, and the impetus is again likely to have come from some major landowner acting as patron. Château-Renaud can be considered a replacement for the village of Virton, but there is a chronological gap between the latest finds from the old village and the earliest from the fort.[11] Sometimes sanctuaries were fortified, on the analogy of the official fortlet at Strimmig, built under Victorinus. The clearest examples are Deneuvre in the Meurthe valley and Belval-Bois-des-Dames in the Argonne; other possible sites are Montcy St. Pierre overlooking the Meuse near Mezières, le Châtelet on the Marne, Gérouville and Velosnes (an old hillfort) in the south-western Treveri, Sion and Mt. Avison among the Leuci.[12] A passage in Ausonius' *Mosella* may guardedly mention unofficial as well as official strongholds before hastening to assure the reader that the purpose of both was now purely storage. Later Salvian refers to flight to *castella* as a normal part of rural life. Further fifth-century texts, epigraphical and literary, show us the piously named Theopolis in the Basses-Alpes (erected by a Praetorian Prefect) and, in Aquitania, variations on the same theme (*montana castella*) belonging to friends of Sidonius Apollinaris.[13] If the trend perhaps started in Belgica, it did not stop there.

One category of fortifications is clearly different. These had carefully built walls of small well-laid blocks, and show many more traces of occupation including an astonishing number of coins for the small space; they tend moreover to overlook roads or rivers. The cemeteries include belt-buckles, spearheads or axes, giving the appearance of military contingents – also the only feasible explanation for the coins. The classic sites are Furfooz, Epraves and Dourbes (in Tungrian territory, hence now part of Germania II). While a permanent garrison is only clearly visible from the late fourth century, the earlier, third-century wall at Furfooz was already built in the same manner.[14] Such sites were then official, while bearing little resemblance to the normal *castra* on the roads, the inhabitants being soldier-farmers whose origins will require further discussion. Williers-Chamleux and perhaps Steinfort, clearly guarding the main road from Trier to Reims, are probably to be put in this category; it remains to be seen whether the hillforts above the Mosel should also be included. In the absence of excavations, the line between the two types of site cannot always be drawn with clarity, though they represent, at least initially, two very different concepts springing on the one hand from private, on the other from official, initiatives. Surprises are doubtless still in store. At Tholey, south of Trier, site of a major villa, there is an irregular fortification on the hilltop and indications of a block-house type of structure below. Further work may lead to the discovery of whole systems hitherto unsuspected.[15]

While in origin so diverse, the fortifications nonetheless had common functions, and the differentiation may have grown less marked with time. True, the official posts formed headquarters for soldiers who, to judge from the rich coin finds, were well-remunerated. But priority must also have been given to working the surrounding land so that the unit was self-sufficient. Common sense suggests such a programme, quite apart from the evidence that the line between soldier and farmer was very much less strictly drawn in the Later Empire.[16] Likewise, the inhabitants of the unofficial hillforts, whether seeking temporary refuge or longer-term quarters, must primarily have been communities of peasants, normally from the estates of a big landowner. Occasionally traces of iron-working are found within the walls ('Alteburg' near Zell on the Mosel, Vireux-Molhain on the Meuse); this could be either estate production or more official in nature.

A different class of evidence also suggests a diminishing differentiation between the inhabitants of 'official' hillforts and other rural settlements. The characteristic late-fourth-century graves with weapons or other military insignia and accoutrements are not normally found beside the obviously private fortifications, though there are ambivalent examples (Ortho on the

Ourthe, Völklingen above the Saar). Burials with weapons have been found, not surprisingly, outside cities and villages (Amiens, Boulogne, Hermes, Daméry, Vermand, Namur, Ciney). They also occur isolated or in small groups at numerous points throughout the countryside of both Belgic provinces (but especially Belgica II) and even beyond the Seine. Normally, these scattered burials belonged to unfortified settlements, villas or villages. Clearly, the soldier-farmers were by no means restricted to the vicinity of a few hilltop fortifications. The known hillforts are geographically restricted, and occur only in certain of the suitable areas – the Ardennes, Eifel, Saarland, and Lorraine. Whether they will also be discovered in the Marne and Somme valleys remains to be seen (inhumations at l'Etoile near Amiens suggest an affirmative answer).[17] Other solutions to the problem of security, such as the strengthening of the perimeter wall of a villa and farmyard (Goeblingen-Nospelt), or the building of earth ramparts round small villages, existed. No obvious towers or *burgi* of the type recognized for the Rhineland (Froitzheim) are as yet known in Belgica.[18] While the true extent of fortifications remains to be determined, attention was certainly paid not only to the main roads but to the Meuse valley and the minor roads which crossed the Ardennes to the frontier.

Overall, an increasing militarization of rural communities is clearly visible in the second half of the fourth century, and it is important to know the nature and identity of these soldier-farmers, and to enquire into the information given by cemeteries both with and without weapon-burials.

2   **The contribution of cemeteries**

Cemeteries always form an important adjunct to habitations in any study of settlement patterns, giving complementary and sometimes clearer information on the society and the social differentiations within it. In late Roman Belgica, their contribution is an important one not at present duplicated by other sources.

The first striking feature is the general lack of continuity from the Early Empire. For every site where Late Empire inhumations are found beside or among earlier incinerations, some ten or more show an Early Empire cemetery going out of use, or late inhumations occurring only after an extended hiatus.[19] Of course, the evidence inevitably allows for impressions rather than hard data. Moreover, the change from cremation to inhumation, which had started in the later second century but became the rural norm only from the later third, might cause a shift of the cemetery. Such a minor dislocation is attested at the villa of Köln-Müngersdorf, where the inhumation cemetery is closer to the habitation. Yet the examples of Grevenmacherberg and Newel show that inhumations might be placed alongside the earlier burials, at Grevenmacherberg in spite of damage to the central sculptured monument. Such continuity might be expected if the same family worked the land, and is found in poorer rural cemeteries like the tiny 'Grabgärten' enclosures near a farmhouse in the Mayener Stadtwald.[20] Even minor changes in location may then denote new occupants or some slight break in continuity. A simple extrapolation to habitations of the figures derived from the cemeteries, suggesting less than 10 per cent continuity, is, however, misleading in that minor changes can appear as ruptures. Very few cemeteries with continuity are reported from the Treveran area, precisely the one where a high number of earlier villas were occupied.

Secondly, the number of known late Roman cemeteries is much smaller than for the Earlier Empire. While a lower number of individual burials might occasion no surprise (the period under review is shorter), the smaller number of cemeteries demands explanation. Bias may admittedly spring from the frequently greater depth of inhumations, which renders them less liable to chance discovery; simple graves without stone coffins or grave-goods are also liable to go unreported. Some bias is strongly suggested by figures from around Trier, where the Late Empire cemeteries form barely 10 per cent of the total, whereas up to 40 per cent of known early villas were reoccupied. In Belgium conclusions based on cemeteries also suggest a lower population than those based on villas, though the discrepancy is less (about 8 per cent for cemeteries, 15 per cent for villas).[21] Meanwhile the Somme, where villa survival appears low, has produced a relatively high proportion of inhumation burials. Nonetheless, pending further study, the cemeteries remain useful, provided the bluntness of the instrument is understood. Where cemeteries and settlements show the same pattern, results can be accepted with greater confidence: around Trier, both combine to indicate that late occupation was densest in certain restricted areas, particularly the Eifel, the Mosel valley and the immediate environs of the city.

A noteworthy feature of some late rural cemeteries is their large size. Most Roman cemeteries are quite small with some 20 to 40 burials. Exceptions, such as the 600 cremations at Cutry or 300 at Flavion, which either belonged to unknown villages or else formed the burial place of several dispersed settlements, are admittedly known. In general, the small early cemeteries go with the dispersal of settlements. The late evidence suggests a slight yet perceptible trend in the opposite direction, at least in certain areas. When continuity of cemeteries is found among the Suessiones, as at Breny or Caranda-Cièrges (Aisne), inhumations outnumber cremations. Existing rural nuclei increased, and new ones such as Vron (Somme), Liévin (Pas-de-Calais) of Sissy (Aisne) were created. In Belgian Luxembourg and Hainaut, on the other hand, where several large cemeteries are found near early villas, later burials are few.[22] A geographical shift may thus be at work.

This tendency towards nucleation is often combined with other factors. Large cemeteries normally contain at least a few weapon-burials, and they also often show continuity not only into the fifth century but beyond. Weapon-burials are, however, not confined either to large cemeteries or to those showing continuity.[23]

One further group of cemeteries reflects changes in rural settlement. In several places among the Suessiones or south-western Remi early cemeteries with roots in the late Iron Age show re-use after a gap of 200 to 250 years. Just as their abandonment in the first century AD is connected with the dispersal of settlement, so the re-use should indicate regrouping. These do not all include weapon-burials, so that regrouping does not depend on a military element; at Vert-la-Gravelle, however, some weapons were found.[24]

The cemeteries containing weapon-burials along with ornamented buckles, strap-ends and brooches form a remarkable group, and their communities were clearly an important new rural element from at least the middle of the fourth century. Size is variable; frequently they are large (75 graves or more), but the graves with weapons may be only a small proportion. Coins and glassware are found in the same graves, while the poorer ones may lack them entirely. It thus becomes clear that the communities had social stratification, and that the men buried with weapons belonged to the upper reaches of it (one rich grave at Vermand has been called that of a 'chef militaire'). Yet when a comparison is made with the cemetery of a regular fort, Oudenburg, the latter is distinguished precisely by a comparative lack of weapons (along with a lower percentage of female burials). Who then are the men buried with their weapons, and why are they so widely scattered?[25]

It has been suggested that burial with military accoutrements in graves frequently oriented north-south was a Germanic custom, formed in the Rhineland between the third and fourth centuries as the Germans learned inhumation from the Romans. Any continuity from the old indigenous northern Gaulish custom of cremating with weapons, still occasionally found in early Roman times, seems extremely dubious and it may be accepted that the fourth century weapon-graves are a new phenomenon (or at most reflect the return of broadly similar social conditions). The Germanic nature of the persons involved can be doubted, for the often elaborately carved buckles, while indeed showing Germanic stylistic traits, are the normal accoutrements of the later Roman army. Certain types are widely spread along the Rhine-Danube frontier, and a Roman provincial manufacture, perhaps in one or other of the state factories, can be taken as likely. Other buckles and strap-ends are widely found on both sides of the frontier, with clusters on the lower Elbe and Weser, and the link with the frontier army is more dubious. It is, however, the grave-goods from the female burials that render the Germanic nature of the provincial graves incontrovertible. Various fibulae, along with ear-rings and decorated hairpins are of types normal between Elbe and Rhine, as are the decorated bone combs found in both female and male graves.[26]

Since comparison with Oudenburg, together with the other factors, raises doubts against regular army units, the Germanic component remains to be identified. It is at once too widespread and too integrated into rural life to be a matter of individual veterans who had kept their arms. The wide variety of sites also requires explanation.

There are literary references to the settlement of outsiders including barbarian captives on the depopulated lands of Nervii, Treveri, Bellovaci and Ambiani (as well as the Lingones and Tricasses of Lugdunensis). The settlement was made on condition that these men would be available for military service when required: otherwise, they were to provide new *coloni* for landowners. Thus the wild barbarian was doubly tamed, by working land otherwise deserted and by Roman army discipline: one orator gives a vivid picture of multitudes of captives awaiting distribution. Also from a panegyric comes the earliest reference to Laeti, distinguished from ordinary Frankish prisoners by the fact that they had been brought back into the Empire from captivity outside. Later, Ammianus refers to the Laeti as if they were a specific Germanic people. The panegyrist's reference is, however, perfectly consistent with their being, or including, Gallo-Roman peasants who had been carried off across the Rhine, or had joined the Bagaudae and later been captured. If Germanic, they must have been originally settled earlier, under Aurelian, Probus or the Gallic emperors (the name Laeti may or may not be of Germanic origin). By the end of the fourth century, *praefecti Laetorum* were established at Arras, Amiens, Beauvais, Senlis, Reims as well as Yvois-Carignan and Famars, and the *terrae laeticae* thus settled had a special controlled status. It is possible that the Laeti had become increasingly Germanicized; a Germanic origin is betrayed by some of the names (e.g. Laeti Franci), though those of Belgica are neutral apart from one group of Sarmatae. Most scholars agree that they were of low social status, though it is not clear that they were always *dediticii* (surrendered enemies) and their military service raised them a notch above ordinary *coloni*.[27]

Three problems arise if the weapon-graves are identified with the Laeti. The first is one of date, since the burials begin around the mid-fourth century and the Laeti are attested from the late third. The second is inconsistency between the low social status of the Laeti and the wealth of the graves; the identification can only be supported if it is supposed that a considerable social development had occurred.

An alternative identification has therefore been sought in the *foederati*, groups of Germans, especially Franks, who settled inside the Empire as a result of a treaty, hence on freer terms and keeping their own social structure. The literary evidence is poor, and the area of Toxandria, where federate Franks are definitely attested, is bereft of weapon-burials. Either considerably more, and rather different settlements have to be envisaged, or yet another group of people, such as the *gentiles*, brought in. But since the status of the *gentiles* is not free from dispute, the substitution achieves little.[28]

A discrepancy between the literary sources and the archaeological record is best acknowledged. The phenomenon behind the material remains is simply not one that received full literary comment. It is clear that Germanic families, in smaller or larger groups, were settled at over forty sites in the Belgicas and had started to form a new type of minor rural aristocracy by the later fourth

42 Map of late Belgica. Numbers refer to forts and cemeteries mentioned in the text. Contours at 100 m, 200 m, 400 m, 800 m

1 Liesenich (Strimmig)	6 Vireux-Molhain
2 Brunehaut-Liberchies	7 Grevenmacherberg
3 Château-Renaud	8 Furfooz
4 Nismes-Viroinval	9 Epraves
5 Hontheim-Pünderich	10 Dourbes

Legend in map:

LATE BELGICA

Official Factories:
- shields
- weapons
- catapult
- weaving
- AR gold and silver work
- P praefectus   L laetorum
- G gentilium   S sarmatarum
- approximate later coastline

0   50   100 KMS
0   10   50 Miles

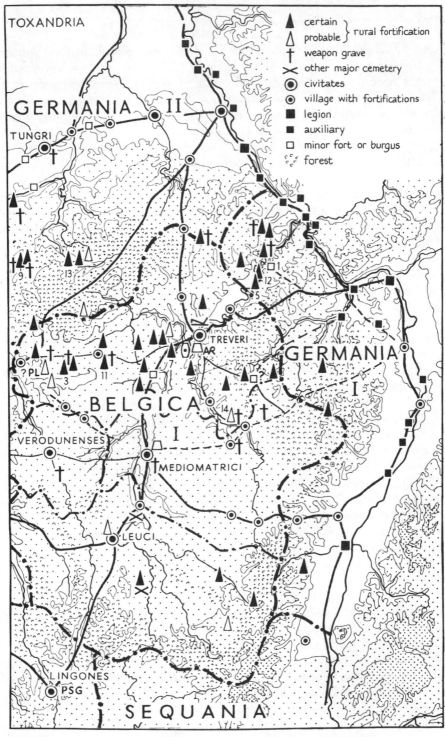

certain ⟩ rural fortification
probable ⟩
weapon grave
other major cemetery
civitates
village with fortifications
legion
auxiliary
minor fort or burgus
forest

GERMANIA II

TUNGRI

GERMANIA I

TREVERI

BELGICA

VERODUNENSES

MEDIOMATRICI

LEUCI

LINGONES
PSG

SEQUANIA

11	Steinfort	16	Caranda-Cièrges	21	Vermand-Marteville
12	Zell	17	Vron	22	Abbeville-Homblières
13	Ortho	18	Liévin	23	Fère-en-Tardenois
14	Völklingen	19	Sissy	24	Limé
15	Breny	20	Vert-la-Gravelle	25	Chouy

century: on the other hand the cemeteries do not suggest entire tribes. Some of them were previously used by an ordinary Gallo-Roman population, while others were new. Burial with full military accoutrements was probably a deliberate expression of status, while the gold and silver coins sometimes found (another adopted Gallo-Roman custom) depict wealth, and a military service remunerated in cash as well as settlement rights.[29]

The communities varied in size from over a hundred (a minimum for Vermand, and there was another contingent at nearby Marteville) to less than 20 (Vert-la-Gravelle). Hamlets consisting of several families can also be envisaged on the basis of Abbeville-Homblières, near St. Quentin, where the majority of a late fourth-century community of some 40–50 persons was Germanic. How the land was divided between Germans and Gallo-Romans remains totally unknown. Settlement on the deserted land mentioned in literary sources is the simplest solution, with rights of ownership (if no owner was known) or as *coloni*. There is no evidence of a system of enforced division of the land itself or the taxes due on it as is later found for Visigoths and Burgundians further south.[30]

The full extent of Germanic settlement is however not reflected in the record. If the above arguments are accepted, the weapon-graves are not to be identified in any simple way with the Laeti, of whose presence and of whose Germanic nature (at least from the mid-fourth century) there can, nonetheless, be no doubt. If the Laeti retained their low status, then they were presumably absorbed into the rural population at a level too poor to leave distinctive traces.

The weapon-grave cemeteries are found only in certain areas. Though present along the lower Mosel they are missing from the lower Eifel and the region surrounding Trier, precisely the area where the highest proportion of reoccupation of old sites is attested (they are equally missing from Lorraine). The Sarmatians seen by Ausonius (probably using the word for any barbarian) in the Hunsrück were in a zone showing little evidence for continued occupation.[31] Germanic soldier-farmers were to be found only where they were needed in one or other of their capacities. The orators' references to depopulated land receiving them were not entirely empty rhetoric.

To sum up, the cemeteries suggest a general drop in the rural population, the possible renewal of a trend towards nucleated rural settlement and the formation in the second half of the fourth century of a new minor élite of German origin, sometimes intermarrying with provincials. The three phenomena are connected, and at the base of the third lay imperial policy. Together they reflect gradual transformations of rural society and settlement, slight in some regions, more profound in others. Though further changes would take place, the pattern for the fifth century at least was being formed, and over much of Belgica, it will be argued, the fifth century caused no more disruption, perhaps indeed less, than the third.

3   Continuity and revival: Late Empire villas and settlements

If cemeteries emphasize the changes that were taking place in the countryside, to what extent is this upheld or modified if the evidence for habitations is laid alongside?

No single answer can be given, for the evidence must rather be taken region by region. The different impressions gained may be partially due to accidents of discovery or research, but it can be argued that genuine reflections of diverse ancient realities do exist among them.

A useful yardstick is provided by the environs of Trier, where the investigation of Roman villas has a long history. Within the early reign of Constantine, recovery of the countryside, as represented by occupation of villas, appears very considerable. Most sites have produced coins and pottery, and to make up for those that have not (e.g. Stahl near Bitburg), there are new sites such as Schweich, or Leiwen (where the latter part of the third century is particularly strongly represented). Moreover, alterations and improvement took place to the villas, whether minor or major (e.g. turning Leiwen into an altogether more luxurious place, or adding a second house at Goeblingen-Nospelt).[32]

Qualifications must however be made. A general survey of sites just north of Trier showed 40 per cent to be occupied in the Later Empire. In the Hunsrück, there are fewer signs of occupation, and if the rural sanctuary at Drohnecken continued in use, Gusenburg, Hottenbach and Hochscheid were abandoned. While this area had already declined from a peak in the late Iron Age, there is no doubt that a further demographic fall took place, and reforestation of part of the area may be envisaged.[33]

Among the western Treveri the situation is less clear. Some villas were not occupied (Robelmont), while others (Florenville, Thiaumont) clearly were, and sanctuaries also vary.[34] It would not be surprising if fewer sites saw late occupation than immediately around Trier. This is certainly true of the lower Ardennes, Condroz, and Entre-Sambre-et-Meuse region, even though a recent re-evaluation, relying whenever possible on pottery as well as coins, shows 20 per cent (rather than 10 per cent or less) and the discovery of a villa and temple precinct at Matagne showing intense use in the late third and fourth centuries has demonstrated a limited renewal.[35] More often the evidence suggests habitation on a much reduced scale, possibly temporary or intermittent (Haccourt), and entailing a change in function for the buildings; hearths are found in living-rooms and a poor quality floor of re-used materials over a cellar where débris had never been cleared out. At several sites late material has come from shallow oval pits which may represent sunken huts (clearest at Neerharen-Rekem), and wooden buildings, set within ditches, have been observed at Warnach.[36] Besides a drop in rural population a return to something closer to subsistence level must be envisaged, with purely utilitarian use of what had been status-granting structures. Fourth-century occupation was also geographically limited, with the central Ardennes virtually abandoned and a preference shown for good soils and for the Meuse and Sambre valleys. Further west, among the Nervii, a certain concentration along the Sambre and the Cambrai-Bavay-Köln road has also been observed.

The Trier area must then itself be further evaluated. The comparative abandonment of the Hunsrück appears natural when compared with the Ardennes, and it is rather for the dense occupation in the lower Eifel that a special reason must be sought. This is of course not hard to find. More important even than the favourable soils of the limestone area is the proximity of Trier, the one city with a population which had not shrunk and which now included a higher proportion of non-producers. While many of the provisions necessary for the court and administrators could have been supplied by way of taxation, the large number of Constantinian coins reaching rural sites suggests the marketing of produce. Court and army thus indeed acted as stimuli, but either the effect was narrower or a lowered rural population was less able to profit from what might have seemed a seller's market. Even in the better known areas, more modern excavations, or careful re-evaluations of old ones, are needed to give a detailed view of the type of occupation. At Newel, the various out-buildings went out of use, so that here too all functions were concentrated in the original dwelling, where the formerly open portico was blocked by walls, either to give more enclosed space or for protective purposes.[37]

Forming a contrast with this evidence for more purely functional and less pretentious buildings are the villas of luxurious, even palatial proportions that were built anew or enlarged and adorned with mosaics in the fourth century. Euren and Ehrang, and probably also Schweich, should be seen as suburban villas like the ones to the north or south of the city. Whether they belonged to local notables or the wealthy incomers, they should be seen as the immediate effect of the court. For the rich remains at Konz, like the remarkable three-storey semi-fortified dwelling at Pfalzel, wholly turned inwards around its court-yard, there is a hint of imperial ownership. The same can be argued for Welschbillig, with its fine ornamental pools balustraded by sculptured busts representing an eclectic selection of subjects from classical Greek philosophers to more contemporary Germanic imperial bodyguards.[38] Here we have the class of building over which Ausonius rhapsodized in his *Mosella*, in which he paints the renewed peace and prosperity resulting from the emperors Valentinian and Gratian – villas such as he himself or his senatorial colleagues might have inhabited. A fine example above Trier at Remerschen was unfortunately destroyed by gravel-digging. Downstream, the exquisite glass cage-cup from a grave at Niederemmel suggests the location of another. Nennig was also occupied in the fourth century, as was the equally huge villa near Echternach. The latter was indeed somewhat reduced in size, but still luxurious, and the baths were actually extended by the addition of a covered swimming-pool.[39]

Ausonius was then telling the truth, but a truth selected and edited, well seen in his casual reference to the walls or fortifications which now served purely as granaries; the humbler *coloni* are shown as happy figures in a smiling landscape. There is of course no mention of a phenomenon that almost certainly lies behind the luxurious villas – the passing of land around Trier into the hands of the wealthy few, the increasing depression of the peasant. Yet an excellent example of the former was to hand only a few miles away in the area, over 220 km^2 in extent, enclosed by the so-called Landmauer to form one vast estate, with Welschbillig its likely centre – clearly a senatorial, if not an imperial estate, and including at least 40 occupied villas and sites. And while Ausonius does imply hard times in the recent past, the reader would not know that many places flourishing in the time of Constantine were now abandoned. Yet at many sites coins cease after the middle of the century, and they include at least one major villa of the type he describes, that overlooking the Lieser near Wittlich.[40]

The stimulus given to the Mediomatrican countryside by the city of Metz, combined with the Rhine frontier, also deserves evaluation. If a number of recent investigations give a representative sample, as many as one half of the known villas were still occupied in the Later Empire, though a regional study of the Sarre valley suggests a third to a quarter. If these examples are added to what can be gleaned from older accounts, a preference for the vicinity of roads and river valleys is again visible, though the sites are well scattered and there is no cluster around Metz. The most noteworthy group lies near Sarrebourg, close to the road to Strasbourg, while another is detectable near the confluence of Saar with Blies and the road leading by way of le Héraple to Worms. This suggests that the direct east–west roads to the Rhine had a greater effect than the city or the Moselle. Both small (Berthelming) and large (Rouhling, Teting, St. Ulrich) villas were occupied, but the latter may well have been less grand than formerly. There is a marked fall-off in numbers of sites after the middle of the fourth century, though a few (e.g. Berthelming) continue. The hilltop Vosges villages did not survive into the fourth century, and may indeed have already been in decline throughout the third. Further north at Sarreinsming, however, the small hamlet (in all probability dependent on a nearby villa) which produced 'imitation' coins of Tetricus survived into the fourth century and continued to work bronze.[41]

Among the Leuci, conclusions cannot yet be drawn. One extensive rural settlement perched on a hill above St. Dié (la Bûre) simply continued, apparently a self-sufficient community with metal-working joined to agriculture.[42]

At the opposite end of the provinces, only a few of the Somme villas have been even trenched, but the collection of surface material suggests that few of them continued into the Later Empire, and surface survey in the Cambrésis also suggests a low survival rate. The Roman villas of Picardie are wholly at odds with the fields and roads that developed in the Middle Ages, a fact that suggests profound disruption at some point. Since depopulation is unlikely to have occurred on quite the dramatic scale of villa disappearances (in view of the inhumation cemeteries) hypotheses that attempt to locate the missing population have been developed.[43] To begin with, there is the possibility that some saw late occupation at a poor level, producing no recognizable fine pottery or coins. Secondly, considerable depopulation is indicated on other grounds. The Merovingian period was in general characterized by a very sparse population, and this state of affairs is easier to understand if the start of a trend be dated to the third rather than to the fifth and sixth centuries. Nor is depopulation inconsistent with the one known item which the north-west produced for export, wool, since extensive sheep-farming at the expense of arable could have been achieved with fewer hands. The brief description by Paulinus of Nola of a northern wasteland peopled only by heathen bandits, while hardly objective, is consistent with sheep rearing, for shepherds, especially when mounted, were normally considered to be on the lawless fringe of society. Some farms and estate centres there must still have been; sites with late pottery as well as late cemeteries are indeed known among Nervii, Atrebates and Morini – some well illustrating the tendency to continuity into and beyond the fifth century (Liévin, Vron).[44]

At present two divergent views hold the field. The first is that the villas which continued into the fourth century lie below and are concealed by later villages. Some villas (e.g. Daméry and Laboissière) lie so close to villages which precisely follow their orientation that it is easy to suppose a connection. Some 20 modern villages are known to be on the site of Roman remains, and other Roman sites have been found below deserted medieval villages. The later Merovingian palace at Athies makes a villa below the village an attractive if hypothetical addition to the one in the same commune which excavation shows to have been abandoned. Here as elsewhere real continuity remains to be demonstrated. Village over Roman villa is a common occurrence and while some villages (e.g. Welschbillig) undoubtedly overlie late sites it has not yet been demonstrated that this is normally caused by uninterrupted settlement, and is not simply the haphazard result of the villa's providing a quarry. A study of later parish boundaries could have a contribution to make here. Roman sites are frequently found on or near the boundaries of parishes, and bear no obvious relationship to the central village; these might be the villas that did not continue, whereas the village masks the one that did, or else a dependent settlement.[45]

The second view suggests that Late Empire habitations did not take the form of villas, but were essentially hamlets formed of buildings purely in wood and clay ('pisé') which inevitably leave less clear traces. In fact, numerous 'anomalies' of unknown date and type, but consistent with use of clay for construction, have been found. Proof that they indeed represent late settlements is again awaited. More than one pattern may eventually be found. At Warfusée-Sud, possible huts have been detected on the site of the villa: at some point, this villa along with five others in the neighbourhood may have given birth to the village which lies on the Roman road, in the middle of them all. To judge by cemeteries, there may have been various pockets of Late Empire occupation – near Amiens itself, around Montdidier and Roiglise and near the mouth of the Somme (Abbeville, St. Valéry, Nouvion).[46]

South of the Ambiani, rural change may or may not have been as radical. The Département Oise has its share of cemeteries with weapon-graves, both isolated and grouped around the village of Hermes. Those at Bailleul-sur-Thérain may be connected with a later re-use of the old fortification on the Mt. César. Insufficient villas are known to draw conclusions.[47]

A territory where additional knowledge would be especially interesting is that of the Remi. The re-use of earlier cemeteries, once at least (Vert-la-Gravelle) with weapon-graves, is confined to the southern part of the *civitas*, where it borders on Suessiones and Catalauni: preliminary evidence from the last area suggests a healthy proportion of sites occupied. The Ardennes, not surprisingly, have the low survival rate of sites that is found elsewhere in marginal areas. Nearer Reims, there is tantalizingly little archaeological evidence that can be satisfactorily joined to the snippets known from later documents and from place-names. A local place-name 'les Lètes' occurs some 6 km north-east of Reims near the village Crépy (derived from Crispiacus, a Gallo-Roman or early medieval estate name). Like the estate of Gothi mentioned in the ninth-century *polyptyque* of the church St. Remy, it could owe its origins to settlement of barbarians in the later Roman period. Another village, Beine, has a Celtic name and a small cemetery of the Early Empire; but the same village has a 'lieu dit' in the form of 'la Noue Jouvin', which raises a possible connection with the *magister militum* Jovinus. The testament of St. Remigius, of early sixth-century date, mentions the bishop's share in four different estates that had belonged to his family, as well as some scattered vineyards and other holdings, which gives some idea of the holdings of his father, a medium fifth-century landowner.[48]

Finally, the Suessiones. Here the archaeological evidence consists largely of mosaics and cemeteries. Nonetheless, the assortment is curiously informative. The cemeteries are large, and some (Breny, Fère-en-Tardenois) show continuity from early Roman (even pre-Roman) times, while others start afresh (Limé, Chouy) in the second or late third century, or start again after a break (perhaps Caranda). Though sites are said to show signs of destruction, the cemeteries suggest a higher than average degree of continuity, and a number of sites likewise were occupied from the first to the fourth century or beyond (Oulchy-le-Château, Limé-Villa d'Ancy, Mercin-et-Vaux). Weapon-graves appear in all kinds of cemeteries, always as an addition to the existing population. Problems remain over distinguishing villas and villages in the three main zones of Roman sites – the valleys of the Marne, of its tributary the Ourcq and of the Vesle along with the Aisne (the last doubled by the road coming from Reims). It may be that this whole area always had dependent rural villages.[49] The site of Blanzy-les-Fismes, near yet above a roadside *vicus*, has produced a very remarkable mosaic – depicting Orpheus charming the animals; it is of fourth-century date and the handiwork of south Gaulish or even north African mosaicists. Outside of Trier and the area around it, this and another fragment at Vailly are the only late Roman mosaics known in Belgica. The Blanzy mosaic might, it is true, have been laid for some wealthy official or administrator who was not a native of the region: a governor of Belgica II is an obvious possibility, the more so since the spot is equidistant from Reims and Soissons.[50]

It appears then that the *civitas* Suessionum was an area which did not suffer from depopulation (though some redistribution may have taken place) and where the Germanic element was grafted onto a relatively healthy indigenous growth. It is an area where great landowners with a wealth of *coloni* can be readily imagined: perhaps a powerful aristocracy was able to secure the Germanic settlers for its own ends. It may be no accident that the family of the Syagrii – whatever their original homeland – flourished there.[51] The Suessiones, along with the Treveri, come closest to producing what might be expected from the pages of Ausonius (or later Sidonius). But the Suessiones – and perhaps the Remi should be linked with them – achieved this without the wholly artificial world of the court.

4 Settlement patterns and society

A history of rural settlement patterns and their implications for the society of late Roman Belgica cannot as yet be fully written. It is, however, valuable for working hypotheses to be stated as coherently as possible, so that future investigations have a point from which to proceed.

Even the case for depopulation rests on evidence which is far from solid if any one aspect of it be examined in isolation. However, the mutual support of the various classes of material lends credibility, bolstered by the fact that the regional variations are consistent with geography and common sense. Weight must also be allowed to arguments looking back from the early Middle Ages, and reversion to forest of marginal areas is necessary to explain the later enormous forest cover and the existence of Roman villa sites in woodland that has remained uncleared for a millennium. Certainly, the encroachment of scrubby woodland, beech and oak forest is the logical counterpart to the archaeological evidence, and can be imagined in the Vosges, Lorraine, Argonne, Hunsrück and above all Ardennes. The later Forêt Charbonnière may have started to take on its later form north of the Sambre, now virtually a frontier zone, and, moreover, an area where intensive agriculture might have worn out the rather light sandy soils.[52] Further south the forests of St. Gobain and Compiègne probably grew between Remi and Suessiones and their neighbours across the Oise, that of Arrouaise divided Viromandui from Nervii while more open, poorer woodland spread in Flanders. The result would be to increase the physical separation between the provinces, and between the north and south of Belgica II.

Changes in crops and diet perhaps also took place, the counterpart of those of the Early Empire; the medieval period saw a general swing away from bread-wheat in favour of the hardier grains, and eventually the reintroduction of buckwheat. If the climate indeed worsened within the late Roman period, that in itself would have rendered the cultivation of bread-wheat on marginal lands more difficult. Invasions and their aftermath would naturally have a deleterious effect on fruit-trees and exotic species. Yet the fig-trees that the emperor Julian saw near Paris and the existence of early medieval vineyards in areas other than the Mosel valley and Champagne warn against exaggeration.[53] Wealth rather than geography was certainly the most important determining factor in any individual diet.

Until analyses of bones from stratified habitation layers, or from sites occupied only in the Later Empire have been undertaken, ignorance of animal husbandry and the supplementing of this by hunting and fishing will also remain. In agrarian technology, a steady state can be assumed, unless iron became harder to obtain. Great series of water-mills for grinding grain, like those of Barbégal near Arles, remain unknown in Belgica.[54]

To these various unknowns must be added the usual ignorance of such basic matters as family sizes, age of marriage, fertility and average life span. For some idea of the percentage of *coloni* to slaves we can however go to the testament of bishop Remigius of Reims (assuming its authenticity). Out of 52 males and 29 females listed, 12 are specifically called *coloni* and 16 slaves; the fourth century, with numerous campaigns across the Rhine, probably increased the numbers of rural slaves. While the distance between them and *coloni* was narrowing in many respects, they were still less free to marry.[55] In view of all this uncertainty, it may seem surprising that a great deal has been written on late Gallo-Roman estates. The reasons are however twofold – Gaul was after all part of the Empire, so that evidence for other areas may (with caution) be applied, while medieval kingdoms about which there is documentary evidence, grew out of Frankish and hence out of late Roman Gaul. Moreover, France is dotted with commune-names and lesser place-names ('lieux-dits') which appear to be derived from estate names formed in the Roman period.[56]

The last point may be considered first. The place-names concerned end in -y, -ay, -ey from an original -acus or -acum, which is a normal Gallo-Roman ending derived from earlier Celtic usage: in Lucaniacus and Avitacum (to take well known examples from Ausonius and Sidonius) it denotes an estate when appended as a suffix to the name of a one-time owner. If anything like a one-to-one correspondence could be indicated between such names and the centres of Gallo-Roman estates we would come near to having a cadastral map of estates with a record of names of owners.

The situation is not so simple.[57] The first part of the name to which -acum was appended may be Celtic, Roman or Germanic and is by no means always a personal name. Place-names derived from Roman or Gallo-Roman personal names form just over 10 per cent of the category ending in -y. Frequently it is a word describing the appearance, vegetation or topography of the place – trees or woods, valleys, gravelly soil, even mud. Moreover, such place-names were still formed throughout the early Middle Ages, using first Latin, later Germanic roots or names. A Latin root is thus not in itself proof of the existence of the place-name in Roman times. While certain types of names do seem to be typical for the various periods, intensive work on a regional basis must first be undertaken to allot them to the proper categories. The one area of Belgica where this has been undertaken is the Oise, roughly corresponding with the *civitas* of the Bellovaci, unfortunately an area where the archaeological record is poor enough to inhibit detailed comparison.

This is the more unfortunate since, if it could be shown that communes with Gallo-Roman names were descended from late Roman estates, they might illustrate a step in the consolidation of these out of smaller units. As it is, later communes normally contain several Roman sites. It is not unreasonable to suppose that some of the really large, consolidated estates encountered in later documents – examples are Mersch, Tholey and Annappes – were already formed, or in process of formation, in late Roman times.[58] The evidence does not all speak with a single voice. It is true that both Ausonius and Sidonius appear to have estates that are consolidated, in the sense that they formed a single tract of land around a central villa which was the administrative centre as well as home of the owner. The only estate of which we actually know the size, Ausonius' 'little inheritance' is in fact not enormous (a little over 200 ha); the most favoured estates may well have been at least ten times larger. It is, however, likely that the holdings of these men were made up both of large consolidated areas and of smaller patches. The testament of Remigius (barely a generation younger than Sidonius), shows that the splitting up of estates among brothers was still practised among fairly substantial landowners.[59] It also gives a valuable indication that an *-acum* name (Passiacum, Passy near Laon) might belong to a *colonica* or dependent farm. Obviously, the wealthier a family was, the more likely its members were to own consolidated estates and to maintain rather than divide them. The taxation system favoured the rich in this respect, while small and medium landowners often could not maintain their independence, but had to sell their property. They thus became *coloni*, tied to the estates of richer landowners for whom they were so many low-grade clients, only just above slaves. A large landowner could hope to acquire areas surrounding his own estate, whether by simple pressure, by colluding at an unfair division of taxes, or by offering a treacherous and often short-lived protection in return for title to the land. It was not safe, says Salvian, for a poor man to live next to a rich one – and despite Salvian's bias, the devices he describes are all too credible.[60]

Consolidation of large tracts may have been most noticeable in the properties of the imperial fisc. The most direct evidence for this in Belgica may be the Landmauer north of Trier, enclosing some 22,000 ha, that was later (arguably) the property of Merovingian kings. This is certainly true of huge portions of the Ardennes, and of many scattered estates elsewhere, such as those based on Athies and Witry-en-Artois.[61] While Merovingian kings may have acquired land by other means, the normally envisaged continuity of organization from Roman into Frankish times is inherently probable. Arguing from the earlier end it also seems likely that the imperial fisc took over unoccupied land where ownership could not be established, in addition to any bequests or confiscations.

Apart from the physical consolidation of estates, it is reasonable to ask whether they were moving closer in organization to the medieval manor, with demesne surrounded by (or inter-leaved with) dependent tenures which also formed a subsidiary labour supply for the demesne. It has been argued that certain features of this organization were a natural outcome of Gaulish social stratification, and are likely to have existed throughout the Roman period, with low grade *coloni* grouped in either hamlets or farmsteads and higher grade tenants occupying separate farms with small villas.[62] Very little is known as yet about the spatial organization of late Roman villa-farms. If an archaeological picture showed the small villas surrounding a big one going out of use and being replaced by clusters of poor houses, it would be reasonably clear that this represented originally high grade *coloni* or small landowners being reduced in status, becoming or being replaced by cottagers. With this would naturally go an increase in the area of farmland directly worked from the big villa for the profit of the owner, with a corresponding decrease in the holdings of *coloni*.

The late Roman writers from Gaul of course make reference to bailiffs, *coloni* and slaves, but tell us relatively little about the organization of estates. They do show that the patronage of large landowners might extend over whole communities, and illustrate fortification – Ausonius' Lucaniacus can be called an *oppidum*, Sidonius describes Burgus, the luxury castle of the Pontii Leontii (hinting that it was for display as much as for defence). Sidonius also metes out summary justice to grave-robbers and illegally upgrades clients, as did Remigius when he freed *coloni* along with slaves in his will. But the growth of seigneurial power was limited by the scattering of estates and the dependence – at least until the mid-fifth century – of the senatorial land-owner's status on the emperor and his agents.[63]

The relevance of the authors, all except Salvian from the south, may be at best partial. The north may have seen more medium landowners, caught between upper and nether millstone. Either this or a high degree of absenteeism is strongly suggested by the general lack of mosaics and other luxuries. Such a pattern still supposes that the remaining villas functioned as estate centres. In northern Belgica the system may have broken down further, to give villa occupation of a squatter type without continuity of function. This would have caused grave problems for the establishment of ownership and the collection of taxes. It also denotes a reversal of Early Empire trends, an abandonment of the values previously adopted as appropriate, of an overtly Romanized lifestyle and the type of organization which had supported it. The Germanic settlers give an additional reason for supposing that the psychological distance between Belgica and the Mediterranean world had greatly increased. Their nucleated settlements must gradually have given rise to a *de facto* peasant ownership of the land, and to a new growth of village headmen. Even when they were integrated into existing rural communities they were not assimilated to a Graeco-Roman view of civilization. Despite many remaining Mediterranean features, Belgica, and especially its northern part, now shared in a cultural continuum which stretched from the Elbe to the Loire. Always caught between the two worlds, the region was increasingly turning its face towards the north-east.

12

PRODUCTION, MARKETING AND TRADE IN LATE ROMAN BELGICA

1   The context

The literary sources available for the late Roman provinces – in some ways more reminiscent of the first century AD than of the intervening centuries – include official documents pertinent to the economy – the Maximum Prices Edict of Diocletian, the *Notitia Dignitatum* and *Notitia Galliarum* and some of the imperial edicts collected in the Theodosian Code. A few vivid and pertinent statements come from the pens of Gallic writers; among these, Ausonius and his grandson Paulinus of Pella are the outstanding figures for the late fourth century, Salvian and Sidonius Apollinaris for the fifth. Palladius, the late writer on agriculture, may have been a rich Gallic landowner contemporary with Sidonius. Of these, only Salvian and Ausonius in his *Mosella* speak directly for the north. By contrast with this increase in literary sources the body of epigraphic material is much smaller than for the preceding period.

This change in the available information is not an unmixed blessing, since the written sources present their own problems. A good example is afforded by the ostensibly straightforward story of Julian's building a fleet on the Rhine to bring over grain from Britain in the late 350s. Zosimus shows this as an extraordinary measure necessitated by the aftermath of extensive Germanic raids, while Libanius and (less clearly) Ammianus imply that it was a restoration of the *status quo*.[1] Normally the latter two authors are accepted, since Zosimus is not always reliable on details. We thus apparently have a striking illustration of the inability of fourth-century Gaul and Germany to support the Rhine army – confirmation of the gloomy picture extracted from archaeological sources for the state of the northern countryside, while going beyond what archaeology alone could provide.

Yet many questions are unanswered. We have no idea when it became necessary (or simply preferable) to furnish part of the Rhine army grain supply from Britain. Interpretation partially depends on the relative size of the army;

here, recent estimates suggest a moderate (not more than one and a half) rather than a dramatic (double or more) increase in size.[2] It is in the context of other information suggesting a shift in the relative prosperity of the continent and Britain that the statement takes on its true value. Other considerations must also be taken into account – for instance the resources drained off towards court and administrators at Trier. In addition, the marine transgressions must have interrupted channel coast salt production and the shipping routes that were connected with it, by which grain too may previously have travelled. The shipping of grain from Britain could principally reflect a change in army supply routes.

Problems of a different order are caused by the decline in epigraphic material, especially the absence of evidence for traders – the solitary *negotiator* Silvanus from Trier only highlights the surrounding blank. *Negotiatores*, or their equivalent, can hardly have disappeared completely, even if a larger proportion of goods may have been moved by requisitioned transport. Is the change caused by the disappearance of a class of persons, by changes in shipping patterns, or simply by the cessation of old commemorative habits? When the literary sources make reference to traders they are either the agents of landowners like Ausonius, or the oriental foreigners lamented by Salvian in the early fifth century.[3] Another difficult problem is that of tracing the distinction between trade and taxation, and between private and state-owned production.

Late Roman taxation is a subject where much is known but little securely understood. Diocletian (along with his colleague and successor Galerius) was held in considerable odium for revising the system and holding fresh censuses. To Diocletian, the need for reorganization after a long period of turmoil when taxes must have been collected on an *ad hoc* basis would be obvious. The unpopularity was doubtless partly due to increased central surveillance in an area previously left to local authorities. From Constantine onwards we find a series of laws dealing with aspects of taxation, and on the other hand laments about its severity. A marked tendency for Christian writers to blame Diocletian and for pagan writers to cast Constantine as villain does, however, cast doubt on the accuracy, if not the sincerity, of the statements. Both men were responsible for army reforms that were necessarily linked with taxation, and Constantine introduced a highly unpopular tax (the *collatio lustralis*) on traders. Diocletian's other reforms also created a somewhat larger administrative staff, even if it remained small by the standards of almost any other large territorial empire.[4]

Each separately assessed area (in Gaul the *civitas*) was seen as a multiplicity of fiscal units which were identified and totalled on the basis of the census. When taxes for the year were set (the *praefectus praetorio* acting as agent of the emperor) the amount due per unit, and hence per assessed area, was established. The decurions, now forming a hereditary class, were, as before, responsible for the collection (their own lands might be forfeit in case of a deficiency). The name of the fiscal unit, and the manner in which it was calculated, varied from province to province. In Gaul the unit was the *caput*, but this denoted an artificial composite of land, people and material goods. It is an attractive, if unprovable, assumption that in Gaul the *caput* bore some resemblance to a small independent household and the amount of land that such a group normally cultivated; an amount of 25 ha arable (or equivalent in other types) has in fact been suggested, but remains very hypothetical.[5] Regardless of contentious details, two questions are of importance. The first is whether taxation in the Later Empire was, as the chorus of articulate laments and the evident attempts at evasion might suggest, particularly onerous, and the second the extent to which taxation was levied in kind rather than money.

Any calculations of the real level of taxation are inevitably tentative. According to Ammianus, Julian reduced the indiction for Gaul from 25 *solidi* to 7 (*per caput*?); this only helps inasmuch as it shows that enormous fluctuations were possible. It is not known whether the 25 *solidi* rate was ever effectively collected, nor whether the reduction was valid only for the few *civitates* of Belgica worst affected by invasions. Tentative calculations have suggested that regular taxation should not on average have exceeded one tenth of the normal product of the land.[6] So little is known about taxation in the Earlier Empire that it is not clear whether any significant increase is involved, though the larger army leaves a *prima facie* case for the affirmative. Moreover, all sorts of extraordinary levies, for instance towards the upkeep of journeying officials, were often imposed.

Much depended on the rigour and fairness of the collection. Almost certainly it was normally neither efficient nor just, since the lack of a regular civil service still precluded efficiency, and corruption was endemic. Julian's aim was to show that efficient collection of a lower figure could produce as much revenue as a theoretical higher rate. The new census was careful in its enumeration of livestock, trees, stored grain, slaves and *coloni*, who (unless they were also landowners in their own right) were counted as part of the estate on which they lived. An impression of rigour was certainly given, and fresh censuses theoretically held every five years. Proprietors may have found their possessions assessed higher, but those of curial or higher rank were also often in a position either to evade tax collection or to bias it in their favour. Salvian shows some of the possible methods, as do the laws by forbidding them. News of the annual total reached the wealthy first, and they could band together to pass an unfairly high proportion of it onto the less fortunate. Extra amounts could be (illegally) passed on to *coloni* in the form of rent increases, and extraordinary indictions levied (also illegally) from the defenceless. Senators could be notoriously lax over paying taxes.[7]

Even if the absolute amount of taxes was not significantly higher than before, this still could only be raised without hardship if population and productivity were constant.[8] In northern Gaul, neither condition seems to have been met, and unless the tax schedules for the northern *civitates* were reduced taxation must indeed have been more burdensome. It is, however, safe to assume that those for whom the burden was heaviest were not the ones who had the wealth and education to complain.

Even when taxes were assessed in money, that was only one of various modes of payment. Others included corvée labour, hospitality to officials and soldiers, the provision of ships or wheeled vehicles to transport official cargoes, and payment in produce. Taxes in the Later Empire seem to have been mostly assessed in kind, but might be paid partly in cash. It is often maintained that from the time of the Severi taxes were increasingly collected in kind. There are, however, strong arguments for dating the significant increase of this custom to the mid-third century, when army needs and lack of central control necessitated *ad hoc* arrangements. The importance of taxes in kind during the Later Empire is certainly clear from legal sources and is reflected in the provision of fortified stores bases. Commutation into money seems to have been mostly favoured by the rich, especially in the later fourth century.[9] It is inherently likely that there was an increase in the requisitioning of transport, and that essential army supplies were more than ever moved around without being objects of trade.

A higher taxation level, combined with the collection of more taxes in kind, could not but affect production and trade. First, a greater percentage of annual agrarian surplus was directly claimed by the state. Second, there was less incentive to market surpluses in return for cash to pay taxes. This in turn meant less stimulus for artisans in market centres to produce goods that they could sell while living off the marketed agrarian surplus. Evidence for a general lowering of production and marketing of ordinary goods might therefore be expected.

Further inroads into the sector producing goods for profit were made by the establishment of state factories. At the end of the third century, the Maximum Prices Edict of Diocletian mentions Atrebatic wool and woollen garments from Ambiani, Nervii and Treveri, suggesting a production that had either survived the crisis or had revived.[10] But the same emperor was responsible for the establishment of the imperial weaving factories whose job it was to supply garments for army and court. The actual work need not have been concentrated in a single building or even within city walls, but could have been dispersed among rural households, whether or not on imperial estates. The *Notitia Galliarum* shows officials in charge of such 'factories' situated at Tournai, Reims, Trier and Metz; the last two cities had two, one of them connected with an imperial estate. Trier and Reims also had the workers who produced richly decorated ceremonial armour and vestments for high officials. While it cannot be formally shown that private production for the market declined through this diversion of materials and labour, it does seem inevitable.[11]

Alongside the trend towards state-organized production should be placed the tendency to self-sufficiency on the part of large landowners. Whereas earlier agricultural writers commend buying and selling, Palladius advises the production of necessary goods within the estate, to prevent journeys to market. While an element of this may always have been normal on the larger Gallic estates, it is now explicitly commended, and this is certainly consistent with the decline of the old villages. Moreover, rather than buying and selling produce locally, large landowners such as Ausonius might transfer goods from one estate to another.[12]

If then there is an impression of lowered activity and fewer goods circulating, this need not be entirely due to problems in the evidence or lack of study. Rather, it may be a real reflection of changes which were inimical to production and trade.

Belgica, it will be seen, really does seem to have experienced an overall drop in economic activity in the Later Empire. In this it resembles the other Gallic provinces, but forms a marked contrast with Britain, where levels of population and productivity appear if anything higher than before and rural life was flourishing. Britain must however be seen as a special case. It had been spared the vicious combination of invasions followed by internal unrest and the consequent actions of the imperial army; the episode of Carausius probably did more harm to northern Belgica. Britain's slower development had avoided the precocious and arguably excessive growth of villas in the second century. The logic of the north-western provinces' economy, whereby industrial development crept outwards by stages from Italy towards the periphery, found Britain able to meet the challenge caused by the failure of the Gallic industries. Changes in the provisioning system for the lower Rhine armies may have helped. The possibility that many northern Gauls had made their way to Britain, following an age-old pattern, must be seriously considered, even if the arguments usually advanced fall short of proof.[13]

2   Products and production

On the subject of agrarian produce, knowledge on many basic matters is, as seen, scanty. The settlement of barbarians on the land was clearly aimed at keeping up agrarian productivity, but it is unlikely that the levels of the Early Empire were in fact maintained. Assuming that Palladius' description of the Gallo-Roman reaping machine really does belong to his own day, its use can more convincingly than before be seen as an attempt to save labour.[14]

The main result of taxation reforms was that a greater percentage of surplus – wool and hides as well as grain – was creamed off at source without ever entering the market. The requisitioning of transport meant that this need not only apply to the areas nearest the frontier, since produce could be hauled any distance without extra cost to the government. There was also a long-term effect on rural society. In order to ensure constant flow of taxes, officialdom had to see that all land had a registered owner and, as far as possible, that there was a sufficiency of peasants to work it. This led to legislation on *agri deserti*, land that was not invariably unworked but where an owner responsible for tax could not be located; some areas of Belgica may have fallen into this category.[15] More important was the string of legislation that turned *coloni*, originally (at least in theory) free tenants who could move from one place to another, into serfs. Already in the Earlier Empire there was a tendency to treat rural workers as chattels – hence a ruling that they could not be bequeathed separately from the land which they worked – and in Gaul, customary tenancies would naturally give rise to such a state of affairs. From Constantine on, imperial legislation removed any residual freedom on the part of *coloni*, while also denying landowners the right to move them at will.

While the legislation was often honoured in the breach, there was a cumulative long-term effect. By the end of the century, an emperor talked of *coloni* as slaves, not of the landowner but of the land itself. At the same time, agricultural slaves were increasingly assimilated to *coloni*, since they too were tied: by the fifth century, if not before, landowners like Sidonius or Remigius were barely sensitive to the distinction.[16] Meanwhile, their power was on balance enhanced as the weight of imperial legislation was added to authority derived from customary sources. The whole system worked to the detriment of all except the *potentes*. Peasants were unable to derive any advantage from the relative scarcity of labour, which under different circumstances could have ameliorated their condition. It is perhaps natural that some of the richer rural burials of northern Belgica should belong to the new partly Germanic aristocracy, who in addition to receiving pay for military service, may have been exempt from certain taxes.[17]

Quarrying and mining may also have been affected, since private quarries and mines were taxable assets. Regrettably little is known about such operations, but it is hard to avoid the conclusion that productivity was lower, though with some bursts of intense activity. More than one boom of quarrying must have been occasioned by the erection of city walls. The quarries of Tournai were certainly still in operation, since they provided limestone for the fortification at Oudenburg. The question of private or imperial ownership of quarries remains, as ever, a difficult one, but this apart, it is clear that there was nothing like the steady quarrying of stone for new buildings that took place from the late first to early third centuries. Except for Trier and its surroundings, new buildings are comparatively rare, and re-use of earlier material probably quite widespread (an example is the villa at Mercin-et-Vaux). Nonetheless, the building of the Kaiserthermen at Trier seems to have occasioned the opening of new quarries in the Eifel.[18] The various marbles used for decoration (especially of the palace) probably came from imperial quarries in other provinces.

Did the use of stone for purposes other than building also decline? Certainly, there was a marked difference in the uses to which it was put. The sculptured votive or funerary monument is now rare. A few undatable votive stones from the Vosges could belong to the end of the third century, and there is the occasional inelegant small marble from a villa. The small sculptured funerary stele is now reserved for soldiers, for instance at Amiens. At Trier, the incorporation of relief panels, pagan or Christian, in sarcophagi lingered for a time but died out early in the fourth century. The plain stone sarcophagus becomes the norm, its overall numbers and spread throughout the social spectrum hard to analyze because of its monotony. The fixing of a special panel with an inscription was not abnormal: this was whenever possible of marble, sometimes certainly re-utilized.[19] Even here the level of luxury and skill is not particularly high, and the carved marble sarcophagus of either Italian or Pyrenaean marble so frequent in southern Gaul is not found. Given its absence at Trier, the vast marble relief sarcophagus with hunting scenes at Reims is the more remarkable.[20] Completely absent from the Late Empire scene is the village or itinerant stone worker producing figured or epigraphic memorials. This is certainly consistent with reduced demand stemming partly from the lack of incentive to market goods for cash, but it is extremely hard to distinguish this from the very real changes in taste that the Later Empire brought.

Trier also had the only active mosaic workshops. The one certain late mosaic not from Trier, Blanzy-les-Fismes, is thought to be a southern product.[21] Thus another craft based on stone had virtually died out. A further loss can be documented in the lava quern-stones from the Mayen area which, if still made, were no longer so widely exported.

Mining, together with the production of metals and metal objects obviously continued. Knowledge is again just sufficient to suggest changes. Gone is the Early Empire picture where every village had artisans busy producing objects in iron and bronze. The unavoidable impression is again of diminished activity, reflecting lessened demand and a concentration on essentials. One marked exception is the bronze cauldrons (the so-called 'Vestland' type) which appear from their distribution to have been manufactured in the middle Meuse valley, from where they spread widely afield, as far as Scandinavia. The excavated evidence for continued activity in villages such as Huy raises the possibility that these objects were made in, or marketed through, one or other of the Meuse *vici*.[22]

As for the smelting of iron ores, the continued (if reduced) occupation of villages such as Waasmunster and Destelbergen suggests that exploitation of the Flanders ores was not abandoned. Otherwise, the evidence is of two kinds. The first is exemplified by the small bowl-furnace inserted into a room of the villa at Horath in a period of fourth-century reoccupation, illustrating home production and an increasingly *ad hoc* use of space. Another possible example is the furnace at Hochscheid, in a now abandoned sanctuary of Apollo and Sirona; this is reminiscent of the ill-defined activity (perhaps connected with cloth) on the sanctuary site at Ribemont-sur-Ancre. The Hochscheid furnace is of a larger, more developed type where a wide shaft-furnace was strengthened by the addition of a stone packing. This same type has been found near Bengel (Wittlich), where examples excavated may belong to larger-scale operations, similar to a complex known at Bellaires in the Jura, where over 20 late Roman furnaces have been identified. A few other examples – though undated – are known, for instance near Longwy. As for the huge slag-heaps of the Condroz and Entre-Sambre-et-Meuse area (many reworked in the nineteenth century), limited evidence for late Roman occupation in these areas gives a *prima facie* case for an earlier date.[23] Further discoveries may strengthen the hypothesis that production was either at household level (as at Horath) or else on a considerable scale, with the larger furnaces denoting a slight advance in technology; it is to be noted that the forested area near Bengel was later royal land, and may have been imperial.

The mining and smelting of the iron needed for the armament factories may well have taken place on imperial estates, but no close connection can at present be observed between the location of the factories (Trier, Reims, Amiens and possibly Soissons) and the distribution of late iron-working. For copper (and hence bronze), the picture is even dimmer, with no active mines known. While it is highly likely that the distinctive military bronze belt-buckles and strap adornments were produced in state factories, no precise attribution has as yet been made. The one fact rendered virtually certain by recent discoveries at Amiens is that the armament factories were located in the cities, and that earlier public buildings might be re-utilized for this purpose.[24] Industrial production in some cities may thus have been as high as before, while being entirely unrelated to commerce.

Lead may have been mined around Metz and the Saarland, where lead coffins are relatively common. Those at Amiens, on the other hand, are mostly ascribed to the second and third centuries.[25] The exploitation of other natural resources is wrapped in darkness. The old North Sea salt-pans were out of commission, and it is possible that the marine transgressions along with a lowered population and the increased risk of piracy precluded the re-formation of the industry in Morinian and Menapian territory. Salt must then have been sought either from coastal areas of Gaul not so affected, or from Britain. There is no evidence for any complementary upsurge in production from the Lorraine salt-springs.

On the use of the woodlands, probably now more extensive than at any point since the conquest, only hypotheses are possible. In apparent contradiction to the inferred regrowth of forest is the use for the scaffolding employed in the erection of the Trier cathedral of many types of wood, mostly from young trees. This is very different from the massive piles and planks hewn from mature oaks for the building of the earlier bridges, and it has been suggested that there was by now an absence of mature woodland.[26] It may however be doubted whether mature trees were considered necessary for scaffolding, and the saplings employed may in fact testify to the convenient regrowth of young forest.

Imperishable products such as tiles, pottery and glass are, as always, over-represented in the record. Tiles and pottery are linked by methods of production, pottery and glass by function. If manufacture and distribution of all three classes of objects present similar patterns, general conclusions are the better warranted.

With tiles, the first obvious feature is the lack of the great variety of tile-stamps which testified to small or medium sized workshops. The comparative absence of new buildings is of course explanation enough, and the few stamped tiles from fortifications such as Furfooz and Brunehaut-Liberchies are almost certainly re-used material. The one area with production of stamped tiles in great quantities is the Mosel Valley. Most come from clearly official buildings, particularly the Baths and Basilica at Trier. Similar stamps are found in the forum area at Trier, the apsed hall at Metz, a scatter of urban and rural sites between Metz and Koblenz, and the Constantinian fortress at Köln-Deutz. One group (not found at Deutz) consists of personal names, some of which have also been found in the area of the Barbarathermen. These may be of earlier date, but repairs to the Barbarathermen are certainly conceivable. The main group, clearly datable to the Tetrarchy or Constantine, give place-names. Of these, ARMO or ARMOTRIACI, CAPIENACI or KAPIONNACO are not yet securely identified, while ADIVTEX or ADIVTECE may refer to Yutz, and Temmels (Tamaltio in the eighth century) is a candidate for TAMAL (though excavation of a kiln has not brought confirmation). The general distribution makes it clear that kiln-sites were on or near the river.[27]

Over a generation or so, vast numbers of tiles must have been produced for the Trier palace and associated buildings, especially since, for the Basilica, tiles (flat bricks) were the exclusive building material. Whereas earlier the demand might have been met by many small private concerns, it looks as if a limited number of very large ones were now employed. The question inevitably arises of whether the tileries were imperial property, arguments being the change from personal names, the sheer numbers required and their employment in official buildings. Against imperial ownership is the scatter of subsidiary sites and the lack of explicit reference to the emperor. If not imperial, the enterprises must have belonged to wealthy landowners, and it is of interest that one location is the village of Yutz. Once the great buildings were up, demand stopped as suddenly as it arose. In the Gratianic rebuilding of the Cathedral, military tile-stamps are found.

It is, of course, likely that other tile-kilns produced unstamped tiles on a small scale. It is equally possible that re-used tiles from old buildings were sufficient for the limited building almost everywhere except Trier, Metz and Reims. Production was either on a huge scale, for specific projects, or on one so small as to escape detection.

Whereas tiles are inevitably linked to building activity, the distributing of pottery is a better indicator of commodity demand and commercial activity at an everyday level. Knowledge of the types and the centres of production has been growing rapidly. Once again, a striking feature is the smaller number of village kilns producing coarse to medium-fine pottery for local or intermediate distribution. The gap is not total, for late kilns are known from Pachten and Port-à-Binson.[28] Given the emphasis on the self-contained estate, kilns for the supply of immediate needs on villas might be anticipated. This remains to be substantiated, and the overwhelming impression is of wide dispersal of pottery both fine and coarse from a limited number of big production centres, together with a general diminution both in variety and in total amount.

For fine wares, the one big remaining centre was the Argonne. Even here, a decline followed by a revival is probable.[29] Certainly there was a great change in style, as the use of figured stamps gave way in the third century to plain forms decorated, if at all, in barbotine technique, and to a variety of fine-walled beakers not always readily distinguishable from those manufactured elsewhere. This change has to some extent obscured the record, making the degree of continuity difficult to determine. The subsequent revival further strengthened the traditional element in decoration, as extensive use was made of roller-stamps with simple patterns of a kind used in the late Iron Age and early Roman periods. The date of the revival is uncertain, with some scholars putting it before 300, others as much as a generation later – the stylistic criteria often used for analysis need not correspond exactly to chronological divisions.[30] Forms continued to be a mixture of more Romanized forms – largely open, including *mortaria* but also various jugs – along with indigenous beakers.

Not all of the earlier potteries participated in the revival, but only a group of which Lavoye, Avocourt, les Allieux and Châtel-Chéhéry were the most important. With the lack of competition from central Gaul, exports now covered a wider area, without ever capturing markets to the south-west. The whole of Belgica and the Germanies was, however, now within their range. A greater amount was also exported to Britain, despite the competition from products of the Oxfordshire potteries. While the main receiving area was the Thames estuary, suggesting traffic down the Meuse, find-spots in central southern England may indicate the Seine or Somme valleys. The quantity exported to Britain actually increased towards the end of the fourth century, and continued a little into the fifth. Noteworthy products of this period are vases with Christian motifs produced at Châtel-Chéhéry.[31] Production continued into the Frankish period with gradual changes in shape, decoration and firing techniques.

The Argonne still could not rival the earlier central Gaulish production in sheer quantity. Signatures again show a mixture of Roman and native elements, but are now found in the form of graffiti on the cylindrical supports used in the kiln, and are fewer.

The production of fine wares, while centred on one area, was thus on a reduced scale, a phenomenon partly explained by competition from glass. The same holds good for the reduced quality and quantity of the black beakers still produced in Trier. On the other hand, the Earlier Empire offers no real parallel for the enormous production of coarse wares at Mayen. Once only a normal small-to-medium scale producer, this centre (in Germania I) now supplied coarse wares for the military and civilian sites of the middle and lower Rhine. Smaller quantities travelled westwards to Trier, southwards to the upper Rhine and also to Britain. While the idea of state ownership has been mooted, the supplying of civilian markets perhaps tells against it, as does the survival of the industry in the fifth century.[32]

Of the other important centres for coarse pottery, none served so wide a market. One was Speicher, which lay within the Landmauer north of Trier and specialized in a mottled ware with sponge-applied decoration. While it supplied a greater proportion of the Trier demand, and for a longer period than used to be thought, unlike Mayen it did not continue throughout the fifth century.[33] The products of another big centre, probably Villeneuve-au-Châtelot (Aube, thus Lugdunensis), shared with those of Mayen and Speicher the technical feature of firing at a very high temperature. While Mayen ware often, and Speicher ware sometimes, has a dark semi-vitrified surface, the other, widely distributed in Champagne, has a crackled bluish-grey finish. The Argonne also produced coarse pottery, another centre is in the neighbourhood of Champlieu, and further north there was limited production at earlier centres.[34]

Taken together, these few centres must have made up for the disappearance of many village kilns. Yet the range of goods was narrower and more standardized. Actual production may well have been more efficient, but it resulted in limited choice. Moreover, although lamps and a limited range of small busts and figures were still made by the Trier potteries, gone for the most part – well in advance of the pagan cults they served – was the wide range of votive terracottas.[35] Overall, the quantity as well as the variety was reduced.

The one product for which this is untrue is glass, which not only had a very wide range but included masterpieces of technical ingenuity. At the very top come the *diatreta* or cage-cups, laboriously carved from a single thick-walled beaker to give the impression of an outer lacy net attached to the inner wall by the finest glass stems. These fall into the highest category of luxury, matched only by the vessels carved at Trier from semi-precious stones such as agate.[36] Below such extravagancies existed a whole range of vessels, from the elaborate with cut decoration or various trailed protuberances to the relatively simple.

Again, one production centre, Köln, towered above all.[37] Production on a smaller scale at a number of other centres is suspected, but unconfirmed. Compared with pottery kilns, glass furnaces are tiny and leave little débris. Only the plotting of glass vessels not Köln products can locate these subsidiary centres. One near the middle of Meuse is postulated, while Amiens and Trier are suspected, but unproven. One strange form, the glass barrel-shaped flask, persisted from the third century (sometimes still bearing the stamp Frontinus) and had a wide distribution in the north of Gaul.[38]

While hard to transport, glass was cheap to produce, and there can be no doubt that it largely replaced pottery as fine table ware. Little profit was made by the actual glass-blowers. The unlocated workshop of Frontinus, which used the name for over a century and perhaps had branch plants, hints at an organization that might bring profit to the owner of the workshop, who was presumably responsible for some stages of the marketing. Similarly, it is hard not to see big landowners behind the successful pottery businesses. The lack of epigraphic and literary testimony is not surprising, for the ambitious land-owner of the fourth century would consider it less worthy of mention than previously. There is, however, no reason why the freedman of Ausonius, who trafficked on his own account while also attending to the transport of goods between Ausonius' estates, should not have also carried other goods manufactured on the estates. The fact that such trafficking was not subject to the tax on traders, if it did not constitute an incentive, at least removed an obstacle.[39]

The production of tiles, pottery and glass thus proceeded on generally similar, though not identical, lines. Tile production fell sharply after an artificial boost, while only the glass industry still shows signs of expansion. In all, a few large centres dominated the market, and there is comparatively little sign of operation between this and the highly localized level.

3 Trade and traders

The conclusion is inescapable that the volume of production generally, and production for export especially, was substantially lower in the Later Empire. The supply of Argonne ware to the German frontier and Britain was a trickle compared with the earlier broad stream from central Gaul. Moreover, some pottery from the kilns of Oxfordshire, the New Forest and Alice Holt reached the Somme and Seine valleys, so that even in this commodity the traffic was not all one way.[40]

That the Belgic provinces still exported more than the other Gallic provinces is possible, though pottery from near the Loire mouth was also reaching Britain. Much depends on commodities that are hard to trace, such as woollen goods and Mosel valley wine. The suggestion that even wool was now imported from Britain is interesting, if incapable of proof. The general balance sheet changes perceptibly if the German provinces are added, and the Mayen pottery thereby included, along with glass from Köln, probably the whole region's biggest single export.

One conclusion arising from a number of separate observations is the increased importance of the middle Meuse valley both as a trade route and as an area of continued production. The export of Argonne ware by this route and the settlement of military or semi-military units among the Tungri naturally helped. Failure to keep the road system in the best state of repair perhaps led to a greater use of river traffic. In the other direction there is the decline of Xanten and Nijmegen, and the problem of ensuring safe transport along the lower Rhine, highlighted during Julian's time; the Meuse and the roads leading eastwards from it thus gained in importance as army supply routes.[41]

The ensuring of army supplies was always a major factor, and it may be surmised that in the Later Empire a higher proportion of total production was thus channelled. Much could be done through taxation (including requisitioned transport) or directly by the army itself. The latter solution was, however, wasteful of manpower, and taxation did not supply everything required. There was then still space for traders even in the military context. Unfortunately, virtually nothing is known of them, since the rich source of inscriptions dried up completely in the Late Empire. A satisfactory explanation must probably envisage a change both in society and its values. If the earlier *nautae* and *negotiatores* were for the most part landowners of second rather than first rank, changes to this segment of society would not be without results. As a group, they probably weathered the late third century less well than the larger landowners. The shrinkage of Gallic industries was itself linked to the absence of their patronage, and in turn rendered their former way of life impracticable or unprofitable. Meanwhile, if the *nautae* were indeed, like the Mediterranean *navicularii*, a corporate enterprise sanctioned by the state, members would now find their profession turned into a hereditary *munus*, a source for no particular pride, even if it won freedom from the (even less attractive) obligation of curial rank. Some traders were of a status too low to record themselves, like the landless Arvernian who plied between Marseille and Clermont and sometimes carried letters for Sidonius. Others would be badly affected by the tax on traders, unless the patronage of aristocratic friends enabled them to escape it. Legislation of around 400 shows that the city guilds of Gaul were losing members who fled to the anonymity of the countryside, preferring to marry *colonae* and live under the shelter of a rich rural patron rather than carry out their hereditary duties and pay the proper taxes.[42]

Nonetheless, some equivalent of the former *nautae* and *negotiatores* there must have been to account for the dispersion of goods. An attractive hypothesis is that the pottery which crossed the Channel southwards did so as a subsidiary cargo on ships which were mostly carrying grain, wool, salt or other cargoes for the state, and may also have carried pottery, glass and wine in the other direction. The main difference in this typical mixture of state control and private enterprise would be the volume of officially required goods now moving from Britain to the continent, rather than *vice versa*.

Sidonius' letter carrier was a small-scale trader of a different sort, for he distributed goods of foreign origin which he had bought on credit at Marseille. The range of goods that might be anticipated is confirmed by various stray literary references – items such as ivory, fine textiles, incense, precious stones, papyrus, fruits, oil and fish–sauce. Most of these fall clearly into the luxury class (though the odd piece of probably Alexandrian glass might find its way to such a remote settlement as la Bûre in the southern Vosges, and a small amount of African pottery is known from Rhineland sites).[43] The dimensions of the luxury trade are hard to estimate. Many such goods may have made their way to Trier after arriving at Arles, which is stressed as a port by both Ausonius and the geographical *Expositio totius mundi* (Arles and Trier between them now cut out Lyon). Rich men elsewhere certainly came by their share, but owners of Spanish estates might dispense precious fish-sauce to their friends without it entering the market.[44]

The extent to which the luxury trade was from start to finish in the hands of oriental traders is the next question. Salvian complained that the cities were full of Syrian merchants no less rapacious than the tax-rigging *curiales*, and in the sixth century both Syrians and Jews are mentioned by Gregory of Tours. Had orientals taken over from Gauls already in the fourth century? It is possible that they were always involved in the luxury trade, which is not the sector on which the epigraphic sources are most informative. An increase in their numbers in the late fourth and early fifth century is perhaps suggested by epitaphs belonging to orientals at Trier (not specifically traders, but equally too late to have been attracted and held there by the court) as well as by the complaints of Salvian. From that time on their activities are one of the threads linking late Roman with Merovingian Gaul.[45]

The import of luxury items into Gaul does not seem to have increased, unless in selected commodities like ivory and fine quality textiles, where Trier may have created a demand. In northern Gaul at least, the absence of exotic marbles for private use is indicative. By the time of Gratian, even at Trier the mighty stone monoliths for the cathedral were of granite from the Odenwald, not Mediterranean marble.

Indications of lowered trade are in line with the observed shrinkage in the size of merchant ships in the Later Empire and with the reduction in numbers of known shipwrecks.[46] It is of some interest to attempt a comparison not so much with the second and third century, when northern Gaulish exports reached their peak, as with the first century. At that point imports were probably higher, if glass, metalware and bronze statuary are added to the staples of wine and oil and the luxuries of perfumes, ointments, spices and fruit. Exports may have been at a level comparable to those of the later period, though that of woollen cloth to Italy was rapidly expanding. Late oriental traders might be seen as analogous to earlier Italian ones. The late pottery centres have, however, little in common with the rapidly expanding mobile businesses of the earlier period, and in place of a growing movement to supplant imports with local products there is at best a maintenance of the *status quo*. Only Britain presents some of the dynamic qualities which were earlier seen in Gaul.

This move to a more static self-sufficiency does not however denote what is often termed a 'natural' economy. While taxation in kind and the lowered commodity market suggest that the economy was less monetized, this does not mean a wholesale return to systems of barter: coins as well as goods circulated. Doubtless coins were used in many ways that fall short of full monetization, being sometimes only a measure of value, or exchanged to make up the difference between two products. Typically, the mass of circulating coinage was bronze of very small denominations, so that the sheer number of coins from sites occupied in the Later Empire can, at first sight, mislead in a direction precisely contrary to impressions based on the comparative paucity of other objects.

The fundamental mechanism behind the circulation of coinage must still have been payments to the troops and to the increased number of government officials. It might therefore be anticipated that coins would circulate at a higher density in the neighbourhood of the army and of capital cities, most of all Trier. Future work may show whether or not this is the case: if it is not, then a more important role must be assigned to secondary circulation through commercial exchange. That trade was not closely linked with the output of coinage from the mint at Trier is shown by the upsurge in pottery exports in the later fourth century, a time of reduced bronze minting.[47] From future studies increased understanding of the function of coinage should emerge. For instance, many fourth-century coins are found at those sanctuaries which continued in use, and it may be possible to determine from their location and density whether they were used largely as votive gifts or were lost in the course of transactions which denote the continuance of local fairs or markets.

If pertinent analogies can perhaps be drawn with the very earliest period of Romanization, when native bronze coins of small denomination circulated in large numbers, the contrast is no less instructive. The accepted reason for the early proliferation of small change is the need to pay services and taxes in coin, along with an expanding commodity market. By the later fourth century, both coins and commodities were rapidly diminishing, and the level that was eventually reached in the ensuing centuries was lower than immediately after the conquest, when inclusion within the Empire had just begun to affect provincial life.

13

THE CHRISTIANIZATION OF BELGICA

1 Late antique paganism

Although attention naturally focuses on the rise of Christianity, there can be no doubt that pagan cults remained the dominant mode of religious adherence in the north of Gaul. For the majority, the reasons for adopting the new faith were insufficiently strong. Even in court circles, where exposure to both knowledge and persuasion were strongest, not everyone adopted the faith which was, after Constantine (Julian apart), that of the emperors.

The continuation of pagan beliefs and practices can be readily detected at a variety of levels. Some of the most persistent are ageless, and leave little or no physical trace. Accounts are preserved in sermons, saints' lives and the acts of councils. The consulting of soothsayers, the wearing of apotropaic charms, the pronouncement of incantations, the leaving of offerings by rocks, trees, springs or crossroads, were all connected with placating malevolent spirits and warding off catastrophes. The placing of replicas of parts of the body by trees in the search for healing continued practices for which there is sometimes archaeological evidence. It was natural that the sign of the cross should eventually spread in rural areas as a novel way of warding off diseases in cattle.[1]

Sometimes a link with cults known from archaeology is detectable. Books of penance mention the Parcae or fates, and the idea of supernatural women, sometimes benevolent, sometimes presaging death, often in triplicate (when two may be benevolent and the third not) has remained strong in folklore. Christianized as Faith, Hope and Charity, they appear in wayside shrines and are the source of the name les Trois Vierges (Luxembourg). The observance of particular days – the fifth of the week as Jove's day, the first of the month, certain phases of the moon – shows that the pagan priesthood kept some control over the calendar. The celebrations of the first of January were particularly abhorrent, since they involved disguise of humans as bulls or stags and an element of transvestism.[2]

Sacred springs, stones, and trees might also be the spatial focus of more organized cults that included temples. One story of Martin of Tours is illuminating, for it shows that the building might be less important than the tree outside it: destruction of the first caused little protest, attack on the tree an uproar. The lives of Martin and later saints make it clear that many cult statues were also venerated. These included columns, some of which might well have been crowned by seated Jupiter or riding god with giant. Destruction of the visible representation was tantamount to defeat of the god.[3]

Temples naturally remained important focal points of human social geography, and archaeology can testify to their continued use. If only a certain proportion of the sanctuaries were still functioning, this should not be seen, except in very specific circumstances, as the triumph of Christianity. Rather, shrines continued to be used so long as there was a population in the neighbourhood which they could serve.[4] Their neglect need not, however, necessarily reflect total depopulation. A shift away from a more organized cult, dependent on a previous rural pattern, to others more purely domestic or superstitious in character might be indicated. Moreover, it is unclear what religious beliefs and practices were observed by Germanic groups settled in the countryside, and whether they involved Gallo-Roman temples.

It is of interest to see which sanctuaries remained in use, and which areas show greatest continuity of the earlier divine geography. The absence of evidence for late activity among shrines of the Menapii and Nervii and its presence at less than half of known Ambianic sites (Eu, perhaps Vendeuil-Caply and Ribemont-sur-Ancre) is to be put alongside the changed rural society in these areas. Among the Mediomatrici, at the other end of the scale, the few excavated sanctuaries (with the exception of those in the Vosges villages) all show signs of continued use (Bierbacher Klosterwald, le Héraple, Mackwiller, Niedaltdorf, Ste. Ruffine). Among the Treveri, between one half and two thirds of the shrines were still in use, with a marked concentration in the lower Eifel north of Trier and in the 'Gutland' of Luxembourg (e.g. Möhn, Newel, Odrang, Altrier). There is a marked divergence between sites where, as at Heckenmünster, evidence for late use is extremely slight, and others such as Möhn or Drohnecken (Hunsrück) where most coins are of the fourth century. At some hilltop sites (e.g. Velosnes-la Romanette) it is not clear whether the sanctuary was still functioning or had been turned into a refuge.

The desertion of some of the very large sanctuaries is noteworthy. The best documented is Fontaine-Valmont, but the Donon, le Châtelet and Champlieu are (with varying degrees of certainty) to be added, and use of Vendeuil-Caply was limited. At Ribemont-sur-Ancre the baths were not used, though the temple was visited and artisans worked close by.[5] If sanctuaries had also served as the focus for the imperial cult in rural areas, such observances (which did not stop with Christianity, except for the sacrifice) must have been drastically reduced or else focused on the remaining road-village sanctuaries (e.g. Héraple, Versigny, Mouzon). Perhaps more surprising is the virtual cessation of activity at Hochscheid and Heckenmünster, where one main function had been healing. Here either depopulation or the psychological impact of destruction was responsible. Other healing shrines, including those of Lenus Mars opposite Trier, remained in use.

While some sanctuaries show particularly abundant coin-lists for the fourth century, this need not mean that use was intensified. The majority of the coins were of very low value, and coins may have been frequent votive gifts in the absence of other choices such as figurines. The more expensive forms of votive offering, inscriptions and sculpture, are virtually unknown. The shrines then, even when visited, were only in a restricted sense flourishing, and there is limited evidence in the Belgicas for new building at this date. Sorcy-St. Martin west of Toul, and Möhn north of Trier are the best documented. The most striking examples lie in Germania Secunda, at Matagne-la-Petite and Matagne-la-Grande, and at Pesch in the higher Eifel. It remains clear however that the type of rural patronage which produced and ornamented the plethora of earlier temples was not generally available in the fourth century, or was not taking that particular form.

In surviving villages and in cities there is limited evidence for continued use of sanctuaries and, occasionally, for building. Rebuilding was certainly involved at Trier, where the Altbachtal had seen extensive destruction in the later third century. The extent of the changes depends on the dating of the theatre's destruction and the erection above it of five strip-houses. If these belong to the middle of the third century, then only minor changes took place later. If the destruction layer over the theatre is part of a general one of later third-century date (which slender coin evidence suggests), then they were more major. Use of the Altbachtal, as measured by coin loss, was certainly considerable, even if no cult statues or reliefs (with the possible exception of those from the Mithraeum) belong to this period. The big reduction in use, involving destruction and perhaps wholesale secularization of the area, came with Gratian, when roads were driven over a number of the temples, and the buildings remaining were, with one important exception, domestic in character.[6]

The mithraeum introduces another aspect of late pagan practices. Built into one of the strip-houses by a proprietor with rank of *pater*, it shows that areas of the great sanctuary might be privately owned by individuals or cult groups. There is no doubt that the fourth century was the main period of its use, and nothing to suggest that this stopped even in the reign of Gratian. The mithraeum at Sarrebourg was also frequented throughout the fourth century, and a mithraic votive plaque at fortified Deneuvre is also late. At Mackwiller, on the other hand, the site was converted back into an ordinary Gallo-Roman temple.[7]

The fate of the Mackwiller mithraeum is a reminder that Mithras was different from normal Gallo-Roman gods, even if he rubbed shoulders with them. His cult remained sporadic, originally that of a small number of relatively high class devotees who deliberately set themselves apart from the masses: thus the mithraeum of one generation might not be required by the next, because the cult was not deeply rooted in local tradition. The same is probably true for others, including that of Sol, originally a distinct deity but sometimes conflated with either Apollo Grannus (as at Grand) or with Mithras. Enjoying the imperial patronage of Aurelian and (more important) Constantius, this cult probably attracted an increasing number of educated adherents. The vaguer syncretistic cults (vague perhaps only because their identity is not clear to us) are well represented by the earlier reliefs of the Igel monument with its emphasis on the zodiac and a symbolism showing the soul ascending in triumph. These have every appearance of being the beliefs of a self-conscious élite, the same people who might, after army experience, seek the reassurance of mithraism with its progress through the ranks.[8]

Had the production of votive inscriptions and reliefs been frequent in the fourth century, there would be much more evidence for adherence to mystery cults. The one area left for major religious display was the medium of mosaic, and here northern Gaul has a poor record compared to Britain. Only two pavements are relevant, one from a rural location, the other from Trier. The Blanzy-lez-Fismes mosaic, which decorated a very large room with three apses, surrounded a central water-basin. Orpheus charming the beasts on one side was probably balanced by Arion and the fishes on the other. While this might be merely a tastefully decorated dining room, the reasons for believing that such mosaics mirror the owners' beliefs, or even decorate a cult room, have grown with recent studies.[9] The Trier mosaic is both more extraordinary and more specific, with scenes that connect a ritual egg (symbol of rebirth) with the mythical one that contained Castor, Pollux, and Helen of Troy. An epigram of Ausonius suggests that he had seen the mosaic, and he drops the clue that the cult was connected with Nemesis. The mosaic may stand for the educated people at Trier who, right up to the reign of Gratian and even beyond, were following one of the various pagan religious options open to them.[10] With the peasants they shared only the fact that this option was not the Christian one. Some members of this higher stratum of society, however, underwent conversion during their time in Trier.

The overview is perforce a partial one. Among the many unknowns are the types of pagan cult practised by the high-ranking Germans who remained pagan, such as Arbogast and Bauto. Given their intense desire for Romanization, it could well have been closer to the Nemesis cult than to less sophisticated rustic religions.

Eventually, measures were taken to suppress pagan cult practices. Officially, these culminated in edicts of Theodosius that outlawed pagan sacrifices. In actuality, things went their own way at their own local speed. Certainly, many pagan statues and reliefs were at some indeterminable point mutilated, and not infrequently thrown down wells. Many cult images from the Altbachtal were found headless. This is one of the few places where the activity can be dated, though it remains unclear whether a fiat from on high or (more likely) a mob roused by preaching was responsible. The lives of the early Trier bishops contain recollections of an enormous site with a hundred idols which were eventually destroyed, although the third-century date implied is wrong.[11] If the work was that of St. Martin, who certainly spent enough time in Trier, it is strange that there is no mention of it. His influence could, however, have been indirectly responsible for later actions. The higher, more private forms of pagan practices were still unaffected by the destructive forces.

The rural shrines meanwhile were frequented until the end of the fourth century, sometimes till at least the mid-fifth. Many rural areas were not thoroughly Christianized till the eighth and ninth centuries. Some shrines were in due course sanctified for Christian use and gave way to churches, or holy wells. Others were seen as the haunts of demons. Some, perhaps those that were simply deserted as rural society changed, gave rise to legends like the Seven Sleepers, occasioned by half-buried remnants of buildings and cult images.[12]

2 Bishops and cathedrals

Obviously both archaeological and written evidence must be used for evaluation of the spread of Christianity in northern Gaul. On the other hand, the types of information afforded are for the most part so different that it can be advantageous to consider them separately. Only written evidence can tell us about the organization of the church, the men who were its bishops and leaders, the changing forms of Christianity and the missionary activities of prominent individuals. Archaeological data, on the other hand, are needed to provide checks on the rather rosy view which can be generated by medieval foundation legends, even after critical sifting.

The beginnings of the church in northern Gaul are shrouded in mystery. The comments of Irenaeus of Lyon on the spread of Christianity among the Germanies has been taken to imply the existence of Christian communities on Mosel and Rhine in the second century. But the passage is rhetorical, and a small community at Besançon would be a sufficient factual basis, if one is needed. It is not until the later third century that there is evidence for bishops in the north, although actual communities of Christians may have preceded them.[13]

Bishop lists present their own problems. Fictitious saintly evangelisers, introduced later in an attempt to provide higher antiquity for the community concerned, can however be identified. Thus St. Firminus of Amiens is very likely a seventh- or eighth-century discovery, at best based on some Christian tombstone with that name. Even reliable lists, for instance that of Trier (where many bishops are mentioned in other sources) can still present problems. Maternus, the third bishop, also figures on the lists of Köln and Tongeren, and was probably 'borrowed' from Köln by the clergy of Trier in the course of later ecclesiastical rivalries. The initial names are often uncheckable. Fixed points are however provided by those bishops who attended councils (e.g. Arles in 314) or whose names are found on the apparently genuine list appended to the fictitious council of Köln. The pattern that emerges from a scrutiny of the lists is in general plausible.[14]

A considerable time lag between the north and the south of Gaul is evident. To start with, the north had no genuine martyrs from the period of the prosecutions, although some were in due course 'discovered'. Timotheus and Apollinaris at Reims were brought from northern Italy (there may have been relics). Neither Quintinus of St. Quentin nor Crispinus and Crispinianus of Soissons have solid claims to historical reality, though mentioned by Gregory of Tours. Likewise the elaborate Theban legion cycle with its soldier–martyrs is a patent, if fascinating, fabrication of the seventh or eighth century; any historical kernel it may have had was unconnected with Trier and the north.[15] Among real figures, only Trier and Reims had bishops present at Arles in 314 (though Soissons, at first included within the diocese of Reims, was arguably independent by this time). For each city this was the third or fourth bishop, which would put the origin of the sees in the second half of the third century. Metz may also have had a bishop by the early fourth century but this list is a little uncertain. By the mid-fourth century, Verdun and probably Châlons were added to the group, and Amiens with Cambrai formed outposts in the north. Even in Belgica Prima, however, the ecclesiastical organization still did not fully parallel the secular one, since the bishopric of Toul belongs at earliest to the late fourth century (despite the existence of Christians in the family that produced Lupus, fifth–century bishop of Troyes).[16]

The northern part of Belgica Secunda poses particular problems. No fourth-century bishops are known at Tournai, St. Quentin, Arras, Beauvais or Thérouanne, and the first part of the Senlis list is unverifiable. The single bishop of the Nervii known for the mid-fourth century has no immediate successors. Consistent with the church making little headway in this whole area is the later missionary activity among Nervii and Morini of Victricius of Rouen. This is rhetorically described by Paulinus of Nola (writing in 399) as a victory for civilization, which turned bandit-ridden wasteland into organized civic and religious communities. The solid evidence for ecclesiastical organization is thus very slight.[17] If further progress had been made, the memory of it was erased by the effects of the barbarian invasions in the fifth century. Much depends on the interpretation of the so-called *Notitia Galliarum*, of late fourth- or early fifth-century date. If this was compiled or used for ecclesiastical purposes, listing *civitates* only because they were bishoprics, then indeed each *civitas* capital must have had its bishop, even if some were to lose him. On balance, the evidence from the north is less consistent with this view than with a time lag in evangelization.[18]

The names given by the bishop lists all too frequently give little information on the people involved. A few, such as Eucharius and Agricius (Agroecius) of Trier or Eulogius of Amiens sound of eastern origin. The majority of names

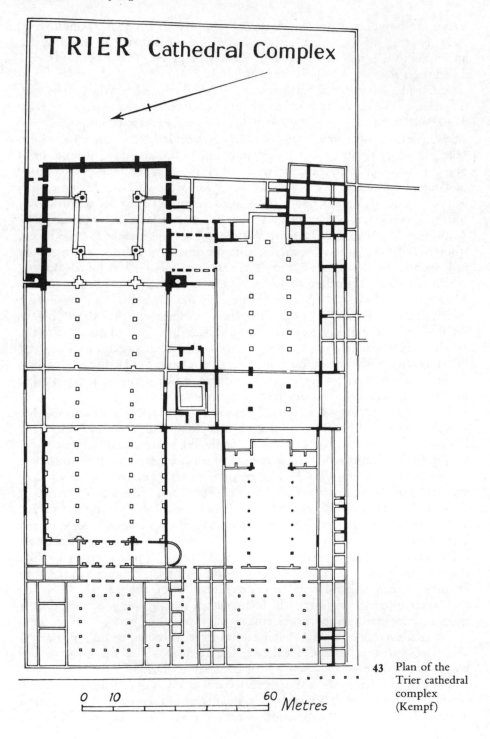

TRIER Cathedral Complex

0 10   60 Metres

43 Plan of the Trier cathedral complex (Kempf)

are very neutral – Valerius, Victor, Mansuetus – and could equally well be of Gauls or foreigners. Stranger ones like Imbetausius of Reims are without obvious context. The suggestion that Maximinus and Paulinus of Trier were from an Aquitanian family is not implausible, but is based on later Lives. The powerful local landowner-bishop seems to be a creation of the fifth century, at a time when the administrative grip of Rome was already weakening. Even then, the best example from Belgica, Remigius of Reims, came from a family whose wealth could not compare with that of Sidonius Apollinaris, and the same is likely to be true of the scholarly Auspicius of Toul.[19]

If a few bishops of Trier emerge from the shadows, it is because of the imperial court and their involvement in questions concerning heresy. Even so, during the time of Constantine, the court had ecclesiastical advisers and tutors in Hosius and Lactantius to keep the limelight off the local figures. The relationship between Agricius and Helena, mother of Constantine, must remain partly a matter of conjecture, despite the apparent fit between pious legend, in which Helena was persuaded to donate her house for a cathedral, and the discovery of the Trier church above part of the imperial palace.[20] Maximus and Paulinus both befriended Athanasius when the latter was in exile in Trier, and Paulinus' active support for the orthodox cause earned him exile. Felix played no very distinguished role when the Priscillianist heretics were condemned by a civil court under Maximus, but tamely supported the emperor in a fashion that contrasts with the intransigent Martin of Tours.[21] He may have been responsible for a more positive and original action – the bringing back of the body of Paulinus from Asia Minor, and his burial in a church in the northern cemetery of Trier. The late and confused literary evidence would hardly inspire confidence but for the complete consistency of the discoveries below the church of St. Paulin – the eastern cedar-wood coffin adorned with metal plaques that belong to the repertoire of western provincial Christian art.[22] Paulinus' translation stands at the beginning of the process whereby certain bishops were elevated to the rank of saints and their places of burial became the principal *foci* of local cult. By the end of the fourth century, the importance of relics from non-local saints is also visible in the writings of Victricius of Rouen, who saw them forming the city's best protection against evil.[23]

It is only with Martin and Victricius that evangelizing fervour is found, lavished for the most part on other areas of Gaul, though Martin's conversion (and perhaps baptism) took place at Amiens. Martin's healing miracles show how Christian holy men might offer a real alternative to pagan cults in a central area of human life. The result could be conversion at the very highest social level, as happened with Tetradius at Trier, and growing power for the Pannonian ex-soldier Martin, of moderate social standing and a foreigner to the area. Only with Martin was any attempt made to spread Christianity outside of the urban communities. Yet even he probably did not touch the depths of the countryside, for his miracles and his tearing down of shrines and images occurred in the context of his journeying, hence in villages along the roads.[24]

Roughly the same period saw the first growth of monasticism in northern Gaul. This was confined to Trier, and was the direct result of the exile thither of Athanasius. A community outside the walls of Trier was discovered by two *agentes in rebus* known to a friend of Augustine, and who were themselves converted to this new way of life. Nothing substantiates the suggestion that one of them might have been Jerome, though he spent a few years at Trier and was attracted to the ascetic life.[25]

By the sixth century it could be taken for granted that each bishop had a permanent episcopal church, part of a complex that included a bishop's residence. To judge from medieval topography, there was a relatively stereotyped position for this, normally just inside the walls. The cathedrals, once fixed, never changed position, and this strong element of continuity has led to the supposition that all cities had intra-mural cathedrals from a time shortly after the creation of the see.[26] When local church tradition, as at Metz, testifies to the first cathedral having been outside the walls, it is confused. The question may be divided into two parts, whether early cathedrals were always intra-mural and whether early bishops had in fact fixed seats in the sense of later cathedrals.

In an ideal situation, archaeology could make a clear contribution to this question. In practice, of course, excavation below cathedrals is not simple. It is moreover extremely hard to regard the evidence impartially; a synthesis of archaeological and written evidence is nowhere more important, and nowhere more difficult. Archaeologically, the best-known cathedral complex by far is that of Trier. The great double church in its final state took up four *insulae*, almost 100 by 200 m. Though doubts can be expressed on the precise dating of some of the various phases, large-scale building in the reign of Constantine seems certain enough. It is also reasonably sure that the south church was the earlier of the two. The north church, which overlies part of the palace with its ceiling painting of the imperial family, was (from coin evidence) started after 326 and may safely be identified with the church that Athanasius saw still unfinished in the 340s. The plans were altered more than once, to incorporate within an enlarged east end the raised, polygonal element that is thought to have enclosed some particularly precious relic connected with the life of Christ. While this may have happened under the sons of Constantine, military tile-stamps show that the building did not attain its final form until Valentinian and Gratian. Yet it was this second church, so long in the building, which acted as cathedral. Athanasius says the church was already in use when half-finished, but the baptistery, which lay between the two churches, was not one of the earliest elements, and even at Trier episcopal control may have taken time to establish. The south church is variously seen as a palace church or a separate church for catechumens.[27]

The earliest bishops, up to and including Agricius, must therefore have preached and baptized elsewhere. The claim that an earlier church lay to the west of the south church remains to be demonstrated, and it may be doubted whether a substantial building with a basilical plan was feasible before Constantine. More probably the Christians gathered in a meeting room that did not have the features later associated with church architecture. Private rooms, on the analogy of the Nemesis mosaic, or a bath-house as at Cimiez, may have been converted for the purpose. While there must have been arrangements for baptism, these may have been *ad hoc* and it may be questioned whether the bishop used one church as a fixed seat.

Evidence elsewhere is meagre. At Metz, the existence of a cathedral on its present location from the early fifth century depends on its identity with the *oratorium* of St. Stephen described by Gregory as miraculously surviving the Hunnic raids of 451. A tradition that placed the earlier cathedral outside the walls could be a recollection of a period when there was no cathedral as such. No archaeological evidence substantiates the claim of St. Stephen, though the existence until the eighteenth century of an apparently Roman building in the courtyard of the episcopal palace is to be noted.[28] At Reims, the remains of early buildings have indeed been found below the cathedral, but cannot be dated; they may or may not be of the period of Nicasius, traditionally supposed to have built the cathedral around 400. Other cathedrals, including that of Amiens, need not be earlier than the Merovingian period.[29] The lack of baptisteries remains a problem; it must be concluded that they took a non-monumental form. A lengthy period of rather informal development must be seriously considered.

The evidence for intra-mural churches of any kind before the fifth century is in fact quite meagre. The *patrocinium* of two Metz churches, both dedicated to the Holy Cross, has led to the suggestion that they might be Roman. With the later St. Pierre-aux-Nonnains, it is the function, not the date, that is in question. While a round water basin has been interpreted as the *piscina* of a baptistery, the balance of opinion at present is in favour of a secular function for the complex. At Reims, hagiographical tradition has it that the cathedral was the second intra-mural church. Churches dedicated to St. Martin at Boulogne and Amiens could be either late Roman or Merovingian, though at Amiens the very close connection with Martin's conversion, and the situation of the church close to one of the gates make a late Roman foundation likely.[30]

The difficulties of proving late Roman dates make it likely that a sceptical approach will fall short of the truth, just as the following of tradition may overshoot it. The truth is sure to lie between, and one man with the stature of Martin or Victricius could make a great difference. It would be surprising if Trier and Reims did not have recognizable Christian meeting places, equivalents of the mithraeum or the room of the Nemesis cult. But it would not be astonishing if only a few cities had intra-mural cathedrals before the fifth century, and if some in the north did not get them till the sixth or even seventh.

3 Cemeteries, churches and Christians

Many churches grew over the real or supposed tombs of martyrs or bishops, and each in due course gathered a tradition unto itself. Mentions of churches by Gregory of Tours are valuable, since they bring testimony from the sixth century rather than later. Even by Gregory's time, however, perceptions of the church and of the tombs of saints had undergone development which can cause distortions. Archaeology is therefore again left with the difficult task of bridging, when possible, the gap between the fourth and the sixth century.[31]

The cemeteries at Trier, Metz and Reims are those that provide most information and problems. The southern cemetery at Trier by Late Empire times stretched to engulf at least one earlier suburban site (probably a villa) at St. Matthias. Besides simple burials and a few definitely pagan sarcophagi, inscriptions show that the cemetery here was predominantly used by Christians. It was here that the first bishops (Eucharius and Valerius) were believed buried. There are indeed burial chambers immediately to the north of the abbey, but none that can be incontrovertibly connected with the early bishops. Such excavations as have been possible are also insufficient to show any of these developing into churches, though this cannot be ruled out. One chamber proved on investigation to contain a fine third-century pagan sculptured sarcophagus; special pleading is required to claim that it was moved to one side of the chamber to make way for the bodies of Eucharius and Valerius. Firmer ground is reached in the interior of the medieval church, where remains of a decorated screen could be fifth-century in date, and point to a church on a larger scale than a tiny chapel or oratory. The text of a metric inscription refers to a building erected by Cyrillus, bishop in the mid-fifth century, in connection with the veneration of Eucharius and Valerius. For Gregory of Tours, St. Eucharius guarded the south gate of the city. The gap between the early bishop's death and the work of Cyrillus cannot however be wholly bridged.[32]

Although the north cemetery at Trier seems, on the basis of the inscriptions, to have been Christianized rather later than the southern one, it provides more clues to the growing veneration of departed bishops. Again, at least one separate complex was engulfed by the cemetery, for near the later St. Maximin were found the remains of a richly decorated building. By the time of Gregory, Maximinus was believed buried not far outside the north gate, protecting the city as did Eucharius to the south, and Gregory's description supposes a large-scale church. Just within the apse of the tenth-century church lay a funerary vault with two late Roman sarcophagi, one of them sculpted on three sides with biblical scenes. Since figured sarcophagi are rare, it is not improbable that this might have been the tomb of a bishop. There is however no clear indication of the period when the grave became an object of special attention.[33]

The organization of cults around bishops' tombs may in fact begin with

Paulinus. His body was richly clad with gold and purple silks, the cedar-wood must have come from the east while the silver ornamental plaques with short statements in Latin are clearly western. Sixth-century tombstones from near the church refer to burial *ad sanctos*. Quite unclear, however, is whether Felix buried Paulinus in an existing church, as tradition would have it, or had a church constructed round the tomb. Even more uncertain is whether the church was a large congregational one, a forerunner of Cyrillus' church in the south, or merely a small oratory. Not far from St Maximin lies a group of burials which did not give rise to a church but which can give some idea of a modest oratory's appearance – a small apsidal building with vestibule.[34] The status of Paulinus and the politics of his homecoming (it is described by the medieval source as resembling an imperial *adventus*) should have ensured something more elaborate, akin to the Church of Jovinus at Reims or the remarkable late Roman kernel of St. Gereon at Köln. A metrical inscription found at St. Maximin and testifying to the cult of Agnes, a Roman martyr, is a reminder that there were other options besides the veneration of local bishops, and that the medieval churches of each city represent the eventual formation of a canon.[35] Rivalry can be imagined between the various centres of adherence.

At Metz, Christian tombstones did not become customary until the fifth century, a period when the Trier stone-carvers were also producing a greater number than previously. The presence of tombstones in the larger amphitheatre, then, does not confirm the tradition that this was the site of the earliest church of the city, later known as St. Peter *in arena*. As seen, it is unlikely that a church was set up there in the late third century, since the amphitheatre shows signs of a Constantinian reconstruction. The central cellar for housing machinery was at some later point converted, with the help of re-used columns, into an aisled building that resembles a church. The church may thus pre-date the tombs. The other extramural church whose existence in the fifth century is reasonably certain is St. Arnoul, originally the Holy Apostles but later called after Bishop Arnolfus. A crypt with sarcophagi, one with an epitaph of late fifth-century date, was discovered by excavation around 1900. In contrast with these two for which there is some archaeological testimony, a study based on *patrocinia* (dedications) has suggested as many as eight late Roman churches in the southern cemetery alone, but some of these are more probably of sixth-century date.[36]

One church in the southern cemetery at Reims is of the highest interest. Although it is preserved only in the text of Flodoard, no doubts have been raised against the authenticity of the metrical inscription which records in allusive literary phrases the career of the *magister militum* Jovinus and his erection of a church as his burial place. An analysis of his career suggests that he was converted late in life. The inscription served both as his own epitaph and as the *titulus* recording the founder of the church.[37] All sorts of doubts, on the other hand, surround the great marble lion-hunt sarcophagus which long stood in the medieval church and was traditionally considered his tomb.

Probably prepared in some Rome workshop in the mid-third century, it had a curious history, since the portrait heads of the central figures were not finished until the fourth century (though hardly as late as the career of Jovinus). That it was brought by him from either Rome or Arles is not beyond the bounds of possibility, nor is the lion-hunt theme incompatible with selection by a Christian. At the same time, it is known that sarcophagi were sometimes brought at a later date to provide suitable housing for the remains of saints. Soissons cathedral had two such, and originally there was a second one with Christian themes in Jovinus' church. In the history of this church only two people and one set of relics seem important – Jovinus the founder, Nicasius (bishop in the fifth century) and the relics of St. Agricola, which could have reached Gaul in the very late fourth or early fifth century (after 'discovery' at Bologna in 393). That the two sarcophagi housed (or were believed to house) the remains of founder and saint is not impossible, but the date of transportation is a separate question.[38]

The church of Jovinus at Reims is thus the best example of a cemetery church dated within the fourth century. Yet since it is a *titulus* church, donated by a patron who was not a bishop (unique in Belgica), general conclusions cannot be drawn from it. Tradition believed another cemetery church at Reims to be connected with the first bishop, but there is no corroborative evidence; Jovinus' church could well have been the first.

It may be assumed that developments in other cities were not ahead of those in Trier, Metz, and Reims. At Amiens, the suburban church of St. Acheul is later than the cemetery with inscriptions in which it lies. At Tournai, graves were marked out by a simple building or *memoria*, but the first church is of sixth-century date. A conservative view suggests that the major developments came a little later, in the fifth or sixth century. Concern for the resting place of bishops was perhaps generally contemporary with the veneration of relics that reached prominence only at the very end of the fourth century with Victricius, to spread wider in the fifth century after the dispersal of the relics of St. Stephen.[39]

The evidence for churches in communities other than cities is also very slight. A Christian tombstone at Pachten may not be earlier than the sixth century, while others are of uncertain origin. The supposed church at Arlon may be only a building that was used for burials in Frankish times.[40] Although the *vici* or *castella* would be the logical places to develop churches and become separate parishes, the archaeological evidence adds little except a sixth-century church at Famars. Only one metrical inscription from Sion suggests Christian faith among rural aristocracy. There is also literary evidence of the Christianization (or destruction) of a sanctuary of Apollo among the Leuci, probably that of Grand, but the verse of an early fifth-century poet who describes Christ as god of the cities is on the whole borne out.[41]

Archaeological evidence for private chapels or oratories is also lacking, though many people, especially at or near Trier, may have had them. The poet

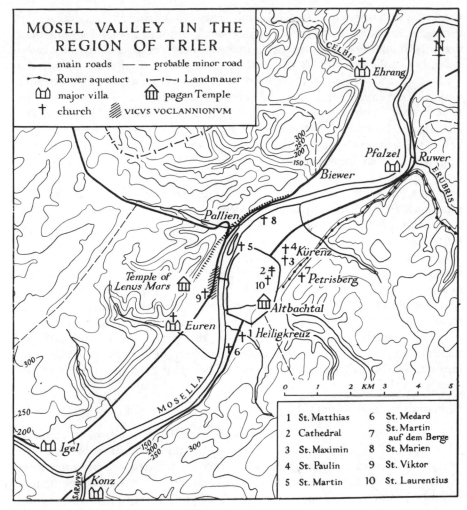

44 Late Roman sites and early churches in the region of Trier

Ausonius probably offered his rather literary prayers in such a room. In contrast to Britain, there is an absence of Christian mosaics or paintings, unless (but it is unlikely) the Orpheus mosaic at Blanzy-les-Fismes be so interpreted. Near Trier, a number of churches were founded on top of Roman villas showing possible continuity between Roman and Merovingian times – St. Martin to the north of the city (sometimes thought to be the site of one of Martin's miracles) and St. Medard to the south, St. Helena at Euren, St. Martin on the Petrisberg behind the city and St. Peter at Ehrang. Although these are all early *patrocinia*, they remain, for the late Roman period, possible rather than proven examples.[42]

Christianity otherwise usually manifests itself in small portable objects.

Glass cups or bowls with Christian symbolism – the chrism, or scenes from the bible – were produced by the Köln glass workshops, probably the same ones that turned out the pagan symbolism that is equally frequent. Other unlocated workshops followed suit. While costly gold-glass is virtually confined to the Rhineland and Trier, mould-blown or engraved vessels are found more widely. One rather early example comes from a Boulogne cemetery. The appearance of later types (for instance at Vermand, Abbeville-Homblières or Armentières) is the only evidence for Christian beliefs in rural areas at a level below the aristocracy that produced the Sion epitaph. It is moreover the only sign that Christian ideas might have percolated before the fifth or sixth century into the communities that were partly Germanic.[43]

In the many minor arts which saw the development of a Christian provincial art, such as decorative metal-work and ivories, Belgica has rather less to show than the Rhineland. One fine carved ivory pyxis from Trier, portraying scenes from the Old Testament, could be of fifth-century date, and was found in the cellar of the amphitheatre. A dendrochronological date for wood that may be associated suggests a somewhat later period of use, but it is not really clear that the pyxis was connected with an amphitheatre church as at Metz. Pottery lamps with Christian motifs are reasonably common, and some seem to be North African imports rather than indigenous products. From the very late fourth century or early fifth, the potters at Châtel-Chéhéry specialized in roulette-decorated pottery with simple Christian motifs, but the meaning of this in terms of the spread of beliefs is hard to estimate.[44]

4   Christianity and society

The introduction of Christianity into the cities of Belgica remains mysterious. That its knowledge was spread by people who came from Italy or the east is likely, but even this assumes that the northerly Christian communities were similar to that of Lyon, where half of the martyrs of 177 had Greek names. Possibly indigenous Gauls, converted at Lyon, carried the new beliefs northwards. The social status of the early converts is unfortunately not determinable, though Christianity had a potential appeal to all ranks, allowing slaves to feel themselves full members of a community and the *potentes* to develop new forms of communication with the heavenly powers. Communities of Christians there must have been in an age when it was still a dangerous adherence, yet we hear of none who were forced to tread the grim but glorious path to public martyrdom.[45]

There were doubtless more Gauls able to accept Constantine's reported vision of Apollo (depicted by the panegyrist as a kind of heavenly companion and even doublet of the handsome young emperor), than could understand his adoption of Christianity. Conceivably, since it became public only by stages, there were many who did not fully realize the difference. The presence of men such as Lactantius at the court would make more impact than the actual conversion of the emperor. Christianization of the court circles could not but cause a number of nominal conversions among men whose expectations could be as well met by Christianity as by any other religion, and who valued a closer connection with court society. At a later date, Ausonius well represents the educated but non-fervid Christian, who pays his respects to the Christian God but is more at home with the literary paraphernalia inherited from the pagan past, and did not see a conflict between the two. Evidence that might allow a study of the rate of conversion in the Belgicas has not come down to us. Analogies from other societies suggest that a slow start would be followed by a steadily increasing rate until a high point was reached. If the funerary inscriptions reflect the trend, then the marked increase came after Constantine, for the earliest examples have forms of the chrism which can hardly be earlier than the 330s. Moreover there are more late fourth-century stones than mid-fourth, and the number goes on increasing into the fifth century.[46]

Unfortunately, the inscriptions tell more about habits of nomenclature in late Roman and Merovingian Trier than they do about social status. Mention of the profession *negotiator* suggests that inscriptions need not be confined to the very highest social levels. Mention of imperial offices is rare, though including two men *a veste sacra* and a *cursor dominicus*. The senatorial rank of one fifth-century lady is carefully recorded. Church officials, including a presbyter and sub-deacon, are probably earlier but still surprisingly few in number.[47] In nomenclature the overwhelming element is the emphasis accorded to names of good omen or denoting desirable moral qualities – Bonosa, Sedulus, Exsuperantia, Faustus, also Elpidius, Eusebius, Nicetia. Names of Greek origin in Latin inscriptions are quite frequent, almost 25 per cent, contrasting with the mere 2 per cent of inscriptions actually written in Greek. Most such names were wholly at home in the body of late Roman western nomenclature, so that little can be concluded from them. Only a few geographical names, such as Maurus, may in fact denote external origin, in this case African, but such a conclusion can only be reached because of other common African names in the same family. Apart from a number of relatively neutral names, only a very few, like Treverius, are derived from the old Gallo-Roman pool. Perhaps more surprisingly, there are more names derived from pagan deities (Iovina, Veneria) than specifically Christian forms like Adeodatus, Revocatus, Quodvultdeus. Of the small stock of German names, only Flavius Gabso, of the imperial bodyguard, is of Roman date.[48]

The formulae of the inscriptions, *hic iacet*, *hic pausat*, *hic quiescit*, are very standardized. They show the same ambiguity over the dead as is found in pagan rituals with, on the face of it, a strong presumption that the dead were present in the grave. Illustration is provided by stories of vengeance being taken (by haunting) on people who had stolen others' sarcophagi. Glimpses of bridges between pagan and Christian customs are also given by the graffiti made in the plaster of the low chancel screen of the southern great church, which was more than once renewed. Except for the fact that they are followed by a chrism, or by *in deo*, expressions like *Victor vivas* are close counterparts to the *vivas* or *pie zeses* found on pottery and glass, and also to the cries of *tu vincas* with which the emperor was greeted.[49]

Against this evidence from Trier must be put the relative silence from elsewhere. Given the bishop lists, the Christian communities, however modest, presumably grew along similar lines but progress, in the absence of the stimulus provided by the court, was slower. Jovinus of Reims remains an intriguing figure, especially if converted only after his service to Julian. Martin's conversion took place, probably in the late 330s, when he was still a serving soldier at Amiens, and it was at one of that city's gates that he gave half of his cloak to a beggar. With his career as bishop of Tours a more assertive movement against paganism is seen, and his attacks on old ways proved a more successful way of building up power and patronage than the bishops' intervention in questions of orthodoxy. His main way of effecting conversions was to demonstrate the powerlessness of pagan gods by destroying their sanctuaries and images. Another was through miraculous healing. Some of the details suggest that his actions were in line with contemporary medical practices, to which his overwhelming *potentia* lent extra efficacy. He could moreover adapt himself to any social class, dealing with demons in a senator's slave or madness in cattle. He thus in his own person rendered the old pagan healing shrines otiose, and so blazed a trail that, except for his disciple Victricius of Rouen, was not really followed until much later.[50]

The veneration of deceased bishops and the cult of relics became increasingly important about the time of Martin's death in the 390s. The writings of Sulpicius Severus on Martin are a landmark in the developing cult of the holy man, as they are in the turning of pagan deities into major or minor devils. The tomb of Paulinus at Trier can be seen as a precursor of a major phenomenon in the life of the Gallic church. It gave a fixed geographical focus for cult at a time when a frontal attack was being made on the pagan sanctuaries. But these new focal points were inevitably urban in nature, since they depended on the actual or supposed location of the saint's body in the city cemeteries. While important for the growth of episcopal power in the urban community, they had no bearing on the countryside. Firmly embedded in city life, Christianity can only have increased the urban–rural division.[51]

The destruction or desertion of rural sanctuaries took place gradually. Basically two options were open to the rural missionary. A traditionally sacred place might be destroyed, the resident spirits demonstrated to be weak and contemptible, so that people had to look to the destroyer's stronger god. Alternatively, the site might be taken over and Christianized. The two processes can be observed in the distinction between springs or wells that were deemed holy, sacred to some saint, and those that were considered accursed, the haunt of the demons. One bishop who could not stop customary sacrifices at a sacred lake wisely diverted them by building a church.[52] This was the work of centuries, for it was not easy to persuade country people that the new religion could accommodate their concerns for the seasons, the weather, diseases in animals – hence the sermons, the pronouncements of councils and the penances for old religious customs. Eventually the church was the victor, its victory also ensuring that a Latin-derived language would prevail even in rural areas (except for the eastern and northern fringes of the provinces). Parish churches are not uncommonly built over Gallo-Roman shrines or habitations. Sometimes this represents the phenomenon of Christianization, which can also be expressed by the re-utilization of pagan cult statues as a church altar. Sometimes there is a demonstrable gap of centuries between the Roman building and the church, and no relationship can be assumed.[53]

The church, despite political upheavals, continued to gain strength between the fourth and fifth centuries, creating new forms of specifically northern Christianity as it went. It was the fifth century that saw the growth of cathedrals and other large churches. The number of datable inscriptions at Trier, if spread out on a per annum basis, is higher than in the preceding century. Links have been detected between the fifth-century bishops of Trier and Toul and the dynamic centres of Christian teaching in southern Gaul, especially the monastery of Lerins. As these links died out towards the end of the century, so did the north's last strong intellectual links with the south. As the organization of the Empire loosened, however, the bishops were well placed to profit, as more and more the civic affairs of the various cities came to rest in their hands. Only in the north of Belgica Secunda, an area increasingly isolated by regrowth of forests and perpetually insecure, was the fifth century perhaps a time of retrogression, for church along with cities.

Christianity, based as it was on the Roman municipal organization, was the last legacy of the Roman Mediterranean world to the north. The church was now left to continue the forms of urban structure first introduced by the Romans, as well as a system of beliefs which, while developing some specifically northern forms, provided continuing if sometimes tenuous links with the world that lay to the south.

14

THE FIFTH CENTURY: A TIME OF TRANSITION

1   The loosening of control

For the Empire as a whole, the year 395 is often seen as a turning point, because after the death of Theodosius east and west were definitively separated. For the north of Gaul, two other factors were more important. The first was the withdrawal of the imperial court and that of the *praefectus praetorio* from Trier, so that administrative services and court paraphernalia were now centred in the south, at Arles. The second was that after the invasion of 406/7, the military and administrative control of the north was at best intermittent and precarious.

The transitional nature of the period is reflected in the written sources, the more strongly after the cessation of Zosimus' narrative in 410. Sources thereafter are fragmentary, compressed into the form of brief chronicles, or else take the form of poetry, panegyric or letters. Increasingly, too, we have to deal with religious tracts, with hagiographies or with Gregory of Tours, who looks back from the world of the sixth century.[1]

No precise estimate of Rome's military strength in early fifth-century Gaul and Germany can be made. The commands mentioned in the *Notitia* should still have functioned, but at no regular forts (e.g. Oudenburg or Liberchies) can occupation be shown to continue beyond 400. In any case the keeping of the *status quo* depended as much or more on the Franks, who now formed a real frontier civilization. The most important group (usually called the Salii after one of their attested components) was settled north of Tongeren, while another was established on both sides of the lower Rhine. Little is heard of the Alamanni, perhaps because of internal weaknesses. The first great disruption was the work of wandering eastern Germans, the Vandals, Alans and Suebi. These were not mere raiders anxious for booty but migrating peoples in search of land inside the Empire. They crossed a frozen Rhine near Mainz on 31 December 406, and despite help from one group of Franks the Dux Mogontiacensis was unable to stop them. The first push was westwards and then northwards by Metz and Reims into the north of Belgica II (perhaps because settlement in the north seemed likely to bring desirable federate status). At Reims, the bishop Nicasius was traditionally believed to have perished. Not improbably the Salian Franks took the opportunity to infiltrate quietly westwards from their original base in Toxandria.[2]

Accounts are more dramatic than clear. In a letter to a Gaulish widow, Jerome, who adds Quadi, Sarmatians, Gepids, Heruli, Saxons and Burgundians to the list of invaders, depicts Reims, Amiens, Arras, Thérouanne and Tournai wholly taken over by Germans. A poet has all Gaul smoking in a common funeral pyre.[3]

Immediate action came from a source that was perhaps unexpected, although consistent with the past history of the north-west. Constantine III was the last of three imperial candidates to be hailed in quick succession by the armies of Britain. Probably chosen in part because of his auspicious name, he crossed to Gaul in 407, almost exactly a century after his illustrious homonym. He is credited with victory, albeit difficult and not wholly decisive, over the invaders in the north.[4] But he marched south without delay (though he has been credited with settling some Alans in the Aisne valley) and once at Arles was quickly caught up in the complicated affairs of the Central Empire. Zosimus hints that disturbances in northern Gaul led to the expulsion of officials; the scope is a matter for conjecture, but implies a further weakening of the Roman hold.[5] The eventual suppression of Constantine by the general Constantius in 411 brought for the northern Gauls insufficient reassurance that the central court was in control. A new imperial candidate, Jovinus, arose from the ranks of the Gallo-Romans who had been promoted by Constantine and was declared emperor at Mainz. While supported by some Gallo-Roman aristocrats, his real strength came from the Burgundians along the middle Rhine, the Alans under a chief Goar and some of the Franks. The power of the frontier people was becoming ever more evident, the distinction between Romans and barbarians more blurred. For the north it signified an emperor present in person, and a mint at Trier, which had struck for Constantine, continued for Jovinus. He may not have been without his challengers, however, for from about this time we again hear of Bagaudae, usually thought to have been in Armorica, but not in fact closely located by the sources; the times were ripe for such disturbances as *potentes* sought local advantages from central weakness.[6]

For the next decade, Constantius as *magister militum* represented the Central Empire. Besides suppressing Jovinus, he had to deal with the usurper's barbarian supporters. Reconstruction of events is difficult. Salvian's second sack of Trier, taken together with Gregory's information that the city was sacked by Franks, fits well with these people taking action against Jovinus' conqueror around 413.[7] At first, Constantius could not control the north, and the Trier mint struck in 414–416 for Priscus Attalus, puppet emperor of the Visigoths under Athaulf. Perhaps about the same time Exsuperantius, a noble native of Poitiers, and relative of the poet Rutilius Namatianus, was busy settling affairs in Armorica, but whether he acted in public or private capacity is unclear.[8] The Goths were also still causing problems, and only after Constantius' settlement of them in southern Gaul in 417 could a measure of stability return. At a council of the Gallic provinces called by Constantius in 418 the northern provinces were not represented. Whether, given his marriage to the emperor's half-sister Galla Placidia and his official elevation to the purple in 421, he could with time have controlled and reorganized the north is a matter for debate.

Some of the features, of an administration based firmly on Arles can be detected. Constantine III had a policy of appointing Gallic aristocrats to the prefecture of the Gauls, and this continued. Some of the types of patronage customary in the fourth century were thus restored, giving Constantius a sound base on which to build.[9] Many features of the early fifth century bear a generic resemblance to the conditions of the later third, and arguably Constantius could have proved a new restorer of the Gauls. Conditions were however now more complicated, with an increased number of Germanic peoples to be held in balance and a new focus of power present in the Visigothic kingdom in Aquitania. Jealousies between Gallic magnates could also be serious, as illustrated by ill feeling against Claudius Postumus Dardanus for his part in the murder of Jovinus. The southern focus of the court was a considerable disadvantage for controlling the north. Moreover, there are signs that northern aristocrats, who might have played their part in adminstration, were drifting south, whether like Protadius of Trier to leisure on Italian estates or like Salvian and Honoratus to religious life at Marseille and Lérins.[10]

The deaths of Constantius in 421 (soon after his elevation) and of Honorius in 423 opened a new chapter. For the central administration it started uncertainly, with the usurpation of Johannes at Ravenna. The ensuing defeat of the western army that supported him by that of Theodosius II may have caused ripples in Gaul. Bagaudae are heard of again, and the third sack of Trier by Franks may belong here. Soon there was a new strongman in the shape of Aetius, a native of the lower Danube whose rise was occasioned partly by his relationship with the Huns. Sent to Gaul by the new emperor Valentinian III as *comes* and *magister militum*, he was intermittently present for the next 25 years. For the Belgicas, his work was mostly with the Franks. Chronicles record victories in 428 and again in 431–2, followed by new treaties (probably made after yet another sack of Trier, which continued to bear the brunt of offensives from the Franks). These apparently recognized Rhineland Frankish kings, further testimony to the growing autonomy of the frontier zone. At some stage the Trier mint struck for Valentinian III, and since the coins are mostly found in graves east of the Rhine they represent some such settlement.[11]

The Frankish peoples were in an expansionist phase, and required the continued attention of Aetius when he was not dealing with Goths, the Alans under Goar (now if not before settled in Armorica) or Bagaudae. There is no sign that the numbers of the barbarians were ever very high: rather it was the extreme mobility of their warriors and the possibilities for quiet, steady infiltration that caused perpetual problems. Localization and dating of events becomes very uncertain. The battle at which Aetius and the future emperor Majorian defeated the Salian Franks is mentioned only by Sidonius, and has been variously dated between 428 and 448, with a date in the 440s preferred by most. The site of the battle, *vicus* Helena, must lie east of Arras, not far from Lens and Douai, to fit the topography of marshes and hills.[12] It is an important landmark, since it shows the Franks' advance westwards and the progress of a familiar pattern whereby the leader, the chief Chlodio or Chlogio, was recognized after defeat as an independent federate king. Probably for the price of abandoning Cambrai and Arras, he was allowed to keep Tournai. It is by no means clear that there was anything like a unified Frankish kingdom: more likely, Chlodio was one of a number of petty kings trying to establish paramountcy. The victory (the result of the Franks' celebration of a marriage feast when Majorian arrived), and the use to which it was put, may show a continued concern to keep the Bavay-Köln road in Roman control. The order and dating of Aetius' victories are bound up with the controversial chronology of St. Germanus, bishop of Auxerre. If his death is as early as 445, then Aetius's settlement of the Rhine frontier also has to be brought back, and the peace that is celebrated in the panegyric of 446 by Merobaudes (an educated Frank of senatorial rank who had property near Troyes as well as in Spain) would then be a general peace on all fronts. The traditional chronology stretches events out rather longer, with Germanus' appeal to Ravenna (against Aetius' Armorican settlement of Alans) in 448.[13]

Aetius' final service came a few years later, when he rallied all the various barbarians (including the Franks) to defeat the invading Huns under Attila. The invasion was due to a familiar cause – the blocking after negotiation of the barbarian's burning ambition for high office and service within the Roman Empire. Crossing the Rhine between Mainz and Koblenz, the Huns with their Germanic allies advanced by way of the Mosel valley (sacking perhaps Trier and more definitely Metz) to Reims and thence westwards, probably planning to join the Alans of Armorica. Aetius raised Attila's siege of Orléans, and the battle of the Catalaunian fields took place as the Huns retreated eastwards, at a site called Mauriacum, probably an estate near Châlons. It is a sign of the times that the battle was in part between the German auxiliaries of Aetius and those of Attila, ironic also that Aetius, who had had good relations with the Huns, should be the man who finally curbed them. Also not untypically, Aetius was killed a few years later by the jealous and fearful Valentinian III. Thus ended the career of a man who had spent much energy to keep the Gauls peaceful, and the north as far as possible within the control of the Empire.[14]

Obvious stages in the loosening of the bonds came soon afterwards. The death of Valentinian III brought the brief rule of a powerful Italian, but this ended in chaos which included the sack of Rome by Vandals. In southern Gaul the Arvernian Eparchius Avitus, newly appointed as *magister militum per*

Gallias, was proclaimed emperor in 455 by a mixture of Visigoths and Gallic aristocrats, and in turn appointed other Gauls to office, including Aegidius (of Lyon and Soissons) as *magister militum*. Avitus' rule was short, ending with his defeat in Italy at the hands of the Suebian Ricimer, the new military strongman. The next emperor, Majorian, forced back Visigoths and Burgundians to their previous limits and attempted to rally the Gallic nobility behind him. Aegidius' position was confirmed, and an embarrassed Sidonius, despite his close relationship with Avitus, delivered a panegyric.[15] Not impossibly, the situation in Gaul might have been held. But Majorian was murdered in 461 and Aegidius refused to accept either the next imperial candidate, or Ricimer's attempts to appoint another *magister militum*. Instead he retired northwards, creating a private capital at Soissons, thus controlling an area where archaeology suggests continuity in rural society, with a warrior element well assimilated. He continued to check barbarian expansion – with varying success, since the Rhineland Franks captured and held Köln as well as besieging Trier. He was now acting on his own initiative, not as a representative of the Roman government, and the Salian Franks of Tournai may even have briefly recognized him as king. His son Syagrius, inheriting his father's position, was to Gregory *rex Romanorum*, and there is no record of his having an appointment from the emperor in Italy (now Anthemius). Yet either the father or the son (the dates are uncertain) may have co-operated for a time with a *comes* Paulus, who fought Visigoths and Saxons in alliance with the Salian Franks of Tournai, and who may have been Anthemius' *magister militum*.[16]

Greater doubt surrounds the position of Arbogast at Trier, also styled *comes*. Descendant of the fourth-century Arbogast who had married into the Gallo-Roman aristocracy, he corresponded with Sidonius and bishop Auspicius of Toul in the 470s. Some see him as an official of an expanded Rhineland Frankish kingdom, but more likely, given the emphasis which Sidonius puts on his Roman culture, he saw himself as an upholder of Roman authority. Later, some change in the situation (takeover of Trier by the Rhineland Franks?) probably caused his flight, since he is very likely the same man found as bishop of Chartres. The bishop of Trier, Iamlychus, may also have fled, for he died near Chalon-sur-Saône.[17]

The Mosel valley certainly lay in due course within the orbit of the Rhineland Franks. Otherwise, Belgica was now divided between the Gallo-Roman kingdom of Syagrius at Soissons and the Frankish kingdom of Childeric based on Tournai. The boundary between them was roughly the Ardennes, and Childeric's kingdom by now probably included the Somme valley – more or less the area of the northern Belgic peoples some centuries ago. To the west, Armorica, which had shown a trend to independence throughout the century, had a king, Riothamus. To the south-west was the expanding Visigothic kingdom of Euric and further east the somewhat less aggressive Alamanni and Burgundians. Despite the nominally federate status of the barbarians, administrative control from the centre had effectively vanished, and with it the old sense of identities and boundaries. After 476, even Italy had a Gothic king in Odoacer; the centre of the Empire was now in theory Constantinople, and there was no longer a prefecture of the Gauls.

Of all the federate barbarians, the Salian Franks had, despite occasional lapses, the best record for loyalty, perhaps partly because their remote location caused minimal trouble. Childeric died and was buried at Tournai with great splendour – the fibula and cloak of a Roman federate, the weapons and accoutrements (decorated with garnets set in gold) of a noble Frank.[18] His successor, Clovis (Chlodovechus) had different ideas. A decade after the deposition of Romulus Augustulus in Italy, he defeated Syagrius and set out on the path of conquest that was to make him master of Gaul after the defeat of the Visigoths at Vouillé in 507. Like Constantine, to whom Gregory compares him, he was converted to Christianity, and since his wife was a Catholic Burgundian, it was the Catholic faith (not the Arian variety of the Visigoths) that he embraced. To Remigius of Reims, who had written to congratulate him on his succession to the throne of Childeric, and to urge him to rule in a conciliatory fashion, fell the task of baptizing the new ruler of Gaul.[19] Clovis well symbolizes the ambivalent state of his country as the controlling hand of Rome slackened. At the common sense level, as he carved out a great kingdom which he proceeded to treat as personal property to be divided among his heirs, he spells the end of Roman rule. Yet after Vouillé he happily accepted from Anastasius the titles of patrician and honorary consul, trappings of authority from a source still recognized as higher. He struck coins with the emperor's portrait and titles, and promoted the codification of Frankish customary law – in Latin.[20]

The fifth-century Germans could never have been beaten back across the Rhine or satisfied with minor adjustments to the frontier area. Though their absolute numbers were probably much lower than the sources would have us believe, they were of too firm purpose to be summarily dealt with. Only the more flexible arrangement of allowing them to settle on negotiated terms – which had seen a lengthy experimentation in the north – offered a possible solution. It gave them what they most wanted, land and (for the high born) a function within the Empire more honourable than among their own small folk. But if the balance between the various groups and the Gallo-Roman landowners was to be kept, the stable presence of an emperor or an emperor's right-hand man was required. The conditions were not met, and increasingly the erstwhile armies of state, regardless of origins, became private war-bands defending individual territories and rights. In such an age, it was fitting that the new Constantine should emerge from a Germanic frontier society.

2   Society, town and country

One way in which fifth-century Gaul shows continuity with its past is the presence of a land-owning aristocracy which still sought senatorial offices. True, there are signs of its ranks suffering attrition; their importance remains indisputable, for they towered above all others in wealth, education and power. One of the effects of the loss of a court was the absence of the careers at intermediate levels which had drawn teachers, lawyers and minor officials into the orbit of court patronage; a fifth-century Ausonius was unthinkable.

In the absence of court and of stable conditions, the church increasingly provided an arena for patronage, and the fifth century produced landowner-bishops whose career was crowned by church office. From such a position a noble could permanently dominate local affairs and use his influence, as occasion demanded, well outside. Germanus of Auxerre and Sidonius' of Clermont well illustrate the peculiar patterns of authority that could occur. Even Germanus' first visit to Britain with Lupus of Troyes in 429, nominally to settle ecclesiastical affairs, saw him embroiled in the local political and military situation. His second visit in the 440s, when he was accompanied by Severus of Trier, may have been undertaken at the behest of Aetius, who saw in the bishop the best available form of aid to the Britons.[21]

Society in the Belgicas may have been rather less distinguished. The exodus of some known members of the senatorial nobility has been noted, and among their number was perhaps one Aelianus, native of Reims but buried at Lyon. Trier did not lose all of its senatorial aristocracy, since there is one fifth-century epitaph of a senatorial lady, and a few noble families are thought to have survived longer. The north certainly produced fewer cultured figures than the south, and it is unlikely that the schools of Trier continued to function. The culture that Sidonius admired in Arbogast had probably been acquired elsewhere.[22]

The noble landowner-bishop, patron of his whole community, did not develop so quickly in the north. Severus of Trier was a disciple of Lupus of Troyes and through him was linked to the southern monastic community of Lérins, and thus to current trends in church life and thought. But though important for these connections, he was not comparable to Germanus in his combination of wealth and offices. Remigius of Reims, though said by his biographer to be of noble birth, was only a medium landowner. Knowledge of other bishops is slight, but the north apparently had to wait for the sixth century to produce a truly dominating figure in Nicetius of Trier.[23] The major figures of fifth-century Belgica are still secular, Aegidius, Syagrius and Arbogast; the last indeed ended as a bishop, but in Chartres rather than in the city of his family.

Salvian makes it clear that in the first half of the fifth century there were still families around Trier that could be styled 'noble'; indeed, there were enough old families to supply bishops until a new nobility of mixed Gallo-Roman and Frankish descent arose in the sixth century. Decent-sized rather than vast land-holdings, and a status below senatorial rank perhaps characterized this northern aristocracy, and with it the bishops. Aegidius, a clear exception, came from a family prominent for several generations, holding property originally near Lyon.

Salvian is also the best source on the urban backdrop against which some still played. His castigation of the *curiales* shows that municipal administrative structures still existed (at least at Trier), and that taxes went on being collected. In due course they swelled the coffers of the Frankish kings, and indeed it may be questioned whether taxes reached the official treasury from the Nervii, Menapii and Morini in the fifth century. Still, the administrative machinery kept on turning, if creakily, and the Merovingians simply took over as much as possible; Childeric's cloak, to take a concrete example, may have come from the *gynaecium* of Tournai.[24]

Further information can be gleaned from Salvian's description, however lurid, of Trier. He lavishes scorn on those who continued to live their accustomed lives of comfort while dead and dying littered the streets, and special vituperation on those who asked the emperor for shows and circuses. Thereby, he shows that some forms of city life continued, and the appeal to the emperor may have been a recognition of the very real need for a stability that only imperial presence could ensure.[25] The continuation of city life at Trier is also demonstrated by the cemeteries, with their increased numbers of gravestones and churches. Continued literacy is also thus attested (even if spelling and grammar become gradually more erratic) together with continuity of a Gallo-Roman population. Moreover the cathedral, after a mid-century destruction uncertainly attributed to the Huns, was rebuilt, if not quite to its former splendour, since the great columns around the polygonal shrine could not be replaced.[26]

The great church is the only monumental building inside the city which certainly kept its original function. Evidence for the use of public buildings comes from the Kaiserthermen, the amphitheatre, the Barbarathermen and an area south-west of the cathedral (Palais Kesselstadt). Recent discoveries confirm Fredegar's account of the amphitheatre being turned into a defensive structure, showing a gateway blocking the entrance on the city side. The Barbarathermen were most probably a strong-point guarding access to the city from the bridge. The area around the cathedral may have begun to take the form of a defensible citadel which it certainly had later.[27] In none of these areas does the pottery at present take us beyond the middle of the century, and the various destruction levels that have been noted cannot be ascribed to any particular sack. Only the churches (including that of Cyrillus in the southern cemetery) and the continuing gravestones testify to the latter part of the fifth century.[28] Trier by then had shrunk and changed form, and continuity was ensured by the elements of late Roman city life that it shared with other cities, not by special imperial patronage or strategic geography linked to a frontier.

A bleak picture for the cities after 450 may in general be correct. Both Reims and Metz, however, show signs of church building, Christian inscriptions start in Metz in the second half of the century, and the present blank at Soissons is probably only apparent. The person of the bishop, and his staff and surrounding organization, were clearly of great importance in ensuring continued city life. It is not inconceivable that life in Arras or Thérouanne, in the absence of bishops, sank to a level below anything that could reasonably be called urban. Continuity could thus have been of the site alone, with topography and the enduring communications network favouring eventual rebirth.[29]

The Mediterranean ideal implanted – with varying degrees of success – by the Romans was no longer a reality, even at Trier, where the great public buildings, symbol of Graeco-Roman urbanism, were adapted to new needs. The result, viewed from a distance sufficient to obscure physical detail, is functionally not far removed from pre-Roman hillfort towns. The town's immediate patron and protector was now the bishop, who enjoyed the authority of permanent magistracy and priesthood combined. City-based, his responsibilities nonetheless stretched over the whole territory, and increasingly he administered, on behalf of the church, a considerable area of donated land. His own original standing in the community was also derived partly from ownership of land, which was, as always, the basic underpinning without which no urbanism could exist.

What can be said of the land in the fifth century? The question of continuity, or lack of it, must be considered at various levels – sites, population, estates and other forms of rural organization. Destruction of sites by invaders may be taken first. Some villas indeed suffered violence, while at many the evidence is more consistent with desertion; one such is Berthelming, abandoned early in the century with much equipment still in place.[30] The very small number of sites where fifth-century occupation is positively attested may be due to loss of the latest levels, or failure to recognize the material. For the time being they are diverse and scattered – the village of Bitburg, the great villa at Echternach (connected with the nearby fortification), a miserable hut at Mercin-et-Vaux (Aisne) which at some point went up in flames, and a few scattered villas. To these should be added a handful of sanctuaries, for instance Steinsel and Altrier (Luxembourg), and some of the irregular fortifications.[31]

The cemeteries are more helpful, though study is hampered by the comparative absence of grave-goods, a phenomenon explained either by a change in customs or by the general impoverishment in material goods. Fortunately, grave-goods are still usually present in the cemeteries of Germanic military settlers, and it is here that we see continuity of rural communities best expressed, even if some do stop in the late fourth century (e.g. Vermand as well as the more officially military Oudenburg). Cemeteries showing continuity are those of some Ardennes fortifications, various scattered examples in the North – e.g. Hermes and Vron – and a number near Soissons and in Lorraine – Caranda, Chouy, Sion.[32] Most of these go on in use into the sixth or seventh century. The impression of rural continuity is thus higher for the fifth century than for the late third, and it is tempting to conclude that the effect of the fifth-century invasions was felt more on city life, trade and marketing.

Nonetheless, detailed studies have shown that continuity was, in some areas, very tenuous. The French Ardennes, a southern extension of the main massif, were for instance considerably depopulated. In none of the cemeteries, even those where the Merovingian cemetery is so close as to appear a continuation, can the fifth century be convincingly bridged.[33] The clearest feature is the start of a series of new cemeteries, with Frankish rather than Gallo-Roman characteristics, in the late fifth or early sixth centuries. Even in the Eifel, where continuity of sites through early infiltration of Franks might be expected, the fifth century remains dark, until we find new cemeteries with the burials neatly arranged in the fashion that has earned the name of 'Reihengräber' (row-grave cemeteries).[34] Population was probably at an even lower ebb than before; whether epidemics played a significant role in diminishing numbers remains to be shown.

When the quest for continuity is expanded to forms of rural organization, the picture becomes more positive. At almost every level from the *pagus* to the individual estate there are some signs of continuity, although not always simple or complete. The Merovingian *pagi* are usually centred on a Gallo-Roman *vicus* – Bitburg, Mouzon, Voncq – and thus are the continuation of Gallo-Roman divisions. Geography and ecclesiastical organization play a role here, for the *pagi* also correspond to the archdeaconates that grew as churches became established in the various *vici*. In areas such as the Ardennes, boundaries were more fluid, but this area exhibits another form of continuity, that of imperial estates into royal fiscs.[35]

Estates are a more difficult area, often involving a leap of faith. The hard evidence for continuity at Echternach does not go beyond the fifth century, leaving in doubt continuity between Roman villa and Merovingian Epternacum. Places mentioned in the testament of Remigius have Gallo-Roman names some of which (Passiacum/Passy) can readily be located, but archaeological evidence is lacking; both this and the testament of Adalgisel-Grimo of Tholey (late seventh century) mention places which are not estates but merely vineyards, meadows or plots.[36]

In the Mosel valley and Eifel, the piecing together of evidence from cemeteries, remains of villas and the *patrocinia* of village churches suggests that various patterns might be found. One is simple continuity of Gallo-Roman occupation of a site, and therefore presumably of the estate which was centred on it (Ehrang, Nennig, Wiltingen and others). The second is the establishment of a Frankish settlement with its own separate cemetery alongside of continuing Roman settlement and cemetery (Temmels, Palzem, Wintersdorf), perhaps implying some division of the estate. From such an arrangement might stem the villages Audun-le-Tiche (= Deutsch) and Audun-le-Roman in northern Lorraine. Sometimes the Frankish burials are actually within the Gallo-Roman cemetery, as at Welschbillig, probably here indicating the taking over by Franks of an erstwhile imperial estate. In many instances the Franks founded settlements, often in the valleys which Gallo-Roman villas had tended to avoid.[37] Toponymy certainly suggests considerable continuity. In the area of Trier, there is a very clear distinction between the Eifel, where most names were Germanicized, and the Mosel valley with its high percentage of obviously Gallo-Roman names. Further case-studies should illumine the relationship between villa, village, estate and parish boundaries.[38]

Estate organization remains a controversial area, though a measure of continuity is inherently likely. The system of demesne and dependant tenures is a practical method of exploiting the land in a hierarchical society, and belongs to the category of nearly permanent rural structures. It is then very likely that the late Roman tenant holding evolved into the one-family *mansus* which is found in later documents. This need not mean that organization remained static, nor that the documents which record ecclesiastical holdings, the *polyptyques*, are the direct descendants of Roman ones. To define the degree and direction of change against the background of permanent realities remains an exciting challenge.[39] One subtle change was in the function of land, for it once more primarily served to provide subsistence for the poor and status for the rich; the incentive for organized production was greatly reduced.

The fifth century also saw two opposing linguistic trends, both inimical to any survival of Celtic. Latin, long dominant in educated and urban society, now had the authority of the church behind it to aid its conquest of residual rural enclaves. Meanwhile Frankish conquest and colonization spread Germanic dialects wherever resistance was not too strong. A remarkable feature is the enclave of Romance dialects in and around Tournai, which retained enough Roman features not to adopt the Germanic tongue of the incomers who made it their capital. Otherwise, by stages that are still much debated, the Frankish tongue spread southwards to meet with that of the Alamanni in Lorraine, and westwards beyond the Somme to the Paris basin. In the Somme, some toponyms may point to Saxon settlers. The eventual boundary between the languages was the effect of centuries of symbiosis and fluctuation. There were for a long time pockets of Romance language in the Mosel valley, and many areas may have been in practical terms bilingual.[40]

The material which complicates the archaeological study of the fifth century is another result of the conditions of the period. Long ago, the frontier army's insatiable demand for supplies and its ability to pay in coin had created favourable opportunities for increased production and marketing. Self-sufficient soldier-farmers, or the war-bands of individual aristocrats, had no such dynamic effect; Childeric's garnered gold was used in the manner of a pre-Roman chief. The *limitanei* had either disappeared or merged quietly into the low-level economy of the surrounding frontier people – the cemetery of Krefeld-Gellep shows how Frankish groups might take over an erstwhile Roman fort site. Yet goods were still produced for those that could acquire them (as witness the fine glass in many of the scattered military graves), and the appearance at Trier of ivories with Christian iconography shows that there was still a trickle of long-distance luxury trade in portable objects.[41] Both Moselle and Meuse retained importance for long-distance trade, while the old strategic roads became relatively insignificant.

The transitional, twilight quality of the fifth century lends it an interest that compensates for the dimness of the material. Northern Belgica once again very obviously played its old role as interface area between the coastal zones and the interior. The influence of Rome was great enough, the region itself remote enough to allow the Franks to develop from unruly bands to a more centralized political entity.[42] The fact that Romanization was in decline helped to draw Franks and Gallo-Romans together and encouraged the forging of a mixed nobility. Trier, island of Romanity and Mediterranean culture, played its part in forming a new Gallo-Germanic aristocracy which by the fifth century produced men like Arbogast. The church continued to take a firmer hold, though slowly and perhaps intermittently in the far north. The final upshot was not the taking over of the Empire by Romanized Gauls but the formation within the north itself of a new order no longer dependant on a southern metropolitan culture. The legacy of Rome was of course immensely important, and the Roman period cannot be dismissed as an episode that disrupted natural development. Most cities proved permanent, though a new rank of importance would be created by a changed strategic geography which, for instance, placed Metz above Trier. The roads too remained, though they might for a time lose in importance to the natural routes, the great northern rivers. The result was a country built on foundations that were at least half Roman, but now – the church excepted – stripped of Mediterranean superstructure.

Abbreviations

AC	*Antiquité Classique*
AE	*Année Epigraphique*
AIALux	*Annales de l'Institut archéologique du Luxembourg* (Belgium)
AKorr	*Archäologisches Korrespondenzblatt*
ANRW	*Aufstieg und Niedergang der Römischen Welt*
AntJ	*Antiquaries Journal*
Arch	*Archéologie*
Arch Belg	*Archaeologia Belgica*
ASHAL	*Annales de la Société d'histoire et d'archéologie de la Lorraine*
BAR	*British Archaeological Reports* (S = Supplementary series)
BCPdeC	*Bulletin de la Commission départementale, Pas de Calais*
BJ	*Bonner Jahrbücher*
BRGK	*Bericht der Römisch-Germanischen Kommission*
BROB	*Berichten van de Rijksdienst voor oudheidkundig Bodemonderzoek*
BSAChamp	*Bulletin de la Société archéologique champenoise*
BSAF	*Bulletin de la Société nationale des Antiquaires de France*
BSDS	*Bericht der staatlichen Denkmalpflege im Saarland* (*Beiträge zur Saarländischen Archäologie und Kunstgeschichte*)
Bull ARB	*Bulletin de l'Académie royale de Belgique*
CAAAH	*Cahiers alsaciens d'archéologie, d'art et d'histoire*
CAPic	*Cahiers archéologique de la Picardie*
CRAI	*Comptes rendues de l'Académie des Inscriptions et Belles-Lettres*
EC	*Etudes Celtiques*
Führer (RGZM)	*Führer zu vor- und frühgeschichtlichen Denkmälern, Römisch-Germanisches Zentralmuseum, Mainz*
JRGZM	*Jahrbuch des Römisch-Germanischen Zentralmuseum, Mainz*
JRS	*Journal of Roman Studies*
JS	*Journal des Savants*
JSGU	*Jahrbuch der Schweizerischen Gesellschaft für Ur- und Frühgeschichte*
K Vl Ak	*Koninklijke Vlaamse Akademie*

LEC	*Les Etudes Classiques*
MGH	*Monumenta Germaniae Historica* (AA, auctores antiquissimi)
MSAMarne	*Mémoires de la Société d'Agriculture, Commerce, Science, et Arts du Département de la Marne*
PSH	*Publications de la Section historique de l'Institut grand-ducal de Luxembourg*
RA	*Revue archéologique*
RAE	*Revue archéologique de l'Est et du Centre-Est*
RBN	*Revue Belge de numismatique*
RBPH	*Revue Belge de philologie et d'histoire*
RCRFA	*Rei Cretariae Romanae Fautorum Acta*
REA	*Revue des études anciennes*
REL	*Revue des études latines*
RhM	*Rheinisches Museum für Philologie*
RN	*Revue numismatique*
RNord	*Revue du Nord*
TZ	*Trierer Zeitschrift*

See also bibliography on inscriptions, coins etc. for other abbreviations

Select Bibliography

General Works, History and Archaeology

H. d'Arbois de Jubainville, *Recherches sur l'origine de la propriété foncière et des noms de lieux habités en France* (Paris 1890)

Atti del colloquio sul tema: La Gallia Romana (Roma 1973; Accad. Naz. Lincei)

J. Breuer, *La Belgique romaine* (Brussels 1944)

O. Brogan, *Roman Gaul* (London 1953)

A.W. Byvanck, *Nederland in de Romeinsche Tijd* (Leiden 1943)

F. Cumont, 'Comment la Belgique fut romanisée', *Ann. Soc. Arch. Brux.* 28 (1914–19) 77–181

E. Desjardins, *Géographie de la Gaule d'après la table de Peutinger* (Paris 1869)

J.F. Drinkwater, *Roman Gaul: the Three Provinces 58 BC-AD 260* (Beckenham 1983)

G. Duby (ed.), *Histoire de la France rurale* vol. 1 (Paris 1977)

G. Duby (ed.), *Histoire de la France urbaine* vol. 1 (Paris 1980)

P.-M. Duval, *La vie quotidienne en Gaule romaine* (Paris 1955)

W.A. van Es, *De Romeinen in Nederland* (Bussum 1972)

A. Grenier, *Manuel d'archéologie gallo-romaine* 4 vols. (Paris 1931–60)

J.-J. Hatt, *Histoire de la Gaule Romaine (120 av. JC-451 après JC). Colonisation ou colonialisme?* (Paris 1966)

E. Hollstein, *Mitteleuropäische Eichendendrochronologie* (Mainz 1980; *Trier. Grab. und Forsch.* 11)

C. Jullian, *Histoire de la Gaule* 8 vols. (Paris 1920–26)

La Belgique de César à Clovis, Les dossiers de l'archéologie no. 21, *mars-avril* 1977

M.E. Mariën, *Belgica Antiqua* (Antwerpen 1980)

H. von Petrikovits, *Rheinische Geschichte* (eds. F. Petri, G. Droege) vol. 1 *Altertum* (Düsseldorf 1978)

C.-M. Ternes, *La vie quotidienne en Rhénanie romaine* (Paris 1972)

Major Regional Studies

R. Agache, 'Détection aérienne de vestiges protohistoriques, gallo-romains et médiévaux dans le bassin de la Somme et ses abords', *Bull. Soc. Préhist. Nord* No. 7 (1970)

R. Agache, B. Bréart, *Atlas d'Archéologie aérienne de Picardie* (Amiens 1975)

R. Agache, *La Somme pré-romaine et romaine* (Amiens 1978)

R. Agache, 'Nouveaux apports des prospections aériennes en archéologie pré-romaine et romaine de la Picardie', *CAPic* 6 (1979) 33–90

J.L. Cadoux, 'La Picardie ancienne', *CAPic* 6 (1979) 91–107

G. Coolen, *La Morinie ancienne* (Saint-Omer 1969)

R. Delmaire, *Etude archéologique de la partie orientale de la cité des Morins (civitas Morinorum)* (Arras 1976)

W. Drack (ed.), *Ur- und frühgeschichtliche Archäologie der Schweiz* vol. 4 *Die Eisenzeit* (Basel 1974), vol. 5 *Die römische Epoche* (Basel 1975)

R. Kaiser, *Untersuchungen zur Geschichte der Civitas und Diözese Soissons in römischer und merowingischer Zeit* (Bonn 1973; *Rheinisches Archiv* 89)

J.B. Keune, 'Gallo-römischer Kultur in Lothringen und den benachbarten Gebiete', *Jahrb. Lothr. Gesch. u. Altertumsk.* 9 (1897) 155–201

R. Laufner (ed.), *Geschichte des Trierer Landes* (Trier 1964)

M. Roblin, *Le terroir de l'Oise aux époques gallo-romaine et franque* (Paris 1978)

P. Roosens, 'Taxandria in de Romeinse en Merovingsische tijden', *Taxandria* 30 (1958) 33–131

J. Sommé, *Les Plaines du Nord de la France et leur bordure. Etude morphologique* (Paris 1977)

J. Steinhausen, *Archäologische Siedlungskunde des Trierer Landes* (Trier 1936)

C.-M. Ternes, 'Die römerzeitliche Civitas Treverorum im Bilde der Nachkriegsforschung. I: Von der Gründung bis zum Ende des dritten Jahrhunderts', *ANRW* 4 (1975) 320–424

C.-M. Ternes, *Das römische Luxemburg* (Zürich 1973)

H. Thoen, *De Belgische kustvlakte in de Romeinse tijd* (Brussels 1978; *K Vl Ak Lett* 98)

M. Toussaint, *La Lorraine à l'époque gallo-romaine* (Nancy 1928)

Vallée de l'Aisne: cinq années de fouilles protohistoriques (Amiens 1982; *Rev. Arch. Picardie*, numéro spécial)

E.M. Wightman, *Roman Trier and the Treveri* (London 1970)

(N.B. Older local studies omitted)

Archaeological Maps

Archaeologische kaarten van België/Cartes archéologiques de la Belgique; 1–2, ed. J. Mertens, A. Despy-Meyer (Brussels 1968); 3, ed. R. Laurent, D. Callebaut, H. Roosens (Brussels 1972); scale 1:500,000

Carte archéologique du Grand-Duché de Luxembourg (Luxembourg 1973–). Various eds., scale 1:20,000

Tabula Imperii Romani. Sheet L31: *Lugdunum.* Sheet M32: *Mogontiacum.* Sheet M31: *Lutetia-Atuatuca-Ulpia Noviomagus.* Sheet L32: *Mediolanum*

Bibliography and Repertories

M.–Th. and G. Raepsaet-Charlier, 'Gallia Belgica et Germania Inferior. Vingt-cinq années de recherches historiques et archéologiques', in *ANRW* 2.4 (1975) 3–299. Very comprehensive: can be used throughout to supplement references given here (except for Late Empire)

M.-H. Corbiau, *Répertoire bibliographique des trouvailles archéologiques de la province de Luxembourg* (Brussels 1978; *Répertoires archéologiques* Série A 11). (Add to list in *ANRW* 2.4, 16)

A. van Doorselaer, *Repertorium van de begraafplaatsen uit de Romeinse tijd in Noord-Gallië/Répertoire des nécropoles d'époque romaine en Gaule Septentrionale/ Repertorium der römerzeitliche Gräber in Nord-Gallien* (Brussels 1964)

J. Steinhausen, *Ortskunde Trier-Mettendorf* (Bonn 1932; *Archäologische Karte der Rheinprovinz* 1)

M. Toussaint, *Répertoire archéologique du département de la Meuse (période gallo-romaine)* (Bar-le-Duc 1946)

M. Toussaint, *Répertoire archéologique du département de Meurthe-et-Moselle (période gallo-romaine)* (Nancy 1947)

M. Toussaint, *Répertoire archéologique du département des Vosges (période gallo-romaine)* (Epinal 1948)

M. Toussaint, *Répertoire archéologique du département de la Moselle (période gallo-romaine)* (Nancy 1950)

Ancient Sources

A.W. Byvanck, *Excerpta Romana, de bronnen der Romeinsche Geschiedenis van Nederland 1–3* ('s Gravenhage 1931–47)

P.-M. Duval, *La Gaule jusqu'au milieu du Ve siècle* (Paris 1971; *Sources de l'histoire de France* 1)

A. Riese, *Das Rheinische Germanien in der antiken Litteratur* (Leipzig 1892, repr. Groningen 1969)

Major Catalogues

Childeric-Clovis 1500e anniversaire 482–1982 (Tournai 1982)

G. Collot, *Musée archéologique de Metz. La civilisation gallo-romaine dans la cité des Médiomatriques* 1 and 2 (Metz 1964, 1976)

Gallien in der Spätantike/A l'aube de la France (Mainz/Paris 1981)

La civilisation gallo-romaine dans la cité des Médiomatriques vols. 1–3 (Metz 1964–)

A. De Loë, *Belgique ancienne, Catalogue descriptif et raisonné, III. La période romaine* (Brussels 1937)

W. Reusch (ed.), *Frühchristliche Zeugnisse im Einzugsgebiet von Rhein und Mosel* (Trier 1965)

R. Schindler, *Landesmuseum Trier. Führer durch die vorgeschichtliche und römische Abteilung* (Trier 1970)

P. Stuart et al., *Deae Nehalenniae, gids bij de Tentoonstelling* (Middelburg 1971)

G. Thill, *Les époques gallo-romaine et mérovingienne au Musée d'histoire et d'art de Luxembourg* (2nd ed. Luxembourg 1972)

Inscriptions and Relief Sculpture

CIL = Corpus Inscriptionum Latinarum vol. 13 (especially *pars* 1, *fasc.* 2), and the following supplements: H. Finke in *BRGK* 17 (1927) 1–107, 198–231; H. Nesselhauf in *BRGK* 27 (1937) 51–134; H. Nesselhauf, H. Lieb in *BRGK* 40 (1959) 120–229; V. Schillinger-Häfele in *BRGK* 58 (1977) 447–604

ILTG = P. Wuilleumier, *Inscriptions Latines des Trois Gaules* (Paris 1963; *Gallia* suppl. 17)

RICG = N. Gauthier, *Recueil des inscriptions chrétiennes de la Gaule* vol. 1 (Paris 1975)

Esp. = E. Espérandieu *et al.*, *Recueil général des bas-reliefs, statues et bustes de la Gaule romaine* 1–16 (Paris 1907–1981)

E. Gose, *Katalog der frühchristliche Inschriften aus Trier* (Berlin 1958)

F. Hettner, *Die römischen Steindenkmäler des Provinzialmuseum zu Trier* (Trier 1893)

K. Krämer, *Die frühchristliche Grabinschriften Triers* (Trier 1974; *Trier. Grab. u. Forsch.* 8)

A. Riese, *Das Rheinische Germanien in den antiken Inschriften* (Leipzig 1914)

Ch. Ternes, 'Inscriptions antiques du Luxembourg', *Hémecht* 17 (1965) 3/4

E. Wilhelm, *Pierres sculptées et inscriptions de l'époque romaine* (Luxembourg 1974)

Bronzes, Mosaics, Glass, Coins

G. Faider-Feytmans, *Recueil des Bronzes de Bavai* (Paris 1957; *Gallia* suppl. 8)

G. Faider-Feytmans, *Les bronzes figurés de Belgique* (Mainz 1979)

FMRD = *Fundmünzen der römischen Zeit in Deutschland* 3. Saarland by D. Kienast (Berlin 1963); 4. 3/1 Trier 3001–3002 by M.R. Alföldi

K. Goethert-Polaschek, *Katalog der römischen Gläser des Rheinischen Landesmuseum Trier* (Trier 1977; *Trier Grab. u. Forsch.* 9)

H. Menzel, *Die römischen Bronzen aus Deutschland 2. Trier* (Mainz 1966)

J. Moreau-Maréchal, 'La céramique gallo-romaine du Musée d'Arlon', *AIAL* 110/11 (1979/80) 3–197

K. Parlasca, *Die römischen Mosaiken in Deutschland* (Berlin 1959)

S. Reinach, *Bronzes figurés de la Gaule romaine* (Paris 1894)

RIC = *Roman Imperial Coinage* (ed. H. Mattingly *et al.*)

H. Stern, *Recueil général des mosaïques de la Gaule I. Province de Belgique* 1–3 (Paris 1957–63; *Gallia* suppl. 10)

R. Weiller, *Die Fundmünzen der römischen Zeit im Grossherzogtum Luxemburg/ Monnaies antiques découvertes au Grand-Duché de Luxembourg* (Berlin 1972)

Toponymy and Onomastics *(see also Chapter 7, section 3)*

A. Dauzat, C. Rostaing, *Dictionnaire étymologique des noms de lieux de la France* (Paris 1963)

A. Dauzat, *La toponymie française* (Paris 1971)

F. Falc'hun, *Les noms de lieux celtiques* (Rennes 1966–1970)

M. Gysseling, A.E. Verhulst, *Nederzettingsnamen en nederzettings-geschiedenis in de Nederlanden, Noord-Frankrijk en Noord-West Duitsland* (Amsterdam/Leuven 1969)

A. Holder, *Alt-Celtischer Sprachschatz* (Leipzig 1896, repr. Graz 1961)

A. Longnon, *Les noms de lieu de la France* (1920–29)

A. Vincent, *Toponymie de la France* (Brussels 1937)

J. Whatmough, *The Dialects of Ancient Gaul* (Cambridge, Mass. 1970)

1 Before the Romans
Sections 1 and 2

L'Age du fer en France Septentrionale (Reims 1981: *Mém. Soc. Arch. Champenoise* 2)

P.-P. Bonenfant, *Des premiers cultivateurs aux premières villes* (Brussels 1969; *Etudes d'histoire Wallonne* 2)

D. Bretz-Mahler, *La civilisation de la Tène I en Champagne. Le facies marnien* (Paris 1971; *Gallia* suppl. 23)

J. Déchelette, *Manuel d'archéologie préhistorique, celtique et gallo-romaine* vols. 2.2 and 2.3 (Paris 1913, 1927)

P.-M. Duval, *Les Celtes* (Paris 1967)

J. Guilaine (ed.), *La préhistoire française* vol. 2 (Paris 1976)

A. Haffner, *Die westliche Hunsrück-Eifel-Kultur* (Berlin 1976)

J. Harmand, *Les Celtes au second âge du fer* (Paris 1970)

R. Joffroy, *L'oppidum de Vix et la civilisation hallstattienne finale dans l'Est de la France* (Dijon 1960; *Publ. Univ. Dijon* 20)

J. Keller, *Das keltische Fürstengrab von Reinheim, I. Ausgrabungs-bericht und Katalog der Funde* (Mainz 1965)

S.J. de Laet, 'Native and Celt in the Iron Age of the Low Countries', in J.V.S. Megaw (ed.), *To Illustrate the Monuments. Essays on Archaeology Presented to Stuart Piggott* (London 1976) 191–198

S.J. de Laet, *Prehistorische Kulturen in het Zuiden der Lage Landen* (2nd ed. Wetteren 1979)

S.J. de Laet, *La Belgique d'avant les Romains* (Wetteren 1982)

M.E. Mariën, *La période de la Tène en Belgique. Le Groupe de la Haine* (Brussels 1961)

J.V.S. Megaw, *Art of the European Iron Age. A Study of the Elusive Image* (Bath 1970)

J.P. Millotte, *Le Jura et les plaines de Saône aux âges des métaux* (Paris 1963; *Ann. litt. Univ. Besançon* 16)

J.P. Millotte, *Carte archéologique de la Lorraine* (Paris 1965; *Ann. litt. Univ. Besançon* 73)

J. Nenquin, *Salt: A Study in Economic Prehistory* (Brugge 1961; *Diss. Arch. Gandenses* 6)

P.S. Wells, *Culture Contact and Culture Change. Early Iron Age Europe and the Mediterranean World* (Cambridge 1980)

Section 3

H. Birkhahn, *Germanen und Kelten bis zum Ausgang der Römerzeit* (Vienna 1970)

R. Hachmann, G. Kossack, H. Kuhn, *Völker zwischen Germanen und Kelten* (Neumünster 1962)

R. Hachmann, 'Germains, Celtes et Belges dans la France du nord et en Belgique à l'époque de Jules César', *RA* (1975) 166–176

Chr. Hawkes, G.C. Dunning, 'The Belgae of Gaul and Britain', *Arch. Journ.* 87 (1930) 150–335

C.F.C. Hawkes, 'Celtes, Gaulois, Germains, Belges', *Celticum* 12 (1964) 1–7

C.F.C. Hawkes, 'New Thoughts on the Belgae', *Antiquity* 42 (1968) 6–16

S.J. de Laet, A. van Doorselaer, 'Groupes culturels et chronologie de l'époque de la Tène en Belgique', *EC* 13 (1972) 571–582

M.E. Mariën, 'Tribes and Archaeological Groupings of the La Tène Period in Belgium: Some Observations', in *The European Community in Later Prehistory. Studies in Honour of C.F.C. Hawkes* (London 1971) 211–241

Sections 4 and 6

J.A. Brongers, *Air Photography and Celtic Field Research in the Netherlands* (Amersfoort 1976)

A.T. Clason, *Animal and Man in Holland's Past* (Groningen 1967; *Palaeohistoria* 13)

J. Collis, *Defended Sites of the Late La Tène in Central and Western Europe* (Oxford 1975; *BAR* S-2)

B. Cunliffe, T. Rowley (eds.), *Oppida: The Beginnings of Urbanisation in Barbarian Europe* (Oxford 1976; *BAR* S-11)

A. Haffner, *Das keltisch-römische Gräberfeld von Wederath-Belginum* vols. 1–3 (Mainz 1971–1978; *Trier. Grab. u. Forsch.* 6)

S.J. de Laet, 'Fortifications de l'époque de La Tène en Belgique', *Archeologické rozhledy* 23 (1971) 432–450

G. Leman-Delerive, G. Lefranc, *Forteresses gauloises et gisements de l'âge du fer dans le Nord – Pas-de-Calais* (Lille 1980)

G. Mahr, *Die jüngere Latènekultur des Trierer Landes* (Berlin 1967)

M. E. Mariën, *Le Trou de l'Ambre au Bois de Wérimont, Eprave* (Brussels 1970)

H. Mueller-Wille, 'Baüerliche Siedlungen der Bronze- und Eisenzeit in den Nord-Seegebieten', in H. Jankuhn, R.R. Schützeichel, F. Schwind (eds.), *Das Dorf der Eisenzeit und des frühen Mittelalters* (Göttingen 1977) 153–218

T. Poulain-Josien, *Les animaux domestiques et sauvages en France du Néolithique au gallo-romain. Thèse III cycle* (Paris 1964)

H. Roosens, G.V. Lux, 'De nederzetting uit de ijzertijd op de Staberg te Rosmeer', *Arch Belg* 109 (1969)

R. Schindler, *Studien zum vorgeschichtlichen Siedlungs- und Befestigungswesen des Saarlandes* (Trier 1968)

R. Schindler, K.-H. Koch, *Vor- und Frühgeschichtliche Burgwälle des Grossherzogtum Luxemburg* (Mainz 1977; *Trier. Grab. u. Forsch.* 13)

R. Schindler, 'Die Altburg von Bundenbach und andere spätkeltische Befestigungen im Trevererland', in *Ausgrabungen in Deutschland* vol. 1 (Mainz 1975) 273–286

R. Schindler, *Die Altburg von Bundenbach* (Mainz 1977; *Trier. Grab. u. Forsch.* 10)

R.E.M. Wheeler, *Hillforts of Northern France* (London 1957)

Section 5

D.F. Allen, 'Wealth, Money and Coinage in a Celtic Society', in J.V.S. Megaw (ed.), *To Illustrate the Monuments. Essays on Archaeology Presented to Stuart Piggott* (London 1976) 199–208

D.F. Allen (ed. D. Nash), *The Coins of the Ancient Celts* (Edinburgh 1980)

J.-B. Colbert de Beaulieu, 'La monnaie de Caletedu et les zones du statère et du denier en Gaule', *RAE* 5 (1966) 101–129

J.-B. Colbert de Beaulieu, 'Les monnaies gauloises au nom de Togirix', *RAE* 13 (1962) 98–118

L. Reding, *Les monnaies gauloises du Tetelbierg* (Luxembourg 1971)

S. Scheers, *Les monnaies de la Gaule inspirées de celles de la République romaine* (Leuven 1969)

S. Scheers, *Traité de numismatique celtique, II. La Gaule Belgique* (Paris 1977; *Ann. litt. Univ. Besançon* 195)

2 The Conquest

Sections 1–3

P. Bonenfant, 'Du Belgium de César à la Belgique de 1830', *Ann. Soc. roy. d'arch. Bruxelles* 50 (1961) 31–58

César, *Bellum Gallicum* ed. M. Rambaud, bks. 2–5 (Paris 1965, 1967, 1974; *Coll. 'Erasme'*)

J.-B. Colbert de Beaulieu, 'Les monnaies gauloises au nom des chefs mentionnés dans les "Commentaires" de César', in *Hommages à Albert Grenier* (Brussels 1962; *coll. Latomus* 58) 419–447

J.-B. Colbert de Beaulieu, 'Peut-on dater par la numismatique l'occupation d'un oppidum? L'exemple de Pommiers (Aisne)', *RAE* 6 (1955) 260–270

R. Dion, *Les frontières de la France* (Paris 1947)

Dom. J. Dubois, 'La carte des diocèses de France avant la Révolution', *Annales* 20 (1965) 680–691

R. Hachmann, 'Die Treverer und die Belger zur Zeit Caesars I. Die literarische Quellen', *BSDS* 23 (1976) 85–116

J. Harmand, 'Une composante scientifique du Corpus Caesarianum: le portrait de la Gaule dans le De Bello Gallico', *ANRW* 1.3 523–595

S. Lewuillon, 'Histoire, Société et Lutte des classes en Gaule', *ANRW* 2.4, 425–583

M. Rambaud, *La déformation historique dans les 'Commentaires' de César* (Paris 1966)

T. Rice Holmes, *Caesar's Conquest of Gaul* 2nd ed. (Oxford 1911)

G. Schulte-Holtey, *Untersuchungen zum gallischen Widerstand gegen Caesar* (Diss. Münster 1969)

M. Sordi, 'La simpolitia presso i Galli', *Parola del Passato* 29 (1953) 111–125

C.E. Stevens, 'The *Bellum Gallicum* as a Work of Propaganda', *Latomus* 11 (1951) 3–18, 165–179

V. Tourneur, *Les Belges avant César* (Brussels 1944)

J. Werner, 'Zur Bronzekanne von Kelheim. Rückblick und Ausblick', *Bayer. Vorgeschbl.* 43 (1978) 1–18, repr. in *Spätes Keltentum zwischen Rom und Germanien* (München 1979) 198–222

E.M. Wightman, 'Il y avait en Gaule deux sortes de Gaulois', in *Travaux du VIe congrès international d'études classiques* (Madrid 1974) 407–419

Section 4

A. Haffner, 'Zum Ende der Latènezeit im Mittelrheingebiet unter besondere Berücksichtigung des Trierer Landes', *AKorr* 4 (1974) 59–72

K. Kraft, 'Die Rolle der "Colonia Julia Equestris" und die römische Auxiliar-Rekrutierung', *JRGZM* 4 (1957) 81–107, *Gesammelte Aufsätze* (Darmstadt 1973) 181–208

E. Ritterling, 'Zur Geschichte des römischen Heeres in Gallien unter Augustus', *BJ* 114/5 (1906) 159–188

V. Tourneur, 'La Belgique pendant l'occupation militaire romaine (49–27 av. JC)', *Latomus* 5 (1946) 175–180

E.M. Wightman, 'La Gaule Chevelue entre César et Auguste', in *Actes du IXe Congrès international d'études sur les frontières romaines, Mamaia 1972* (Bucureşti/ Köln/Wien 1974) 472–483; also published in *Cahiers numismatiques* no. 39 (mars 1974) 9–18

E.M. Wightman, 'Military Arrangements, Native Settlements and Related Developments in Early Roman Gaul', *Helinium* 17 (1977) 105–126

E.M. Wightman, 'Soldier and Civilian in Early Roman Gaul', in *Akten des XI Internationalen Limeskongresses* (Budapest 1978) 75–86

N.J. de Witt, *Urbanization and the Franchise in Roman Gaul* (Lancaster 1940)

3 The Foundations of Roman Belgica
Sections 1–2

G. Alföldy, *Die Hilfstruppen der römischen Provinz Germania Inferior* (Düsseldorf 1968; *Epig. Stud.* 6)

J.E. Bogaers, 'Germania inferior, Gallia Belgica en de civitates van de Frisiavones en de Tungri', *Helinium* 11 (1971) 228–237

A.J. Christopherson, 'The Provincial Assembly of the Three Gauls in the Julio-Claudian Period', *Historia* 17 (1968) 351–366

J. Deininger, *Die Provinziallandtage der römischen Kaiserzeit von Augustus bis zum Ende des dritten Jahrhunderts n. Chr.* (München 1965; *Vestigia* 6)

R. Delmaire, 'Civitas Morinorum, pagus Gesoriacus, civitas Bononensium', *Latomus* 33 (1974) 265–279

H. Draye, 'Die civitates und ihre Capita in Gallia Belgica während der frühen Kaiserzeit', *Ancient Society* 2 (1971) 228–237

B. Galsterer-Kröll, 'Zum *ius Latii* in den keltischen Provinzen des Imperium Romanum', *Chiron* 3 (1973) 277–306

O. Hirschfeld, 'Die Organization der drei Gallien durch Augustus', *Klio* 8 (1908) 464–476 (*Kleine Schriften* 479 ff)

S.J. de Laet, *Portorium. Etude sur l'organisation douanière chez les Romains, surtout à l'époque du Haut-Empire* (Bruges 1949)

W. Meyers, *L'administration de la province romaine de Belgique* (Brugge 1964; *Diss. arch. Gand.* 7) 134; additions and corrections by H.G. Pflaum, *Gnomon* 37 (1965) 388–396

E. Ritterling, *Fasti des römischen Deutschland unter dem Prinzipat* (Wien 1932)

E. Ritterling, E. Stein, *Die kaiserliche Beamten und Truppenkörper in römischen Deutschland unter dem Prinzipat* (Wien 1932, repr. Amsterdam 1965)

Chr. Rüger, *Germania Inferior: Untersuchungen zur Territorial- und Verwaltungs-geschichte Niedergermaniens in der Prinzipatszeit* (Köln/Graz 1968; *BJ Beiheft* 30)

G. Rupprecht, *Untersuchungen zum Dekurionenstand in den nordwestlichen Provinzen des römischen Reiches* (Kallmünz 1975)

L. van de Weerd, 'Civitas Tungrorum en Germania inferior', *AC* 4 (1934) 175–189

E.M. Wightman, 'The Lingones: Belgica, Lugdunensis or Germania Superior?', in *Studien zu den Militärgrenzen Roms II* (Köln/Bonn 1977) 207–217

H. Wolff, 'Kriterien für lateinische und römische Städte in Gallien und Germanien und die "Verfassung" der gallischen Stammesgemeinden', *BJ* 176 (1976) 45–54

H. Wolff, 'Civitas und Colonia Treverorum', *Historia* 26 (1977) 204–242

Sections 3–4

G. Alföldy, 'La politique provinciale de Tibère', *Latomus* 24 (1965) 824–844

P.A. Brunt, 'Tacitus on the Batavian Revolt', *Latomus* 19 (1960) 494–517

J.F. Drinkwater, 'The Rise and Fall of the Gallic Julii: Aspects of the Development of the Aristocracy of the Three Gauls under the Early Empire', *Latomus* 37 (1978) 817–850

J.F. Drinkwater, 'A Note on Local Careers in the Three Gauls under the Empire', *Britannia* 10 (1979) 89–100

S. Dyson, 'Native Revolt Patterns in the Roman Empire', in *ANRW* 2.3 138–175

K. Kraft, *Zur Rekrutierung der Alen und Kohorten* (Bern 1951)

J. Krier, *Die Treverer ausserhalb ihrer Civitas. Mobilität und Aufstieg* (Trier 1981; *TZ* Beiheft 5)

S.J. de Laet, 'Claude et la romanisation de la Gaule septentrionale', *Mélanges . . . A. Piganiol* (Paris 1966) 951–961

P.G. van Soesbergen, 'The Phases of the Batavian Revolt', *Helinium* 11 (1971) 238–256

R. Syme, 'Tacitus on Gaul', *Latomus* 12 (1953) 25–37, repr. in *Ten Studies in Tacitus* (Oxford 1970) 19–29

4 Urbanization

Sections 1–3, 5

B. Ancien, M. Tuffreau-Libre, *Soissons gallo-romain, découvertes anciennes et récentes* (Soissons 1980)

D. Bayard, J.-L. Massy, 'Amiens romain: étude sur le développement urbain du Ier siècle av. JC au Ve siècle ap. JC', *RNord* 44 (1982) 5–26

H. Bievelet, *Etudes bavaisiennes* (Lille 1975)

H. Bögli, 'Aventicum', *BJ* 172 (1972) 175–184

Colloque international d'archéologie urbaine, Tours, novembre 1980: rapport préliminaire (Paris 1980; Ministère de Culture).

Les cryptoportiques dans l'architecture romaine (Rome 1973; *Coll. Ec. franç. de Rome* n. 14)

H. Cüppers, *Die Trierer Römerbrücken* (Mainz 1969; *Trier. Grab. u. Forsch.* 5)

G. Duby (ed.), *Histoire de la France urbaine* 1. *La ville antique* (Paris 1980)

Festschrift 100 Jahre Rheinisches Landesmuseum Trier (Mainz 1979; *Trier Grab. u. Forsch.* 14)

S.S. Frere, 'Town Planning in the Western provinces', in *Festschrift zum 75 jährigen Bestehen der Röm.-Germ. Komm.* (Mainz 1979) 87–104

Führer RGZM 32 *Trier* (Mainz 1977)

E. Gose, L. Hussong, W. Jovy, S. Loeschcke, *Der Tempelbezirk im Altbachtal zu Trier* vols. 1–2 (Berlin 1938, 1942)

E. Gose, *Der Tempelbezirk des Lenus Mars in Trier* (Berlin 1955; *Trier. Grab. u. Forsch.* 2)

E. Gose (ed.), *Die Porta Nigra in Trier* (Berlin 1969; *Trier. Grab. u. Forsch.* 4)

E. Gose, *Der gallo-römische Tempelbezirk im Altbachtal bei Trier* (Mainz 1972; *Trier. Grab. u. Forsch.* 7)

J.B. Keune, 'Zur Geschichte von Metz in römischer Zeit', *Jahrb. Lothring. Gesch. u. Altertumsk.* 10 (1898) 1–71

J.B. Keune, 'Sablon in römischer Zeit', *Jahrb. Lothring. Gesch. u. Altertumsk.* 15 (1903) 324–460

S.J. de Laet, 'Schets van het onstaan en de ontwikkeling van stedelijke agglomeraties in noord-Gallië in de romeinse tijd', *Med. K Vl Ak Lett.* 22 (1960) no. 6

P. Leman, 'Les villes romaines de la région Nord et Pas-de-Calais à la lumière des fouilles récentes', *RA* (1979) 168 ff

P. Leman, 'Un quartier romain de Beauvais (Oise)', *Gallia* 40 (1982) 195–217

M. Lesenne, *Bibliografisch repertorium van de oudheidkundige overblijfselen te Tongeren* (Brussels 1975; Nationaal Centrum voor oudheidkundige navorsingen, Reeks A, 10)

J.-L. Massy, *Samarobriva Ambianorum (Diss. Univ. de Paris IV*; Paris-Sorbonne 1977)

Thèmes de recherches sur les villes antiques d'Occident ed. P.-M. Duval, E. Frézouls (Paris 1977; *Colloques internationaux du CNRS* 542)

M. Toussaint, *Metz à l'époque gallo-romaine* (Metz 1948)

W. Vanvinckenroye, *Tongeren Romeinse stad* (Tongeren 1975)

A. Wankenne, *La Belgique à l'époque romaine: sites urbains, villageois, religieux et militaires* (Brussels 1972; Centre national de recherches archéologiques en Belgique, Série C, no. 3)

E. Will, 'Recherches sur le développement urbain sous l'Empire romain dans le Nord de la France', *Gallia* 20 (1962) 79–101

Section 4

Actes du colloque, Le vicus gallo-romain (Caesarodunum 11, *numéro spécial* 1976)

M. Amand, M.I. Eykens-Dierickx, *Tournai romain* (Brugge 1960; *Diss. arch. Gand.* 5)

M. Amand, 'Un nouveau quartier romain à Tournai. Les fouilles du Luchet d'Antoing', *Arch Belg* 102 (1968)

A. Bertrang, *Histoire d'Arlon* (2nd ed. Arlon 1953)

L. Bonnard, *La Gaule thermale, sources et stations thermales et minérales de la Gaule à l'époque gallo-romaine* (Paris 1908)

R. Brulet, *Liberchies gallo-romain. Rempart de la Romanité* (Gembloux 1975)

R. Brulet, *Braives gallo-romain.* 1. *La zone centrale* (Louvain-la-Neuve 1981)

C. Dubois, *Vieux-Virton romain* (Gembloux 1970)

A. Kolling, 'Schwarzenacker an der Blies', *BJ* 172 (1972) 238–257

M. Mangin, *Un quartier de commerçants et d'artisans d'Alésia: contributions à l'histoire de l'habitat urbain en Gaule* (Paris 1981; *Publ. Univ. Dijon* 60)

J. Mertens, A. Cahen-Delhaye, 'Saint-Mard, fouilles dans le vicus romain de Vertunum', *Arch Belg* 119 (1970)

J. Mertens, H. Rémy, 'Tournai, fouilles à la Loucherie', *Arch Belg* 165 (1974)

H. von Petrikovits, 'Kleinstädte und nichtstädtische Siedlungen im Nordwesten des römischen Reiches', in *Das Dorf der Eisenzeit und des frühen Mittelalters* (Göttingen 1977) 86–135

M. Thirion, *Le trésor de Liberchies. Aurei des I^e et IIe siècles* (Brussels 1972)

5 Rural Belgica in the Early Roman Empire

Sections 1–3

Actes du colloque, La villa romaine dans les provinces du Nord-Ouest (*Caesarodunum* 17, num. spéc. 1982)

R. Agache, 'La campagne à l'époque romaine dans les grandes plaines du Nord de la France d'après les photographies aériennes', in *ANRW* 2.4 (1975) 658–713

R. Agache, 'Les fermes indigènes d'époque pré-romaine et romaine dans le bassin de la Somme', *CAPic* 3 (1976) 117–138

A. Barbet, 'Mercin et Vaux (Aisne). Un habitat gallo-romain', *CAPic* 8 (1981) 65–92

G. de Boe, 'De stand van het onderzoek der Romeinse Villa's in België', *Arch Belg* 132 (1971)

G. de Boe, 'Haccourt I–III', *Arch Belg* 168 (1974), 174 (1975), 182 (1976)

G. de Boe, F. Lauwerijs, 'Een inheemse nederzetting uit de Romeinse tijd te Oelegem', *Arch Belg* 228 (1980)

G. de Boe, 'De Gallo-Romeinse nederzetting op de Steenakker te Mortsel (Antwerpen)', *Arch Belg* 94 (1966)

G. de Boe, L. van Impe, 'Nederzetting uit de Ijzertijd en Romeinse villa te Rosmeer', *Arch Belg* 216 (1979)

H. Cüppers, A. Neyses, 'Der römerzeitliche Gutshof mit Grabbezirk und Tempel bei Newel (Kreis Trier-Land)', *TZ* 34 (1971) 143–225

F. Fremersdorf, *Der römische Gutshof Köln-Müngersdorf* (Berlin 1933)

M. le Glay, 'La Gaule romanisée', in G. Duby (ed.), *L'Histoire de la France rurale* (Paris 1972)

A. Grenier, *Habitations Gauloises et villas latines* (Paris 1906)

H. Lambert, 'Vestiges superposés d'une villa gallo-romaine en matériaux dur et d'une habitation en bois à Velaines–Popuelles', *Arch Belg* 133 (Brussels 1971)

R. de Maeyer, *De romeinsche Villa's in België* (Antwerpen 1937)

R. de Maeyer, *De Overblijfselen der Romeinsche Villa's in België* (Antwerpen 1940)

J. Metzler, J. Zimmer, L. Bakker, *Ausgrabungen in Echternach* (Luxembourg 1981)

E. Oelmann, 'Ein Gallorömischer Bauernhof bei Mayen', *BJ* 133 (1928) 51–140

J. Percival, *The Roman Villa: An Historical Introduction* (London 1976)

G. Raepsaet, 'Quelques aspects de la division du sol en pays tongre', in *Studien zu den Militärgrenzen Roms* 2 (Köln 1977; *Vorträge des 10 Internationalen Limeskongresses*)

P. Steiner, *Römische Villen im Treverer Gebiet, I: Die Villa von Bollendorf* (Trier 1922)

Ch.-M. Ternes, 'Les villas romaines du Grand-Duché de Luxembourg. Etat de la question', *Helinium* 7 (1967) 121–143

La Villa Romana. Giornata di Studi Russi (Faenza 1971)

E.M. Wightman, 'The Pattern of Rural Settlement in Roman Gaul', in *ANRW* 2.4 584–657

Sections 4–5

M. Coûteaux, 'Recherches palynologiques en Gaume, en pays d'Arlon, en Ardenne méridionale (Lux. Belge) et au Gutland (G.-D. Lux.)', *Acta Geol. Louvanensia* 8 (1969)

J. Kolendo, 'Origine et diffusion de l'araire à avant-train en Gaule et en Bretagne', *Cah. Hist.* 24 (1979) 61–73

U. Körber-Grohne, *Nutzpflanzen und Umwelt im römischen Germanien* (Aalen 1979; *Limesmuseum Aalen Kleine Schriften* 21)

M. Renard, *Technique et agriculture en pays trévire et rémois* (Brussels 1959; *Coll. Latomus* 38)

J.T. Smith, 'Villas as a Key to Social Structure', in M. Todd (ed.), *Studies in the Romano-British Villa* (Leicester 1978) 149–185

K.D. White, 'The Economics of the Gallo-Roman Harvesting Machines', in *Hommages à M. Renard* (Brussels 1969) 804–809

A. Valet, 'Mercin et Vaux (Aisne): l'étude des ossements animaux', *CAPic* 8 (1981) 115–156

E.M. Wightman, 'Peasants and Potentates in Roman Gaul', *Amer. Journ. Anc. Hist.* 3 (1978) 43–63

W. van Zeist, 'Prehistoric and Early Historic Food Plants in the Netherlands', *Palaeohistoria* 14 (1970) 41–173

6 The Materials and Structures of Economic Life

Sections 1, 3–4

A. Aubin, 'Der Rheinhandel in römischer Zeit', *BJ* 130 (1925) 1–37

M.R. Alföldi (ed.), *Studien zu Fundmünzen der Antike I, Ergebnisse des FMRD-Colloquium 8–13 Feb. Frankfurt-am-Main* (Bad Homburg/Berlin 1979)

G. de Boe, Fr. Hubert, 'Une installation portuaire d'époque romaine à Pommeroeul', *Arch Belg* 192 (1977)

L. Bonnard, *La navigation intérieure de la Gaule à l'époque gallo-romaine* (Paris 1913)

R. Chevallier, *Les routes romaines* (Paris 1972) = *Roman Roads* (London 1976)

L. Cracco Ruggini, 'Les structures de la société et de l'économie lyonnaises au IIe siècle par rapport à la politique locale et impériale', in *Les Martyrs de Lyon* (Paris 1978; *Colloque internat. CNRS*)

R. Dion, *Histoire de la vigne et du vin en France des origines au XIXe. siècle* (Paris 1959)

H. Dragendorff, E. Krüger, *Das Grabmal von Igel* (Trier 1924)

J.F. Drinkwater, 'Die Secundinier von Igel und die Woll- und Textilindustrie in Gallia Belgica: Fragen und Hypothesen', *TZ* 40/41 (1977/8) 107–125

A. Grenier, 'La Gaule romaine', in T. Frank (ed.), *An Economic Survey of Ancient Rome* vol. 3 (1937) 379ff

J. Hagen, *Römerstrassen der Rheinprovinz* (2nd ed. Bonn 1931)

H. Heinen, 'Grundzüge der wirtschaftlichen Entwicklung des Moselraumes zur Römerzeit', *TZ* 39 (1976) 75–118

K. Hopkins, 'Taxes and Trade in the Roman Empire', *JRS* 70 (1980) 101–125

S.J. de Laet, A. van Doorselaer *et al.*, 'Lokale ijzerwinning in westelijke België in de romeinse tijd', *Med. K Vl Ak* 31 (1969)

P. Lambrechts, 'Gallië en de Middellandsche zee', *Tijdschr. voor Econ. en Sociologie* 4 (1938) 47ff

W. von Massow, *Die Grabmäler von Neumagen* (Berlin 1932)

P. Middleton, 'Army Supply in Roman Gaul', in B.L. Burnham, H.B. Johnson (eds.), *Invasion and Response* (Oxford 1979: *BAR* 73) 81–98

R. Pleiner, 'Die Eisenverhüttung in der "Germania Magna" zur römischen Kaiserzeit', *BRGK* 45 (1964) 11–86

J. du Plat Taylor and H. Cleere (ed.), *Roman Shipping and Trade: Britain and the Rhine Provinces* (London 1978; *CBA Research Report* 24)

M. Rostovtzeff, *Social and Economic History of the Roman Empire* 2nd ed. rev. P.M. Fraser (Oxford 1957)

O. Schlippschuh, *Die Händler im römischen Kaiserreich in Gallien, Germanien und den Donauprovinzen Rätien, Noricum und Pannonia* (Amsterdam 1974)

H. van de Weerd, 'Het economisch bloeitijdperk van Noord-Gallië in den Romeinschen Tijd', *Med. K Vl Ak* (1940) no. 4

L. West, *Roman Gaul, the Objects of Trade* (Oxford 1935)

J.P. Wild, 'Clothing in the North-western Provinces of the Roman Empire', *BJ* 168 (1968) 116–234

J.P. Wild, *Textile Manufacture in the Northern Roman Provinces* (Cambridge 1970)

Section 2

G. Chenet, G. Gaudron, *La céramique sigillée d'Argonne des IIe et IIIe siècles* (Paris 1955; *Gallia* suppl. 6)

E. Fölzer, *Die Bilderschüsseln der ostgallischen Sigillata-Manufakturen* (Bonn 1913: *Römische Keramik in Trier* I)

J.J. Hatt, 'Aperçu sur l'évolution de la céramique commune gallo-romaine principalement dans le nord-est de la Gaule', *REA* 51 (1949) 100–128

I. Huld-Zetsche, *Trierer Reliefsigillata Werkstatt I* (Bonn 1972)

L. Lerat, Y. Jeannin, *La céramique sigillée de Luxeuil* (Paris 1960; *Ann. Litt. Univ. Besançon* 31)

M. Lutz, 'Etat actuel de nos connaissances sur la céramique sigillée de l'Est de la Gaule', *RAE* 5 (1966) 130–157

M. Lutz, *L'atelier de Saturninus et de Satto à Mittelbronn (Moselle)* (Paris 1970; *Gallia* suppl. 22)

M. Lutz, *La sigillée de Boucheporn* (Paris 1977; *Gallia* suppl. 32)

M. Lutz, 'La céramique belge en Gaule de l'Est', *RCRFA* 19/20 (1979) 64–71

H. von Petrikovits, 'Der Wandel römischer Gefässkeramik in der Rheinzone', in *Landschaft u. Geschichte, Festschrift H. Petri* (Bonn 1970) 383–404

G. Raepsaet, 'L'organisation du commerce de la céramique sigillée en Gaule Belgique et en Germanie supérieure', in *ANRW* 2.12 (forthcoming)

M. Tuffreau-Libre, *La céramique commune gallo-romaine dans le nord de la France* (Lille 1980)

7 Romanized Belgica

Sections 1 and 5

J. Colin, 'Sénateurs gaulois à Rome et gouverneurs romains en Gaule au IIIe siècle', *Latomus* 13 (1954) 218–228

G. Drioux, 'Les Nerviens dans l'armée romaine', *REA* 48 (1946) 80–90

L. Flam-Zuckermann, 'A propos d'une inscription de Suisse (*CIL* XIII 5010): étude du phénomène de brigandage dans l'Empire romain', *Latomus* 29 (1970) 451–473

F. Jacques, 'Les cens en Gaule au IIe siècle et dans la première moitié du IIIe siècle', *Ktema* 2 (1977) 285–328

Y. de Kisch, 'Tarifs de donations en Gaule romaine d'après les inscriptions', *Ktema* 4 (1979) 259–280

L. van de Weerd, 'De Belgen in het Romeinsche leger', *AC* 5 (1936) 341–372; 6 (1937) 71–92

J.C. Wilmanns, 'Die Doppelurkunde von Rottweil. Beitrag zum Städtewesen in Obergermanien', *Epig. Stud.* 12 (1981) 1–183

Sections 2 and 3

A. van Doorselaer, *Les Nécropoles d'époque romaine en Gaule septentrionale* (Brugge 1967; *Diss. arch. Gand.* 10)

L. Hahl, *Zur Stilentwicklung der Provinzialrömischen Plastik in Germanien und Galliën* (Darmstadt, 1937)

J.-J. Hatt, 'Esquisse d'une histoire de la sculpture régionale de la Gaule romaine, principalement dans le nord-est de la Gaule', *REA* 59 (1957) 76–107

J.-J. Hatt, *La tombe gallo-romaine* (Paris 1951)

H. Koethe, 'La sculpture romaine au pays des Trévires', *RA* (1937) 199ff

P. Lambrechts, 'La persistance des éléments indigènes dans l'art de la Gaule Belgique', in *Le rayonnement des civilisations grecque et romaine sur les cultures périphériques* (Paris 1965; *Actes VIIe Cong. internat. d'arch. class.*) 153–163

E. Linckenheld, *Les stèles funéraires en forme de maison chez les Médiomatriques et en Gaule* (Paris/Oxford 1927)

M.E. Mariën, 'Les monuments funéraires de l'Arlon romain', *AIAL* 76 (1945) 1–157

M.E. Mariën, 'Les monuments funéraires de Buzenol', *Bull. Mus. roy. d'Art et d'Hist.*, 15 (1943) 2ff, 58ff, 104ff; 16 (1944) 28ff, 59ff

J. Mertens, 'Nouvelles sculptures romaines d'Arlon', *Arch Belg* 103 (1968)

J. Mertens, 'Sculptures romaines de Buzenol', *Arch Belg* 42 (1958)

E. Misciatelli, 'Les monuments funéraires de Reims gallo-romain. Catalogue des monuments figurés du Musée St Rémi et d'autres collections', *BSAChamp* 74 (1981) 3–48

J. Morris, 'Changing Fashions in Roman Nomenclature in the Early Empire', *Listy Filologické* 86 (1963) 34–46

R. Nierhaus, 'Römerzeitliche Bestattungssitten im nördlichen Gallien: Autochthones und Mittelmeerländisches', *Helinium* 9 (1969) 245–262

H. Roosens, 'Bestattungsritual und Grabinhalt einiger tumuli im Limburger Haspengouw', *Arch Belg* 191 (1976)

L. Weisgerber, 'Sprachwissenschaftlishe Beiträge zur frührheinischen Siedlungs- und Kulturgeschichte I': 'Die sprachliche Schichtung der Mediomatriker-namen', and 'Zum Namengut der Germani cisrhenani', in *Rhenania Germano-Celtica, Gesammelte Abhandlungen* (Bonn 1969)

Section 4

Actes du colloque La géographie sacrée de la Gaule, Caesarodunum 8 (1973)

F. Drexel, 'Götterverehrung im römischen Germanien', *BRGK* 14 (1922) 1–68

G. Drioux, *Cultes indigènes des Lingons* (Paris/Langres 1934)

P.-M. Duval, *Les dieux de la Gaule* (2nd ed. Paris 1976)

J.-J. Hatt, 'Essai sur l'évolution de la réligion gauloise', *REA* 67 (1965) 80–125

J.-J. Hatt, 'Divinités orientales et dieux gaulois', in *Mélanges offerts à Marcel Simon* (Paris 1978) 277–294

P. Horne, A.C. King, 'Romano-Celtic Temples in Continental Europe: A Gazetteer of Those with Known Plans', in W. Rodwell (ed.), *Temples, Churches and Religion. Recent Research in Roman Britain* (Oxford 1980; *BAR* 77) 369–556

H. Koethe, 'Die Keltischen Rund- und Vielecktempel der Kaiserzeit', *BRGK* 23 (1933) 10–108

P. Lambrechts, *Contributions à l'étude des divinités celtiques* (Gand 1942)

R. Schindler, 'Gallo-römische Götter, Kulte und Heiligtümer im Saarland', *BSDS* 12 (1965) 79

W. Schleiermacher, 'Studien an Göttertypen der römischen Rhienprovinzen', *BRGK* 23 (1933) 109–143

E. Schwertheim, *Die Denkmäler orientalischer Gottheiten im Deutschland* (Leiden 1974)

J. Toutain, *Les cultes païens dans l'Empire romain (Provinces latines)* 1–3 (Paris 1905–1917, repr. Rome 1967)

G. Weisgerber, *Das Pilgerheiligtum des Apollo und Sirona von Hochscheid im Hunsrück* (Bonn 1975)

V. Walters, *The Cult of Mithras in the Roman Province of Gaul* (Leiden 1974)

J. Zwicker, *Fontes historiae religionis Celticae* (Berlin 1934–36)

8 The Gallic Empire

P. Bastien, *Le monnayage de bronze de Postume* (Wetteren 1967)

P. Bastien, C. Meleger, *Le trésor de Beaurains (dit d'Arras)* (Wetteren 1977)

P. Bastien, 'Trésors de la Gaule septentrionale. La circulation monétaire à la fin du 3e et au début du 4e siècles', *RN* 60 (1978) 789–812

P. Brown, *The Making of Late Antiquity* (Cambridge, Mass./London 1978)

P.J. Casey, 'Carausius and Allectus, rulers in Gaul?', *Britannia* 8 (1977) 283–301

M. Crawford, 'Finance, Coinage and Money from the Severans to Constantine', in *ANRW* 2.2 560–593

B. Czuth, *Die Quellen der Geschichte der Bagauden* (Szeged 1965; *Acta Universitatis de Attila Jozsef Nominatae*)

E. Demougeot, *La formation de l'Europe et les invasions barbares I. Des origines germaniques à l'avènement de Dioclétien* (Paris 1969)

G. Elmer, 'Die Münzprägung der gallischen Kaiser in Köln, Trier und Mailand', *BJ* 146 (1941) 1–106

J.B. Giard, 'La monnaie locale en Gaule à la fin du IIIe siècle. Reflet de la vie économique', *JS* (1969) 5–34

J. Gricourt, G. Fabre, M. Mainjouet, J. Lafaurie, *Trésors monétaires et plaques-boucles de la Gaule romaine* (Paris 1948; *Gallia* suppl. 12)

J. Gricourt, 'Les évènements de 289–292 en Gaule d'après les trésors de monnaies', *REA* 56 (1954) 366–376

I. Koenig, *Die gallischen Usurpatoren von Postumus bis Tetricus* (München 1981; *Vestigia* 31)

H. Koethe, 'Zur Geschichte Galliens im dritten Viertel des 3. Jahrhunderts', *BRGK* 32 (1942) 199–224

J. Lafaurie, 'L'Empire Gaulois. Apport de la numismatique', in *ANRW* 2.2, 853–1012

329

J. Lallemand, M. Thirion, *Le trésor de St. Mard I* (Wetteren 1970)

H.-G. Pflaum, *Le marbre de Thorigny* (Paris 1948)

M. Thirion, *Les trésors monétaires gaulois et romains trouvés en Belgique* (Brussels 1967)

F. Vasselle, 'Les trésors monétaires gallo-romains du département de la Somme', *RNord* 36 (1954) 447–469

9 Northern Gaul and the Later Empire

Section 1

L. Harmand, *Un aspect social et politique du monde romain: le patronat public sur les collectivités locales des origines au Bas-Empire* (Paris 1958)

A.H.M. Jones, *The Later Roman Empire 284–602. A Social, Economic and Administrative Survey* (Oxford 1964)

H. Nesselhauf, *Die spätrömische Verwaltung der gallisch-germanischen Länder* (Berlin 1938; Preuss. Akad. Wiss.)

M. Rouche, 'Le changement de nom des chefs-lieux de cité en Gaule au Bas-Empire', *Mém. Soc. nat. Antiq. France* 9e s. 4 (1968) 47–64

P. Veyne, 'Clientèle et corruption au service de l'état: la vénalité des offices dans le Bas-Empire romain', *Annales* 36 (1981) 339–360

Section 2

R. MacMullen, *Soldier and Civilian in the Later Roman Empire* (Cambridge Mass. 1963)

E. Demougeot, *La formation de l'Europe et les invasions barbares II. De l'avènement de Dioclétien à l'occupation germanique de l'Empire romain d'Occident* (Paris 1979)

D. Hoffmann, *Das Spätrömische Bewegungsheer und die Notitia Dignitatum* (Düsseldorf 1969/70)

D. Hoffmann, 'Die Gallienarmee und der Grenzschutz am Rhein in der Spätantike', *Nassau. Ann.* 84 (1973) 1–18

D. Hoffmann, 'Die Neubesetzung des Grenzschutzes am Rhein, an der gallischen Atlantikküste und in Britannien unter Valentinian I um 369', in *Roman Frontier Studies 1969* (Cardiff 1974) 168–173

S. Johnson, *The Roman Forts of the Saxon Shore* (London 1976)

R. MacMullen, 'Barbarian Enclaves in the Northern Roman Empire', *AC* 32 (1963) 552–561

J. Mertens, 'Oudenburg and the Northern Sector of the Continental Litus Saxonicum', in *The Saxon Shore* (London 1977; *CBA Research Report* 18) 51–62

J. Mertens, 'Recherches récentes sur le limes en Gaule Belgique', in *Roman Frontier Studies 1979* (Oxford 1980; *BAR* S-71)

Section 3

M.R. Alföldi, *Die constantinische Goldprägung. Untersuchungen zu ihrer Bedeutung für Kaiserpolitik und Hofkunst* (Mainz 1963)

M.R. Alföldi, 'Die constantinische Goldprägung in Trier', *Jahrb. Num. u. Geldgesch.* 9 (1958) 99–139

M.R. Alföldi, 'Zum Datum der Aufgabe der Residenz Treviri unter Stilicho', *Jahrb. Num. u. Geldgesch.* 20 (1970) 241–249

P. Bastien, *Le monnayage de Magnence* (Wetteren 1964)

P. Basticn, F. Vasselle, *Les trésors monétaires de Fresnoy-les-Roye (Somme)* (Amiens 1971)

R. Beck, *Die 'Tres Galliae' und das 'Imperium' im 4. Jahrhundert* (Zürich 1969)

T. J. Haarhoff, *Schools of Gaul: A Study of Pagan and Christian Education in the Last Century of the Western Empire* (Oxford 1920, repr. Johannesburg 1958)

A.H.M. Jones *et al.*, *Prosopography of the Later Roman Empire* vols. 1–2 (Cambridge 1971)

J. Matthews, *Western Aristocracies and Imperial Court* AD *364–425* (Oxford 1975)

J. Steinhausen, 'Hieronymus und Laktanz in Trier', *TZ* 20 (1951) 126–134

J. Steinhausen, 'Die Hochschulen im römischen Trier', in *Rhein. Verein. f. Denkmalpflege* (1952) 47–64

K. Stroheker, *Der senatorische Adel in spätantiken Gallien* (Tübingen 1948)

M. Waas, *Germanen im römischen Dienst (im 4. Jh. n. Chr.)* (2nd ed. Bonn 1971)

H. Wrede, *Die spätantike Hermengalerie von Welschbillig* (Berlin 1972)

10 The Late Roman Cities

B. Beaujard, 'Les vici des Médiomatriques au Bas-Empire', *Caesarodunum* 11 (1975) 296–308

R. Brulet, G. Coulon, *La nécropole gallo-romaine de la Rue Perdue à Tournai* (Louvain 1977)

A. Blanchet, *Les enceintes romaines de la Gaule* (Paris 1907)

C. Brühl, *Palatium und Civitas, I: Gallien. Studien zur Profantopographie spätantiker Civitates vom 3. bis zum 13. Jahrhundert* (Köln/Wien 1975)

R.M. Butler, 'Late Roman Town Walls in Gaul', *Arch. Journ.* 116 (1959) 25–50

N. Duval, P.-A. Février, C. Pietri, *La topographie chrétienne des cités de la Gaule fasc. 1–2* (Paris-Sorbonne 1980)

H. Eiden, 'Ausgrabungen im spätantiken Trier', in *Neue Ausgrabungen in Deutschland* (Berlin 1958) 340–367

L. Hussong, H. Cüppers, *Die Trierer Kaiserthermen. Die spätrömische und frühmittelalterliche Keramik* (Mainz 1971; *Trier. Grab. u. Forsch.* 1, 2)

S. Johnson, 'A Group of Late Roman City Walls in Gallia Belgica', *Britannia* 4 (1973) 210–223

D. Krencker, E. Krüger, H. Lehmann, H. Wächtler, *Die Trierer Kaiserthermen* (Augsburg 1929; *Trier. Grab. u. Forsch.* 1, 1)

A. Lombard-Jourdan, 'Oppidum et banlieue. Sur l'origine et les dimensions du térritoire urbain', *Annales* 27 (1972) 373–395

H. von Petrikovits, 'Fortifications in the North-western Roman Empire from the Third to the Fifth Centuries, AD', *JRS* 61 (1971) 178–219

M. Roblin, 'Cités ou citadelles? Les enceintes romaines du Bas-Empire d'après l'exemple de Paris', *REA* 53 (1951) 301–311

M. Roblin, 'Cités ou citadelles? Les enceintes romaines du Bas-Empire d'après l'exemple de Senlis', *REA* 67 (1965) 368–391

F. Vercauteren, *Etudes sur les civitates de la Belgique seconde* (Brussels 1934)

F. Vittinghoff, 'Zur Verfassung der spätantiken Stadt', in *Vorträge und Forschungen* 4 (1958) 11–40

W. Schlesinger, H. Steuer (eds.), *Vor- und Frühformen der europäischen Stadt im Mittelalter* (Göttingen 1973)

K. Weidemann, 'Zur Topographie von Metz in der Römerzeit und im frühen Mittelalter', *JRGZM* 17 (1970) 147–171

E.M. Wightman, 'The Fate of Gallo-Roman Villages in the Third Century' in A. King, M. Henig (eds.), *The Roman West in the Third Century* (Oxford 1981; *BAR* S-109) 235–243

11 The Countryside in the Later Empire

Sections 1, 3, 4

S. Applebaum, 'The Late Gallo-Roman Rural Pattern in the Light of the Carolingian Cartularies', *Latomus* 23 (1964) 774–787

R. Brulet, *La fortification de Hauterecenne à Furfooz* (Louvain 1978)

R. Brulet, *Recherches archéologiques sur le Bas-Empire romain dans les civitates Turnacensium, Camaracensium et Tungrorum*. Diss. Louvain 1975: summary in *Rev. Arch. et Hist. d'Art Louvain* 9 (1976) 260–264

J. Chapelot, R. Fossier, *Le village et la maison au Moyen Age* (Paris 1980, London 1985)

J. Mertens, 'Le Luxembourg méridional au Bas-Empire. Documents anciens et nouveau', *Arch Belg* 76 (1964)

P. van Ossel, 'Les établissements ruraux au Bas-Empire dans la partie méridionale de la Civitas Tungrorum', *Rev. Arch. et Hist. d'art Louvain* 12 (1979) 9–27

J. Percival, 'Ninth Century Polyptyques and the Villa-system: A Reply', *Latomus* 25 (1966) 134–138

J. Percival, 'Seigneurial Aspects of Late Roman Estate Management', *Eng. Hist. Rev.* 84 (1969) 449–473

P. Perin, 'Le peuplement rural de la région ardennaise', *Actes du 95e Cong. soc. sav. Reims 1970* (Paris 1974) 347–365

V.A. Sirago, 'L'agricoltura Gallica sotto la Tetrarchia', in *Hommages à M. Renard* (Brussels 1969; *coll. Latomus*) vol. 1 687–699

E.M. Wightman, 'Some Aspects of the Late Roman Defensive System in Gaul' in *Roman Frontier Studies 1967* (Tel Aviv 1971; *7th Internat. Congr. Roman Frontier Studies*) 46–51

E.M. Wightman, 'North-eastern Gaul in Late Antiquity: The Testimony of Settlement Patterns in an Age of Transition', *BROB* 28 (1978) 241–250

Section 2

H.W. Böhme, *Germanische Grabfunde des 4. and 5. Jahrhunderts zwischen unterer Elbe und Loire* (München 1974)

K. Böhner, 'Zur historichen Interpretation der sogenannten Laetengräber', *JRGZM* 10 (1963) 139–67

E. Demougeot, 'A propos des lètes gaulois du IVe siècle', in *Beiträge zur alten Geschichte, Festschrift Franz Altheim* (Berlin 1970) 101–113

R. Gunther, 'Laeti, Foederati und Gentilen im Nord-und Nordostgallien im Zusammenhang mit der sogennanten Laetenzivilisation', *Zeitschr. f. Arch.* 5 (1971) 19–38

R. Gunther, 'Die socialen Träger der frühen Reihengräberkultur in Belgien und Nordfrankreich im 4./5. Jahrhundert', *Helinium* 12 (1972) 268–272

E. James, 'Cemeteries and the Problem of Frankish Settlement in Gaul', in P.H. Sawyer (ed.), *Early Medieval Settlement* (Leeds 1979)

S.J. de Laet, J. Dhondt and J. Nenquin, 'Les Laeti du Namurois et l'origine de la civilisation mérovingienne', in *Etudes d'histoire et d'archéologie dédiées à F. Courtroy* (1952)

H. Roosens, 'Laeti, Foederati und andere spätrömische Bevolkerungsniederschläge im belgischen Raum', *Arch Belg* 104 (1968)

E. Salin, *Le haut Moyen-Age en Lorraine d'après le mobilier funeraire* (Paris 1939)

J. Werner, 'Zur Entstehung der Reihengräberzivilisation', *Arch. Geograph.* 1 (1950) 23–32

12 Production, Marketing and Trade in Late Roman Belgica

Section 1

M.T.W. Arnheim, *The Senatorial Aristocracy in the Later Roman Empire* (Oxford 1972)

A.R. Birley, 'The Economic Effects of Roman Frontier Policy', in A. King, M. Henig (eds.), *The Roman West in the Third Century* (Oxford 1981; *BAR* S-109) 39–54

A. Cérati, *Caractère annonaire et assiette de l'impôt foncier au Bas-Empire* (Aix-en-Provence 1969); review by A. Chastagnol in *Latomus* 30 (1971) 495–501

R. Clausing, *The Roman Colonate* (New York 1925, repr. Rome 1965)

A. Déléage, *La capitation du Bas-Empire* (Mâcon 1945)

E. Faure, 'Etude de la capitation de Dioclétien d'après le Panégyrique VIII', in *Varia, études de droit romain* 4 (Paris 1961) 1–153

W. Goffart, *Caput and Colonate* (Toronto 1974)

A.H.M. Jones (ed. P.A. Brunt), *The Roman Economy* (Oxford 1974) especially 'Capitatio and Iugatio' 280–292 and 'The Roman Colonate' 293–307

C.R. Whittaker, 'Inflation and the Economy in the Fourth Century AD in C.E. King (ed.), *Imperial Revenue, Expenditure and Monetary Policy in the Fourth Century* AD (Oxford 1980; *BAR* S-76) 1–22

Section 2

G. Chenet, *La céramique gallo-romaine d'Argonne du IVe siècle et la terre sigillée décorée à la molette* (Mâcon 1941)

M. Fulford, 'Pottery and Britain's Foreign Trade in the Later Roman Period', in D. Peacock (ed.), *Pottery and Early Commerce* (London/New York/ San Francisco 1977) 35–84

M. Fulford, 'The Interpretation of Britain's Late Roman Trade: The Scope of Medieval Historical and Archaeological Analogy', in *Roman Shipping and Trade: Britain and the Rhine Provinces* (London 1978; *C.B.A. Research Report* no. 24) 59–69

M. Fulford and J. Bird, 'Imported Pottery from Germany in Late Roman Britain', *Britannia* 6 (1975) 171–181

W. Hübener, 'Eine Studie zur spätrömischen Rädchensigillata', *BJ* 168 (1968) 241–299

R. Schindler, 'Fragen zur römischen Eisenverhüttung im Moselland', *TZ* 39 (1976) 45–59

F. Steiner, 'Einige Bemerkungen an den römischen Ziegelstempeln aus Trier', *Trier. Jahresber.* 10/11 (1917/18) 15–31

J. Werner, 'Die Herkunft und Zeitstellung der Hemmoorer Eimer', *BJ* 140/41 (1936) 395–410; for distribution also *BJ* 153 (1953) 126–127

Section 3

C.E. King, 'The Sacrae Largitiones, Revenues, Expenditure and the Production of Coin', in C.E. King (ed.), *Imperial Revenue, Expenditure and Monetary Policy in the Fourth Century* AD (Oxford 1980; *BAR* S-76) 141–174

J. Lallemand, 'La circulation sur le territoire de la Belgique actuelle des monnaies romaines émises de 346/8 à 363', in M.R. Alföldi (ed.), *Studien zu Fundmünzen der Antike 1* (Berlin 1979) 121–135

J. Lallemand, 'La circulation sur le territoire de la Belgique actuelle des monnaies romaines en bronze émises de 379 à 402', in *Mélanges de numismatique, d'archéologie et d'histoire offerts à J. Lafaurie* (Paris 1980) 117–123

P. Lambrechts, 'Le commerce des "syriens" en Gaule du haut-empire à l'époque mérovingienne', *AC* 6 (1937) 35–61

R. Latouche, 'De la Gaule romaine à la Gaule franque', *Settimane di Studio sull' alto Medioevo* 9 (1961) 379ff

J. Rougé, *Recherches sur l'organisation du commerce maritime en Méditerranée sous l'Empire romain* (Paris 1966)

13 The Christianization of Belgica
Section 1

C. Clemen, *Fontes Historiae Religionis Germanicae* (Berlin 1928)

N. Kyll, 'Zum Fortleben vorchristlichen Volksglauben im Trierer Lande', *Kurtrier. Jahrb.* 5 (1965) 11–19

N. Kyll, 'Trierer Volksglaube und römerzeitliche Überreste', *TZ* 32 (1969) 333–340

J. Moreau, *Das Trierer Kornmarktmosaik* (Köln 1960)

W. Schleiermacher, 'Zum Beharrungsvermögen des keltischen Heidentums gegenüber der christlichen Religion', in *Rome et le Christianisme dans la région rhénane. Colloque du centre de recherches d'histoire des religions de l'Université de Strasbourg 1960* (Paris 1963) 127–137

J. Zwicker, *Fontes historiae religionis Celticae* vol. 2 (Berlin 1936)

Sections 2–4

P. Brown, *The Cult of the Saints* (Chicago/London 1981)

P. Clemen (ed.), *Kunstdenkmäler der Rheinprovinz* espec. vol. 13 (Düsseldorf 1938)

L. Duchesne, *Fastes episcopaux de l'ancienne Gaule* vol. 3 (Paris 1915)

E. Ewig, *Trier im Merowingerreich, Civitas, Stadt, Bistum* (Trier 1954)

N. Gauthier, *L'évangélisation des pays de la Moselle* (Paris 1980)

F. Gerke, 'Die Trierer Agricius-Sarkophag. Ein Beitrag zur Geschichte der altchristlichen Kunst in den Rheinlanden', *TZ* 18 (1949 *Beiheft*)

E. Griffe, *La Gaule chrétienne à l'époque romaine* (Paris 1964–66; 3 vols.)

N. Kyll, 'Die Einführung des Christentums bei der Landbevölkerung des Trierer Landes', *Pastor Bonus* 48 (1937) 189–197; 241–250; 286–296; 329–341

N. Kyll, 'Siedlung, Christianisierung und kirchliche Organisation der Westeifel', *Rhein. Vierteljahrsbl.* 26 (1961) 159–241

E. de Moreau, *Histoire de l'Eglise en Belgique 1* (1940; 2nd ed. Bruxelles 1945)

W. Neuss, *Die Anfänge des Christentums im Rheinlande* (2nd ed. Bonn 1933)

F.J. Ronig (ed.), *Der Trierer Dom (Jahrb. Rhein. Verein Denkmalpflege u. Landschaftsschutz 1978/9)*

A. Rousselle, 'Du sanctuaire au thaumaturge: la guérison en Gaule au IVe siècle', *Annales* 31 (1976) 1085–1107

M. Vieillard-Troiëkouroff, *Les monuments de la Gaule d'après les oeuvres de Grégoire de Tours* (Paris 1976)

14 The Fifth Century: A Time of Transition

K. Böhner, *Die fränkischen Altertümer des Trierer Landes* (Berlin 1958)

K. Böhner, 'Urban and Rural Settlement in the Frankish Kingdom', in M. Barley (ed.), *European Towns, Their Archaeology and Early History* (London 1977) 185–202

A. Dasnoy, 'Les Germains dans la Romanité', in *La Wallonie, le pays et les hommes 1* (Brussels 1975) 36–60

E. Demougeot, 'La Gaule nord-orientale à la veille de la grande invasion germanique de 407', *Rev. Hist.* (1966) 27–34

E. Demougeot, 'La Notitia dignitatum et l'histoire de l'Empire d'Occident au début du Ve siècle', *Latomus* 34 (1975) 1079–1134

E. Demougeot, *La formation de l'Europe et les invasions barbares* vol. 2 pt. 2 (Paris 1979)

E. Ewig, 'Das Fortleben römischer Institutionen in Gallien und Germanien', in *Francia* 3.1 (1976) 409–434

E. Ewig, 'Les Ardennes au haut moyen-âge', in *Francia* 3.1 (1976) 523–552

E. Ewig, 'Observations sur la grandeur et la décadence de Trèves la Romaine', in *Economies et sociétés du Moyen Age, hommages à E. Perroy* (Paris 1973) repr. in *Francia* 3.2 (1976) 21–32

M. Gysseling, 'La genèse de la frontière linguistique', *RNord* 44 (1962) 22ff

A. Longnon, *Etudes sur les pagi de la Gaule 1–2* (Paris 1869–72)

J.R. Martindale, *Prosopography of the Later Roman Empire* vol. 2 (Cambridge 1980)

F. Petri (ed.), *Siedlung, Sprache und Bevölkerungsstruktur im Frankenreich* (Darmstadt 1973)

J. Stengers, 'Les origines de la frontière linguistique ou de la légitimité de l'hypothèse historique', *Latomus* 18 (1959) 366–395, 593–611

E.M. Wightman, 'The Towns of Gaul with Special Reference to the North-east', in M. Barley (ed.), *European Towns, Their Archaeology and Early History* (London 1977) 303–313

E. Will, 'Remarques sur la fin de la domination romaine dans la Nord de la Gaule', *RNord* 48 (1966) 517–534

E. Will, 'Boulogne et la fin de l'Empire romain d'Occident', in *Hommages à M. Renard* (Brussels 1969; *coll. Latomus* 101–103) 820–827

E. Zöllner, *Geschichte der Franken bis zur Mitte des sechsten Jahrhunderts* (München 1970)

NOTES *(consult bibliography for fuller references)*

1 Before the Romans

1 General overview hard. Simplified regional summaries in the appropriate *Guides Michelins*; see also *Carte géologique de la France, feuille nord* at 1:1,000,000. For greater detail, Steinhausen, *Siedlungskunde* and Thoen, *Kustvlakte* (Regional Studies); more technical, Sommé, *Les Plaines* (Regional Studies) and S. Jelgersma *et al.*, *Mededel. Rijks. geolog. Dienst* 21 (1970) 94–167

2 W. van Zeist, M.R. van der Spoel-Walvins, *Palaeohistoria* 22 (1980) 67–109; J. de Heinzelin, P. Haesaerts, S.J. de Laet, *Le gué du Plantin (Neufvilles, Hainaut), site néolithique et romain* (Brugge 1977; *Diss. Arch. Gand.* 17); M. Coûteaux, 'Recherches palynologiques' (chap. 5); J. Harmand, *Bull. Soc. Préhist. Franç.* 46 (1949) 229–30

3 H. Jankuhn, *Einführung in die Siedlungsarchäologie* (Berlin/New York 1977) 52–7 and in *ANRW* 2.5.1 65–126

4 De Laet, *Prehistorische Kulturen* 476–8; consult this, or *Cultures Préhistoriques* for further bibliography

5 M.E. Mariën, *Trouvailles du champs d'urnes et des tombelles hallstattiennes de Court-Saint-Etienne* (Brussels 1958); de Laet, 'Native and Celt'

6 For Belgium, de Laet (n. 4); A. Thenot, in Guilaine (ed.) 826–36; Millotte, *La Lorraine*; Haffner, *Hunsrück-Eifel-Kultur*

7 R. Joffroy, *Le trésor de Vix (Côte d'Or)* (Paris 1954) and *L'Oppidum de Vix*; W. Kimmig in *Ausgrabungen in Deutschland 1950–1975* (Mainz, RGZM 1975)

8 Wells, *Culture Contact*

9 For the Jura, J.-P. Millotte in Guilaine (ed.) 724–33; for the Hunsrück-Eifel, Haffner (n. 6), also in *Führer (RGZM)* vols. 5 (*Saarland*), 33 (*Südwestliche Eifel*), 34 (*Westlicher Hunsrück*); for Champagne, Bretz-Mahler

10 Mariën, *La Haine*

11 See Megaw, *Art* 80 no. 84 and for further references Wells, *Culture Contact* 133

12 G. Thill, *Hémecht* 24 (1972) 487–98; silk unconfirmed, but see Wells, *Culture Contact* 18 and 134

13 Haffner, *Hunsrück-Eifel-Kultur* 162–4, also in *Festschrift Trier* (chap. 4);
Schindler, *Saarland* (chap. 1.4) 112–35

14 Wells, *Culture Contact* 130ff; L. Pauli, *Der Dürrnberg bei Hallein III:
Auswertung der Grabfunde* (München 1978) 464; cf. Pliny *nat. hist.* 12.5

15 To refs. in n. 9 add A. Cahen-Delhaye, *AKorr* 5 (1975) 47–58 and *Tombelles
de l'âge du fer en Ardenne* (Brussels 1978; *Arch. Belg. Speculum* 8); A. van
Doorselaer, J. de Meulenmeester, R. Putnam, *Arch Belg* 161 (1974); Mariën,
La Haine and *Eigenbilzen et Hallein* (Brussels 1962; *Coll. Latomus* 58)

16 Keller, *Reinheim*; Megaw, *Art* and P.-M. Duval, *Les Celtes* for the objects

17 Herodotus *hist.* 2.53. Summary and discussion of this and other references in
P.-M. Duval, *Sources*; cf. also Riese, *Litteratur* (Ancient Sources)

18 Avienus, *ora maritima* 130ff

19 E.g. by Cassius Dio

20 De Laet, 'Native and Celt'; W. Jungandreas, *TZ* 22 (1955) 1–12; cf. C.F.C.
Hawkes, *EC* 13 (1972) 607–28

21 Caesar *bell. gall.* 1.1

22 De Laet, 'Fortifications' (chap. 1.4); Hachmann in Hachmann, Kossack, Kuhn

23 Kuhn in Hachmann, Kossack, Kuhn; L. Weisgerber, *Rhenania Germano-Celtica*
(chap. 7.2–3) 275–95

24 Hawkes, 'New thoughts'; Hachmann, 'Germains, Celtes et Belges'. See also
W.S. Cooter in D.H. Miller, J.O. Steffen (eds.), *The Frontier. Comparative
Studies* (Oklahoma 1977) 81–108

25 Caesar, *bell. gall.* 2.3, 6.2, 6.32; for Posidonius, F. Jacoby, *Die Fragmente der
griechischen Historiker* (Berlin 1923–) II C 169. On Posidonius and Caesar, see
D. Nash, *Britannia* 7 (1976) 111–26

26 Hawkes and Dunning, 'The Belgae'

27 Mariën, 'Tribes and archaeological groupings', also (summary) in *Belgica
Antiqua* (General Works)

28 Hawkes, 'Celtes, Gaulois'

29 De Laet, 'Native and Celt'
Haffner, *TZ* 32 (1969) 71–127, and *AKorr* 9 (1979) 405–9. See also Haffner,
as mercenaries, Jullian, *La Gaule* (General Works) vol. 1 324–8. References to
Bolgios (or Belgius) and Viridomarus in Holder, *Sprachschatz* (Onomastics)

31 G. Lobjois, *Celticum* 18 (1969) 1–284

32 J.-L. Flouest, I.M. Stead, *BSAChamp* 67 (1974) 59–67; Thenot (above n. 6); de
Laet (above n. 4); Megaw, *Art* no. 173

33 A. Duval, O. Buchsenschutz in Guilaine (ed.) 789–801; G. Leman-Delerive,
CAPic 3 (1976)

34 The low chronology of Mahr, *Die jüngere Latènekultur* has been countered by
Haffner, *TZ* 32 (1969) 71–127, and *AKorr* 9 (1979) 405–9. See also Haffner,
Wederath and G. Mahr, A. Miron, 'Kr. Bernkastel-Wittlich', *TZ* 43/4 (1980–
81) 7–262

35 See now J. Chapelot, *Arch. Médiévale* 10 (1980) 5–57 and A. Villes,
BSAChamp 75 (1982) 2–114; Agache, *La Somme* (Regional Studies) 120–68

36 G. Leman-Delerive, J.F. Piningre in *L'âge du fer en France Septentrionale* (chap.
1.2) 319–37; R. Schindler, *Bundenbach*

37 A. Villes in *L'âge du fer en France Septentrionale* 49–90; R.M. Rowlett, E.S.J.
Rowlett, M. Boureux, *World Arch.* 1 (1969) 106–35

38 G.J. Verwers, *Das Kamps Veld in Haps in Neolithikum, Bronzezeit und Eisenzeit* (Leiden 1972; *Analecta Praehist. Leiden.* 5); A. Gautier, *Helinium* 8 (1968) 241–58 (cf. Mariën in *Belgica Antiqua*); H. Roosens, G.V. Lux, 'Staberg te Rosmeer'; R. de Ceunynck, H. Thoen, *Helinium* 21 (1981) 21–42 (de Panne not la Tène III)

39 F. Oelmann, 'Mayen' (chap. 5); M. Mueller-Wille, 'Baüerliche Siedlungen'

40 Schindler, *Saarland* 136–46; see also summaries in the various *Führer* (*RGZM*)

41 Schindler, 'Bundenbach', also *TZ* 39 (1976) 5–22

42 A. Deyber, *RAE* 23 (1972) 55–76; G. Tronquart, *Gallia* 34 (1976) 201–13

43 On *muri gallici*, M.A. Cotton in Wheeler, *Hillforts* 159–226; W. Dehn, *Germania* 47 (1969) 165–8

44 G. Lobjois, *Celticum* 15 (1966) 1–26; cf. O. Buchsenschutz, *RA* (1981) 45–66

45 R.M. Rowlett, E. Rowlett, H. Thomas, *Hémecht* 26 (1974) 377–80 and *Journ. Field Arch.* 3 (1976) 241–59; K. Bittel, *Der Donnersberg, eine keltische Stadtanlage* (Mainz 1981; *Akad. Wiss. u. Lit. Mainz*)

46 For further bibliography, Mariën, *Belgica Antiqua* (General Works) and de Laet, *Cultures préhistoriques*

47 Wheeler, *Hillforts* and Leman-Delerive, Lefranc, *Forteresses gauloises*

48 J.-L. Brunaux, P. Meniel, A. Rapin, *Gallia* 38 (1980) 1–25

49 Polyaenus *strategemata* 4.17. The most accessible modern introduction to the subject is now Allen (ed. Nash)

50 D.F. Allen, *Schweiz. num. Rundschau* 53 (1974) 42–74; S. Scheers, *RBN* 114 (1968) 43–73. This and other articles by Scheers are now incorporated in her *Traité*. Coins are quoted according to her categories; the Tarentine imitations are Scheers 1–7

51 Strabo 4.2.3; Allen, 'Wealth, Money and Coinage', cf. *The Coins* 35–6

52 D.F. Allen, *Germania* 49 (1971) 91–100; Scheers 16–20. Pegasus, Scheers 23; Janus head, Scheers 34

53 Scheers 8

54 Allen's Gallo-Belgic B is Scheers 10–10a (*à lignes entremêlées*); his C is Scheers 9 (*Ambiani biface*); D is 13 (*à bateau*); E is 24 (*Ambiani uniface*). On B, E. Huysecom, *Bull. Cercle Et. Num.* 18 (1981) 77–81

55 Allen's F is Scheers 26 (*Suessiones anépigraphique*). The type with Criciru is Scheers 27; on this, J.-B. Colbert de Beaulieu, *RBN* 110 (1964) 69–132 and Scheers, *Ancient Society* 1 (1970) 135–61

56 Scheers 25, 29, 30 respectively

57 Low dating in Scheers, *Brit. Num. Journ.* (1972) 1–6. Allen's higher date has been vindicated by new discoveries, notably the hoard at Thuin; E. Huysecom, *Arch* (1981) 24

58 Scheers 21

59 Colbert de Beaulieu, 'La monnaie de Caletedu'; Scheers, *Les monnaies* 87–1:6

60 The two latter types are Scheers 186 and 191. Allen argued for a high date for the earliest potins; for a potin coin in the second rampart at Vieux-Laon, Lobjois (above n. 44)

61 Scheers 48, 49, 54–7; also Scheers, *Bull. Antiq. Lux.* 8 (1977) 15–55

62 Useful summary in U. Körber-Grohne, *Nutzpflanzen und Umwelt* (chap. 5)

63 H. Reichstein, *TZ* 39 (1976) 31–7; Brunaux, Meniel, Rapin (above n. 48); T. Poulain in *L'Age du fer* (chap. 1.2) 365–6; more generally, Clason, *Animal and Man*

64 Brongers, 'Celtic Field Research'; Agache, *La Somme* (Regional Studies) 120–68; Roosens and Lux, 'Staberg te Rosmeer'. Plough from la Tène in Drack (ed.) *Schweiz* vol. 4 (Regional Studies)

65 D. Nash and C. Haselgrove in Cunliffe and Rowley (eds.), *Oppida*

66 Livy 5.34.1; above n. 30

67 For one recent study, J.-P. Guillaumet, *Gallia* 35 (1977) 239–48

68 See Wightman in *ANRW* 2.4 (chap. 5); cf. A. Daubigney, *Dial. Hist. Anc.* 5 (1979) 145–89

69 De Laet, *Prehistorische Kulturen* 597

70 Caesar *bell. gall.* 2.4

71 M. Sordi, 'La simpolitia' (chap. 2.1)

72 Nash (above n. 65)

73 Mariën, *Le Trou de l'Ambre*

2 The Conquest

1 Dion, *Frontières passim*; Dubois, 'La carte des diocèses'

2 For place-names derived from *Fines*, Grenier, *Manuel* vol. 1 (General Works) 168; consult also *Tabula Imperii Romani, Lutetia*

3 M. Mangard, *Rev. Soc. Savantes Haute Normandie* 40 (1965) 73–5. On the name Ambiani, C.J. Guyonvarc'h, *Celticum* 15 (1965) 385–400

4 Compare Caesar *bell. gall.* 2.4 with 7.75

5 Roblin, *Oise* (Regional Studies) subsuming earlier articles. For Gournay, chap. 1 n. 48

6 Caesar *bell. gall.* 2.3.5, 2.4.7, 2.5.4

7 Werner, 'Kelheim'; D. Peacock in M. Jesson, D. Hill (eds.), *The Iron Age and its Hill-forts* (Southampton 1971) 161–79; Nash, in Cunliffe and Rowley (eds.), *Oppida*

8 Caesar *bell. gall.* 2.4.8; J.M. Desbordes in *Mélanges d'archéologie et d'histoire offerts à A. Piganiol* vol. 2 (Paris 1966) 936–76; Colbert de Beaulieu, 'Pommiers'. See also Agache, *La Somme* (Regional Studies) 227–9 and (here as elsewhere) Wheeler, *Hillforts* (chap. 1.4). G. Leman-Delerive, *CAPic* 4 (1977) 103–9 for a possible predecessor to Amiens at St.-Acheul-Cagny

9 C.J. Guyonvarc'h, *Celticum* 18 (1967) 299–314; Caesar *bell. gall.* 2.3

10 A. Birchall, *Proc. Prehist. Soc.* 30 (1964) 241–367 espec. 295; C. Constantin, B. Illet-Fleury in *Vallée de l'Aisne* (Regional Studies) 265–76 (not certainly pre-Caesar)

11 Guyonvarc'h (above n. 9); Caesar *bell. gall.* 2.3.1

12 Guyonvarc'h (above ns. 3 and 9); Caesar *bell. gall.* 8.46.7

13 H. Marriette, *Celticum* 18 (1967) 53–96

14 Caesar *bell. gall.* 4.22; Thoen, *Kustvlakte* (Regional Studies) 50–1; E. Trips, *De Duinen* 6 (1968) 159–71

15 Caesar *bell. gall.* 4.4; Thoen, *Kustvlakte* 53ff; S.J. de Laet, *Helinium* 1 (1961) 20–34; Y. Graff, P. Lenoir, *Romana Contact* 18 (1980) 5–72 (the area is in fact smaller)

16 Caesar *bell. gall.* 2.23, 2.28; Mariën, 'Tribes and archaeological groupings' (chap. 1.3); G. Faider-Feytmans, *AC* 21 (1952) 338–58; J.-L. Boucly, *LEC* 46 (1978) 247–9. See also Wheeler, *Hillforts* (chap. 1.4) and Leman-Delerive, *Forteresses* (chap. 1.4)

17 Caesar *bell. gall.* 6.32; Mariën, *Le Trou de l'Ambre* (chap. 1.4); F. Ulrix in
   Hommages à M. Renard vol. 2 (Brussels 1969, *coll. Latomus* 101–3) 726–32
18 Scheers 31
19 R. Thurneysen, *RhM* 84 (1935) 188–92; but see W. Jungandreas (chap. 1 n.
   20)
20 R. Hachmann, 'Die Treverer'; Reding, *Tetelbierg* (chap. 1.5); see also *Führer*
   (*RGZM*) 33 and 34
21 Millotte, *La Lorraine* (chap. 1.2)
22 Discussion in Harmand, *Les Celtes* (chap. 1.2) 62–3
23 The events are in Caesar *bell. gall.* 1. Rice Holmes still valuable, but consult
   also Rambaud's edition of Caesar
24 The events of 57 are in Caesar *bell. gall.* 2. Modern bibliography (1949–1974)
   will be found in Raepsaet-Charlier, *ANRW* 2.4
25 J.B. Giard, *RN* 10 (1968) 76–130, 11 (1969) 62–97
26 Most recently M.A. Arnould, R. Verdière, *RBPH* 53 (1975) 48–58
27 Recently, A. Wankenne, *LEC* 45 (1977) 63–6
28 L. Richard, *LEC* 36 (1968) 223–46
29 The events are in Caesar *bell. gall.* 3; E. Mensching, *Latomus* 38 (1979) 902–31
30 Caesar *bell. gall.* 4.1–5; A. Grisart, *LEC* 28 (1960) 129–204
31 R. Dion, *REL* 41 (1963) 186–209
32 R. Dion, *Latomus* 22 (1963) 191–208; R. Delmaire, 'Civitas Morinorum'
   (chap. 3.1)
33 To the discussion by Rice Holmes, add G. Peyre, *REL* 66 (1978) 175–215
34 Agache, *La Somme* (Regional Works) 207–44
35 Colbert de Beaulieu, 'Les monnaies gauloises au nom des chefs' and *RBN* 101
   (1955) 55–83
36 Wightman, 'Soldier and civilian' (chap. 2.4)
37 Obverse with three heads, perhaps triple monetary magistrates, legend
   Remo-: Scheers 146. Appearance at Alesia may mean a date before 52 BC
38 The events are in Caesar *bell. gall.* 5. For coins, see discussion in Reding,
   Tetelbierg and Scheers, *Traité* (chap. 1.5)
39 See graphs in Hollstein, *Eichendendrochronologie* (General Works)
40 A. Grisart, *Romana Contact* 12 (1972) 4–16; for Liercourt-Hérondelle, Agache,
   La Somme (Regional Works) 218–27
41 Scheers 31
42 Cicero *epist.* 13.7.2
43 Dio 40.31.3; for Odenbach and other hoards, Scheers, *Traité* (chap. 1.5) 872ff
44 Caesar *bell. gall.* 6.11–28; Dio 40.32.2
45 Caesar *bell. gall.* 7.75
46 Caesar *bell. gall.* 8.6–21; J. Harmand, *BSAF* (1959) 263–81
47 Caesar *bell. gall.* 8.47–8; Frontinus *strategemata* 13.11
48 K. Castelin, *Cahiers Num.* 53 (Sept. 1977) 62–8; Suetonius *Div. Jul.* 54; cf.
   Strabo 4.1.13
49 Caesar *bell. gall.* 8.49.2; Orosius 6.12
50 Scheers, *Les monnaies* (chap. 1.5) 106; Drinkwater, 'Rise and fall of the Gallic
   Julii' (chap. 3.4), espec. 824ff
51 Reding, *Tetelbierg* (chap. 1.5); Wightman, 'Il y avait en Gaule', espec. 415ff
52 Appian *bell. civ.* 2.49; Caesar *bell. civ.* 1.39.2; Livy *epit.* 141

53 The main literary sources are collected in Wightman, 'La Gaule chevelue', and (less fully) in 'Military arrangements'. Cf. Tourneur, 'La Belgique pendant l'occupation militaire'

54 Scheers 154

55 Drinkwater, *Roman Gaul* argues for the earlier date, von Petrikovits, *Rheinische Geschichte* (General Works) 54 for a later one

56 For Kaster-Kanne, Hollstein, *Eichendendrochronologie* (General Works); for Otzenhausen, St. Dié (la Bûre) and Donnersberg above chap. 1 ns. 40ff; R. Schindler, *TZ* 34 (1971) 43–82; A. Haffner, *AKorr* 4 (1974) 53–8 and 59–72

57 Reding, *Tetelbierg* (chap. 1.5); J. Metzler, *PSH* 91 (1977) 15–88; the Carrinas coin is Scheers 162

58 E. Hollstein in *Festschrift Trier* (chap. 4) 313–8

59 J. Debord and C. Constantin, A. Coudart, J.P. Demoule in *Vallée de l'Aisne* (Regional Studies) 213–64 and 195–210; J. Debord, *CAPic* 5 (1978) 110–1 and *Cahiers Num.* 64 (1980) 47–8

60 R. Neiss, *BSAChamp* 69 (1976) 47–62

61 J.-L. Cadoux, G.-W. Woimant, *CAPic* 4 (1977) 111–23; E. Huysecom, *RBN* 126 (1980) 45–68; L.P. Delestrée, *La circulation monétaire gauloise dans l'ouest du Belgium après la conquête romaine: les monnaies gauloises de Bois-l'Abbé* (*Thèse 3e cycle*, Univ. Hte. Bretagne 1974)

62 Scheers 186, 191 (cf. 194), 190, 185

63 Scheers 41

64 Scheers 146, 147, 30a, 137, 138

65 Scheers 198, 163

66 Scheers *Traité* (chap. 1.5) 184–5

67 Suetonius *Div. Jul.* 25

68 Wightman, 'Soldier and civilian'

69 H. Horn, *Foederati* (Frankfurt 1930) 58ff; Kraft, 'Colonia Julia Equestris'

70 H. Müller-Beck, E. Ettlinger, *BRGK* 43/4 (1962/3) 148–53; Metzler (above n. 57); Agache, *La Somme* (Regional Studies) 237–9; A. Furger-Gunti, *Die Ausgrabungen im Basler Münster I. Spätkeltische und augusteische Zeit* (Basel 1979) and *AKorr* 11 (1981) 231–46

71 The basic statement remains that of Ritterling, 'Zur Geschichte'; recently, Wightman, 'Military arrangements'

72 Above n. 59; Reding, *Tetelbierg* (chap. 1.5); publication of Pommeroeul coins forthcoming by E. Huysecom

73 Clear discussion by S. von Schnurbein, *Die unverzierte terra sigillata aus Haltern* (Münster 1982; *Bodenaltertümer Westfalens* 19) 86ff; cf. C.M. Wells, *RCRFA* 17/18 (1977) 152–60; J. Lasfargues, *RAE* 24 (1973) 525ff

74 Hollstein, above n. 58

75 References to Gallo-Belgic wares are in chap. 6.2; G. Thill, *Hémecht* 18 (1966) 483–91 and 19 (1967) 199–213

76 *Panegyrici latini* 8.7 (ed. Galletier); P. Claes, *Helinium* 9 (1969) 138–50

77 Wightman, *Roman Trier* (Regional Studies) 36; R. Schindler in *Festschrift Trier* (chap. 4) 121–210, espec. 137; see also Hollstein, *Eichendendrochronologie* (General Works); J.L. Massy, *CAPic* 7 (1980) 115–36

78 Agache, *La Somme* (Regional Studies) 231ff; Goguey, *BSAF* (1967) 159–71; M. Rogge, *Hermeneus, Tijdschrift voor antieke cultuur* 52 (1980) 135–9

79 E. Will, 'Le développement urbain' (chap. 4); P. Leman, *Caesarodunum* 10 (1975) 102–8 and *CAPic* 2 (1975) 63–8
80 M. Vanderhoeven, *Helinium* 7 (1967) 32–64, 193–228; J. Mertens, W. Vanvinckenroye, *Arch Belg* 180 (1975)
81 Dio 54.21.2-8; J. Benabou, *REA* (1967) 221–7
82 Scheers 216, 217; for post conquest coinages also D. Nash in R.A.G. Carson, C.M. Kraay (eds.), *Scripta Nummaria Romana, essays presented to Humphrey Sutherland* (London 1978) 12–31
83 Livy *epit.* 139
84 Quintilian *inst. orat.* 6.3.79

3 The Foundations of Roman Belgica

1 *ILTG* 357; A. Piganiol, *CRAI* (1959) 450–7; Leman, *CAPic* 2 (1975) 63–8; Ptolemy *geog.* 2.9.11
2 Pliny *nat. hist.* 4.101; on meaning, Birkhahn, *Germanen und Kelten* (chap. 1.3)
3 Birkhahn (above n. 2); Roosens, 'Taxandria' (Regional Studies)
4 Rüger, *Germania Inferior* 22ff; H. Klumbach in *Limes-Studien 1957* (Basel 1959) 69–76; H. Instinsky, *Germania* 50 (1972) 133–6; Caesar *bell. gall.* 4.10, cf. 6.2.5; Pliny *nat. hist.* 4.101; Strabo 4.3.4
5 Delmaire, 'Civitas Morinorum'
6 M. Mangard, *Rev. Soc. Savantes Haute Normandie* 40 (1965) 73–5
7 Wightman, 'The Lingones', but see comments by Wilmanns (chap. 7.1) 78ff; J. Braun, *CAAAH* 2 (1959) 47–52; cf. M. Toussaint, 'Le térritoire et les limites de la "Civitas Leucorum"', *Bull. Arch. du Comité* (1941–2) 413–28
8 Bogaers, 'Germania Inferior' wants even the Tungri in Germania Inferior, rejecting the arguments of van de Weerd, 'Civitas Tungrorum'; for brief discussion with further bibliography, Raepsaet-Charlier *ANRW* 2.4 56–7. Batavian magistrate, *CIL* 13. 8771; pagus Vellaus *CIL* 7.1072 (*RIB* 2107); J.A. Huisman, *Bijdr. en Mededel. Naamkunde* 12 (1958) 9–24
9 Rüger, *Germania Inferior* 104ff; cf. Wilmanns (chap. 7.1)
10 A. Grenier, *REL* 14 (1936) 73ff
11 Tacitus *ann.* 3.43; T. Haarhoff, *The Schools of Gaul* (Oxford 1920) 33ff
12 Plutarch *Caes.* 15; Josephus *bell. jud.* 2.16
13 H. Lieb, *Chiron* 4 (1974) 415–23
14 *BRGK* 17.322; *CIL* 13. 1048, cf. 8771
15 Tacitus *hist.* 5.19
16 G. Alföldy, *Latomus* 25 (1966) 37–57; Wolff, 'Kriterien'; Galsterer-Kroll, 'Zum *ius Latii*'
17 As argued by Wolff, 'Kriterien'
18 Tacitus *ann.* 11.24, cf. *CIL* 13.1668; A. Chastagnol, *BSAF* (1971) 282–310
19 Morini, *CIL* 8727 (was use of the title *colonia* prompted by the place of dedication, Nijmegen in Germania Inferior?); Mediomatrici, *CIL* 13.4325, 4335, 11358, 11359; for Treveri, Wightman, *Roman Trier* (Regional Studies) 39ff; and the further discussion of *BRGK* 58, 84 (*AE* 1968, 321) by Krier in *Die Treverer* (chap. 3.4) 92–6; cf. Wolff, 'Civitas und Colonia'
20 Recently, D. van Berchem, *Chiron* 11 (1981) 221–8
21 Wightman, *TZ* 39 (1976) 61–8; also Krier (above n. 19)

22 R. Delmaire, *Septentrion* 8 (1978) 25–8

23 Cf. Draye, 'Die civitates'

24 Treveri, *CIL* 13.3648–3650, 11316; Mediomatrici, *CIL* 13.4301, 4303

25 *Pagi*, above n. 8; *CIL* 13.4143, *BRGK* 17.13, 14, 238 (Treveri); *CIL* 13.4316 (Mediomatrici), 4636, 4679–80 (Leuci); 3459 (Remi). Drinkwater, 'Local Careers' (chap. 3.4)

26 Deininger, *Provinziallandtage*; D. Fishwick in *Les Martyrs de Lyon* (Paris 1978; *colloque internat. CNRS*) 33ff

27 Ritterling, Stein, *Die kaiserliche Beamten*; Meyers, *L'Administration*

28 Above n. 7 and below chap. 3.3

29 Benabou (chap. 2 n. 81)

30 R. Syme, *Harvard Stud. Class. Philol.* 73 (1969) 201–36

31 *CIL* 3. 5215, Meyers, *L'Administration* 76, 96ff; P.R.C. Weaver, *Latomus* 25 (1966) 910–1

32 *CIL* 10. 1705, 6331, Meyers, *L'Administration* 63

33 De Laet, *Portorium*; H. Cüppers, *TZ* 37 (1974) 149–73

34 Frontinus *strategemata* 1.1.8

35 H.-G. Pflaum, *BJ* 171 (1971) 349–66; see above n. 8

36 J. Heurgon, *REA* 50 (1948) 101–11 and 51 (1949) 324ff

37 Heurgon, *AC* 17 (1948) 322–30; *CIL* 13. 3570

38 T.D. Barnes, *JRS* 64 (1974) 21–6

39 K. Polaschek, *TZ* 35 (1972) 141–99; *CIL* 13. 1036, 3026, 4635 (Naix), 4481 (le Héraple)

40 Above n. 10 and Alföldy, 'La politique provinciale'

41 Tacitus *ann.* 3.42-47

42 Discussion in Krier, *Die Treverer* 179ff

43 R. Schindler, *TZ* 37 (1974) 71–97 (though Schindler favours the revolt of 70); J.-J. Hatt, *ASHAL* 49 (1959) 5–15; J.-J. Hatt, M. Lutz, *ASHAL* 49 (1959) 41–64

44 For an alternative explanation, Krier, *Die Treverer* 182–3 (ignoring *CIL* 13. 3076 and 3077, with the implication that the Turones also lost 'free' status)

45 Suetonius *Calig.* 8

46 Fr. d'Erce, *RA* (1966) 89–96

47 Suetonius *Claud.* 2; Alföldy, *Hilfstruppen* 40–1; for Tournai ditches, J. Mertens, H. Remy, *Arch Belg* 165 (1974)

48 See chap. 4.1

49 Above n. 1 and *CIL* 13. 4565

50 Pliny *nat. hist.* 33.54

51 Suetonius *Claud.* 25.3

52 Above n. 18

53 Suetonius *Claud.* 25.5; Pliny *nat. hist.* 29.3.12; G. Cherrière, *RAE* 17 (1966) 88–94

54 Tacitus *ann.* 4.51; *hist.* 2.61; P.A. Brunt, *Latomus* 18 (1959) 531–59; S. Mazzarino in *Atti del colloquio La Gallia Romana* (General Works)

55 Tacitus *hist.* 1.8 and 53; above n. 22

56 Tacitus *hist.* 1.63; above n. 43

57 Brunt and van Soesbergen, 'Batavian revolt'; Tacitus *hist.* 4.12-36

58 Tacitus *hist.* 4.54-79, on Reims, Neiss (chap. 2 n. 60)

59 Tacitus *hist*. 5.14–26
60 On Arlaines, M. Reddé in *Cahiers du groupe de recherches sur l'armée romaine et les provinces* 1 (Paris 1977) 35–70; on Mauchamps, Peyre (chap. 2 n. 33)
61 Above n. 43; Vanvinckenroye, *Tongeren* (chap. 4.1) 28–9
62 Cicero *de divin*. 1.41
63 Drinkwater, 'Gallic Julii', 824ff
64 Livy *epit*. 141
65 I.e. the view of Kraft, *Rekrutierung*; against this, Alföldy, *Hilfstruppen* 86–91
66 Drinkwater, 'Gallic Julii', 848–50; J. Krier, L. Schwinden, *TZ* 37 (1974) 123–47
67 Krier, *Die Treverer* 92ff
68 *BRGK* 17. 322; Alföldy, *Hilfstruppen*
69 *CIL* 13. 11353, 8727
70 Drinkwater, 'Local careers'
71 Drinkwater, 'Gallic Julii'
72 H. Gabelmann in U. Hockmann, A. Krug (eds.), *Festschrift für Franz Brommer* (Mainz 1977) 101–17; G. Thill, *AKorr* 5 (1975) 69–79
73 L. Weisgerber, *Germania* 17 (1933) 14–22
74 *Esp*. 5815, 4929, 4103; Mariën, *Belgica Antiqua* 97; G. Precht, Chr. Rüger, *Zeitschr. f. Papyr. u. Epig*. 43 (1981) 329–35
75 Mariën, *Belgica Antiqua* 153, 204, 246, 253, 259

4 Urbanization

1 See above chap. 2.1 and 2.4 for references to pre-Roman sites; generally, Leman 'Les villes romaines', and D. van Berchem in *Thèmes de recherches* 21–28; for Metz, Toussaint, *Metz* 21–22; for Senlis, G. Matherat in *Hommages à M. Renard* (chap. 2 n. 17) 418–30 (but this thesis lacks substantiation); for Trier, Schindler (chap. 2 n. 56). Late Gaulish coin-moulds at Bavay do not imply a pre-Roman site; H. Biévelet, *RNord* 49 (1967) 623–5
2 For general discussion, J.C. Mann, *Latomus* 22 (1963) 777–82 and B. Galsterer-Kröll in *Epig. Stud*. 9 (Bonn 1972) 44–145; cf. A.L.F. Rivet, C. Smith, *The Place-names of Roman Britain* (London, Princeton 1979) 22ff
3 Tetelbierg best illustrated in Reding, *Tetelbierg* (chap. 1.5). For Boviolles, Grenier, *Manuel* (General Works) vol. 1.1, 255 (a modern publication much desired)
4 *CIL* 13. 4630, 4636
5 J. Krier, *PSH* 94 (1980) 139–94; Hollstein, *Eichendendrochronologie* (General Works) under Stadtbredimus
6 J.L. Massy, 'Les origines d'Amiens', *CAPic* 7 (1980) 115–36
7 R. Schindler in *Festschrift Trier* 121–210; Bögli, 'Aventicum'
8 *CIL* 13. 3671; *Esp*. 3960; cf. 3254 (Reims)
9 Vanvinckenroye, *Tongeren* 26ff; J.-C. Carmelez, *Septentrion* 10 (1980) 20–24
10 For Reims, see R. Neiss in *Colloque . . . urbaine*; for Thérouanne, H. Bernard, *Septentrion* 10 (1980) 41–60. On *cardo* and *decumanus*, J. le Gall, *BSAF* (1970) 292–307

11 Frere, 'Town-planning'; Massy, *Samarobriva*; C.V. Walthew, *Britannia* 12 (1981) 298–302

12 Summary by Cüppers in *Führer (RGZM) Trier* 3ff

13 Plan in Déchelette, *Manuel* (chap. 1.1) vol. 2.3, 949

14 Hollstein, *Eichendendrochronologie* (General Works) 135ff, superseding earlier defective dates; Cüppers, *Römerbrücken* and, in summary, *Führer (RGZM) Trier* 209

15 *Mela* 3.20; above ns. 7 and 12; Bayard and Massy, 'Amiens romain'; Carmelez and Neiss (above ns. 9 and 10)

16 H. Cüppers, H. Biévelet, *TZ* 28 (1965) 53–68; Cüppers in *Festschrift Trier* 211–62

17 E. Frézouls and E. Will in *Les cryptoportiques* 293–313, 342ff

18 D. Bayard, J.-L. Massy, *CAPic* 6 (1979) 131–52

19 Brief accounts by Wightman in *Roman Trier* (Regional Studies) 82–5 and by Cüppers in *Führer (RGZM) Trier* 198–208

20 Toussaint, *Metz* 168–77; recently, *Gallia* 34 (1976) 363 and in *Colloque . . urbaine. CIL* 13. 4324

21 Ancien and Tuffreau-Libre, *Soissons* 11–14

22 Toussaint, *Metz* 176–7; *CIL* 13. 4325

23 R. Jolin, *Bull. Cercle Arch. Mons* 62 (1950/53) 79–93

24 For amphitheatres generally, Grenier, *Manuel* (General Works) vol. 3.2. For Trier, Cüppers in *Führer (RGZM)* 165–77; for Metz, Toussaint, *Metz* 180–186; for Amiens, F. Vasselle in *Hommages à A. Grenier* vol. 3 (Brussels 1962; coll. *Latomus* 58) 1586–600

25 For theatres generally, Grenier, *Manuel* (General Works) vol. 3. Gose, *Altbachtal* and *Lenus Mars*; Bögli, 'Aventicum'

26 *BRGK* 58.12

27 W. von Massow, *TZ* 18 (1949) 149–69. For Soissons, Greg. Tur. *hist. franc.* 2.17

28 E. Gose, *TZ* 30 (1967) 81–100. *CIL* 13. 3694, 3707

29 Gose, *Altbachtal* and *Lenus Mars*

30 Grenier, *Manuel* (General Works) vols. 3.1, 416; J. Mertens, *Köln. Jahrb.* 9 (1967/8) 101–6

31 Leman, 'Un quartier romain'; J.-P. Adam, *RNord* 61 (1979) 823–33; G. Picard, *Actes Congrès nat. Soc. Sav.* 95 (*Reims 1970*) (Paris 1974) 59–73; R. Neiss, *Etudes Champ.* 2 (1976) 5–26; Th. Kraus, *Röm. Mitteil.* 72 (1965) 171–81

32 Summary of evidence for Trier palace by K.-P. Goethert, in *Führer (RGZM) Trier* 152–3; for Reims, C.-R. Brühl, *Palatium und Civitas* (chap. 10); for Tongeren, J. Mertens, W. Vanvinckenroye, *Arch Belg* 180 (1975)

33 Cüppers, *Römerbrücken* 154ff and *TZ* 36 (1973) 133–222; Gose, *Porta Nigra*

34 Vanvinckenroye, *Tongeren* 29ff; chap. 10.1

35 Bögli, 'Aventicum', and below chap. 4.4

36 Wightman, *Roman Trier* 72–3, 89ff; Cüppers in *Führer (RGZM) Trier* 182ff; Bögli, 'Aventicum'; Leman, 'Un quartier romain'; R. Neiss, *BSAChamp* 71 (1977) 71–9 and 72 (1979) 33–54

37 For mosaics, Parlasca and Stern (Mosaics etc.); for Amiens, Bayard and Massy; for Trier, W. Reusch, *TZ* 29 (1966) 187–235 and in *Ausgrabungen in Deutschland* (chap. 1 n. 7) 461–9

38 Cüppers (n. 36) and Neiss (ns. 31 and 36); *Esp.* 3608, cf. 3469
39 Summary of Trier potteries by Binsfeld in *Führer (RGZM) Trier* 232ff; see map in Vanvinckenroye, *Tongeren*; Reims material largely unpublished
40 Faider-Feytmans, *Bronzes de Bavai* (Bronzes etc.)
41 For Trier, Wightman, *Roman Trier* 91f; Toussaint, *Metz* 164f, cf. Keune, 'Sablon'; for Arras, G. Jelski, *Septentrion* 1 (1970) 135–46; for Soissons, Kaiser, *Soissons* (Regional Studies)
42 Chap. 3 n. 24
43 Bayard and Massy, 'Amiens romain'; Cüppers, *TZ* 36 (1973) 133–222
44 *CIL* 13. 9158; H. Baillien, *Limburg* 37 (1958) 1–10; A. Deman, *Das Altertum* 11 (1965) 115–24
45 Convenient overview by Haffner and Binsfeld in *Führer (RGZM) Westlicher Hunsrück* 180ff
46 Metzler, 'Titelberg' (chap. 2 n. 57) and R. Weiller, *PSH* 91 (1977) 17–116, 119–87; Tronquart, 'la Bûre' (chap. 1 n. 42)
47 For Velzeke, see Rogge (chap. 2 n. 78); for sites along Bavay-Köln road see generally Wankenne, *La Belgique*; also Brulet, *Liberchies* and *Braives*; for Dalheim, Krier (above n. 5); and J. Metzler, J. Zimmer, *Hémecht* 30 (1978) 351–82; J. Harmand in *Colloque sur le vicus*
48 H. Roosens, *Arch Belg* 21 (1954) and 20 (1954)
49 Destelbergen, definitive report to come; H. Thoen, *De gallo-romeinse nederzetting van Waasmunster-Pontrave* (Brussels 1967); Pommeroeul, G. de Boe, F. Hubert, *Arch Belg* 207 (1978); Dieulouard, *Gallia* 30 (1972) 349–54
50 Generally, consult Wankenne, *La Belgique*; Raepsaet-Charlier, *ANRW* 2.4; and *Tabula Imperii Romani, Lutetia* for detailed bibliography. For Bourbonne, Bonnard, *La Gaule thermale*
51 J. Heurgon in *Hommages à J. Bidez et à Fr. Cumont* (Brussels 1949; *coll. Latomus* 2); J.Y. Gosselin, C. Seillier, P. Leclercq, *Septentrion* 6 (1976) 5–15; Gosselin *et al.*, *Septentrion* 8 (1978) 18–22; C. Seillier, *Septentrion* 10 (1980) 25–9; see above chap. 3 n. 22
52 J. Mertens, *Le relais romain de Chameleux* (Brussels 1968)
53 *CIL* 13. 4132, *BRGK* 40.8 (Bitburg); *CIL* 13. 7555a (Belginum); 3450 (Nizy); 4565 (Marsal); 4310 (Vic); above chap. 3 n. 25
54 For Vendeuil-Caply, see plan in Agache, *La Somme* 240; Le Héraple, *CIL* 13. 4481 and Grenier, *Manuel* (General Works) vol. 1, 436; Pachten, R. Schindler, *BSDS* 11 (1964) 5–50
55 M. Cabal, *RNord* 55 (1973) 17–28
56 See below chap. 6.1.3; additional bibliography in Raepsaet-Charlier, *ANRW* 2.4
57 G.-Ch. Picard in *ANRW* 2.3 90–111; von Petrikovits, 'Kleinstädte'
58 See above n. 53
59 J. Metzler, J. Zimmer, *Hémecht* 27 (1975) 429–66; Kolling, 'Schwarzenacker'; H. Guillaume, *RNord* 42 (1960) 353–62; M. Amand, *Arch. Belg.* 143 (1973)
60 Belginum, W. Binsfeld, *AKorr* 6 (1976) 39–42, and for the cemeteries Haffner, *Wederath-Belginum* (chap. 1.4); old plan of Naix in Grenier, *Manuel* (General Works) vol. 1, 254; for Tournai, Wankenne, *La Belgique* or Amand, *Tournai*; Kolling, 'Schwarzenacker'
61 Discussions of urban population in P.-M. Duval, *Paris Antique* (Paris 1961) 249

and P. Broise, *Genève et son térritoire dans l'Antiquité* (Brussels 1974; *coll.*
Latomus 129), discussing the *vicus* at Fins d'Annecy
62 On the schools of Trier, Steinhausen, 'Hochschulen' (chap. 9.3)
63 See below chap. 7.2-3
64 For the Secundinii, below chap. 5.4 and 7.3
65 For Reims, Neiss (above n. 36); for Trier, Parlasca, *Mosaiken* and Reusch
(above n. 37); for Amiens forum, Bayard and Massy (above n. 18)

5 Rural Belgica in the Early Roman Empire

1 Oelmann, 'Mayen'; but see now D. Vermeersch, *CAPic* 8 (1981) 147ff
2 De Boe, 'Haccourt I'; Auve, *Gallia* 25 (1967) 184–5; Agache, 'Les fermes
indigènes'; Condé-Folie, Agache, *La Somme* 154, 169
3 *Gallia* 32 (1973) 333–5; de Boe, 'De stand van het onderzoek'
4 De Boe, *Acta Arch. Lovanesia* 4 (1971); A. Deyber, *RAE* 24 (1973) 129–43; H.
Cüppers, *TZ* 30 (1967) 114–43; Conchil-le-Temple, above chap. 1 n. 36
5 A. Brisson, J.-J. Hatt, *RAE* 6 (1955) 313–33; Brisson, Hatt, P. Roualet,
MSAMarne 82 (1967) 30–50; *Gallia* 12 (1954) 151; *Gallia* 27 (1969) 304, A.
Kolling, *BSDS* 18 (1971) 27–45; K. Klein, *BSDS* 3 (1929) 29–58 and 4 (1930)
13–54; further bibliography in Wightman, *Roman Trier* (Regional Studies)
279; R. Schindler, *BJ* 159 (1969) 281–9; A. Haffner, chap. 1 n. 34; de Boe,
van Impe, 'Rosmeer', cf. also R. Brulet, *La nécropole gallo-romaine de la Thure*
à Solre-sur-Sambre (Brussels 1972)
6 Lambert, 'Velaines-Popuelles'; H. Brunsting, in *Nieuws-bull. konink. Nederland.*
Oudheidkund. Bond 3 (1950) 112–4; W. Drack, *Der römische Gutshof bei Seeb*
(Basel 1969; *Arch. Führer der Schweiz* 1)
7 See discussion in Wightman, 'Pattern of rural settlement'
8 Percival, *Roman Villa* 31–3; but see E. Thevenot and M. Roblin, *RAE* 4
(1953) 78–85, 269–71, 271–2
9 C.E. Stevens, *RA* 9 (1937) 26–37; H. von Petrikovits, *Das römische Rheinland*
(Köln 1960) 109–24
10 O. Dilke, *The Roman Land Surveyors* (Newton Abbot 1971)
11 J. Mertens, *Arch Belg* 75 (1964); R. Fossier, *La terre et les hommes en Picardie*
(Paris/Louvain 1968) 138; F. Jacques, *RNord* 61 (1979) 783–823 and, with J.-L.
Pierre, *RNord* 63 (1981) 901–28; G. Grosjean, *JSGU* 50 (1963) 7–25
12 G. Raepsaet, 'La division du sol'; Dilke (above n. 10)
13 De Boe, 'Haccourt I'; for an overview of villa-building consult Raepsaet-
Charlier, *ANRW* 2.4 107ff
14 A. Kolling, *AKorr* 3 (1973) 219–22; Steinhausen, *Siedlungskunde* (Regional
Studies) 325ff
15 De Boe, 'Steenakker te Mortsel'
16 Anthée, de Maeyer, *Overblijfselen* and P. Spitaels, *Helinium* 10 (1970) 209–41;
Fliessem and Oberweis now conveniently in *Führer (RGZM) Südwestliche*
Eifel 127, 279; Fremersdorf, *Köln-Müngersdorf*
17 Agache, *La Somme* (Regional Studies); for Nennig and Wittlich *Führer*
(RGZM) Saarland and *Südwestliche Eifel*
18 Agache, 'La campagne' and *La Somme* 251ff
19 De Maeyer, *Overblifselen* or Mariën, *Belgica Antiqua* 482 for Rognée; *Führer*

(RGZM) Westlicher Hunsrück 104 for Weitersbach; J. Metzler, G. Thill, R. Weiller, 'Ein umwallter gallo-römischer Gutshof in "Miécher" bei Goeblingen', *Hémecht* 25 (1973) 375–99. For older or minor bibliography on Treveran villas, Wightman, *Roman Trier* (Regional Studies) 279ff; for Newel, Cüppers, Neyses, 'Newel'

20 For Belgian villas, de Maeyer, *Overblijfselen* and for Somme ones Agache, *La Somme*; Smith, 'Social structure'

21 De Boe, 'Haccourt II' and 'III'; for Téting, Grenier, *Habitations gauloises*

22 M. Lutz, *Gallia* 30 (1972) 41–82; for Bous, Stern, *Mosaïques* no. 175; Seeb, above n. 6; Oberentfelden, R. Laur-Belart, *Ur-Schweiz* 22 (1958) 33ff; D. Paunier, *JSGU* 56 (1971) 139–49

23 Metzler, Zimmer, Bakker, *Echternach*; G. Thill, *Hémecht* 19 (1967) 477–82

24 Somme mosaics in R. Agache, F. Vasselle, E. Will, *RNord* 11 (1965) 541–76

25 See below chap. 7.1; de Maeyer, *De romeinsche Villa's* 255; E. de Marmol, *Ann. Soc. arch. Namur* 15 (1881) 220–4. Villas are still little known in Champagne, F. Lefevre, *MSAMarne* 93 (1978) 49–57

26 For Wollersheim, H. von Petrikovits, *Germania* 34 (1956) 99–123

27 De Boe, 'Steenakker te Mortsel' and, with Lauwerijs, 'Oelegem'; W.E. van Es, *Wijster, a native village beyond the Imperial Frontier* (Amersfoort 1967); J.H.F. Bloemers, *Rijswijk (Z.H.), 'De Bult'. Eine Siedlung der Cananefaten* (Amersfoort 1978). For settlements in 'Free Germany', Jankuhn in *ANRW* 2.5.1 (chap. 1 n. 3); for Beaufort, R. Schindler, *Hémecht* 21 (1969) 37–50

28 Grenier, *Habitations gauloises* (with references to earlier work); Steinhausen, *Siedlungskunde* (Regional Studies) 262ff; R. Agache, *BSAPic* 52 (1967) 6–22

29 Stevens (above n. 9); M. Lutz, *ASHAL* 64 (1964) 25–39 and, with B. Babault, *ASHAL* 70 (1970) 1–13

30 Landscheid, R. Schindler, above n. 5 and *TZ* 36 (1973) 57–76; for Oelegem, above n. 27

31 Morville, de Marmol (above n. 25); Vellereille-le-Brayeux, de Maeyer, *Romeinsche Villa's* 107–8

32 J. Noel, *Arch Belg* 106 (1968), and with M. Amand, R.F. Jessup, *Arch Belg* 134 (1971); Cutry, *Gallia* 32 (1974) 335–8; cf. Y. Fremault, *Les cimetières gallo-romains de Remagne et Ste-Marie-Laneuville* (Brussels 1966)

33 Agache, *La Somme* (Regional Studies)

34 *CIL* 13. 4228; *BRGK* 17. 89 (*ILTG* 379); *CIL* 13. 3631; Chr. Rüger, *Epig. Stud.* 9 (1972) 251–60

35 For Hainaut, van Doorselaer, *Repertorium* (e.g. Rouveroy, Flavion, Rognée, Treignes); Soissonais, E. Moreau, *Album Caranda* (St. Quentin 1878–93); summary in Kaiser, *Soissons* (Regional Studies) 120ff and *CAPic* 1 (1974) 115–22

36 K.A. Seel, *BJ* 163 (1963) 317–41

37 For a useful summary of pollen evidence, Körber-Grohne, *Nutzpflanzen*; more specific to the area, Coûteaux, 'Recherches palynologiques'; cf. also chap. 1 n. 2

38 For a drop in population after conquest, see R.A. Oliver in B.C. Burnham, H.B. Johnson (eds.) *Invasion and Response: The Case of Roman Britain* (Oxford 1979; *BAR* 73)

39 Van Doorselaer, *Les nécropoles* (chap. 7.3); the time periods vary in length, and only a rough impression can be gained

40 Above n. 14

41 M.E. Jones in P.J. Casey (ed.), *The End of Roman Britain* (Oxford 1979; *BAR* 71) 231–51; cf. P. Salway, *Roman Britain* (Oxford 1981) 542ff and P. Fowler in *The Agricultural History of England and Wales* (ed. H.P. Finberg) vol. 1.1 (Cambridge 1981) 84ff

42 *SHA Marcus* 13.3; 17.2; cf. S.J. de Laet, H. Thoen, A. van Doorselaer, *Helinium* 10 (1970) 31–8

43 A. Verhulst in *L'archéologie du village médiéval* (Louvain/Gand 1967; Centre Belge d'histoire rurale); Roosens and Lux, 'Staberg te Rosmeer' (above chap. 1.4) 10ff; M. Born, *BSDS* 19 (1972) 73–88; cf. Landscheid and Mayen, above ns. 30, 36

44 Pliny *nat. hist.* 18.172; the most enlightening discussion is Kolendo, 'Origine et diffusion'

45 There is much need for a publication of plough-shares from museums. Saarbrücken and Sarrebourg have interesting examples: M. Lutz, *BSDS* 18 (1971) 53–6

46 *Esp.* 4092, 4044

47 Pliny *nat. hist.* 18.261; P. Lebel, *RAE* 11 (1960) 72–5

48 E. Delort, *Cahiers lorrains* (1951) 41–8

49 Pliny *nat. hist.* 18.296; Palladius 7.2.2-4; White, 'The economics' and J. Kolendo in R. Günther, G. Schrot (eds.), *Sozialökonomische Verhältnisse im Alten Orient und im klassischen Altertum* (Berlin 1961); R. Legros, *Latomus* 30 (1971) 696–702

50 Körber-Grohne, *Nutzpflanzen*; K.-H. Knörzer, *Novaesium V. Römerzeitliche Pflanzenfunde aus Neuss* (Berlin 1970; *Limesforschungen* 10) 128ff; Schindler, *Bundenbach* (chap. 1.4) 72ff

51 Pliny *nat. hist.* 18. 183; cf. 17. 42; P.J. Reynolds, *Farming in the Iron Age* (Cambridge 1976)

52 Generally, Körber-Grohne; for fruits, Pliny *nat. hist.* 15.39, 15.103; Julian, *Misopogon* 8. 342; for flax, Pliny *nat. hist.* 19.9

53 K. Schroeder, *TZ* 34 (1971) 97–117; cf. J. Baas, *Saalburg Jahrb.* 36 (1979) 45–82

54 Evidence for climate (still disputed) best summarized by Jankuhn in *ANRW* 2.5.1, 65ff. Low points in Hollstein's graphs for 54 BC and AD 68/9, Hollstein, *Eichendendrochronologie* (General Works); deteriorations in Denmark, K. Randsborg, *The Viking Age in Denmark: The Formation of a State* (London 1980) 48ff

55 Pliny *nat. hist.* 10.53; J.P. Wild, 'Clothing' and *Textile Manufacture* (chap. 6)

56 Generally, Clason, *Animal and Man* (chap. 1.6); see analysis in S. Martin-Kilcher, *Die Funde aus dem römischen Gutshof von Laufen-Müschhag* (Bern 1980) and (summary) *AKorr* 10 (1980) 185–94

57 Colum. 2.12.7; Auson. 3.1 (ed. Pieper); A. Daubigney, F. Favory, in *Actes du Colloque 1972 sur l'esclavage* (Paris 1974) 315–18 (includes comments on Marxist theories that relate slave supply to the growth of villas)

58 R. Bargeton, *BCPdeC* 10 (1976) 33–53

59 Bloemers, *Rijswijk* (above n. 27); cf. S. Applebaum, *Britannia* 6 (1975) 118ff

60 *Digest* 33. 7. 8 etc.; A. Steinwenter, *Sitzungsber. Wien. Ak. Wiss.* 221 (1942) 1–103

61 Daubigney, Favory (above n. 57); *CIL* 13. 4665. For a Marxist view, N. N.

Belova, summarized in *Bull. anal. d'hist. rom.* 9 (1970) 538–9, no. 1676
62 Wightman, 'Peasants and Potentates'
63 Above n. 23; both places appear as villas in Merovingian or Carolingian documents
64 Whatever the precise interpretation; see J.F. Drinkwater in A. King, M. Henig (eds.), *The Roman West in the Third Century* (Oxford 1981; *BAR* S–109) 215–34
65 On 'Grabgärten', E.M. Wightman, *BJ* 170 (1970) 211–32

6 The Materials and Structures of Economic Life

1 For references to clothing, Wild, 'Clothing' and *Textile Manufacture*
2 For a reaction to the views of M.I. Finley, *The Ancient Economy* (London 1973) see for example J. Gillam, K. Greene in A.C. and A.S. Anderson (eds.), *Roman Pottery Research in Britain and North-Western Europe: Papers presented to Graham Webster* (Oxford 1981; *BAR* S-123) 1–24
3 *CIL* 13. 4623–5, *BRGK* 17.90 (*ILTG* 387); Aubin, 'Rheinhandel'; P. Lebel, *RAE* 6 (1953) 360–5; Amand, 'Tournai' (chap. 4.4)
4 Y. Burnand, *RNord* 44 (1962) 409–12; M. Lutz, *ASHAL* 64 (1964), 25–39; H. Thoen in *The Roman West in the Third Century* (chap. 5 n. 64) 245–57
5 P.F. Hörter, *TZ* 40/41 (1977/8) 75–82; P. den Dooven, *Bull. soc. Verviétoise d'arch. et d'hist.* 53 (1966) 115–59
6 J. Röder in *Neue Ausgrabungen in Deutschland* (Berlin 1958) 268–85; Cüppers, *Römerbrücken* (above chap. 4.2) 154ff
7 Lebel (above n. 3); *Gallia* 22 (1964) 356–7 and 24 (1966) 288
8 A. Grenier in H. von Petrikovits, A. Steeger (eds.), *Festschrift A. Oxé* (Darmstadt 1938)
9 Gabelmann (above chap. 3 n.72); T. Panhuysen, *AKorr* 10 (1980) 63–5: *Esp.* 4376, 4382, 4397 and others, 4698, 4569ff
10 M.E. Mariën, 'Les monuments . . . d'Arlon' and E. Misciatelli, 'Les monuments . . . de Reims' (chap. 7.3); von Massow, *Neumagen*; Soulosse, *Esp.* 4845ff, Til-Châtel 3602ff; J. Röder, *BJ* 160 (1960) 137–60; cf. F. Braemer, J. Mallon, *BSAF* (1971) 35–48
11 For the Vosges, E. Linckenheld, *Les stèles funéraires* (chap. 7.2)
12 But see P. Horne in *The Roman West in the Third Century* (chap. 5 n. 64)
13 Stern, *Mosaïques* and Parlasca, *Mosaiken* (Mosaics etc.); for a different view, T.F.C. Blagg in *The Roman West in the Third Century* (chap. 5 n. 64) 167–88
14 R. Pleiner, 'Die Eisenverhüttung'
15 P. Pelet, *JSGU* 48 (1960/1) 104–6; de Maeyer, *Romeinsche Villa's* 45ff; for Morville, chap. 5 n. 25; A. van Doorselaer in *Römer und Germanen in Mitteleuropa* (Berlin 1975) 149–60
16 De Laet, van Doorselaer, 'Lokale ijzerwinning'; G. Stiller, *ASHAL* 70 (1970) 13–30; detailed publication from Tetelbierg awaited. For Laufen-Müschhag, Martin-Kilcher (chap. 5 n. 56)
17 P.-M. Duval, *Gallia* 10 (1952) 43–57; *Esp.* 5006, 4606, 4563, 7710, 4433, 5127, 5235, 5139 (cf. 4423, 5136); *CIL* 13. 5476; S. de Vaugirard, *RAE* 10 (1959) 202–9
18 H. von Petrikovits, *Zeitschr. f. Erzbergbau und Metallhüttenwesen*' 11 (1958) 594–600; Massy, *Samarobriva* (chap. 4); for British lead pigs near the mouth of the Aa, R. Delmaire, *Septentrion* 9 (1979) 19

19 Schindler in *Studien . . . Saarlandes* (chap. 1.4) 24ff, and *Kurtrier. Jahrb.* 7 (1967) 5–11

20 Y. Gaillet, *Cahiers hautmarnais* 85 (1966) 75–91; M. Amand, *Arch Belg* 171 (1975); Faider-Feytmans, *Les Bronzes*; Schindler, *BSDS* 11 (1964) 5–49

21 J. Werner, *BJ* 153 (1953) 126–7

22 Generally, J. Nenquin, *Salt* (chap. 1.1); H. Thoen in *Salt, the Study of an ancient Industry* (Colchester 1975) 56–60

23 E. Will in *Hommages à A. Grenier* (chap. 4 n. 24) 1649–57; for Colijnsplaat, *Deae Nehalenniae* (Catalogues)

24 *Esp.* 7249, *CIL* 13. 4543

25 For an overview, von Petrikovits, 'Der Wandel'

26 de Maeyer, *Romeinsche Villa's* 107–8, 203ff; *Arch* (1975) 40; H. Biévelet in *Etudes F. Courtoy* (Namur 1952) 83–94; D. Peacock in A. McWhirr (ed.) *Roman Brick and Tile* (Oxford 1979; *BAR* S–68) 5–10; P. Leman, *Caesarodunum* 12 (1977) 426–9

27 A. Kolling, *AKorr* 4 (1974) 81–7; *Gallia* 18 (1960) 233–4; J. Krier, *Hémecht* 33 (1981) 483–6; *TZ* 24/6 (1956/8) 561–3; S. Loeschcke, *TZ* 6 (1931) 1–7

28 Martin-Kilcher (chap. 5 n. 56); K. Hartley in J. Dore and K. Greene (eds.), *Roman Pottery Studies in Britain and Beyond* (Oxford 1977; *BAR* S–30) 5–18; R. Delmaire, *Septentrion* 2 (1972) 46–54

29 S.J. de Laet, H. Thoen, *Helinium* 4 (1964) 193–218 (cf. subsequent articles); M. Amand, *Arch Belg* 127 (1971); consult Raepsaet-Charlier, *ANRW* 2.4 for Braives, Amay, Clavier-Vervoz and Liberchies

30 M. Tuffreau-Libre, *La céramique commune*; J. Coupe, M. Tuffreau-Libre, F. Vincent, *RNord* 59 (1977) 501–44; G. Vion, *BCPdeC* 10 (1977) 87–100; D. Bayard, *CAPic* 7 (1980) 147–209; S. Loeschcke, *Trier. Heimatblätter* 1 (1922) 5–13

31 J. Dheedene, *Helinium* 1 (1961) 211–22

32 W. Drack, *Die helvetische Terra sigillata-Imitation* (Basel 1945); J. Fromols, *BSAChamp* (1939) 31ff; M. Bry, *Gallia* 3 (1944) 229ff; M. Tuffreau-Libre, *BSAChamp* 74 (1981) 81–93; J.H. Holwerda, *De Belgische Waar in Nijmegen* (Nijmegen 1941); A. Laufer, *La Péniche, un atelier de céramique à Lousonna* (Lausanne 1980)

33 H. Koethe in *Festschrift Oxé* (above n. 8) 89ff; W. Reusch, *Germania* 27 (1943) 146ff; S.J. de Laet, H. Thoen, *Helinium* 8 (1968) 3–21; Lutz, 'La céramique belge'

34 F. Maier, *RCRFA* 1 (1967) 54–61

35 S. Loeschcke, *Denkmäler vom Weinbau aus der Zeit der Römerherrschaft an Mosel, Saar and Ruwer* (Trier 1933); Chenet, Gaudron, *Argonne*

36 Lutz, 'Etat actuel' *Mittelbronn* and *Boucheporn*; J.-J. Hatt, *RCRFA* 19/20 (1979) 72–6

37 G. Stiller, H. Muller, H. Zumstein, J.-J. Hatt, *ASHAL* 60 (1960) 5–40; M. Lutz, *BSDS* 19 (1972) 65–72; M. Lutz, P. Weiller, *Cahiers lorrains* (1981) 33–50

38 Chenet. Gaudron, *Argonne*

39 Fölzer, *Bilderschüsseln*; Huld-Zetsche, *Werkstatt I*

40 Grenier (above n. 8); J.-P. Jacob, H. Leredde, *RCRFA* 21/22 (1982) 89–104; H. Cockle, *JRS* 71 (1981) 87–97; note a villa with mosaic near Boucheporn (Stern, *Mosaïques* 60); *Esp.* 4387, *CIL* 13. 11361

41 M. Lutz, *Mém. de l'Acad. de Metz* (1976) 63–74

42 Lerat, Jeannin, *Luxeuil*; B. Hofmann, *RCRFA* 19/20 (1979) 214–25; A. King in *The Roman West in the Third Century* (chap. 5 n. 64); D. Bayard (above n. 30)

43 M.M. Chassaing, *RAE* 12 (1961) 89–106; for small scale manufacture, G. Thill, *Hémecht* 20 (1968) 521–7

44 K. Hopkins, 'Taxes and Trade'

45 Dion, *La vigne*; Loeschcke, *Weinbau* (n. 35); A. Neyses, *AKorr* 7 (1977) 217–24; but see P. Kneissel, *BJ* 181 (1981) 169–204

46 *Esp.* 4148, 5193, 5216; Loeschcke, *Weinbau* (n. 35); J. Vierin, Ch. Léva, *Latomus* 20 (1961) 759–84

47 *Esp.* 3232, 4148; *BRGK* 17.41, *CIL* 13. 11319, *Esp.* 4049

48 D. Manacorda, *JRS* 68 (1978) 122ff

49 Martial 13.54; Pliny *nat. hist.* 10.53, 11.262; Varro *de re rust.* 2.4.10

50 Wild, *Textile Manufacture*; Strabo 4.4.3; Pliny *nat. hist.* 8. 191–3; Juvenal 9.30; Martial 6.11.7; *Edict. Diocl.* 19.32, 45, 46, 48, 54, 60; *Esp.* 5069, 5123, 7556, 4210, 5261, 4043, 3683, 3786; Dragendorff, Krüger, *Igel*; E. Zahn, *Die Igeler Säule bei Trier* (Neuss 1976)

51 Kolling, 'Schwarzenacker' (chap. 4.4); M. Cabal, *RNord* 55 (1973) 17–28; Wild, *Textile Manufacture* 69ff

52 *CIL* 13. 4564

53 Drinkwater, 'Die Sekundinier'; *CIL* 5.5929

54 Strabo 4.1.2 and 14

55 H. Sec, *Caesarodunum* 12 (1977); generally, Bonnard, *La navigation*

56 De Boe and Hubert, 'Pommeroeul', also *AKorr* 6 (1976) 227–34

57 G. Raepsaet, *AC* 48 (1979) 171–6

58 *Gallia* 30 (1972) 351

59 *Esp.* 5833, 5261, 4120, 5264, 3232; von Massow, *Neumagen*; Dragendorff, Krüger, *Igel*

60 *CIL* 13. 4335, *BRGK* 58.1, *CIL* 13. 2839; for the *utriclarii* as shippers of wine and other liquids in skins, Kneissl (above n. 45)

61 Hofmann (above n. 42)

62 G. Raepsaet, 'L'organisation du commerce' and, with M. Th. Raepsaet-Charlier, R. Clausse, *Le Pays Gaumais* 18/19 (1977/8) 23–105

63 K. Greene and D.P.S. Peacock in *Roman Shipping and Trade* 52–58, 59–61 (but the absence of amphorae in the west of Gaul is exaggerated); cf. I. Hodder, *Britannia* 5 (1974) 340–59

64 P.R. Frank, *BSDS* 16 (1969) 161–3; H. Cüppers, *TZ* 37 (1974) 149–73

65 Grenier, 'La Gaule romaine' 539 for classic statement on 'bourgeoisie'; see also Rostovtzeff, *Social and Economic History,* and, *contra*, Finley, *The Roman Economy passim*

66 E.g. de Boe, 'De stand von het onderzoek' (chap. 5)

67 *CIL* 13. 1911. 1688; P. Middleton, 'Army supply'; Cracco Ruggini, 'Les structures'; A. Hondius-Crone, *The temple of Nehalennia at Domburg* (Amsterdam 1955); Stuart, *Deae Nehalenniae* (Catalogues). Negotiatores etc.: Treveri, *CIL* 13. 2029, 2033, 1911; 634, 2839, *falsae* 450, *BRGK* 48. 3, *BRGK* 58. 106, *Deae Nehalenniae* nos. 1, 22; Mediomatrici, *CIL* 13. 4335, 4336, 11360, *CIL* 5. 5929; Nervii, *CIL* 13. 8338, 8725, 1056; Tungri, *CIL* 13. 8815; Viromandui, *CIL* 13. 1688

68 M. Hassall in *Roman Shipping and Trade* 41–8

69 Middleton (above n. 67); Drinkwater, 'The Gallic Julii' (chap. 3.4); against any idea of direction, Schlippschuh, *Die Händler*

70 J.-B. Giard, *JS* (1975) 81–102; for site finds, consult the various *Fundmünzen* volumes (Coins)

71 Van de Weerd, 'Het economische bloeitijdperk'

7 Romanized Belgica

1 Tac. *hist.* 4. 74

2 G. Alföldy, *Die Legionslegaten der römischen Rheinarmeen* (Köln/Graz 1967; *Epig. Stud.* 3) 11ff; Wightman, 'The Lingones' (chap. 3.1); Eutropius 8.2, Orosius 7.12; above chap. 3 n. 61; *CIL* 13. 4290

3 Meyers, *L'administration* (chap. 3.2); F. Jacques, 'Les cens'

4 Jullian, *La Gaule* (General Works) vol. 4, 470ff; *SHA Hadrian* 10–12, Aurel. Victor *epit.* 14.5

5 *CIL* 2. 6278, *CIL* 13. 1688

6 *SHA Marcus* 24.5, *Did. Julianus* 1.7–8

7 Thirion, *Trésors* (chap. 8), 16; Amiens, Bayard and Massy, 'Amiens romain' (chap. 4.2); Arras, J. Jelski, *RNord* 62 (1980) 832–56; M. Amand, *Arch Belg* 102 (1968); J. Mertens, *Arch Belg* 206 (1978) 73–76

8 *SHA Marcus* 22.10; Herodian 1.10; G. Alföldy, *BJ* 171 (1971) 367–76; *CIL* 11. 6053; Wilmanns, 'Die Doppelurkunde'; cf. Aurelius Victor 16.13; L. Flam-Zuckermann, 'Le phénomène du brigandage'

9 Chap. 5 n. 42; Orosius 7. 27, 7–12 for various 'plagues', some spreading to the west

10 *CIL* 13. 6800; *CIL* 3. 10471–3, cf. 13. 7945; R. Saxer, *Untersuchungen zu den Vexillationen des römischen Kaiserheeres von Augustus bis Diocletian* (Köln/Graz 1967; *Epig. Stud.* 1) 48–9; Alföldy, *Legionslegaten* (above n. 2) 51

11 Meyers, *L'administration*

12 For league-stones, *CIL* 13. 9028, 9031, 9129, 9158 (*miliarium Tongrense*)

13 Galsterer-Kröll, 'Zum *ius Latii*' (chap. 3.2)

14 *CIL* 13. 3528, 1688

15 Colin, 'Sénateurs gaulois'; Pflaum, *Thorigny* (chap. 8), *CIL* 13. 3162

16 *CIL* 13. 2669, 1949; Krier, *Die Treverer* (chap. 3.4) 36, 61

17 *Contra*, Drinkwater, 'The Gallic Julii' (chap. 3.4); cf. Cracco Ruggini (chap. 6.1); *CIL* 13. 11179, Krier, *Die Treverer* (chap. 3.4) 32

18 *CIL* 13. 2029, 542; Krier, *Die Treverer* (chap. 3.4) 48, 16

19 H.G. Horn, *AKorr* 3 (1973) 47–9; K. Polaschek, *TZ* 34 (1971) 119–42; *Esp.* 4831, 4839, 4678; for later workshops, see Koethe, Mariën, Hatt, also *TZ* 27 (1964) 130–8

20 Hahl, *Stilentwicklung*; G. Bauchhenss, *Die Juppitersaülen der Provinz Germania Superior* (Bonn 1981; *BJ Beiheft* 41); H. Walter, *La sculpture funéraire gallo-romaine en Franche-Comté* (Paris 1974)

21 For inscriptions, *CIL* 13. 3596, *BRGK* 17.3; Roosens, 'Bestattungsritual'

22 Linckenheld, *Stèles funéraires*

23 E.g. A. Mócsy, *Gesellschaft und Romanisation in der römischen Provinz Moesia Superior* (Budapest 1970)

24 *CIL* 13. 1036, 5071, 11179, 4103, 4350, 4325, 11454; an example of a Belgic family (all with single names) in *CIL* 13. 8342, 8409, 8341
25 *CIL* 13. 3636, 4623–5, 4346, 4380, 634 (cf. 3979), 11313, 4142
26 Morris, 'Changing fashions'; *CIL* 13. 3645, 3547
27 M. Hassall (chap. 6 n. 68); *Deae Nehalenniae* (Catalogues) no. 45; *CIL* 13. 3620
28 *CIL* 13. 11385, 4385
29 *CIL* 13. 3700, 4344, (*BRGK* 17. 26), 3649, 3986
30 *CIL* 13. 4016, 4403
31 See articles of Weisgerber and cf. J. Guerrier, *RAE* 30 (1979) 219–32
32 *CIL* 13. 3707, 3652, 4159, 4113, 11644, 4350, 5995, 4555, 4534
33 R. G. Collingwood, *The Roman Inscriptions of Britain* I (Oxford 1965) no. 12; *CIL* 13. 5708; von Massow, *Neumagen*; Dragendorff and Krüger, *Igel* (chap. 6); E. Will in *Actes du colloque sur les influences helléniques en Gaule* (Dijon 1958) 123–31
34 *BRGK* 17.3, cf. G.V. Lux, H. Roosens, *Arch Belg* 121 (1970) and 128 (1970); *Esp.* 3851, 3791, 3926, 3956, 3986 for marble sarcophagi, which were sometimes moved in medieval times; for the objects from tumuli, Mariën, *Belgica Antiqua*; Roman chariot burial, M.E. Mariën, *AKorr* 9 (1979) 91–5; chapels, D. Krencker, *Germania* 6 (1922) 8–10
35 Cüppers, Neyses, 'Newel' (chap. 5); H. Roosens, G.V. Lux, *Arch Belg* 147 (1973)
36 E.g. *Esp.* 4045 (4147), 4043 (3786), 7249, 4221, 8442, 4387, 4611, 4295. The monuments from Metz well illustrate trades; to those in Espérandieu should be added the ones in *Gallia* 34 (1976) 362ff; cf. also the stones from Reims, Arlon and Soulosse; M. Reddé, *Gallia* 36 (1978) 43–63 (not in fact complete)
37 E.g. at Wederath: Haffner, *Wederath-Belginum* (chap. 1.6)
38 Linckenheld, *Les stèles funéraires*; cf. F. Oelmann in *Studi Aquileiesi offerti a Giovanni Brusin* (Aquileia 1953) 177ff
39 Caesar *bell. gall.* 6.13, Tacitus *Germania* 43; *AE* (1894) 18; the most pragmatic introduction is Duval, *Les dieux*; bibliography is enormous; consult also Raepsaet-Charlier, *ANRW* 2.4 and Wightman in *ANRW* 2.18
40 Hatt, 'L'évolution'; A. Ross, *EC* 9 (1961) 405–38
41 Lucan 1. 441ff; commentaries in Zwicker, *Fontes* vol. 1, 49f
42 Luxeuil, *Esp.* 5347; S. Deyts, *RAE* 17 (1966) 198–211; for bronzes, see especially Faider-Feytmans, *Les Bronzes*
43 Terracottas not extensively studied, but see G. Weisgerber, *BSDS* 21 (1974) 77–94
44 *Esp.* 3133, 4929; *CIL* 13. 3026 (cf. *ILTG* 331), 3656
45 *Esp.* 4831, 4839, 4678, 7702
46 *Esp.* 3653, 4195, 3666, 2067, 7700, 3137, 7234, 4937; P.F. Bober, *Amer. Journ. Arch.* 55 (1951) 13–51; on stags, E. Linckenheld, *CAAAH* 9 (1947–50) 67–114
47 *Esp.* 7800, 4591, 4793; P. Lambrechts, *De geestelijke weerstand van de westelijke provincies tegen Rom* (Brussels 1966; *K Vl Ak Lett.* 28); G. Sander, *Helinium* 6 (1966) 139–45, cf. R. MacMullen, *Historia* 14 (1965) 93–104
48 *CIL* 13. 1444, 4651, 4294–7; *Esp.* 4566 (*CIL* 13. 4542), *CIL* 13. 3632, 3653, 3969 (examples only); on Sucellus, W. Binsfeld, in *Festschrift Landesmuseum Trier* (chap. 4) 263–70
49 *CIL* 13. 4113, 7848, *BRGK* 17.5, *Esp.* 4442; *BRGK* 17.5, *Esp.* 3796 (3930,

3992 etc.); *CIL* 13. 3585, 8789, and see *Deae Nehalenniae* (Catalogues); *Esp.* 4350–6, 4449, 4479, *CIL* 13. 7555a, *CIL* 6. 32799

50 E.g. *BRGK* 40. 9, *CIL* 13. 4192–3, *BRGK* 17.69, *CIL* 4542–3 (*Esp.* 4566, 4568); on Apollo and Sirona, Schleiermacher, 'Studien'

51 *CIL* 13. 4257, *BRGK* 17. 80, *CIL* 13. 11346, 4507, 3970, 4049, 3635, 4564, 4130; *BRGK* 17. 20–21 etc., *ILTG* 351, *CIL* 13. 5340

52 *BRGK* 17. 15–16, *CIL* 13. 4256; *Esp.* 4664 (*CIL* 13. 4668), cf. *Esp.* 4668

53 *Esp.* 7217, cf. *CIL* 3527; M. Green, *Latomus* 38 (1979) 345–67

54 List of Jupiter-giant groups in Lambrechts, *Contributions* 98–9 (he does not include bases); perhaps the most striking is *Esp.* 4425 (Merten); G.C. Picard, *Gallia* 35 (1977) 89–113; G. Bauchhenss, *AKorr* 4 (1974) 359–64

55 Walter, *The Cult of Mithras*; G. Faider-Feytmans, *Bull. ARB Beaux-Arts* 57 (1975) 156–8; Schwertheim, *Orientalische Gottheiten*; Faider-Feytmans, *Les Bronzes*

56 *Seviri Augustales*, of native and/or freedman origin, at Metz and Trier, *CIL* 13. 2669, 4325, 4192, 11353, 4335, 1949, 4153, 4154, 4208 (*AE* 1966. 256), 4251, 4325, 11358, *CIL* 3. 5797; R. Duthoy, *AC* 39 (1970) 88–101; J. Harmand, *Latomus* 26 (1967) 957–86; M.-Th. Raepsaet-Charlier in *ANRW* 2.3 232–82; for gods and cults among the Treveri, see Wightman, *Roman Trier* (Regional Studies)

57 Above, chap. 4.2; *CIL* 13. 3636, 3647; J.-L. Cadoux, *Latomus* 37 (1978) 325–60

58 R. Daviet in *Mélanges A. Piganiol* (chap. 2 n. 8) 337–42; G. Faider-Feytmans, *Bull. ARB Beaux-Arts* 61 (1979) 20–41

59 B. Bodson, *Rev. d'arch. et d'hist. d'art Louvain* 11 (1978) 191–2; *CIL* 13. 4132, *BRGK* 40.8 (Bitburg), *BRGK* 17. 238 (Wederath), *CIL* 13. 3450 (Nizy-le-Comte); W. Schleiermacher, *Germania* 41 (1963) 38–53; Cadoux (above n. 57); R. Agache, *Caesarodunum* 8 (1973) 50–5 (Rouvroy, Eu, Vendeuil-Caply); Metzler *et al.*, *Echternach* (chap. 5) 312; W. Binsfeld, *TZ* 32 (1969) 239–68

60 R. Billoret, *Grand la gallo-romaine* (Nancy 1972); F. Braemer, *Caesarodunum* 8 (1973) 144–50

61 Horne and King, 'Romano-Celtic temples'; M. Lutz, *Caesarodunum* 8 (1973) 108–13

62 Asclepius, *CIL* 13. 3636; soldiers, *CIL* 13. 3605, 3645, 4630, 3592; Mithras, *ILTG* 380, *BRGK* 17. 24; high-ranking men, *ILTG* 351, *CIL* 13. 4030, 3528; *collegia*, *BRGK* 27. 1, 7, *CIL* 13. 11313

63 *BRGK* 40.8; E. Thevenot in *Hommages à A. Grenier* (chap. 4 n. 24) 1476–90

64 On 'religious' names, J.-J. Hatt, *La Tombe* 43ff (though with untrustworthy precision); for a limited sector of the population R. Duthoy, *AC* 39 (1970) 88–101

65 Krier, *Die Treverer* (chap. 3.4); Drioux, 'Les Nerviens'; van de Weerd, 'De Belgen'; H.G. Pflaum, *BSAF* (1965) 268–70

66 Above n. 46

67 *CIL* 13. 4132 (Bitburg); G. Faider-Feytmans, *Helinium* 20 (1980) 3–43

68 For a view of 'capitalism' that may fit the situation, F. Braudel, *Afterthoughts on Material Civilization and Capitalism* (Baltimore 1977)

8   The Gallic Empire

1 J.V. Buttrey, *Amer. Num. Soc. Mus. Notes* 18 (1972) 33–58; J.-M. Carrié in *Armées et fiscalité dans le monde antique* (Paris 1977; *Colloque internat. CNRS* 936) 373–94; S. Mrozek, *Prix et rémunération dans l'occident romain* (Gdansk 1975)

2 Flam-Zuckermann (chap. 7.1); R. MacMullen, *Rev. int. droits de l'antiq.* 10 (1963) 221–5; ideas taken further by R. van Dam, *Heretics, Bandits and Bishops: studies in the religion and society of late Roman Gaul and Spain* diss. Cambridge (1974)

3 For appointment of magistrates, W. Seston, *BSAF* (1962) 314–25; generally, P. Garnsey in *ANRW* 2.1 229–52; on changing ambitions, Brown, *Late Antiquity* chap. 2; *CIL* 13. 11350 for implied *praeses*

4 H.-G. Pflaum, *Thorigny* with comments by Carcopino, *REA* (1948) 336–47 (*CIL* 13. 3162); for Timesitheus, *CIL* 13. 1807, also Pflaum, *Les Carrières procuratoriennes équestres* (Paris 1962) vol. 2 no. 317; Eutropius 9.4; *RIC* vol. 4, pt. 3, 66–7

5 Demougeot, *La formation* vol. 1, 257–312; on the political implications, H. von Petrikovits in *Festschrift A. Oxé* (chap. 6 n. 8) 247ff

6 Demougeot, *La formation* 242–56, 465–92; literary sources conveniently collected in Riese, *Litteratur* (Sources). On the mints, M. Christol in *Armées et Fiscalité* (above n. 1) 235–78

7 On the chronology and political aims of the Gallic Empire, Koenig, *Usurpatoren*; readable short account (with outdated chronology and a certain patriotic fervour) in Jullian, *La Gaule* (General Works) vol. 4, 470–92 (575 n. 2 for the 'choice' of the Gauls); on the social context, J.F. Drinkwater, *The Gallic Empire* diss. Oxford

8 P. Bastien, *RN* (1958) 59–78; B. Stolte, *Brabantia* (1954) 50–53

9 Eutrop. 9.10; Orosius 7.22.10ff (Jullian vol. 4, 586 n. 4)

10 Eutrop. 9.10 (*seditiones multas*); Polem. Silv. *Laterc.* 3 (*Chron. min.* ed. Mommsen 522)

11 On the literary problems, T.D. Barnes, *The sources of the Historia Augusta* (Brussels 1978; *coll. Latomus* 155)

12 *CIL* 13. 11975/6 (*burgus* at Liesenich); for fortifications generally, chap. 11.1

13 Koenig, *Usurpatoren* 172–81; *CIL* 6. 1641; H.-G. Pflaum in *Actes du congrès international de numismatique* (Paris 1953) vol. 2, 273–80 (*Scripta Varia* vol. 2, 68–75); P. le Gentilhomme, *BSAF* (1943/4) 69ff; I. Koenig, *Latomus* 33 (1974) 51–6

14 Use of the hoards to reconstruct history especially by Koethe, 'Zur Geschichte Galliens' based on A. Blanchet, *Les trésors de monnaies romaines et les invasions germaniques en Gaule* (Paris 1900); P. van Gansbeke, *RBN* 98 (1952) 8–22 and *Latomus* 14 (1955) 404–25 tried for even greater precision

15 J.P.C. Kent in P.J. Casey, R. Reece (eds.), *Coins and the Archaeologist* (Oxford 1974; *BAR* 4) 184–200; cf. the very small number of hoards that can be connected with the troubles of 69/70, Thirion, *Trésors*, 11ff

16 In addition to discussion in Thirion, *Trésors*, the following studies of individual hoards are of importance: 1. hoards ending with Postumus: P. Bastien (Muirancourt), *Gazette num. Suisse* 15 (1965) 137–342; M. Thirion (Basècles),

Helinium 6 (1966) 193–217; J. Lallemand (Oombergen), *Helinium* 11 (1974) 48–60; W. Binsfeld (Trier), *TZ* 35 (1972) 127–33: 2. hoards containing coins of Tetricus and imitations, but dated by coins of the Central Empire: P. le Gentilhomme (la Vineuse), *RN* (1942) 37ff and (Coesmes), *Gallia* 5 (1947) 319–49; R. Weiller (Burmerange), *Helinium* 8 (1968) 131–48 and (Tetelbierg), *Num. Chron.* (1969) 163–76; Lallemand and Thirion, *St. Mard I*

17 H. Mattingly in *Studies in Roman Economic and Social History in Honour of A.C. Johnson* (Princeton 1951) 275–89; C.E. King in *The Roman West in the Third Century* (chap. 5 n. 64)

18 J. Lallemand in *Mélanges de numismatique, d'archéologie et d'histoire offerts à Jean Lafaurie* (Paris 1980) 117–23

19 Legends conveniently to hand in Lafaurie, 'L'empire gaulois'; J.F. Drinkwater, *Num. Chron.* (1971) 325–6; Bastien, *Le monnayage de bronze*

20 Lallemand and Thirion, *St. Mard I*; Giard, 'La monnaie locale'; King (above n. 17)

21 J. Hiernard in M.R. Alföldi (ed.), *Studien zu Fundmünzen der Antike I* (Bad Homburg/Berlin 1979) 39–78

22 Schindler, *BSDS* 11 (1964) espec. 15–24

23 F. Baratte, *Gallia* 38 (1980) 253–64; for hoards in Chaourse (Aisne) and Trier, D.E. Strong, *Greek and Roman Silver Plate* (London 1966); Bastien, 'Trésors de la Gaule septentrionale'

24 Overview of sources best obtained from Jullian, *La Gaule* (General Works) vol. 4 598–602, or Riese, *Litteratur* (Sources); main ones are Eutropius 9.17; Zosimus 1.67, Julian *Caesares* 403.H, *SHA Probus* 13; Orosius 7.24.2 (but cf. 7.22.7 and 7.41.2); Aurel. Vict. *Caes.* 37 (but cf. 33)

25 For walls, chap. 10.1; *SHA Probus* 15.1, 18.8

26 Zosimus 1.67; cf. the strange 'rain' of wool among the Atrebates, Orosius 7.32.18

27 A. Chatagnol, *BSAF* (1969) 78–98

28 *SHA Firmus* 2

29 Paneg. 2.4.3; 2.6.1 (ed. Galletier); Czuth, *Die Quellen*

30 E.A. Thompson, *Past and Present* 2 (1952) 11ff

31 *RIC* vol. 5 pt. 2, 578–9; Auson. *epist.* 17.1, cf. 14.1

32 Strongly argued by Van Dam (above n. 2)

33 Bauchhenss, *Die Jupitersäulen* and Hahl, *Stilentwicklung* (chap. 7.2 and n. 20)

34 Gricourt, 'Les événements'; Bastien, Metzger, *Beaurains*; Casey, 'Carausius and Allectus'

9 Northern Gaul and the Later Empire

1 Lactantius *mort. pers.* 7.4 (*provinciae quoque in frusta concisae*); Verona List conveniently summarized in Jones, *Later Roman Empire* vol. 2, 1451ff; for general background, Jones vol. 1, and for the Gallic provinces, Nesselhauf, *Verwaltung*

2 Nesselhauf, *Verwaltung* 88, citing *Cod. Theod.* 7.20.1.2

3 Seston, *BSAF* (1962) 314–25, citing Ulpian in *Digest* 49.4.1; *CIL* 13. 3693

4 Veyne, 'Clientèle et corruption'

5 Harmand, *Le patronat* 462ff; *Cod. Theod.* 1.28.1, 1.29.6

6 A.L.F. Rivet in R. Goodburn, P. Bartholomew (eds.), *Aspects of the Notitia Dignitatum* (Oxford 1976; *BAR* S–15) 119–42; on Boulogne, Delmaire, 'Civitas Morinorum' (chap. 3.1); C. Seillier in *The Saxon Shore* (London 1977; *CBA Research Report* 18) 31–4

7 Hoffmann, *Bewegungsheer* 160ff

8 Jullian, *La Gaule* vol. 7, 107 n. 2; J.-J. Hatt, *Latomus* 9 (1950) 427ff; R. Billoret, *RAE* 20 (1969) 219–33

9 For a somewhat different conclusion, Rouche, 'Le changement de nom'; note also Laeti Nemetacenses at Arras, *Not. Dig. Occ.* 42.40

10 Cf. Ausonius' house just outside Bordeaux, Auson. *epist.* 25. 90–98; R. Etienne, *Bordeaux Antique* (Bordeaux 1962) 357–8

11 Salvian, *gub. Dei* 5.28ff; see below chap. 12.1

12 Veyne (above n. 4)

13 Ammianus, bks. 16–18 for Julian's campaigns; J.C. Mann in *Aspects of the Notitia Dignitatum* (above n. 6) 1–10; on the army, Hoffmann, *Bewegungsheer* and 'Die Gallienarmee'

14 Generally, Jones and Nesselhauf (n. 1); Birley, 'The economic effects' (chap. 12); Zosimus 2.34; Lactantius *mort. pers.* 7.2

15 MacMullen, *Soldier and Civilian*; R. Tomlin in *Aspects of the Notitia Dignitatum* (above n. 6)

16 I. Creus, *Arch Belg* 179 (1975); J. Mertens, L. van Impe, *Arch Belg* 206 (1978) 73–76; Mertens, 'Oudenburg and the northern sector'; D. de Vries, *BROB* 17 (1967) 227–60; H. Dijkstra, F.C. Ketelaar, *Brittenburg* (Bussum 1965); cf. Johnson, *Saxon Shore* 83ff

17 Johnson, *Saxon Shore* 87ff; and in *The Saxon Shore* (above n. 6); for Boulogne, Seillier (above n. 6); Mertens, 'Oudenburg and the northern sector'

18 Mertens, 'Recherches récentes' gives bibliography on individual sites; Liesenich (chap. 8 n. 12); T. Bechert, *AKorr* 8 (1978) 127–32; E.M. Wightman in *Roman Frontier Studies* (Tel Aviv 1971) 46–51

19 J. Mertens, R. Brulet, *Arch Belg* 163 (1974) 61–120; J. Lallemand, *RBN* 120 (1974) 35–72

20 Hoffmann, *Bewegungsheer* 149, 160, 180ff

21 Mertens, 'Recherches récentes'; older views of a frontier in J. Vannérus, *Le Limes et les fortifications gallo-romains de Belgique; enquête toponymique* (Brussels 1943); von Petrikovits, (chap. 8 n. 5), and more recently in *Rheinische Geschichte* (General Works) 196, 218ff; on Toxandria, Roosens (Regional Studies) and C.E. Stevens in *RE* VIA

22 *Paneg.* 2 (10) 5 (ed. Galletier)

23 Treaties best discussed by von Petrikovits (chap. 8 n. 5) and less handily in Demougeot, *La formation* vol. 2.1; von Petrikovits, *Rheinische Geschichte* (General Works) 340; Eusebius, *vita Const.* 1.5; Ammianus 17.8.3, cf. Libanius *Orat.* 18.75

24 *Paneg.* 6.11.5; 6.12.3; E. Demougeot, 'A propos des lètes' and other references in chap. 11.2; for auxiliary units, Hoffmann, *Bewegungsheer* 149, 160

25 Ammianus 14.10. 8–14

26 Julian *ad Athen.* 278d–279b; J. Schwartz, *CAAAH* 1 (1957) 33–49; W. Binsfeld, *TZ* 36 (1973) 119–32 and 38 (1975) 101–8; K.-J. Gilles, *TZ* 43/4 (1980/81) 317–39

27 Zosimus 2.53.4; for additional sources, here and elsewhere, Jullian, *La Gaule* (General Works) vol. 7 (156), or Riese, *Litteratur*
28 Besides Jullian, von Petrikovits, (chap. 8 n. 5) and *Rheinische Geschichte* (General Works) 202ff
29 See Waas, *Germanen* (chap. 9.3) and individual entries in Jones etc., *Prosopography*
30 See the introduction to Galletier's edition; Haarhoff, *Schools of Gaul*
31 *Paneg.* 4.12.2 (to Constantius, after the final victory)
32 *Paneg.* 4.21.2; 5, *passim*, espec. 18.1–2
33 See chap. 10.3; *Paneg.* 6.22.4 for Trier's birthday; *Paneg.* 7 for the jealousy of Autun; on the schools of Trier, Haarhoff, *Schools of Gaul* and Steinhausen, 'Hochschulen'; also Galletier's introduction to each panegyric
34 Bastien, Metzger, *Le trésor de Beaurains* (chap. 8); *Paneg.* 4.2.2; 4.4.3
35 Jones, *Later Roman Empire* 266ff gives lower figures than Nesselhauf, *Verwaltung*, 83. On Eumenius and Mamertinus, Galletier's introduction to *Paneg.* 5. 2 and 11, or Jones etc., *Prosopography*. *Paneg.* 7.23 for the shameless commendation of the orator's sons to Constantine in 310
36 *Paneg.* 7.21.4 (above n. 8)
37 Jones, *Later Roman Empire* 366ff
38 For a Gallic perspective, Jullian, *La Gaule* vol. 7, 144ff
39 Zosimus 2.42.2ff; for detailed sources, Jullian, *La Gaule* (General Works) vol. 7, 150ff; Bastien, *Le monnayage de Magnence*; J.P.C. Kent, *Num. Chron.* (1959) 105–8
40 Demougeot, *La formation* vol. 2 86ff; for coin hoards, above n. 26
41 Ammianus, bks. 16–18; brief account in G.W. Bowersock, *Julian the Apostate* (Cambridge, Mass. 1978) 33ff; for archaeological evidence, von Petrikovits, *Rheinische Geschichte* (General Works) 196ff; for fortifications in Lorraine, chap. 10.1
42 Ammianus 16.5.14–15, cf. 17.3.4–5
43 For the careers of these individuals, Jones etc., *Prosopography*
44 Jullian, *La Gaule* vol. 7, 176, 209
45 Ammianus 10.9.6–7; 21.1.4; Jones etc., *Prosopography*
46 Ammianus 17.6.1–3
47 For Trier, below chap. 10.3; Symmachus, *orat.* 1.15 (*MGH AA* 6 pt. 1, 322); Steinhausen, 'Hieronymus und Lactanz'; Keune, in *TZ* 1 (1926) 141–3; Wightman, *Roman Trier* (Regional Studies) 62ff
48 For the influence of Ausonius, Matthews, *Western Aristocracies* 56ff; Beck, *Die 'Tres Galliae'*
49 Waas, *Germanen* and Jones etc., *Prosopography*; see also the more controversial Bappo, possibly the person mentioned by Ausonius in *Mosella* 409–10, refs. in edition of C.-M. Ternes (Paris 1972)
50 Jones etc., *Prosopography*; J.F. Matthews, *Latomus* 30 (1971) 1073–99; L. Pietri, *RNord* 52 (1970) 443–53
51 Ausonius *Mosella* 400 and 18.13 (ed. Peiper, 243)
52 *Paneg.* 12.23.28; for a discussion of the other contradictory sources, Jullian, *La Gaule* vol. 7, 219ff
53 *Paneg.* 12.26.1–5; Sulp. Sev. *chron.* 2.50, *dialog.* 2 (3) 11.3
54 Sulp. Sev. *dial.* 1 (2) 5–7, 2 (3) 13.3

55 H. Bloch in A. Momigliano (ed.), *The Conflict Between Paganism and Christianity in the Fourth Century* (Oxford 1963)
56 R. Alföldi, 'Zum Datum der Aufgabe'
57 Symmachus *epist.* 4.33; A. Chastagnol, *Rev. Hist.* 249 (1973) 23–40; J.-R. Palanque, *Provence hist.* 23 (1973) 29–38
58 Matthews (above n. 50)
59 For discussion old and new, Jullian, *La Gaule* vol. 7, 317ff and von Petrikovits, *Rheinische Geschichte* 271ff (General Works)
60 Salvian *gub. Dei* 5.18

10   The Late Roman Cities

1 Roblin, 'Cités ou citadelles?'; above chap. 9.1 for administrative changes
2 Above chap. 8.3
3 G. Thill, J. Metzler, R. Weiller, *Hémecht* 23 (1971) 79–91; G. Thill, *Hémecht* 31 (1979) 113–27; G. de Boe, *Arch Belg* 197 (1977); *Gallia* 31 (1973) 394–99
4 Vanvinckenroye, *Tongeren* (chap. 4) 44; S. Loeschcke, *Trier. Jahresber.* 12 (1921) *Beilage* 2, 103–7 (pottery now dated later); Schindler in *Festschrift Trier* (chap. 4) 133; Amiens evidence will be found in D. Bayard, J.-L. Massy, *Samarobriva Ambianorum* (forthcoming); Reims, see forthcoming report by R. Neiss on excavations by the Porte Bazée; Leman, 'Beauvais' (chap. 4); H. Thoen, *Septentrion* 1 (1970) 123–34
5 Kolling, 'Schwarzenacker' (chap. 4); F. Vasselle, E. Will, *RNord* 49 (1958) 467–82
6 D. Bayard, D. Piton, *CAPic* 6 (1979) 153ff; E. Will, *RNord* 44 (1962) 391–401 (also for Famars); Vasselle and Will (above n. 5)
7 Bayard and Massy, 'Amiens romain' (chap. 4)
8 For Grand, *Gallia* 36 (1978) 311 (but note that topography may suggest an even larger initial circuit of some kind)
9 J. Mertens, Ch. Léva in *Mélanges offerts à A. Piganiol* (Paris 1966) 1063–74; Brulet, *Liberchies* (chap. 4); and Braives (chap. 4. 4), also *Arch* (1977) 93; Ch. Léva, *Arch Belg* 45 (1958); *CIL* 13. 4131, and MacMullen, *Soldier and Civilian* (chap. 9) 137 for the suggestion of a memorial tower; Grenier, *Manuel* (General Works) vol. 1, 447ff for Senon etc., also H. Reiner, *Eine Römersiedlung vor Verdun* (München 1918)
10 Dating evidence summarized in von Petrikovits, 'Fortifications', 190; *Gallia* 20 (1962) 84; J. Choux, A. Liéger, *Gallia* 7 (1949) 88–101 (espec. 95); a later date for Beauvais is now being supported by Leman, 'Beauvais' (chap. 4) 213, on the basis of coins of Maximian and Licinius in a fill cut by the wall; Greg. Tur. *hist. franc.* 3. 19
11 J. Mertens, *Arch Belg* 196 (1977) 49–54; Eutropius 9.23; H. Koethe, *TZ* 11 (1936) *Beiheft* 50–106 and *TZ* 10 (1935) 1–5; Ausonius *Mosella* 11, H. Cüppers in *Führer (RGZM) Westlicher Hunsrück* 246ff; Gent and Brugge still much debated, see e.g. S.J. de Laet, *Spiegel Historiael* 4.3 (1969) 133–40
12 For walls as 'gifts', Brown, *Making of Late Antiquity* (chap. 8) 46; Cl. Seillier in *The Saxon Shore* (chap. 9 n. 6) 35–7
13 In general, Blanchet, *Les Enceintes* 237ff; *Cod. Theod.* 1.9.17.2–4; 1.16.10.3; 1.16.10.19; J. Metzler, G. Thill, *Hémecht* 26 (1974) 119–63

14 Johnson, 'A group of late Roman city walls'; for Amiens, Bayard and Massy (above n. 4). (*Paneg.* 15.18.4 may refer to ramparts)

15 Blanchet, *Les Enceintes*; Grenier, *Manuel* (General Works) vol. 1; Vercauteren, *Etudes*; above ns. 4, 5, 6, 10; Ch. Biévelet, *RNord* 46 (1964) 183–204; Ancien and Tuffreau-Libre, *Soissons* (chap. 4); J.-M. Desbordes, J.-L. Massy, *CAPic* 2 (1975) 55–61; best plan of Tournai in Wankenne, *La Belgique* (chap. 4); G. Bersu, W. Unverzagt, *Gallia* 19 (1961) 159–90; R. Schindler in *Varia Archaeologica, Festschrift W. Unverzagt* (Berlin 1964) 184–91

16 The 20–30 ha given by Vercauteren for Reims is an error; publication by R. Neiss awaited

17 Above ns. 9 and 15; H. Bernard, *Septentrion* 10 (1980) 41–60; R. Schindler, *BSDS* 9 (1962) 12–21; *Gallia* 30 (1972) 351 (Scarpone); Beaujard, 'Les vici des Médiomatriques'; Arlon conveniently in Wankenne, *La Belgique* (chap. 4)

18 J. Mertens, L. van Impe, *Arch Belg* 135 (1971); Seillier (above n. 12); E. Will, *RNord* 36 (1954) 141–5 (*CIL* 13. 3492, 3293, 3295); M. Chossenot, F. Lefevre, *MSAMarne* 96 (1981) 45–62 (*CIL* 13. 3457–8)

19 Roblin, 'Cités ou citadelles?'; Lombard-Jourdain, 'Oppidum et banlieue'

20 See, besides Roblin, discussion in Brühl, *Palatium und Civitas*; also M. Fleury in *Paris, Croissance d'une capitale* (Paris 1961) 73–96

21 Bayard and Massy, forthcoming (n. 4); Ammianus 15.11.10

22 See discussion in Brühl, *Palatium und Civitas*; in Metz, *Gallia* 38 (1980) 409; J. and F. Cartier, *RNord* 49 (1967) 637–57; Brulet, Coulon, *La rue Perdue*; Wightman, *Roman Trier* (Regional Studies) 120, cf. 233

23 Amiens, see above n. 4; Reims evidence poorer, but see discussion in Duval etc., *La Topographie chrétienne* vol. 1; Trier cemeteries summarized in *Führer (RGZM) Trier*

24 Wightman, 'The fate of Gallo-roman villages'; information from Raepsaet-Charlier, *ANRW* 2.4 and other scattered sources; for the north, H. Thoen, *Helinium* 6 (1966) 97–166; Kaiser, *Untersuchungen . . Soissons* (Regional Studies) for Soissonais; J. Metzler, J. Zimmer, *Hémecht* 27 (1975) 429–75; Tetelbierg, above n. 3; Schwarzenacker, above n. 5; W. Binsfeld, *AKorr* 6 (1976) 39–42; A. Haffner, *Kurtrier. Jahrb.* 20 (1980) 16–40; for coins, consult *Fundmünzen* vols. (Coins etc.)

25 E. Huber, *Le Héraple* (Strasbourg 1907–11) and Grenier, *Manuel* (General Works) vol. 1, 434ff; Scarpone, *Gallia* 30 (1972) 351; Daméry, A. Brisson, J.-J. Hatt, P. Roualet, *MSAMarne* 84 (1969) 39–55; Pachten, Schindler, *BSDS* 11 (1964) 5–50; for a Picardie *vicus* at Andéchy which escaped aerial photography because without stone foundations, Agache, *La Somme* (Regional Studies) 422

26 J. Mertens, *Le relais romain de Chameleux* (Brussels 1968); A. Cahen-Delhaye, H. Gratia, *Arch Belg* 213 (1979) 112–16; J.-L. Cadoux, *Latomus* 37 (1978) 325–60

27 Systematic but much (perhaps wrongly) criticized attempt by F. Lot, *Recherches sur la population et la superficie des cités remontant à la période gallo-romaine* 4 vols. (Paris 1945–53)

28 Beauvais, above n. 4; Bavay, *Gallia* 35 (1977) 279ff; Amiens, Bayard and Piton, above n. 6

29 Arguments for early cathedrals and continuity by Brühl, *Palatium und Civitas*

and in M. Barley (ed.), *European Towns* (London/New York 1977);
Vanvinckenroye, *Tongeren* 84ff, and see below chap. 13. 2

30 F. Oswald, *Frühmittelalt. Stud.* 1 (1967) 156–69; J.-J. Hatt, *ASHAL* 75 (1961)
15–27; Weidemann, 'Metz'; Gauthier, *L'évangélisation* (chap. 13.2) 32–3; R.
Egger, *Das Praetorium als Amtsitz und Quartier römischer Spitzenfunktionäre*
(Köln/Wien 1966)
31 Leman (above n. 4); R. Neiss, *BSAChamp* 4 (1979); Bavay, above n. 28;
paved streets at Reims, *Vita S. Rigoberti* (*MGH SS rer. Merov.* 7, 69)
32 *CIL* 13. 3255; baths themselves not known
33 See above chap. 4.2
34 E. Schramm, G. Wolfram, J.B. Keune, *Jahrb. Ges. Lothr. Gesch.* 14 (1902)
340–430; plan conveniently in Gauthier, *L'évangélisation* (chap. 13.2) 19, with
discussion
35 See below chap. 13.2–3; Greg. Tur. *hist. franc.* 10.31 for a *vicus Christianorum*
at Tours, widely generalized by Vercauteren and others
36 For 'black earth' over Roman layers, R. Neiss, *BSAChamp* 70 (1977) 71–9
and G. Jelski, *RNord* 62 (1980) 832–56; for cemeteries, Duval etc., *La
Topographie chrétienne*
37 Ammianus 15.11.6; Julian *epist.* 26 (18) 414 b–d; Symmachus *orat.* 1.15
38 See above chap. 8.2; in general, Wightman, *Roman Trier and the Treveri*
(Regional Studies) chap. 3.4 and *Führer (RGZM) Trier*
39 See chap. 4 n. 33 and above n. 4; *Paneg.* 7.22.4 (ed. Galletier)
40 *RIC* vols. 6 and 7; *Paneg.* 7.22.5
41 Reusch (chap. 4 n. 37); Krencker etc., *Kaiserthermen* and, for summary, *Führer
(RGZM) Trier* 178ff
42 Hollstein, *Eichendendrochronologie* (General Works); *Paneg.* 7.11.5, 6.12.3
43 *Paneg* 7.22.5; to earlier bibliography add R. Krautheimer, *Dumbarton Oaks
Papers* 21 (1967) 117ff
44 For tiles, P. Steiner, in *Trierer Jahresber.* 10/11 (1917/18) 18ff; *CIL* 13. 3672
45 K.-P. Goethert, K. Goethert-Polaschek in *Festschrift Trier* (chap. 4) 69–96
46 See now F.J. Ronig (ed.), *Der Trierer Dom* (chap. 13.2); new ceiling paintings
are not all yet published, but see Th. K. Kempf, *AKorr* 7 (1977) 147ff
47 *Paneg.* 7.22.7
48 In general, Parlasca, *Mosaïken*; above n. 45 for a debated date
49 Below chap. 12.2
50 Cüppers, in *Festschrift Trier* (above chap. 4)
51 References to suburban villas as scattered, Wightman, *Roman Trier* (Regional
Studies) 233; see also maps in *Führer (RGZM) Trier*; on cemeteries, below
chap. 13.3
52 Ausonius, *Ordo Urbium Nobilium*
53 *Trierer Jahresber.* 12 (1919/20) *Beilage* 56–8; see also discussion in Hussong and
Cüppers, *Kaiserthermen*
54 Gose, *Altbachtal* (chap. 4); for paved streets generally, Schindler in *Festschrift
Trier* (chap. 4)
55 Eiden, 'Ausgrabungen'; for fifth-century destruction levels, above n. 45 and
W. Binsfeld, 'Das Mosaik von der Fausenburg', *TZ* 31 (1968) 235–42; above
chap. 9.3
56 *Cod. Theod.* 15.1.32–33

57 Above chap. 9.1; for the Syagrii, Stroheker, *Senatorische Adel* (chap. 9), or Jones etc., *Prosopography*

58 E.g. Ausonius *epist.* 25. 90–98

59 Pachten, above n. 25; J. Willems, *Arch Belg* 148 (1973); Binson, *Gallia* 15 (1957) 324; Loeschche, *Denkmäler vom Weinbau* (chap. 7 n. 35)

60 *Not. Dig. Occ.* 11.35, 58, 77; 12.26; 11.59; 12.27; 11.34, 56, 76

61 *Gallien in der Spätantike* (Catalogues) 6, no. 93

62 Wightman, 'The towns of Gaul' (chap. 14); E. Perroy, *RNord* 29 (1947) 49–63

11 The Countryside in the Later Empire

1 De Maeyer, *Romeische Villa's* (chap. 5) 289ff read too much from the coins (chap. 5)

2 P. Steiner (Bollendorf), *Trier. Jahresber.* 12 (1923) 1–59; A. Kolling (Sotzweiler), *BSDS* 10 (1963) 71–86; H. Cüppers, A. Neyses, 'Newel' (chap. 5), *TZ* 34 (1971) 143–225; Weitersbach, *TZ* 24/6 (1956/8) 511–26; Cüppers (Horath), *TZ* 30 (1967) 114–43; H. Koethe (Oberweis), *TZ* 9 (1934) 20–56; G. Raepsaet, *La céramique en terre sigillée de la villa belgo-romain de Robelmont* (Brussels 1974); Metzler etc., *Echternach* (chap. 5) 96; de Boe (Haccourt), *Arch Belg* 174 (1975) 45; Sarreinsming, *Gallia* 36 (1978) 308–9

3 R. Schindler, *BSDS* 10 (1963) 107–17; Metzler, G. Thill, R. Weiller, *Hémecht* 25 (1973) 375–99; Lutz, *Gallia* 29 (1971) 17–44

4 Agache, *La Somme* (Regional Studies) 374; J.-M. Bastien, P. Demolon, *Septentrion* 5 (1975) 1–36; Soignies, preliminary report in *L'Archéologie en Wallonie* 39; Irsch, *TZ* 14 (1939) 248–53; Newel, above n. 2

5 P. van Ossel, 'Les établissements ruraux'; rough estimates can be made by assuming that the sites in Raepsaet-Charlier, *ANRW* 2.4 are a representative sample; cf. A. Vanderschelden, G. Raepsaet, *RNord* 56 (1974) 533–69; M. Lutz, *ASHAL* 78 (1978) 11–39

6 Thoen, *De Belgische Kustvlakte*; M. Cabal, *RNord* 55 (1973) 17–23

7 S. Walker, *Récentes recherches en archéologie gallo-romaine et paléochrétienne sur Lyon et sa région* (Oxford 1981; *BAR* S–108); cf. Martin-Kilcher, *Laufen-Müschhag* (chap. 5 n. 56); J. de Heinzelin etc., *Le gué du Plantin* (chap. 1 n. 2) 54; M. Coûteaux, 'Recherches palynologiques' (chap. 5) 76

8 J. Mertens, 'Le Luxembourg méridional'; for Nismes-Viroinval, *Arch* (1979) 19ff; Treignes, *Arch* (1980) 94; Matagne-la-Grande, *Arch* (1980) 111, cf. G. de Boe, 'Le sanctuaire gallo-romain de Matagne-la-Petite', *Arch Belg* 213 (1979) 93ff; for third-century fortifications elsewhere, von Petrikovits, 'Fortifications' (chap. 10) 191ff

9 K.-J. Gilles, *AKorr* 3 (1973) 67–74 and *TZ* 37 (1974) 99–122; for supposed medieval sites being late Roman, Schindler, *Studien . . Saarlandes* (chap. 1.4); A. Cahen-Delhaye, *Arch Belg* 206 (1978) 82–6; J.-P. Lemant, *BSAChamp.* 71 (1968) 87–91

10 Metzler and Thill, chap. 10 n. 13; J. Mertens, *Arch Belg* 42 (1958)

11 Bekker, in Metzler etc., *Echternach* (chap. 5) 269ff; R. Linden, *Hémecht* 29 (1977) 575–90

12 Deneuvre, Blanchet, *Les Enceintes* (chap. 10) 228, 243; L. Déroche, *Gallia* 23

(1965) 242–4; cf. Salin, *Le haut Moyen-Age*; Mt. Avison, *Gallia* 26 (1968) 391; other hypotheses built on topography and the existence of sculptures, perhaps from foundations – see index to Espérandieu

13 Auson. *Mosella* 446ff; Sidon. *epist.* 14.1; Salvian *gub. Dei* 5.44, suggesting flight from taxes as much as external foes; cf. *Paneg.* 2.25.1; Theopolis, *CIL* 12. 1524, was a Christian stronghold – does le Héraple (or Hieraple) represent a pagan Hierapolis, or is the name more recent?

14 R. Brulet, *La fortification de la Hauterecenne à Furfooz* (Louvain 1978) and *Arch Belg* 160 (1974); J. Mertens, H. Remy, *Arch Belg* 144 (1973)

15 Mertens, *Chameleux* (chap. 4 n. 52); Steinfort, A. Namur, *PSH* 5 (1850) 45ff; A. Kolling, *BSDS* 20 (1973) 5–49; cf. A. Matthys, G. Hossey, *Arch Belg* 146 (1973); J. Mertens, H. Remy, *Arch Belg* 129 (1971); J. Mertens, R. Brulet, *Acta Arch. Lovaniensia* 9 (1974); R. Seyler, *BSDS* 11 (1964) 87–119; R. Krantz, L. Koeperich, *Hémecht* 32 (1980) 185–200: cf. Schindler, Koch, *Burgwälle . . Luxemburg* (chap. 1. 4)

16 Generally, MacMullen, *Soldier and Civilian* (chap. 9.2)

17 See list in Böhne, *Germanische Grabfunde* (chap. 11.2); also van Doorselaer, *Repertorium* (Repertories)

18 L.H. Barfield in *Rheinische Ausgrabungen* (Düsseldorf 1968), 9ff; Metzler etc., 'Goeblingen-Nospelt' (n. 3)

19 In general, van Doorselaer, *Repertorium* (the omission of the Département Marne is unfortunate); for cemeteries with late reuse after a gap, see chap. 5 n. 5

20 Fremersdorf, *Köln-Müngersdorf* (chap. 5), cf. the separate cremation and inhumation cemeteries of the villa at Villeneuve d'Ascq, *Gallia* 33 (1975) 278–80; for Grevenmacherberg, Newel and Mayener Stadtwald, above chap. 10 n. 13, chap. 5 n. 36

21 Figures are based on van Doorselaer, *Repertorium* (Repertories) and van Ossel 'Les établissements ruraux'

22 Cutry, *Gallia* 32 (1974) 335–8; Flavion and Sissy, van Doorselaer, *Repertorium*; Breny and Caranda-Cierges, F. Moreau, *Album Caranda* (St. Quentin 1878–93); C. Seillier (Vron), *RNord* 60 (1978) 873–82; F. Roger (Liévin), *RNord* 49 (1967) 741–70; D. Piton, R. Schuler (Nouvion-en-Ponthieu), *CAPic* 8 (1981) 219ff; chap. 5 n. 32 (other large early cemeteries that die out are Hatrival, Hollange, Thiaumont, Witry, Rouveroy)

23 Böhme, *Germanische Grabfunde* for weapons; Cl. Seillier, *Septentrion* 10 (1980) 30–34

24 R. Lantier (Vert-la-Gravelle) in *Mélanges van de Weerd* (Brussels 1948)

25 For Vermand, Böhme, *Germanische Grabfunde*; cf. M. Loizel, J. Coquelle, *CAPic* 4 (1977) 161ff; Mertens, van Impe, 'Oudenburg' (chap. 10 n. 18)

26 Werner, 'Zur Entstehung'; James, 'Cemeteries and Frankish Settlement'; see distribution maps in Böhme, *Germanische Grabfunde*

27 *SHA Probus* 15.6; *Paneg.* 4.9; 4.21; 7.6; Ammianus 16.11.4; 20.8.12; *Not. Dig. Occ.* 42.33–44; *Cod. Theod.* 13.11.10 for *terrae Laeticae*, cf. *Sev. novellae* 2; Demougeot, 'A propos des Lètes'; C.J. Simpson, *Latomus* 36 (1977) 169–70 and 519–21

28 See items by Roosens, Böhner, Gunther and Böhme

29 James, 'Cemeteries and Frankish Settlement'

30 Above n. 25; W. Goffart, *Barbarians and Romans* AD *418–584: the techniques of accommodation* (Princeton 1980)

31 Ausonius *Mosella* 9; presence of Sarmatians often deduced from place-names, e.g. Sermaise, but see M. Roblin in *Hommages à M. Renard* (chap. 2 n. 17) vol. 2, 663–74

32 E. Aus'm Weerth (Stahl), *BJ* 62 (1878) 1ff, or summary in Steinhausen, *Ortskunde Trier-Mettendorf* (Repertories); Leiwen, *TZ* 24/6 (1956/8) 583–93; Schweich, Steinhausen, *Ortskunde* 287; above n. 3

33 H. Cüppers, A. Neyses, *TZ* 34 (1971) 227–32; for Hunsrück, Steinhausen, *Siedlungskunde* (Regional Studies) 401; F. Hettner, *Drei Tempelbezirke im Trevererlande* (Trier 1901); P. Steiner (Hottenbach), *TZ* 6 (1931) 139–41; Weisgerber, *Hochscheid* (chap. 7.4); Ausonius *Mosella* 5

34 Robelmont, above n. 2; for others, Corbiau, *Répertoire* (Repertories)

35 For old figure, de Maeyer, *Romeinsche Villa's* (chap. 5) 289ff; recently, van Ossel and de Boe (above ns. 5, 8)

36 Van Ossel, 'Les établissements ruraux'; M.-H. Corbiau, *Arch Belg* 196 (1977) 44–8; G. de Boe, *Arch Belg* 247 (1982) 70–4

37 Cüppers, Neyses, 'Newel' (chap. 5); cf. the concentration of fourth-century sites in parts of the Rhineland near Köln, H. Hinz, *Archäologische Funde und Denkmäler des Rheinlandes, Kreis Bergheim* (Düsseldorf 1969) 48ff

38 Euren etc., Steinhausen, *Ortskunde* (Repertories) and, for mosaics, Parlasca, *Mosaiken* (Mosaics etc.); Pfalzel, also H. Cüppers in *Frühchristliche Zeugnisse* (Catalogues) 152–62; E. Gose, *Germania* 19 (1961) 204–6, or Reusch in *Frühchristliche Zeugnisse* 150–2

39 Ausonius *Mosella* (ed. Ternes) 300ff; Ch.-M. Ternes, *REL* 48 (1970) 376–97; G. Thill, *Hémecht* 22 (1970) 455–67; Metzler etc., *Echternach* (chap. 5) 109ff; H. Eiden, *TZ* 19 (1950) 26–40; Nennig, *Führer (RGZM) Saarland* 185ff

40 Ausonius *Mosella* 455ff; Landmauer, Steinhausen, *Siedlungskunde* (Regional Studies) 440ff; Wrede, *Welschbillig* (chap. 9); Wittlich, *TZ* 16/17 (1941/2) 229–35 and *Führer (RGZM) Südwestlicher Eifel* 236ff; for effects of Alamanni, H. Bernhard, *Mitteil. Hist. Verein Pfalz* 79 (1981) 5–103; consult also *Fundmünzen* volumes

41 For modern discoveries, Raepsaet-Charlier, *ANRW* 2.4 109ff; Lutz, (above n. 5) and *RAE* 1 (1950) 180–4; Grenier, *Habitations gauloises* (chap. 5) (but he dates the large villas too late); *Gallia* 36 (1978) 328–9

42 G. Tronquart, *Gallia* 34 (1976) 201–13

43 Agache, *La Somme* (Regional Studies) 366ff, 419ff; Vanderschelden and Raepsaet (above n. 5); cf. R. Fossier, *La Terre et les Hommes en Picardie* (Paris/Louvain 1968) vol. 1, 132ff

44 Diocletian *Edict* 19, 27 etc.; Paulinus *epist.* 18.4; Liévin, Vron etc., above n. 22; for low population, R. Doehaerd, *Le haut moyen âge occidental* (Paris 1971) 86ff but contrast Fossier (above n. 43) 203ff (speaking however of a later period)

45 Essentially the view of Agache

46 Chapelot and Fossier, *Le village* 50ff; Agache, *La Somme* 449; for cemeteries, van Doorselaer, *Repertorium*

47 Böhme, *Germanische Grabfunde*; M. Roblin, *Caesarodunum* 8 (1973) 128ff and *l'Oise* (Regional Studies) 245ff

48 Preliminary information on Catalauni in M. Chossenot, *La civilisation gallo-romaine en Champagne Sèche, Sites ruraux* (Châlons-sur-Marne n.d.); P. Perin, 'Le peuplement rural'; Applebaum, 'The late Gallo-Roman rural pattern' and

Percival, 'Polyptyques'; A.H.M. Jones, P. Grierson, J.A. Crook, *RBPh* 35 (1957) 370–3 (*MGH SS rer. Merov.* 3, 336–47)

49 Summary in Kaiser, *Soissons* (Regional Studies); see above n. 22 and chap. 5 n. 5; only major villa publication is Barbet etc., 'Mercin et Vaux' (above chap. 5) *CAPic* 8 (1981) 65–146

50 Stern, *Mosaïques* no. 77 and *Gallia* 13 (1955) 41–77

51 Stroheker, *Senatorische Adel* (chap. 9)

52 Steinhausen, *Siedlungskunde* (Regional Studies) 325 drew attention to Roman remains in woodland; only the discovery of Roman villas showed that the Forêt Charbonnière was not a permanent feature of the landscape until modern times

53 Julian *Misopogon* 8, 342 b; Dion, *La vigne* (chap. 6)

54 Ausonius *Mosella* 361–4

55 Above n. 48

56 Convenient introduction in Percival, *The Roman Villa* (chap. 5) 30ff and 172ff; H. d'Arbois de Jubainville, *Recherches* (General Works); Falc'hun, *Les noms de lieux* (Toponymy)

57 M. Roblin, *Le terroir de Paris aux époques gallo-romaine et franque* (2nd ed. 1971) and *l'Oise* (Regional Studies) 79ff

58 Grenier, *Manuel* (General Works) vol. 2, 884ff; H.-W. Hermann, *BSDS* 22 (1975) 67–89; P. Grierson, *RBPh* 18 (1939) 437–61; there is no convenient study on Mersch, but see Doehaerd (above n. 44) 177–8

59 Ausonius 3.1 (ed. Pieper) ('de herediolo'); G. Fouet, *La villa gallo-romaine de Montmaurin* (Haute-Garonne) (Paris 1969; *Gallia* suppl. 20); above n. 48

60 Salv. *gub. Dei* 4.20, 4.30; A.H.M. Jones, *Past and Present* 13 (1958) 1–13, repr. in P. Brunt (ed.), *The Roman Economy* (Oxford 1974) 293–307

61 Above n. 40; E. Ewig, 'Les Ardennes' (chap. 14)

62 Wightman, 'Peasants and Potentates'; J. Percival, 'Seigneurial Aspects'; I. Hahn, *Klio* 50 (1968) 260–76

63 Auson. *epist.* 26; Sidonius *carm.* 22, *epist.* 3.12 and 5.19; generally, Jullian, *La Gaule* (General Works) vol. 8, 139ff

12   Production, Marketing and Trade in Late Roman Belgica

1 Zosimus 3.5; Ammianus 18.2.3; Libanius *epitaph.* 549; cf. Julian *ad Athen.* 360 h

2 Birley, 'The economic effects'

3 *CIL* 13. 3704, *RICG* 1.561; Auson. *epist.* 26; Salvian *gub. Dei* 4.69; Lambrechts, 'Le commerce des Syriens' (chap. 12.3); Rougé, *Commerce maritime* (chap. 12.3) 486ff

4 See listed works by Cérati, Chastagnol, Déléage, Goffart, Jones

5 *Paneg.* 8.11; Jullian, *La Gaule* (General Works) vol. 8, 36ff; Faure, 'Etude'

6 Ammianus, 16.5.14, 17.3.1–6

7 Salvian *gub. Dei* 5.29–35; cf. *Cod. Theod.* 10.1.16, 11.3.1–5, 12.1.173; that taxes were passed on as higher rents is only implicit in Salvian but see *Cod. Just.* 11.50.1; on senators' taxes, Arnheim, *Senatorial Aristocracy* 161

8 C.R. Whittaker, 'Inflation'

9 Cérati, *Caractère annonaire passim*; D. van Berchem in *Armées et Fiscalité* (above chap. 8 n. 1) 331–9 (and comments by Carrié and Corbier)

10 Diocletian *edict*. 19.32, 54; 25.9 (ed. S. Lauffer)

11 *Not. Dig. Occ.* 11.34, 39, 57; 12.26, 27; 11.36–39

12 Pallad. 1.6.3 (ed. Martin); Auson. *epist*. 7 and 26 (suggestive rather than explicit); for senatorial estates, Arnheim, *Senatorial Aristocracy* 143ff

13 K. Branigan, *Trans. Bristol and Gloucs. Arch. Soc.* 92 (1973) 82–95

14 Pallad. 7.2.2–4; see above chap. 5 n. 49

15 Chap. 11.4; C.R. Whittaker in M.I. Finley (ed.), *Studies in Roman Property* (Cambridge 1976) 137–207

16 *Digest* 30.1.112, 50.15.4.8, cf. Paulus *sententiae* 3.6.48; *Cod. Theod.* 11.1.7, cf. 11.1.14, 11.1.26, 11.53.1 and 11.52.1 (*servi terrae ipsius*); 11.48.7 for the forbidding of the sale of rural slaves; for Sidonius and Remigius, chap. 11 ns. 48, 63

17 On patronage, Salvian *gub. Dei* 5. 42ff, cf. *Cod. Theod.* 12.1.146 (addressed to the praeses of Lugdunensis I); on tax exemptions for veterans, Goffart, *Caput and Colonate* 24–25; tax status of settled barbarians is not so clear – they are sometimes *tributarii* (Ammianus 18.5.15), but *terrae laeticae* had special status (*Cod. Theod.* 13.11.10)

18 Mertens, *Arch Belg* 206 (1978); Barbet, *CAPic* 8 (1981) 88ff; Krencker etc., *Kaiserthermen* (chap. 10)

19 E.g. the inelegant *Esp.* 5263 (Pölich), 3940–3 (Amiens); sarcophagi, plain and sculptured, best seen in *Frühchristliche Zeugnisse* (Catalogues), inscriptions in either Gose or Gauthier (chap. 13); for marbles in the Basilika, Reusch in *Die Basilika in Trier* (Trier 1956) 33f

20 *Esp.* 3677; see below chap. 13

21 Chap. 11 n. 50, chap. 10 n. 45, and Parlasca, *Mosaïken* (Mosaics etc.)

22 *Gallien in der Spätantike* (Catalogues) 127; for Huy, Willems (chap. 10 n. 59)

23 Thoen (chap. 4 n. 49); to references in chap. 6 ns. 14–16 add Cüppers, *TZ* 30 (1967) 114–43 espec. 129–32; R. Schindler, 'Eisenverhüttung' (with discussion of various sites); for Ribemont, Cadoux (chap. 7.4)

24 Bayard, Piton (chap. 10 n. 6)

25 There is no convenient collection either of the coffins or of other evidence on lead

26 Hollstein, *Eichendendrochronologie* under Trier, Dom

27 Steiner in *Trier. Jahresber.* 10/11 (1917/18) 18ff; see map in Wightman, *Roman Trier* (Regional Studies) 178–9; *TZ* 24/6 (1956/8) 569–71; see chap. 10.1 and 2 on Metz and Trier

28 Chap. 10 n. 59

29 Chenet and Gaudron (chap. 6.2); Hofmann (chap. 6 n. 42); Chenet, *Argonne du IVe siècle*

30 Hübener, 'Rädchensigillata'; M. Fulford, 'Pottery and Britain's Foreign Trade'

31 Fulford (n. 30) and 'The interpretation'; recent articles on distribution within Belgica include J. Nicolle, *Gallia* 23 (1965) 245–9; C. Robert, *Gallia* 27 (1969) 135–48; D. Piton, D. Bayard, *CAPic* 4 (1977) 205ff

32 Von Petrikovits, 'Der Wandel' (above chap. 6.2); Fulford and Bird, 'Imported pottery'; R. Nierhaus, *Germania* 24 (1940) 47–54

33 Hussong and Cüppers, *Kaiserthermen* (chap. 10), discussion of coarse wares

34 'Céramique craquelée-bleutée' little studied as yet; Chenet, *Argonne du IVe siècle* 97, 107
35 Detailed study still required
36 *Gallien in der Spätantike* 72ff; W. Reusch, *TZ* 32 (1969) 295–317; Eiden (above chap. 11 n. 39)
37 F. Fremersdorf, *Denkmäler des römischen Köln* (various volumes)
38 *Gallien in der Spätantike* for glass generally, and 122 for 'barillets'; Chassaing (chap. 6 n. 43); cf. Chenet, *Argonne du IVe siècle* 107ff
39 Ausonius *epist.* 7 and 26; Jones, *Later Roman Empire* (chap. 9) 431 for exemption of peasants and landowners
40 Above ns. 30–31
41 Van de Weerd, 'Het economische bloeitijdperk' (chap. 6.1), Wightman, 'The towns of Gaul' (chap. 14); von Petrikovits, *Rheinische Geschichte* (General Works) 250
42 Nautae, J.F. Drinkwater, 'The Gallic Julii' (chap. 3. 4); Rougé, *Commerce maritime* 486ff, and in *Settimane di Studio sull' alto Medioevo* 25 (1977/78) 67–124; Sidonius *epist.* 6.8 and 7.7; *Cod. Theod.* 12.19.1–3
43 References in West, *Objects of Trade* (chap. 6); Tronquart, 'La Bûre' (chap. 1 n. 42); for African Red Slip, Hussong and Cüppers, *Kaiserthermen* (chap. 10)
44 *Expositio totius mundi* (ed. Rougé) 58; because of the court, everything is available, but at a high price; Ausonius *epist.* 25, cf. 18
45 Lambrechts, 'Le commerce des "syriens"'; Salvian 4 (14) 69; Gose, *Frühchristliche Inschriften* 402, 402A, *RICG* 1.10, 168
46 Rougé, in *Settimane di studio* (above n. 42); Hopkins, 'Taxes and trade' (above chap. 6)
47 King, 'The Sacrae Largitiones'; Lallemand, 'La circulation'; M. Fulford, *Arch. Journ.* 135 (1978) 67–114

13 The Christianization of Belgica

1 Passages from *Concilium Rothomagense, Vita S. Eligii, Vita S. Pirmini*, Caesarius of Arles etc. collected in Zwicker, vol. 2, 136, 196–7, 221, 305; for cattle disease, Endelechius *de mortibus boum* (Buecheler-Riese, *Anthologia* 2 no. 893, 105–12); Forêt de Halatte, *Esp.* 3864–9
2 N. Kyll, 'Trier Volksglaube' for *Parcae*, Clemen, *Fontes* 65; for ritual observances, Zwicker, *Fontes* vol. 2 136, 174, 221 (*Concilium Rothomagense, Concilium Narbonense, Vita S. Pirmini*)
3 Sulpicius Severus *Vita S. Martini* 13.1 (Zwicker 118–9); *dialogi* 2(3) 9.1 (Zwicker 121); Greg. Tur. *de passione S. Iuliani* (Zwicker 177); *Vita S. Magnerici* (Zwicker 242); P. Lambrechts, *Latomus* 13 (1954) 207–14
4 For re-use of shrines, consult lists in Raepsaet-Charlier, *ANRW* 2.4 and in Horne and King, 'Romano-Celtic temples' (chap. 7.4). The map in *Gallien in der Spätantike* indicates more continued use than my own researches
5 Recently, Bayard and Cadoux, *Gallia* 40 (1982) 83–105; otherwise, bibliography in Horne and King (n. 4)
6 In Gose, *Altbachtal* (1972; chap. 4.2) Schindler's dating in the summary does not agree with the detailed description but is supported by the coin evidence as given in *Fundmüzen* 4.3.1 (Coins etc.)

7 See Walters, *The cult of Mithras* (chap. 7.4) and J.-J. Hatt, *CRAI* (1958) 94–6, *Gallia* 16 (1958) 336–9

8 See generally chap. 7.4; symbolism extensively explored by F. Cumont, *Recherches sur le symbolisme funéraire des Romains* (Paris 1942), though not all his conclusions are still accepted

9 See above chap. 11 n. 50; J.M.C. Toynbee, *Britannia* 12 (1981) 1–5

10 Ausonius, *epig.* 66 ('de Castore, Polluce et Helena'); Moreau, *Kornmarktmosaik*

11 Zwicker, *Fontes* vol. 2, 205 (*Vita S. Echarii* and *Vita S. Valerii*). Esp. 4665 for one of many stones found in wells

12 Kyll, 'Volksglaube'; J. Hubert, *CRAI* (1967) 567–73; cf. Schleiermacher, 'Zum Beharrungsvermögen' and R. Wirtz, *PSH* 61 (1926) 405ff; for a temple (Steinsel) with particularly numerous coins of the late fourth century, J. Metzler, *Hémecht* 26 (1974) 491ff

13 Irenaeus *adv. haereses* 1.102; Tertullian *adv. Iudanos* 7; see discussion by Gauthier, *L'évangélisation* 9–10

14 Discussion by Duchesne, *Fastes épiscopaux passim*; de Moreau, *L'église en Belgique* chap. 1; Gauthier, *L'évangélisation* 10ff

15 Clearest general discussion in Duchesne, *Fastes*; for Theban martyrs, also Gauthier, *L'évangélisation* 67ff

16 As noted by Gauthier, 91 and 103

17 Paulinus *epist.* 12.18 (*Corpus script. eccles. Lat.* 29.1, 130–33), generally, Duchesne and de Moreau

18 Recently, suggesting an ecclesiastical origin, Rivet in *Aspects of the Notitia Dignitatum* (chap. 9 n. 6). There is indeed a gap in the Tongeren/Maastricht list, which starts up again in the late fifth or early sixth century with Falco

19 Ewig, *Trier in Merowingerreich* for Aquitanian connections; above chap. 11 n. 48 for Remigius; C.E. Stevens, *Sidonius Apollinaris* (Oxford 1933)

20 Griffe, *La Gaule chrétienne* 175ff; Steinhausen, 'Hieronymus und Laktanz' (chap. 9.3); Ewig, *TZ* 24/6 (1956/8) 147–86; T.D. Barnes, *Constantine and Eusebius* (Cambridge, Mass. 1981) 47

21 For Trier bishops, Ewig, *Trier im Merowingerreich* and Gauthier, *L'évangélisation*; Gauthier 61ff on Priscillianists; main text in Sulpic. Sev. *chron.* 2.49; see also Matthews, *Western Aristocracies* (above chap. 9) 164ff

22 Gauthier, *L'évangélisation* 67ff for discussion of texts; for objects, *Frühchristliche Zeugnisse* (Catalogues) 71–2, 179

23 Victricius *de laude sanctorum* (Migne, *P.L.* 20, 443–58); Brown, *The Saints* 95–6

24 Sulp. Sev. *vita Martini* 3.17 (ed. J. Fontaine); C.E. Stancliffe in *Studies in Church History* vol. 16 (1979) 43–59; Brown, *The Saints* 124 for urban context

25 Griffe, *La Gaule chrétienne* 366ff; Augustine, *confess.* 8.6; Jerome *epist.* 3.5

26 Brühl (see above chap. 10 n. 29)

27 Th. K. Kempf, *Germania* 42 (1964) 126–41; recently, articles by J. Zink, H. Cüppers, Th. K. Kempf in Ronig (ed.), *Der Trierer Dom*

28 Gauthier, *L'évangélisation* 32, 139; cf. Vieillard-Troiëkouroff, *Les monuments* under Metz; generally, Duval etc., *Topographie chrétienne* (chap. 10)

29 Besides Duval etc. (n. 28), Brühl, *Palatium und Civitas* (chap. 10), but the latter tends to assume the existence of cathedrals

30 For Metz, Weidemann, 'Metz' (above chap. 10); but see remarks by Gauthier, *L'évangélisation* 32–3; above chap. 10 n. 30; churches at Amiens, in Bayard and

Massy, *Samarobriva Ambianorum* (chap. 4); P. Heliot, *RA* (1958) 158–82

31 Flodoard, *Historia Remensis ecclesiae* (*MGH SS* 13); Vieillard-Troiëkouroff, *Les monuments*; *RICG* for inscriptions

32 H. Cüppers, in *Frühchristliche Zeugnisse* (Catalogues) 165ff and *Führer (RGZM) Trier* 226ff; also *TZ* 31 (1968) 177–90 and 32 (1969) 269–93; Greg. Tur. *Vitae Patrum* 17.4

33 *RICG* 103; Gerke, *Die Trierer Agricius-Sarkophag* (Trier 1949; *TZ Beiheft* 2); W. Sanderson, *TZ* 31 (1968) 7–172

34 Gauthier, *L'évangélisation* 67ff, and see also Vieillard-Troiëkouroff; Eiden, in *Neue Ausgrabungen* (chap. 10)

35 M. Guarducci, in *Frühchristliche Zeugnisse* (Catalogues) 54ff

36 Above n. 30; *RICG* for dating of inscriptions

37 Duval etc., *La topographie chrétienne*; L. Pietri, *RNord* 52 (1970) 443–53

38 E. le Blant, *Sarcophages chrétiens de la Gaule* (Paris 1886) 14–17; B. Andreae, *Die römische Jagdsarkophage 2. Die Sarkophage mit Darstellungen aus dem Menschenleben* (Berlin 1980) 46–9, no. 75

39 Above n. 23; M. Amand, H. Lambert, *Arch Belg* 222 (1980) 11–43

40 *RICG* 1.238–241; J. Krier, *Hémecht* 33 (1981) 375–80; Gauthier, *L'évangélisation* 154–5; contrast the evidence from Alesia, J. la Gall in *Mélanges . . J. Carcopino* (Paris 1966) 613–28

41 *RICG* 1.258; P.-M. Duval in *Hommages à M. Renard* (chap. 2 n. 17) 256–61; Endelechius (above n. 1); for Famars, *Gallia* 33 (1975) 271ff

42 See above n. 9 and chap. 10 n. 51; K. Böhner in *Führer (RGZM) Trier* 29–42

43 See *Frühchristliche Zeugnisse* and *Gallien in der Spätantike* (Catalogues)

44 *Frühchristliche Zeugnisse* no. 54; Chenet, *La céramique d'Argonne du IVe siècle* (chap. 12.2)

45 On the role of the *potentes* in the fourth century, Brown, *The Saints passim*

46 Cf. R.W. Bulliet, *Conversion to Islam in the medieval period: an essay in quantitative history* (Cambridge, Mass. 1979); Gauthier, *L'évangélisation* 100ff

47 *RICG* 1.56; 1.37; 126; 1.138; 1.177; 1.192; 1.109, 170; 1.199, 142A, 214

48 *RICG* 79ff; for a pagan German Hariulfus the Burgundian, *CIL* 13. 3682

49 *RICG* 37ff; Greg. Tur. *gloria confess.* 17; *Frühchristliche Zeugnisse* (Catalogues) 223ff

50 A. Rouselle, 'Du sanctuaire au thaumaturge'

51 Brown, *The Saints* 121ff

52 Above n. 12; Brown, *The Saints* may underestimate the range of possible accommodations in the countryside, both then and earlier

53 See e.g. K. List, *AKorr* 2 (1972) 225–30 (gap between villa and church). On other aspects of rural Christianity, M. Roblin, *Caesarodunum* 8 (1973) 128ff and *BSAF* (1963) 138–40, but cf. F. Jacques, *Ann. Féd. arch. hist. de Belgique* 38 (1961) 253–65

14 The Fifth Century: A Time of Transition

1 Not all sources cited here. For continuous accounts: from the Roman angle Jones, *Later Roman Empire* (chap. 9); for Romans and barbarians, Demougeot, *La formation* vol. 2; for the Gallo-Roman aristocracy, Stroheker, *Senatorische Adel* (chap. 9); for the Franks, Zöllner, *Geschichte*. Most sources in Riese, *Litteratur*, not all later ones in Duval, *La Gaule* (Sources)

2 For Oudenburg and Liberchies, chap. 9 ns. 16, 19; E. Will, 'Boulogne'; Flodoard 1.6; Demougeot, 'La Gaule nord-orientale' and 'La Notitia Dignitatum'

3 Jerome *epist.* 123.156; Salvian 7.12.2; Orientius *commonitorium* 2.184; see also P. Courcelle, *Histoire littéraire des grandes invasions germaniques* (3rd ed. Paris 1964) 80ff

4 Zosimus 6.3.1–3; C.E. Stevens, *Athenaeum* 35 (1957) 316–47; for Alans, B.S. Bachrach, *Traditio* 23 (1967) 476–89

5 Zosimus 6.10.2; for a traditional view, essentially following Thompson (chap. 8 n. 30), Demougeot, *La formation* vol. 2, 442; see now P. Bartholomew, *Britannia* 13 (1982) 261–70

6 On Bagaudae, consult Czuth, *Bagauden* (chap. 8); chap. 8 generally for an alternative view of the Bagaudae; for Trier mint, H. von Koblitz, *TZ* 3 (1928) 14–47

7 Demougeot, *La formation* 483ff; Greg. Tur. *hist.* 2.9, Salvian 6.72 and 6.75

8 The meaning of the passage of Rutil. Namat. *de reditu* 1.213–16 is now challenged by Bartholomew (above n. 5) as well as by van Dam (chap. 8 n. 2)

9 For patronage around Constantine III and Constantius, Matthews, *Western Aristocracies* (chap. 9.3) 308ff

10 Matthews, *Western Aristocracies* 333ff; Stroheker, *Senatorische Adel* (chap. 9) 183; Gauthier, *L'évangélisation* (chap. 13. 2) 123ff

11 Demougeot, *La formation* 485ff; M.F. Clover, *Historia* 20 (1971) 354ff and *Trans. Amer. Philos. Soc.* n.s. 61.1 (1971); A. Loyen, *REA* 74 (1972) 153–74

12 Sidon. *carm.* 5. 210–30; A. Loyen, *REA* 46 (1944) 121–34

13 For chronology, Clover, *Trans. Amer. Philos. Soc.* (above n. 11) 44ff; for the suggestions that the routes taken by S. Germanus reflect the insecurity of the north, R. Borins, *Journées arch. internat. de Compiègne, mai 1964* 9–14

14 Demougeot, *La formation* 521, 546ff, and *MSAMarne* 73 (1958) 25–31

15 Stevens, *Sidonius* (above chap. 13 n. 19)

16 For these figures, Martindale, *Prosopography* vol. 2; Demougeot, *La formation* vol. 2, 625ff, 641ff

17 Sidon. *epist.* 4. 17; for recent discussion, Gauthier, *L'évangélisation* 118ff, cf. Ewig, *Trier im Merowingerreich* (chap. 13.2)

18 See *Childeric-Clovis* (Catalogues) 69ff

19 See Zöllner, *Franken* 44ff

20 J. Lafaurie, in *Childeric-Clovis* 72ff

21 Clover (above n. 13) 44ff

22 Generally, Stroheker, *Senatorische Adel* (chap. 9) and Ewig, *Trier im Merowingerreich*; Arbogast, above n. 17; chap. 13 n. 47

23 *Vita S. Remigii* (*MGH AA* 4.2.64) and above chap. 11 n. 48; for others, consult Gauthier, *L'évangélisation*

24 Ewig, 'Das Fortleben'

25 Salvian, *gub. Dei* 6.72ff, 85ff

26 See summary by Kempf in Ronig (ed.), *Der Trierer Dom* (chap. 13.2); also Hussong and Cüppers, *Kaiserthermen* (chap. 10) 127

27 Best discussion in Hussong and Cüppers, *Kaiserthermen* 126ff; Trier may thus have resembled some North African cities with their various fortified points or 'blockhouses'. Summary by Böhner in *Führer (RGZM) Trier* 29ff

28 Above chap. 13.3–4; E. Ewig, 'Observations'
29 Above chap. 13.2–3; for Metz cemeteries, *RICG*; for Noyon etc., Duchesne, *Fastes* (chap. 13.2)
30 M. Lutz, *RAE* 1 (1950) 180–4 (Berthelming)
31 W. Binsfeld (Bitburg), *AKorr.* 9 (1979) 431–4; Metzler etc., *Echternach* (chap. 5) 110, and (for the fortification), 290; Barbet, 'Mercin-et-Vaux' (chap. 5) 92; Metzler (Steinsel), *Hémecht* 26 (1974) 491ff
32 See chap. 11 n. 22 and Salin, *Le haut moyen-âge en Lorraine* (chap. 11)
33 Perin, 'Le peuplement rural' (chap. 11.1) and James, 'Frankish settlement' (chap. 11.2); generally, Longnon, *Pagi*
34 Böhner, *Fränkischen Altertümer*
35 Ewig, 'Les Ardennes'; P. Rolland, *Annales* 7 (1935) 245–84
36 Metzler etc., *Echternach* (chap. 5); chap. 11 ns. 48, 58
37 Böhner, *Fränkischen Altertümer*
38 Böhner makes a start in *Fränkischen Altertümer*; on place-names, H. Engels, *Die Ortsnamen an Mosel, Sauer und Saar* (Trier 1961)
39 Much depends on the definition of 'continuity'; for two extreme views, Percival in *The Roman Villa* (high degree of continuity) and A. Verhulst in *Settimani di Studi* 13 (1965) 135–60
40 Enormous and contentious bibliography; for purposes here, Stengers, Gysseling and Petri; for Mosel valley, above n. 38
41 On ivories at Trier (but arguing for a local workshop) W. Sanderson in *Festschrift Trier* (chap. 4), 319–46
42 Böhner, 'Urban and rural settlement'; Ewig, 'Résidence et capitale'; cf. Dasnoy, Dollinger-Léonard and Stroheker

General Index

aerial photography 15, 22, 38, 49, 94, 107, 114, 141, 244
Agri Decumates 193
agriculture 4, 95, 96, 118, 123–8, 148
altars 51, 55, 59, 156, 174, 175
amber 9, 175
amphitheatres 59, 84, 88, 232, 235, 237, 307
  used as cemeteries 293
amphorae 93, 134, 142, 148, 154
  from Italy 28–30, 48
Antonine Edict 170, 172
Antonine Itinerary 91–3, map xii–xiii
aqueducts 83, 183
archaeology 13, 14, 33, 37, 38, 44–6, 48, 49, 65, 68, 69,
    77, 88, 90–92, 99, 101, 102, 107, 110, 119, 121, 134,
    150, 158–60, 178, 189, 206, 220, 229–33, 240, 243,
    253, 259–62, 265, 267, 273, 282, 290–4, 309–10
architecture at Trier 235
Arianism 214
armament factories 240, 275
Arretine pottery 48
artisans 91, 187, 188
Attic pottery 7, 8, 10
Augustan History 198–9
Augustan period 76, 77, 80, 135, 163
  pottery 92, 142, 144

baptisteries 291
Barbarathermen 83, 87, 136, 235, 275, 277, 307
barbarians see Alans, Franks, Germans, Suebi, Vandals
barrels 134, 142, 148
basalt 136
Basilika (audience chamber) at Trier 235, 236, 275
Batavian revolt 88, 104
baths 81, 83, 232, 237, 283
  see Barbarathermen, Kaiserthermen
beakers 145, 147
beer 148, 155
bishops see Christianity
boats and barges 152, 153, 156
bone combs 252
brass 140
bricks 94, 142
bridges 41, 136, 161
  Mosel 49, 66, 69, 76, 80, 159
  Rhine 41, 69
  Saar 66, 76
bronze 48, 140, 175
  Etruscan 7–9, 28, 29
  Greek 7
  cauldrons 273
  figurines 178, 189
brooches 8, 252 and see fibulae
building materials see bricks, chalk, clay, marble,
  plaster, stone, tuff, wood
building traditions 16, 17
burgus 208
burial customs and burials 45, 48, 229
  pre-Roman 6–10, 13–15
  Roman 90, 91
  Gallo-Roman 90, 174–6, 188
  late-Roman 272
  inhumation 250
  weapon burials 249–53, 256, 261

cage-cups 258, 277
calendars 187
Campanian pottery 28

canals 60, 66, 151
castella 21, 248
castra 240, 249
cathedral, at Trier 236, 274, 289, 290, 307; plan 288
cemeteries
  pre-Roman 14, 15, 101, 102
  Roman 90–3, 96, 97, 100, 116, 119, 121, 129, 131,
    229, 230
  late-Roman 250–6, 261
  Christian 292–6, 308–10
  re-use 229–33, 238, 252
censuses 45, 51, 60, 103, 104, 159, 160, 268, 269
chalk 110
Champagne chalk-lands 1
Christianity 282–310
  bishop lists 286, 287, bishoprics, medieval 26
  bishops 286, 287, 289, 290–3, 306, 308
  bishops as landowners 306
  cemeteries 292–4, 308–9
  cults, shrines, sanctuaries 232, 282, 283, 286, 292, 294
churches
  built over pagan structures 231, 232, 236, 291–3, 298
  in cemeteries 233, 294
  in cities 231, 241, 242
circus 235
civitas 39, 75, 76, 91–100 passim, 140, 142, 149, 165, 204,
    245, 264
  late-Roman 219–28, 261, 262, 268, 287
  re-use of stone 223–7
civitates 24, 26, 37, 39, 44, 47, 49, 51, 53, 58, 59, 66, 68,
    103, 104, 118, 168, 202, 204, 205, 219, 239, 240,
    241, 269, 287
  as seats of bishops 242, 307
classis Britannica 93, 227
classis Sambrica 207
clay 110
Claudian period 77, 78, 80
  pottery 92
  villas 105
claviculae 38, 69
climate 2, 4, 5, 126, 148, 160
cloth and clothing 134, 149, 150, 155, 189
  production 270
coal 141
coffins 140, 233, 273
coins and coinage
  army 192, 197, 280, 281
  debasement 191
  forgeries 156, 159, 197, 200
  hoards 38, 41, 45, 46, 159, 195–8, 200, 221, 245
  mints 43, 46, 48, 193–6, 201, 212, 213, 217, 235, 239,
    281, 301, 302
  pre-Roman 11, 12, 18–21, 24, 25, 27–32, 39–41
  post conquest 43–9, 51, 68, 92, 94, 95, 130, 191, 194,
    208, 209, 220, 230, 235, 236, 238, 243–6, 252,
    256–9, 284, 305, 310
collatio lustralis 268
collegia 82, 97, 153, 154, 161, 162, 185, 279
coloni 264, 265, 269, 272
colonies 56, 58, 59, 69
commerce 94–6 passim
Concilium Galliarum 51, 52, 59, 60, 140, 161
copper 140
coral 9
craftsmen see artisans
cults
  imperial 58, 181, 183, 283, 285

Index of Names and Places